Statistical Functions in Excel	*Description*
AVERAGE(*data range*)	Computes the average value (arithmetic mean) of a set of data.
BETADIST(*x, alpha, beta, A, B*)	Returns the cumulative beta density function.
BINOMDIST(*number_s, trials, probability_s, cumulative*)	Returns the individual term binomial distribution.
CHITEST(*actual_range, expected_range*)	Returns the test for independence; the value of the chi-square distribution and the appropriate degrees of freedom.
CONFIDENCE(*alpha, standard_dev, size*)	Returns the confidence interval for a population mean.
CORREL(*arrayl, array2*)	Computes the correlation coefficient between two data sets.
EXPONDIST(*x, lambda, cumulative*)	Returns the exponential distribution.
FORECAST(*x, known_y's, known_x's*)	Calculates a future value along a linear trend.
GAMMADIST(*x, alpha, beta, cumulative*)	Returns the gamma distribution.
GROWTH(*known_y's, known_x's, new_x's, constant*)	Calculates predicted exponential growth.
LINEST(*known_y's, known_x's, new_x's, constant, stats*)	Returns an array that describes a straight line that best fits the data.
LOGNORMDIST(*x, mean, standard_deviation*)	Returns the cumulative lognormal distribution of x, where $\ln(x)$ is normally distributed with parameters mean and standard deviation.
MEDIAN(*data range*)	Computes the median (middle value) of a set of data.
MODE(*data range*)	Computes the mode (most frequently occurring) of a set of data.
NORMDIST(*x, mean, standard_deviation, cumulative*)	Returns the normal cumulative distribution for the specified mean and standard deviation.
NORMSDIST(*z*)	Returns the standard normal cumulative distribution (mean = 0, standard deviation = 1).
PERCENTILE(*array, k*)	Computes the kth percentile of data in a range.
POISSON(*x, mean, cumulative*)	Returns the Poisson distribution.
QUARTILE(*array, quart*)	Computes the quartile of a distribution.
SKEW(*data range*)	Computes the skewness, a measure of the degree to which a distribution is not symmetric around its mean.
STANDARDIZE(*x, mean, standard_deviation*)	Returns a normalized value for a distribution characterized by a mean and standard deviation.
STDEV(*data range*)	Computes the standard deviation of a set of data, assumed to be a sample.
STDEVP(*data range*)	Computes the standard deviation of a set of data, assumed to be an entire population.
TREND(*known_y's, known_x's, new_x's, constant*)	Returns values along a linear trend line.
TTEST(*arrayl, array2, tails, type*)	Returns the probability associated with a *t*-test.
VAR(*data range*)	Computes the variance of a set of data, assumed to be a sample.
VARP(*data range*)	Computes the variance of a set of data, assumed to be an entire population.
WEIBULL(*x, alpha, beta, cumulative*)	Returns the Weibull distribution.
ZTEST(*array, x, sigma*)	Returns the two-tailed *p*-value of a *z*-test.

STATISTICS, DATA ANALYSIS, AND DECISION MODELING

Second Edition

James R. Evans
University of Cincinnati

David L. Olson
University of Nebraska

PRENTICE HALL
UPPER SADDLE RIVER, NJ 07458

Library of Congress Cataloging-in-Publication Data

Evans, James R. (James Robert), [date]
    Statistics, data analysis, and decision modeling/James R. Evans,
      David L. Olson. —2nd ed.
        p. cm.
    Includes index.
    ISBN 0-13-067553-9
    1. Industrial management—Statistical methods.   2. Statistical decision.
    I. Olson, David
  Louis. II. Title.
  HD30.215 .E93 2003
  658.4'033—dc21

2002024248

Acquisitions Editor: Tom Tucker
Editor-in-Chief: PJ Boardman
Assistant Editor: Erika Rusnak
Editorial Assistant: Jisun Lee
Media Project Manager: Nancy Welcher
Marketing Manager: Debbie Clare
Managing Editor (Production): John Roberts
Production Editor: Renata Butera
Production Assistant: Dianne Falcone
Permissions Coordinator: Suzanne Grappi
Associate Director, Manufacturing: Vincent Scelta
Production Manager: Arnold Vila
Manufacturing Buyer: Michelle Klein
Art Director: Jayne Conte
Cover Design: Bruce Kenselaar
Cover Illustration/Photo: Kiwi Design
Composition: Progressive Information Technology
Full-Service Project Management: Progressive Publishing Alternatives
Printer/Binder: Hamilton Printing Company

To our wives, Beverly and Meri, for all their encouragement and understanding.

—James R. Evans and David L. Olson

Credits and acknowledgments borrowed from other sources and reproduced, with permission, in this textbook appear on appropriate page within text. Microsoft Excel, Solver, and Windows are registered trademarks of Microsoft Corporation in the U.S.A. and other countries. Screen shots and icons reprinted with permission from the Microsoft Corporation. This book is not sponsored or endorsed by or affiliated with Microsoft Corporation.

Pearson Education LTD.
Pearson Education Australia PTY, Limited
Pearson Education Singapore, Pte. Ltd
Pearson Education North Asia Ltd
Pearson Education, Canada, Ltd
Pearson Educación de Mexico, S.A. de C.V.
Pearson Education–Japan
Pearson Education Malaysia, Pte. Ltd

1 0 9 8 7 6 5
ISBN 0-13-067553-9

Brief Contents

Contents

Preface

In recent years, we have seen a rather significant trend in business schools as Microsoft Excel and other spreadsheet add-ins have become the principal tool for applications of quantitative methods. *Statistics, Data Analysis, and Decision Modeling* was initially written to meet the need for an introductory text that provides a basic introduction to business statistics, focusing on practical applications of data analysis and decision modeling. To support this purpose, we have integrated fundamental theory and practical applications in a spreadsheet environment. Spreadsheet add-ins, specifically *PHStat*, a collection of statistical tools that enhance the capabilities of Excel, published by Pearson Education; the student version of *Crystal Ball* (including *CBPredictor* for forecasting and *OptQuest* for optimization), the most popular commercial package for risk analysis; *TreePlan*, a decision analysis add-in; and *Premium Solver*, a more powerful version of Excel's *Solver*, are used for additional analysis capability.

The second edition of this book has been updated and expanded to better meet the needs of our users and provide more flexibility for use in shorter, modular courses. The most significant changes are

1. Increased coverage of simulation and optimization, resulting in the net addition of three chapters
2. A more complete coverage of important statistical topics, better aligned with the capabilities of *PHStat2*
3. An assortment of new data sets for both illustrative examples and problems
4. Many new problems and exercises from a variety of disciplines

Users of the first edition will also note that the Tracway scenario and database have been converted to case problems and exercises at the end of each chapter.

The book consists of 12 chapters. The first seven chapters deal with statistical and data analysis topics, while the last five chapters deal with decision modeling and applications.

- Chapter 1, "Data and Business Decisions," describes the importance of, and types of data used in, business decision making. This chapter also provides the foundation for working with Excel and other add-ins and introduces some fundamental concepts of measurement, sample data, and decision models. The coverage of basic Excel skills has been increased, and new topics such as data tables and *PivotTables* have been included.
- Chapter 2, "Displaying and Summarizing Data," focuses on data visualization and descriptive statistics. We have added a new section on contingency tables and cross tabulations, as well as many new examples.
- Chapter 3, "Random Variables and Probability Distributions," introduces basic concepts of probability distributions, random sampling, sampling distributions, and sampling error. *Crystal Ball* is introduced and used as a tool for simulating sampling distributions to gain insight into their nature. New material on probability and probability calculations has been added in this edition, as well as a revised treatment of Monte Carlo methods in statistics.

- Chapter 4, "Sampling and Statistical Inference," addresses sampling methods, statistical analysis of sample data, estimation, and hypothesis testing. This edition provides increased coverage of confidence intervals and hypothesis testing. It also provides an introduction to analysis of variance and distribution fitting using *Crystal Ball*.
- Chapter 5, "Regression Analysis," introduces fundamental concepts and methods of both single and multiple regression. Stepwise regression is included in this edition.
- Chapter 6, "Forecasting," discusses both qualitative and quantitative forecasting methods. These include statistical time series models and applications of regression analysis to forecasting. The topics are arranged to facilitate the use of *CBPredictor* as an Excel-based tool.
- Chapter 7, "Statistical Quality Control," develops some applications of statistical concepts presented in the previous chapters to the design and use of control charts and process capability studies.
- Chapter 8, "Risk Analysis and Monte Carlo Simulation," is the first of two chapters that deal with simulation. In this edition we provide a more complete coverage of Monte Carlo simulation with *Crystal Ball* and its applications to risk analysis.
- Chapter 9, "System Simulation Modeling and Analysis," is new to this edition and provides a basic introduction to concepts of dynamic simulation, all within a spreadsheet environment. This provides students with the ability to gain a solid understanding of simulation concepts, while not requiring additional time to learn a commercial simulation language or software package.
- Chapter 10, "Selection Models and Decision Analysis," is expanded in this edition to provide a more complete coverage of decision trees (using *TreePlan*). Other new topics include scoring models, the analytic hierarchy process, and portfolio risk.
- Chapter 11, "Optimization Modeling," introduces basic concepts of linear, integer, and nonlinear optimization models and spreadsheet formulations. A variety of new examples such as blending, media selection, cash management, distribution center location, and Markowitz portfolio models are included in this edition to provide better insight into the modeling process and applications of optimization.
- Chapter 12, "Solving and Analyzing Optimization Models," describes the use of Excel *Solver* and *Premium Solver* for solving linear, integer, and nonlinear optimization models. This chapter also illustrates how Monte Carlo simulation can provide additional insight about optimization results and how search procedures such as *OptQuest* can be used in stochastic problem environments.

The first six or seven chapters can be used for a one-quarter or shorter module for introductory statistics. The second part of the book can be used for a follow-up course on decision models and optimization. The book can also be used for a semester course on both topics.

Throughout the book we have placed boxed "Notes" for Excel, *PHStat,* and *Crystal Ball* that provide procedural details of using specific functions, tools, or techniques. These provide key information for the student to apply the tools but do not disrupt from the flow of the discussion. The CD-ROM accompanying this book contains all the data and model files used throughout the book, *PHStat,* the student version of *Crystal Ball, TreePlan* software and documentation, and *Premium Solver.*

We would like to thank the following individuals who have provided reviews, suggestions, and guidance during the development of both editions of this book: Samir

Barman, University of Oklahoma; James Cochran, University of Cincinnati; Lillian Fok, University of New Orleans; Soumen Ghosh, Georgia Institute of Technology; Jim Grayson, Augusta State University; Peter Jurkat, Stevens Institute of Technology; Ina Markham, James Madison University; Tom McCullough, University of California at Berkeley; David Pentico, Duquesne University; Barbara Price, Georgia Southern University; Jeffrey Rummell, University of Connecticut at Storrs; Barbara Russell, Saint Bonaventure University; and Lee Tangedahl, University of Montana.

In addition, we thank our students who provided numerous suggestions, data sets and problem ideas, and insights into how to better present the material. Finally, we express our appreciation to our editor Tom Tucker, and the entire production staff at Pearson Education for their dedication in developing and producing this book. If you have any suggestions or corrections, please contact us care of james.evans@uc.edu.

James R. Evans
David L. Olson

PART

I

STATISTICS AND DATA ANALYSIS

CHAPTER

1

DATA AND BUSINESS DECISIONS

INTRODUCTION

A phrase one often hears in many companies today is "In God we trust; all others use data." Modern organizations truly manage by fact—they depend upon complete and accurate data for performance evaluation, improvement, and decision making. However, many organizations ignore the most important data they need to make good decisions. This may occur for several reasons:

1. They may not fully understand what to measure or how to measure.
2. They may be reluctant to spend the required time and effort.
3. They may feel they can make decisions by instinct and do not need data.
4. They may fear discovering problems or poor performance that data may uncover.

Even if organizations do gather data, they may not interpret them properly.

Information derives from analysis of data. *Analysis* refers to extracting larger meaning from data to support evaluation and decision making. One of the most important tools for analyzing data in business is **statistics,** which is the science of *collecting, organizing, analyzing, interpreting,* and *presenting* data. Modern spreadsheet technology, such as Microsoft Excel, has made it quite easy to organize, analyze, and present data.

Data also provide key inputs to decision models. A **decision model** is a logical or mathematical representation of a problem or business situation. Decision models establish a relationship between actions that a decision maker might take and results that he or she might expect, thereby allowing the decision maker to predict what might happen based on the model assumptions. For instance, the manager of a grocery store might want to know how best to use price promotions, coupon programs, and advertising to increase sales. In the past, grocers have studied the relationship of sales volume to programs such as these by conducting controlled experiments to identify the relationship between actions and sales volumes.[1] That is, they implement different combinations of price promotions, coupon programs, and advertising (the decision variables), and then observe the sales that result. Using the data from these experiments and a statistical technique known as *regression analysis* (which we cover in Chapter 5), we can develop a predictive model of sales as a function of the decision variables. Such a model might look like the following:

$$\text{Sales} = a + b \cdot \text{Price} + c \cdot \text{Coupons} + d \cdot \text{Advertising} + e \cdot \text{Price} \cdot \text{Advertising}$$

where a, b, c, d, and e are constants that are estimated from the data. By setting levels for price, coupons, and advertising, the model estimates a level of sales. The manager can use the model to identify effective pricing, promotion, and advertising strategies.

Statistics and data analysis have long been critical to business decisions, but they are becoming more important as an increasing amount of electronic information becomes available. These techniques help managers to determine trends, projections, cause-and-effect relationships, and other significant meanings of data that might not be evident. The purpose of this book is to introduce you to practical approaches for analyzing data, ways of using data effectively to make informed decisions, and approaches for developing, analyzing, and solving models of decision problems. Part I of this book (Chapters 1–7) focuses on key issues of data analysis, and Part II (Chapters 8–12) introduces you to various types of decision models that rely on good data analysis.

In this chapter we discuss the roles of data analysis and decision models in business, discuss how data are used in evaluating business performance, introduce some fundamental issues of statistics and measurement, and introduce spreadsheets as a support tool for data analysis and decision modeling. The key concepts we will discuss are

- The importance of statistical thinking in business
- The scope of business performance data and the concept of a "balanced scorecard," as well as the use of data outside the business environment
- The role of statistics: using sample data to understand and draw inferences about populations and monitor the effectiveness of business processes
- Classification of data and common types of measurement scales
- The notion of a decision model and various types that you will learn about in later chapters
- Basic Microsoft Excel skills, and add-ins that are supplied with this book
- Using Excel to manipulate data

STATISTICAL THINKING IN BUSINESS

The importance of applying statistical concepts to make good business decisions and improve performance cannot be overemphasized. **Statistical thinking** is a philosophy of learning and action for improvement that is based on the principles that

---

[1] "Flanking in a Price War," *Interfaces,* Vol. 19, No. 2, 1989, 1–12.

1. All work occurs in a system of interconnected processes.
2. Variation exists in all processes.
3. Understanding and reducing variation are keys to success.[2]

Work gets done in any organization through **processes**—systematic ways of doing things that achieve desired results. Understanding processes provides the context for determining the effects of variation and the proper type of action to be taken. Any process contains many sources of variation. In manufacturing, for example, different lots of material vary in strength, thickness, or moisture content. Cutting tools have inherent variation in their strength and composition. During manufacturing, tools experience wear, vibrations cause changes in machine settings, and electrical fluctuations cause variations in power. Workers do not position parts on fixtures consistently, and physical and emotional stress affect workers' consistency. In addition, measurement gauges and human inspection capabilities are not uniform, resulting in variation in measurements even when the true value is constant. The complex interactions of these variations in materials, tools, machines, operators, and the environment are not easily understood and are often referred to as *common causes* of variation. Other variations, which we generally call *special causes,* arise from external sources that are not inherent in the process. Common factors that lead to special causes are a bad batch of material from a supplier, a poorly trained substitute machine operator, a broken or worn tool, or miscalibration of measuring instruments. These typically result in unusual variation that disrupts the statistical pattern of common causes.

While variation exists everywhere, many business decisions do not often account for it, and managers frequently confuse common and special causes of variation and try to take action to eliminate a perceived special cause when it in fact is simply common-cause variation. For example, if sales in some region fell from the previous year, the regional manager might quickly blame her sales staff for not working hard. If a new advertising campaign happens to coincide with a drop in sales, some managers would quickly drop the ad campaign without any further analysis. How often do managers make decisions based on a single data point or two, seeing trends when they don't exist, or manipulate financial figures they cannot truly control? Usually, it is simply a matter of ignorance of how to deal with data and information. A better approach would be to formulate a theory ("Certain ad campaigns positively affect sales") and test this theory in some way, either by collecting and analyzing some data ("Measure change in sales when advertising is adopted") and perhaps developing a model of the situation that will provide better insight ("When advertising is increased by 10 percent, sales increase by 15 percent"). Using statistical thinking in this fashion can provide much better insight into the true facts and nature of relationships among the many factors that may have contributed to the event.

The lack of broad and sustained use of statistical thinking in many organizations is due to two reasons.[3] First, statisticians historically have functioned as problem solvers in manufacturing, research, and development and thereby have focused on individual clients rather than on organizations. Second, statisticians have focused primarily on technical aspects of statistics rather than emphasizing process definition, measurement, control, and improvement—the key activities that will lead to bottom-line results. Recently, however, many organizations, including General Electric, Allied Signal, and Ford Motor Company just to name a few, are implementing "Six Sigma"

---

[2] Galen Britz, Don Emerling, Lynne Hare, Roger Hoerl, and Janice Shade, "How to Teach Others to Apply Statistical Thinking," *Quality Progress,* June 1997, 67–79.
[3] Ronald D. Snee, "Getting Better Business Results: Using Statistical Thinking and Methods to Shape the Bottom Line," *Quality Progress,* June 1998, 102–106.

initiatives and training all employees in statistical thinking and other problem-solving tools and techniques to improve organizational effectiveness and financial performance. The material in this book will provide the foundation for more advanced topics found in Six Sigma training.

DATA IN THE BUSINESS ENVIRONMENT

A recent example from Boeing Corporation shows the value of good data analysis.[4] In the early 1990s, Boeing's assembly lines were morasses of inefficiency. A manual numbering system dating back to World War II bomber days was used to keep track of an airplane's four million parts and 170 miles of wiring; changing a part on a 737's landing gear meant renumbering 464 pages of drawings. Factory floors were covered with huge tubs of spare parts worth millions of dollars. In an attempt to grab market share from rival Airbus, the company discounted planes deeply and was buried by an onslaught of orders. The attempt to double production rates, coupled with implementation of a new production control system, resulted in Boeing being forced to shut down its 737 and 747 lines for 27 days in October 1997, leading to a $178 million loss and a shakeup of top management. Much of the blame was focused on Boeing's financial practices and lack of real-time financial data. With a new CFO and finance team, the company created a "control panel" of vital measures, such as material costs, inventory turns, overtime, and defects, using a color-coded spreadsheet. For the first time, Boeing was able to generate a series of bar charts showing which of its programs were creating value and which were destroying it. The results were eye-opening and helped formulate a growth plan. As one manager noted, "The data will set you free."

Data and analysis support a variety of company purposes, such as planning, reviewing company performance, improving operations, and comparing company performance with competitors' or "best practices" benchmarks. Data that organizations use should focus on critical success factors that lead to competitive advantage. Most organizations have traditionally focused on financial and market information, such as profit, sales volume, and market share. Today, however, many organizations create a "balanced scorecard" of measures that provide a comprehensive view of business performance. Such a scorecard is balanced by the interests of all stakeholders—customers, employees, stockholders, suppliers and partners, and the community—and allows organizations to focus on the critical success factors that lead to competitive advantage.

The term **balanced scorecard** was coined by Robert Kaplan and David Norton of the Harvard Business School in response to the limitations of traditional accounting measures.[5] Its purpose is "to translate strategy into measures that uniquely communicate your vision to the organization." Their version of the balanced scorecard consists of four perspectives:

- *Financial Perspective.*   Measures the ultimate results that the business provides to its shareholders. This includes profitability, revenue growth, return on investment, asset utilization, operating margins, earnings per share, economic value added (EVA), shareholder value, and other relevant measures.
- *Internal Perspective.*   Focuses attention on the performance of the key internal processes that drive the business. This includes such measures as quality levels, productivity, process yields, cycle time, cost, and legal compliance.

---

[4] Jerry Useem, "Boeing Versus Boeing," *Fortune,* October 2, 2000, 148–160.
[5] Robert S. Kaplan and David P. Norton, *The Balanced Scorecard* (Boston: Harvard Business School Press, 1996).

- *Customer Perspective.*   Focuses on customer needs and satisfaction as well as market share. This includes service levels, satisfaction ratings, repeat business, and other indicators such as complaints.
- *Innovation and Learning Perspective.*   Directs attention to the basis of a future success—the organization's people and infrastructure. Key measures might include intellectual assets such as patent filings, employee satisfaction, turnover, market innovation, training effectiveness, skills development, environmental improvements, and supplier performance.

Many organizations have adopted the **dashboard** as an alternative to a balanced scorecard. The term stems from the analogy to an automobile's dashboard—a collection of indicators (speed, RPM, oil pressure, temperature, etc.) that summarizes performance. Whatever the terminology, a good balanced scorecard contains both leading and lagging measures and indicators. **Lagging measures** (outcomes) tell what has happened; **leading measures** (performance drivers) predict what *will* happen. For example, customer survey results about recent transactions might be a leading indicator for customer retention (a lagging indicator), employee satisfaction might be a leading indicator for turnover, and so on.

Two examples illustrate how data can lead to useful decision models. IBM Rochester developed a model to quantify the causal relationships among the key measures in its balanced scorecard. This model suggests that improving internal capabilities such as people skills, product/service quality, and products and channels will lead to improved customer satisfaction and loyalty, which, in turn, lead to improved financial and market share performance. Another example is Sears Roebuck, Inc., which provided a consulting group with 13 financial measures, hundreds of thousands of employee satisfaction data points, and millions of data points on customer satisfaction. Using advanced statistical tools, the analysts discovered that employee attitudes about the job and the company are key factors that predict their behavior with customers, which, in turn, predicts the likelihood of customer retention and recommendations, which, in turn, predict financial performance. Sears can now predict that if a store increases its employee satisfaction score by five units, customer satisfaction scores will go up by 2 units and revenue growth will beat the stores' national average by 0.5 percent.[6] Such an analysis can help managers to make decisions, for instance, on improved human resource policies.

We will illustrate the nature of data and information used in a business by describing their role in Solectron Corporation, a two-time winner of the Malcolm Baldrige National Quality Award.[7] Solectron, based in Milpitas, California, is an independent provider of customized design and manufacturing services to electronics original equipment manufacturers (OEMs). In 1997, the company had 19 global locations and 20,000 employees and annual revenues of $3.7 billion. Among Solectron's services are product design and development, electrical design, concurrent engineering, prototype building, component and packaging selection, printed circuit board assembly, and software and documentation packaging. Figure 1.1 shows how Solectron's performance measures link to their key business processes, business drivers, and company beliefs. These performance measures—an aggregation of raw data collected throughout the firm—are analyzed and evaluated by various managers as a basis for their business decisions. For example, the board of directors reviews customer, business, operational, human resource, and strategy data on a bimonthly basis; all managers review a

---

[6] "Bringing Sears Into the New World," *Fortune,* October 13, 1997, 183–184.
[7] Adapted from Solectron's 1997 Malcolm Baldrige National Quality Award Application Summary. Solectron won the Baldrige Award in 1991 and 1997, becoming the first repeat winner.

Mission	Beliefs	Business Driver	Key Business Processes	Performance Measures
• Custom-integrated services • Worldwide responsiveness • Long-term partnerships • Ethical business practices	1. Customer First (stakeholder— Customer)	• Customer satisfaction	• Market and customer requirements determination • Annual customer survey • Customer satisfaction assurance process	• Overall evaluation of Solectron • Customer satisfaction index (CSI) • Customer return rate • Market share
	2. Respect for the Individual (stakeholder— Employee)	• Employee satisfaction	• Performance planning and evaluation • Training and development • Customer focus team deployment	• EOS • Absenteeism • Lost time per employee • Turnover
Vision Be the best and continuously improve.	3. Quality (stakeholders— Customer and Stockholder)	• Product quality • Process capability	• Continuous improvement • Benchmark industry performance • Hoshin planning	• Test and inspection yields • Manufacturing performance and delivery
	4. Supplier Partnership (stakeholder— Supplier)	• Supply quality and assurance	• Supply base management	• Supplier reject rates • Strategic supplier relationships
	5. Business Ethics (all stakeholders)	• Customer confidence	• Ethical behavior • Understanding customer requirements and Solectron capabilities and then meeting commitments	• Customer likely to recommend Solectron • CSI
	6. Shareholder Value (stakeholder— Stockholder)	• Stockholder satisfaction	• Execute to the long-range plan (LRP) and annual operating plan (AOP) • EMS competitor analysis	• Revenue • PBT • ROA • EPS • PBT per employee
	7. Social Responsibility (stakeholder— Community)	• Environmental friendliness • Employee health and safety • Community involvement	• Environmental regulation compliance and proactive environmental action • Health and safety training, audits, and improvement • Proactive support for Solectron's communities	• Compliance • Recycling • Contributions • Involvement

FIGURE 1.1   Solectron's Information and Data

Source: Solectron 1997 Malcolm Baldrige National Quality Award Application Summary

comprehensive Corporate Scorecard quarterly; and site managers review more detailed performance data daily, weekly, and quarterly. Solectron focuses on timely and actionable information to address the needs of their stakeholders.

SOURCES AND TYPES OF DATA

Business data may come from a variety of sources: internal, external, and generated. Internal data are routinely collected by accounting, marketing, and operations functions of a business. Much of this data might be gathered using modern technology such as bar coding or automated transaction reporting. External data might include competitive performance acquired from annual reports, Standard & Poor's Compustat data sets, or industry trade associations, and government data from the Bureau of Commerce statistics [http://www.tcb-indicators.org/], the Bureau of the Census or the Bureau of Labor, and other cabinet departments. Other data must be generated through special efforts. For example, customer satisfaction data are often acquired by mail or telephone surveys, personal interviews, or focus groups.

The use of statistics, data analysis, and decision models is not limited to business. Science, engineering, medicine, and sports, to name just a few, are examples of professions that rely heavily on these tools. Many of these types of data or statistical results pop up in the daily newspapers and magazines and provide the layperson with some basic notions (which are often flawed!) about statistics. Table 1.1 provides a list of data files that are available in the Statistics Data Files folder on the CD-ROM accompanying this book. All are saved in Microsoft Excel 97-2000 & 5.0/95 Workbook format. These data files will be used throughout the first seven chapters to illustrate various issues associated with statistics and data analysis and also for many of the questions and problems at the end of the chapters. They show but a sample of the wide variety of applications for which statistics and data analysis techniques may be used.

Data Classification

When we deal with data sets, it is important to understand the nature of the data in order to select the appropriate statistical tool or procedure. One classification of data is the following:

1. Type of data
   - *Cross-sectional*—data that are collected over a single period of time
   - *Time series*—data collected over time
2. Number of variables
   - *Univariate*—data consisting of a single variable
   - *Multivariate*—data consisting of two or more (often related) variables

Figures 1.2–1.5 show examples of data sets from Table 1.1 representing each combination from this classification.

Another classification of data is by the type of measurement scale. Failure to understand the differences in measurement scales can easily result in erroneous or misleading analysis. Data may be classified into four groups:

1. **Categorical (nominal) data,** which are sorted into categories according to specified characteristics. For example, a firm's customers might be classified by their geographical region (North America, South America, Europe, and Pacific); employees might be classified as managers, supervisors, and associates. The categories bear no quantitative relationship to one another, but we usually assign an arbitrary number to each category to ease the process of managing the data and computing statistics. Categorical

TABLE 1.1   Data Files Available on CD-ROM

Business and Economics

30 Year Mortgage Rates.xls	*Energy Production & Consumption.xls*
Accounting Professionals.xls	*Gas & Electric.xls*
Automobile Quality.xls	*HATCO.xls*
Baldrige.xls	*House Sales Data.xls*
California Disposable Income.xls	*Housing Starts.xls*
Call Center Data.xls	*Market Value.xls*
Coal Consumption.xls	*Prime Rate.xls*
Computer and Software Sales.xls	*Room Inspection.xls*
Consumer Price Index.xls	*Salary Data.xls*
Customer Support Survey Data.xls	*Syringe Data.xls*
Economic Indexes.xls	*Tracway Database.xls*

Social Sciences

Arizona Population.xls	*Ohio Education Performance.xls*
Burglaries.xls	*Ohio Prison Population.xls*
Census Education Data.xls	*Self Esteem.xls*
Demographics.xls	*TV Viewing.xls*
Infant Mortality.xls	*Unions and Labor Law Data.xls*

Health and Medicine

Blood Pressure.xls	*Smoking and Cancer.xls*
Cereal Data.xls	*Surgeries.xls*

Physical Sciences

US Average Temperatures.xls	*Weather.xls*
Washington DC Weather.xls	

Engineering

Pile Foundation.xls	*Surface Finish.xls*

Sports

1999 Baseball Data.xls	*NASCAR Track Data.xls*
2000 NFL Data.xls	*Olympic Track and Field Data.xls*
Baseball Attendance.xls	

data are usually counted or expressed as percents; statistics such as averages are difficult to interpret and are usually meaningless.

2.   **Ordinal data,** which are ordered or ranked according to some relationship to one another. For instance, J. D. Power and Associates' Initial Quality Study ranks new cars and trucks according to how many problems per 100 vehicles that owners report experiencing in the first 90 days. Other examples include ranking regions according to sales levels each month and NCAA basketball rankings. Ordinal data are more meaningful than categorical data because data in different categories can be compared to one another according to some characteristic. In the 2001 Initial Quality Study, the top five were Lexus, Jaguar, Acura, BMW, and Saab; this ordinal ranking means that Lexus had lower rates of reported problems than the makes that follow. However, like categorical data, averages are generally meaningless, because ordinal data have no fixed units of

	A	B	C	D
1	2001 J.D. Powers Initial Quality Study Rankings			
2	Rank	Brand	Problems per 100 vehicles	
3	1	Lexus	85	
4	2	Jaguar	108	
5	3	Acura	118	
6	4	BMW	119	
7	5	Saab	121	
8	6	Toyota	121	
9	7	Buick	123	
10	8	Infinity	123	
11	9	Cadillac	126	
12	10	Mercedes	129	
13	11	honda	135	
14	12	Chrysler	137	
15	13	Saturn	139	
16	14	Audi	140	
17	15	Porsche	140	

FIGURE 1.2 Example of Cross-Sectional, Univariate Data (portion of file *Automobile Quality.xls*)

measurement. In addition, meaningful numerical statements about differences between categories cannot be made. For example, comparing the average rank of U.S. models versus imports does not meaningfully compare differences in reported problem rates.

3. **Interval data,** which are ordered, have a specified measure of the distance between observations but have no natural zero. A common example is temperature: Both the Fahrenheit and Celsius scales represent a specified measure of distance—degrees—but have no natural zero. Thus we cannot say that 50 degrees is twice as hot as 25 degrees. Nevertheless, in contrast to ordinal data, interval data allow meaningful comparison of ranges, averages, and other statistics.

In business, data from satisfaction and attribute rating scales (for example, 1 = poor, 2 = average, 3 = good, 4 = very good, 5 = excellent) are often considered to be interval data. Strictly speaking, this is not correct, as the numerical "distance" between categories on the measurement scale, such as between *good* and *very good,* is meaningless. If respondents select their response on the basis of the category description, the data are ordinal. However, if respondents clearly understand that response categories are associated with the numerical measurement scale, then the data are interval. Usually, this is a very tenuous assumption but, nevertheless, most users of

FIGURE 1.3 Example of Cross-Sectional, Multivariate Data (portion of file *2000 NFL Data.xls*)

	A	B	C	D	E	F	G
1	Team	Yards Gained	Takeaways	Giveaways	Yards Allowed	Points Scored	Games Won
2	Tennessee	5,350	30	30	3,813	346	13
3	Baltimore	5,014	49	26	3,967	333	12
4	New York Giants	6,376	31	24	4,546	328	12
5	Oakland	5,776	37	20	5,249	479	12
6	Minnesota	5,961	18	28	5,701	397	11
7	Philadelphia	5,006	31	29	4,820	351	11
8	Denver	6,567	44	25	5,544	485	11
9	Miami	4,461	41	26	4,636	323	11
10	Indianapolis	6,141	22	29	5,357	429	10

	A	B
1		
2	Year	Attendance
3	1958	1273
4	1959	1422
5	1960	1795
6	1961	1391
7	1962	1593
8	1963	1571
9	1964	1504
10	1965	1546
11	1966	1657
12	1967	1242
13	1968	1674
14	1969	1652
15	1970	1519
16	1971	2021
17	1972	1569
18	1973	1835
19	1974	1366
20	1975	1601
21	1976	1408
22	1977	1196
23	1978	2267

FIGURE 1.4 Example of Time Series, Univariate Data (portion of file *Baseball Attendance.xls*)

survey data treat such data as interval, and we will make this assumption also in examples and problems. You should remember, however, that care must be taken when collecting and interpreting survey data as interval data.

4. **Ratio data,** which have a natural zero. For example, sales dollars has an absolute zero (no sales activity at all). Knowing that the Seattle region sold $12 million in March while the Tampa region sold $6 million means that Seattle sold twice as much as Tampa. Most business and economic data fall into this category, and statistical methods are the most widely applicable to them.

This classification is hierarchical in that each level includes all of the information content of the one preceding it. For example, ratio information can be converted to any

FIGURE 1.5 Example of Time Series, Multivariate Data (portion of file *Energy Production & Consumption.xls*)

	A	B	C	D	E	F	G	H	I
1	Year	Fossil Fuels Production	Total Energy Production	Petroleum Imports	Total Energy Imports	Coal Exports	Total Energy Exports	Fossil Fuels Consumption	Total Energy Consumption
4	1949	28,748,176	31,722,160	1,427,346	1,468,655	877,294	1,593,798	29,002,098	31,999,960
5	1950	32,562,667	35,540,385	1,886,296	1,933,411	786,496	1,466,882	31,631,956	34,634,733
6	1951	35,792,151	38,750,615	1,872,278	1,916,838	1,682,779	2,623,589	34,008,105	36,996,399
7	1952	34,976,732	37,916,913	2,114,304	2,170,913	1,402,980	2,367,492	33,799,902	36,770,393
8	1953	35,349,337	38,180,797	2,284,823	2,336,137	980,726	1,870,074	34,826,155	37,683,501
9	1954	33,764,330	36,518,429	2,323,614	2,371,442	910,509	1,699,351	33,877,300	36,659,898
10	1955	37,363,679	40,147,666	2,751,505	2,827,756	1,464,521	2,289,649	37,410,105	40,241,679
11	1956	39,771,452	42,622,034	3,166,178	3,248,404	1,984,106	2,950,451	38,888,151	41,790,841
12	1957	40,133,484	42,982,790	3,461,019	3,567,599	2,174,059	3,449,417	38,925,592	41,815,828
13	1958	37,216,322	40,133,327	3,719,106	3,915,660	1,415,843	2,055,669	38,716,703	41,670,485
14	1959	39,045,215	41,948,741	3,910,109	4,109,477	1,051,257	1,540,144	40,550,067	43,492,583
15	1960	39,869,116	42,803,761	3,998,694	4,226,742	1,023,170	1,483,266	42,136,752	45,120,196

	A	B	C	D	E	F	G
1	New Store Financial Analysis Model						
2							
3	Model Assumptions		Year 1	Year 2	Year 3	Year 4	Year 5
4	Annual Growth Rate			20%	12%	9%	5%
5	Sales Revenue		$ 800,000				
6							
7	Cost of Merchandise (% of sales)	30%					
8	Operating Expenses						
9	Labor Cost	$ 200,000					
10	Rent Per Square Foot	$ 28					
11	Other Expenses	$ 325,000					
12							
13	Inflation Rate	2%					
14	Store Size (square feet)	$ 5,000					
15	Total Fixed Assets	$ 300,000					
16	Depreciation period (straight line)	5					
17	Discount Rate	10%					
18	Tax Rate	34%					
19							
20	Model Outputs	Year	1	2	3	4	5
21	Sales Revenue		$ 800,000	$ 960,000	$1,075,200	$1,171,968	$1,230,566
22	Cost of Merchandise		$ 240,000	$ 288,000	$ 322,560	$ 351,590	$ 369,170
23	Operating Expenses						
24	Labor Cost		$ 200,000	$ 204,000	$ 208,080	$ 212,242	$ 216,486
25	Rent Per Square Foot		$ 140,000	$ 142,800	$ 145,656	$ 148,569	$ 151,541
26	Other Expenses		$ 325,000	$ 331,500	$ 338,130	$ 344,893	$ 351,790
27	Net Operating Income		$ (105,000)	$ (6,300)	$ 60,774	$ 114,674	$ 141,579
28	Depreciation Expense		$ 60,000	$ 60,000	$ 60,000	$ 60,000	$ 60,000
29	Net Income Before Tax		$ (165,000)	$ (66,300)	$ 774	$ 54,674	$ 81,579
30	Income Tax		$ (56,100)	$ (22,542)	$ 263	$ 18,589	$ 27,737
31	Net After Tax Income		$ (108,900)	$ (43,758)	$ 511	$ 36,085	$ 53,842
32	Plus Depreciation Expense		$ 60,000	$ 60,000	$ 60,000	$ 60,000	$ 60,000
33	Annual Cash Flow		$ (48,900)	$ 16,242	$ 60,511	$ 96,085	$ 113,842
34	Discounted Cash Flow		(44,454.55)	13,423.14	45,462.69	65,627.36	70,687.05
35	Cumulative Discounted Cash Flow		(44,454.55)	(31,031.40)	14,431.28	80,058.65	150,745.70

FIGURE 1.7 New Store Financial Analysis Model Spreadsheet

Spreadsheets are ideal vehicles for implementing decision models because of their versatility in managing data, evaluating different scenarios, and presenting results in a meaningful fashion. Figure 1.7 shows an example of a financial spreadsheet for evaluating the cash flow of a proposed retail store in a shopping mall, not unlike what you may have seen in accounting and finance classes. This is available in the Decision Models folder on the CD-ROM. The model assumptions are given in rows 4 through 18. The key inputs are the first-year sales, annual growth rates, various cost factors, associated inflation assumptions, and so on. Formulas for computing the model outputs are entered in the lower section of the spreadsheet. Calculating the outputs basically consists of "stepping through" the formulas. The user may experiment with the model by using different assumptions, for example, changing inflation factors or baseline values to answer a variety of "what if?" questions. We will introduce the use of Excel shortly.

Decision models take many different forms. In this book, we introduce five generic types of decision models: *regression, risk analysis, decision analysis, simulation,* and *optimization.* We gave an example of a regression model at the beginning of this chapter. The other types of decision models are briefly explained here:

- **Risk analysis models** support the important business need of assessing risks in the face of uncertainty.
- **Decision analysis models** assist a decision maker in comparing a small number of alternative options and seeking the best choice. Selection models might be used to choose where to build a new factory, how and when to expand capacity, or which new products to develop.

- **Simulation models** help to analyze business decisions that involve high levels of uncertainty. They are used to explain the behavior of systems, to gain better understanding of risks associated with decisions, and to assist decision makers in choosing the best solution or systems design. These might include financial models for which future estimates of sales or costs may vary substantially or models of waiting line systems with random arrivals. A spreadsheet is essentially a deterministic simulation.
- **Optimization models** assist decision makers to identify the best course of action to take, usually when faced with limited resources or other restrictions that must be satisfied. Such decision models have been very useful in problems such as product and process selection, operations scheduling, portfolio design, advertising planning, and many others.

USING MICROSOFT EXCEL

Spreadsheet software for personal computers has become an indispensable tool for business analysis, particularly for the manipulation of numerical data and the development and analysis of decision models. In this text, we will use Microsoft Excel to perform most calculations and analyses.

Basic Excel Skills

To be able to apply statistical procedures and decision modeling techniques in this book, it is necessary for you to know many of the basic capabilities of Excel. We will assume that you are familiar with the most elementary spreadsheet concepts and procedures, such as

- Opening, saving, and printing files
- Moving around a spreadsheet
- Selecting ranges
- Inserting/deleting rows and columns
- Entering and editing text, numerical data, and formulas
- Formatting data (number, currency, decimal places, etc.)
- Working with text strings
- Performing basic arithmetic calculations
- Formatting data and text
- Modifying the appearance of the spreadsheet

Excel has extensive online help, and many good manuals and training guides are available both in print and online, and we urge you to take advantage of these. However, to facilitate your understanding and ability, we will review some of the more important topics in Excel that you may not have used. Other tools and procedures in Excel, such as creating graphs and charts, will be introduced as we need them throughout this book.

Copying Formulas and Cell References

Excel provides several ways of copying formulas to different cells. This is extremely useful in building decision models, since many models required replication of formulas for different trials. One way is to select a cell, choose *Edit . . . Copy* from the menu bar (or click on the *Copy* icon or simply press Ctrl-C on your keyboard), click on the cell you wish to copy to, and then choose *Edit . . . Paste* (or click on the *Paste* icon or press Ctrl-V). To copy a formula from a single cell or range of cells down a column or across a row, first select the cell or range, then click and hold the mouse on the small square in the lower right-hand corner of the cell (the "drag handle"), and drag the formula to the "target" cells you wish to copy to (see Figures 1.8 and 1.9 for an example of copying

Year	1	2	3	4	5
	$ 800,000	$ 960,000			
	$ 240,000	$ 288,000			
	$ 200,000	$ 204,000			
	$ 140,000	$ 142,800			
	$ 325,000	$ 331,500			
	$ (105,000)	$ (6,300)			
	$ 60,000	$ 60,000			
	$ (165,000)	$ (66,300)			
	$ (56,100)	$ (22,542)			
	$ (108,900)	$ (43,758)			
	$ 60,000	$ 60,000			
	$ (48,900)	$ 16,242			
	(44,454.55)	13,423.14			
	(44,454.55)	(31,031.40)			

Click here and drag to the right

FIGURE 1.8 Highlighting a Range of Formulas to Copy

the formulas for years 3 through 5 in the financial spreadsheet model introduced in Figure 1.7). You may enter a formula directly in a range of cells without copying and pasting by selecting the range, typing in the formula, and then pressing Ctrl-Enter.

In any of these procedures, the *structure* of the formula is the same as in the original cell, but the cell references have been changed to reflect the *relative addresses* of the formula in the new cells. That is, the new cell references have the same relative relationship to the new formula cell(s) as they did in the original formula cell. Thus, if a formula is copied (or moved) one cell to the right, the relative cell addresses will have their column label increased by one; if we copy or move the formula two cells down, the row number is increased by 2. Figure 1.10 shows the formulas for the financial spreadsheet model. For example, note that the formulas in row 21 for years 3, 4, and 5 are the same as for year 2, except for the column reference.

Sometimes, however, you do not want to change the relative addressing because you would like all the copied formulas to point to a certain cell. We do this by using a $ before the column or row address of the cell. This is called an *absolute address*. For example, in Figure 1.10, we want to use the same inflation factor for all years; therefore, we define the reference to the inflation factor in cell B13 as $B$13. Then, if we copy this formula in rows 24 through 26 in column D across to columns E, F, and G, the reference will still point to cell B13. If we had not used an absolute address and copied the formulas, then the reference to cell B13 in column E, for instance, would have been changed to C13, resulting in an incorrect formula. You should be very careful to use

FIGURE 1.9 Result of Copying a Range of Formulas

Year	1	2	3	4	5
	$ 800,000	$ 960,000	$1,075,200	$1,171,968	$1,230,566
	$ 240,000	$ 288,000	$ 322,560	$ 351,590	$ 369,170
	$ 200,000	$ 204,000	$ 208,080	$ 212,242	$ 216,486
	$ 140,000	$ 142,800	$ 145,656	$ 148,569	$ 151,541
	$ 325,000	$ 331,500	$ 338,130	$ 344,893	$ 351,790
	$ (105,000)	$ (6,300)	$ 60,774	$ 114,674	$ 141,579
	$ 60,000	$ 60,000	$ 60,000	$ 60,000	$ 60,000
	$ (165,000)	$ (66,300)	$ 774	$ 54,674	$ 81,579
	$ (56,100)	$ (22,542)	$ 263	$ 18,589	$ 27,737
	$ (108,900)	$ (43,758)	$ 511	$ 36,085	$ 53,842
	$ 60,000	$ 60,000	$ 60,000	$ 60,000	$ 60,000
	$ (48,900)	$ 16,242	$ 60,511	$ 96,085	$ 113,842
	(44,454.55)	13,423.14	45,462.69	65,627.36	70,687.05
	(44,454.55)	(31,031.40)	14,431.28	80,058.65	150,745.70

	C	D	E	F	G
20	1	2	3	4	5
21	=C5	=C21*(1+D4)	=D21*(1+E4)	=E21*(1+F4)	=F21*(1+G4)
22	=$B$7*C21	=$B$7*D21	=$B$7*E21	=$B$7*F21	=$B$7*G21
23					
24	=B9	=C24*(1+$B$13)	=D24*(1+$B$13)	=E24*(1+$B$13)	=F24*(1+$B$13)
25	=$B$10*$B$14	=C25*(1+$B$13)	=D25*(1+$B$13)	=E25*(1+$B$13)	=F25*(1+$B$13)
26	=B11	=C26*(1+$B$13)	=D26*(1+$B$13)	=E26*(1+$B$13)	=F26*(1+$B$13)
27	=C21-C22-C24-C25-C26	=D21-D22-D24-D25-D26	=E21-E22-E24-E25-E26	=F21-F22-F24-F25-F26	=G21-G22-G24-G25-G26
28	=$B$15/$B$16	=$B$15/$B$16	=$B$15/$B$16	=$B$15/$B$16	=$B$15/$B$16
29	=C27-C28	=D27-D28	=E27-E28	=F27-F28	=G27-G28
30	=C29*$B$18	=D29*$B$18	=E29*$B$18	=F29*$B$18	=G29*$B$18
31	=C29-C30	=D29-D30	=E29-E30	=F29-F30	=G29-G30
32	=C28	=D28	=E28	=F28	=G28
33	=C31+C32	=D31+D32	=E31+E32	=F31+F32	=G31+G32
34	=C33/(1+$B$17)^C20	=D33/(1+$B$17)^D20	=E33/(1+$B$17)^E20	=F33/(1+$B$17)^F20	=G33/(1+$B$17)^G20
35	=C34	=C35+D34	=D35+E34	=E35+F34	=F35+G34

FIGURE 1.10   Financial Spreadsheet Model Formulas

relative and absolute addressing appropriately in your models. An easy way to make a cell reference absolute or partially absolute is to press the F4 key after entering the cell reference in a formula. For instance, if you enter =A1 in a cell and press F4 repeatedly, the formula changes to $A$1, then A$1, then $A1, and then back to A1.

Functions

Functions are used to perform special calculations in cells. Some of the more common functions that we will see are:

MIN(*range*)—finds the smallest value in a range of cells

MAX(*range*)—finds the largest value in a range of cells

SUM(*range*)—finds the sum of values in a range of cells

AVERAGE(*range*)—finds the average of the values in a range of cells

AND(*condition 1, condition 2, . . .*)—a logical function that returns TRUE if all conditions are true, and FALSE if not

OR(*condition 1, condition 2, . . .*)—a logical function that returns TRUE if any condition is true, and FALSE if not

IF(*condition, value if true, value if false*)—a logical function that returns one value if the condition is true and another if the condition is false

VLOOKUP(*value, table range, column number*)—looks up a value in a table

Excel has many other functions for statistical, financial and other applications, many of which we will use throughout the text. The easiest way to locate a particular function is to select a cell and then click on the *Paste function* button "f_x" on the toolbar. This is particularly useful even if you know what function to use but you are not sure of what arguments to enter. Figure 1.11 shows the dialog box from which you may select the function you wish to use, in this case, the AVERAGE function. Once this is selected, the dialog box in Figure 1.12 appears. When you click in an input cell, a description of the argument is shown. Thus, if you were not sure what to enter for the argument Number 1, the explanation in Figure 1.12 will help you. For further information, you could click on the Help button in the lower left-hand corner.

The IF function, *IF(condition, value if true, value if false),* allows you to choose one of two values to enter into a cell. If the specified *condition* is true, value A will be put in the cell. If the condition is false, value B will be entered. For example, if cell C2 contains the function =IF(A8=2,7,12), it states that if the value in cell A8 is 2, the number 7 will be assigned to cell C2; if the value in cell A8 is not 2, the number 12 will be assigned to cell C2. "Conditions" may include

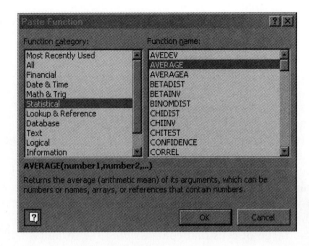

FIGURE 1.11   *Paste Function* Dialog Box

=   equal to
\>   greater than
\<   less than
\>=   greater than or equal to
\<=   less than or equal to
\<\>   not equal to

You may "nest" IF functions by replacing *value-if-true* or *value-if-false* in an IF function with another IF function; for example:

$$=IF(A8=2, IF(B3=5,(("YES",""),15)$$

This says that if cell A8 equals 2, then check the contents of cell B3. If cell B3 is 5, then the value of the function is the text string YES; if not, it is a blank space (a text string that is blank). However, if cell A8 is not 2, then the value of the function is 15 no matter what cell B3 is. You may use AND and OR functions as the *condition* within an IF function, for example: IF(AND(B1=3,C1=5),12,22). Here, if cell B1=3 and cell C1=5, then the value of the function is 12, otherwise it is 22.

Data Tables
Excel allows you to construct two types of data tables. Data tables are useful for performing **sensitivity analyses** on key variables in decision models. Sensitivity analysis asks the question: How does a change in one or more input variables affect the output

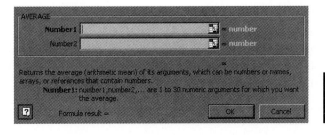

FIGURE 1.12   AVERAGE *Paste Function* Input Dialog Box

of the model? A **one-way data table** evaluates an output variable over a range of values for a single input variable. The input values must be listed either down a column (column-oriented) or across a row (row-oriented). Formulas used in a one-way data table must refer to an input cell, that is, a cell to which the input values in the data table refer.

1. Type the list of values you want to substitute in the input cell either down one column or across one row.
2. If the input values are listed down a column, type the formula (or reference a cell in your model) in the row above the first value and one cell to the right of the column of values. Type any additional formulas to the right of the first formula. If the input values are listed across a row, type the formula in the column to the left of the first value and one cell below the row of values. Type any additional formulas below the first formula.
3. Select the range of cells that contains *both* the formulas and values you want to substitute.
4. On the *Data* menu, click *Table*.
5. If the data table is column-oriented, type the cell reference for the input cell in the *Column input cell* box. If the data table is row-oriented, type the cell reference for the input cell in the *Row input cell* box.

I	J
	192,471.13
2.00%	
2.10%	
2.20%	
2.30%	
2.40%	
2.50%	
2.60%	
2.70%	
2.80%	
2.90%	
3.00%	
3.10%	
3.20%	
3.30%	
3.40%	
3.50%	
3.60%	
3.70%	
3.80%	
3.90%	
4.00%	

FIGURE 1.13
Creating a One-Way Data Table

To illustrate this, suppose we wish to evaluate the cumulative discounted cash flow in the new store model in Figure 1.7 (cell G35) for inflation rates from 2 to 4 percent in increments of 0.1 percent. We first create a column of these values in cells I3 to I23 and enter the formula =G35 in cell J2, as shown in Figure 1.13. Then highlight the range I2:J23, choose *Table* from the *Data* menu, and enter B13 for the *Column input cell*. The result is shown in Figure 1.14.

Two-way data tables use only one formula with two lists of input values. The formula must refer to two different input cells.

1. In a cell on the worksheet, enter the formula that refers to the two input cells.
2. Type one list of input values in the same column, below the formula. Type the second list in the same row, to the right of the formula.
3. Select the range of cells that contains the formula and both the row and column of values.
4. On the *Data* menu, click *Table*.
5. In the *Row input cell* box, enter the reference for the input cell for the input values in the row.
6. In the *Column input cell* box, enter the reference for the input cell for the input values in the column.

An example of a two-way data table that varies the inflation rate and the store size is shown in Figure 1.15. To create this table, we enter B14 as the *Row input cell* and B13 as the *Column input cell*.

FIGURE 1.14
One-Way Data Table Result

I	J
	$192,471.13
2.00%	$192,471.13
2.10%	$188,692.84
2.20%	$184,907.06
2.30%	$181,113.79
2.40%	$177,313.01
2.50%	$173,504.72
2.60%	$169,688.89
2.70%	$165,865.52
2.80%	$162,034.61
2.90%	$158,196.13
3.00%	$154,350.07
3.10%	$150,496.43
3.20%	$146,635.20
3.30%	$142,766.35
3.40%	$138,889.89
3.50%	$135,005.80
3.60%	$131,114.07
3.70%	$127,214.69
3.80%	$123,307.64
3.90%	$119,392.92
4.00%	$115,470.51

Other Useful Excel Tips

- *Split Screen.* You may split the worksheet horizontally and/or vertically to view different parts of the worksheet at the same time. The vertical splitter bar is just to the right of the bottom scroll bar, and the horizontal splitter bar is just above the right-hand scroll bar. Position your cursor over one of these until it changes shape, click, and drag the splitter bar to the left or down.

- *Paste Special.* When you normally copy (one or more) cells and paste them in a worksheet, Excel places an exact copy of the formulas or data in the cells (except for

L	M	N	O	P	Q
$192,471.13	4000	4500	5000	5500	6000
2.00%	$273,478.29	$232,974.71	$192,471.13	$151,967.55	$111,463.97
2.10%	$269,859.08	$229,275.96	$188,692.84	$148,109.72	$107,526.59
2.20%	$266,232.71	$225,569.89	$184,907.06	$144,244.24	$103,581.42
2.30%	$262,599.15	$221,856.47	$181,113.79	$140,371.11	$ 99,628.43
2.40%	$258,958.41	$218,135.71	$177,313.01	$136,490.32	$ 95,667.62
2.50%	$255,310.46	$214,407.59	$173,504.72	$132,601.84	$ 91,698.97
2.60%	$251,655.30	$210,672.10	$169,688.89	$128,705.69	$ 87,722.48
2.70%	$247,992.92	$206,929.22	$165,865.52	$124,801.83	$ 83,738.13
2.80%	$244,323.30	$203,178.95	$162,034.61	$120,890.26	$ 79,745.91
2.90%	$240,646.44	$199,421.28	$158,196.13	$116,970.97	$ 75,745.81
3.00%	$236,962.33	$195,656.20	$154,350.07	$113,043.94	$ 71,737.81
3.10%	$233,270.95	$191,883.69	$150,496.43	$109,109.17	$ 67,721.92
3.20%	$229,572.29	$188,103.74	$146,635.20	$105,166.65	$ 63,698.10
3.30%	$225,866.34	$184,316.35	$142,766.35	$101,216.36	$ 59,666.36
3.40%	$222,153.10	$180,521.50	$138,889.89	$ 97,258.29	$ 55,626.68
3.50%	$218,432.55	$176,719.18	$135,005.80	$ 93,292.43	$ 51,579.05
3.60%	$214,704.68	$172,909.38	$131,114.07	$ 89,318.76	$ 47,523.46
3.70%	$210,969.49	$169,092.09	$127,214.69	$ 85,337.29	$ 43,459.89
3.80%	$207,226.95	$165,267.29	$123,307.64	$ 81,347.99	$ 39,388.33
3.90%	$203,477.06	$161,434.99	$119,392.92	$ 77,350.85	$ 35,308.78
4.00%	$199,719.80	$157,595.16	$115,470.51	$ 73,345.87	$ 31,221.22

FIGURE 1.15   Two-Way Data Table

relative addressing). Often you simply want the *result* of formulas so that the data will remain constant even if other parameters used in the formulas change. To do this, use the *Edit . . . Paste Special* option shown in Figure 1.16 instead of the typical *Edit . . . Paste* command. Checking the box for *Values* will paste the result of the formulas from which the data were calculated.

•   *Column and Row Widths.*   Many times a cell contains a number that is too large to display properly because the column width is too small. You may change the column width from the menu option *Format . . . Column . . . Width.* However, an easier way to change a column width to fit the largest value or text string anywhere in the column is to position the cursor to the right of the column label so that it changes to a cross with

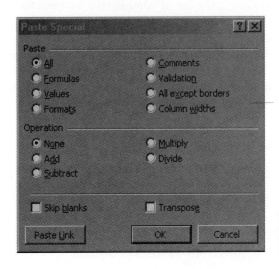

FIGURE 1.16   *Edit . . .
Paste Special* Dialog Box

horizontal arrows, and then double click. You may also move the arrow to the left or right to manually change the column width. You may change the row heights in a similar fashion by moving the cursor below the row number label. This can be especially useful if you have a very long formula to display. To break a formula within a cell, position the cursor at the break point in the formula bar and press Alt and Enter simultaneously.

- *Displaying Formulas in Worksheets.*   Choose *Tools . . . Options* from the menu bar and click on the *View* tab. Check the box for *Formulas.* You will probably need to change the column width to display the formulas properly.

- *Displaying Grid Lines and Row and Column Headers for Printing.*   Choose *File . . . Page Setup* from the menu and click on the *Sheet* tab. Check the boxes for *Gridlines* and *Row and column headings.*

- *Filling a Range with a Series of Numbers.*   Suppose you want to build a worksheet for entering 100 data values. It would be tedious to have to enter the numbers from 1 to 100 one at a time. Filling in a column of numbers in a series can be done using the *Edit . . . Fill . . . Series* command. Simply fill in the first few values in the series and highlight them. Now click and hold the mouse and drag the small square in the lower right-hand corner down until you have filled in the column to 100; then release the mouse. Excel will show a small pop-up window that tells you the last value in the range.

- *Comment Boxes.*   You may add "hidden" comment text boxes by clicking on some cell (that is perhaps labeled "Comment" or "Formulas," for example), and then selecting *Insert . . . Comment* from the menu. This allows you to include descriptive comments about the spreadsheet to assist other users without taking up valuable space on the worksheet itself. Comment cells are identified by a small red triangle in the upper right-hand corner of the cell. By positioning the cursor over the cell, the comment box is displayed.

Excel Add-Ins

Microsoft Excel will provide most of the computational support required for the material in this book. Excel provides an add-in called the *Analysis Toolpak,* which contains a variety of tools for statistical computation. The *Analysis Toolpak* is not included in a standard Excel installation. To install it, select the *Add-Ins* option from the *Tools* menu. If *Analysis Toolpak* is not checked, simply check the box and click OK. You will not have to repeat this procedure every time you run Excel in the future. If *Analysis Toolpak* does not appear in the list of add-ins, then you will have to run the Microsoft Excel setup procedure from your original distribution disk to make it available, choosing a "Custom" installation instead of "Typical."

Four other add-ins available with this book provide additional capabilities and features not found in Excel. Prentice-Hall's *PHStat* add-in provides useful additional statistical support that extends the capabilities of Excel.[8] (We do caution you that *PHStat* is not a commercial statistical package nor intended to replace such packages as SAS or SPSS for serious statistical work. Nevertheless, it is a useful tool for most practical applications as well as a good learning device.) The student version of *Crystal Ball,* introduced in Chapter 3, provides added ability to sample from probability distributions and perform risk analysis simulations (which we will study in Chapter 8). *TreePlan* provides Excel support for decision trees (see Chapter 10). You should install these add-ins now on your computer. Refer to the installation procedures on the

---

[8] The latest version of *PHStat, PHStat2,* is included on the CD-ROM. Enhanced versions and updates may be published on the PHStat Web site at [www.prenhall.com/phstat].

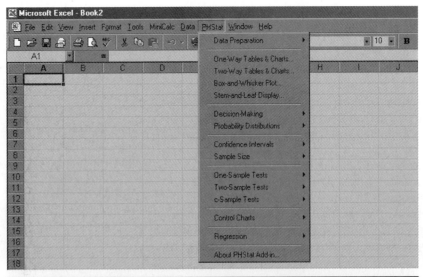

FIGURE 1.17   *PHStat* menu

CD-ROM in the back of this book. When *PHStat* is loaded, Excel will display a new menu item on the menu bar, as shown in Figure 1.17. *Crystal Ball* also creates additional menu items as well as a new button bar. Finally, Frontline Systems' *Premium Solver for Education* is included as a replacement for the default Solver in Excel. This add-in provides a more stable and accurate solution algorithm for optimization problems than Excel's default tool.

Throughout this book we will provide many "Notes" that describe how to use specific features of Microsoft Excel, *PHStat,* or *Crystal Ball.* These are introduced as needed to supplement examples and discussions of applications. It is important to read these notes and apply the procedures described in them in order to gain a working knowledge of the software features to which they refer.

WORKING WITH DATA IN EXCEL

In many cases, data on Excel worksheets may not be in the proper form to use a statistical tool. Figure 1.18, for instance, shows a worksheet from *Tracway.xls,* which we use as a case problem in this and other chapters. Some tools in the *Analysis Toolpak,*

	A	B	C	D	E	F
1	Defects After Delivery					
2						
3		1998	1999	2000	2001	2002
4	January	812	828	824	782	771
5	February	810	832	836	795	775
6	March	813	847	818	792	747
7	April	823	839	825	786	742
8	May	832	832	804	773	766
9	June	848	840	812	781	749
10	July	837	849	806	796	743
11	August	831	857	798	788	751
12	September	827	839	804	784	741
13	October	838	842	813	772	745
14	November	826	828	805	777	738
15	December	819	816	786	769	736

FIGURE 1.18 Worksheet *Defects After Delivery* in *Tracway.xls*

PHSTAT NOTE

USING THE *STACK DATA* AND *UNSTACK DATA* TOOLS

From the *PHStat* menu, select *Data Preparation,* and then either *Stack Data* (to create a single column from multiple columns) or *Unstack Data* (to split a single column into multiple columns according to a grouping label). Figure 1.19 shows the dialog boxes that appear. To stack data in columns (with optional column labels), enter the range of the data in the *Unstacked Data Cell Range.* If the first row of the range contains a label, check the box *First cells contain group*

labels. These labels will appear in the first column of the stacked data to help you identify the data, if appropriate.

To unstack data in a single column and group them according to a set of labels in another column, enter the range of the column that contains the labels for the grouping variable in the *Grouping variable cell range box,* and the range of the data in the *Stacked data cell range box.* If the top row contains descriptive labels, check the *First cells contain labels* box. This tool is useful when you wish to sort data into different groups.

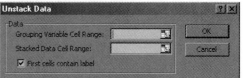

FIGURE 1.19 *PHStat* Dialog boxes for Stack Data and Unstack Data

however, require that the data be listed in a single column in the worksheet. As a user, you have two choices. You can manually move the data within the worksheet, or you can used a *PHStat* utility from the *Data Preparation* option in the *PHStat* menu called *Stack Data* (see the *PHStat Note: Using the Stack Data and Unstack Data Tools*).

Figure 1.20 shows the use of the *Stack Data* tool in *PHStat* for the defect data. The tool creates a new worksheet called "Stacked" in your Excel workbook, a portion of

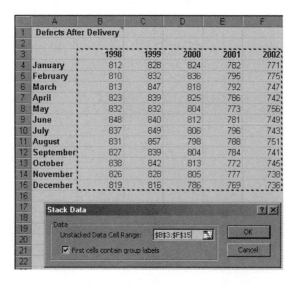

FIGURE 1.20 *PHStat* Stack Data Application

	A	B
1	Group	Value
2	1998	812
3	1998	810
4	1998	813
5	1998	823
6	1998	832
7	1998	848
8	1998	837
9	1998	831
10	1998	827
11	1998	838
12	1998	826
13	1998	819
14	1999	828
15	1999	832
16	1999	847
17	1999	839

FIGURE 1.21   Portion of the Worksheet *Stacked* for Defect Delivery Data

which is shown in Figure 1.21. The column labeled "Group" shows the original column (year) from which the data came. If you apply the *Unstack Data* tool to Figure 1.21, you will put the data in its original form (although the month labels will not be included in the worksheet).

PivotTables

Excel provides a powerful tool for distilling a complex data set into meaningful information: PivotTables. PivotTables allows you to create custom summaries and charts (see Chapter 2) of key information in the data. To apply PivotTables, you need a data set with column labels in the first row. The data set in the Excel file *Accounting Professionals.xls,* shown in Figure 1.22, providing the results of a survey of 27 employees in a tax division of a Fortune 100 company satisfies this condition. Select any cell in

---

EXCEL NOTE

CREATING PIVOTTABLES

Step 1 of the PivotTable and *PivotChart Wizard* (see Figure 1.23) asks you for the location of the data, which is typically a Microsoft Excel list. You may create PivotTables alone or PivotCharts along with PivotTables by clicking on the appropriate button. Step 2 asks you for the range of the data. If your data are in organized rows and columns, Excel will generally default to the complete range of your list. Finally, step 3 asks you where to put the PivotTable,

either into a new worksheet or in a blank range of the existing worksheet. The result is shown in Figure 1.24.

You may create other PivotTables without repeating all the steps in the wizard. Simply copy and paste the first table. Point and click on the upper-left cell of the PivotTable, and copy. Click a new cell in the spreadsheet, and then paste. Then point to the upper-left cell of the duplicate table, right click *Select Wizard,* and then replace the variables you wish to analyze.

	A	B	C	D	E	F	G
1	Employee	Gender	Years of Service.	Years Undergraduate Study	Graduate Degree?	CPA?	Age Group
2	1	F	17	4	N	Y	5
3	2	F	6	2	N	N	2
4	3	M	8	4	Y	Y	3
5	4	F	8	4	Y	N	3
6	5	M	16	4	Y	Y	4
7	6	F	21	1	N	Y	7
8	7	M	27	4	N	N	7
9	8	F	7	4	Y	Y	2
10	9	M	8	4	N	N	3
11	10	M	23	2	N	Y	5
12	11	F	9	4	Y	Y	3
13	12	F	8	2	N	N	2
14	13	F	8	4	Y	N	2
15	14	M	26	4	N	Y	6
16	15	F	9	4	N	Y	2
17	16	F	9	2	N	N	2
18	17	M	19	2	Y	Y	4
19	18	M	5	4	N	N	4
20	19	M	19	4	Y	N	7
21	20	M	20	4	N	N	6
22	21	F	14	4	Y	Y	4
23	22	M	31	4	N	N	7
24	23	F	10	0	N	N	7
25	24	F	10	4	N	Y	3
26	25	M	26	4	Y	Y	6
27	26	M	28	4	N	N	7
28	27	F	5	4	N	Y	1

FIGURE 1.22   *Accounting Professionals.xls* Data Set

the data set and choose *PivotTable and PivotChart Report* from the *Data* menu and follow the steps of the wizard (see the *Excel Note: Creating PivotTables*).

You should first decide on what types of tables you wish to create. For example, in the data set in Figure 1.22, suppose you wish to count the average number of years of service for males and females with and without a graduate degree. If you drag the variable *Gender* from the PivotTable toolbar in Figure 1.24 to the Row Field area, the

FIGURE 1.23 (*a, b, c*)   Steps in the PivotTable and PivotChart Wizard

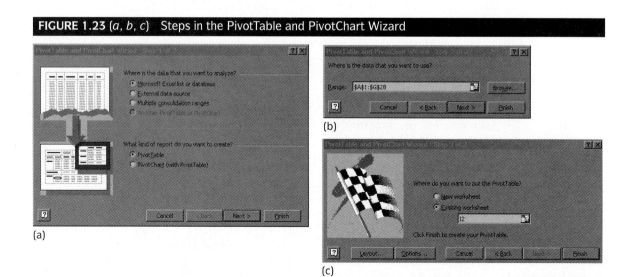

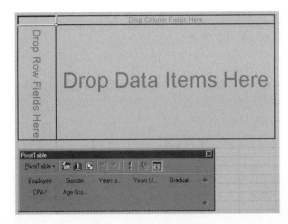

FIGURE 1.24   PivotTable Structure

variable *Graduat . . .* (Graduate Degree—shorter variable names are better!) into the Column Field area, and the variable *Years o . . .* (Years of Service) into the Data Items area, you will have created the PivotTable shown in Figure 1.25. However, the sum of years of service (default) is probably not what you would want. If you right click inside the table and select *Field Settings,* you will be able to change the summarization method in the PivotTable. Selecting *Average* results in the PivotTable shown in Figure 1.26. We see that average years is not much different for holders of graduate degrees, but that females have much fewer years of service than males.

The beauty of PivotTables is that if you wish to change the analysis, you can simply drag the shaded variable names out of the PivotTable and replace them with different ones. Figure 1.27 shows a count of Years of Service by Gender and Age Group. You

FIGURE 1.25   PivotTable for Sum of Years of Service

Sum of Years of Service.	Graduate Degree?		
Gender	N	Y	Grand Total
F	95	46	141
M	168	88	256
Grand Total	263	134	397

FIGURE 1.26   PivotTable for Average of Years of Service

Average of Years of Service.	Graduate Degree?		
Gender	N	Y	Grand Total
F	10.55555556	9.2	10.07142857
M	21	17.6	19.69230769
Grand Total	15.47058824	13.4	14.7037037

FIGURE 1.27   PivotTable for Count of Years of Service by Gender and Age Group

Count of Years of Service.	Age Group							
Gender	1	2	3	4	5	6	7	Grand Total
F	1	6	3	1	1		2	14
M			2	3	1	3	4	13
Grand Total	1	6	5	4	2	3	6	27

Count of Years of Service.		Graduate Degree?		
Gender	Age Group	N	Y	Grand Total
F	1	1		1
	2	4	2	6
	3	1	2	3
	4		1	1
	5	1		1
	7	2		2
F Total		9	5	14
M	3	1	1	2
	4	1	2	3
	5	1		1
	6	2	1	3
	7	3	1	4
M Total		8	5	13
Grand Total		17	10	27

FIGURE 1.28 PivotTable with Multiple Field Variables

may easily add multiple variables in the fields to create different views of the data. For instance, by adding the Graduate Degree variable to the Row Field area, we create the table shown in Figure 1.28. The best way to learn about PivotTables is simply to experiment with them!

PHStat includes two procedures that facilitate the process of creating certain types of PivotTables by simplifying the input process and automatically creating charts (see the *PHStat Note: One- and Two-Way Tables and Charts*).

PHSTAT NOTE

ONE- AND TWO-WAY TABLES AND CHARTS

To generate a one-way PivotTable for a set of categorical data, select *Descriptive Statistics* from the *PHStat* menu, and then *One-Way Tables & Charts*. The dialog box in Figure 1.29 prompts you for the type and location of the data and optional charts that you would like to create (which we discuss further in Chapter 2). The type of data may be

- *Raw Categorical Data.* If selected, the single-column cell range entered in the dialog box contains raw, unsummarized data. Selected by default.

- *Table of Frequencies.* If selected, the two-column cell range entered in the dialog box contains a frequency table containing categories and frequency counts for each category.

Enter the single-column (raw data) or two-column (frequency table) cell range containing the categorical data to be summarized in the *Raw Data Cell Range* field, and check *First cell contains label* if the contents of the first cell (or first row) is treated as a descriptive label and not as a data value. Figure 1.30 shows the table generated for Years of Undergraduate Study in *Accounting Professionals.xls* and a pie chart of these data.

A two-way table may also be constructed by selecting *Two-Way Tables & Charts* from the menu. However, we note that the PivotTables created by this tool only include the variables selected, and not all the variables in the data set, thus limiting the flexibility of creating different views of PivotTables as can be done using the Excel PivotTable tool.

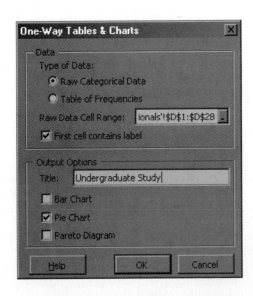

FIGURE 1.29 *PHStat*
One-Way Tables
and Charts Dialog Box

FIGURE 1.30 One-Way Tables and Charts Output

	A	B
1	Undergraduate Study	
2		
3	Count of Years Undergraduate Study	
4	Years Undergraduate Study	Total
5	0	1
6	1	1
7	2	5
8	4	20
9	Grand Total	27

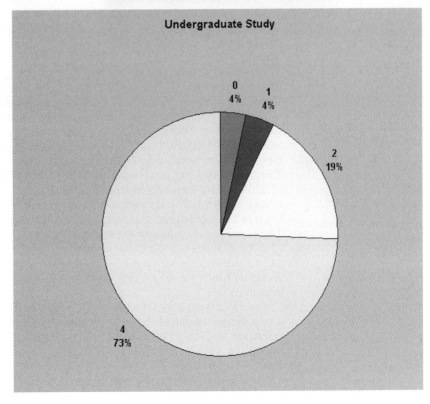

Undergraduate Study

0 4%
1 4%
2 19%
4 73%

29

Questions and Problems

1. Explain the concept of statistical thinking. How might it be used in dealing with the stock market?
2. How can managers develop theories about the relationship between their actions and results?
3. Propose a managerial theory that might logically relate the following variables to a company's market share: productivity, customer satisfaction, costs due to poor quality, employee satisfaction, satisfaction with managers, job satisfaction, and satisfaction with having the right job skills.
4. What is a balanced scorecard? Explain the difference between leading and lagging measures.
5. Read recent annual reports on selected Fortune 500 companies (most can be found on the Internet) to determine what information these companies use for evaluating and analyzing their business performance. How prevalent is nonfinancial information?
6. Explain the difference between data and information.
7. Provide additional examples of categorical, ordinal, interval, and ratio data not described in this chapter.
8. Examine each of the following data sets on the CD-ROM accompanying this book. Which ones represent cross-sectional data? Time series data? Univariate data? Multivariate data?
   a. *Blood Pressure*
   b. *Customer Support Survey Data*
   c. *Economic Indexes*
   d. *Market Value*
   e. *Olympic Track and Field Data*
   f. *TV Viewing*
   g. *Washington DC Weather*
   h. *NASCAR Track Data*
9. Which of the data files in Table 1.1 represent populations and not samples?
10. Would surveying the first 100 customers of the day provide a useful sample of a retailing firm's client base?
11. What is a decision model?
12. What sort of factors (variables) might be important in developing a decision model of the sales of an exclusive restaurant?
13. Construct a one-way data table for evaluating the effect of the assumption of the Year 1 Sales Revenue (cell C5) in the New Store Financial Model spreadsheet on Year 5 Cumulative Discounted Cash Flow (cell G35) for values from $500,000 to $1,000,000 in increments of $50,000.
14. Construct a two-way data table for evaluating the effect of Year 1 Sales Revenue (cell C5) for values from $500,000 to $1,000,000 in increments of $50,000, and Rent Per Square Foot (cell B10) for values of $25 to $30 in increments of $1 on Year 5 Cumulative Discounted Cash Flow (cell G35) in the New Store Financial Model spreadsheet.
15. The Excel file *Accounting Professionals.xls* provides the results of a survey of 27 employees in a tax division of a Fortune 100 company. Use PivotTables to find the average number of years of undergraduate study of each age group with or without a CPA. What conclusions might you reach from this information?
16. Call centers have high turnover rates because of the stressful environment. The national average is approximately 50 percent. The director of human resources for a large bank has compiled data about 70 former employees at one of the bank's call centers (see the Excel file *Call Center Data.xls*). Use PivotTables to find
   a. The average length of service for males and females in the sample

    b. The average length of service for individuals with and without a college degree

    c. The average length of service for males and females with and without prior call center experience.

What conclusions might you reach from this information?

17. The file *1999 Baseball Data.xls* contains data for professional baseball teams for 1999, including their total payroll, winning percentage, batting average, home runs, runs, runs batted in, earned run average, and pitching saves. Use PivotTables to find the average payroll, winning percentage, and batting average for teams in each league. What conclusions might you reach from this information?

18. A national homebuilder builds single-family homes and condominium-style townhouses. The Excel file *House Sales Data.xls* provides information on the selling price, lot cost, type of home, and region of the country (M = Midwest, S = South) for closings during one month. Use PivotTables to find the average selling price and lot cost for each type of home in each region of the market. What conclusions might you reach from this information?

19. The Excel file *Cereal Data.xls* provides a variety of nutritional information about 67 cereals and their shelf location in a supermarket. Use PivotTables to determine if there appear to be differences in nutritional values among cereal manufacturers.

20. A mental health agency measured the self-esteem score for randomly selected individuals with disabilities who were involved in some work activity within the past year. The Excel file *Self Esteem.xls* provides the data, including the individuals' marital status, length of work, type of support received (direct support includes job-related services such as job coaching and counseling), education, and age. Use PivotTables to find the average length of work and self-esteem score for individuals in each classification of marital status and support level. What conclusions might you reach from this information?

21. The Excel file *Unions and Labor Law Data.xls* reports the percent of public and private sector employees in unions in 1982 for each state, along with indicators whether the states had a bargaining law that covered public employees or right-to-work laws. Use PivotTables to find

    a. The average percent of public and private sector employees in unions for states with and without bargaining laws

    b. The average percent of public and private sector employees in unions for states with and without right-to-work laws

    c. The average percent of public and private sector employees in unions for states that have both bargaining laws and right-to-work laws, and those that have neither

What conclusions might you reach from this information?

CASE

THE TRACWAY BALANCED SCORECARD

Data, whether gathered from internal, external, or generated sources, are usually maintained in a computer database. A well-designed computer database allows managers to easily access necessary data, obtain answers to specific queries, and link data to decision models through a comprehensive decision support system. We will use a database for a fictitious company, Tracway International, Inc.,[9] as a case exercise in many chapters of this book. To put the database in perspective, we will first provide some background about the company, so that the applications of data analysis and decision modeling tools will be more meaningful.

Tracway is a privately owned designer and producer of traditional lawn mowers used by homeowners. Since homeowners are more often using lawn cover or hiring lawn services (or in California and Arizona relying more on natural sand for their front yards), the lawn mower market has not experienced high growth. In the past ten years Tracway has added another key product, a medium-size diesel power lawn tractor (21–50 hp) with front and rear power takeoffs (PTOs), class I three-point hitches, four-wheel drive, power steering, and full hydraulics. This equipment is built primarily for a niche market consisting of large estates, including golf and country clubs, resorts, private estates, city parks, and large commercial complexes, and lawn care service providers, private homeowners with five or more acres, and government (federal, state, and local) parks, building complexes, and military bases. The company is headquartered in St. Louis, Missouri, with manufacturing plants in St. Louis, Missouri; Greenwood, South Carolina; Camarillo, California; and Providence, Rhode Island.

In the United States, the focus of sales is on the Eastern Seaboard, California, the Southeast, and the South Central states, which have the greatest concentration of estates. Outside the United States, Tracway's sales include a declining European market, a growing South American market, and developing markets in the Pacific Rim and China. The market is cyclical, but the different products and regions balance some of this, with just less than 30 percent of total sales in the spring and summer (in the United States), about 25 percent in the fall, and about 20 percent in the winter. Annual sales are approximately $180 million.

Tracway provides most of the products to owner dealerships, which in turn sell directly to end users. The owner dealerships are also maintenance and repair facilities for customers, including support for federal and foreign governments. Because of the importance of the dealerships to the company's success, special steps are taken to ensure that they are successful. To minimize their inventory costs, the company guarantees delivery within five working days of replacement tractors for those sold and replacement equipment within three days for U.S. dealers. For dealers outside of the United States, replacement tractors will be shipped within 48 hours and equipment within 24 hours of notification of sale. This approach has enabled the dealerships' inventory costs to be 57 percent below other dealers' and demonstrates the commitment Tracway is making to dealers. Tracway also involves the dealers in the yearly planning process, new and upgrade design processes, pricing strategy, sales, and other meetings to fully integrate them into the business. When new products are designed, the dealers pilot use of the maintenance and support documentation for validation before finalization. Training of dealers in the operation and maintenance of new and modified tractors and equipment is always a top priority.

Tracway employs 1660 people worldwide. About half the workforce is based in St. Louis; the remainder is split among the Camarillo, Greenwood, and Providence sites. Of the total workforce, 100 are classified as management, 1150 as design and production, and the remaining as sales/administrative support.

Both end users and dealers have been established as important customers for Tracway. Collection and analysis of end-user data showed

---

[9] This scenario was adapted from Gateway Estate Lawn Equipment Co. Case Study, used for the 1997 Malcolm Baldrige National Quality Award Examiner Training course. This material is in the public domain. The database, however, was developed by the authors.

that satisfaction with the products depends on high quality, easy attachment/dismount of implements, low maintenance, price value, and service. For dealers, key requirements are high quality, parts and feature availability, rapid restock, discounts, and timeliness of support.

Tracway has several key suppliers: Mitsitsiu, Inc., the sole source of all diesel engines; LANTO Axles, Inc., which provides tractor axles; Schorst Fabrication, which provides subassembles; Cuberillo, Inc., supplier of transmissions; and Specialty Machining, Inc., a supplier of precision machine parts.

To help manage this enterprise, Tracway has developed a balanced scorecard of customer, financial, internal, and innovation and learning measures. These data, which are summarized here, are stored in the form of a Microsoft Excel workbook (*Tracway.xls*) that is included on the CD-ROM accompanying this book. Figure 1.31 shows the Excel screen for the Tracway database. Data for each of the key measures are stored in one of the worksheets. By clicking on any of the worksheet tabs, you may access the particular data sets. The navigation buttons allow you to move through the worksheets in the workbook (similar to moving through tracks on a compact disk!). A small red triangle in the upper right-hand corner of a cell indicates a comment. By positioning the cursor over that cell, you may view the comment. The comments in the Tracway database describe the nature of the data on each worksheet.

CUSTOMER PERSPECTIVE

Customer and stakeholder satisfaction is a key strategic factor for Tracway. Measures obtained to assist Tracway in this perspective of the balanced

FIGURE 1.31   Portion of the Tracway Database in Microsoft Excel

	A	B	C	D	E	F	G	H (Sample Size)
1	Dealer Satisfaction		This worksheet provides dealer survey results of perceived Tracway product quality by year					
3	Survey Scale:	0						
4	North America							
5	1998	1	0	2	13			
6	1999	0	0	2	14			
7	2000	1	1	1	6	36	15	60
8	2001	1	2	6	13	38	40	100
9	2002	2	3	5	15	44	56	125
10								
11	South America							
12	1998	0	0	0	2	6	2	10
13	1999	0	0	0	2	6	2	10
14	2000	0	0	1	4	9	14	28
15	2001	0	1	1	3	12	30	47
16	2002	1	1	2	4	21	48	77
17								
18	Europe							
19	1998	0	0	1	3	7	4	15
20	1999	0	0	1	2	8	4	15
21	2000	0	0	1	2	8	4	15
22	2001	0	0	1	2	8	4	15
23	2002	0	0	1	2	8	4	15
24								
25	Pacific Rim							
26	1998	0	0	1	2	2	0	5
27	1999	0	0	1	1	3	0	5
28	2000	0	0	1	1	3	1	6
29	2001	0	0	0	2	3	1	6
30	2002	0	0	1	2	3	2	8
31								
32	China							
33	2000	0	0	0	1	0	0	1
34	2						0	2
35	2					3	0	5

C1 Dealer Satisfaction   C2 End-User Satisfaction   C3 2002 Customer Survey   C4 Complaints

scorecard are provided here, along with measures of sales and market share.

1. *C1 Dealer Satisfaction,* measured on a scale of 1–5 (1 = poor, 2 = less than average, 3 = average, 4 = above average, and 5 = excellent). Each year, dealers in each region are surveyed about their overall satisfaction with Tracway. The worksheet contains summary data from surveys for the past five years.

2. *C2 End-User Satisfaction,* measured on the same scale as dealers. Each year, 100 users from each region are surveyed. The worksheet contains summary data for the past five years.

3. *C3 2002 Customer Survey* is the result of a new survey conducted in 2002 for customer ratings of specific attributes of Tracway tractors: quality, ease of use, price, and service on the same 1–5 scale. This sheet contains 200 observations of customer ratings.

4. *C4 Complaints* shows the number of complaints registered by all customers each month in each of Tracway's five regions (North America, South America, Europe, the Pacific, and China).

5. *C5 Mower Unit Sales* and *C6 Tractor Unit Sales* provides Tracway sales by product by region on a monthly basis. Unit sales for each region are aggregated to obtain Tracway world sales.

6. The market within which Tracway operates is monitored monthly by region. Units sold by all producers are recorded in *C7 Industry Mower Total Sales* and *C8 Industry Tractor Total Sales.*

7. Tracway market share is calculated for each product by dividing the unit sales by the industry total sales. Market share by month by region is shown on sheet *C9 Mktshare Mowers* and sheet *C10 Mktshare Tractors.*

FINANCIAL PERSPECTIVE

Tracway measures several key financial indicators in the Financial Perspective of its balanced scorecard:

1. *F1 Revenues* shows sales in dollars per month for each product (tractors and mowers) in each market region.

2. *F2 Pre-Tax Earnings* provides pre-tax earnings, calculated with the following assumptions. We will assume that production is essentially a make-to-order environment (only minimal inventories are kept), so the quantity sold is equal to the quantity produced. Overhead expenses are allocated equally to each month. Dealers selling Tracway products all receive 20 percent of sales revenue for their part of doing business. Tracway pays 5 percent of revenues in taxes and shipping expenses. Profit is the net of revenue minus these expenses. For example, the profit for January 1998 is computed as follows:

January 1998 Revenues				$5,472,000
Production costs		Tractors	Mowers	
	Unit cost	$1750	$50	
	Units produced	1590	7020	
		$2,782,500	$351,000	($3,133,500)
Overhead				($773,540)
Dealer return				($1,094,400)
Tax and shipping				($273,600)
Profit				$196,960

INTERNAL PERSPECTIVE

Tracway's key measures here include supplier performance, quality, and response time.

1. *I1 On-Time Delivery* provides results for delivery-to-need date (1 day early or 0 days late), a critical measure to maintain the flow of the assembly lines. Tracway measures on a monthly basis the percent of all shipments from suppliers that meet the delivery-to-need date for each of its major suppliers.

2. *I2 Defects After Delivery* shows the number of defects in supplier-provided material found in all shipments received from suppliers.

3. *I3 Time To Pay Suppliers* provides measurements in days from the time the invoice is received until payment is sent.
4. *I4 Response Time* gives samples of the times by quarter beginning in 2001 taken by Tracway customer service personnel to respond to service calls.

INNOVATION AND LEARNING PERSPECTIVE

Tracway has only one measure in this category.

1. *L1 Employee Satisfaction* provides data for the past four years of Tracway surveys of its employees to determine their overall satisfaction with their jobs with the same scale used for customers. Employees are surveyed quarterly and results are stratified by employee category: design and production, managerial, and sales/administrative support.

SPECIAL STUDIES

In addition to the balanced scorecard measures, the Tracway database contains worksheets with data from special studies. These include:

1. *S1 Engines* gives 50 samples of the time required to produce a lawn mower blade using a new technology.
2. *S2 Transmission Costs* provides the results of 30 samples each for the current process used to produce Tracway tractor transmissions and two proposed new processes.
3. *S3 Blade Weight* provides samples of mower blade weights to evaluate the consistency of the production process.
4. *S4 Mower Test* gives 30 samples of 100 test results of mower functional performance after assembly.
5. *S5 Process Capability* gives samples of blade weights taken from a controlled process.
6. *S6 Employee Retention* is data from a study of employee duration (length of hire) with

Tracway. The 40 subjects were identified by reviewing hires from ten years prior and identifying those who were involved in managerial positions (either hired into management or promoted into management) at some time in this ten-year period.

Henry Hudson has recently joined the Tracway International, Inc. management team to oversee Tracway's production operations. He has reviewed the types of data that the company collects and has assigned you the responsibility to be his chief analyst in the coming weeks. To prepare for this task, you have decided to review each worksheet and determine whether the data were gathered from internal sources, external sources, or generated. Also, you need to know which data sets contain attributes data and which contain only variables data.

Henry has asked you to do some preliminary calculations. First, he wants to know the total number of responses to the survey in the worksheet *C1 Dealer Satisfaction* for all regions for each year. Modify the worksheet to compute this. Second, he wants to know the average responses for each of the customer attributes in the worksheet *C3 2002 Customer Survey* for each market region. Use PivotTables to accomplish this task. Third, he wants a count of the number of failures in the Tracway worksheet *S4 Mower Test*. Stack the data into a single column and use the Excel function COUNTIF to find this. Finally, Henry has provided you with prices for Tracway products in the following table. Create a new worksheet in the Tracway database to compute gross revenues by month and region, as well as worldwide totals, for each product using the data in *C5 Mower Unit Sales* and *C6 Tractor Unit Sales*. Summarize all your findings in a report to him.

Year	Mower Price	Tractor Price
1998	$100	$3000
1999	$105	$3100
2000	$110	$3250
2001	$115	$3400
2002	$125	$3600

CHAPTER

2

DISPLAYING AND SUMMARIZING DATA

INTRODUCTION

In Chapter 1 we discussed the role of data in modern organizations, ways of extracting meaningful information from data using PivotTables, and rudimentary concepts of statistics. In this chapter, we discuss how to effectively display and summarize data quantitatively for useful managerial information and insight. Because of the ease with which data can be generated and transmitted today, managers, supervisors, and even frontline workers can be overwhelmed. Hence, it is vital that critical data be aggregated, summarized, and displayed in as succinct a fashion as possible. Various charts and plots are simple communication vehicles that all employees can easily understand. Statistical summaries, such as measures of central tendency, dispersion, and relationships among variables, provide more precise quantitative information on which to base decisions. Spreadsheet software makes it possible to easily create visual displays and compute statistical measures. Our focus is on learning how to understand and incorporate these tools into making better decisions, as well as becoming proficient with the capabilities of Microsoft Excel.

The key concepts that we will discuss in this chapter are

- Visual data display: using line charts, bar charts, pie charts, area charts, scatter plots, box-and-whisker plots, and stem-and-leaf displays to understand data
- Descriptive statistics: computing and understanding measures of central tendency (mean, median, mode), dispersion (range and variance), shape (skewness), fractiles (quartiles, deciles, and percentiles), and the coefficient of variation
- Statistical relationships: understanding linear relationships between two variables through correlation and covariance measures

EXCEL NOTE

USING THE *CHART WIZARD*[1]

The Excel *Chart Wizard* is accessed from either the *Insert...Chart...* menu selection or by clicking on the *Chart Wizard* icon (the colored bar chart on the menu bar). The *Chart Wizard* guides you through four dialog boxes; the first is shown in Figure 2.1. The following steps outline the process of creating a chart:

1. Select the chart type from the list (e.g., *Bar*) and then click on the specific chart subtype option. Click *Next* or press *Enter* to continue.

2. The second dialog box asks you to define the data to plot. You may enter the data range directly or highlight it in your spreadsheet with your mouse. You also need to define whether the data are stored by rows or columns. (Note: If the data you wish to plot are not stored in contiguous columns, hold down the Ctrl key while selecting each block of data; then start the *Chart Wizard*.) The *Series* tab allows you to check and modify the names and values of the data series in your chart.

3. The third dialog box allows you specify details to customize the chart and make it easy to read and understand. You may specify titles for the chart and each axis, axis labels, style of gridlines, placement of the legend to describe the data series,

data labels, and even a data table of values from which the chart is derived.

4. Finally, the last dialog box allows you to specify whether to place the chart as an object in an existing worksheet or as a new sheet in the workbook.

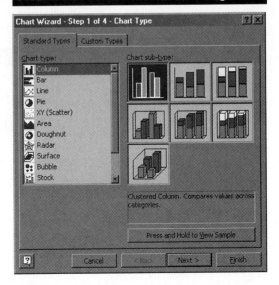

FIGURE 2.1 Excel *Chart Wizard* Dialog Box

---

[1] In this and other Excel Notes in this book we provide some basic information about using key features in Excel. More detail can be found using Excel's Help files, and we encourage you to do so.

DISPLAYING DATA WITH CHARTS AND GRAPHS

Graphs and charts provide a convenient way to communicate information. Microsoft Excel offers a variety of options to express data visually. These include vertical and horizontal bar charts, line charts, pie charts, area charts, scatter plots, three-dimensional charts, and many other special types of charts. The Excel *Chart Wizard* (see *Excel Note: Using the Chart Wizard*) provides an easy way to create charts within your spreadsheet.

Column and Bar Charts

Excel distinguishes between vertical and horizontal bar charts, calling the former *column charts* and the latter *bar charts*. Figure 2.2 shows a column chart for displaying the 1999 payroll of baseball teams from the worksheet *1999 Baseball Data.xls*. The *Excel Note: Creating a Column Chart* describes the step-by-step procedure to develop Figure 2.2. We generally will not guide you through every application, but will provide some guidance for new procedures as appropriate. Column charts may include multiple sets of data; for example, you could plot home runs and pitching saves together on one chart for American League teams (hint: first sort the data by league using the *Sort* option in the *Data* menu) as shown in Figure 2.4. To select noncontiguous columns of data, hold down the Ctrl key while selecting additional ranges.

Bar charts present information in a similar fashion, only horizontally instead of vertically. A *stacked bar chart* displays multiple values consecutively instead of side-by-side as in a clustered chart. Figure 2.5 shows one Excel option, a 100 percent stacked bar chart, which compares the percent each value contributes to a total across categories for the civilian labor force in the worksheet *Census Education Data.xls*, which is shown in Figure 2.6. We see that higher levels of education correspond to increasingly higher percentages of employment.

Line Charts

Line charts provide a useful means for displaying data over time. For instance, a line chart showing the one-year average yield of Treasury bills from the worksheet *Economic Indexes.xls* is shown in Figure 2.7. This chart clearly shows the trend of rising

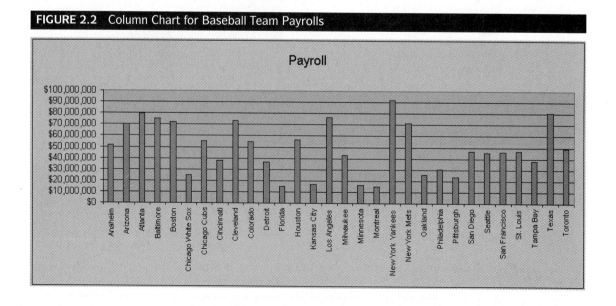

FIGURE 2.2   Column Chart for Baseball Team Payrolls

EXCEL NOTE

CREATING A COLUMN CHART

1. The first step is to access the data. In the worksheet *1999 Baseball Data.xls,* payroll data are found in column C; column A lists the data labels (teams). See Figure 2.3 for this worksheet.
2. The next step is to select the data to be plotted: cells C3 through C32.
3. Access the *Chart Wizard* by clicking on the chart icon on the menu bar.
   a. Use the default *Column chart type,* which should be *clustered column* style. Click on *Next.*
   b. The next dialog box is *Chart Source Data.* Since you selected the data you want to graph, you can see what the chart will look like in the viewing window. The columns radio button is checked by default, because that is how the highlighted data was stored. In the *Series* tab, you can specify a name for the data series highlighted ("Payroll") and define the range for the *Category (X) axis labels.* Here we want the labels to be the team names, so select the range A3:A32. If the chart looks correct, click on *Next.*
   c. The *Chart Options* dialog box appears next. You may also specify a title for the Category (X) Axis Value (Y) Axis; however, because the axis values are self-evident, we left this option out. You may also modify the gridlines, the placement or existence of the legend, and other customized options. We deleted the legend because there is only one data series; with multiple series, we recommend keeping the legend. Click on *Next.*
   d. The last dialog box is *Chart Location.* You have the option of placing your chart on its own sheet or inserting it into the current sheet as an object. Either way, the chart can be copied to insert it in a Microsoft Word document or other applications.

FIGURE 2.3 Worksheet *1999 Baseball Data.xls*

	A	B	C	D	E	F	G	H	I	J
1					Batting					Pitching
2	Team	League	Payroll	Winning %	Avg	HR	R	RBI	ERA	Saves
3	Anaheim	American	$51,340,297	0.432	0.256	158	711	673	4.79	37
4	Arizona	National	$70,046,818	0.617	0.277	216	908	865	3.77	42
5	Atlanta	National	$79,256,599	0.636	0.266	197	840	791	3.65	45
6	Baltimore	American	$75,443,363	0.481	0.279	203	851	804	4.77	33
7	Boston	American	$72,330,656	0.580	0.278	176	836	808	4.00	50
8	Chicago White Sox	American	$24,535,000	0.466	0.277	162	777	742	4.92	39
9	Chicago Cubs	National	$55,419,648	0.414	0.257	189	747	717	5.27	32
10	Cincinnati	National	$38,031,285	0.589	0.272	209	865	820	3.99	55
11	Cleveland	American	$73,531,692	0.599	0.289	209	1009	960	4.91	46
12	Colorado	National	$54,367,504	0.444	0.288	223	906	863	6.03	33
13	Detroit	American	$36,954,666	0.429	0.261	212	747	704	5.22	33
14	Florida	National	$14,650,000	0.395	0.263	128	691	655	4.90	33
15	Houston	National	$56,389,000	0.599	0.267	168	823	784	3.84	48
16	Kansas City	American	$16,557,000	0.398	0.282	151	856	800	5.35	29
17	Los Angeles	National	$76,607,247	0.475	0.266	187	793	761	4.45	37
18	Milwaukee	National	$42,976,575	0.460	0.273	165	815	777	5.08	40
19	Minnesota	American	$15,845,000	0.394	0.264	105	686	643	5.03	34
20	Montreal	National	$15,015,250	0.420	0.265	163	718	680	4.69	44
21	New York Yankees	American	$91,990,955	0.605	0.282	193	900	855	4.16	50
22	New York Mets	National	$71,510,523	0.595	0.279	181	853	814	4.27	49
23	Oakland	American	$25,208,858	0.537	0.259	235	893	845	4.76	48
24	Philadelphia	National	$30,441,500	0.475	0.275	161	841	797	4.93	32
25	Pittsburgh	National	$23,682,420	0.484	0.259	171	775	735	4.35	34
26	San Diego	National	$46,507,179	0.457	0.252	153	710	671	4.47	43
27	Seattle	American	$45,351,254	0.488	0.269	244	859	825	5.25	40
28	San Francisco	National	$45,991,934	0.531	0.271	188	872	828	4.71	42
29	St. Louis	National	$46,337,129	0.466	0.262	194	809	763	4.76	38
30	Tampa Bay	American	$37,860,451	0.426	0.274	145	772	728	5.06	45
31	Texas	American	$80,801,598	0.586	0.293	230	945	897	5.07	47
32	Toronto	American	$48,847,300	0.519	0.280	212	883	856	4.93	39

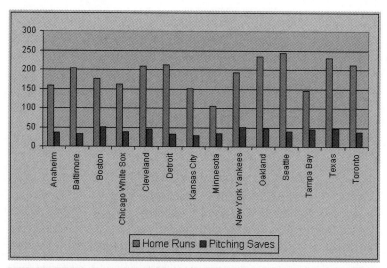

FIGURE 2.4   Column Chart for Home Runs and Pitching Saves

rates through 1981, followed by a period of falling rates. You may plot multiple data series in line charts; however, the information can be difficult to interpret if the magnitude of the data values differs greatly. In this case, it would be advisable to create separate charts for each data series.

Pie Charts

For many types of data, we are interested in understanding the relative proportion of each data source to the total. For example, consider the marital status of individuals in the U.S. population in the worksheet *Census Education Data.xls* (cells A18:B23 in Figure 2.6). To show the relative proportion in each category of marital status, we can use a *pie chart,* as shown in Figure 2.8. In this chart, we selected *Show label* in the *Data Labels* tab of the *Chart Options* dialog box; this is often better than showing a legend, as it clearly identifies the different categories in the chart.

FIGURE 2.5   100 Percent Stacked Bar Chart
for Civilian Employment

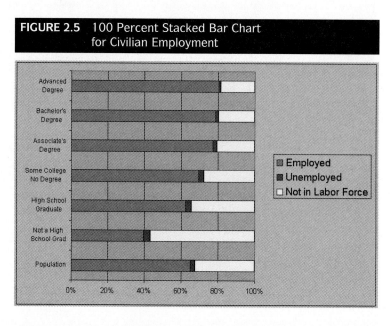

	A	B	Not a High School Grad	High School Graduate	Some College No Degree	Associate's Degree	Bachelor's Degree	Advanced Degree
1		Population						
2	Total Persons	172,211,000	29,620,292	58,207,318	29,620,292	12,915,825	28,242,604	13,604,669
3	Age							
4	25-34	39,354,000	4,683,126	12,553,926	7,792,092	3,423,798	8,382,402	2,439,948
5	35-44	44,462,000	5,335,440	15,117,080	8,136,546	4,134,966	8,136,546	3,556,960
6	45-54	34,058,000	4,427,540	10,932,618	6,062,324	2,894,930	5,960,150	3,848,554
7	55-64	22,255,000	4,562,275	8,301,115	3,338,250	1,157,260	2,893,150	2,047,460
8	65-74	17,873,000	5,165,297	6,505,772	2,466,474	768,539	1,787,300	1,179,618
9	75 and older	14,209,000	5,399,420	4,717,388	1,847,170	454,688	1,150,929	625,196
10	Sex							
11	Male	82,376,006	14,168,672	26,607,448	14,086,296	5,683,944	14,086,296	7,743,344
12	Female	89,835,000	15,361,785	31,621,920	15,541,455	7,186,800	14,193,930	5,929,110
13	Race							
14	White	145,078,000	23,647,714	49,181,442	24,953,416	11,171,006	24,373,104	11,751,318
15	Black	19,376,000	4,650,240	6,975,360	3,700,816	1,201,312	1,995,728	852,544
16	Other	7,756,000	1,279,740	1,977,780	1,047,060	550,676	1,915,732	992,768
17	Marital Status							
18	Never Married	25,752,000	4,120,320	7,777,104	4,789,872	1,828,392	5,124,648	2,137,416
19	Married, spouse present	107,008,000	15,516,160	36,382,720	18,084,352	8,346,624	19,154,432	9,523,712
20	Married, spouse absent	6,844,000	1,847,880	2,368,024	1,184,012	465,392	670,712	301,136
21	Separated	4,605,000	1,188,090	1,667,010	842,715	336,165	405,240	165,780
22	Widowed	13,577,000	5,145,683	4,670,488	1,765,010	556,657	977,544	475,195
23	Divorced	19,030,000	2,968,680	7,003,040	3,806,000	1,674,640	2,340,690	1,217,920
24	Civilian Labor Force							
25	Employed	111,131,000	11,668,755	36,228,706	20,448,104	9,890,659	22,115,069	10,890,838
26	Unemployed	4,597,000	1,057,310	1,783,636	809,072	317,193	455,103	170,089
27	Not in Labor Force	55,822,000	16,858,244	20,040,098	8,205,834	2,623,634	5,582,200	2,511,990

FIGURE 2.6 *Census Education Data.xls* Worksheet

Area Charts

An *area chart* combines the features of a pie chart with those of line charts. For example, Figure 2.9 displays energy consumption from fossil fuels and other energy sources from the worksheet *Energy Production & Consumption.xls*. This chart shows that total energy consumption has grown since 1949, and by stacking the two sources on one chart, we can clearly see that the proportion of fossil fuel consumption has gotten smaller. Area charts present more information than pie or line charts alone but suffer from the potential to clutter the observer's mind with too many details; thus, they should be used with care.

FIGURE 2.7 Line Chart for Treasury Bill Yield Over Time

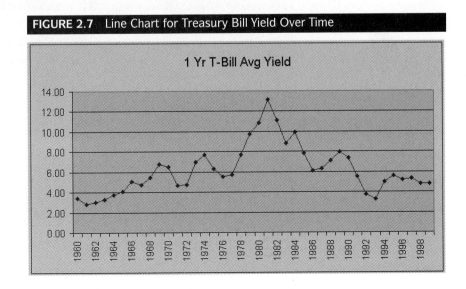

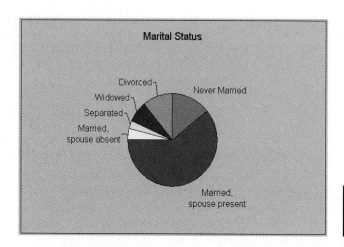

FIGURE 2.8 Pie Chart for Marital Status of U.S. Population

FIGURE 2.9 Area Chart for Energy Consumption

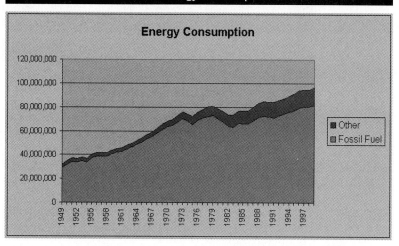

FIGURE 2.10 Scatter Diagram of NFL Statistics

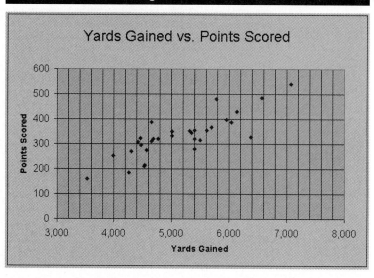

Scatter Diagrams

Scatter diagrams show the relationship between two variables. Figure 2.10 shows a scatter diagram of yards gained versus points scored for National Football League teams in 2000 from the worksheet *2000 NFL Data.xls*. Each point on the chart represents one team; thus, a scatter diagram plots pairs of observations and displays the value of one variable against the corresponding value of the other. We see that a clear relationship appears to exist between these variables—larger numbers of yards gained corresponds to larger number of points scored. In fact, the relationship appears to be linear. Later in this chapter we shall see how to describe such a relationship numerically.

Miscellaneous Excel Charts

Excel provides several additional charts for special applications. A *radar chart* (sometimes known as a *spider chart*) allows you to plot multiple dimensions of several data series. An example is shown in Figure 2.11. Using the *Cereal Data.xls* worksheet, we plotted the values of fiber, carbohydrates, and sugars for three cereals in the database. This chart clearly shows the differences in nutritional attributes. A *bubble chart* is a type of scatter chart in which the size of the data marker corresponds to the value of a third variable; consequently, it is a way to plot three variables in two dimensions. A *doughnut chart* is similar to a pie chart but can contain more than one data series. Finally, a *stock chart* allows you to plot stock prices, such as the daily high, low, and close. It may also be used for scientific data such as temperature changes. Examples of these additional charts are shown in Figure 2.12. We encourage you to experiment with different charts in displaying and interpreting data.

Summary of Graphical Display Methods

In summary, tables of numbers often hide more than they inform. Graphical displays clearly make it easier to gain insights about the data. Thus, graphs and charts are a means of converting raw data into useful managerial information. However, it can be easy to distort data by manipulating the scale on the chart. For example, Figure 2.13 shows the average T-bill yield in Figure 2.7 displayed on a different scale. The pattern looks much flatter and does not suggest as dramatic a rise and fall in rates. It is not

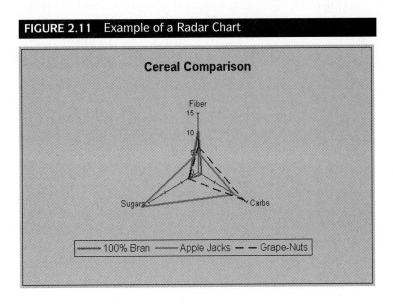

FIGURE 2.11   Example of a Radar Chart

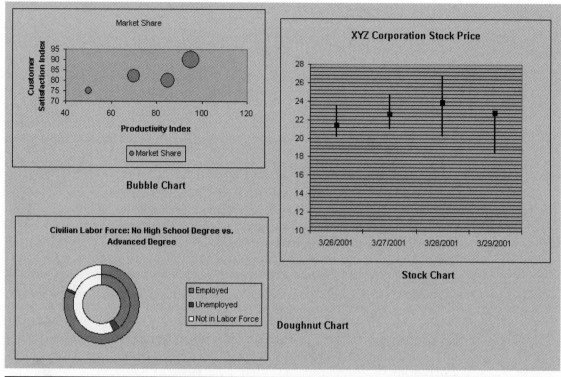

FIGURE 2.12   Additional Charts Available in Excel

unusual to see distorted graphs in newspapers and magazines that are intended to support the author's conclusions. Creators of statistical displays have an ethical obligation to report data honestly and without attempts to distort the truth. Another drawback of visual displays is that they provide no *quantitative* summaries of the data. We will discuss statistical measures useful to convey information for decision making later in this chapter.

FIGURE 2.13   Another View of T-Bill Yields

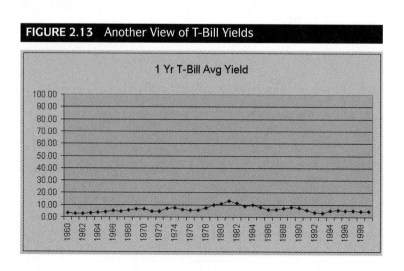

CONTINGENCY TABLES AND CROSS TABULATIONS

One of the most basic statistical tools used to summarize categorical data and examine the relationship between two variables is cross tabulation. A **cross tabulation** is a tabular method that displays the number of observations in a data set for different subcategories of two categorical variables. For example, suppose we wish to count the number of employees of each gender within each age group in the *Accounting Professionals.xls* data set (see Figure 1.22). We may construct a matrix, with the rows representing the gender classification and the columns the age groups, as shown:

Count of Employee	Age Group							Grand Total
Gender	1	2	3	4	5	6	7	
F	1	6	3	1	1		2	14
M			2	3	1	3	4	13
Grand Total	1	6	5	4	2	3	6	27

We see that there are roughly an equal number of males and females in the sample; however, males tend to be older. Excel PivotTables, which are described in Chapter 1, provide an easy method of constructing cross tabulations. For this example, we dropped the Employee variable in the Data Item field and changed its Field Setting to "Count."

A cross tabulation table is often called a **contingency table.** Note that the subcategories of the variables must be mutually exclusive and exhaustive, meaning that each observation can only be classified into one subcategory and, taken together over all subcategories, they must constitute the complete data set. We might also wish to convert the counts to percents by dividing each cell value by the total (27). This can help in interpreting the data more easily; we leave this to you as an exercise. The *PHStat* tool *Two-Way Tables & Charts,* described in Chapter 1, provides a quick method of creating cross tabulations in the form of Excel PivotTables.

DESCRIPTIVE STATISTICS

Statistical measures provide an effective and efficient way of obtaining meaningful information from data that are useful for making decisions. **Descriptive statistics** refers to a collection of quantitative measures and ways of describing data. This includes frequency distributions and histograms, measures of central tendency (mean, median, mode, proportion), and measures of dispersion (range, variance, standard deviation). Statistical support within Microsoft Excel can be accomplished in three ways:

1. Using statistical functions that are entered in worksheet cells directly or embedded in formulas,
2. Using the Excel *Analysis Toolpak* add-in to perform more complex statistical computations, or
3. Using the *Prentice-Hall Statistics* add-in, *PHStat,* available with this book to perform analyses not designed into Excel.

TABLE 2.1 Excel Statistical Functions and Tools	
Excel Function	*Description*
AVERAGE(*data range*)	Computes the average value (arithmetic mean) of a set of data
MEDIAN(*data range*)	Computes the median (middle value) of a set of data
MODE(*data range*)	Computes the mode (most frequently occurring) of a set of data
VAR(*data range*)	Computes the variance of a set of data, assumed to be a sample
VARP(*data range*)	Computes the variance of a set of data, assumed to be an entire population
STDEV(*data range*)	Computes the standard deviation of a set of data, assumed to be a sample
STDEVP(*data range*)	Computes the standard deviation of a set of data, assumed to be an entire population
SKEW(*data range*)	Computes the skewness, a measure of the degree to which a distribution is not symmetric around its mean
PERCENTILE(*array, k*)	Computes the kth percentile of data in a range
QUARTILE(*array, quart*)	Computes the quartile of a distribution
CORREL(*array1, array2*)	Computes the correlation coefficient between two data sets
Analysis Toolpak *Tools*	*Description*
Descriptive Statistics	Provides a summary of a variety of basic statistical measures
Histogram	Creates a frequency distribution and graphical histogram for a set of data
Rank and Percentile	Computes the ordinal and percentage rank of each value in a data set
Correlation	Computes the correlation coefficient between two data sets
Prentice-Hall Statistics *Add-In*	*Description*
Box-and-Whisker Plot	Creates a box-and-whisker plot of a data set
Stem-and-Leaf Display	Creates a stem-and-leaf display of a data set
Dot Scale Diagram	Creates a dot scale diagram of a data set
Frequency Distribution	Creates a table of frequency counts and percentage frequency values
Histogram & Polygons	Creates a frequency table and histogram and optional frequency polygons

Table 2.1 summarizes the descriptive statistics functions and tools available.

To illustrate the use of descriptive statistics, we will examine the data in the worksheets *1999 Baseball Data.xls* (shown in Figure 2.3, which represents a population), and the worksheet *TV Viewing.xls* (a portion of which is shown in Figure 2.14, which represents a sample).

Frequency Distributions and Histograms

Before computing any statistical measures, it is helpful to summarize the data in a **frequency distribution,** a tabular summary showing the frequency of observations in each of several nonoverlapping classes, or cells. A graphical depiction of a frequency distribution in the form of a column chart is called a **histogram.** A frequency distribution and histogram

18-24 Age Group		25-34 Age Group		35-44 Age Group		45-54 Age Group		55-64 Age Group		65+ Age Group	
Age	TV hours/week	Age	TV hours/week	Age	TV hours/week	Age	TV hours/week	Age	TV hours/week	Age	TV hours/week
21	48	30	61	36	76	49	95	63	103	79	117
21	47	28	78	35	75	54	80	61	110	80	113
18	73	26	72	42	69	52	105	55	99	78	117
23	65	30	65	36	70	48	83	56	109	76	124
19	74	34	73	35	70	49	89	57	93	70	126
19	50	34	69	43	64	51	90	62	95	67	120
20	57	29	54	39	53	49	72	61	116	76	119
24	64	34	74	37	78	51	94	56	103	69	116
21	70	29	70	37	71	48	72	56	93	74	113
23	51	30	57	36	70	45	103	59	91	71	116
20	54	33	86	40	76	50	99	59	74	68	113
21	63	30	55	43	75	50	84	61	81	77	110
23	67	30	64	40	66	50	93	60	74	67	128
24	75	26	67	42	61	47	108	60	95	73	107
19	61	32	71	44	70	47	82	56	111	79	110
24	51	33	57	37	77	54	88	57	108	71	116
23	47	27	71	44	72	54	93	59	88	74	123
18	76	27	70	40	63	53	82	58	92	80	124
20	63	29	87	38	61	52	106	59	101	77	113
19	72	31	58	38	74	46	89	64	90	75	116
22	59	34	62	40	64	51	110	64	109		
18	57	33	91	40	63	49	87	62	87		
20	51	29	63	44	71	51	94	59	92		
24	62	25	69	36	64	46	76	56	86		
22	68	28	79	43	62	49	74	60	135		
20	46	32	75	37	62	46	90	61	87		
21	64	32	56	44	76	52	83	55	90		
20	69	26	77	40	55	45	91	63	90		
19	57	30	86	44	73	46	98	59	80		

FIGURE 2.14 Portion of the Worksheet *TV Viewing.xls*

EXCEL NOTE

CREATING A HISTOGRAM

Access the Histogram tool by clicking on *Tools . . . Data Analysis* and select *Histogram* from the list. In the dialog box (Figure 2.15), specify the *Input Range* corresponding to the home run data as F3:F32. If you include the column header in cell F2, then also check the *Labels* box so that Excel

FIGURE 2.15 Dialog Box for Histogram Tool

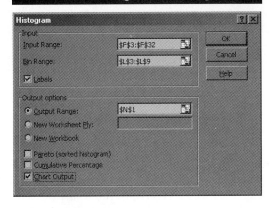

knows that the range contains a label. If you do not specify a *Bin Range,* Excel will automatically determine cell ranges for the frequency distribution and histogram. Usually it is best to define the cell ranges by specifying the upper cell limits of each range in a column in your worksheet. (If you check the *Data Labels* box, be sure you include a column label such as "Bin" or "Upper Limit.") In our example, we specified the *Bin Range* as L3:L9, with cell values 100, 125, 150, 175, 200, 225, and 250 in this range. We determined these by first finding the smallest and largest values of the data using Excel functions *MIN(range)* and *MAX(range).* You should use at least 5 but no more than 15 cells; the more data you have, the more intervals you should generally use. Note that with fewer cells, the cell widths will be wider. Wider cell widths provide a "coarse" histogram. Sometimes you need to experiment to find the best number of cells that provide a useful picture of the data. Check the *Chart Output* box to create a histogram in addition to the frequency distribution.

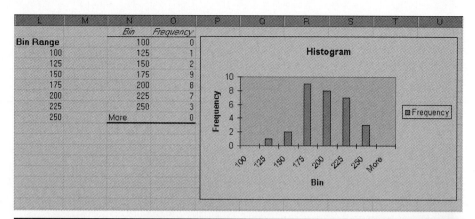

Bin Range		Bin	Frequency
100		100	0
125		125	1
150		150	2
175		175	9
200		200	8
225		225	7
250		250	3
		More	0

FIGURE 2.16   Frequency Distribution and Histogram of Home Run Totals

of 1999 baseball team home run totals was created by using the *Analysis Toolpak* in Excel (see the *Excel Note: Creating a Histogram*). *PHStat* also provides tools for creating frequency distributions and histograms in the *Descriptive Statistics* menu option.

Figure 2.16 shows the bin range, frequency distribution, and histogram. The frequency distribution is the table in the range N1:O9. *Bin* refers to the upper limit of each cell in which the data fall. For example, the first cell includes all data below or equal to 100; we see that no observations fall in this cell. The second cell includes all observations greater than 100 and less than or equal to 125; this cell has one observation; and so on. Although Excel does not provide the total, you can easily modify the spreadsheet to count the total number of observations and compute the fraction that falls within each interval—called the **relative frequency.** By summing all the relative frequencies at or below each upper limit, we have the **cumulative relative frequency.** The cumulative frequency represents the proportion of the sample that falls below the upper limit value. Note that relative frequencies must be between zero and one and must add to one over all cells. This also means that the cumulative frequency for the last cell must equal one. We have done these computations in the following table.

Upper Limit	Frequency	Relative Frequency	Cumulative Relative Frequency
100	0	0.000	0.000
125	1	0.033	0.033
150	2	0.067	0.100
175	9	0.300	0.400
200	8	0.267	0.667
225	7	0.233	0.900
250	3	0.100	1.000
Sum	30	1.000	

We see that the majority of teams had between 150 and 225 home runs during the season. Only 10% hit 150 or fewer home runs, and only 10% hit more than 225 home runs.

A serious limitation of the Excel Histogram tool is that the frequency distribution and histogram are not linked to the data; thus, if you change any of the data, you must repeat the entire procedure to construct a new frequency distribution and histogram. An alternative is to use Excel's FREQUENCY function and the *Chart Wizard*. First, define the bins as you would using the Histogram tool. Select the range of cells adjacent to the bin range and add one additional empty cell below it (this provides an overflow cell). Then enter the formula =FREQUENCY(*range of data, range of bins*) and press Ctrl-Shift-Enter simultaneously. This is necessary because FREQUENCY is an array function in Excel. This will create the frequency distribution. You may then construct a histogram using the *Chart Wizard* for a column chart, customizing it as appropriate. Now, if the data are changed, the frequency distribution and histogram will be updated automatically. We encourage you to try this on the home run data in *1999 Baseball Data.xls* and compare your result to Figure 2.16.

Measures of Central Tendency

In viewing a histogram, you can generally tell approximately where the data are centered. Measures of central tendency provide estimates of a single value that in some fashion represents "centering" of the entire set of data. The most common is the *average,* formally called the **arithmetic mean** (or simply the *mean*), which is the sum of the observations divided by the number of observations. We all use averages routinely in our lives, for example, to measure student accomplishment in a curriculum, to measure the scoring ability of sports figures, and, as we show here, to measure performance in business. It is common practice in statistics to use Greek letters to represent population parameters and Roman letters to represent sample statistics. Thus, if a population consists of N observations $x_1, \ldots, x_N$, the population mean, μ, is

$$\mu = \frac{\sum_{i=1}^{N} x_i}{N}$$

The mean of a sample of n observations is

$$\bar{x} = \frac{\sum_{i=1}^{n} x_i}{n}$$

For example, if we consider only the American League teams in the *1999 Baseball Data.xls* worksheet, the sum of the team payrolls is shown below.

Team	League	Payroll
Anaheim	American	$51,340,297
Baltimore	American	$75,443,363
Boston	American	$72,330,656
Chicago White Sox	American	$24,535,000
Cleveland	American	$73,531,692
Detroit	American	$36,954,666
Kansas City	American	$16,557,000
Minnesota	American	$15,845,000
New York Yankees	American	$91,990,955
Oakland	American	$25,208,858
Seattle	American	$45,351,254
Tampa Bay	American	$37,860,451
Texas	American	$80,801,598
Toronto	American	$48,847,300
	Sum	$696,598,090

Therefore, the average American League payroll is \$696,598,090/14 = \$49,757,006.43. Similarly, the average number of TV hours/week for the 65+ Age Group in the *TV Viewing.xls* data set is computed by dividing the sum, 2341 by the number of samples, 20, or:

65+ AGE GROUP

Age	TV hours/week	Age	TV hours/week
79	117	77	110
80	113	67	128
78	117	73	107
76	124	79	110
70	126	71	116
67	120	74	123
76	119	80	124
69	116	77	113
74	113	75	116
71	116	Sum	2341
68	113	Mean	117.05

The mean is unique for every set of data and is meaningful for both interval and ratio data. However, it can be affected by **outliers**—rare observations that are radically different from the rest. One property of the mean is that the sum of the deviations from each observation is zero:

$$\sum_i (x_i - \bar{x}) = 0$$

Another measure of central tendency is the **median,** the middle value when the data are arranged from smallest to largest. For an odd number of observations, the median is the middle of the sorted numbers. For an even number of observations, the median is the arithmetic mean of the two middle numbers. We could use the *Sort* option in Excel to rank order the payroll values in column C of the baseball data. Since we have 14 observations, the median would be the average of the 7th and 8th observation, or (\$45,351,254 + \$48,847,300)/2 = \$47,099,277. The Excel function MEDIAN(*data range*) would also provide this result. The median is meaningful for ratio, interval, and ordinal data. As opposed to the mean, the median is *not* affected by outliers.

A third measure of central tendency is the **mode.** The mode is the observation that occurs most frequently. This statistic is not affected by order or differences in scale, but only by the count for each observation. The mode is more useful for large numbers of observations that consist of a relatively small number of unique values. In our examples, the data are continuous, and few values occur more than once. For example, no value in the baseball data occurs more than once. In the *TV Viewing* data set for the 65+ Age Group, we find that both 113 and 116 occur the most—only four times each. Thus, the mode is not unique, and we say that the data are **multimodal.** (If the data have exactly two modes, we call it **bimodal.**) The Excel function MODE(*data range*) can be used to compute the mode.

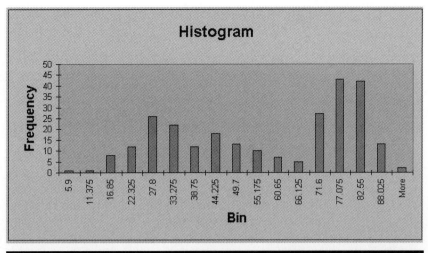

FIGURE 2.17   Example of a Bimodal Distribution

The mode is more useful for grouped data. For example, in the histogram in Figure 2.16, we see that the mode corresponds to the highest column of the histogram, namely, the bin [150, 175]. In this case, the mode is near the center of the distribution and all columns of the histogram become progressively smaller as you move away from the mode in either direction. Now consider the histogram in Figure 2.17. It appears that the data have two "centers," characterized by modes corresponding to the bins [22.325, 27.8] and [71.6, 77.075]. This is an example of a bimodal distribution. This often occurs when data from two different populations are mixed. In fact, Figure 2.17 represents the distribution of both the mean January temperature and mean July temperature of cities in the data set *Weather.xls.*

Another measure of central tendency is the **midrange.** This is simply the average of the largest and smallest values in the data set. For the American League payroll data, the maximum value is $91,990,955 and the minimum value is $15,845,000. Thus the midrange is ($91,990,955 − $15,845,000)/2 = $38,072,977.50. Caution must be exercised when using this statistic because extreme values easily distort the result, as we see in this example; the midrange is quite different from the values of the mean and median. Outliers can dramatically affect the midrange. Note that the midrange uses only two pieces of data while the mean uses *all* the data; thus, it is usually only used for very small sample sizes.

MEASURES OF DISPERSION

Dispersion refers to the degree of variation in the data, that is, the numerical spread (or compactness) of the data. For instance, a cursory examination of the baseball data clearly shows more variation in the payroll data than in the batting average data. Several statistical measures characterize dispersion: the *range, variance,* and *standard deviation.* The **range** is the simplest and is computed as the difference between the maximum value and the minimum value in the data set. Although Excel does not provide a function for the range, it can be computed easily by the formula =MAX(*data* *range*) − MIN(*data range*). In the case of the American League payroll data, the range is ($91,990,955 − $15,845,000) = $71,145,955. Like the midrange, the range is affected by outliers.

A more commonly used measure of dispersion is the **variance,** whose computation depends on *all* the data. The formula for the variance of a population is:

$$\sigma^2 = \frac{\sum\limits_{i=1}^{N}(x_i - \mu)^2}{N}$$

where x_i is the value of the *i*th item, N is the number of items in the population, and μ is the population mean. Using this formula, the calculations for the variance of the American League payroll data are:

Team	League	Payroll	Payroll − Mean	(Payroll − Mean)^2
Minnesota	American	$15,845,000	− $33,912,006	$1,150,024,180,011,470
Kansas City	American	$16,557,000	− $33,200,006	$1,102,240,426,857,180
Chicago White Sox	American	$24,535,000	− $25,222,006	$ 636,149,608,282,898
Oakland	American	$25,208,858	− $24,548,148	$ 602,611,591,271,174
Detroit	American	$36,954,666	− $12,802,340	$ 163,899,920,449,034
Tampa Bay	American	$37,860,451	− $11,896,555	$ 141,528,031,065,072
Seattle	American	$45,351,254	− $ 4,405,752	$ 19,410,654,461,863
Toronto	American	$48,847,300	− $ 909,706	$ 827,565,786,184
Anaheim	American	$51,340,297	$ 1,583,291	$ 2,506,809,033,575
Boston	American	$72,330,656	$22,573,650	$ 509,569,654,973,657
Cleveland	American	$73,531,692	$23,774,686	$ 565,235,674,020,294
Baltimore	American	$75,443,363	$25,686,357	$ 659,788,913,914,572
Texas	American	$80,801,598	$31,044,592	$ 963,766,665,836,814
New York Yankees	American	$91,990,955	$42,233,949	$1,783,706,411,934,070
			Sum	$8,301,266,107,897,870

The variance is $8,301,266,107,897,870/14 = $592,947,579,135,562. The Excel function VARP(*data range*) may be used to compute the population variance.

The variance of a set of sample data is calculated using the formula:

$$s^2 = \frac{\sum\limits_{i=1}^{n}(x_i - \bar{x})^2}{n - 1}$$

where n is the number of items in the sample, and $\bar{x}$ is the sample mean. It may seem peculiar to use a different "average" for populations and samples, but statisticians have shown that the sample variance provides a more accurate representation of the true population variance when computed in this way. For the 65+ Age Group in *TV Viewing.xls,* the calculations for the sample variance are:

TV Hours/Week	Hours − Mean	(Hours − Mean)^2
117	−0.05	0.0025
113	−4.05	16.4025
117	−0.05	0.0025
124	6.95	48.3025
126	8.95	80.1025
120	2.95	8.7025
119	1.95	3.8025
116	−1.05	1.1025
113	−4.05	16.4025
116	−1.05	1.1025
113	−4.05	16.4025
110	−7.05	49.7025
128	10.95	119.9025
107	−10.05	101.0025
110	−7.05	49.7025
116	−1.05	1.1025
123	5.95	35.4025
124	6.95	48.3025
113	−4.05	16.4025
116	−1.05	1.1025
	Sum	614.95

The variance is $614.95/(20 - 1) = 32.366$. The Excel function VAR(*data range*) may be used to compute the sample variance.

Perhaps the most popular and useful measure of dispersion is the **standard deviation,** which is defined as the square root of the variance. For a population, the standard deviation is computed as:

$$\sigma = \sqrt{\frac{\sum_{i=1}^{N}(x_i - \mu)^2}{N}}$$

and for samples, it is:

$$s = \sqrt{\frac{\sum_{i=1}^{n}(x_i - \bar{x})^2}{n - 1}}$$

For the American League payroll data, the standard deviation is computed as $\sqrt{\$592,947,579,135,562} = \$24,350,515$. For the 65+ Age Group in the *TV Viewing* data, the standard deviation is $\sqrt{32.366} = 5.689$. The Excel function STDEVP(*data range*) calculates the standard deviation for a population; the function STDEV(*data range*) calculates it for a sample. The standard deviation is generally easier to interpret than the variance because its units of measure are the same as the units of the data.

Thus, it can be more easily related to the mean or other statistics measured in the same units.

Importance of the Standard Deviation

The standard deviation provides an indication of where the majority of data are clustered around the mean. For example, if we add and subtract 1 standard deviation from the mean of the baseball data, we obtain the interval [$25,406,491, $74,107,521]. You may verify that half the data actually fall within this range. One of the most important results in statistics is **Chebyshev's theorem,** which states that for *any set of data,* the proportion of values that lie within k standard deviations ($k > 1$) of the mean is at least $1 - 1/k^2$. Thus, for $k = 2$, at least 3/4 of the data lie within 2 standard deviations of the mean; for $k = 3$, at least 8/9, or 89 percent, of the data lie within 3 standard deviations of the mean. For the American League payroll data, this range is [−$23,294,539, $122,808,551], and you can easily see that all data fall into this interval. For symmetric, unimodal distributions, these percentages are generally much higher than Chebyshev's theorem specifies. Three standard deviations around the mean is commonly used to describe the range of most distributions. For example, the capability of a manufacturing process, that is, the expected variation of output, is generally quantified as the mean plus or minus three standard deviations.

The larger the standard deviation, the more the data are "spread out" from the mean. Thus, the standard deviation is a useful measure of risk, particularly in financial analysis. Figure 2.18 shows the distributions of potential returns of two investments. Both distributions have similar means, 6.66 percent and 6.39 percent. However, the standard deviations are quite different: 1.02 percent versus 2.79 percent. The first investment has the smaller standard deviation, and therefore little risk exists that the return will vary substantially from the mean. However, the larger standard deviation for the second investment implies that there is greater risk of achieving a significantly

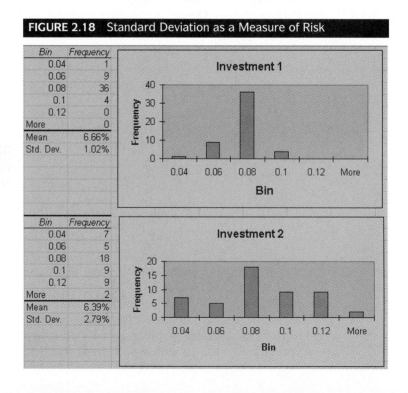

FIGURE 2.18   Standard Deviation as a Measure of Risk

Bin	Frequency
0.04	1
0.06	9
0.08	36
0.1	4
0.12	0
More	0
Mean	6.66%
Std. Dev.	1.02%

Bin	Frequency
0.04	7
0.06	5
0.08	18
0.1	9
0.12	9
More	2
Mean	6.39%
Std. Dev.	2.79%

lower return, while at the same time, a greater potential exists of a higher return. This is easily seen by examining the histograms shown in the figure.

CALCULATIONS FOR GROUPED DATA

When sample data are summarized in a frequency distribution, a simple formula for computing the mean is:

$$\bar{x} = \frac{\sum_{i=1}^{n} f_i x_i}{n}$$

where f_i is the frequency of the observation x_i in the ith class. This provides an exact value of the mean if the data are discrete. To illustrate, consider the 65+ Age Group in *TV Viewing.xls*. The calculations are shown below:

Data Value	Frequency	Value × Frequency
107	1	107
110	2	220
113	4	452
116	4	464
117	2	234
119	1	119
120	1	120
123	1	123
124	2	248
126	1	126
128	1	128
	20	2341

The mean is $2341/20 = 117.05$. For populations, the formula is similar:

$$\mu = \frac{\sum_{i=1}^{N} f_i x_i}{N}$$

If the data are grouped into k cells in a frequency distribution, we can use modified versions of these formulas to estimate the mean by replacing x_i with a representative value for all the observations in each cell (such as the midpoint), $\hat{x}_i$. For the home run totals in Figure 2.16, we have:

Bin Range	Midpoint	Frequency	Midpoint × Frequency
100–125	112.5	1	112.5
125–150	137.5	2	275
150–175	162.5	9	1462.5
175–200	187.5	8	1500
200–225	212.5	7	1487.5
225–250	237.5	3	712.5
		Sum	5550

Thus, the mean is computed as $5550/30 = 185$. Note that this is not identical, but is very close, to the true mean of 184.27. This is because we have not used all the original data, but only five representative values. Although most statistics are simple concepts, they must be applied correctly, and we need to understand how to interpret them properly.

We use similar formulas to compute the population variance:

$$\sigma^2 = \frac{\sum\limits_{i=1}^{N} f_i\,(x_i - \mu)^2}{N}$$

and sample variance:

$$s^2 = \frac{\sum\limits_{i=1}^{n} f_i\,(x_i - \bar{x})^2}{n - 1}$$

COEFFICIENT OF VARIATION

The **coefficient of variation** provides a relative measure of the dispersion in data relative to the mean and is defined as

Coefficient of Variation (CV) = Standard Deviation/Mean

This statistic is useful when comparing the variability of two or more data sets when their scales differ. For example, the following table shows the calculations for the coefficients of variation for each age group in *TV Viewing.xls*. Note that while the 45–54 and 55–64 Age Groups have higher standard deviations than the 18–24 Age Group, the relative dispersion of the 18–24 Age Group is actually larger as evidenced by the larger CV.

	18–24 Age Group	25–34 Age Group	35–44 Age Group	45–54 Age Group	55–64 Age Group	65+ Age Group
Mean	60.16	70.28	67.40	89.06	95.93	117.05
Standard Deviation	10.09	9.85	6.35	11.06	13.25	5.69
Coefficient of Variation	0.168	0.140	0.094	0.124	0.138	0.049

Sometimes the coefficient of variation is multiplied by 100 to express it as a percent. For example, suppose that the standard deviation of a stock whose average price is $2 is $0.40, whereas the standard deviation of another stock whose average price is $80 is $6. You would expect the standard deviation of the $2 stock to be smaller; thus comparing standard deviations directly provides little information. However, looking at the CVs, $0.4/2 = 0.2$, or 20 percent, versus $6/80 = 0.075$, or 7.5 percent, shows that the $2 stock shows much larger relative variation, indicating a higher relative level of risk. Note that when the mean is close to zero, the magnitude of CV will tend to be large and must be interpreted with caution.

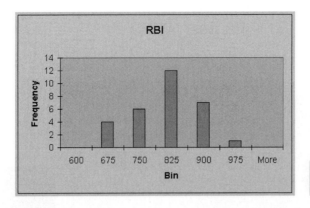

FIGURE 2.19 Example of a Symmetric Distribution

MEASURES OF SHAPE

Histograms of sample data can take on a variety of different shapes as we saw in Figures 2.16 and 2.17. A distribution that is unimodal with a peak in the center and which falls away from the center in roughly the same fashion on either side is called *symmetric*. Figure 2.19 shows a histogram of runs batted in from the *1999 Baseball Data* worksheet. We see that this distribution is quite symmetric. In Figure 2.20, we show histograms for two statistics in the *2000 NFL Data* worksheet. Note that the histogram of giveaways is asymmetrical, or *skewed;* that is, more of its mass is concentrated on the left side and the distribution "tails off" to the right. The distribution for yards allowed tails off distinctly to the left. Distributions that tail off to the left are said to be *negatively skewed*, while those that tail off to the right are *positively skewed*. The **coefficient of skewness,** which can be found using an Excel function in Table 2.1, measures the degree of asymmetry of a distribution around its mean. For a population, this is computed as:

$$CS = \frac{\frac{1}{n} \sum_{i=1}^{n} (x_i - \mu)^3}{\sigma^3}$$

FIGURE 2.20 Examples of Skewed Distributions

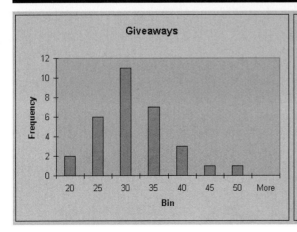

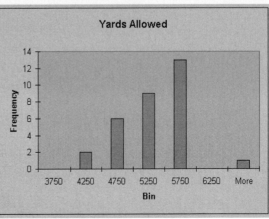

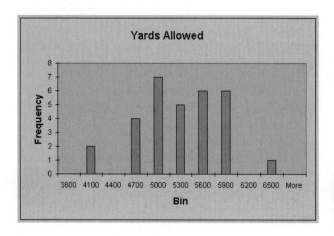

FIGURE 2.21 An Alternative Histogram of Yards Allowed

(For sample data, replace the population mean and standard deviation with the corresponding sample statistics.) If the coefficient is positive, the distribution is positively skewed; if negative, it is negatively skewed. The closer the coefficient is to zero, the less the degree of skewness in the distribution. A distribution whose coefficient of skewness is greater than 1 or less than −1 is highly skewed. A value between 0.5 and 1 or between −0.5 and −1 is moderately skewed. Coefficients between 0.5 and −0.5 indicate relative symmetry. The coefficient of skewness for the RBI data in Figure 2.19 is 0.0. The skewness measure for the giveaways is 0.86, indicating a moderate positive skewness. Although the distribution for yards allowed appears to be highly negatively skewed—its skewness measure is only −0.27, indicating relative symmetry. Why is this so? The answer lies in how the bin ranges are defined. Figure 2.21 shows an alternative histogram for the same data. We see that the distribution does look much more symmetric than in Figure 2.20. Therefore, you must be careful when drawing conclusions on the basis of visual histograms alone!

Comparing measures of central tendency can sometimes reveal information about the shape of a distribution. For example, in a perfectly symmetrical unimodal distribution, the mean, median, and mode would all be the same. For a highly negatively skewed distribution, we would generally find that mean < median < mode, while for a highly positively skewed distribution, mode < median < mean.

Kurtosis refers to the peakedness (i.e., high, narrow) or flatness (i.e., short, flat-topped) of a distribution. The **coefficient of kurtosis** measures the degree of kurtosis of a population and is computed as:

$$CK = \frac{\frac{1}{n} \sum_{i=1}^{n} (x_i - \mu)^4}{\sigma^4}$$

(Again, for sample data, use the sample statistics instead of the population parameters.) If the value of CK is less than 3, the distribution is relatively flat with a very wide degree of dispersion. As the values of CK get farther from 3, the distribution becomes more peaked with less dispersion.

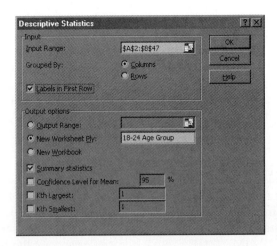

FIGURE 2.22 *Descriptive Statistics* Dialog Box

EXCEL'S DESCRIPTIVE STATISTICS TOOL

Excel provides a useful tool for basic data analysis, which is available in the *Data Analysis Toolpak* from the *Tools* menu. The Descriptive Statistics tool provides a variety of statistical measures for one or more data sets: the mean, standard error, median, mode, standard deviation, sample variance, kurtosis, skewness, range, minimum, maximum, sum, count, *k*th largest and smallest values (for any value of *k* you specify), and the confidence level for the mean. We will discuss the standard error and confidence level in Chapters 3 and 4, respectively, so you may ignore them for now.

To illustrate the use of this tool, we will apply it to the data for the 18–24 Age Group in *TV Viewing.xls*. If you select *Descriptive Statistics,* the dialog box shown in Figure 2.22 will appear. You need only enter the range of the data, which must be in a *single row or column*. If the data are in multiple columns, the tool treats each row or column as a separate data set, depending on which you specify. In this example, we have two samples, one in column A (Age) and the second in column B (TV hours/week). Thus, the tool will treat these as two independent data sets. The results are shown in Figure 2.23.

	A	B	C	D
1	Age		TV hours/week	
2				
3	Mean	21.2	Mean	60.15555556
4	Standard Error	0.281769302	Standard Error	1.504859319
5	Median	21	Median	62
6	Mode	21	Mode	57
7	Standard Deviation	1.890165938	Standard Deviation	10.0949032
8	Sample Variance	3.572727273	Sample Variance	101.9070707
9	Kurtosis	-1.114446513	Kurtosis	-0.693445522
10	Skewness	-0.090445425	Skewness	-0.15711463
11	Range	6	Range	41
12	Minimum	18	Minimum	37
13	Maximum	24	Maximum	78
14	Sum	954	Sum	2707
15	Count	45	Count	45

FIGURE 2.23 Descriptive Statistics Results for TV Viewing Data

One important point to note about the use of the tools in the *Analysis Toolpak* versus Excel functions is that while functions dynamically change as the data in the spreadsheet are changed, the results of the tools do not. For example, if you compute the mean and standard deviation directly using the functions AVERAGE(*range*) and STDEV(*range*), then changing the data in the range will automatically update these statistics. However, you would have to re-run the Descriptive Statistics tool to find new values after changing the data.

DATA PROFILES AND PROPORTIONS

Data profiles (or **fractiles**) describe the location and spread of data over its range. These measures include percentiles and quartiles. You are no doubt familiar with percentiles from standardized tests used for college or graduate school entrance examinations (SAT, ACT, GMAT, GRE, etc.). Percentiles specify the percent of other test takers who scored at or below the score of a particular individual. Specifically, the *kth percentile* is a value at or below which at least *k* percent of the observations lie. *Quartiles* divide the sorted data into four sets, representing the 25th percentile, 50th percentile, 75th percentile, and 100th percentile. Note that the median is actually the second quartile, with two-fourths of the data below the median and two-fourths of the data above the median. One-fourth of the data is below the first quartile, and three-fourths of the data is below the third quartile. Similarly, *deciles* divide the data into 10 sets: the 10th percentile, 20th percentile, and so on.

Figure 2.24 shows the dialog box for this tool, using the 55–64 Age Group in the *TV Viewing* data set; results are shown in Figure 2.25. While the Rank and Percentile tool sorts the data into percentiles, the column labeled Percent *does not correctly* display the percent at or below the given value. For example, while 100 percent of the data fall at or below 135, the correct percentage of the data falling at or below 116 is 28/29 = 96.55 percent, not 96.40 percent, and clearly 0 percent of the data do not fall at or below 74. This is a flaw in Excel, and one that Microsoft has yet to correct.

Other fractiles can be calculated as well. For example, the quartiles for these data are:

QUARTILE	VALUE
First	88
Second	93
Third	103
Fourth	135

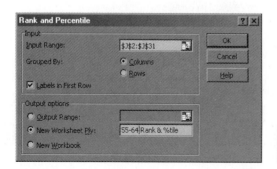

FIGURE 2.24   Rank and Percentile Dialog Box

	A	B	C	D
1	Point	TV hours/week	Rank	Percent
2	25	135	1	100.00%
3	7	116	2	96.40%
4	15	111	3	92.80%
5	2	110	4	89.20%
6	4	109	5	82.10%
7	21	109	5	82.10%
8	16	108	7	78.50%
9	1	103	8	71.40%
10	8	103	8	71.40%
11	19	101	10	67.80%
12	3	99	11	64.20%
13	6	95	12	57.10%
14	14	95	12	57.10%
15	5	93	14	50.00%
16	9	93	14	50.00%
17	18	92	16	42.80%
18	23	92	16	42.80%
19	10	91	18	39.20%
20	20	90	19	28.50%
21	27	90	19	28.50%
22	28	90	19	28.50%
23	17	88	22	25.00%
24	22	87	23	17.80%
25	26	87	23	17.80%
26	24	86	25	14.20%
27	12	81	26	10.70%
28	29	80	27	7.10%
29	11	74	28	.00%
30	13	74	28	.00%

FIGURE 2.25   Rank and Percentile Results

A **proportion** is the fraction of data that has a certain characteristic. For example, in the *1999 Baseball* data, 14 teams had more than 40 pitching saves during the year. Thus, the proportion of teams is $14/30 = 0.466$. The Excel function COUNTIF(*data range, criteria*) is useful in determining how many observations meet specified characteristics. For instance, to find the number of teams with more than 40 pitching saves, we used the function =COUNTIF(J3:J32,">40"). Proportions are key descriptive statistics for attribute data, such as defects or errors in quality control applications or consumer preferences in market research.

VISUAL DISPLAY OF STATISTICAL MEASURES

Statisticians use other types of graphs to visually display the dispersion in a data set. Three useful tools are *box-and-whisker plots, stem-and-leaf displays,* and *dot scale diagrams,* all of which are available in the *PHStat* Excel add-in. When *PHStat* is installed, it opens a new menu item on the Excel menu bar called *PHStat*. All procedures are accessed from this menu.

Box-and-Whisker Plots
Box-and-whisker plots graphically display five key statistics of a data set—the minimum, first quartile, median, third quartile, and maximum—and are very useful in identifying the shape of a distribution and outliers in the data. Box-and-whisker plots can be created in Excel using *PHStat* (see *PHStat Note: Creating Box-and-Whisker Plots*).

PHSTAT NOTE

CREATING BOX-AND-WHISKER PLOTS

From the *PHStat* menu, select *Descriptive Statistics* and then *Box-and-Whisker Plot.* The dialog box is shown in Figure 2.26. In the *Raw Data Cell Range* box, enter the range of the data; if the first cell contains a label, check the box below. For a single data set, check the *Single Group Variable* radio button. For multiple groups of data, check the appropriate button (see the *PHStat* note on stacked and unstacked data in Chapter 1). In the *Output Options* section, you may enter a title for the chart. Checking the *Five-Number Summary* box will provide a worksheet with the minimum, first quartile, median, third quartile, and maximum values of the data set(s).

FIGURE 2.26 *Box-and-Whisker* Dialog Box

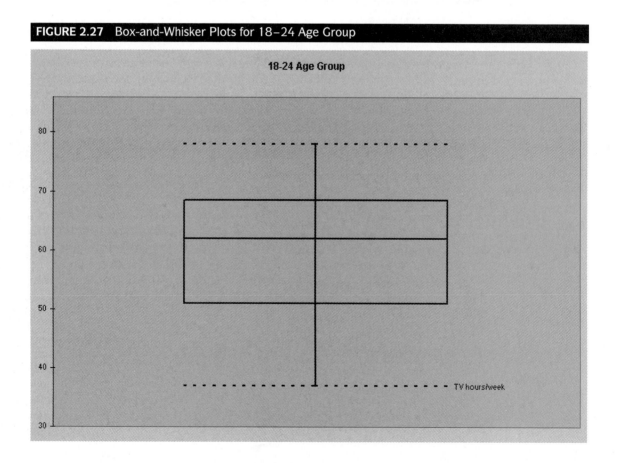

FIGURE 2.27 Box-and-Whisker Plots for 18–24 Age Group

PHSTAT NOTE

CREATING STEM-AND-LEAF DISPLAYS

From the *PHStat* menu, select *Descriptive Statistics* and then *Stem-and-Leaf Display.* The dialog box is shown in Figure 2.28. Enter the range of the data in the first box, checking the *First cell contains label* box if appropriate. You may have the tool automatically calculate the stem unit, or you may specify it as a power of 10. For example, if the numbers are large, say in the range of 800 to 900, then you might wish to specify the stem unit as 100 so that the stem values are 800, 900, and so on, and leaves represent values after the first digit. The stem-and-leaf routine also provides summary statistics if the box is checked.

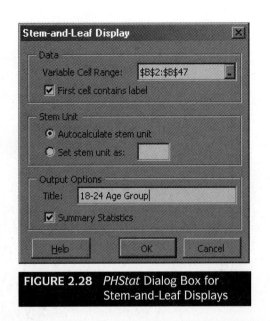

FIGURE 2.28 *PHStat* Dialog Box for Stem-and-Leaf Displays

A box-and-whisker plot for TV viewing hours for the 18–24 Age Group in the *TV Viewing.xls* worksheet is shown in Figure 2.27. Box-and-whisker plots use dashed lines to represent the minimum and maximum values in a data set, and a box encloses the first and third quartiles, with a line representing the median inside the box. There do not appear to be any extreme outliers, as neither whisker is very long relative to the box (remember that the horizontal lines divide the data into quartiles). Box-and-whisker plots that have very large whiskers help identify outliers. Also, since the median is somewhat above the center of the box, the distribution is slightly negatively skewed (from Figure 2.23, the coefficient of skewness is −0.157). The closer the median line is to the ends of the box, the higher is the degree of skewness.

The difference between the first and third quartiles, $Q_3 - Q_1$, which is represented by the box in a box-and-whisker plot, is often called the **interquartile range,** or the **mid-spread.** This includes only the middle 50 percent of the data and therefore is not influenced by extreme values. Thus it is sometimes used as an alternative measure of dispersion instead of the standard deviation.

Stem-and-Leaf Displays

Another useful tool for visually displaying data is a *stem-and-leaf display.* The concept behind the stem-and-leaf display is to classify the data into cells, similar to a histogram, but at different levels of aggregation as defined by the stem unit. Each observation is represented by two numbers: $x \mid y$, where x is the stem and y is the leaf. The stem indicates the cell, while the leaf indicates the value within the cell. For example, consider the numbers 117, 113, 124, and 126. If we define the stem to be the first two digits (i.e., a stem unit of 10), then each number can be represented as

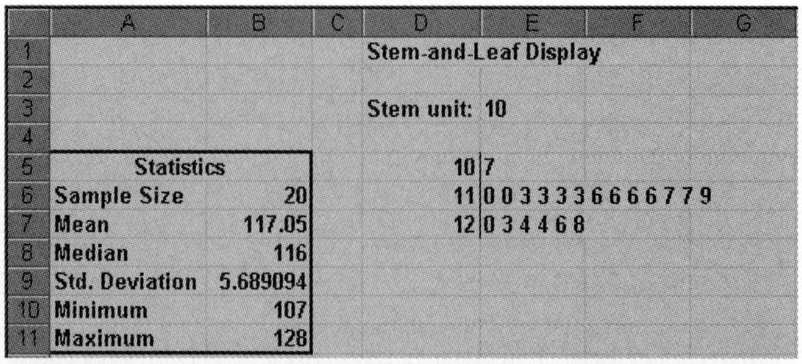

FIGURE 2.29   Stem-and-Leaf Display, Stem Unit = 10 (65+ Age Group)

NUMBER	STEM | LEAF
117	11 | 7
113	11 | 3
124	12 | 4
125	12 | 6

A stem-and-leaf display aggregates and sorts all leaves within the same stem, for example:

$$11 \mid 37$$
$$12 \mid 46$$

Figure 2.29 shows a stem-and-leaf display for the 65+ Age Group *TV Viewing* data expressed in this fashion (see the *PHStat Note: Creating Stem-and-Leaf Displays*).

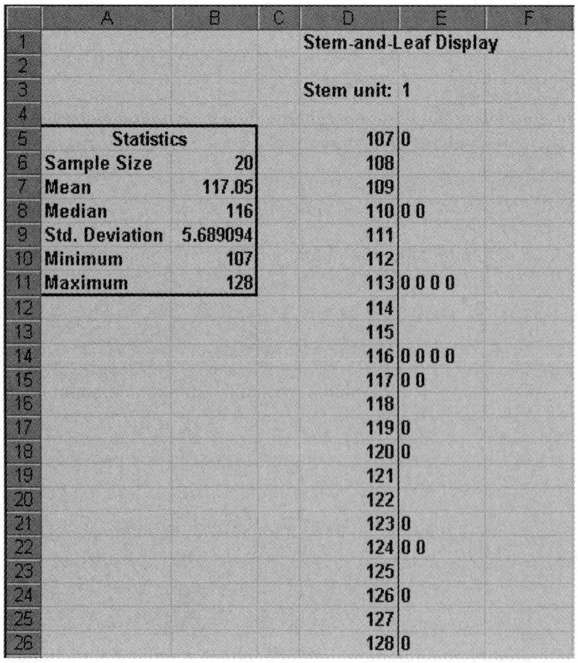

FIGURE 2.30   Stem-and-Leaf Display, Stem Unit = 1 (65+ Age Group)

	A	B	C	D	E	F	G
1				Stem-and-Leaf Display			
2							
3				Stem unit: 100			
4							
5		Statistics		6	9 9		
6	Sample Size	30		7	1 1 2 5 5 7 8 8 9		
7	Mean	823.033		8	1 2 2 4 4 4 5 5 6 6 7 7 8 9		
8	Median	838		9	0 1 1 5		
9	Std. Deviation	78.6312		10	1		
10	Minimum	686					
11	Maximum	1009					

FIGURE 2.31 Stem-and-Leaf Display, Stem Unit = 100 (Runs Scored)

The stem unit is a power of 10; the higher the stem unit, the higher the degree of aggregation of the data. A stem unit of 1 creates essentially a histogram of the individual observations. Zeros are used to indicate the number of observations (leaves) for each value (stem). Turned sideways, this looks like an ordinary histogram. Figure 2.30 shows the TV data represented in this fashion. A stem unit of 10 (as in Figure 2.29) defines the last digit as the leaf and sets all other leading digits as the stem.

Figure 2.31 shows a stem-and-leaf display for runs scored in the *1999 Baseball Data* worksheet using a stem unit of 100. Note that each leaf corresponds to the last two digits of the observations. For example, the four observations in the 900 range are 900, 906, 908, and 945. Each leaf value rounds up the last two digits to the 10s value: 00 becomes 0, 06 becomes 1, 08 becomes 1, and 45 becomes 5. Thus, in the stem-and-leaf display at this level of aggregation, we do not know the exact values of the observations. To estimate the values, multiply the stems by the stem unit, and then add the leaves multiplied by 1 if the stem is positive or −1 if the stem is negative to the next 10s digit. Thus,

$$9 \mid 0\ 1\ 1\ 5$$

provides estimates of 900, 910, 910, and 950.

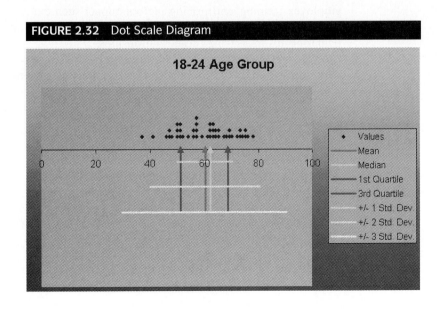

FIGURE 2.32 Dot Scale Diagram

Dot Scale Diagrams

A *dot scale diagram* is another visual display that shows the distribution of data values, along with the mean, median, first and third quartiles, and $\pm 1, 2$, and 3 standard deviation ranges from the mean. The mean essentially acts as a fulcrum as if the data were balanced along an axis. Figure 2.32 shows a dot scale diagram for the 18–24 Age Group generated by *PHStat* from the *Descriptive Statistics* menu item. Dot scale diagrams provide a visual picture as well as key statistical measures in a more detailed fashion than either box-and-whisker plots or stem-and-leaf displays.

Visual displays such as box-and-whisker plots, stem-and-leaf displays, and dot scale diagrams give more complete pictures of data sets. They are highly useful tools in exploring the characteristics of data before computing other statistical measures.

STATISTICAL RELATIONSHIPS

Two variables have a strong statistical relationship with one another if they appear to move together. For example, Figure 2.10 showed a scatter diagram of Yards Gained versus Points Scored for NFL teams. This chart suggests that an increase in yards gained corresponds to higher scoring. We see other examples on a daily basis; for instance, attendance at baseball games is often closely related to the win percentage of the team, and ice cream sales likely have a strong relationship with daily temperature. In these cases, you might suspect a definite cause-and-effect relationship. Sometimes, however, statistical relationships exist even though a change in one variable is not caused by a change in the other. For example, the *New York Times* reported a strong relationship between the golf handicaps of corporate CEOs and their companies' stock market performance over three years. CEOs that were better-than-average golfers were likely to deliver above-average returns to shareholders![2] You must be cautious in drawing inferences about *causal* relationships based solely on *statistical* relationships. (On the other hand, you might want to spend more time out on the course!)

Understanding the relationships between variables is extremely important in making good business decisions, particularly when cause-and-effect relationships can be justified. When a company understands how internal factors such as product quality, employee training, and pricing factors impact such external measures as profitability and customer satisfaction, it can make better decisions. Thus, it is helpful to have statistical tools for measuring these relationships.

Correlation is a measure of a linear relationship between two variables, X and Y, and is measured by the (population) **correlation coefficient:**

$$\rho_{x,y} = \frac{\text{cov}(X, Y)}{\sigma_x \sigma_y}$$

The numerator is called the **covariance** and is the average of the products of deviations of each observation from its respective mean:

$$\text{cov}(X, Y) = \frac{\displaystyle\sum_{i=1}^{N}(x_i - \mu_x)(y_i - \mu_y)}{N}$$

[2] Adam Bryant, "CEOs' golf games linked to companies' performance," *Cincinnati Enquirer,* June 7, 1998, p. E1.

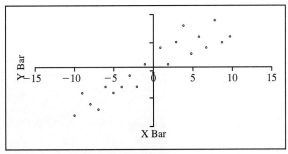

a. Positive Correlation

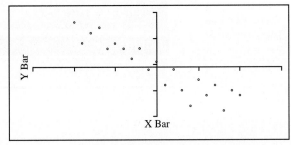

b. Negative Correlation

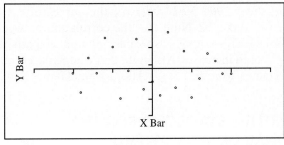

c. No Correlation

FIGURE 2.33 Examples of Correlation

Similarly, the sample correlation coefficient is computed as:

$$r = \frac{\sum\limits_{i=1}^{n}(x_i - \bar{x})(y_i - \bar{y})}{(n - 1)s_x s_y}$$

Correlation coefficients will range from -1 to $+1$. A correlation of 0 indicates that the two variables have no linear relationship to each other. Thus, if one changes, we cannot reasonably predict what the other variable might do using a linear equation (we might, however, have a well-defined nonlinear relationship). A correlation coefficient of $+1$ indicates a perfect positive linear relationship; as one variable increases, the other will also increase. A correlation coefficient of -1 also shows a perfect linear relationship, except that as one variable increases, the other decreases. In economics, for instance, a perfectly price-elastic product has a correlation between price and sales of -1; as price increases, sales decrease, and vice versa. These relationships are illustrated in Figure 2.33.

EXCEL NOTE

USING THE CORRELATION TOOL

Select *Correlation* from the *Tools/Data Analysis* menu option. The dialog box is shown in Figure 2.34. You need only input the range of the data (which must be in contiguous columns), specify whether the data are grouped by rows or columns (most applications will be grouped by columns), and indicate whether the first row contains data labels. Output options are the standard ones as for other tools we have discussed. The output of this tool is a matrix giving the correlation between each pair of variables.

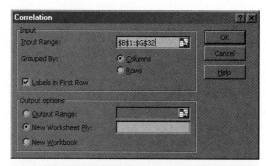

FIGURE 2.34　Correlation Tool Dialog Box

Using the Correlation tool (see *Excel Note: Using the Correlation Tool*) and the data in the worksheet *2000 NFL Data.xls,* the correlation matrix among all the variables is given in Table 2.2. Note that the correlation between Yards Gained and Points Scored is 0.83. This strong positive correlation suggests that as Yards Gained increases, Points Scored increases. Also note that a negative correlation exists between Giveaways and Games Won, and Yards Allowed and Games Won.

CASE STUDY: USING DESCRIPTIVE STATISTICS FOR THE MALCOLM BALDRIGE NATIONAL QUALITY AWARD

The Malcolm Baldrige National Quality Award recognizes U.S. companies that excel in high-performance management practice and have achieved outstanding business results. The award is a public–private partnership, funded primarily through a private foundation and administered through the National Institute of Standards and Technology (NIST) in cooperation with the American Society for Quality (ASQ). It was created to increase the awareness of American business for quality and good business practices and has become a worldwide standard for business excellence.

The award examination is based on a rigorous set of criteria, called the *Criteria for Performance Excellence,* which consists of seven major categories:

TABLE 2.2　Correlation Matrix for NFL DATA

	A	B	C	D	E	F	G
1		Yards Gained	Takeaways	Giveaways	Yards Allowed	Points Scored	Games Won
2	Yards Gained	1					
3	Takeaways	0.054527278	1				
4	Giveaways	-0.328911463	-0.31702097	1			
5	Yards Allowed	-0.092363341	-0.46593399	0.243849975	1		
6	Points Scored	0.830526921	0.298211056	-0.359934561	-0.035998535	1	
7	Games Won	0.601483569	0.58259747	-0.541538751	-0.513343889	0.68135208	1

Leadership

Strategic Planning

Customer and Market Focus

Information and Analysis

Human Resource Focus

Process Management

Business Results

Each category consists of several *items* that focus on major requirements on which businesses should focus. For example, the three items in the Process Management category are 6.1, Product and Service Processes; 6.2, Business Processes; and 6.3, Support Processes. Each item, in turn, consists of a small number of *areas to address,* which seek specific information on approaches used to ensure and improve competitive performance, the deployment of these approaches, or results obtained from such deployment. The criteria may be downloaded from the National Quality Program Web site [http://www.quality.nist.gov/ or www.baldrige.org].

Applicants submit a 50-page document that describes their management practices and business results that respond to the criteria. The evaluation of applicants for the award is conducted by a volunteer board of examiners selected by NIST. In the first stage, each application is reviewed by a team of examiners. They evaluate the applicant's response to each criteria item, listing major strengths and opportunities for improvement relative to the criteria. Based on these comments, a score from 0 to 100 in increments of 10 is given to each item. Scores for each examination item are computed by multiplying the examiner's score by the maximum point value that can be earned for that item, which varies by item. These point values weight the importance of each item in the criteria. The scores are reviewed by a panel of nine judges without knowledge of the specific companies. The higher-scoring applications enter a *consensus stage* in which a selected group of examiners discuss, via telephone conferencing, variations in individual assessments and scores and arrive at consensus comments and scores for each item. The panel of judges then reviews the scores and selects the highest-scoring applicants for site visits. At this point, six or seven examiners visit the company for up to a week to verify information contained in the written application and resolve issues that are unclear. The judges use the site visit reports to recommend award recipients.

The consensus stage is an extremely important step of the process. It is designed to smooth out variations in examiners' scores, which inevitably arise because of different perceptions of the applicants' responses relative to the criteria, and provide useful feedback to the applicants. Statistics and data analysis tools are used to provide a summary of the examiners' scoring profiles and to help schedule the order of discussion based on the variation in the scores and the point values of the items. Specifically, the standard deviation of each item's scores is multiplied by the point value to arrive at a weighted standard deviation. The discussion priorities of the items is based on these weighted standard deviations. Thus, items having higher point values as well as larger variation among examiners will be discussed earlier in the consensus call, so that sufficient time can be allotted to their discussion and so that important items not be affected by fatigue during the conference call (which may last up to 5 hours).

Figures 2.35 through 2.37 illustrate a hypothetical example (all data and calculations may be found in the Excel workbook *Baldrige.xls*).[3] The distribution of

---

[3] The criteria undergo periodic revision, so the items and maximum points will not necessarily coincide with the current year's criteria.

	A	B	C	D	E	F	G	H	I	J
1	Item	Maximum	Examiner	Examiner	Examiner	Examiner	Examiner	Examiner	Examiner	Examiner
2		Points	1	2	3	4	5	6	7	8
3	1.1	80	80	80	50	60	60	70	70	50
4	1.2	30	30	50	30	40	40	60	60	50
5	2.1	40	50	70	50	50	40	60	70	40
6	2.2	40	30	40	50	50	60	30	30	50
7	3.1	40	30	60	40	60	50	30	50	30
8	3.2	40	30	50	60	60	60	50	30	60
9	4.1	25	40	70	50	60	40	30	20	50
10	4.2	15	30	20	40	40	30	30	10	30
11	4.3	40	20	20	30	50	30	30	20	30
12	5.1	40	70	50	60	40	40	60	60	50
13	5.2	30	50	30	40	40	30	50	50	50
14	5.3	30	50	20	40	40	70	40	40	20
15	6.1	60	50	60	50	50	50	40	30	40
16	6.2	20	30	40	30	50	40	30	20	30
17	6.3	20	20	30	30	40	20	10	10	30
18	7.1	125	60	70	70	70	80	70	70	70
19	7.2	125	50	60	70	50	70	50	70	70
20	7.3	50	50	40	50	50	70	30	30	50
21	7.4	25	40	50	50	50	50	40	20	60
22	7.5	125	60	80	70	60	70	40	60	70
23	Weighted score		497	575.5	549.5	539.5	581	474	505.5	535.5

FIGURE 2.35   Examiner Scores for a Hypothetical Baldrige Consensus Analysis

examiner scores is shown in Figure 2.35. The weighted score is obtained by adding the product of the maximum point column entry times the examiner score for that item divided by 100. Thus each examiner score is the percent of the maximum points awarded for that item. The box-and-whisker plot in Figure 2.36 shows the variation among item scores in a graphical fashion. On item 7.1, the examiners were very consistent, with most examiners assigning a score of 70; Examiner 1 gave a score of 60, and Examiner 5 a score of 80. The greatest range of scores awarded was for item 4.1,

FIGURE 2.36   Box-and-Whisker Plot of Examiner Scores

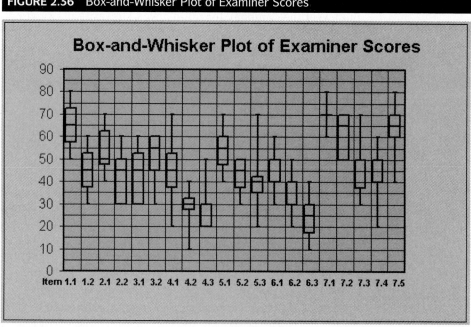

	A	B	C	D	E	F	G	H
1	Item	Maximum	Average	Median		Standard	Weighted	
2		Points	Score	Score	Range	Deviation	Std. Dev.	Rank
3	7.5	125	63.8	65	30	11.9	1484.7	1
4	7.2	125	61.3	65	20	9.9	1238.8	2
5	1.1	80	65.0	65	30	12.0	956.2	3
6	7.1	125	70.0	70	10	5.3	668.2	4
7	7.3	50	46.3	50	20	13.0	651.2	5
8	6.1	60	46.3	50	20	9.2	549.7	6
9	3.2	40	50.0	55	30	13.1	523.7	7
10	3.1	40	43.8	45	0	13.0	521.0	8
11	5.3	30	40.0	40	30	16.0	481.1	9
12	2.1	40	53.8	50	10	11.9	475.1	10
13	2.2	40	42.5	45	20	11.6	466.0	11
14	5.1	40	53.8	55	30	10.6	424.3	12
15	4.1	25	45.0	45	30	16.0	400.9	13
16	4.3	40	28.8	30	10	9.9	396.4	14
17	1.2	30	45.0	45	20	12.0	358.6	15
18	7.4	25	45.0	50	40	12.0	298.8	16
19	5.2	30	42.5	45	20	8.9	265.9	17
20	6.3	20	23.8	25	20	10.6	212.1	18
21	6.2	20	33.8	30	10	9.2	183.2	19
22	4.2	15	28.8	30	20	9.9	148.7	20
23	Weighted Score		453.2	470.3				

FIGURE 2.37   Statistical Analysis and Weighted Ranks of Consensus Scores

with Examiner 7 assigning a score of 20, and Examiner 2 giving a score of 70. Item 7.2 had less range, but more variance, as examiners for the most part assigned a score of either 50 or 70. In Figure 2.37, we show the key statistics of the distribution, including the averages, medians, ranges, and standard deviations. The weighted standard deviation is used to establish the ranking of each item (using the Excel function RANK). As shown, the data are sorted according to these rankings using the *Sort* command in the *Data* menu.

The Baldrige scoring example demonstrates the value of statistical tools first to provide a basis for ranking but also to examine specifics as to why a company was ranked wherever it was ranked. The analysis provided by the box-and-whisker plot, as well as the basic data in Figure 2.35, shows where examiners differed the most and which items had the most impact in company ratings.

Questions and Problems

1. How can a cost accountant or financial analyst use charts to aid in understanding firm operations?
2. Data from the 2000 U.S. Census show the following distribution of ages for residents of Ohio:

TOTAL HOUSEHOLDS	4,445,773
Family households (families)	2,993,023
With own children under 18 years	1,409,912
Married-couple family	2,285,798
With own children under 18 years	996,042
Female householder, no husband present	536,878
With own children under 18 years	323,095

Nonfamily households	1,452,750
Householder living alone	1,215,614
Householder 65 years and over	446,396

    a. Construct a column chart to visually represent these data.

    b. Construct a stacked bar chart to display the subcategories where relevant. (Note that you will have to compute additional subcategories, for instance, under Family households, the number of families without children under 18, so that the total of the subcategories equals the major category total. The sum of all categories does not equal the total.)

    c. Construct a pie chart showing the proportion of households in each category.

3. The Excel file *Energy Production & Consumption.xls* provides various energy data from 1949 through 1999.

    a. Construct an area chart showing the fossil fuel production as a proportion of total energy production.

    b. Construct line charts for each of the variables.

    c. Construct a line chart showing both the total energy production and consumption during these years.

    d. Construct a scatter diagram for total energy exports and total energy production.

4. The Excel file *Economic Indexes.xls* provides data on the annual percent change in the Dow Jones Industrial average, Consumer Price Index, Standard & Poor's 500, and average yield for one-year Treasury bills from 1960 through 1999.

    a. Construct line charts for each of these data series.

    b. Compute the mean and variance for the percent changes in the DJIA and S&P 500 indexes.

5. The Excel file *Accounting Professionals.xls* provides the results of a survey of 27 employees in a tax division of a Fortune 100 company. Use PivotTables to find a cross tabulation of

    a. The number of employees of each gender who have or do not have a CPA.

    b. The number of employees in each age group who have or do not have a CPA.

6. A mental health agency measured the self-esteem score for randomly selected individuals with disabilities who were involved in some work activity within the past year. The Excel file *Self Esteem.xls* provides the data, including the individuals' marital status, length of work, type of support received (direct support includes job-related services such as job coaching and counseling), education, and age. Use PivotTables to find a cross tabulation of the number of individuals within each classification of marital status and support level.

7. The Excel file *Unions and Labor Law Data.xls* reports the percent of public and private sector employees in unions in 1982 for each state, along with indicators of whether the states had a bargaining law that covered public employees or right-to-work laws. Use PivotTables to find a cross tabulation of the number of states within each classification of having or not having bargaining laws and right-to-work laws.

8. Construct frequency distributions and histograms for the number of TV hours/week for each age group in the data set *TV Viewing.xls*. Also compute the relative frequency and cumulative relative frequency for each.

9. A producer of computer-aided design software for the aerospace industry receives numerous calls for technical support. Tracking software is used to monitor response and resolution times. In addition, the company surveys customers who request support using the following scale:

> 0—Did not exceed expectations
> 1—Marginally met expectations
> 2—Met expectations
> 3—Exceeded expectations
> 4—Greatly exceeded expectations

The questions are:

> Q1: Did the support representative explain the process for resolving your problem?
> Q2: Did the support representative keep you informed about the status of progress in resolving your problem?
> Q3: Was the support representative courteous and professional?
> Q4: Was your problem resolved?
> Q5: Was your problem resolved in an acceptable amount of time?
> Q6: Overall, how did you find the service provided by our technical support department?

A final question asks the customer to rate the overall quality of the product using a scale of

> 0—Very poor
> 1—Poor
> 2—Good
> 3—Very good
> 4—Excellent

A sample of survey responses and associated resolution and response data are provided in the Excel file *Customer Support Survey Data.xls.*
   a. Construct frequency distributions and histograms for the responses to each of these questions.
   b. Compute the relative frequency and cumulative relative frequency for each of the distributions in part (a).
10. The Excel file *Baseball Attendance.xls* shows the attendance in thousands at San Francisco Giants baseball games for the 10 years before the Oakland A's moved to the Bay Area in 1968, as well as the combined attendance for both teams for the next 11 years. What is the mean and standard deviation of the number of baseball fans attending before and after the A's move to the San Francisco area? What conclusions might you draw?
11. Data obtained from a county auditor (see the file *Market Value.xls*) provides information about the age, square footage, and current market value of houses along one street in a particular subdivision.
   a. Considering these data as describing the population of homeowners on this street, compute the mean, median, variance, and standard deviation for each of these variables using the formulas presented in this chapter.
   b. Use the appropriate Excel functions to compute these statistics and compare your results.
   c. Compute the coefficient of variation for each variable. Which has the least and greatest relative dispersion?
   d. Show that Chebyshev's theorem holds for these data for $k = 3$.
12. Compute the mean, variance, and standard deviation of the National League payroll in the file *1999 Baseball Data.xls* using the formulas presented in this chapter. Use the appropriate Excel functions to compute these statistics and compare your results. How do they compare to those of the American League?

13. A marketing study of adults in the 18–34 age group reported the following information:

> Spent under $100 on children's clothing per year: 9.3 percent
> Spent $100–$499 on children's clothing per year: 24.6 percent
> Spent $500–$999 on children's clothing per year: 3 percent

The remainder reported spending nothing. Estimate the sample mean and sample variance of spending on children's clothing for this age group.

14. A marketing study found that 6.1 percent of adults 35 and older spent under $100 on cameras or accessories last year, 2.7 percent spent between $100 and $249, 4.0 percent spent between $250 and $499, and 2.4 percent spent between $500 and $999. The rest of the sample reported no spending on cameras and accessories.
    a. What is the estimate of the mean and standard deviation of the amount spent by adults 35 and older?
    b. Of those who purchased cameras and accessories, what is the mean amount spent?

15. Data from the 2000 U.S. Census show the following distribution of ages for residents of California:

	Number	Percent
Under 5 years	2,486,981	7.3
5 to 9 years	2,725,880	8
10 to 14 years	2,570,822	7.6
15 to 19 years	2,450,888	7.2
20 to 24 years	2,381,288	7
25 to 34 years	5,229,062	15.4
35 to 44 years	5,485,341	16.2
45 to 54 years	4,331,635	12.8
55 to 59 years	1,467,252	4.3
60 to 64 years	1,146,841	3.4
65 to 74 years	1,887,823	5.6
75 to 84 years	1,282,178	3.8
85 years and over	425,657	1.3

Estimate the mean age and standard deviation of age for California residents, assuming these data represent a sample of current residents.

16. Data from the 2000 U.S. Census show the following distribution of ages for residents of New York:

	Number	Percent
Under 5 years	1,239,417	6.5
5 to 9 years	1,351,857	7.1
10 to 14 years	1,332,433	7
15 to 19 years	1,287,544	6.8
20 to 24 years	1,244,309	6.6
25 to 34 years	2,757,324	14.5
35 to 44 years	3,074,298	16.2

45 to 54 years	2,552,936	13.5
55 to 59 years	932,008	4.9
60 to 64 years	755,979	4
65 to 74 years	1,276,046	6.7
75 to 84 years	860,818	4.5
85 years and over	311,488	1.6

Estimate the mean age and standard deviation of age for New York residents, assuming these data represent a sample of current residents.

17. The following data were reported on annual giving for a church. Estimate the mean and standard deviation of the annual contributions, assuming these data represent the entire population of parishioners.

Church Contributions		
	All Parishoners	No. of Families with Children in Parish School
Did Not Contribute	861	14
$ — to $ 100.00	431	43
$ 100.00 to $ 200.00	227	61
$ 200.00 to $ 300.00	218	58
$ 300.00 to $ 400.00	186	54
$ 400.00 to $ 500.00	145	41
$ 500.00 to $ 600.00	122	41
$ 600.00 to $ 700.00	90	28
$ 700.00 to $ 800.00	72	27
$ 800.00 to $ 900.00	62	26
$ 900.00 to $ 1,000.00	57	20
$ 1,000.00 to $ 1,500.00	191	63
$ 1,500.00 to $ 2,000.00	83	21
$ 2,000.00 to $ 2,500.00	45	16
$ 2,500.00 to $ 3,000.00	20	5
$ 3,000.00 to $ 3,500.00	13	4
$ 3,500.00 to $ 4,000.00	6	2
$ 4,000.00 to $ 4,500.00	5	3
$ 4,500.00 to $ 5,000.00	4	2
$ 5,000.00 to $10,000.00	7	1
$10,000.00 to $15,000.00	2	0

18. Use the Descriptive Statistics tool for the number of TV viewing hours/week for the remaining age groups in the data set *TV Viewing.xls* not computed in Figure 2.23. Clearly explain each of the statistics. What conclusions do you draw with respect to differences?

19. The Excel file *Weather.xls* contains mean temperatures for January and July and average annual precipitation for selected cities across the United States.
   a. Apply the Descriptive Statistics tool to these data. What differences are evident?
   b. Explain the coefficients of skewness and kurtosis (use a histogram to illustrate their meaning).

20. Find the first and third quartiles for each of the performance statistics in the data set *Ohio Education Performance.xls.*
21. Find the 10th and 90th percentile of home prices in the data set *Market Value.xls.*
22. Find the first and third quartiles and the 10th and 90th percentiles of each of the variables in the data set *Weather.xls.*
23. The Excel file *Unions and Labor Law Data.xls* reports the percent of public and private sector employees in unions in 1982 for each state, along with indicators of whether the states had a bargaining law that covered public employees or right-to-work laws.
    a. Compute the proportion of employees in unions in each of the four categories: public sector with bargaining laws, public sector without bargaining laws, private sector with bargaining laws, and private sector without bargaining laws.
    b. Compute the proportion of employees in unions in each of the four categories: public sector with right-to-work laws, public sector without right-to-work laws, private sector with right-to-work laws, and private sector without right-to-work laws.
24. Construct box-and-whisker plots and dot scale diagrams for each of the variables in the data set *Weather.xls.* What conclusions can you draw from them?
25. Construct box-and-whisker plots and dot scale diagrams for each of the variables in the data set *Ohio Education Performance.xls.* What conclusions can you draw from them?
26. Construct stem-and-leaf displays for the following statistics in the *1999 Baseball Data.xls* file:
    a. Home runs scored using a stem unit of 10.
    b. ERA using a stem unit of 1 (each leaf will represent the decimal value).
    c. Pitching saves using a stem unit of 10.
    d. Pitching saves using a stem unit of 1.
27. What are the approximate values of the data represented by the stem-and-leaf display in Figure 2.38?

	A	B	C
1	Stem-and-Leaf Display		
2			
3	Stem unit: 1000		
4			
5	9	8	
6	10		
7	11		
8	12	0 0 8	
9	13	2 5 5 5	
10	14	3	
11	15		
12	16	5 8	
13	17		
14	18	8 8	
15	19		
16	20		
17	21	0	
18	22		
19	23		
20	24		
21	25		
22	26		
23	27	0	

FIGURE 2.38   Stem-and-Leaf Display Example

28. A deep foundation engineering contractor has bid on a foundation system for a new world headquarters building for a Fortune 500 company. A part of the project consists of installing 311 augercast piles. The contractor was given bid information for cost estimating purposes, which consisted of the estimated depth of each pile; however, actual drill footage of each pile could not be determined exactly until construction was performed. The Excel file *Pile Foundation.xls* contains the estimates and actual pile lengths after the project was completed. Compute the correlation coefficient between the estimated and actual pile lengths. What does this tell you?

29. Call centers have high turnover rates because of the stressful environment. The national average is approximately 50 percent. The director of human resources for a large bank has compiled data about 70 former employees at one of the bank's call centers (see the Excel file *Call Center Data.xls*). For this sample, how strongly is length of service correlated with starting age?

30. A national homebuilder builds single-family homes and condominium-style townhouses. The Excel file *House Sales Data.xls* provides information on the selling price, lot cost, type of home, and region of the country (M = Midwest, S = South) for closings during one month.
    a. Construct a scatter diagram showing the relationship between sales price and lot cost and compute the correlation coefficient.
    b. Construct scatter diagrams showing the relationship between sales price and lot cost *for each region* and compute the correlation coefficient.
    c. Construct scatter diagrams showing the relationship between sales price and lot cost for each type of house and compute the correlation coefficient.

31. The Excel file *Salary Data.xls* provides information on current salary, beginning salary, previous experience in months when hired, and total years of education for a sample of 100 employees in a firm. Find the correlation matrix for these data. What conclusions can you draw?

32. The Excel file *Infant Mortality.xls* provides data on infant mortality rate (deaths per 1000 births), female literacy (percent who read), and population density (people per square kilometer) for 85 countries. Compute the correlation matrix for these three variables. What conclusions can you draw?

C A S E

DESCRIPTIVE STATISTICAL ANALYSIS OF TRACWAY DATA

Tracway originally produced lawn mowers, but a significant portion of sales volume over the past ten years has come from the growing small tractor market. As we noted in Chapter 1, Tracway sells their products worldwide, with sales regions including North America, South America, Europe, and the Pacific Rim. Three years ago a new region was opened to serve China, where a booming market for small tractors has been established. Tracway has always emphasized quality and considers the quality it builds into its products as its primary selling point. In the last two years Tracway has also emphasized the ease-of-use of their products.

Before digging into the details of operations, Henry Hudson wants to gain an overview of Tracway's overall business performance and market position by examining the data in the balanced scorecard provided in the *Tracway.xls* database. Specifically, he is asking you to

1. Construct appropriate charts for the data in the following worksheets and summarize your conclusions from analysis of these charts.

   a. *C1 Dealer Satisfaction*
   b. *C2 End-User Satisfaction*
   c. *C4 Complaints*
   d. *C5 Mower Unit Sales*
   e. *C6 Tractor Unit Sales*
   f. *F1 Revenues*

   g. *I1 On-Time Delivery*
   h. *I2 Defects After Delivery*
   i. *I4 Response Time*

2. Construct frequency distributions and histograms for the entire data in the worksheet *C3 2002 Customer Survey,* and individually by region. What are your conclusions from examining these?

3. Determine how sales of mowers and tractors compare with industry totals. How strongly are monthly product sales correlated with industry sales?

4. Compute the mean satisfaction ratings and standard deviations by year and region in the worksheets *C1 Dealer Satisfaction* and *C2 End-User Satisfaction.* What conclusions can you reach?

5. Find the proportion of complaints from North America. Has this changed over time?

6. Evaluate the differences in each quarter of the worksheet *I4 Response Time.*

7. Determine how defects after delivery (worksheet *I2 Defects After Delivery*) have changed over these five years. (Use stem-and-leaf displays.)

8. Draw conclusions for the process study data in the worksheet *S2 Transmission Costs.* (Compute key descriptive statistics and construct box-and-whisker plots.) ■

CHAPTER

3

RANDOM VARIABLES AND PROBABILITY DISTRIBUTIONS

INTRODUCTION

Most business decisions involve some elements of uncertainty and randomness. For example, in models of manufacturing operations, times of job arrivals, job types, processing times, times between machine breakdowns, and repair times all involve uncertainty. Similarly, a model to predict the future return of an investment portfolio requires a variety of assumptions about uncertain economic conditions and market behavior. Specifying the nature of such assumptions is a key modeling task that relies on fundamental knowledge of random variables and probability distributions—the subject of this chapter. Random variables and probability distributions are also important in applying statistics to analyze sample data from business processes, because sample data are usually assumed to stem from some underlying probability distribution. Thus, we will also examine characteristics of sampling distributions in this chapter and introduce simulation as a tool for understanding them and errors associated with sampling. The key concepts and tools that we will study are

- The notion of probability, and the calculation of joint, marginal, and conditional probabilities
- Random variables, including their definition and calculations of expected value and variance
- Probability distributions: discrete and continuous distributions, and their applications in probability modeling
- Simulation techniques for random sampling from probability distributions, the concept of random numbers, and an introduction to the Excel add-in, *Crystal Ball*
- Sampling distributions and sampling error

BASIC CONCEPTS

In this section we define and illustrate fundamental concepts of probability, random variables, and probability distributions. Many of these concepts are similar to ideas we developed in Chapter 2. Here, however, the focus is on theoretical models rather than on sample data.

Probability

The notion of probability is used every day, from casino gambling to weather forecasts to stock market predictions. **Probability** is the likelihood that an event will occur. We can think of an **event** as the collection of one or more outcomes of some experiment, such as rolling dice, observing the weather, or watching the stock market. The outcomes might be values of the sum of the dice, the temperature or amount of precipitation for the next day, or the value of the Dow Jones Industrial Average (DJIA) at the end of a month.

Probability may be viewed in one of three ways. First, if the process that generates the event is known, probabilities can be determined from theoretical arguments; this is the *classical definition* of probability. For example, if we count the possible outcomes associated with rolling two dice, we can easily determine that out of 36 possible outcomes, one outcome will be the number 2, two outcomes will be the number 3, six outcomes will be the number 7, and so on. Thus, the probability of rolling a 7 is 6/36 = 1/6. The second approach to probability, called the *relative frequency definition,* is based on empirical data. For example, a meteorologist knows that on 10 days when certain weather conditions have been observed, it has rained the next day eight times. Thus, the probability of rain the next day would be specified as 0.8, or 80 percent. Clearly, as more data become available, the relative frequency, and hence, the probability, may change. Finally, the *subjective method* of probability is based on judgment, as financial analysts might do in predicting a 75 percent chance that the DJIA will increase 10 percent over the next year, or as sports experts might predict a one in five chance (0.20 probability) of a certain team making it to the Super Bowl at the start of the football season.

Probability Rules and Calculations

There are some basic rules and formulas for computing probabilities associated with events:

Rule 1. The probability associated with any outcome must be between 0 and 1.
Rule 2. The sum of the probabilities over all possible outcomes must be 1.0.

For example, suppose that the outcomes associated with observing the stock market on a particular day along with their estimated probabilities are

1. DJIA up; NASDAQ up, probability = 0.26
2. DJIA down; NASDAQ up, probability = 0.05
3. DJIA unchanged; NASDAQ up, probability = 0.03
4. DJIA up; NASDAQ down, probability = 0.10
5. DJIA down; NASDAQ down, probability = 0.42
6. DJIA unchanged; NASDAQ down, probability = 0.05
7. DJIA up; NASDAQ unchanged, probability = 0.04
8. DJIA down; NASDAQ unchanged, probability = 0.03
9. DJIA unchanged; NASDAQ unchanged, probability = 0.02

We may summarize this in the following table:

Probability	NASDAQ Up	NASDAQ Down	NASDAQ Unchanged
DJIA up	0.26	0.10	0.04
DJIA down	0.05	0.42	0.03
DJIA unchanged	0.03	0.05	0.02

We see that these outcomes are exhaustive (there are no other possibilities) and that the sum of the probabilities is 1.0. Two events are **mutually exclusive** if both cannot occur at the same time. Clearly, any two of the preceding outcomes are mutually exclusive.

Rule 3. The probability of any event is the sum of the probabilities of the outcomes that compose that event.

For instance, consider the event *DJIA goes up*. This event will occur if outcomes 1 or 4 or 7 occurs. Therefore, the probability of this event is $P(DJIA\ goes\ up) = 0.26 + 0.10 + 0.04 = 0.40$—equivalently, the sum of the probabilities in the first row of the table.

Rule 4. If events A and B are mutually exclusive, then $P(A\ or\ B) = P(A) + P(B)$.

To illustrate this, let A be the event *DJIA goes up* and B be the event *DJIA unchanged*. Clearly, these events are mutually exclusive, and $P(DJIA\ unchanged) = 0.03 + 0.05 + 0.02 = 0.10$. Therefore, $P(DJIA\ goes\ up\ or\ DJIA\ unchanged) = 0.40 + 0.10 = 0.50$.

Rule 5. If two events A and B are not mutually exclusive, then $P(A\ or\ B) = P(A) + P(B) - P(A\ and\ B)$.

Consider the event *NASDAQ unchanged*. This occurs if outcome 7 or 8 or 9 occurs, and $P(NASDAQ\ unchanged) = 0.04 + 0.03 + 0.02 = 0.09$. Now consider $P(DJIA\ unchanged\ or\ NASDAQ\ unchanged)$. We see that these events are *not* mutually exclusive since they may occur at the same time (specifically, when outcome 9 occurs). Thus, $P(DJIA\ unchanged\ and\ NASDAQ\ unchanged) = 0.02$. If we simply added $P(DJIA\ unchanged)$ and $P(NASDAQ\ unchanged)$, which represent the last row and last column in the preceding table, then we would be adding the probability $P(DJIA\ unchanged\ and\ NASDAQ\ unchanged)$ twice. Using Rule 5, we have $P(DJIA\ unchanged\ or\ NASDAQ\ unchanged) = 0.10 + 0.09 - 0.02 = 0.17$. Note that this probability is the same as the collection of outcomes 3, 6, 7, 8, and 9, the sum of whose probabilities are $0.03 + 0.05 + 0.04 + 0.03 + 0.02 = 0.17$.

RANDOM VARIABLES

A **random variable** is a numerical description of the outcome of an experiment. Random variables are usually denoted by capital Roman letters, such as X or Y. Some "experiments," like rolling dice or observing the value of the DJIA, naturally have numerical outcomes; for others, like the weather, we might have to associate some arbitrary numerical value to the outcomes, such as $0 =$ sunny, $1 =$ cloudy, $2 =$ rain, and so on.

Random variables may be *discrete* or *continuous*. A **discrete random variable** can have only a countable number of outcomes. For example, the outcome of rolling dice, the weather for the next day, and the number of customers who respond to a telemarketing campaign are discrete random variables. A **continuous random variable** assumes outcomes over a continuous range of real numbers. Examples of continuous random variables include the daily temperature, the time to complete a task, time to repair a failed machine, and the return on an investment. Sometimes the distinction between a discrete and continuous random variable is not clear. For example, stock prices used to be recorded in increments of one-eighth. Technically, this is discrete; however, for practical purposes of building and analyzing decision models, it would be easier to consider these values as continuous random variables. (Now, stock prices are recorded as decimal fractions.)

PROBABILITY DISTRIBUTIONS

A **probability distribution** is a characterization of the possible values that a random variable may assume along with the probability of assuming these values. For a discrete random variable X, the probability of each discrete outcome is characterized by a **probability function, $f(x)$.** A probability function has the properties that (1) the probability of each outcome must be between 0 and 1 and (2) the sum of all probabilities must add to 1; that is,

$$0 \le f(x_i) \le 1$$

$$\sum_i f(x_i) = 1$$

For example, the U.S. Census Bureau 1998 Current Population Reports P20-513 provides data on the educational status of persons 25 years and older. Figure 3.1 shows a portion of the Excel file *Census Education Data.xls*. If we divide the number of individuals in each age bracket in the range B4:B9 by the population in cell B2, we will

FIGURE 3.1   Portion of *Census Education Data.xls*

	A	B	C	D	E	F	G	H
1		Population	Not a High School Grad	High School Graduate	Some College No Degree	Associate's Degree	Bachelor's Degree	Advanced Degree
2	Total Persons	172,211,000	29,620,292	58,207,318	29,620,292	12,915,825	28,242,604	13,604,669
3	Age							
4	25-34	39,354,000	4,683,126	12,553,926	7,792,092	3,423,798	8,382,402	2,439,948
5	35-44	44,462,000	5,335,440	15,117,080	8,136,546	4,134,966	8,136,546	3,556,960
6	45-54	34,058,000	4,427,540	10,932,618	6,062,324	2,894,930	5,960,150	3,848,554
7	55-64	22,255,000	4,562,275	8,301,115	3,338,250	1,157,260	2,893,150	2,047,460
8	65-74	17,873,000	5,165,297	6,505,772	2,466,474	768,539	1,787,300	1,179,618
9	75 and older	14,209,000	5,399,420	4,717,388	1,847,170	454,688	1,150,929	625,196

have constructed a probability distribution for the random variable X, where we associate the value $x = 1$ to an age bracket of 25–34, $x = 2$ to the bracket 35–44, and so on. The probability distribution of age brackets for persons 25 and older is

x	$f(x)$
1	0.2285
2	0.2582
3	0.1978
4	0.1292
5	0.1038
6	0.0825

Note that this probability distribution satisfies the two properties just stated.

A **cumulative distribution function, $F(x)$,** specifies the probability that the random variable X will assume a value less than or equal to a specified value, x. This is also denoted as $P(X \le x)$. In the previous example, the cumulative distribution function is

x	$F(x)$
1	0.2285
2	0.4867
3	0.6845
4	0.8137
5	0.9175
6	1.0000

Many situations involve two or more random variables. For example, in the census education data, not only is an individual's age a random variable, but so also is his or her educational status as shown in row 1 in Figure 3.1. We may define the random variable $Y = 1$ to correspond to Not a High School Grad, $Y = 2$ to High School Graduate, and so on. By dividing the number in each cell by the total population, we construct a **joint probability distribution** for the two random variables:

Age	Not a High School Grad	High School Graduate	Some College No Degree	Associate's Degree	Bachelor's Degree	Advanced Degree	
25–34	0.027	0.073	0.045	0.020	0.049	0.014	0.228
35–44	0.031	0.088	0.047	0.024	0.047	0.021	0.258
45–54	0.026	0.063	0.035	0.017	0.035	0.022	0.198
55–64	0.026	0.048	0.019	0.007	0.017	0.012	0.129
65–74	0.030	0.038	0.014	0.004	0.010	0.007	0.104
75 and older	0.031	0.027	0.011	0.003	0.007	0.004	0.082
	0.172	0.338	0.172	0.075	0.164	0.080	1.000

A joint probability distribution of two random variables X and Y specifies the probability that $X = x$ and $Y = y$, denoted as $P(X = x, Y = y) = f(x,y)$. Thus, the joint probability of being in the 25–34 age bracket and not being a high school graduate is $f(1,1) = 0.027$. (Note that the table we constructed earlier for the DJIA and NASDAQ is a joint probability distribution.) The probabilities in the last row and column are called **marginal probabilities** and represent the probability associated with each random variable regardless of the value of the other. For instance, the probability of having a bachelor's degree, $P(Y = 5)$, is 0.164, and the probability of being 75 and older, $P(X = 6)$, is 0.082. *PHStat* has a tool for computing simple and joint probabilities, but it is limited to 2 × 2 cross tabulations.

Two discrete random variables X and Y are **independent** if the joint probability of X and Y equals the product of the marginal probabilities, that is, $f(x,y) = f(x)f(y)$. In this example, it is easy to see that age bracket and education status are *not* independent, since, for example, $P(X = 1, Y = 1) = 0.027 \neq (0.228)(0.172) = 0.038$. The notion of independence is best understood by noting that if the random variables *were* independent, then the proportion of individuals with a certain education status would be the same for every age bracket. Here, we see, for instance, that 11.9% of the population in the 25–34 age bracket are not high school graduates, while 38% of those 75 and older are not high school graduates. Not being independent means that the probability that one random variable takes on a certain value (e.g., education status) depends on the value of the other random variable (e.g., age bracket). This leads to the concept of conditional probability.

Conditional probabilities are the probabilities of occurrence of one event, given that another event is known to have occurred. For example, suppose we know that an individual has a bachelor's degree. What is the probability that he or she is in the 55–64 age bracket? From Figure 3.1, we see that of the 28,242,604 individuals with bachelor's degrees, 2,893,150 are in the 55–64 age bracket. Therefore, the probability is 2,893,150/28,242,604 = 0.102. We can also find this from the joint and marginal probabilities by dividing the joint probability by the marginal probability. In general,

$$f(x \mid y) = f(x,y)/f(y)$$

where $f(x \mid y)$ is the conditional probability of x given y. Thus, the probability of being in the 55–64 age bracket given that one has a bachelor's degree is 0.017/0.164 = 0.104 (with the difference due to rounding the probabilities first to three decimal places). Similarly, the probability of being a high school graduate only, given that the individual is in the 35–44 age bracket is 0.088/0.258 = 0.341.

This formula provides an alternative way of viewing the notion of independent random variables. Note that

$$f(x,y) = f(x \mid y)f(y)$$

But we stated earlier that if X and Y are independent, then $f(x,y) = f(x)f(y)$, or by substitution, $f(x) = f(x \mid y)$. This simply says that the probability of the random variable X does not depend on the value of the random variable Y. The symmetric statement is also true for independence: $f(y) = f(y \mid x)$, meaning that the probability of the random variable Y does not depend on the value of X.

The probabilities of various outcomes of continuous random variables are characterized by a **probability density function, $f(x)$.** A density function has the properties that $f(x) \geq 0$ for all values of x and that the total area under the function is 1. For continuous random variables, it does not make mathematical sense to attempt to define a probability for a specific value of x, as there are an infinite number of values (if we attempt to add them up, the result will always be larger than one!). For continuous

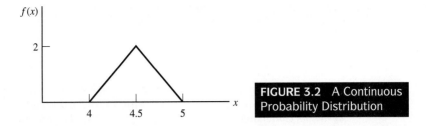

FIGURE 3.2 A Continuous Probability Distribution

random variables, probabilities are defined *over intervals*. The probability that a random variable will assume a value between x_1 and x_2 is given by the area under the density function between x_1 and x_2. As an illustration, Figure 3.2 shows a triangular density function. Using simple geometry, it is easy to see that the total area under the curve is 1.0. Figure 3.3 shows the probability that X is greater than 4.7. Using similar triangles ($0.3/0.5 = h/2$), we see that the height of the function at $x = 4.7$ is 1.2. Therefore, the area of the triangle to the right of 4.7 is 0.5(height)(base) = 0.5(1.2)(0.3) = 0.18.

The cumulative distribution function for a continuous random variable is denoted $F(x)$. Knowing $F(x)$ makes it easy to compute probabilities over intervals. The probability that X is between x_1 and x_2 is equal to the difference of the cumulative distribution function evaluated at these two points; that is,

$$P(x_1 \leq X \leq x_2) = F(x_2) - F(x_1)$$

You probably see the analogy between probability distributions and the frequency distributions we studied in Chapter 2. The key difference is that a frequency distribution characterizes *sample data,* whereas a probability distribution is a theoretical model of all possible values that a random variable may assume. One of the important applications of sample frequency distributions is in gaining insight into the nature of the underlying probability distribution of the population from which the sample came.

A working knowledge of theoretical probability distributions is important for several reasons. First, it can help you to understand the underlying process that generates sample data. We will investigate the relationship between distributions and samples later in this chapter. Second, many phenomena in business and nature follow some theoretical distribution and therefore are useful in building decision models. Finally, working with distributions is essential in computing probabilities of occurrence of outcomes to assess risk and make decisions. Table 3.1 summarizes most of the important Excel functions that relate to this topic.

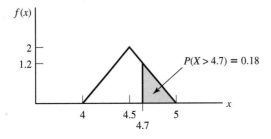

FIGURE 3.3 Probability of the Random Variable X Exceeding 4.7 as an Area

TABLE 3.1	Probability Distribution Support in Excel
Excel Function	**Description**
BINOMDIST(*number_s, trials, probability_s, cumulative*)	Returns the individual term binomial distribution
POISSON(*x, mean, cumulative*)	Returns the Poisson distribution
NORMDIST(*x, mean, standard_deviation, cumulative*)	Returns the normal cumulative distribution for the specified mean and standard deviation
NORMSDIST(*z*)	Returns the standard normal cumulative distribution (mean = 0, standard deviation = 1)
STANDARDIZE(*x, mean, standard_deviation*)	Returns a normalized value for a distribution characterized by a mean and standard deviation
EXPONDIST(*x, lambda, cumulative*)	Returns the exponential distribution
LOGNORMDIST(*x, mean, standard_deviation*)	Returns the cumulative lognormal distribution of *x*, where ln(*x*) is normally distributed with parameters mean and standard deviation
BETADIST(*x, alpha, beta, A, B*)	Returns the cumulative beta density function
GAMMADIST(*x, alpha, beta, cumulative*)	Returns the gamma distribution
WEIBULL(*x, alpha, beta, cumulative*)	Returns the Weibull distribution
Prentice Hall Statistics Add-In	**Description**
Binomial Probabilities	Computes binomial probabilities and histogram
Poisson Probabilities	Computes Poisson probabilities and histogram
Normal Probabilities	Computes normal probabilities
Exponential Probabilities	Computes exponential probabilities
Hypergeometric Probabilities	Computes hypergeometric probabilities
Simple and Joint Probabilities	Computes simple and joint probabilities for a 2 × 2 cross tabulation
Sampling Distribution Simulation	Generates a simulated sampling distribution from a uniform, standardized normal, or discrete population

EXPECTED VALUE AND VARIANCE OF A RANDOM VARIABLE

The **expected value** of a random variable corresponds to the notion of the mean, or average, for a data set. For a discrete random variable X, the expected value is the weighted average of all possible outcomes, where the weights are the probabilities:

$$E[X] = \sum_{i=1}^{\infty} x_i f(x_i)$$

For example, suppose that you play a lottery in which you buy a ticket for $50 and are told you have a 1 in 1000 chance of winning $25,000. The random variable X is your net winnings, and its probability distribution is

x	$P(x)$
−$50	0.999
$24,950	0.001

Your expected value is $-\$50(0.999) + \$24,950(0.001) = -\$25.00$. This means that if you played this game repeatedly over the long run, you would lose an average of $25.00 each time you play. Of course, for any one game you would either lose $50 or win $25,000. The definition of expected value of a continuous random variable is similar; however, it relies on notions of calculus, so we will not discuss it in this book.

The **variance** of a random variable X is defined as

$$\text{Var}[X] = \sum_{j=1}^{\infty} (x_j - E[X])^2 f(x_j)$$

For the previous example, the variance is

$$\text{Var}[X] = (-50 - [-25.00])^2(0.999) + (24{,}950 - [-25.00])^2(0.001) = 624{,}375$$

The variance of a random variable X is often denoted as σ_X^2. Similar to our discussion in Chapter 2, the variance measures the uncertainty of the random variable; the higher the variance, the higher the uncertainty of the outcome. Although variances are easier to work with mathematically, we usually measure the variability of a random variable by the **standard deviation,** σ_X, which is simply the square root of the variance:

$$\sigma_X = \sqrt{\sum_{j=1}^{\infty} (x_j - E[X])^2 f(x_j)}$$

The standard deviation for the lottery example is $\sqrt{624{,}375} = 790.17$. The standard deviation, σ_X, is expressed in the same units as the random variable and thus is a more meaningful measure than the variance. The standard deviation is a measure of risk and therefore is a critical concept in financial modeling.

It is important to understand that the expected value, variance, and standard deviation of random variables are not sample statistics like the mean, sample variance, and sample standard deviation we introduced in Chapter 2. Rather, they are measures associated with the set of all possible outcomes of the random variable.

Two other formulas are often useful. If a is a constant, then $E[aX] = aE[X]$, and $\text{Var}[aX] = a^2\text{Var}[X]$. This simply says that the expected value of a constant times a random variable is equal to the constant times the expected value, and the variance of a constant times a random variable is equal to the constant squared times the variance.

DISCRETE PROBABILITY DISTRIBUTIONS

Three useful discrete distributions are the Bernoulli, binomial, and Poisson.

Bernoulli and Binomial Distributions

The *Bernoulli distribution* characterizes a random variable with two possible outcomes with constant probabilities of occurrence. Typically, these outcomes represent "success" ($x = 1$) or "failure" ($x = 0$). The probability function is

$$f(x) = p \qquad \text{if } x = 1$$
$$= 1 - p \quad \text{if } x = 0$$

where p represents the probability of success. A Bernoulli distribution might be used to model whether an individual responds positively to a telemarketing promotion. For example, if you estimate that 3 percent of customers contacted will make a purchase ($x = 1$), the probability distribution that describes whether or not an individual makes a purchase is

$$f(x) = 0.03 \quad \text{if } x = 1$$
$$= 0.97 \quad \text{if } x = 0$$

A "success" can be any outcome. For example, in attempting to boot a new computer just off the assembly line, we might define a "success" as "does not boot up" in defining a Bernoulli random variable. Thus, "success" need not be a positive result.

The *binomial distribution* models n independent replications of a Bernoulli experiment with probability p of success on each experiment. The random variable x represents the number of successes in these n experiments. The probability function is

$$f(x) = \begin{cases} \binom{n}{x} p^x (1-p)^{n-x}, & \text{for } x = 0, 1, 2, \ldots, n \\ 0, & \text{otherwise} \end{cases}$$

The notation $\binom{n}{x}$ represents the number of ways of choosing x distinct items from a group of n items and is computed as

$$\binom{n}{x} = \frac{n!}{x!(n-x)!}$$

where $n!$ (n factorial) $= n(n-1)(n-2) \ldots (2)(1)$ and $0! = 1$.

The expected value of the binomial distribution is np, and the variance is $np(1-p)$. A binomial distribution might be used to model the results of sampling inspection in a production operation or the effects of drug research on a sample of patients. For example, if the probability that any individual will react positively to a new drug is 0.8, then the probability distribution that x individuals will react positively out of a sample of 10 is

$$f(x) = \begin{cases} \binom{10}{x} (0.8)^x (0.2)^{10-x}, & \text{for } x = 0, 1, 2, \ldots, 10 \\ 0, & \text{otherwise} \end{cases}$$

If $x = 4$, for example, we have

$$f(4) = \binom{10}{4}(0.8)^4(0.2)^{10-4} = \frac{10!}{4!6!}(0.4096)(0.000064) = 0.005505$$

Binomial probabilities are cumbersome to compute by hand but can be computed in Excel using the function BINOMDIST(*number_s, trials, probability_s, cumulative*). If *cumulative* is set to TRUE, then this function will provide cumulative probabilities. Figure 3.4 shows the results of using this function to compute the distribution for this example. From the figure, the probability that exactly 4 individuals will react positively is 0.005505, for example. You should verify that the sum of the probabilities is 1.0 since all possible outcomes are shown in this distribution.

	A	B	C	D	E	F	G
1	Binomial Probabilities						
2	n	10					
3	p	0.8					
4							
5	x	p(x)					
6	0	0.000000	← =BINOMDIST(A6,$B$2,$B$3,FALSE)				
7	1	0.000004					
8	2	0.000074					
9	3	0.000786					
10	4	0.005505					
11	5	0.026424					
12	6	0.088080					
13	7	0.201327					
14	8	0.301990					
15	9	0.268435					
16	10	0.107374					

FIGURE 3.4   Computing Binomial Probabilities Using the Excel Function BINOMDIST

EXCEL NOTE

USING THE EXCEL PASTE FUNCTION BUTTON

Any of the Excel functions in Table 3.1 can be accessed by clicking the Paste function button "f_x" on the toolbar. This is particularly useful if you are not sure of what to enter for the arguments. Figure 3.5 shows the dialog box from which you may select the function you wish to use, in this case, the binomial distribution function. Once this is selected, the dialog box in Figure 3.6 appears. When you click in any empty cell, a description of the argument is shown. Thus, if you were not sure what to enter for the *cumulative* argument, the explanation in Figure 3.6 will help you. For further information, you could click on the Help button in the lower left-hand corner.

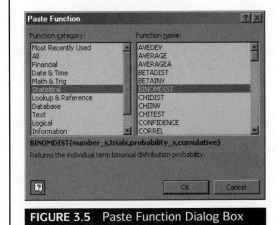

FIGURE 3.5   Paste Function Dialog Box

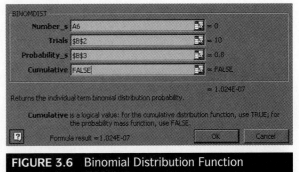

FIGURE 3.6   Binomial Distribution Function Dialog Box

One useful fact that often simplifies calculations involving large values of *n* is

$$P(X < x) + P(X \geq x) = 1 \quad \text{for any permissible value of } x$$

Thus, $P(X < x) = 1 - P(X \geq x)$. For example, the probability that *at least* 4 will react positively, $P(X \geq 4)$ can be found by subtracting the probability of 3 or less, $P(X < 4)$, from 1:

$$P(X \geq 4) = 1 - 0.000000 - 0.000004 - 0.000074 - 0.000786 = 0.99136.$$

See the *Excel Note: Using the Paste Function Button* for some tips on using Excel functions with which you may not be familiar.

Poisson Distribution

The Poisson distribution is a discrete distribution used to model the number of occurrences in some unit of measure; for example, the number of events occurring in an interval of time, number of items demanded per customer from an inventory, or the number of errors per line of software code. The Poisson distribution assumes no limit on the number of occurrences, that occurrences are independent, and that the average number is constant. The probability function is

$$p(x) = \begin{cases} \dfrac{e^{-\lambda}\lambda^x}{x!}, & \text{for } x = 0, 1, 2, \ldots \\ 0, & \text{otherwise} \end{cases}$$

	A	B	C	D	E	F
1	Poisson Distribution					
2	Mean	12				
3						
4	x	p(x)				
5	1	0.00007	=POISSON(A5,$B$2,FALSE)			
6	2	0.00044				
7	3	0.00177				
8	4	0.00531				
9	5	0.01274				
10	6	0.02548				
11	7	0.04368				
12	8	0.06552				
13	9	0.08736				
14	10	0.10484				
15	11	0.11437				
16	12	0.11437				

FIGURE 3.7 Computing Poisson Probabilities Using the Excel Function POISSON

where the mean number of occurrences in the defined unit of measure is λ. The expected value of the Poisson distribution is λ, and the variance also is equal to λ.

For example, suppose that the average number of customers arriving at an ATM during lunch hour is $\lambda = 12$ customers per hour. The probability that exactly x customers will arrive during the hour is

$$p(x) = \begin{cases} \dfrac{e^{-12}12^x}{x!}, & \text{for } x = 0, 1, 2, \ldots \\ 0, & \text{otherwise} \end{cases}$$

It is theoretically possible that any positive number of customers will arrive; however, for values of $x > 30$, the probability is less than 0.000005.

Poisson probabilities are cumbersome to compute by hand. Many books have tables, but probabilities can easily be computed in Excel using the function POISSON (*x, mean, cumulative*). Figure 3.7 shows the results of using this function to compute the distribution for this example. Thus, the probability of exactly 1 arrival during the lunch hour is 0.00007, the probability of 2 arrivals is 0.00044, and so on. Because the possible values of a Poisson random variable are infinite, we have not shown the complete distribution in Figure 3.7.

CONTINUOUS PROBABILITY DISTRIBUTIONS

Continuous probability distributions are defined by their density functions; discrete distributions are defined by probability mass functions. The density and mass functions depend on one or more *parameters*. Many continuous distributions can assume different shapes and sizes, depending on the value of the parameters. There are three basic types of parameters. A **shape parameter** controls the basic shape of the distribution. For certain distributions, changing the shape parameter will cause major changes in the form of the distribution. For others, the changes will be less severe. A **scale parameter** controls the unit of measurement within the range of the distribution. Changing the scale parameter either contracts or expands the distribution along the horizontal axis. Finally, a **location parameter** specifies the location of the distribution relative to zero on the horizontal axis. The location parameter may be the midpoint or the lower endpoint of the range of the distribution. Not all distributions will have all three parameters;

some may have more than one shape parameter. Understanding the effects of these parameters is important in selecting distributions as inputs to decision models.

In this section we review some of the more common types of probability distributions that are used in decision modeling, discuss how shape, scale, and location parameters affect the distributions, and describe typical situations for which each distribution often applies.

Uniform Distribution

The uniform distribution characterizes a random variable for which all outcomes between some minimum and maximum value are equally likely. For a uniform distribution with a minimum value a and a maximum value b, the density function is

$$f(x) = \frac{1}{b - a} \quad \text{if } a \leq x \leq b$$

and is shown in Figure 3.8. The distribution function is

$$F(x) = \begin{cases} 0, & \text{if } x < a \\ \dfrac{x - a}{b - a}, & \text{if } a \leq x \leq b \\ 1, & \text{if } b < x \end{cases}$$

The mean of the uniform distribution is $(a + b)/2$, and the variance is $(b - a)^2/12$. Note that a is a location parameter since it controls the location of the distribution along the horizontal axis. The difference, $b - a$, is a scale parameter. Increasing $b - a$ elongates the distribution; decreasing $b - a$ compresses it. There is no shape parameter since any uniform distribution is flat. The uniform distribution is often used when little knowledge about a random variable is available; the parameters a and b are chosen judgmentally to reflect a modeler's best guess about the range of the random variable. Although Excel does not provide a function to compute uniform probabilities, the formula is simple enough to incorporate into a spreadsheet.

As we noted before, with continuous distributions, it only makes sense to compute probabilities over intervals. For example, suppose that sales revenue for a product varies uniformly each week between $1000 and $2000. Then the probability that sales revenue will be less than $1300 is

$$F(1300) = \frac{1300 - 1000}{2000 - 1000} = 0.3$$

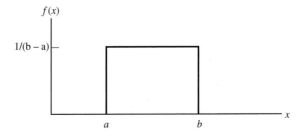

FIGURE 3.8   Uniform Probability Density Function

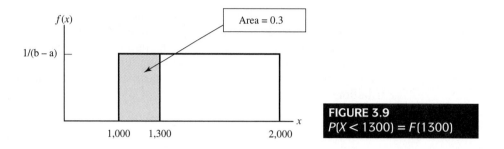

FIGURE 3.9
$P(X < 1300) = F(1300)$

This is shown in Figure 3.9 as the area under the distribution to the left of $x = 1300$. Similarly, the probability that revenue will be between \$1500 and \$1700 is $F(1700) - F(1500) = 0.7 - 0.5 = 0.2$.

Normal Distribution

The *normal distribution* is described by the familiar bell-shaped curve. The normal distribution is symmetric and has the property that the median equals the mean. Thus, half the area falls above the mean and half below it. Although the range of x is unbounded, meaning that the tails of the distribution extend to negative and positive infinity, most of the density is close to the mean. It is characterized by two parameters: the mean, μ (the location parameter), and the variance, σ^2 (the scale parameter). Thus, as μ changes, the location of the distribution on the x axis also changes, and as σ^2 is decreased or increased, the distribution becomes narrower or wider, respectively.

The normal distribution is observed in many natural phenomena. Errors of various types, such as deviation from specifications of machined items, often are normally distributed. Thus, the normal distribution finds extensive applications in quality control. Processing times in some service systems also follow a normal distribution. Another useful application is that the distribution of the averages of random variables having *any* distribution tends to be normal as the number of random variables increases.

The probability density function for the normal distribution is

$$f(x) = \frac{e^{-\frac{(x-\mu)^2}{2\sigma^2}}}{\sqrt{2\pi\sigma^2}}$$

However, the cumulative distribution function cannot be expressed mathematically, only numerically. Figure 3.10 provides a sketch of the **standard normal distribution,** the normal distribution with $\mu = 0$ and $\sigma = 1$. A standard normal random variable is usually denoted by Z, and its density function by $f(z)$. A numerical tabulation of the standard normal distribution is provided in Appendix A at the end of this book in two forms. In Appendix A.1, we have a table of areas from 0 to z; in Appendix A.2, we have a table of the cumulative probabilities from negative infinity to z. In both cases, z represents the number of standard deviations from the mean of zero.

To illustrate the use of these tables, let us find the area under the normal distribution within 1, 2, and 3 standard deviations of the mean, as shown in Figure 3.10. First, consider Table A.1. To find the area from 0 to $z = 1.00$, which is the probability $P(0 \leq Z \leq 1.00)$, identify the proper row and column corresponding to $z = 1.00$. Note that each column corresponds to the second decimal place, so the area corresponding to

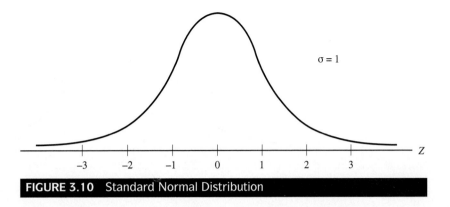

FIGURE 3.10   Standard Normal Distribution

$z = 1.00$ is found in the first column in the row labeled 1.0. This value is 0.3413. Since the distribution is symmetric, the area from 0 to z is the same as the area from $-z$ to 0. Therefore, the area within 1 standard deviation of the mean—that is, $P(-1.00 \leq Z \leq 1.00)$—is $2(0.3413) = 0.6826$. In a similar fashion, verify that the area within 2 standard deviations of the mean is 0.9544 and the area within 3 standard deviations of the mean is 0.9973.

Table A.2 tabulates the cumulative probabilities from $-\infty$ to z. Observe that $P(Z \leq 0)$ is 0.5. Therefore, when z is positive, $P(Z \leq z) = P(Z \leq 0) + P(0 \leq Z \leq z) = 0.5 +$ the area found in Table A.1. So, for instance, when $z = 1.00$, Table A.2 provides the cumulative probability 0.8413. Subtracting 0.5 yields the same value as in Table A.1. Therefore, both tables provide essentially the same information, only in different forms. The key in using either of them is to first sketch the area you are seeking, and then apply the symmetry property to find the appropriate area.

Any normal distribution with an arbitrary mean μ and standard deviation σ may be transformed to a standard normal distribution by applying the following formula:

$$z = \frac{x - \mu}{\sigma}$$

This is particularly useful to solve problems involving normal distributions and allows us to find probabilities using the standard normal tables A.1 or A.2. For example, suppose that we determine that the distribution of customer demand (X) is normal with a mean of 750 units/month and a standard deviation of 100 units/month. Figure 3.11(a) shows the probability that demand will exceed 900 units as the area under the normal distribution. To find this probability using the tables in Appendix A, we transform this into a standard normal distribution by finding the z-value that corresponds to $x = 900$ (Figure 3.11(b)):

$$z = \frac{900 - 750}{100} = 1.5$$

From Appendix A.1, the area between 0 and 1.5 is 0.4332; thus the area from 1.5 to infinity is $0.5 - 0.4332 = 0.0668$. Alternatively, from Appendix A.2, the cumulative probability for $z = 1.5$ is 0.9332. Therefore, the probability that Z exceeds 1.5 (equivalently, the probability that X exceeds 900) is $1 - 0.9332 = 0.0668$. To summarize,

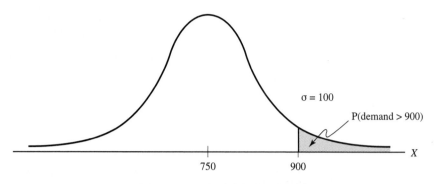

$\sigma = 100$

$P(\text{demand} > 900)$

750   900   X

(a)   Original normal distribution

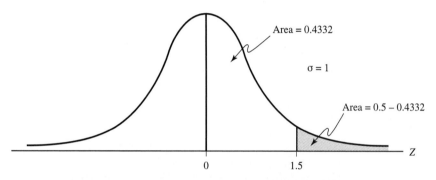

Area = 0.4332

$\sigma = 1$

Area = 0.5 − 0.4332

0   1.5   Z

(b)   Transformed standard normal distribution

FIGURE 3.11   Computing $P(\text{Demand} > 900)$

$$P(X > 900) = P(Z > 1.5) = 1 - P(Z < 1.5) = 1 - 0.9332 = 0.0668$$

Probabilities for negative values of z are found by symmetry of the distribution. For instance, suppose we want to find $P(X > 700)$, as shown in Figure 3.12. Transforming this into a standard normal distribution yields the z-value

$$z = \frac{700 - 750}{100} = -0.5$$

FIGURE 3.12   Computing $P(\text{Demand} > 700)$

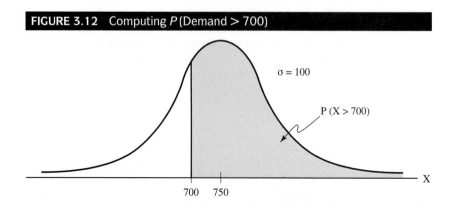

$\sigma = 100$

$P(X > 700)$

700   750   X

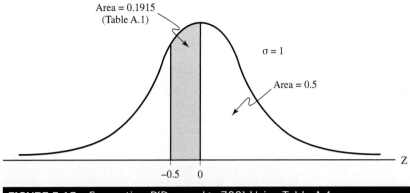

FIGURE 3.13   Computing *P*(Demand > 700) Using Table A.1

Therefore, $P(X > 700) = P(Z > -0.5) = 1 - P(Z < -0.5)$. From Appendix A.2, $P(Z < -0.5) = 0.3085$. Thus, $P(X > 700) = 1 - 0.3085 = 0.6915$. Alternatively, we could use Table A.1. Note that by symmetry, $P(-0.5 \le Z \le 0) = P(0 \le Z \le 0.5) = 0.1915$. Since $P(Z > 0) = 0.5$, the required area is $0.1915 + 0.5 = 0.6915$ (see Figure 3.13). Both approaches yield the same result; however, you must be careful to add and subtract the correct areas.

As a third example, consider finding the probability that *X* is between 700 and 900 (Figure 3.14). Using Table A.1, we see that

$$P(700 \le X \le 900) = P(-0.5 \le Z \le 0) + P(0 \le Z \le 1.5)$$
$$= P(0 \le Z \le -0.5) + P(0 \le Z \le 1.5)$$
$$= 0.1915 + 0.4332 = 0.6247$$

Using Table A.2, we have

$$P(700 \le X \le 900) = P(Z \le 1.5) - P(Z \le -0.5)$$
$$= 0.9332 - 0.3085 = 0.6247$$

Another common calculation involving the normal distribution is to find the value of *x* corresponding to a specified probability, or area. For the same example of customer demand, suppose that we wish to find the level of demand that will be exceeded only 10 percent of the time; that is, find the value of *x* so that $P(X \ge x) = 0.10$. This is illustrated in Figure 3.15. An upper tail probability of 0.10 is equivalent to a cumulative

FIGURE 3.14   Finding $P(700 \le X \le 900)$

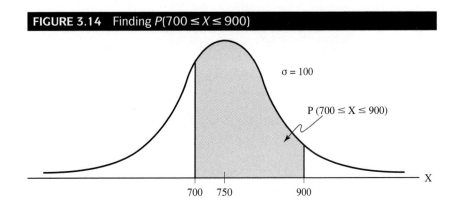

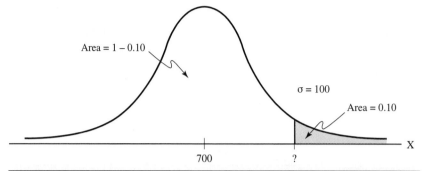

FIGURE 3.15   Finding the Level of Demand Satisfying *P*(Demand > *x*) = 0.10

probability of 0.90. Using Appendix A.2, and finding 0.90 as close as possible in the *body* of the table, we obtain $z = 1.28$, corresponding to 0.8997. This means that a value of Z that is 1.28 standard deviations above the mean has an upper tail area of approximately 0.10. Using the standard normal transformation,

$$z = \frac{x - 750}{100} = 1.28$$

or $x = 878$. How would you use Table A.1 to solve this? Which table you use to solve problems is a matter of personal preference. We encourage you to use both tables until you feel confident about your approach. *And always draw a picture!*

Two Excel functions are used to compute normal probabilities: NORMDIST (*x, mean, standard_deviation, cumulative*), and NORMSDIST(*z*). NORMSDIST(*z*) generates the same values as Table A.2. Figure 3.16 shows the application of NORMDIST. For the cumulative distribution, the last argument of the function, *cumulative,* must be set to TRUE. The Excel function STANDARDIZE(*x, mean, standard_deviation*) can be used to compute *z*-values within a spreadsheet using the standard normal transformation. Thus, STANDARDIZE(*700, 750, 100*) = −0.5 as in the earlier example.

The normal distribution is often used as an approximation to the binomial distribution with $\mu = np$ and $\sigma^2 = np(1 - p)$ when the sample sizes are large or p is small, to simplify calculations. This approximation holds well when $np \geq 5$ and $n(1 - p) \geq 5$.

Triangular Distribution

The triangular distribution is defined by three parameters: the minimum, *a*; maximum, *b*; and most likely, *c*. Outcomes near the most likely value have a higher chance of

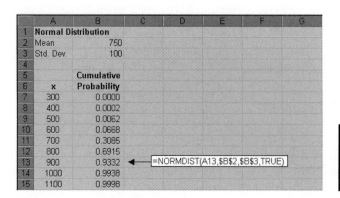

FIGURE 3.16   Computing Normal Probabilities Using the Excel Function NORMDIST

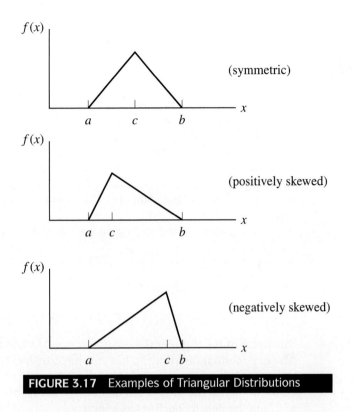

FIGURE 3.17   Examples of Triangular Distributions

occurring than those at the extremes. By varying the position of the most likely value relative to the extremes, the triangular distribution can be symmetric or skewed in either direction, as shown in Figure 3.17. The probability density function is given by

$$f(x) = \begin{cases} \dfrac{2(x-a)}{(b-a)(c-a)}, & \text{if } a \leq x \leq c \\ \dfrac{2(b-x)}{(b-a)(b-c)}, & \text{if } c < x \leq b \\ 0, & \text{otherwise} \end{cases}$$

From Figure 3.17, you can see that a is the location parameter, $(b-a)$ is the scale parameter, and c is the shape parameter. The cumulative distribution function is

$$F(x) = \begin{cases} 0, & \text{if } x < a \\ \dfrac{(x-a)^2}{(b-a)(c-a)}, & \text{if } a \leq x \leq c \\ 1 - \dfrac{(b-x)^2}{(b-a)(b-c)}, & \text{if } c < x \leq b \\ 1, & \text{if } b < x \end{cases}$$

The mean is computed as $(a + b + c)/3$ and the variance is $(a^2 + b^2 + c^2 - ab - ac - bc)/18$.

The triangular distribution is often used as a rough approximation of other distributions, such as the normal, or in the absence of more complete data. Because it depends on three simple parameters and can assume a variety of shapes—for instance, it can be skewed in either direction by changing the value of c—it is very flexible in modeling a wide variety of assumptions. One drawback, however, is that it is bounded, thereby eliminating the possibility of extreme outlying values that might possibly occur. Excel does not have a function to return triangular probabilities, but the formulas can easily be used in a spreadsheet.

Exponential Distribution

The exponential distribution models events that recur randomly over time. Thus, it is often used to model the time between customer arrivals to a service system and the time to failure of machines, light bulbs, and other mechanical or electrical components. A key property of the exponential distribution is that it is *memoryless*; that is, the current time has no effect on future outcomes. For example, the length of time until a machine failure has the same distribution no matter how long the machine has been running.

The exponential distribution has the density function

$$f(x) = \lambda e^{-\lambda x}, \ x \geq 0$$

and cumulative distribution function

$$F(x) = 1 - e^{-\lambda x}, \ x \geq 0$$

The mean of the exponential distribution $= 1/\lambda$ and the variance $= (1/\lambda)^2 = (\text{mean})^2$. The exponential distribution has no shape or location parameters; λ is the scale parameter. Figure 3.18 provides a sketch of the exponential distribution. The exponential distribution has the properties that it is bounded below by 0, it has its greatest density at 0, and the density declines as x increases.

To illustrate the exponential distribution, suppose that the mean time to failure of a critical component of an engine is 8000 hours. The probability that the component will fail before x hours is given by the cumulative distribution function. Thus, the probability of failing before 5000 hours is

$$F(5000) = 1 - e^{-(1/8000)(5000)} = 1 - e^{-5/8} = 0.465$$

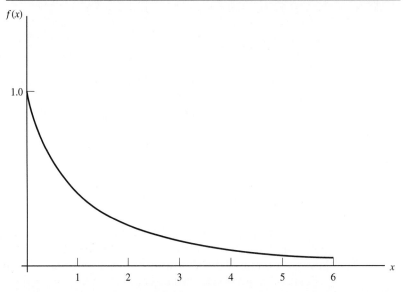

FIGURE 3.18   Exponential Distribution ($\mu = 1$)

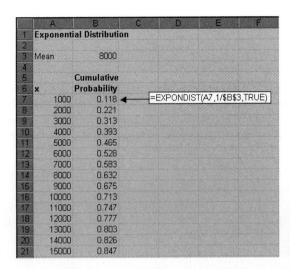

FIGURE 3.19 Computing Exponential Probabilities Using the Excel Function EXPONDIST

The Excel function EXPONDIST(*x, lambda, cumulative*) can be used to compute exponential probabilities. Figure 3.19 shows the cumulative distribution for this example. Note that the mean is *not* the same as the parameter lambda; thus, in the Excel function, lambda is set equal to the reciprocal of the mean.

The exponential distribution has an important relationship with the Poisson: If the number of occurrences of some phenomenon has a Poisson distribution, then the time between occurrences has an exponential distribution. For instance, if the number of arrivals at a bank is Poisson distributed, say with mean 12/hour, then the time between arrivals is exponential, with mean 1/12 hour, or 5 minutes.

OTHER USEFUL DISTRIBUTIONS

Many other probability distributions find application in decision modeling, especially those distributions that assume a wide variety of shapes. Such distributions provide a great amount of flexibility in representing empirical data that may be available. We provide a brief description of these distributions; further details may be found in more advanced texts on probability and statistics.

- *Lognormal Distribution.* If the natural logarithm of a random variable X is normal, then X has a lognormal distribution. Because the lognormal distribution is positively skewed and bounded below by zero, it finds applications in modeling phenomena that have low probabilities of large values and cannot have negative values, such as the time to complete a task. Other common examples include stock prices and real estate prices. The lognormal distribution is also often used for "spiked" service times, that is, when the probability of zero is very low but the most likely value is just greater than zero.

- *Gamma Distribution.* The gamma distribution is a family of distributions defined by a shape parameter α, a scale parameter β, and a location parameter L. L is the lower limit of the random variable x; that is, the gamma distribution is defined for $x > L$. Gamma distributions are often used to model the time to complete a task, such as customer service or machine repair. It is used to measure the time between the occurrence of events when the event process is not completely random. It also finds application in inventory control and insurance risk theory.

A special case of the gamma distribution when $\alpha = 1$ and $L = 0$ is called the *Erlang distribution.* The Erlang distribution can also be viewed as the sum of k independent and identically distributed exponential random variables. The mean is k/λ, and the variance is k/λ^2. When $k = 1$, the Erlang is identical to the exponential distribution. For $k = 2$, the distribution is highly skewed to the right. For larger values of k, this skewness decreases, until for $k = 20$, the Erlang distribution looks similar to a normal distribution. One common application of the Erlang distribution is for modeling the time to complete a task when it can be broken down into independent tasks, each of which has an exponential distribution.

- *Weibull Distribution.* The Weibull distribution is another probability distribution capable of taking on a number of different shapes defined by a scale parameter α and a shape parameter β. Both α and β must be greater than zero. When the location parameter $L = 0$ and $\beta = 1$, the Weibull distribution is the same as the exponential distribution with $\lambda = 1/\alpha$. By choosing the scale parameter L different from 0, you can model an exponential distribution that has a lower bound different from zero. When $\beta = 3.25$, the Weibull approximates the normal distribution. Weibull distributions are often used to model results from life and fatigue tests, equipment failure times, and times to complete a task.

- *Beta Distribution.* One of the most flexible distributions for modeling variation over a fixed interval from 0 to a positive value s is the beta. The beta distribution is a function of two shape parameters, α and β, both of which must be positive. The parameter s is the scale parameter. Note that s defines the upper limit of the distribution range. If α and β are equal, the distribution is symmetric. If either parameter is 1.0 and the other is greater than 1.0, the distribution is in the shape of a J. If α is less than β, the distribution is positively skewed; otherwise, it is negatively skewed. These properties can help you to select appropriate values for the shape parameters.

- *Geometric Distribution.* This distribution describes the number of trials until the first success where the probability of a success is the same from trial to trial. An example would be the number of parts manufactured until a defect occurs, assuming that the probability of a defect is constant for each part.

- *Negative Binomial Distribution.* Like the geometric distribution, the negative binomial distribution models the distribution of the number of trials until the rth success, for example, the number of sales calls needed to sell 10 orders.

- *Hypergeometric Distribution.* This is similar to the binomial, except that it applies to sampling without replacement. The hypergeometric distribution is often used in quality control inspection applications.

- *Logistic Distribution.* This is commonly used to describe growth of a population over time.

- *Pareto Distribution.* This describes phenomena in which a small proportion of items accounts for a large proportion of some characteristic. For example, a small number of cities constitutes a large proportion of the population. Other examples include the size of companies, personal incomes, and stock price fluctuations.

- *Extreme Value Distribution.* This describes the largest value of a response over a period of time, such as rainfall, earthquakes, and breaking strengths of materials.

Figure 3.20 is a graphical summary of the distributions we have discussed. Understanding the shapes of these distributions makes it easier to select an appropriate

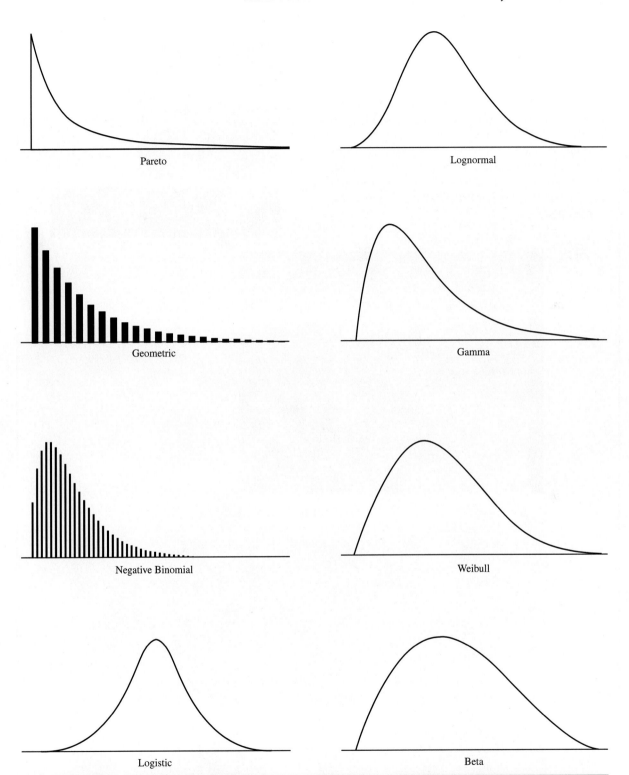

FIGURE 3.20   Shape of Some Probability Distributions

PHSTAT NOTE

GENERATING BINOMIAL PROBABILITIES

From the *PHStat* menu, select *Probability &
Prob. Distributions* and then *Binomial* . . . . The
dialog box in Figure 3.21 prompts you for the distribution's parameters and range of outputs
desired. By checking the boxes for *Cumulative
Probabilities* and *Histogram*, the routine provides
additional information as shown in Figure 3.22,
specifically columns D through G, and the histogram of the probability distribution for the
range specified.

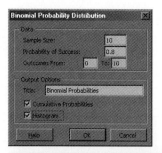

FIGURE 3.21   Binomial Probability
Distribution Dialog Box in
PHStat

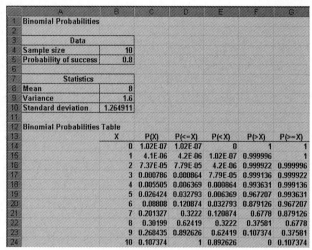

	A	B	C	D	E	F	G
1	Binomial Probabilities						
2							
3		**Data**					
4	Sample size	10					
5	Probability of success	0.8					
6							
7		**Statistics**					
8	Mean	8					
9	Variance	1.6					
10	Standard deviation	1.264911					
11							
12	Binomial Probabilities Table						
13			X	P(X)	P(<=X)	P(<X)	P(>X)	P(>=X)
14			0	1.02E-07	1.02E-07	0	1	1
15			1	4.1E-06	4.2E-06	1.02E-07	0.999996	1
16			2	7.37E-05	7.79E-05	4.2E-06	0.999922	0.999996
17			3	0.000786	0.000864	7.79E-05	0.999136	0.999922
18			4	0.005505	0.006369	0.000864	0.993631	0.999136
19			5	0.026424	0.032793	0.006369	0.967207	0.993631
20			6	0.08808	0.120874	0.032793	0.879126	0.967207
21			7	0.201327	0.3222	0.120874	0.6778	0.879126
22			8	0.30199	0.62419	0.3222	0.37581	0.6778
23			9	0.268435	0.892626	0.62419	0.107374	0.37581
24			10	0.107374	1	0.892626	0	0.107374

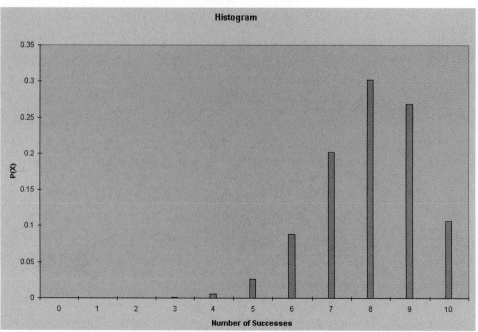

FIGURE 3.22   Output from *PHStat* Binomial Probability Distribution Option

distribution for a decision modeling application. In the next chapter, we will discuss fitting an appropriate distribution to sample data.

Probability Distributions in *PHStat*

PHStat has several routines for generating probabilities of distributions we have discussed. This allows you to compute probabilities without requiring you to develop a detailed worksheet in Excel. The distributions available are

- Normal
- Binomial
- Exponential
- Poisson
- Hypergeometric

The accompanying *PHStat Note* describes the binomial option; other probabilities can be generated in a similar fashion.

MONTE CARLO METHODS IN STATISTICS

Monte Carlo methods involve sampling experiments whose purpose is to estimate the distribution of an outcome variable that depends on several input random variables. Many decision models contain variables of interest that are functions of random variables. For example, in the financial model we introduced in Chapter 1 (Figure 1.7), we might be interested in the distribution of the cumulative discounted cash flow for the fifth year (cell G35) when first-year sales, growth rate, operating expenses, and inflation factor assumptions are uncertain and are characterized by random variables. One approach is to input many different values from the probability distributions of these random variables into the spreadsheet model and record the value of cell G35 for each combination of inputs. If we use many different combinations of inputs in a random fashion, we will have created a distribution of possible values of the cumulative discounted cash flow that provides an indication of the likelihood of what we might expect. This process is often called **Monte Carlo simulation.** The term *Monte Carlo simulation* was first used during the development of the atom bomb as a code name for computer simulations of nuclear fission. Researchers coined this term because of the similarity to random sampling in games of chance such as roulette in the famous casino in Monte Carlo. Although we will discuss the use of Monte Carlo simulation for analyzing risk in decision problems in Chapter 8, Monte Carlo methods are also important in statistics. We will use them to gain insight into important statistical issues involving probability distributions and sample data.

To apply Monte Carlo simulation, we will need to generate outcomes from many different types of probability distributions, such as a discrete distribution or a normal, exponential, or Poisson distribution. Sometimes physical processes can be used to generate random outcomes from specific distributions. For example, rolling a die is a physical experiment that randomly generates a number from a discrete uniform probability distribution between 1 and 6. Other experiments include spinning a roulette wheel, drawing from a deck of shuffled cards, or selecting numbered balls drawn from a cage as is done for state lotteries. While such experiments are highly intuitive, these approaches cannot be used to solve practical problems. We will describe the fundamental concepts of sampling from probability distributions so that you will understand how this is accomplished in Excel and other software programs and then use them to gain insight about sampling distributions.

Random Numbers

The basis for generating samples from probability distributions is the concept of a *random number*. In simulation, a **random number** is defined as one that is *uniformly distributed between 0 and 1*. Technically speaking, computers cannot generate truly random numbers since they must use a predictable algorithm. However, the algorithms are designed to generate a stream of numbers that *appear* to be random. In Excel, we may generate a random number within any cell using the function RAND( ). This function has no arguments; therefore, nothing should be placed within the parentheses. Table 3.2 shows a table of 100 random numbers generated in Excel. You should be aware that unless the automatic recalculation feature is suppressed, whenever any cell in the spreadsheet is modified, the values in any cell containing the RAND( ) function will change. Automatic recalculation can be changed to manual in the *Tools/Options/Calculation* menu. Under manual recalculation mode, the worksheet is recalculated only when the F9 key is pressed.

Random Sampling from Probability Distributions

Sampling from discrete probability distributions using random numbers is quite easy. We will illustrate this process using the example of a discrete probability distribution for individuals' age brackets from the *Census Education Data.xls* worksheet introduced earlier in this chapter. The probability function and cumulative distribution follows.

x	$f(x)$	$F(x)$
1	0.2285	0.2285
2	0.2582	0.4867
3	0.1978	0.6845
4	0.1292	0.8137
5	0.1038	0.9175
6	0.0825	1.0000

Two properties of discrete probability distributions that allow us to use random numbers to generate samples are (1) the probability of any outcome is always between 0 and 1, and (2) the sum of the probabilities of all outcomes adds to 1. We can therefore break up the range from 0 to 1 into intervals that correspond to the probabilities of discrete outcomes. Any random number, then, must fall within one of these intervals. For instance, the interval from 0 up to but not including 0.2285 would correspond to the

TABLE 3.2	One Hundred Random Numbers								
0.007120	0.215576	0.386009	0.201736	0.45799	0.127602	0.387275	0.639298	0.757161	0.285388
0.714281	0.165519	0.768911	0.687736	0.466579	0.481117	0.260391	0.508433	0.528617	0.755016
0.226987	0.454259	0.487024	0.269659	0.531411	0.197874	0.527788	0.613126	0.716988	0.747900
0.339398	0.434496	0.398474	0.622505	0.829964	0.288727	0.801157	0.373983	0.095900	0.041084
0.692488	0.137445	0.054401	0.483937	0.954835	0.643596	0.970131	0.864186	0.384474	0.134890
0.962794	0.808060	0.169243	0.347993	0.848285	0.216635	0.779147	0.216837	0.768370	0.371613
0.824428	0.919011	0.820195	0.345563	0.989111	0.269649	0.43317	0.36907	0.845632	0.158662
0.428903	0.470202	0.064646	0.100007	0.379286	0.183176	0.180715	0.008793	0.569902	0.218078
0.951334	0.258192	0.916104	0.271980	0.330697	0.989264	0.770787	0.107717	0.102653	0.366096
0.635494	0.395185	0.320618	0.003049	0.153551	0.231191	0.73785	0.633932	0.056315	0.281744

outcome $x = 1$; the interval from 0.2285 up to but not including 0.4867 corresponds to $x = 2$; and so on. (To prevent overlap, we do not include the upper limit of an interval in the interval, as well as because of the fact that a random number will never equal 1.0 exactly.) This is summarized as follows:

INTERVAL	OUTCOME, x
0.0 to 0.2285	1
0.2285 to 0.4867	2
0.4867 to 0.6845	3
0.6845 to 0.8137	4
0.8137 to 0.9175	5
0.9175 to 1.0000	6

To generate an outcome from this distribution, all we need to do is to select a random number and determine the interval into which it falls. Suppose we use the first column in Table 3.2. The first random number is 0.007120. This falls in the first interval; thus, the first sample outcome is $x = 1$. The second random number is 0.714281. This number falls in the fourth interval, generating a sample outcome $x = 4$. If this is done repeatedly, the frequency of occurrence of each outcome should be proportional to the size of the random number range (that is, the probability function) because random numbers are uniformly distributed. We can easily use this approach to generate outcomes from *any* discrete distribution; the VLOOKUP function in Excel can be used to implement this on a spreadsheet.

This approach of generating random numbers and transforming them into outcomes from a probability distribution may be used to sample from most any distribution. A value randomly generated from a specified probability distribution is called a **random variate.** For example, it is quite easy to transform a random number into a random variate from a uniform distribution with parameters a and b. Consider the formula:

$$U = a + (b - a)R$$

where R is some random number. Note that when $R = 0$, $U = a$, and when R approaches 1, U approaches b. For any other value of R between 0 and 1, $(b - a)R$ represents the same proportion of the interval (a, b) as R does of the interval $(0, 1)$. Thus all real numbers between a and b can occur. Since R is uniformly distributed, so also is U. However, it is certainly not obvious how to generate random variates from other distributions such as a normal or exponential. We will not describe the technical details of how this is done, but rather just describe the capabilities available in Excel.

Generating Random Variates in Excel

Excel allows you to generate random variates from discrete distributions and certain others using the *Random Number Generation* option in the *Analysis Toolpak* (see *Excel Note: Sampling from Probability Distributions*). However, one disadvantage with using the *Random Number Generation* tool is that you must repeat the process to generate a new set of sample values; pressing the F9 key will not change the values. This can make it difficult to use this tool to analyze decision models.

Excel also has several functions that may be used to generate random variates. The most common ones are

EXCEL NOTE

SAMPLING FROM PROBABILITY DISTRIBUTIONS

From the main toolbar, select *Tools/Data Analysis/Random Number Generation.* The *Random Number Generation* dialog box, shown in Figure 3.23, will appear. From the *Random Number Generation* dialog box, you may select from seven distributions: uniform, normal, Bernoulli, binomial, Poisson, and patterned, as well as discrete. (The patterned distribution is characterized by a lower and upper bound, a step, a repetition rate for values, and a repetition rate for the sequence.) You are asked to specify the upper-left cell reference of the output table that will store the outcomes, the number of variables (columns of values you want generated), number of random numbers (the number of data points you want generated for each variable), and the

type of distribution. The default distribution is the discrete distribution, which we illustrate. To use the discrete distribution, the spreadsheet must contain a table with two columns: the left column containing the outcomes, and the right column containing the probabilities associated with the outcomes (which must sum to 1.0). Figure 3.24 shows an example. The outcomes generated are found in cells C3 through C12.

The dialog box in Figure 3.23 also allows you the option of specifying a *random number seed.* A random number seed is a value from which a stream of random numbers is generated. By specifying the same seed, you can produce the same random numbers at a later time. This is desirable when we wish to reproduce an identical sequence of "random" events in a simulation in order to test the effects of different policies or decision variables under the same circumstances.

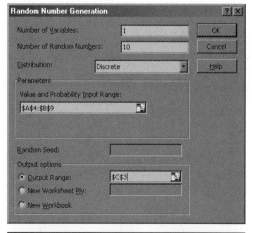

FIGURE 3.23 Excel Random Number Generation Dialog Box

	A	B	C
1			Simulated
2	Age Bracket	Probability	Age Brackets
3	x	p(x)	2
4	1	0.2285	1
5	2	0.2582	3
6	3	0.1978	5
7	4	0.1292	5
8	5	0.1038	6
9	6	0.0825	1
10			2
11			5
12			1

FIGURE 3.24 Result from Excel's Random Number Generation Tool

- NORMINV(*probability, mean, standard_deviation*)—normal distribution
- NORMSINV(*probability*)—standard normal distribution
- LOGINV(*probability, mean, standard_deviation*)—lognormal distribution where $\ln(x)$ has the specified mean and standard deviation

and for some advanced distributions:

- BETAINV(*probability, alpha, beta, A, B*)—beta distribution
- GAMMAINV(*probability, alpha, beta*)—gamma distribution

PHSTAT NOTE

SAMPLING DISTRIBUTIONS SIMULATION

From the *PHStat* menu, select *Probability Distributions,* then *Sampling Distributions Simulation.* The dialog box shown in Figure 3.25 appears. You must enter the number of samples to be generated, the sample size, and the type of distribution (uniform, standard normal, or discrete). If you select the discrete distribution, you also need to enter the range in a worksheet that contains the probability mass function. You may also opt for a histogram as part of the output. The procedure creates a new worksheet with the sample output in columns, along with the mean of each sample, overall mean, and standard error (to be discussed shortly). An example for the standard normal distribution is shown in Figure 3.26.

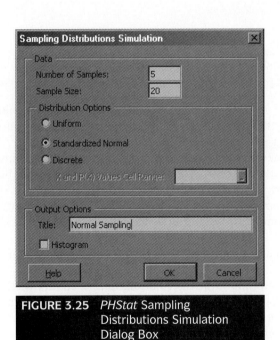

FIGURE 3.25 *PHStat* Sampling Distributions Simulation Dialog Box

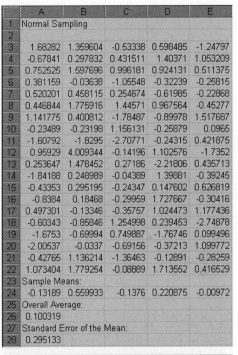

	A	B	C	D	E
1	Normal Sampling				
2					
3	1.68282	1.359604	-0.53338	0.598485	-1.24797
4	-0.67841	0.297832	0.431511	1.40371	1.053209
5	0.752525	1.597696	0.996181	0.924131	0.511375
6	0.381159	-0.03638	-1.05548	-0.32239	-0.25815
7	0.520201	0.458115	0.254674	-0.61985	-0.22868
8	0.446844	1.775916	1.44571	0.967564	-0.45277
9	1.141775	0.400812	-1.78487	-0.89978	1.517687
10	-0.23489	-0.23198	1.156131	-0.25879	0.0965
11	-1.60792	-1.8295	-2.70771	-0.24315	0.421875
12	0.95929	4.009344	-0.14196	1.102576	-1.7352
13	0.253647	1.478452	0.27186	-2.21806	0.435713
14	-1.84188	0.248989	-0.04389	1.39881	-0.39245
15	-0.43353	0.295195	-0.24347	0.147602	0.626819
16	-0.8384	0.18468	-0.29959	1.727667	-0.30416
17	0.497301	-0.13346	-0.35757	1.024473	1.177436
18	-0.60343	-0.85846	1.254998	0.239453	-2.74878
19	-1.6753	-0.69994	0.749887	-1.76746	0.099496
20	-2.00537	-0.0337	-0.69156	-0.37213	1.099772
21	-0.42765	1.136214	-1.36463	-0.12891	-0.28259
22	1.073404	1.779254	-0.08889	1.713552	0.416529
23	Sample Means:				
24	-0.13189	0.559933	-0.1376	0.220875	-0.00972
25	Overall Average:				
26	0.100319				
27	Standard Error of the Mean:				
28	0.295133				

FIGURE 3.26 *PHStat* Output for Normal Distribution Sampling

To use these, simply enter RAND( ) in place of *probability* in the function. For example, NORMINV(RAND( ), 5, 2) will generate random variates from a normal distribution with mean 5 and standard deviation 2. Each time the worksheet is recalculated (for instance, when the F9 key is pressed), a new random number and hence a new random variate are generated. These functions may be embedded in cell formulas and will generate new values whenever the worksheet is recalculated.

PHStat also includes the ability to generate samples from a uniform (0, 1) distribution, standard normal distribution, and an arbitrary discrete distribution (see the *PHStat Note: Sampling Distributions Simulation*). As with the Excel *Random Number Generation* tool, this *PHStat* tool generates the samples "off-line"; that is, they cannot be embedded directly into other cell formulas.

TABLE 3.3 Probability Distribution Functions Available in *Crystal Ball*

CB.BETA(*Alpha, Beta, Scale*)
CB.BINOMIAL(*Probability, Trials*)
CB.CUSTOM(*Cell range*)
CB.EXPONENTIAL(*Rate*)
CB.EXTREMEVALUE(*Mode, Scale*) (for maximum)
CB.EXTREMEVALUE2(*Mode, Scale*) (for minimum)
CB.GAMMA(*Location, Scale, Shape*)
CB.GEOMETRIC(*Probability*)
CB.HYPERGEOMETRIC(*Probability, Trials, Population*)
CB.LOGNORMAL(*Mean, Standard Deviation*)
CB.NEGBINOMIAL(*Probability, Trials*)
CB.NORMAL(*Mean, Standard Deviation*)
CB.PARETO(*Location, Shape*)
CB.POISSON(*Rate*)
CB.TRIANGULAR(*Minimum, Likeliest, Maximum*)
CB.UNIFORM(*Minimum, Maximum*)
CB.WEIBULL(*Location, Scale, Shape*)

The capabilities of Excel and *PHStat* for sampling from probability distributions are rather limited. However, this book also includes a student version of *Crystal Ball,* an Excel add-in that was developed and is published by Decisioneering, Inc., and is designed to facilitate the process of Monte Carlo simulation. *Crystal Ball* allows you to define cells in spreadsheets as random variables with specified distributions, draw samples from these distributions, evaluate the spreadsheet formulas using the sample data, and collect extensive statistical information about the distribution of one or more output cells of interest. *Crystal Ball* is used extensively in analyzing risks associated with decisions, as we will explore further in Chapter 8. However, it can also be a useful tool in understanding probability distributions and statistics.

Crystal Ball provides functions for all of the distributions described in this chapter that can be entered directly into cell formulas in a spreadsheet: uniform, normal, triangular, binomial, Poisson, geometric, hypergeometric, lognormal, exponential, Weibull, beta, gamma, logistic, Pareto, extreme value, and negative binomial, as well as user-defined custom distributions. These are listed in Table 3.3. For example, to generate a sample from a uniform distribution between 10 and 20, you would enter the formula:

$$=CB.UNIFORM(10,20)$$

into the appropriate cell. This is much more flexible than using either the Excel *Random Number Generation* tool or the *PHStat Sampling Distribution Simulation* tool.

In addition to these Excel functions, *Crystal Ball* also provides a point-and-click approach to specifying probability distributions in spreadsheets. To illustrate, we will

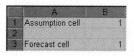

FIGURE 3.27 *Crystal Ball* Model for Sampling

CRYSTAL BALL NOTE

SAMPLING FROM A NORMAL DISTRIBUTION

An **assumption cell** is a value cell in a spreadsheet model that has been defined as a probability distribution. The cell must contain a simple constant and no formula. In Figure 3.27, cell B1 is an assumption cell. To define this cell as a normal distribution, for example, first click on it, select *Define Assumption* from the *Cell* menu, choose the normal distribution from the distribution gallery, and specify the mean as 10 and the standard deviation as 1.0. Click OK to return to the spreadsheet.

A **forecast cell** is a formula cell whose values we want to track during a simulation.

Forecast cells refer either directly or indirectly to assumption cells. In Figure 3.27, cell B3 has the formula =B1 because all we wish to do is capture the samples drawn from the normal distribution assumption cell. Define cell B3 as a forecast cell by first clicking on it, choosing *Define Forecast* from the *Cell* menu, entering a name for the forecast cell ("Sample from normal distribution"), and then clicking OK. Choose *Run Preferences* in the *Run* menu, select *Trials*, and specify either 50 or 500 to run the experiment. Then select *Run* from the *Run* menu.

generate samples from a normal distribution with mean 10 and standard deviation 1.0 using the spreadsheet model in Figure 3.27 (see the *Crystal Ball Note: Sampling from a Normal Distribution*). Figure 3.28 shows one sample of size 50, and Figure 3.29 shows one sample of size 500.

Applications of Monte Carlo Methods in Statistics

Monte Carlo methods are often used when a problem cannot apparently be solved using mathematics. For example, we know that dispersion of sample data can be measured using either the range or the standard deviation. If we use the range, which is a much simpler calculation if done manually, how might we estimate the standard deviation of the data, if we assume the data are normally distributed? (This is actually an important issue in quality control.) Suppose that we conduct an experiment

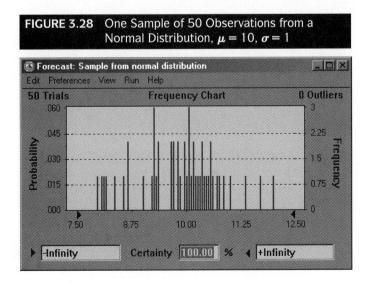

FIGURE 3.28   One Sample of 50 Observations from a Normal Distribution, $\mu = 10$, $\sigma = 1$

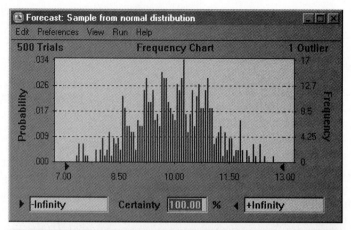

FIGURE 3.29 One Sample of 500 Observations from a Normal Distribution, $\mu = 10$, $\sigma = 1$

in which samples of size n are generated from a normal distribution having a known standard deviation σ. If we compute the range, R, of each sample, we can estimate the distribution of the statistic R/σ. The expected value of this statistic is a factor that statisticians have labeled as d_2. If we know this value, then we can estimate σ by R/d_2.

Figure 3.30 shows a simple spreadsheet for performing this experiment using *Crystal Ball*. We assume a mean of 0 and $n = 5$. Each value in the range B4:B8 is computed using the function =CB.NORMAL(0,$B$1). Cell B10 is defined as a *Crystal Ball* forecast. For each trial, new values of the five samples are generated, and the value of the forecast cell is recorded. Figure 3.31 shows the distribution of R/σ in the *Crystal Ball* Forecast Chart as well as the statistical summary 10,000 trials. (To view the statistics, select *Statistics* from the *View* menu in the *Crystal Ball* Forecast Chart.) We see that the actual distribution of R/σ covers a fairly wide range. The sample mean, that is, the estimate of d_2, is 2.34. Published statistical tables give this value as 2.326, so we see that the simulated value is very close to the value identified by statisticians.

As another example, the current of a simple electrical circuit is computed as

$$I = V/R$$

where V = voltage and R = resistance. Due to random fluctuations in performance, the voltage and resistance may not be constant, resulting in uncertainty of the current.

	A	B
1	Std. Dev.	1
2		
3	Sample	Value
4	1	-0.51515
5	2	0.105171
6	3	0.892567
7	4	1.655972
8	5	-0.46834
9		
10	R/σ	2.171124

FIGURE 3.30 Spreadsheet Model for Estimating d_2

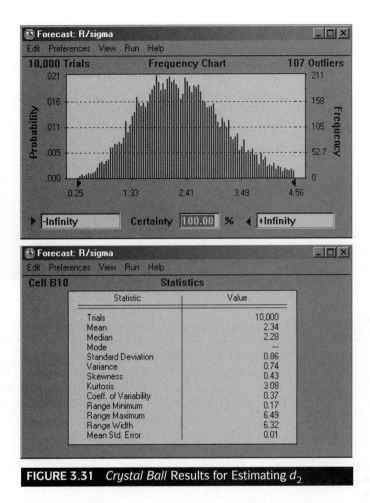

FIGURE 3.31 *Crystal Ball* Results for Estimating d_2

For example, suppose that the voltage is normally distributed with a mean of 12 and a standard deviation of 2.5 and the resistance is also normal with a mean of 3.0 and standard deviation of 0.8. Intuitively, one might believe that the mean current is $12/3 = 4$; however, as we shall see, this is not the case. We can use Monte Carlo simulation to identify the distribution of current for these assumptions. Figure 3.32 shows a simple *Crystal Ball* model. The simulated values in column D are normally distributed assumption cells with the parameters in columns B and C, and cell D8 is the *Crystal Ball* forecast. Figure 3.33 demonstrates that the ratio of two normal distributions is not normally distributed. When the resistance is low, the current increases significantly more than when the resistance is high. Thus, the distribution is skewed to the right, and the mean is larger than 4.

	A	B	C	D
1	**Electrical Circuit Analysis**			
2				
3			Standard	Simulated
4		Mean	Deviation	Values
5	Voltage	12	2.5	1
6	Resistance	3	0.8	1
7				
8			Current	1

FIGURE 3.32 *Crystal Ball* Model for Electrical Circuit Calculations

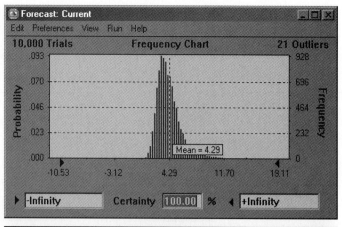

FIGURE 3.33   *Crystal Ball* Results for Distribution of Electrical Current

SAMPLING DISTRIBUTIONS AND SAMPLING ERROR

Whenever we collect data, we are essentially taking a sample from some generally unknown probability distribution. Usually the goal is to estimate a population parameter, such as the mean. An important statistical question is: How good is the estimate obtained from the sample? Let us examine the *Crystal Ball* results in Figures 3.28 and 3.29. Notice that as the sample size gets larger, the frequency distribution begins to assume the shape of the normal distribution.

More revealing, however, are the results shown in Figure 3.34, which shows the results for 10 independent samples of each size. Each of the observations represents the mean of a sample. Two things are evident. First, the average of the 10 sample means for $n = 500$ is closer to the true mean of 10.0 than the average of the sample means for $n = 50$. Second, the standard deviation of the sample means for $n = 500$ is much smaller, indicating that they vary less from the true population mean than those for $n = 50$. In other words, samples of size 500 have *less sampling error* than samples of size 50.

The means of multiple samples of a fixed size n from some population will form a distribution, which we call the **sampling distribution of the mean.** The sampling

D	E	F
Trial	n = 50	n = 500
1	9.6470	9.9246
2	10.0206	9.9800
3	10.3006	10.0658
4	9.9079	10.0909
5	9.9043	10.1273
6	10.1973	9.9552
7	10.3475	9.9375
8	10.0586	10.0801
9	9.9604	9.9748
10	9.8590	10.0327
Mean	10.02031	10.01688
Std. Dev.	0.214332	0.071559

FIGURE 3.34   Results of Sampling Experiment

distribution of the mean characterizes the population of means of *all possible samples* of a given size. (In Figure 3.34 we have 10 samples from the sampling distribution of the mean for each sample size.) From our experiment, we saw that as the sample size increases, the variance of the sampling distribution decreased. This suggests that the estimates we obtain from larger sample sizes provide greater accuracy in estimating the true population mean.

Standard Error of the Mean

The standard deviation of the sampling distribution of the mean is called the **standard error of the mean** and is computed as

$$\text{Standard Error of the Mean} = \sigma/\sqrt{n}$$

where σ is the standard deviation of the distribution of individual observations and n is the sample size. From this formula, we see that as n increases, the standard error decreases, just as our experiment demonstrated.

We may estimate the standard error of the mean by dividing the sample standard deviation (since the true population parameter is unknown) by the square root of n. Figure 3.35 shows the statistics from the last experiment with $n = 500$. We see that the sample standard deviation of the 500 samples is 1.03. Therefore, the standard error of the mean is estimated to be $1.03/\sqrt{500} = 0.05$, which is given on the last line of the chart. The "standard deviations" in the last row of Figure 3.34 are actually different estimates of the standard error—not based on the preceding formula, but based on a limited number of means from each sampling distribution. For $n = 500$, the standard deviation of the sample means is 0.07, which is close to 0.05, the difference due to sampling error.

What about the shape of the sampling distribution of the mean? Statisticians have shown that if the population is normal, then the sampling distribution of the mean will also be normal for *any* sample size and that the mean of the sampling distribution will be the same as that of the population. Furthermore, the **central limit theorem,** one of the most important practical results in statistics, states that if the sample size is large enough, the sampling distribution of the mean can be approximated by a normal distribution, *regardless* of the shape of the population distribution. We can illustrate this easily with a simple experiment in Excel (we invite you to try this). Copy the RAND( ) function into a matrix of 30 rows by 50 columns. This represents 50 samples of size

Statistic	Value
Trials	500
Mean	9.96
Median	9.97
Mode	---
Standard Deviation	1.03
Variance	1.06
Skewness	-0.09
Kurtosis	2.80
Coeff. of Variability	0.10
Range Minimum	6.88
Range Maximum	12.76
Range Width	5.88
Mean Std. Error	0.05

FIGURE 3.35 *Crystal Ball* Statistics Report Summary

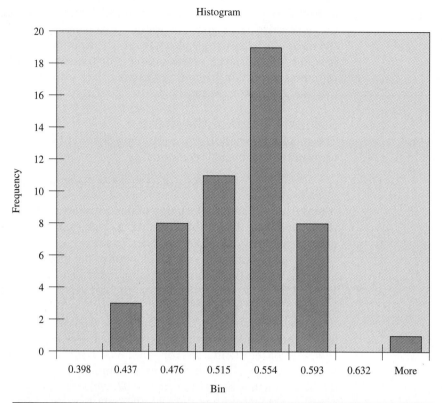

FIGURE 3.36   Distribution of 50 Sample Means from a Uniform Distribution

$n = 30$. Compute the mean of each column, and construct a histogram of the 50 means. Figure 3.36 shows one result. Although the distribution of the individual values is uniform, the distribution of the sample means looks more like a normal distribution. As the sample size and the number of samples increase, the distribution will become closer in shape to a normal distribution.

Understanding the standard error of the mean and characteristics of the sampling distribution is important for designing sampling experiments and performing various statistical tests. We address these issues in other chapters.

Questions and Problems

1. Enumerate the 36 possible outcomes from rolling a pair of dice, and compute the probability of rolling each of the numbers from 2 to 12.
2. Three coins are dropped on a table. List all possible outcomes. What is the probability of finding
   a. Exactly 2 heads?
   b. At most 1 head?
   c. At least 2 heads?
3. In Question 1, suppose the event A = "roll 7 or 11" and the event B = "roll 2, 3, or 12." Are these events mutually exclusive? Find $P(A)$, $P(B)$, and $P(A \text{ or } B)$.
4. In Question 2, suppose the event A = "exactly 2 heads" and event B = "at least 2 heads." Are these events mutually exclusive? Find $P(A \text{ or } B)$.
5. An airline tracks data on its flight arrivals. Over the past six months, 65 flights on one route arrived early, 273 arrived on time, 218 were late, and 44 were cancelled.
   a. What is the probability that a flight is early? On time? Late? Cancelled?
   b. Are these outcomes mutually exclusive?
   c. What is the probability that a flight is either early or on time?
6. A survey of 100 MBA students found that 85 owned mutual funds, 55 owned stocks, and 45 owned both.
   a. What is the probability that a student owns a stock? A mutual fund?
   b. What is the probability that a student owns neither stocks nor mutual funds?
   c. What is the probability that a student owns either a stock or a mutual fund?
7. Roulette is played at a table similar to the one in Figure 3.37. A wheel with the numbers 1 through 36 (evenly distributed with the colors red and black) and two green numbers 0 and 00 rotates in a shallow bowl with a curved wall. A small ball is spun on the inside of the wall and drops into a pocket corresponding to one of the numbers. Players may make 11 different types of bets by placing chips on different areas of the table. These include bets on a single number, two adjacent numbers, a row of three numbers, a block of four numbers, two adjacent rows of six numbers, and the five number combinations of 0, 00, 1, 2, and 3; bets on the numbers 1–18 or 19–36; the first, second, or third group of 12 numbers; a column of 12 numbers; even or odd; and red or black. Payoffs differ by bet. For instance, a single-number bet

FIGURE 3.37 Layout of a Typical Roulette Table

pays 35 to 1 if it wins; a three-number bet pays 11 to 1; a column bet pays 2 to 1; and a color bet pays even money. Define the following events: C1 = column 1 number, C2 = column 2 number, C3 = column 3 number, O = odd number, E = even number, G = green number, F12 = first 12 numbers, S12 = second 12 numbers, and T12 = third 12 numbers.

a. Find the probability of each of these events.

b. Find $P(G$ or $O)$, $P(O$ or $F12)$, $P(C1$ or $C3)$, $P(E$ and $F12)$, $P(E$ or $F12)$, $P(S12$ and $T12)$, $P(O$ or $C2)$

8. Using the data in *Census Education Data.xls,* develop a probability distribution and cumulative distribution function for
   a. Sex
   b. Race
   c. Marital status

9. A consumer products company found that 48 percent of successful products also received favorable results from test market research, while 12 percent had unfavorable results, but nevertheless were successful. Twenty-eight percent of unsuccessful products had unfavorable research results, while 12 percent of them had favorable research results. Construct the joint probability distribution for the two random variables: product success and test market research results.

10. Using the *Census Education Data.xls* worksheet, construct a joint probability distribution for marital status and educational status.
    a. Are these random variables independent?
    b. What is the probability that a divorced person has a bachelor's degree?
    c. What is the probability that someone with an advanced degree is married with spouse present?
    d. What is the probability that an individual who was never married has *at least* an associate's degree?

11. Develop the joint probability distribution of age and educational status in *Census Education.xls* presented in the chapter, if indeed the random variables were independent.

12. Explain the difference between a discrete random variable and a continuous random variable.

13. Explain the difference between a discrete probability function and the probability distribution of a continuous random variable.

14. Verify that the function corresponding to the figure below is a valid probability density function. Then find the probabilities:
    a. $P(X \leq 7)$
    b. $P(X > 9)$
    c. $P(7 \leq X \leq 9)$
    d. $P(9 \leq X \leq 11)$

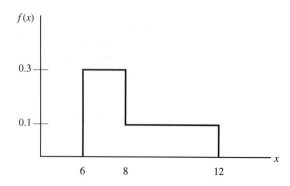

15. The weekly demand of a slow-moving product has the probability function:

DEMAND, x	PROBABILITY, $f(x)$
0	0.1
1	0.2
2	0.4
3	0.3
4 or more	0

Find the expected value, variance, and standard deviation of weekly demand.

16. Develop a probability distribution for the following data using the relative frequency notion, and calculate the expected value, variance, and standard deviation.

VALUE	RELATIVE FREQUENCY
0	56
1	28
2	12
3	3
4	0
5	1

17. A major application of data mining in marketing is determining the attrition of customers. Suppose that the probability of a long-distance carrier's customer leaving for another carrier from one month to the next is 0.2. What distribution models the retention of an individual customer? What is the expected value and standard deviation?

18. If a long-distance carrier conducted a telemarketing campaign to generate new clients, and the probability of successfully gaining a new customer was 0.02, what is the probability that contacting 50 potential customers would result in 0, 1, 2, 3, or 4 new customers?

19. A telephone call center where people place marketing calls to customers has a probability of success of 0.03. The manager is very harsh on those who do not get a successful call each hour. Find the number of calls needed to ensure that there is a probability of 0.70 of obtaining 4 or more successful calls.

20. A financial consultant has an average of 6 customers arrive each day. The consultant's overhead requires that at least 5 customers arrive in order that fees cover expenses. Find the probabilities of 0 through 4 customers arriving in a given day. What is the probability that at least 5 customers arrive?

21. The time required to play a game of Battleship is uniformly distributed between 20 and 60 minutes.
    a. Find the expected value and variance of the time to complete the game.
    b. What is the probability of finishing within 30 minutes?
    c. What is the probability that the game would take longer than 45 minutes?

22. In determining automobile mileage ratings, it was found that the mpg in the city (X) for a certain model is normally distributed, with a mean of 22.5 mpg and a standard deviation of 1.5 mpg. Find:
    a. $P(X < 22.5)$
    b. $P(0 \leq X \leq 24)$
    c. $P(X > 24)$
    d. $P(22 \leq X \leq 22.5)$
    e. $P(X < 22)$
    f. $P(21.5 \leq X \leq 23)$

    g. $P(X > 21)$

    h. The mileage rating that the upper 5% of cars achieve.

23. A popular soft drink is sold in 2 liter (2000 ml) bottles. Because of variation in the filling process, bottles have a mean of 2000 ml and a standard deviation of 25, normally distributed.
    a. If the process fills the bottle by more than 60 ml, the overflow will cause a machine malfunction. What is the probability of this occurring?
    b. What is the probability of underfilling the bottles by at least 30 ml?

24. A supplier contract calls for a key dimension of a part to be between 1.95 and 2.05 cm. The supplier has determined that the standard deviation of its process, which is normally distributed, is 0.10 cm.
    a. If the mean is 1.98, what fraction of parts will meet specifications?
    b. If the mean is adjusted to 2.00, what fraction of parts will meet specifications?
    c. How small must the standard deviation be to ensure that no more than 2 percent of parts are nonconforming, assuming the mean is 2.00?

25. Sketch the triangular distribution, find the probability density function and cumulative distribution function, and compute the mean and variance for each of the following parameter sets.
    a. $a = 0, b = 3, c = 6$
    b. $a = 0, b = 1, c = 6$
    c. $a = 0, b = 4, c = 6$

26. A light bulb is warranted to last for 1000 hours. If the time to failure is exponentially distributed with a true mean of 800 hours, what is the probability that it will last at least 1000 hours?

27. Generate 25 normally distributed random variates from a distribution with a mean of 50 and a standard deviation of 10. Compare the sample mean and variance with the input parameters. Repeat this experiment with 100 random variates, and compare the results. What do you conclude?

28. Generate a set of 200 random numbers and place these in cells A1 through A200 of an Excel worksheet. Convert these to random variates by entering the following formula in the next column to the right of the random numbers. For instance, in cell B1, enter:

$$= -50*LN(1-A1)$$

Copy this formula down through all 200 cells through cell B200. Compute the mean and variance of these values and construct a histogram. From what distribution do these random variates appear to be? Why?

29. Generate 100 uniformly distributed random variates between 0 and 25. Construct a histogram with cells of width 5. Repeat this for 500 random variates. How do the histograms compare?

30. Modify the spreadsheet in Figure 3.30 to estimate the factor d_2 for sample sizes of $n = 2$ through 10. Use 10,000 trials and compare your results to published factors shown here:

N	d_2
2	1.128
3	1.693
4	2.059
5	2.326
6	2.534
7	2.704
8	2.847

N	d_2
9	2.970
10	3.078

31. Devise and implement a Monte Carlo experiment for estimating the standard deviation of the range, σ_R, as a function of the standard deviation of a normal distribution, σ. That is, determine the distribution of σ_R/σ and estimate the expected value, d_3, for sample size 5. Compare your results with the published value 0.864.

32. A government agency is putting a large project out for low bid. Bids are expected from 10 different contractors and will have a normal distribution with a mean of $3.5 million and a standard deviation of 0.25 million. Devise and implement a Monte Carlo experiment for estimating the distribution of the minimum bid and the expected value of the minimum bid.

33. Generate 20 groups of 10 uniformly distributed numbers, and calculate the mean of each group. Compute the mean and variance of all 200 values, as well as the mean and variance of the 20 means. Compute the standard error of the mean using the 20 sample means and compare this to $s/\sqrt{n}$ for the entire sample. Explain your results.

34. Generate three data sets of normally distributed random variates, all with a mean of 80 and a standard deviation of 5. Let data set 1 be 50 groups of 5, data set 2 be 50 groups of 10, and data set 3 be 50 groups of 30. Calculate the mean of each group. Compare the average of the means for each set, as well as their variances. What can you conclude?

35. Repeat the *Crystal Ball* experiment in this chapter using 1000 trials. How do the results compare with Figures 3.28 and 3.29?

36. Consider the situation described in Problem 22. Suppose that the car manufacturer samples 16 cars from its assembly line and tests them for mileage ratings.
    a. What is the distribution of the mean mpg for the sample?
    b. What is the probability that the sample mean will be greater than 21 mpg?
    c. What is the probability that the sample mean will be at least 23?

37. Consider the situation described in Problem 23.
    a. If the manufacturer samples 100 bottles, what is the probability that the mean is less than 1950 ml?
    b. What mean overfill or more will occur only 10 percent of the time?

CASE

PROBABILITY MODELING FOR TRACWAY QUALITY MEASUREMENTS

Tracway collects a variety of data from special studies, many of which are related to quality control. Tracway routinely collects data about functional test performance of its mowers after assembly; results from the last 30 days are given in the worksheet *S4 Mower Test*. In addition, many in-process measurements are taken to ensure that manufacturing processes remain in control and can produce according to design specifications. The worksheet *S5 Process Capability* provides the results of 200 samples of blade weights taken from the manufacturing process that produces mower blades. Henry Hudson has asked you to evaluate these data. Specifically, he has the following questions:

1. What fraction of mowers fails for each of the 30 samples in the worksheet *S4 Mower Test*? What distribution models the failure of an individual mower? Using these data, estimate the sampling distribution of the mean, the overall fraction of failures, and the standard error of the mean. Is a normal distribution an appropriate assumption for the sampling distribution of the mean?

2. What fraction of mowers fails the functional performance test using all the data in the worksheet *S4 Mower Test*? Using this result, what is the probability of having 0, 1, 2, 3, 4, or 5 failures in the next 100 mowers tested?

3. What does the distribution of the data in the worksheet *S5 Process Capability* look like? (Construct a frequency distribution and histogram.) Do the data appear to be normally distributed? Compare your conclusion by constructing a normal probability plot using *PHStat*.

4. Assuming that the process capability data are normal, what are estimates of the mean and standard deviation? What is the probability that blade weights from this process will exceed 5.20? What is the probability that weights will be less than 4.80? What is the percent of weights that exceed 5.20 or are less than 4.80 from the data in the worksheet? How do the normal probability calculations compare? What do you conclude?

Summarize your findings in a report. ■

C H A P T E R

4

SAMPLING AND STATISTICAL INFERENCE

INTRODUCTION

In Chapters 1–3, we discussed the use of data and sampling for managing and decision making, introduced methods for data visualization and descriptive statistics, and gained an understanding of some important probability distributions used in statistics and decision modeling. These topics were focused on how to view data to gain better understanding and insight. However, managers need to go further than simply understanding what data tell; they need to be able to *draw conclusions* about populations from the data to make effective decisions. Sampling methods and statistical analysis of data provide the tools for doing this.

In this chapter we focus on using statistics to estimate important population parameters and make inferences about sample data. The key concepts and tools that we will present are

- Statistical sampling, including sample design, simple random sampling, and other sampling schemes; sampling error; and sample size determination
- Estimation, focusing on point estimates, interval estimates, and confidence intervals
- Principles of hypothesis testing and examples of hypothesis tests for means, variances, and proportions
- An introduction to analysis of variance (ANOVA), which also will be used in later chapters
- The chi-square test for independence
- Distribution fitting and use of *Crystal Ball*

STATISTICAL SAMPLING

Sampling approaches play an important role in providing information for making business decisions. Sampling is a valuable tool in business, because even if the population is finite, it generally is too large to deal with effectively or practically. For instance, it would be impractical as well as too expensive to survey the entire population of TV viewers in the United States. Sampling is also clearly necessary when data must be obtained from destructive testing or from a continuous production process. Thus, the purpose of sampling is to obtain sufficient information to draw a valid inference about a population.

Sample Design

The first step in sampling is to design an effective sampling plan that will yield representative samples of the populations under study. A **sampling plan** is a description of the approach that will be used to obtain samples from a population prior to any data collection activity. A sampling plan states the objectives of the sampling activity, the target population, the population *frame* (the list from which the sample is selected), the method of sampling, the operational procedures for collecting the data, and the statistical tools that will be used to analyze the data. The objectives of a sampling study might be to estimate key parameters of a population, such as a mean, proportion, or standard deviation. For example, *USA Today* reported on May 19, 2000, that the U.S. Census Bureau began a statistical sampling procedure to estimate the number and characteristics of people who might have been missed in the traditional head count. Another application of sampling is to determine if significant differences exist between two populations. For instance, the Excel worksheet *Burglaries.xls* provides data about monthly burglaries in the Hyde Park area of Chicago before and after a citizen–police program was instituted. You might wish to determine whether the program was successful in reducing the number of burglaries.

The ideal frame is a complete list of all members of the target population. However, for practical reasons, a frame may not be the same as the target population. For example, a company's target population might be all golfers in America, which might be impossible to identify, whereas a practical frame might be a list of golfers who have registered handicaps with the United States Golf Association. Understanding how well the frame represents the target population helps us to understand how representative of the target population the actual sample is and hence the validity of any statistical conclusions drawn from the sample. In a classic example, *Literary Digest* polled individuals from telephone lists and membership rolls of country clubs for the 1936 presidential election and predicted that Alf Landon would defeat Franklin D. Roosevelt. The problem was that the frame—individuals who owned telephones and belonged to country clubs—was heavily biased toward Republicans and did not represent the population at large.

Sampling Methods

Sampling methods can be *subjective* or *probabilistic*. Subjective methods include **judgment sampling,** in which expert judgment is used to select the sample (survey the "best" customers), and **convenience sampling,** in which samples are selected based on the ease with which the data can be collected (survey all customers I happen to visit this month). Probabilistic sampling involves selecting the items in the sample using some random procedure. The most common approach is simple random sampling.

Simple random sampling involves selecting items from a population so that every subset of a given size has an equal chance of being selected. If the population data are stored in a database, simple random samples can generally be obtained easily by generating random numbers, as we discussed in Chapter 3. For example, suppose that a telephone book database consists of 400,000 individuals and we wish to sample 250 people. The Excel *Data Analysis* tool *Random Number Generation* (described in Chapter 3) can be used to generate 250 random numbers between 1 and 400,000, and the TRUNC function can be used to remove the decimal fraction and convert the data to whole numbers. This tool, however, does not guarantee that all numbers are unique. If any duplicates are found, they may be discarded and replaced with new numbers. *PHStat* provides a tool to generate a random set of values from a given population size *without replacement,* guaranteeing that each item in the sample will be unique (see the *PHStat Note: Using the Random Sample Generator*). Once the random numbers are generated, you must match the sample numbers generated with the actual data.

If the data are available as a list on an Excel worksheet, the *Data Analysis* tool *Sampling* allows you to select a simple random sample or a systematic sample from a list in the worksheet (see *Excel Note: Using the Sampling Tool*). However, this tool generates random samples *with replacement,* so you must be careful to check for duplicate observations in the sample. The *PHStat Random Sample Generator* also provides the

EXCEL NOTE

USING THE SAMPLING TOOL

The Excel file *Cereal Data.xls* provides information about 67 cereal products, as shown in Figure 4.1. Suppose that we wish to sample 15 products from this list. Click on *Tools,* followed by *Data Analysis,* and *Sampling.* This brings up the dialog box shown in Figure 4.2. In the *Input Range* box, you specify the data range from which the sample will be taken; in this example, the list of product numbers (the tool requires that the data sampled be numeric). The *Labels* box can be checked if the first row is a data set label. There are two options for sampling:

- Sampling can be *periodic* (i.e., systematic), and you will be prompted for the *Period,* which is the interval between sample observations from the beginning of the data set. For instance, if a period of 5 is used, observations 5, 10, 15, etc. will be selected as samples.

- Sampling can also be *random,* and you will be prompted for the *Number of Samples.* Excel will then randomly select this number of samples (with replacement) from the specified data set.

Figure 4.3 shows the output that results. We used the VLOOKUP function in Excel to extract the product names in column L.

FIGURE 4.1 Portion of the Excel File *Cereal Data.xls*

	A	B	C	D	E	F	G	H	I
1	Product	Cereal Name	Manufacturer	Calories	Sodium	Fiber	Carbs	Sugars	Shelf
2	1	100% Bran	Nabisco	70	130	10	5	6	3
3	2	All-Bran	Kellogg	70	260	9	7	5	3
4	3	All-Bran w/Extra Fiber	Kellogg	50	140	14	8	0	3
5	4	Almond Delight	Ralston Purina	110	200	1	14	8	3
6	5	Apple Cinn Cheerios	General Mills	110	180	1.50	10.50	10	1
7	6	Apple Jacks	Kellogg	110	125	1	11	14	2
8	7	Basic 4	General Mills	130	210	2	18	8	3
9	8	Bran Chex	Ralston Purina	90	200	4	15	6	1
10	9	Bran Flakes	Post	90	210	5	13	5	3
11	10	Cap'n'Crunch	Quaker	120	220	0	12	12	2

FIGURE 4.2 Dialog Box for Excel Sampling Tool

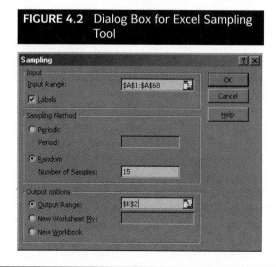

FIGURE 4.3 Sampling Tool Results

K	L
Sample	Product
64	Trix
28	Fruitful Bran
34	Honey Comb
44	Nut & Honey Crunch
61	Total Corn Flakes
27	Fruit & Fibre
60	Strawberry Fruit Wheels
40	Life
14	Cocoa Puffs
19	Cracklin' Oat Bran
32	Grape-Nuts
36	Honey Nut Cheerios
35	Honey Graham Ohs
11	Cheerios
5	Apple Cinn Cheerios

PHSTAT NOTE

USING THE RANDOM SAMPLE GENERATOR

This tool can be used to generate a random list of integers between 1 and a specified population size or to randomly select values from a range of data on a worksheet without replacement. From the *PHStat* menu, select *Sampling,* then *Random Sample Generator*. Figure 4.4 shows the dialog box that appears. Enter the sample size desired in the *Sample Size* box. Click the first radio button if you want a list of random integers, and enter the population size in the box below this option. Click the second radio button to select a sample from data on a worksheet. The range of the data must be entered in the *Values Cell Range* box (checking *First cell contains label* if appropriate). This range must be a single column containing the values from which to draw the random sample.

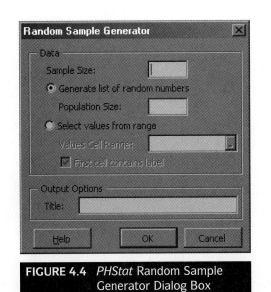

FIGURE 4.4   *PHStat* Random Sample Generator Dialog Box

capability of generating samples from a predefined list in a worksheet, but without replacement.

Other methods of sampling include

- *Systematic sampling.* A sampling plan that selects items periodically from the population. For example, to sample 250 names from a list of 400,000, every 1600th name could be selected. If the first item is selected randomly among the first 1600, then a probabilistic sample results. This approach can be used for telephone sampling when supported by an automatic dialer that is programmed to dial numbers in a systematic manner. However, systematic sampling is not the same as simple random sampling because for any sample, every possible sample of a given size in the population does not have an equal chance of being selected. In some situations, this approach can induce significant bias if the population has some underlying pattern. For instance, sampling orders received every seven days may not yield a representative sample if customers tend to send orders on certain days every week.

- *Stratified sampling.* Applies to populations that are divided into natural subsets (strata) and allocates the appropriate proportion of samples to each stratum. For example, a large city may be divided into political districts called wards. Each ward has a different number of citizens. A stratified sample would choose a sample of individuals in each ward proportionate to its size. This approach ensures that each stratum is weighted by its size relative to the population and can provide better results than simple random sampling if the items in each stratum are not homogeneous. However, issues of cost or significance of certain strata might make a disproportionate sample more useful. For example, the ethnic or racial mix of each ward might be significantly different, making it difficult for a stratified sample to obtain the desired information.

- *Cluster sampling.* Based on dividing a population into subgroups (clusters), sampling a set of clusters, and then usually conducting a complete census within the clusters sampled. For instance, a company might segment its customers into small geographical regions. A cluster sample would consist of a random sample of the geographical regions, and all customers within these regions would be surveyed (which might be easier because regional lists might be easier to produce and mail).

• *Sampling from a continuous process.* Selecting a sample from a continuous manufacturing process can be accomplished in two main ways. First, select a time at random, and then select the next *n* items produced after that time. Second, select *n* times at random, and then select the next item produced after these times. The first approach generally ensures that the observations will come from a homogeneous population; however, the second approach might include items from different populations if the characteristics of the process should change over time, so caution should be used.

Errors in Sampling

The purpose of sampling is to obtain statistics that estimate population parameters. Sample design can lead to two sources of errors. The first type of error, *nonsampling error,* occurs when the sample does not represent the target population adequately. This is generally a result of poor sample design, such as using a systematic sample when a simple random sample would have been more appropriate. *Sampling (statistical) error* occurs because samples are only a subset of the total population. We observed such sampling error with the simulation experiments in Chapter 3. Sampling error is inherent in any sampling process, and while it can be minimized, it cannot be totally avoided.

Sampling error depends on the size of the sample relative to the population. Thus, determining the number of samples to take is essentially a statistical issue that is based on the accuracy of the estimates needed to draw a useful conclusion. We discuss this later in this chapter. However, from a practical standpoint, one must also consider the cost of sampling and sometimes make a trade-off between cost and the information that is obtained.

Sampling from Finite Populations

In most practical applications, samples are drawn from finite populations without replacement. However, the central limit theorem and the calculation of the standard error that we discussed in Chapter 3 assume that samples were selected with replacement. When the sample size, *n*, is less than about 5 percent of the population size, *N*, the difference is insignificant. However, when the sample is larger than this, a correction factor should be used in computing the standard error. Specifically, the standard error should be multiplied by

$$\sqrt{\frac{N-n}{N-1}}$$

Thus, the standard error of the mean would be

$$\sigma_{\bar{x}} = \frac{\sigma}{\sqrt{n}}\sqrt{\frac{N-n}{N-1}}$$

Note that if *n* is small relative to *N*, then the term $\sqrt{(N-n)/(N-1)}$ is approximately 1 and the difference is insignificant.

STATISTICAL ANALYSIS OF SAMPLE DATA

Sample data provide the basis for many useful analyses to support decision making. These include *estimation* of population parameters and development of *confidence intervals* for population parameters, which provide an interval estimate of the parameter

TABLE 4.1 Statistical Analysis Support in Excel

Excel Function	Description
CONFIDENCE(*alpha, standard_dev, size*)	Returns the confidence interval for a population mean
CHITEST(*actual_range, expected_range*)	Returns the test for independence, the value of the chi-square distribution, and the appropriate degrees of freedom
TTEST(*array1, array2, tails, type*)	Returns the probability associated with a *t*-test
ZTEST(*array, x, sigma*)	Returns the two-tailed *p*-value of a *z*-test

Analysis Toolpak Tools	Description
Sampling	Creates a simple random sample with replacement or a systematic sample from a population
t-test: Paired Two-Sample for Means	Performs a paired *t*-test to test a hypothesis for equality of means between two populations for small samples
t-test: Two-Sample Assuming Equal Variances	Performs a test of hypothesis for equality of means between two populations if the populations are assumed to have equal variances
t-test: Two-Sample Assuming Unequal Variances	Performs a test of hypothesis for equality of means between two populations if the populations are assumed to have unequal variances
z-test: Two-Sample for Means	Performs a test of hypothesis for equality of means between two populations for large samples
F-test: Two-Sample for Variances	Performs a test of hypothesis for equality of variances between two populations
ANOVA: Single Factor	Tests hypothesis that means of two or more samples measured on one factor are equal
ANOVA: Two-Factor with Replication	Tests hypothesis that means of two or more samples measured on two factors are equal, more than one sample per group
ANOVA: Two-Factor without Replication	Tests hypothesis that means of two or more samples measured on two factors are equal based on one sampling

Prentice Hall Statistics Add-In	Description
Random Sample Generator	Generates a random sample without replacement
Confidence Intervals	Computes confidence intervals for means with σ known or unknown, proportions, and population total
Sample Size	Determines sample sizes for means and proportions
One-Sample Tests	Performs hypothesis tests for means with σ known or unknown, and for proportions
Two-Sample Tests	Performs *t*-test for difference in means, *F*-test for equality of variances, chi-square and *z*-tests for proportions
Multiple-Sample Tests	Performs chi-square test of independence
Normal Probability Plot	Generates a normal probability plot from a set of data

along with a probability that the interval correctly estimates the true (unknown) population parameter. Statistical sampling also provides a means to compare alternative decisions or systems. For example, in the worksheet *Burglaries.xls,* we find that the average number of monthly burglaries before the citizen–police program is 64.317, while the average after the program began was 60.647. While the average number of monthly burglaries appears to have fallen, we cannot tell whether the difference is significant or simply due to sampling error. *Hypothesis testing* is a tool that allows you to draw valid statistical conclusions about the value of population parameters or differences between them.

A variety of support is available in Microsoft Excel to perform statistical analyses. This includes standard Excel functions, the *Data Analysis* tools, and the *Prentice-Hall Statistics* add-in available with this book. Table 4.1 summarizes these options; we will illustrate many of them in this chapter.

ESTIMATION

Estimation involves assessing the value of a population parameter using sample data. **Point estimates** are single numbers used to estimate the population parameter. However, because of sampling error, it is unlikely that a point estimate will equal the true population parameter. **Interval estimates** provide a range of values between which the population parameter is believed to be and also provide a means of assessing sampling error.

Point Estimates

The most common point estimates are the descriptive statistical measures we described in Chapter 2 and which are summarized in Table 4.2. They are used to estimate the population parameters, also listed in Table 4.2.

Suppose that we performed an experiment in which we repeatedly sampled from a population and computed a point estimate for a population parameter (similar to the *Crystal Ball* experiment we did in Chapter 3). Each individual point estimate will vary from the population parameter; however, we would hope that the average (expected value) of all possible point estimates would equal the population parameter. If the expected value of an estimator equals the population parameter it is intended to estimate, the estimator is said to be **unbiased.** If this is not true, the estimator is called **biased.** Fortunately, all the estimators in Table 4.2 are unbiased and therefore are meaningful for making decisions involving the population parameter. In particular, you may recall a difference in calculating the sample variance versus the population variance. Recall that the sample variance is computed by the formula

$$s^2 = \frac{\sum_{i=1}^{n}(x_i - \bar{x})^2}{n-1}$$

while the population variance is computed by

$$\sigma^2 = \frac{\sum_{i=1}^{n}(x_i - \mu)^2}{N}$$

Statisticians have shown that the denominator $n-1$ used in computing s^2 is necessary to provide an unbiased estimator of σ^2. If we simply divided by the number of observations, the estimator would tend to underestimate the true variance.

TABLE 4.2 Common Point Estimates	
Point Estimate	*Population Parameter*
Sample mean, $\bar{x}$	Population mean, μ
Sample variance, s^2	Population variance, σ^2
Sample standard deviation, s	Population standard deviation, σ
Sample proportion, p	Population proportion, π

To illustrate some important issues regarding point estimation, let us consider the data in *TV Viewing.xls*. Point estimates for the mean, variance, and standard deviation are given next.

Age Group	Sample Mean	Sample Variance	Sample Standard Deviation
18–24	60.16	101.91	10.09
25–34	70.28	97.06	9.85
35–44	67.40	40.30	6.35
45–54	89.06	122.36	11.06
55–64	95.93	175.5 7	13.25
65+	117.05	32.37	5.69

These point estimates indicate that the number of TV viewing hours per week for the 18–24 age group is smaller than, for example, the 25–34 and 35–44 age groups, but the variance and standard deviation are larger. The 65+ age group has the smallest variance of all, but also has the highest average value. Thus, it is not clear how to interpret these values and make an informed decision. Interval estimates, which we discuss next, provide better information than point estimates alone.

INTERVAL ESTIMATES

An interval estimate provides a range within which we believe the true population parameter falls. For example, a Gallup poll might report that 56 percent of voters support a certain candidate with a margin of error of ±3 percent. A **confidence interval (CI)** is an interval estimate that also specifies the likelihood that the interval contains the true population parameter. This probability is called the **level of confidence,** denoted by $1 - \alpha$, and is usually expressed as a percent. For example, we might state that "a 90 percent CI for the mean is 10 ± 2." The value 10 is the point estimate calculated from the sample data, and 2 can be thought of as a margin for error. Thus, the interval estimate is [8, 12]. However, this interval may or may not include the true population mean. If we take a different sample, we will most likely have a different point estimate, say 10.4, which determines the interval estimate [8.4, 12.4]. Again, this may or may not include the true population mean. If we chose 100 samples, leading to 100 different interval estimates, we would expect that 90 percent of them—the level of confidence—would contain the true population mean. We would say we are 90 percent confident that the interval we obtain from sample data contains the true population mean. Commonly used confidence levels are 90, 95, and 99 percent; the higher the confidence level, the more assurance we have that the interval contains the true population parameter. As the confidence level increases, the confidence interval becomes larger to provide higher levels of assurance.

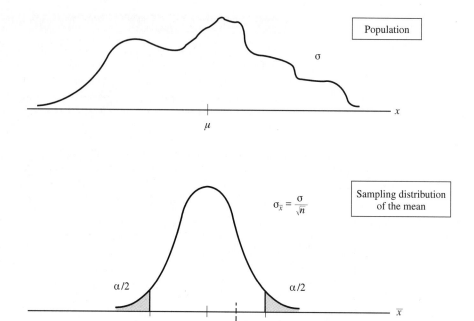

FIGURE 4.5 The Rationale for Confidence Intervals

CONFIDENCE INTERVALS FOR THE MEAN

We stated that the sample mean, $\bar{x}$, is a point estimate for the population mean μ. We can use the central limit theorem (see Chapter 3) to quantify the sampling error in $\bar{x}$. Recall that the central limit theorem states that no matter what the underlying population, the distribution of sample means is approximately normal with mean μ and standard deviation (standard error) $\sigma_{\bar{x}} = \sigma/\sqrt{n}$. The value of α represents the proportion of samples expected to be outside the confidence interval. Therefore, $100(1 - \alpha)$ percent of sample means (for all possible samples of size n) would fall within $\mu \pm z_{\alpha/2}(\sigma/\sqrt{n})$. This is illustrated in Figure 4.5.

Because we do not know μ but estimate it by $\bar{x}$, a $100(1 - \alpha)$ percent confidence interval for the population mean μ is

$$\bar{x} \pm z_{\alpha/2}(\sigma/\sqrt{n})$$

From Figure 4.5, note that whenever the sample mean falls within the interval $\mu \pm z_{\alpha/2}(\sigma/\sqrt{n})$, the confidence interval will contain the true population mean; however, if $\bar{x}$ falls in one of the tails, the confidence interval will not contain the true mean. Thus the CI will contain the true population mean $100(1 - \alpha)$ percent of the time. The value $z_{\alpha/2}$ may be found from a standard normal table (Table A.1 in the appendix at the end of the book) or may be computed in Excel using the function NORMSINV $(1 - \alpha/2)$. For the most common confidence levels used, we have

Confidence Level	$z_{\alpha/2}$
90%	1.645
95%	1.96
99%	2.576

The confidence interval we developed, however, assumes that we know the standard deviation. When the standard deviation is unknown, as would almost always be the case, we need to use the **t-distribution** to compute a confidence interval. The t-distribution is actually a family of probability distributions with a shape similar to the standard normal distribution. Different t-distributions are distinguished by an additional parameter, **degrees of freedom (df).** The t-distribution has a larger variance than the standard normal, thus making confidence intervals wider than those obtained from the standard normal distribution, in essence correcting for the uncertainty about the true standard deviation. As the number of degrees of freedom increases, the t-distribution converges to the standard normal distribution (see Figure 4.6). When sample sizes get to be as large as 120, the distributions are virtually identical; even for sample sizes as low as 30–35, it becomes difficult to distinguish between the two. Thus, for large sample sizes, many people use z-values to establish confidence intervals even when the standard deviation is unknown. We must point out, however, that for any sample size, the *true* sampling distribution of the mean is the t-distribution, so when in doubt, use the t.

The concept of "degrees of freedom" can be puzzling. It can best be explained by examining the formula for the sample variance:

$$s^2 = \frac{\sum_{i=1}^{n}(x_i - \bar{x})^2}{n - 1}$$

Note that to compute s^2 we need to first compute the mean, $\bar{x}$. If we know the value of the mean, then we need only know $n - 1$ distinct observations; the nth is completely determined. (For instance, if the mean of 3 values is 4, and you know that two of the values are 2 and 4, you can easily find the third to be 6.) The number of sample values that are free to vary defines the number of degrees of freedom; in general, *df* equals the number of sample values minus the number of estimated parameters. Because the sample variance uses one estimated parameter, the mean, the t-distribution used in

---

FIGURE 4.6 Convergence of t-Distribution to the Standard Normal Distribution

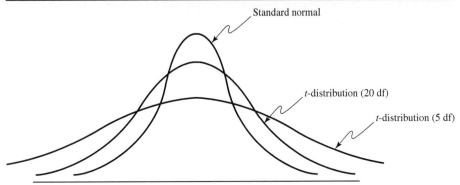

confidence interval calculations has $n - 1$ degrees of freedom. Because the t-distribution explicitly accounts for the effect of the sample size in estimating the population variance, it is the proper one to use for any sample size. However, for large samples, the difference between t- and z-values is very small, as we noted earlier.

Using the t-distribution, a $100(1 - \alpha)$ percent confidence interval for the population mean μ is

$$\bar{x} \pm t_{\alpha/2,n-1}(s/\sqrt{n})$$

where $t_{\alpha/2,n-1}$ is the value from the t-distribution with $n - 1$ degrees of freedom, giving an upper-tail probability of $\alpha/2$. We may find t-values in Table A.3 in the appendix at the end of the book or by using the Excel function TINV(*probability, degrees of freedom*). However, take careful note that "probability" in the function TINV refers to the probability in *both* tails of the distribution. Thus, $t_{\alpha/2,n-1}$ in Table A.3 is equivalent to TINV($\alpha, n - 1$).

In the TV viewing data, suppose we wish to find a 99 percent CI for the mean of the 18–24 age group. A 99 percent CI corresponds to $1 - \alpha = 0.99$. Thus $\alpha/2 = 0.005$. For the 18–24 age group, we have 45 observations, thus the t-distribution has $45 - 1 = 44$ df. Using Table A.3, we find that $t_{0.005, 44} = 2.6923$, yielding a 99 percent CI for the mean of

$$60.16 \pm 2.6923(10.09/\sqrt{45}) = 60.16 \pm 4.05 \quad \text{or} \quad [56.11, 64.21]$$

This means that if we chose 100 samples of size 45, we would expect 99 of the sample means to fall within the computed confidence intervals. Stated less formally, we are 99 percent confident that the true population mean falls between 56.11 and 64.21. We leave it as an exercise to compute confidence intervals for the remaining age groups.

Because we have a sample size of 45, let us compare this confidence interval to that using a normal distribution. From Table A.1, or using the function NORMSINV(.995) in Excel, we find $z = 2.576$. Thus, a 99 percent CI for the mean of the 18–24 age group using the normal distribution would be

$$60.16 \pm 2.576(10.09/\sqrt{45}) = 60.16 \pm 3.87 \quad \text{or} \quad [56.29, 64.03]$$

This confidence interval is close to that found using the t-distribution but is slightly smaller (the width is 95.6 percent of the correct CI).

Now suppose we used only the first 25 samples (having a sample mean of 61.00 and a sample standard deviation of 9.40). Using the t-distribution in Table A.3, or the Excel function TINV(0.01, 24), we have $t_{0.005, 24} = 2.7969$, and the confidence interval is

$$61.00 \pm 2.7969(9.40/\sqrt{25}) = 61.00 \pm 5.26 \quad \text{or} \quad [55.74, 66.26]$$

However, using the normal distribution results in the confidence interval

$$61.00 \pm 2.576(9.40/\sqrt{25}) = 61.00 \pm 4.84 \quad \text{or} \quad [56.16, 65.84]$$

The ratio of the width of this CI to that of the t-distribution is now only 92.0 percent. Thus, as the sample size gets smaller, the errors in using z instead of t magnify.

PHStat provides tools for computing confidence intervals for the mean with the standard deviation either known or unknown (see the *PHStat Note: Confidence Intervals for the Mean*). The Excel function CONFIDENCE(*alpha, standard_dev, size*) can be used to compute the term $z_{\alpha/2}(s/\sqrt{n})$ within a spreadsheet model or report.

PHSTAT NOTE

CONFIDENCE INTERVALS FOR THE MEAN

From the *PHStat* menu, select *Confidence Intervals,* and then *Estimate for the mean, sigma known* . . . , or *Estimate for the mean, sigma unknown* . . . . The dialog box for the case when sigma is unknown is shown in Figure 4.7. First

enter the confidence level. If you know the sample statistics, click the radio button Sample Statistics Known, and enter them in the appropriate boxes. Otherwise, you may have the tool compute them by specifying the range of the data in the second option. If the sample came from a finite population, we suggest that you check the box for *Finite Population Correction* in the output options and enter the population size. This adjusts the standard error using the finite population correction factor discussed earlier in this chapter. Figure 4.8 shows the output yielding the same results for the *TV Viewing.xls* data we have discussed.

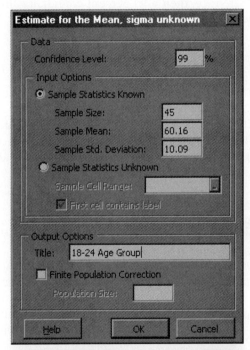

FIGURE 4.7 *PHStat* Dialog Box for Confidence Intervals— Estimate for the Mean, Sigma Unknown

	A	B
1	18-24 Age Group	
2		
3	Data	
4	Sample Standard Deviation	10.09
5	Sample Mean	60.16
6	Sample Size	45
7	Confidence Level	99%
8		
9	Intermediate Calculations	
10	Standard Error of the Mean	1.504128393
11	Degrees of Freedom	44
12	t Value	2.692286216
13	Interval Half Width	4.049544139
14		
15	Confidence Interval	
16	Interval Lower Limit	56.11
17	Interval Upper Limit	64.21

FIGURE 4.8 *PHStat* Output for Confidence Interval Estimation for the Mean

CONFIDENCE INTERVALS FOR PROPORTIONS

For categorical variables having only two possible outcomes, such as good or bad, male or female, and so on, we are usually interested in the *proportion* of observations in a sample that have a certain characteristic. An unbiased estimator of a population proportion π is the statistic $p = x/n$ (sample proportion), where x is the number in the sample having the desired characteristic and n is the sample size. The sampling distribution of p is the probability distribution of all possible values of p. If we are sampling with replacement from a finite population, the sampling distribution of x follows the binomial distribution with mean $n\pi$ and variance $n\pi(1 - \pi)$. It follows that the sampling distribution of $p = x/n$ has mean $n\pi/n = \pi$ and variance $n\pi(1 - \pi)/n^2 = \pi(1 - \pi)/n$.

Thus, the standard error of the proportion is $\sqrt{\pi(1 - \pi)/n}$. When $n\pi$ and $n(1 - \pi)$ are at least 5, the sampling distribution of p approaches the normal distribution as a consequence of the central limit theorem. Therefore, under these conditions, we may use z-values to determine the range of sampling error for a specified confidence level. Using the sample proportion p as a point estimate of the population proportion π, a $100(1 - \alpha)$ confidence interval for the proportion is

$$p \pm z_{\alpha/2}\sqrt{\frac{p(1 - p)}{n}}$$

For example, if a sample of 1000 voters found that 51 percent voted for a particular candidate ($p = 0.51$) in a two-candidate race, then a 90 percent confidence interval ($\alpha/2 = 0.05$) for the population proportion would be

$$0.51 \pm 1.645\sqrt{\frac{0.51 \times 0.49}{1000}} = 0.51 \pm 0.026$$

If the sample represented the overall voting population, there is a 0.90 probability that the true percentage of the vote in favor of the candidate is between 0.484 and 0.536. Because of this uncertainty of the sample data, even though the *point estimate* indicates a majority vote, the candidate might lose because the true population proportion might be less than 0.50! *PHStat* provides a simple tool for finding confidence intervals for proportions in the *Confidence Intervals* option.

CONFIDENCE INTERVALS AND SAMPLE SIZE

In all the formulas for confidence intervals, the sample size plays a critical role in determining the width of the confidence interval. If we have already collected the data, we may be constrained by the amount of data available. However, if we are planning a sampling study, we could determine the appropriate sample size needed to estimate the population parameter within a specified level of precision. For example, consider the confidence interval for the mean with a known population standard deviation:

$$\bar{x} \pm z_{\alpha/2}(\sigma/\sqrt{n})$$

Suppose we want the width of the confidence interval on either side of the mean to be at most E. In other words,

$$E \geq z_{\alpha/2}(\sigma/\sqrt{n})$$

Solving for n, we find

$$n \geq (z_{\alpha/2})^2(\sigma^2)/E^2$$

Of course, we do not know σ^2 since we have not collected any data yet. A common-sense approach would be to take an initial sample to estimate it using the sample variance s^2. If $z_{\alpha/2}(s/\sqrt{n}) \leq E$, then we clearly have achieved our goal. If not, we can use the estimate s^2 to determine n using the preceding formula and collect additional data as needed. Note that if s^2 changes significantly, we still might not have achieved the desired precision and might have to repeat the process. Usually, however, this will be unnecessary.

As an example, consider the problem of estimating the number of TV viewers in the 18–24 age group to develop a 95 percent confidence interval for the mean having a precision of no more than $E = 2$ hours. Note that from the sample of 45 viewers in the data set *TV Viewing.xls,* $z_{\alpha/2}(s/\sqrt{n}) = (1.96)(9.40)/\sqrt{45} = 2.746$. Therefore, this sample size is insufficient to provide the desired precision. Using the preceding formula and the estimated standard deviation based on the sample of 45 viewers, the sample size required is

$$n \geq (1.96)^2(9.40)^2/(2)^2 = 84.86$$

or 85 (always round up). After taking the sample, we should check the actual precision obtained based on the new estimate of the standard deviation, and recalculate n if necessary.

In a similar fashion we can compute the sample size required to achieve a desired confidence interval half-width for a proportion by solving the following equation for n:

$$E \geq z_{\alpha/2}\sqrt{\frac{\pi(1-\pi)}{n}}$$

This yields

$$n \geq \frac{(z_{\alpha/2})^2\pi(1-\pi)}{E^2}$$

In practice, the value of π will not be known. You could use the sample proportion from a preliminary sample as an estimate of π to plan the sample size, but this might require several iterations and additional samples to find the sample size that yields the required precision. When no information is available, the most conservative estimate is to set $\pi = 0.5$. This maximizes the quantity $\pi(1-\pi)$ in the formula, resulting in the sample size that will guarantee the required precision no matter what the true proportion is. For example, to estimate the number of voters to poll to obtain a 90 percent confidence interval on the proportion of voters that choose a particular candidate with a precision of 0.01 or less, we would need

$$n \geq \frac{(1.645)^2 0.5(1-0.5)}{(0.01)^2} = 6765.06$$

or at least 6766 voters. *PHStat* provides a tool for computing sample sizes for estimating both means and proportions (see the *PHStat Note: Determining Sample Size*).

ADDITIONAL TYPES OF CONFIDENCE INTERVALS

Most confidence intervals have the same basic form: a point estimate of the population parameter of interest plus or minus some number of standard errors. Thus, establishing confidence intervals requires choosing the proper point estimate for a population parameter as well as an understanding of the sampling distribution of the parameter being estimated and, in particular, the standard error. In this section we summarize several additional types of confidence intervals and the formulas used to calculate them.

Population Total
In some applications, we might be more interested in the *total* of a population rather than the mean. For instance, an auditor might wish to estimate the total amount of receivables by sampling a small number of accounts. If a population of N items has a

---

PHSTAT NOTE

DETERMINING SAMPLE SIZE

From the *PHStat* menu, select *Sample Size,* and then either *Determination for the Mean* or *Determination for the Proportion*. The dialog box

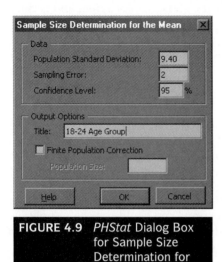

FIGURE 4.9 *PHStat* Dialog Box for Sample Size Determination for the Mean

for the mean is shown in Figure 4.9. You need to enter the standard deviation, sampling error desired, and confidence level. The output options also allow you to incorporate a finite population correction factor. The tool creates a new worksheet with the results for the TV Viewing example shown in Figure 4.10. The tool for determining the sample size for a proportion is similar.

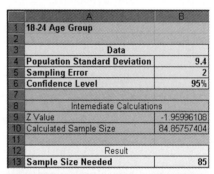

FIGURE 4.10 *PHStat* Results for Sample Size Determination

---

mean μ, then the population total is $N\mu$. We may estimate a population total from a random sample of size n from a population of size N by $N\bar{x}$.

The sampling distribution of $N\bar{x}$ has a standard error equal to

$$N \frac{s}{\sqrt{n}} \sqrt{\frac{N-n}{N-1}}$$

when the finite population correction factor is applied. Therefore, a $100(1 - \alpha)$ percent CI for the total is

$$N\bar{x} \pm t_{\alpha/2,\, n-1} N \frac{s}{\sqrt{n}} \sqrt{\frac{N-n}{N-1}}$$

PHStat has a tool for calculating a CI for a population total. In the *Confidence Intervals* menu, choose *Estimate for the Population Total*. The dialog box is similar to the one used to calculate a confidence interval for a mean.

Differences Between Means

In many situations, we are interested in differences between two populations. For example, in the *Accounting Professionals.xls* data set, we might be interested in the difference in mean years of service between males and females. Similarly, in the *Burglaries.xls* data, we might be interested in the difference between the mean number of burglaries per month before and after the citizen–police program was instituted. In both these examples, the two populations from which samples are drawn are independent. A second situation involves *paired samples*. For example, a deep foundation engineering contractor has bid on a foundation system for a new world headquarters building for a Fortune 500 company. A part of the project consists of installing 311 augercast piles. The contractor was given bid information for cost estimating purposes, which consisted of the estimated depth of each pile; however, actual drill footage of each pile could not be determined exactly until construction was performed. The Excel file *Pile Foundation.xls* contains the estimates and actual pile lengths after the project was completed. The method of constructing confidence intervals differs depending on whether the samples are independent or paired. We will discuss both cases.

We will assume that we have random samples from two populations with the following:

	Population 1	Population 2
Mean	μ_1	μ_2
Standard deviation	σ_1	σ_2
Point estimate	$\bar{x}_1$	$\bar{x}_2$
Sample size	n_1	n_2

A point estimate for the difference in means, $\mu_1 - \mu_2$, is given by $\bar{x}_1 - \bar{x}_2$. We consider two different cases: when the variances of the two populations are unequal, and when they can be assumed to be equal.

Independent Samples with Unequal Variances

A confidence interval for independent samples with unequal variances is

$$\bar{x}_1 - \bar{x}_2 \pm (t_{\alpha/2,\,\mathrm{df}^*}) \sqrt{\frac{s_1^2}{n_1} + \frac{s_2^2}{n_2}}$$

where the degrees of freedom for the *t*-distribution, df*, is computed as

$$\frac{\left[\dfrac{s_1^2}{n_1} + \dfrac{s_2^2}{n_2}\right]^2}{\left[\dfrac{(s_1^2/n_1)^2}{n_1 - 1}\right] + \left[\dfrac{(s_2^2/n_2)^2}{n_2 - 1}\right]}$$

and fractional values are rounded down. This calculation may be eliminated by using a conservative estimate of the number of degrees of freedom as the minimum of n_1 and n_2, which results in a larger confidence interval.

To illustrate, Figure 4.11 shows a portion of the *Accounting Professionals.xls* worksheet after the data were sorted by gender and sample means and standard deviations were calculated. Note that $s_1 = 4.39$ and $n_1 = 14$ (females), and $s_2 = 8.39$ and $n_2 = 13$ (males). Calculating df*, we obtain df* = 17.81, so use 17 as the degrees of freedom. A 95 percent confidence interval for the difference in years of service is

$$10.07 - 19.69 \pm 2.1098 \sqrt{\frac{19.2721}{14} + \frac{70.3921}{13}} = -9.62 \pm 5.026$$

$$\text{or} \quad [-14.646, -4.594]$$

	A	B	C
1	Employee	Gender	Years of Service.
2	1	F	17
3	2	F	6
4	4	F	8
5	6	F	21
6	8	F	7
7	11	F	9
8	12	F	8
9	13	F	8
10	15	F	9
11	16	F	9
12	21	F	14
13	23	F	10
14	24	F	10
15	27	F	5
16		Mean	10.07
17		Std. Dev.	4.39
18	3	M	8
19	5	M	16
20	7	M	27
21	9	M	8
22	10	M	23
23	14	M	26
24	17	M	19
25	18	M	5
26	19	M	19
27	20	M	20
28	22	M	31
29	25	M	26
30	26	M	28
31		Mean	19.69
32		Std. Dev.	8.39

FIGURE 4.11 Accounting Professionals Data Sorted By Gender

Independent Samples with Equal Variances

When we can assume that the variance of the two populations are equal, we can estimate a common ("pooled") standard deviation that is a weighted combination of the individual sample standard deviations, s_p:

$$s_p = \sqrt{\frac{(n_1 - 1)s_1^2 + (n_2 - 1)s_2^2}{n_1 + n_2 - 2}}$$

Then the sampling distribution of $\bar{x}_1 - \bar{x}_2$ has a *t*-distribution with $n_1 + n_2 - 2$ degrees of freedom and standard error

$$s_p \sqrt{\frac{1}{n_1} + \frac{1}{n_2}}$$

Therefore, a $100(1 - \alpha)$ percent confidence interval is

$$\bar{x}_1 - \bar{x}_2 \pm (t_{\alpha/2,\, n_1 + n_2 - 2})\, s_p \sqrt{\frac{1}{n_1} + \frac{1}{n_2}}$$

If we assume equal population variances for the Accounting Professionals data, the pooled standard deviation is

$$s_p = \sqrt{\frac{(14 - 1)(4.39)^2 + (13 - 1)(8.39)^2}{14 + 13 - 2}} = 6.62$$

Then, a 95 percent CI for the difference in mean years of service between females and males is

$$10.07 - 19.69 \pm (2.0595)\, 6.62 \sqrt{\frac{1}{14} + \frac{1}{13}} = -9.62 \pm 5.25 \quad \text{or} \quad [-14.87, -4.37]$$

Note that there is little difference in the CI from the unequal variance case for this example. In general, assume equal population variances unless you have evidence that the variances are significantly different. Neither Excel nor *PHStat* has tools for constructing these confidence intervals, but it would be straightforward to develop an Excel spreadsheet to perform these calculations.

Paired Samples

For paired samples, we first compute the difference between each pair of observations, D_i, for $i = 1, \ldots, n$. $\overline{D}$, the average of these differences, is a point estimate for the mean difference between the populations. The standard deviation of the differences is similar to calculating an ordinary standard deviation:

$$s_D = \sqrt{\frac{\sum_{i=1}^{n} (D_i - \overline{D})^2}{n-1}}$$

A $100(1 - \alpha)$ percent confidence interval is

$$\overline{D} \pm (t_{n-1, \alpha/2})\, s_D / \sqrt{n}$$

For the Pile Foundation data described at the beginning of this section, we computed the difference for each pile by subtracting the estimated value from the actual value, as shown in Figure 4.12. Note that because the sample size is so large, we must use the critical value of t with an infinite number of degrees of freedom in Table A.3. For $\alpha/2 = 0.025$, this value is 1.96, which is the same as the z-value. Thus, a 95 percent confidence interval is

	A	B	C	D
1	Pile	Estimated	Actual	
2	Number	Pile Length (ft.)	Pile Length (ft.)	Actual - Estimated
3	1	10.58	18.58	8.00
4	2	10.58	18.58	8.00
5	3	10.58	18.58	8.00
6	4	10.58	18.58	8.00
7	5	10.58	28.58	18.00
8	6	10.58	26.58	16.00
9	7	10.58	17.58	7.00
10	8	10.58	27.58	17.00
11	9	10.58	27.58	17.00
12	10	10.58	37.58	27.00
13	11	10.58	28.58	18.00
14	12	5.83	1.83	-4.00
15	13	5.83	8.83	3.00
16	14	5.83	8.83	3.00
17	15	5.83	8.83	3.00

FIGURE 4.12 Difference Calculations for Portion of *Pile Foundation.xls*

$$-10.63 \pm 1.96 \, (300.50)/\sqrt{311} = -10.63 \pm 33.40 \quad \text{or} \quad [-44.03, 22.77]$$

This states that the true population difference is likely to be either negative or positive, suggesting that the pile lengths may have been either underestimated or overestimated, despite the fact that the pile lengths in this sample were, on average, overestimated.

Neither *PHStat* nor Excel has tools for this type of confidence interval; however, *PHStat* has a tool to calculate confidence intervals for the *total difference* with paired data and a finite population. Select *Estimate for the Total Difference* from the *Confidence Intervals* menu.

Differences Between Proportions

Let p_1 and p_2 be sample proportions from two populations using sample sizes n_1 and n_2, respectively. For reasonably large sample sizes, that is, when $n_i \, p_i$ and $n_i(1 - p_i)$ are greater than 5 for $i = 1, 2$, the distribution of the statistic $p_1 - p_2$ is approximately normal. A confidence interval for differences between proportions of two populations is computed as follows:

$$p_1 - p_2 \pm z_{\alpha/2} \sqrt{\frac{p_1(1 - p_1)}{n_1} + \frac{p_2(1 - p_2)}{n_2}}$$

For example, in the *Accounting Professionals.xls* worksheet, the proportion of females having a CPA is $8/14 = 0.57$, while the proportion of males having a CPA is $6/13 = 0.46$. A 95 percent confidence interval for the difference in proportions between females and males is

$$0.57 - 0.46 \pm 1.96 \sqrt{\frac{0.57(1 - 0.57)}{14} + \frac{0.46(1 - 0.46)}{13}} = 0.11 \pm 0.072$$

$$\text{or} \quad [0.038, 0.182]$$

Variance and Standard Deviation

Understanding variability is critical to effective business decisions. Thus, in many situations, one is interested in obtaining point and interval estimates for the variance or standard deviation. Although we use the sample standard deviation s as a point estimate for σ, the sampling distribution of s is not normal, but is a special distribution called the **chi-square (χ^2) distribution.** The chi-square distribution is characterized by degrees of freedom, similar to the t-distribution. A χ^2 random variable with n degrees of freedom is the sum of the squares of n independent standard normal random variables. Table A.4 in the back of this book provides critical values of the chi-square distribution for selected values of α. The Excel function CHIDIST $(x, deg\_freedom)$ returns the probability to the right of x for a given value of degrees of freedom. Also, the Excel function CHIINV($probability, deg\_freedom$) returns the value of x that has a right-tail area equal to $probability$ for a specified degrees of freedom. However, unlike the normal or t-distributions, the chi-square distribution is not symmetric, which means that the confidence interval is not simply s plus or minus some number of standard errors. The point estimate is always closer to the left endpoint of the interval.

PHSTAT NOTE

CONFIDENCE INTERVALS FOR THE POPULATION VARIANCE

From the *PHStat* menu, select *Confidence Intervals,* and then *Estimate for the Population Variance.* The dialog box for the mean is shown in Figure 4.13. You need to enter the sample size, sample standard deviation, and confidence level. The tool creates a new worksheet with the upper and lower limits for confidence intervals for both the variance and standard deviation. Results for the 18–24 age group in the TV Viewing data are shown in Figure 4.14.

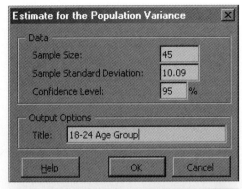

FIGURE 4.13 *PHStat* Dialog Box for Estimating Population Variance

	A	B	C	D	E
1	18-24 Age Group				
2					
3	Data				
4	Sample Size	45			
5	Sample Standard Deviation	10.09			
6	Confidence Level	95%			
7					
8	Intermediate Calculations				
9	Degrees of Freedom	44			
10	Sum of Squares	4479.556			
11	Single Tail Area	0.025			
12	Lower Chi-Square Value	27.57454			
13	Upper Chi-Square Value	64.20141			
14					
15	Results				
16	Interval Lower Limit for Variance	69.77348			
17	Interval Upper Limit for Variance	162.4526			
18					
19	Interval Lower Limit for Standard Deviation	8.353052			
20	Interval Upper Limit for Standard Deviation	12.74569			
21					
22	Assumption:				
23	Population from which sample was drawn has an approximate normal distribution.				

FIGURE 4.14 Results for TV Viewing Example

A $100(1 - \alpha)$ percent confidence interval for the variance is

$$\left[\frac{(n-1)s^2}{\chi^2_{n-1,\alpha/2}}, \frac{(n-1)s^2}{\chi^2_{n-1,1-\alpha/2}} \right]$$

We will illustrate this by finding a 95 percent CI for the variance of the 18–24 age group in the TV Viewing data. Since Table A.4 provides values only for up to 30 degrees of freedom, we find $\chi^2_{44,\,0.025}$ using the Excel function CHIINV(0.025, 44) = 64.201 and

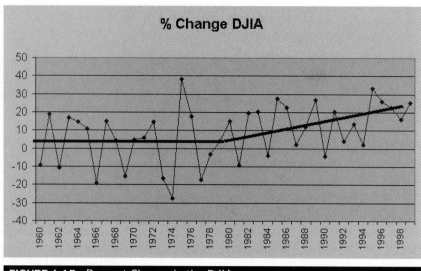

FIGURE 4.15   Percent Change in the DJIA

$\chi^2_{44,0.975}$ by CHIINV(0.975, 44) = 27.575. With a sample standard deviation of 10.09, the confidence interval is

$$[(44)(10.09)^2/64.201, (44)(10.09)^2/27.575] \quad \text{or} \quad [69.77, 162.45]$$

PHStat has a tool for computing confidence intervals for the variance as well as the standard deviation. This is explained in the *PHStat Note: Confidence Intervals for the Population Variance.* The calculations assume that the population from which the sample was drawn has an approximate normal distribution. If this assumption is not met, the confidence interval may not be accurate for the confidence level chosen.

Time Series Data

In general, confidence intervals for time series data make little sense because the mean and/or variance of such data typically change over time. However, for the case in which time series data are *stationary*—that is, they exhibit a constant mean and constant variance—then confidence intervals make sense. A simple way of determining whether time series data are stationary is to plot them on a line chart. If the data do not show any trends or patterns, and the variation remains relatively constant over time, then it is reasonable to assume the data are stationary. For example, Figure 4.15 shows the percent change in the Dow Jones Industrial Average from 1960 through 1999 in the worksheet *Economic Indexes.xls*. To compute a confidence interval for the mean change would be inappropriate, as the data appear to show an increasing trend during the economic boom in the 1980s and 1990s. However, during the 1960s and 1970s, the data appear to be relatively stationary (as economists have noted, the Dow went nowhere), and it would be appropriate to compute a confidence interval for this period.

Summary and Conclusions About Confidence Intervals

Table 4.3 summarizes formulas for confidence intervals. In viewing the formulas used to compute confidence intervals, we can observe the following:

TABLE 4.3 Summary of Confidence Interval Formulas

Type of Confidence Interval	Formula
Mean, standard deviation known	$\bar{x} \pm z_{\alpha/2}(\sigma/\sqrt{n})$
Mean, standard deviation unknown	$\bar{x} \pm t_{\alpha/2,\, n-1}(s/\sqrt{n})$
Proportion	$p \pm z_{\alpha/2}\sqrt{\dfrac{p(1-p)}{n}}$
Population total	$N\bar{x} \pm t_{\alpha/2,\, n-1}N\dfrac{s}{\sqrt{n}}\sqrt{\dfrac{N-n}{N-1}}$
Difference between means, independent samples, equal variance	$\bar{x}_1 - \bar{x}_2 \pm (t_{\alpha/2,\, n_1+n_2-2})s_p\sqrt{\dfrac{1}{n_1}+\dfrac{1}{n_2}}$
Difference between means, independent samples, unequal variance	$\bar{x}_1 - \bar{x}_2 \pm (t_{\alpha/2,\, \mathrm{df}*})\sqrt{\dfrac{s_1^2}{n_1}+\dfrac{s_2^2}{n_2}}$
	$\mathrm{df}* = \dfrac{\left[\dfrac{s_1^2}{n_1}+\dfrac{s_2^2}{n_2}\right]^2}{\left[\dfrac{(s_1^2/n_1)^2}{n_1-1}\right]+\left[\dfrac{(s_2^2/n_2)^2}{n_2-1}\right]}$
Difference between means, paired samples	$\bar{D} \pm (t_{n-1,\,\alpha/2})\, s_D/\sqrt{n}$
Differences between proportions	$p_1 - p_2 \pm z_{\alpha/2}\sqrt{\dfrac{p_1(1-p_1)}{n_1}+\dfrac{p_2(1-p_2)}{n_2}}$
Variance	$\left[\dfrac{(n-1)s^2}{\chi_{n-1,\,\alpha/2}^2},\dfrac{(n-1)s^2}{\chi_{n-1,\,1-\alpha/2}^2}\right]$

- As the confidence level $(1 - \alpha)$ increases, the width of the confidence interval also increases. Essentially this means that to have a higher confidence that the interval estimate actually contains the true population parameter, we must sacrifice some precision.
- As the sample size increases, the width of the confidence interval decreases. This is because the standard error decreases with increasing sample size, thereby increasing the accuracy of the estimate.

We may conclude that if you wish to increase the confidence level, you should also increase the sample size to maintain a level of precision in your estimate.

Confidence Intervals and Probability Intervals

It is important not to confuse a confidence interval with a probability interval. A 100 $(1 - \alpha)$ percent **probability interval** for a random variable X is any interval $[A, B]$ such that $P(A \leq X \leq B) = 1 - \alpha$. A probability interval describes the probability that the random variable falls within the interval and is often used in describing risk. Probability intervals are often centered on the mean. For instance, in a normal distribution, the mean plus or minus 1 standard deviation describes an approximate 68 percent probability interval around the mean. As another example, the 5th and 95th percentiles in a data set constitute a 90 percent probability interval. A confidence interval provides an interval estimate of a population parameter, such as the mean. A confidence interval is a probability interval associated with the *sampling distribution* of a statistic, but it is not the same as a probability interval associated with the distribution of the random variable itself. We will work with probability intervals extensively in Chapter 8.

HYPOTHESIS TESTING

Hypothesis testing involves drawing inferences about two contrasting propositions (hypotheses) relating to the value of a population parameter, one of which is assumed to be true in the absence of contradictory data. In conducting an hypothesis test, we seek evidence to determine if the assumed hypothesis can be rejected; if not, we can only assume it to be true. For instance, a producer of computer-aided design software for the aerospace industry receives numerous calls for technical support. Tracking software is used to monitor response and resolution times (see the worksheet *Customer Support Survey Data.xls*). The company has a goal of responding to customers in less than 30 minutes on average of the call. Without data to suggest that the mean response time is less than 30 minutes, the company would have to assume that it is not meeting its goal. Similarly, in the worksheet *Burglaries.xls,* we might wish to determine whether the citizen–police program had a significant effect in reducing the rate of burglaries. Without data to suggest that the rate was reduced, we could only conclude that the rate was at least the same as before.

The evidence we seek is based on sample data. For example, if we have sample data that statistically demonstrates that the rate of burglaries is reduced, we would conclude that the program had a positive effect. However, what does "statistically demonstrates" mean? In looking at descriptive statistics of the data, we find that the average number of burglaries before the program was 64.32/month, while the average after the program began was 60.65/month. Can we draw the conclusion that the program was beneficial based simply on these averages? Absolutely not! We need to consider the variability of sampling in our decision, recognizing that each sample mean is only one from an infinite number of possibilities that can be drawn from the sampling distribution of the mean.

An hypothesis test involves

1. Formulating the hypotheses to test.
2. Selecting a *level of significance,* which defines the risk of drawing an incorrect conclusion about the assumed hypothesis that is actually true.
3. Determining a decision rule on which to base a conclusion.
4. Collecting data and calculating a test statistic.
5. Applying the decision rule to the test statistic and drawing a conclusion.

Hypothesis Formulation

Hypothesis testing begins by defining two alternative, mutually exclusive propositions. The first is called the **null hypothesis,** denoted by H_0, which represents a theory or statement about the status quo that is accepted as correct. The second is called the **alternative hypothesis,** denoted by H_1, which must be true if we conclude that the null hypothesis is false. In the Customer Support Survey Data example, the null and alternative hypotheses would be

H_0: *mean response time* $\geq$ *30 minutes*
H_1: *mean response time* $<$ *30 minutes*

TABLE 4.4   Types of Hypothesis Tests

One-Sample Tests
H_0: test statistic $\geq$ constant vs. H_1: test statistic $<$ constant
H_0: test statistic $\leq$ constant vs. H_1: test statistic $>$ constant
H_0: test statistic $=$ constant vs. H_1: test statistic $\neq$ constant

Two-Sample Tests
H_0: test statistic(1) $\geq$ test statistic(2) vs. H_1: test statistic(1) $<$ test statistic (2)
H_0: test statistic(1) $\leq$ test statistic(2) vs. H_1: test statistic(1) $>$ test statistic (2)
H_0: test statistic(1) $=$ test statistic(2) vs. H_1: test statistic(1) $\neq$ test statistic (2)

This hypothesis test involves a single population parameter—the mean response time—and is called a *one-sample hypothesis test*. We could also formulate hypotheses about the parameters of two populations, called *two-sample tests*. For instance, in the burglaries example, we might define the null hypothesis to be

H_0: *Mean number of burglaries after program $\geq$ mean number of burglaries before program*
H_1: *Mean number of burglaries after program $<$ mean number of burglaries before program*

Table 4.4 summarizes the types of one-sample and two-sample hypothesis tests that we may conduct. Note that the null hypothesis may be expressed as an equality. For example, in the TV Viewing data, we might wish to test the null hypothesis that the mean number of hours/week of TV viewing for the 18–24 age group is the same as that of the 25–34 age group against the alternative hypothesis that the means are not equal.

How do we determine the proper form of the null and alternative hypotheses? Hypothesis testing always *assumes* that H_0 is true, and sample evidence is used to conclude whether H_1 is more likely to be true. Statistically, we cannot "prove" that H_0 is true; we can only fail to reject it. Thus, if we cannot reject the null hypothesis, we have only shown that there is insufficient evidence to conclude that it is not true. However, rejecting the null hypothesis provides proof in a statistical sense that the null hypothesis is not true and that the alternative hypothesis is therefore correct. Therefore, the answer lies in the legal analogy of "burden of proof." In our legal system, an individual is assumed innocent (H_0) unless evidence demonstrates guilt (H_1). Burden of proof revolves around the alternative hypothesis. For example, if we wish to prove statistically that the citizen–police program has had an effect in reducing the rate of burglaries, it would be *incorrect* to state the hypotheses as

H_0: *Mean number of burglaries after program $\leq$ mean number of burglaries before program*
H_1: *Mean number of burglaries after program $>$ mean number of burglaries before program*

If we cannot find evidence to conclude that H_1 is true, we can only assume that H_0 is true, but we have not statistically proven it. However, using the original form of our hypotheses, if we have evidence that shows that the mean number of burglaries after the program began is less than the mean number of burglaries before the program, then we can conclude that the program was beneficial. A useful way of thinking about this is whatever claim is made (i.e., what you would like to prove to be true) should define the *alternative* hypothesis. Thus, in the Customer Support Survey Data example, the claim that the firm is meeting its goal of a mean response time of less than 20 minutes would define H_1.

Significance Level

Hypothesis testing can result in four different outcomes:

1. The null hypothesis is actually true, and the test correctly fails to reject it.
2. The null hypothesis is actually false, and the hypothesis test correctly reaches this conclusion.
3. The null hypothesis is actually true, but the hypothesis test incorrectly rejects it (called **Type I error**).
4. The null hypothesis is actually false, but the hypothesis test incorrectly fails to reject it (called **Type II error**).

The probability of making a Type I error is generally denoted by α and is called the **level of significance** of the test. This probability is essentially the risk that you can afford to take in making the incorrect conclusion that the alternative hypothesis is true when in fact the null hypothesis is true. The **confidence coefficient** is $1 - \alpha$, which is the probability of correctly failing to reject the null hypothesis. For a confidence coefficient of 0.95, we mean that we expect 95 out of 100 cases to support the null hypothesis rather than the alternate hypothesis. Commonly used levels for α are 0.10, 0.05, and 0.01, resulting in confidence levels of 0.90, 0.95, and 0.99, respectively.

The probability of a Type II error is denoted by β. Unlike α, this cannot be specified in advance, but depends on the true value of the (unknown) population parameter. To see this, suppose that our hypotheses are

H_0: *mean response time $\geq$ 30 minutes*
H_1: *mean response time $<$ 30 minutes*

Then if the true mean response is, say, 20 minutes, we would expect to have a much lower probability of incorrectly concluding that the null hypothesis is true than when the true mean response is 28 minutes, for example. In the first case, the sample mean would very likely be much less than 30, leading us to reject H_0. In the second case, however, even though the true mean response is less than 30, we would have a much higher probability of failing to reject H_0 because a higher likelihood exists that the sample mean would be greater than 30 due to sampling error. Thus, the further away the true mean response time is from the hypothesized value, the smaller is β. Generally, as α decreases, β increases, so the decision maker must consider the trade-offs of these risks.

The value $1 - \beta$ is called the **power of the test** and represents the probability of correctly rejecting the null hypothesis when it is indeed false. If the power of the test is deemed to be too small, it can be increased by taking larger samples. Larger samples enable us to detect small differences between the sample statistics and population parameters with more accuracy. However, a larger sample size incurs higher costs, giving more meaning to the adage "There is no such thing as a free lunch." Table 4.5 summarizes this discussion.

TABLE 4.5 Error Types in Hypothesis Testing		
	Test Rejects H_0	*Test Fails to Reject* H_0
Alternative hypothesis (H_1) is true	Correct	Type II error (β)
Null hypothesis (H_0) is true	Type I error (α)	Correct

Decision Rules

The decision to reject or fail to reject a null hypothesis is based on computing a test statistic from sample data that is a function of the mean, variance, or proportion and comparing it to the hypothesized sampling distribution of the test statistic. The sampling distribution is usually the normal distribution, *t*-distribution, chi-square, or some other well-known distribution. The sampling distribution is divided into two parts, a *rejection region,* and a *nonrejection region*. If the null hypothesis is true, it is unlikely that the test statistic will fall into the rejection region. Thus, if the test statistic falls into the rejection region, we reject the null hypothesis; otherwise, we fail to reject it. The probability of falling into the rejection region if H_0 is true is the probability of a Type I error, α.

The rejection region generally occurs in the tails of the sampling distribution of the test statistic. For tests in which we reject the null hypothesis if the test statistic is either significantly high or low—for example, in testing the mean amount of liquid in 32 ounce bottles:

**H_0: *mean volume = 32 ounces*
H_1: *mean volume ≠ 32 ounces***

the rejection region will occur in *both* the upper and lower tail of the distribution (see Figure 4.16(a)). This is called a **two-tailed** test of hypothesis. Because the probability that the test statistic falls into the rejection region, given that H_0 is true, is α, the combined area of both tails must be α. Usually, each tail has an area of $\alpha/2$.

FIGURE 4.16   Illustration of Rejection Regions in Hypothesis Testing

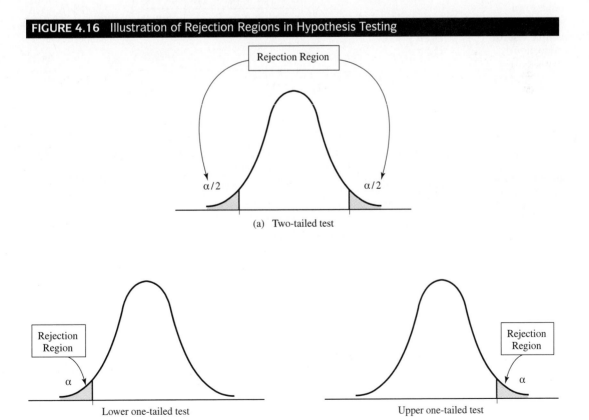

(a) Two-tailed test

(b) One-tailed tests

TABLE 4.6 Common Types of Hypothesis Tests

Type of Test	Representative Hypotheses*	Test Statistic	Representative Decision Rule
One-sample test for mean (two-tailed), σ known	$H_0: \mu = \mu_0$ $H_1: \mu \neq \mu_0$	$z = \dfrac{\bar{x} - \mu_0}{\sigma/\sqrt{n}}$	Reject H_0 if $z < -z_{\alpha/2}$ or $z > z_{\alpha/2}$
One-sample test for mean (two-tailed), σ unknown	$H_0: \mu = \mu_0$ $H_1: \mu \neq \mu_0$	$t = \dfrac{\bar{x} - \mu_0}{s/\sqrt{n}}$	Reject H_0 if $t < -t_{n-1,\alpha/2}$ or $t > t_{n-1,\alpha/2}$
One-sample test for mean (lower one-tailed), σ known	$H_0: \mu \geq \mu_0$ $H_1: \mu < \mu_0$	$z = \dfrac{\bar{x} - \mu_0}{\sigma/\sqrt{n}}$	Reject H_0 if $z < -z_\alpha$
One-sample test for mean (upper one-tailed), σ known	$H_0: \mu \leq \mu_0$ $H_1: \mu > \mu_0$	$z = \dfrac{\bar{x} - \mu_0}{\sigma/\sqrt{n}}$	Reject H_0 if $z > z_\alpha$
One-sample test for mean (lower one-tailed), σ unknown	$H_0: \mu \geq \mu_0$ $H_1: \mu < \mu_0$	$t = \dfrac{\bar{x} - \mu_0}{s/\sqrt{n}}$	Reject H_0 if $t < -t_{n-1,\alpha}$
One-sample test for mean (upper one-tailed), σ unknown	$H_0: \mu \leq \mu_0$ $H_1: \mu > \mu_0$	$t = \dfrac{\bar{x} - \mu_0}{s/\sqrt{n}}$	Reject H_0 if $t > t_{n-1,\alpha}$
Two-sample test for means (two-tailed), σ known	$H_0: \mu_1 - \mu_2 = 0$ $H_1: \mu_1 - \mu_2 \neq 0$	$z = \dfrac{\bar{x}_1 - \bar{x}_2}{\sqrt{\sigma_1^2/n_1 + \sigma_2^2/n_2}}$	Reject H_0 if $z < -z_{\alpha/2}$ or $z > z_{\alpha/2}$
Two-sample test for means (two-tailed), σ unknown, assumed equal	$H_0: \mu_1 - \mu_2 = 0$ $H_1: \mu_1 - \mu_2 \neq 0$	$t = \dfrac{\bar{x}_1 - \bar{x}_2}{\sqrt{\dfrac{(n_1-1)s_1^2 + (n_2-1)s_2^2}{n_1+n_2-2}\left(\dfrac{n_1+n_2}{n_1 n_2}\right)}}$	Reject H_0 if $t < -t_{\mathrm{df},\alpha/2}$ or $t > t_{\mathrm{df},\alpha/2}$ $\mathrm{df} = n_1 + n_2 - 2$
One-sample test for proportion (two-sided)	$H_0: \pi = \pi_0$ $H_1: \pi \neq \pi_0$	$z = \dfrac{p - \pi_0}{\sqrt{\pi_0(1-\pi_0)/n}}$	Reject H_0 if $z < -z_{\alpha/2}$ or $z > z_{\alpha/2}$
Two-sample test for means (one-tailed), σ unknown, unequal	$H_0: \mu_1 - \mu_2 \geq 0$ $H_1: \mu_1 - \mu_2 < 0$	$t = (\bar{x}_1 - \bar{x}_2)/\sqrt{\dfrac{s_1^2}{n_1} + \dfrac{s_2^2}{n_2}}$ $\mathrm{df}^* = \dfrac{\left[\dfrac{s_1^2}{n_1} + \dfrac{s_2^2}{n_2}\right]^2}{\left[\dfrac{(s_1^2/n_1)^2}{n_1-1}\right] + \left[\dfrac{(s_2^2/n_2)^2}{n_2-1}\right]}$	Reject H_0 if $t < -t_{\alpha,\mathrm{df}^*}$
Two-sample test for proportions (two-tailed)	$H_0: \pi_1 - \pi_2 = 0$ $H_1: \pi_1 - \pi_2 \neq 0$	$z = \dfrac{p_1 - p_2}{\sqrt{\bar{p}(1-\bar{p})\left(\dfrac{1}{n_1} + \dfrac{1}{n_2}\right)}}$	Reject H_0 if $z < -z_{\alpha/2}$ or $z > z_{\alpha/2}$
F-test for difference in variances	$H_0: \sigma_1^2 = \sigma_2^2$ $H_1: \sigma_1^2 \neq \sigma_2^2$	$F = \dfrac{s_1^2}{s_2^2}$ (assume $s_1^2 > s_2^2$)	Reject H_0 if $F > F_{\alpha/2,\,n_1-1,\,n_2-1}$

* Note: any of these tests may be stated as upper one-tailed, lower one tailed, or two-tailed tests.

The other type of hypothesis, which specifies a direction of relationship, such as

H_0: *mean response time $\geq$ 30 minutes*
H_1: *mean response time $<$ 30 minutes*

is a one-tailed test of hypothesis. In this case, the rejection region occurs in one tail of the distribution (see Figure 4.16(b)). Determining the correct tail of the distribution to use as the rejection region for a one-tailed test is easy. If H_1 is stated as "<," the rejection region is in the lower tail; if H_1 is stated as ">," the rejection region is in the upper tail (just think of the inequality as an arrow pointing to the proper direction!). The rejection region is defined by a *critical value* of the test statistic. For normal and *t*-distributions, lower-tail critical values are negative; upper-tail critical values are positive.

Table 4.6 summarizes many of the more common types of hypothesis tests. Both Excel and *PHStat* have tools for conducting many (but not all) of these (as summarized in Table 4.1). We will discuss the major types of tests in the next several sections.

ONE-SAMPLE HYPOTHESIS TESTS

In this section we will discuss several hypothesis tests for means, proportions, and variances involving a single sample.

One-Sample Tests for Means

We will first consider one-sample tests for means. The appropriate test statistic depends on whether the population standard deviation is known or unknown. If the population standard deviation is known, then the sampling distribution is normal; if not, we use a *t*-distribution. In most practical applications, the standard deviation will not be known but is estimated from the sample.

For the Customer Support Survey data, we will test the hypotheses

H_0: *mean response time $\geq$ 30 minutes*
H_1: *mean response time < 30 minutes*

with a level of significance of 0.05. This is a one-tailed, one-sample test for the mean with an unknown standard deviation. The test statistic is

$$t = \frac{\bar{x} - \mu_0}{s/\sqrt{n}}$$

where μ_0 is the hypothesized value. From the data in the worksheet *Customer Support Survey Data.xls,* we find that the sample mean is 21.91 and the sample standard deviation is 19.49 for the $n = 44$ observations. Because the rejection region is in the lower tail, the decision rule is to reject H_0 if $t < -t_{n-1, \alpha}$. Note that the critical value is negative because this is a lower one-tailed test. The rationale for this rule is simple. Notice that if the sample mean is much larger than $\mu_0 = 20$, then the value of t will be a large positive number, and it is unlikely that we would reject the null hypothesis. If, however, the true mean response time is less than 30, then the sample mean will most likely be less than 30 also, and the value of t will be negative. If it is "negative enough," that is, if it falls in the lower tail of the *t*-distribution with a 0.05 level of significance, then we would reject H_0. The value of the sample statistic t is computed as follows:

$$t = \frac{\bar{x} - \mu_0}{s/\sqrt{n}} = \frac{21.91 - 30}{19.49/\sqrt{44}} = \frac{-8.09}{2.938} = -2.75$$

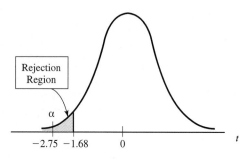

FIGURE 4.17 *t*-Test for Mean Response Time

and the critical value is $-t_{43,0.05} = -1.6811$. Therefore, we reject H_0, and conclude that the mean response time is less than 30 minutes. Figure 4.17 illustrates the conclusion we reached. *PHStat* provides a routine for conducting *t*-tests (see *PHStat Note: Testing Hypotheses for the Mean, Sigma Unknown*). We also note that although the

---

PHSTAT NOTE

TESTING HYPOTHESES FOR THE MEAN, SIGMA UNKNOWN

From the *PHStat* menu, select *One Sample Tests,* then *t-Test For The Mean, Sigma Unknown*. The dialog box, shown in Figure 4.18, first asks you to

FIGURE 4.18 *PHStat* Dialog Box for *t-Test*

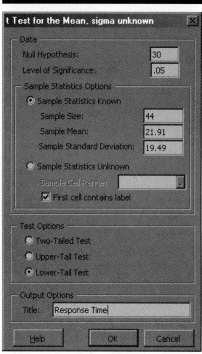

input the value of the null hypothesis and significance level. As with the confidence interval tools, you can either specify the sample statistics or let the tool compute them from the data. The sample statistics for the Customer Support Survey data have been entered in the dialog box shown in Figure 4.18. Under *Test Options,* you may choose among a two-tailed test, upper one-tailed test, or lower one-tailed test. Figure 4.19 shows the output provided by this tool. Key statistics are computed as well as the conclusion of the test.

FIGURE 4.19 *PHStat* Results for *t-Test*

	A	B
1	**Response Time**	
2		
3	**Data**	
4	**Null Hypothesis** μ=	30
5	**Level of Significance**	0.05
6	**Sample Size**	44
7	**Sample Mean**	21.91
8	**Sample Standard Deviation**	19.49
9		
10	Intermediate Calculations	
11	Standard Error of the Mean	2.938228053
12	Degrees of Freedom	43
13	*t* Test Statistic	-2.753360139
14		
15	**Lower-Tail Test**	
16	**Lower Critical Value**	-1.681071353
17	***p*-Value**	0.004303659
18	**Reject the null hypothesis**	

t-distribution is the correct sampling distribution to use whenever the standard deviation is unknown, the normal distribution (*z*-values) can be used for large samples, as the difference is negligible.

Next, we illustrate a two-tailed test using the data in the Excel file *Pile Foundation.xls,* which contains the estimates and actual augercast pile lengths for a foundation engineering project that was introduced in our discussion of confidence intervals. The contractor's past experience suggested that the bid information was generally accurate, so that the average difference between the actual pile lengths and estimated lengths should be close to zero. After this project was completed, the contractor found that the average difference was −10.63. Did he receive poor bid information, or was this difference simply the result of sampling error? The hypothesis to test is

H₀: *average difference = 0*
H₁: *average difference ≠ 0*

Using a two-tailed, one-sample test for means with σ unknown, the test statistic is the same as for the one-tailed test:

$$t = \frac{\bar{x} - \mu_0}{s/\sqrt{n}}$$

However, the decision rule is to reject H₀ if *t* falls below the negative critical value $-t_{n-1,\alpha/2}$, or above the positive critical value, $t_{n-1,\alpha/2}$. Computing the value of *t*, we obtain

$$t = \frac{\bar{x} - \mu_0}{s/\sqrt{n}} = \frac{-10.63 - 0}{300.5/\sqrt{311}} = \frac{-10.63}{17.04} = -0.624$$

Note that because the sample size is so large, we must use the critical value of *t* with an infinite number of degrees of freedom in Table A.3. For a tail area of $\alpha/2 = 0.025$, this value is 1.96, which is the same as the *z*-value for this level of significance. Because the computed value of *t* falls between −1.96 and +1.96, we cannot reject the null hypothesis that the average difference is 0. Figure 4.20 shows the output using the *PHStat* tool

A	B
Pile Foundation Hypothesis Test	
Data	
Null Hypothesis μ=	0
Level of Significance	0.05
Sample Size	311
Sample Mean	-10.63
Sample Standard Deviation	300.5029336
Intermediate Calculations	
Standard Error of the Mean	17.03995806
Degrees of Freedom	310
t Test Statistic	-0.623616483
Two-Tailed Test	
Lower Critical Value	-1.967646313
Upper Critical Value	1.967646313
p-Value	0.533338061
Do not reject the null hypothesis	

FIGURE 4.20 *PHStat* Results for the Pile Foundation Hypothesis Test

for testing hypotheses for the mean with sigma unknown. We see that the true critical value of t is 1.967646313, leading to the same conclusion.

Using *p*-Values

In the *PHStat* output in Figures 4.19 and 4.20, we see something called a *p-value*. An alternative approach to comparing a test statistic to a critical value in hypothesis testing is to find the probability of obtaining a test statistic value equal to or more extreme than that obtained from the sample data when the null hypothesis is true. This probability is commonly called a **p-value.** For example, first consider the one-tailed test for the mean response time in Figure 4.19. The t statistic for the hypothesis test is -2.75. What is the probability of obtaining a test statistic less than -2.75? Using the Excel function TDIST(*x, degrees_freedom, tails*), with $x = 2.75$, *degrees_freedom* $= 43$, and *tails* $= 1$, we find this probability to be 0.0043. The *p*-value represents the probability to the left of the computed test statistic, -2.75, for a lower one-tailed test. In other words, there is less than a half percent chance that the test statistic would be this small if the null hypothesis were true. Since we used a level of significance $\alpha = 0.05$, we reject the null hypothesis.

For the two-tailed test in Figure 4.20, we find TDIST(0.6236, 310, 2) = 0.533. This represents the probability of obtaining a result equal to or more extreme in either tail of the distribution than the computed test statistic. In other words, there is a 0.533 probability that the computed test statistic will be either greater than 0.6236 or less than -0.6236 when the null hypothesis is true. Since this is larger than the chosen significance level of 0.05, we would fail to reject H_0. Figure 4.21 shows the graphical

FIGURE 4.21   Graphical Interpretation of *p*-Values

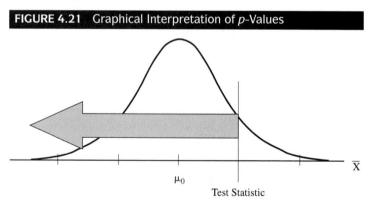

(a) Computing p-value for lower one-tailed test

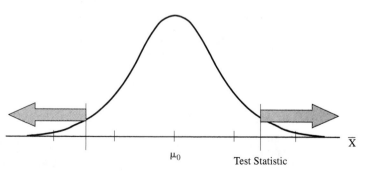

(b) Computing p-value for two-tailed test

interpretation of *p*-values for both one- and two-tailed tests. For a one-tailed test, find the area to the left of the test statistic for a lower-tailed test, or to the right of the test statistic for an upper-tailed test. For a two-tailed test with a symmetric sampling distribution such as a normal or *t*, plot the test statistic and its negative value, and find the area in both tails. The general rule is simple: Whenever the *p*-value is *less* than or equal to the level of significance, α, *reject* H_0; if the *p*-value is *greater* than α, *do not reject* H_0.

One-Sample Test for Proportions

Many important business measures, such as market share or the fraction of deliveries received on time, are expressed as proportions. For example, in the Customer Support Survey data, one question asks the customer to rate the overall quality of the company's software product using a scale of

    0—Very poor
    1—Poor
    2—Good
    3—Very good
    4—Excellent

The firm tracks customer satisfaction of quality by measuring the proportion of responses in the top two categories. Over the past year, this proportion has averaged about 75 percent. For this data, the sample proportion is 68.2 percent. Is there sufficient evidence to conclude that this satisfaction measure has dropped below 75 percent? Answering this question involves testing the hypotheses

H_0: $\pi \geq \pi_0$
H_1: $\pi < \pi_0$

where $\pi_0 = 0.75$. The test statistic for a one-sample test for proportions is

$$z = \frac{p - \pi_0}{\sqrt{\pi_0(1 - \pi_0)/n}}$$

Since this is a lower one-tailed test, reject if $z < -z_\alpha$. For this example,

$$z = \frac{0.682 - 0.75}{\sqrt{0.75(1 - 0.75)/44}} = -1.04$$

For a level of significance of 0.05, the critical value of *z* is -1.645; therefore, we cannot reject the null hypothesis that the proportion is at least 0.75 and attribute the low proportion of responses in the top two boxes to sampling error. *PHStat* has a tool for performing this test (see *PHStat Note: One Sample z-Tests for Proportions*), but Excel does not.

TWO-SAMPLE HYPOTHESIS TESTS

Hypothesis testing finds wide applicability in comparing two populations for differences in means or variances. The hypothesis testing procedures are similar to those previously discussed in the sense of formulating one- or two-tailed tests and identifying

PHSTAT NOTE

ONE SAMPLE *Z*-TESTS FOR PROPORTIONS

One-sample tests involving a proportion can be found by selecting the menu item *One Sample Tests* and choosing *z-Test for the Proportion.* Figure 4.22 shows the dialog box. The tool requires you to enter the value for the null hypothesis, significance level, number of successes, sample size, and the type of test. Note that you cannot enter the proportion alone, because the test depends on the sample size. Figure 4.23 shows the results for the Customer Support Survey data example. Note that the *p*-value is greater than the significance level, leading to the same conclusion of not rejecting the null hypothesis.

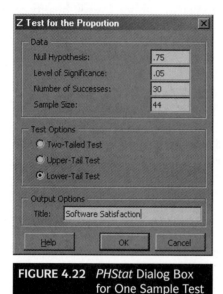

FIGURE 4.22   *PHStat* Dialog Box for One Sample Test for Proportions

	A	B
1	**Software Satisfaction**	
2		
3	**Data**	
4	**Null Hypothesis** *p=*	0.75
5	**Level of Significance**	0.05
6	**Number of Successes**	30
7	**Sample Size**	44
8		
9	Intermediate Calculations	
10	Sample Proportion	0.681818182
11	Standard Error	0.065279121
12	Z Test Statistic	-1.044465936
13		
14	**Lower-Tail Test**	
15	**Lower Critical Value**	-1.644853
16	*p*-Value	0.148134958
17	Do not reject the null hypothesis	

FIGURE 4.23   *PHStat* Results for *z*-Test for Proportion

the critical test statistic and rejection region. In this section we discuss two-sample tests for equality of means and variances.

Two-Sample Tests for Means

In the *Burglaries.xls* data we described earlier, we might wish to test the hypotheses

H_0: *Mean burglaries/month after program (μ_1) − Mean burglaries/month before program (μ_2) ≥ 0*

H_1: *Mean burglaries/month after program (μ_1) − Mean burglaries/month before program (μ_2) < 0*

Rejecting the null hypothesis suggests that the citizen–police program was effective in reducing the number of burglaries. If we cannot reject the null hypothesis, then even though the mean number of monthly burglaries is smaller since the program began, the difference would most likely be due to sampling error.

Selection of the proper test statistic for a two-sample test for means depends on whether the population standard deviations are known, and if not, whether they are assumed to be equal. The test statistics for these three cases are given next.

Standard Deviation Known

$$z = \frac{\bar{x}_1 - \bar{x}_2}{\sqrt{\sigma_1^2/n_1 + \sigma_2^2/n_2}}$$

Standard Deviation Unknown, Assumed Equal

$$t = \frac{\bar{x}_1 - \bar{x}_2}{\sqrt{\dfrac{(n_1 - 1)s_1^2 + (n_2 - 1)s_2^2}{n_1 + n_2 - 2}\left(\dfrac{n_1 + n_2}{n_1 n_2}\right)}}$$

with $n_1 + n_2 - 2$ degrees of freedom.

Standard Deviation Unknown, Unequal

$$t = (\bar{x}_1 - \bar{x}_2)/\sqrt{\frac{s_1^2}{n_1} + \frac{s_2^2}{n_2}}$$

where the degrees of freedom for the *t*-distribution, df*, is computed as

$$\text{df*} = \frac{\left[\dfrac{s_1^2}{n_1} + \dfrac{s_2^2}{n_2}\right]^2}{\left[\dfrac{(s_1^2/n_1)^2}{n_1 - 1}\right] + \left[\dfrac{(s_2^2/n_2)^2}{n_2 - 1}\right]}$$

For the *Burglaries.xls* data, we have $\bar{x}_1 = 64.32$, $s_1^2 = 282.47$, $\bar{x}_2 = 60.65$, and $s_2^2 = 253.87$. Since the magnitudes of the variances of both samples are very close, we will assume that the population variances are equal in conducting the test. (To test statistically whether or not sample variances are equal, we could use the *F*-test, described later.) Computing

$$t = \frac{\bar{x}_1 - \bar{x}_2}{\sqrt{\dfrac{(n_1 - 1)s_1^2 + (n_2 - 1)s_2^2}{n_1 + n_2 - 2}\left(\dfrac{n_1 + n_2}{n_1 n_2}\right)}}$$

$$= \frac{64.32 - 60.65}{\sqrt{\dfrac{(41 - 1)(282.47) + (17 - 1)(253.87)}{56}\left(\dfrac{41 + 17}{(41)(17)}\right)}} = 0.77$$

The critical value of t is $-t_{56,0.05} = -1.6725$ because this is a lower-tailed test; therefore, we cannot reject the null hypothesis. We could also conduct this test using a *PHStat* tool *Two-Sample Tests . . . t-test for Differences in Two Means* or Excel's *Data Analysis* tool *t-Test: Two Sample Assuming Equal Variances* (see the *Excel/PHStat Note: Using Two-Sample t-Test Tools*). Please read this carefully, as care must be taken in interpreting the Excel output.

Two-Sample Tests for Proportions

To test the hypotheses

$H_0: \pi_1 - \pi_2 \;\{=, \geq, \text{ or } \leq\}\; 0$

$H_1: \pi_1 - \pi_2 \;\{\neq, <, \text{ or } >\}\; 0$

EXCEL/*PHSTAT* NOTE

USING TWO-SAMPLE *t*-TEST TOOLS

Excel has tools for two-sample *t*-tests assuming either equal or unequal variances. From the main menu bar, click on *Tools ... Data Analysis* and *t-test: Two Sample Assuming Unequal Variances* or *t-test: Two Sample Assuming Equal Variances*. Data input is straightforward: The dialog box prompts you to enter the ranges for each sample, the hypothesized mean difference, and the level of significance (α), which defaults as 0.05. If you leave the box *Hypothesized Mean Difference* blank or enter zero, the test is for equality of means. However, the tool allows you to specify a value d to test the hypothesis $H_0: \mu_1 - \mu_2 = d$.

The *PHStat* tool *t-test for Differences in Two Means* is selected from the menu for *Two Sample Tests*. This tool conducts the test for equal variances only. You are requested to enter the value for the hypothesized difference and the level of significance, but instead of entering the range of data as in the Excel tools, you must compute and enter the sample mean, sample standard deviation, and sample size for each sample. You can also specify the type of test: two-tailed, upper-tail, or lower-tail. The *PHStat* output will provide the critical value for the test you specify, the *p*-value associated with the test, and the conclusion.

Figure 4.24 shows the output from all three tests for the *Burglaries.xls* data. Although the *PHStat* output is straightforward, you must be *very careful* in interpreting the information from Excel. The one-tailed test output in Excel is provided for an *upper-tail test only*. For a lower-tail test you must do two things. First, you must change the sign on *t Critical one-tail*; thus, the correct value for this example is -1.67252. Second, you must subtract $P(T<=t)$ *one-tail* from 1.0 to find the correct *p*-value. For this example, the correct *p*-value is $1 - 0.2228 = 0.7772$. Note that these are the values shown in the *PHStat* output. Since the *p*-value is greater than 0.05, we cannot reject the null hypothesis. For a two-tail test, the critical value is specified for the upper tail, and you must also realize that the lower-tail critical value is the negative; however, the *p*-value provided is correct.

FIGURE 4.24 Results of Two-Sample *t*-Tests in Excel and *PHStat*

	A	B	C	D	E	F	G
1	Difference in Mean Burglaries/Month				t-Test: Two-Sample Assuming Equal Variances		
2							
3	Data						
4	Hypothesized Difference	0			Mean	64.31707317	60.64705882
5	Level of Significance	0.05			Variance	282.4719512	253.8676471
6	Population 1 Sample				Observations	41	17
7	Sample Size	41			Pooled Variance	274.2992929	
8	Sample Mean	64.32			Hypothesized Mean Difference	0	
9	Sample Standard Deviation	16.81			df	56	
10	Population 2 Sample				t Stat	0.768170828	
11	Sample Size	17			P(T<=t) one-tail	0.222806507	
12	Sample Mean	60.65			t Critical one-tail	1.672522103	
13	Sample Standard Deviation	15.93			P(T<=t) two-tail	0.445613014	
14					t Critical two-tail	2.003239388	
15	Intermediate Calculations						
16	Population 1 Sample Degrees of Freedom	40			t-Test: Two-Sample Assuming Unequal Variances		
17	Population 2 Sample Degrees of Freedom	16					
18	Total Degrees of Freedom	56				Variable 1	Variable 2
19	Pooled Variance	274.3443			Mean	64.31707317	60.64705882
20	Difference in Sample Means	3.67			Variance	282.4719512	253.8676471
21	t-Test Statistic	0.768105			Observations	41	17
22					Hypothesized Mean Difference	0	
23	Lower-Tail Test				df	31	
24	Lower Critical Value	-1.67252			t Stat	0.785617276	
25	p-Value	0.777174			P(T<=t) one-tail	0.219027737	
26	Do not reject the null hypothesis				t Critical one-tail	1.695518677	
27					P(T<=t) two-tail	0.438055473	
28					t Critical two-tail	2.039514584	

use the following test statistic:

$$z = \frac{p_1 - p_2}{\sqrt{\bar{p}(1 - \bar{p})\left(\dfrac{1}{n_1} + \dfrac{1}{n_2}\right)}}$$

where $\bar{p}$ = *Number of Successes in Both Samples*$/(n_1 + n_2)$. This statistic has an approximate standard normal distribution; therefore, the critical value is chosen from a standard normal distribution for the appropriate type of test—two-tail, lower one-tail, or upper one-tail. The *PHStat* tool *Z-Test for Differences in Two Proportions* can be applied to this test.

Hypothesis Tests and Confidence Intervals

You may have been thinking that a relationship exists between hypothesis tests and confidence intervals, since they rely on essentially the same information. For example, we tested the hypotheses for the Customer Support Survey data using a level of significance of 0.05:

H₀: *mean response time ≥ 30 minutes*
H₁: *mean response time < 30 minutes*

We rejected the null hypothesis and concluded that the mean is less than 30 minutes. If we construct a 95 percent confidence interval for the mean response time, we obtain [15.98, 27.84]. Note that the hypothesized value, 30, is *not* contained within this confidence interval. Similarly, we tested the hypotheses in the *Burglaries.xls* data using a level of significance of 0.05:

H₀: *Mean burglaries/month after program (μ_1) − Mean burglaries/month before program (μ_2) ≥ 0*
H₁: *Mean burglaries/month after program (μ_1) − Mean burglaries/month before program (μ_2) < 0*

and concluded that we could not reject H₀. If we compute a 95 percent confidence interval for the difference in means, we would find [−4.30, 11.64]. In this case, the interval contains the hypothesized difference, 0. In general, if a $100(1 - \alpha)$ percent confidence interval *contains* the hypothesized value, then we *do not* reject the null hypothesis based on this value with a level of significance α. If, however, the hypothesized value *is not contained* in the CI, then we *would* reject the null hypothesis at this significance level.

F-Test for Differences in Two Variances

As we have seen, Excel supports two different *t*-tests for differences in means, one assuming equal variances, and the other assuming unequal variances. We can test for equality of variances between two samples using the *F-test*. To use this test, we must assume that both samples are drawn from normal populations. The *F*-test statistic is the ratio of the variances of the two samples:

$$F = \frac{s_1^2}{s_2^2}$$

This statistic is compared to a critical value from the *F*-distribution for a given confidence level. Like the *t*-distribution, the *F*-distribution is characterized by degrees of freedom. However, the *F*-statistic has *two* values of degrees of freedom—one for the sample variance in the numerator, and the other for the sample variance in the denominator. In both cases, the number of degrees of freedom is equal to the respective sample size minus 1.

To illustrate the *F*-test, we will use the *Burglaries.xls* data and test whether the variance in the number of monthly burglaries is the same before and after the citizen–police program began.

$$H_0: \sigma^2_{before} = \sigma^2_{after}$$
$$H_1: \sigma^2_{before} \neq \sigma^2_{after}$$

The test statistic is $F = s_1^2/s_2^2 = 282.47/253.87 = 1.112$. Proper interpretation of the *F*-statistic and finding the correct critical value depends on how we take the ratio of sample variances. In this case, we divided the larger variance by the smaller. Note that when we do this, $F \geq 1$. If the variances differ significantly, we would expect *F* to be much larger than 1; the closer *F* is to 1, the more likely it is that the variances are the same. Therefore, we need only compare *F* to the upper-tail critical value $F_{\alpha/2,df_1,df_2}$ of the *F*-distribution, where df_1 and df_2 are the degrees of freedom in the numerator and denominator, respectively. If $F > F_{\alpha/2,df_1,df_2}$, then we reject H_0. From Table A.5, we find $F_{0.025,40,16} = 2.51$. Since $F = 1.112 < 2.51$, we cannot reject the null hypothesis of equal variances.

In reality, this is a two-tailed test; however, Table A.5 provides only upper-tail critical values, and the distribution is *not* symmetric. To find the lower-tail critical value, reverse the degrees of freedom, find the upper-tail value, and then take the reciprocal. Thus, the lower-tail critical value for this test is approximately $1/F_{0.025,15,40} = 1/1.92 = 0.521$ (we used the numerator df = 15 because 16 is not included in Table A.5). The correct value is 0.464.

Suppose we took the ratio of the smaller variance to the larger one; that is, $F = 253.87/282.47 = 0.899$. In this case, the closer that *F* is to zero, the greater the likelihood that the population variances differ, so we need only compare *F* to the lower-tail critical value and reject if *F* is less than this value. Thus, in this case, with a numerator df = 16 and the denominator df = 40, the lower-tail critical value is $1/F_{0.025,40,16} = 1/2.15 = 0.465$. Since $F = 0.899 > 0.465$ we cannot reject the null hypothesis and reach the same conclusion as before.

The *F*-test can be applied using either the *PHStat* tool found in the menu by choosing *Two Sample Tests . . . F-test for Differences in Two Variances,* or the Excel *Data Analysis* tool *F-test for Equality of Variances* (see the *Excel/PHStat Note: Testing for Equality of Variances*).

ANOVA: TESTING DIFFERENCES OF SEVERAL MEANS

To this point, we have discussed hypothesis tests that compare a population parameter to a constant value or that compare the means of two different populations. Often, we would like to compare the means of several different groups to determine if all are equal, or if any are significantly different from the rest. For example, in the *TV Viewing.xls* data, there appear to be clear differences in TV viewing behavior between younger and older age groups; however, it is not clear, for example, whether any significant differences exist among the 18–24, 25–34, and 35–44 age groups, whose sample means are 60.16, 70.28, and 67.40, respectively. In statistical terminology, the age group is called a **factor**, and we have three categorical levels of this factor. Thus, it would appear that we will have to perform three different pairwise tests to establish whether any significant differences exist among them. As the number of populations increases, you can easily see that the number of pairwise tests grows large very quickly. Fortunately, other statistical tools exist that eliminate the need for such a tedious approach. **Analysis of variance (ANOVA)** provides a tool for doing this.

EXCEL/*PHSTAT* NOTE

TESTING FOR EQUALITY OF VARIANCES

To use the Excel tool, from the main menu bar, click on *Tools,* followed by *Data Analysis,* and *F-test for Equality of Variances.* Specify the *Variable 1 Range* and the *Variable 2 Range* for both data sets and a value for the significance level. Note, however, that Excel provides results for only a one-tailed test. Thus, for a two-tailed test of equality of variances, *you must use $\alpha/2$ for the significance level* in the Excel dialog box. If the variance of variable 1 is greater than the variance of variable 2, the output will specify the upper tail; otherwise, you obtain the lower-tail information.

The *PHStat* tool, *F-test for Differences in Two Variances,* provides both the upper- and lower-tail values for the two-tailed test. In this case, you enter the full level of significance α. As with the *t*-test for differences in means, *PHStat* requires that you compute the sample standard deviations whereas Excel allows you to specify the range of the data and will compute the sample statistics.

Figure 4.25 shows the output from both tests using the ratio $F = s_{\text{before}}^2/s_{\text{after}}^2$. In comparing the results, note that the computed F ratio is the same (to within some rounding differences) and that the upper critical values are both the same. Note that the *p*-values differ, because in *PHStat*, the level of significance is entered as α, while in Excel, the level of significance must be entered as $\alpha/2$ for a two-tailed test. Thus, the *p*-value for Excel is half that of *PHStat*. These are both correct, as long as you realize that you compare the *p*-values to the proper levels of significance; that is, in *PHStat*, $0.847369 > 0.05$, while in Excel, $0.42439 > 0.025$. The same conclusions are reached in both cases.

	A	B	C	D	E	F	G
1	PHStat Output: F-Test for Equality of Variances			Excel Output: F-Test for Equality of Variances			
2							
3	Data				*Variable 1*	*Variable 2*	
4	Level of Significance	0.05		Mean	64.31707317	60.64705882	
5	Population 1 Sample			Variance	282.4719512	253.8676471	
6	Sample Size	41		Observations	41	17	
7	Sample Standard Deviation	16.81		df	40	16	
8	Population 2 Sample			F	1.112674082		
9	Sample Size	17		P(F<=f) one-tail	0.424390536		
10	Sample Standard Deviation	15.93		F Critical one-tail	2.508528496		
11							
12	Intermediate Calculations						
13	F-Test Statistic	1.113535					
14	Population 1 Sample Degrees of Freedom	40					
15	Population 2 Sample Degrees of Freedom	16					
16							
17	Two-Tailed Test						
18	Lower Critical Value	0.464214					
19	Upper Critical Value	2.508528					
20	p-Value	0.847369					
21	Do not reject the null hypothesis						
22							

FIGURE 4.25 Excel and *PHStat* Results for Equality of Variances *F*-test

ANOVA requires assumptions that the *m* groups or factor levels being studied represent populations whose outcome measures are randomly and independently obtained, are normally distributed, and have equal variances. The null hypothesis is that the population means of all groups are equal; the alternative hypothesis is that at least one mean differs from the rest:

H_0: $\mu_1 = \mu_2 = \ldots = \mu_m$
H_1: *at least one mean is different from the others*

Observation	18-24 Age Group	25-34 Age Group	35-44 Age Group
1	48	61	76
2	47	78	75
3	73	72	69
4	65	65	70
5	74	73	70
6	50	69	64
7	57	54	53
8	64	74	78
9	70	70	71
10	51	57	70
11	54	86	76
12	63	55	75
13	67	64	66
14	75	67	61
15	61	71	70
16	51	57	77
17	47	71	72
18	76	70	63
19	63	87	61
20	72	58	74
21	59	62	64
22	57	91	63
23	51	63	71
24	62	69	64
25	68	79	62
26	46	75	62
27	64	56	76
28	69	77	55
29	57	86	73
30	57	80	63
31	56	87	70
32	62	67	71
33	37	63	70
34	69	70	70
35	75	76	69
36	52	70	71
37	78		54
38	63		65
39	41		62
40	50		61
41	65		62
42	62		62
43	73		
44	50		
45	56		
Sample mean	60.16	70.28	67.40
Grand mean	65.59		

FIGURE 4.26 TV Viewing Data for ANOVA

Figure 4.26 shows data extracted from *TV Viewing.xls* for the first three age groups. We will test the hypothesis that the mean viewing hours/week for all groups are equal against the alternative that at least one mean is different.

We define n_j as the number of observations in sample j; thus, in Figure 4.28, $n_1 = 45$, $n_2 = 36$, and $n_3 = 42$. ANOVA examines the variation among and within the m groups or factor levels. Specifically, the total variation in the data is expressed as the variation among groups plus the variation within groups:

$$SST = SSB + SSW$$

where

SST = total variation in the data
SSB = variation between groups
SSW = variation within groups

EXCEL NOTE

SINGLE-FACTOR ANALYSIS OF VARIANCE

To use ANOVA to test for difference in sample means, click on *Tools, Data Analysis,* and select *ANOVA: Single Factor.* This displays the dialog box shown in Figure 4.27. You need only specify the input range of the data and whether it is stored in rows or columns (i.e., whether each factor level or group is a row or column in the range). You must also specify the level of significance (alpha level) and the output options.

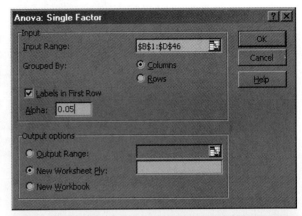

FIGURE 4.27   ANOVA: Single Factor Dialog Box

We compute these terms using the following formulas:

$$\text{SST} = \sum_{j=1}^{n} \sum_{i=1}^{n_j} (X_{ij} - \overline{\overline{X}})^2$$

$$\text{SSB} = \sum_{j=1}^{n} n_j (\overline{X}_j - \overline{\overline{X}})^2$$

$$\text{SSW} = \sum_{j=1}^{n} \sum_{i=1}^{n_j} (X_{ij} - \overline{X}_j)^2$$

where

n = total number of observations
$\overline{\overline{X}}$ = overall or grand mean
X_{ij} = ith observation in group j
$\overline{X}_j$ = sample mean of group j

From these formulas, you can see that each term is a "sum of squares" of elements of the data; hence the notation "SST," which can be thought of as the "Sum of Squares Total," SSB is the "Sum of Squares Between" groups, and SSW is the "Sum of Squares Within" groups. Observe that if the means of each group are indeed equal (H_0 is true), then the sample means of each group will be essentially the same as the overall mean, and SSB would be very small, and most of the total variation in the data is due to sampling variation within groups.

With n total observations, we need to estimate the overall mean to compute SST; thus, SST has $n - 1$ degrees of freedom. Similarly, to compute SSB for the m groups, we need to estimate the overall mean; thus, SSB has $m - 1$ degrees of freedom. This leaves $(n - 1) - (m - 1) = n - m$ degrees of freedom for SSW. By dividing SSB and SSW by their respective degrees of freedom, we obtain variance measures, or *mean squares*:

$$\text{MSB} = \text{SSB}/(m - 1)$$
$$\text{MSW} = \text{SSW}/(n - m)$$

	A	B	C	D	E	F	G
1	Anova: Single Factor						
2							
3	SUMMARY						
4	*Groups*	*Count*	*Sum*	*Average*	*Variance*		
5	18-24 Age Group	45	2707	60.15556	101.9071		
6	25-34 Age Group	36	2530	70.27778	97.06349		
7	35-44 Age Group	42	2831	67.40476	40.29559		
8							
9							
10	ANOVA						
11	*Source of Variation*	*SS*	*df*	*MS*	*F*	*P-value*	*F crit*
12	Between Groups	2258.422	2	1129.211	14.21397	2.88E-06	3.071776
13	Within Groups	9533.252	120	79.44377			
14							
15	Total	11791.67	122				

FIGURE 4.28   ANOVA Results for TV Viewing Hypothesis Test

Because the mean squares are variances, we can use the *F*-test to test for equality of variances using the *F*-statistic

$$F = MSB/MSW$$

This statistic follows an *F*-distribution with $m - 1$ and $n - m$ degrees of freedom. Therefore, if *F* is larger than the critical value from the *F*-distribution, we reject H_0. That is, if the mean square between groups is significantly larger than the mean square within groups, then we would have statistical evidence to conclude that a difference exists among the means.

ANOVA derives its name from the fact that we are analyzing variances in the data. If the null hypothesis is true, the within-group variation should equal the total variation and the *F* statistic ideally will be 1. If the means among groups are different, then MSB will be significantly larger than MSW. If the *F*-statistic is large enough based on the level of significance chosen, we can conclude that the alternative hypothesis is true. However, ANOVA does not provide any information about which mean(s) would be different.

Excel provides a *Data Analysis* tool, *ANOVA: Single Factor* (see the *Excel Note: Single-Factor Analysis of Variance*) to conduct analysis of variance. The results for the TV Viewing data are given in Figure 4.28. The output report begins with a summary report of basic statistics for each group. The ANOVA section reports the details of the hypothesis test. Note that the mean squares are simply the sums of squares, SS, divided by their respective degrees of freedom; that is, MSB = 2258.422416/2 = 1129.211208 and MSW = 9533.252381/120 = 79.44376984. The *F*-ratio is MSB/MSW = 14.21. Since this is larger than the critical value of the *F*-distribution of 3.07 for an α of 0.05, we reject the null hypothesis and conclude that at least one mean is different. The *p*-value reported by Excel is essentially zero, which leads us to the same conclusion.

Tukey–Kramer Multiple Comparison Procedure

Although ANOVA can identify a difference among the means of multiple populations, it cannot determine which of the means are significantly different from the rest. To do this, we may use the **Tukey–Kramer multiple comparison procedure.** This method compares the absolute value of the difference in means for all pairs of groups and compares these to a critical range. Values exceeding the critical range identify those populations whose means differ. *PHStat* provides this procedure (see the *PHStat Note: Using the Tukey–Kramer Multiple Comparison Procedure*), and Figure 4.29 shows the results for our example. We conclude that the mean of the 18–24 age group differs from the other two but that the means of the 25–34 and 35–44 age groups are not significantly different.

PHSTAT NOTE

USING THE TUKEY–KRAMER MULTIPLE COMPARISON PROCEDURE

The Tukey–Kramer procedure is selected from the *Multiple Sample Tests* menu. You need only enter the cell range of the data. However, *PHStat* prompts you to enter a value for "Q Statistic" (see cell B14 in Figure 4.29) manually in the worksheet before displaying the conclusions of the test. This value is based on the numerator df and denominator df and may be found in Table A.6 in the back of this book.

	A	B	C	D	E	F	G	H	I	J	K
1	Tukey-Kramer Test										
2											
3		Sample	Sample			Absolute	Std. Error	Critical			
4	Group	Mean	Size		Comparison	Difference	of Difference	Range	Results		
5	1	60.15556	45		Group 1 to Group 2	10.12222	1.40928856	4.7352	Means are different		
6	2	70.27778	36		Group 1 to Group 3	7.249206	1.35220846	4.5434	Means are different		
7	3	67.40476	42		Group 2 to Group 3	2.873016	1.43148345	4.8098	Means are not different		
8											
9	Other Data										
10	Level of significance	0.05									
11	Numerator d.f.	3									
12	Denominator d.f.	120									
13	MSW	79.44377									
14	Q Statistic	3.36									

FIGURE 4.29 Results of Tukey–Kramer Multiple Comparison Procedure

Analysis of variance may be extended to more than one factor. For example, suppose that a company wants to investigate whether changes in temperature and pressure settings affect output quality or yield in some production process. Temperature and pressure represent two factors, and multiple samples might be selected for each of three different combinations of temperature levels and pressure settings. This would be an example of a two-factor ANOVA and would allow the investigator to test hypotheses about whether differences exist among the levels of each factor individually and also whether any interactions exist between the factors; that is, whether the effect of one factor depends on the level of the other. Further discussion is beyond the scope of this book, but additional information may be found in more comprehensive statistics texts and books devoted exclusively to the subject.

CHI-SQUARE TEST FOR INDEPENDENCE

A common problem is to determine whether two categorical variables are independent. For example, a consumer study might collect data on preferences for three different soft drinks of both male and female high school students. The objective of the study might be to determine if soft drink preferences are independent of gender. Independence would mean that the proportion of individuals who prefer one drink over another would be essentially the same no matter if the individual is male or female. On the other hand, if males have different preferences than females, the variables would be dependent. As another example, a company might collect categorical data on its customer satisfaction survey each month. The company might like to determine if category responses are independent of time.

Such situations can be analyzed using a contingency table and the chi-square test for independence. A **contingency table** is a matrix of *r* rows and *c* columns that shows

	A	B	C	D
1	Accounting Professionals			
2				
3	Count of Gender	CPA?		
4	Gender	N	Y	Grand Total
5	F	6	8	14
6	M	7	6	13
7	Grand Total	13	14	27

FIGURE 4.30 Contingency Table for Accounting *Professionals.xls Data*

the value of two categorical variables together. For example, Figure 4.30 shows an Excel PivotTable for the count of employees in the *Accounting Professionals.xls* data by gender and whether they have a CPA. The chi-square test for independence tests whether the proportion of females who hold a CPA is no different from the proportion of males who hold a CPA. Alternatively, we might pose the question: Is the proportion of CPAs who are male no different from the proportion of CPAs who are female? For instance, of the 14 female accounting professionals, 8, or 57 percent, hold a CPA. If gender and CPA status are indeed independent, we would expect that about 57 percent of the sample of male employees would also hold a CPA. In actuality, only 6 of 13, or 46 percent, hold a CPA. However, we do not know whether this is simply due to sampling error or represents a significant difference. These questions can be expressed as the following hypotheses:

H_0: *the two categorical variables are independent*
H_1: *the two categorical variables are dependent*

We can use the frequencies in the contingency table to compute a test statistic, called a **chi-square statistic,** which is the square of the difference between observed frequency, f_o, and expected frequency, f_e, divided by the expected frequency in each cell:

$$\chi^2 = \sum \frac{(f_o - f_e)^2}{f_e}$$

The expected frequency is what would be expected if the null hypothesis is true. To compute the expected frequency for a particular cell in the table, multiply the row total by the column total and divide by the grand total. Thus, the expected number of females who do not hold a CPA under the null hypothesis is $(14)(13)/27 = 6.74$. The remaining expected frequencies are shown next.

Expected Frequencies	No CPA	CPA	Total
Female	6.74	7.26	14
Male	6.26	6.74	13
Total	13	14	27

One caution: All expected frequencies should be at least 1.0. If not, then you should combine rows or columns to meet this requirement.

The closer the actual counts are to the expected counts, the smaller will be the value of the chi-square statistic. We compare this statistic for a specified level of significance α to the critical value from a chi-square distribution with $(r - 1)(c - 1)$ degrees of freedom. If the test statistic exceeds the critical value for a specified level of significance, we reject H_0. The calculations are shown next.

$$\chi^2 = (6 - 6.74)^2/6.74 + (8 - 7.26)^2/7.26 + (7 - 6.26)^2/6.26$$
$$+ (6 - 6.74)^2/6.74 = 0.33$$

Comparing this to the chi-square critical value of 3.841 from Table A.4 with $\alpha = 0.05$ and $(2 - 1)(2 - 1) = 1$ df, we see that we cannot reject the null hypothesis that the two categorical variables are independent. We could also use a *PHStat* tool (see *PHStat Note: Chi-Square Test for Independence*).

PHSTAT NOTE

CHI-SQUARE TEST FOR INDEPENDENCE

From the *PHStat Multiple Sample Tests* menu, select *Chi-Square Test*. In the dialog box, enter the level of significance, number of rows, and number of columns in the contingency table. *PHStat* will create a worksheet in which you will need to enter the data for the observed frequencies. You may also customize the names of the rows and columns for your specific application. After you complete the table, the calculations are performed automatically. Figure 4.31 shows the results for the Accounting Professionals example. Note that the *p*-value is greater than 0.05, which leads us to fail to reject the null hypothesis.

	A	B	C	D
1	Accounting Professionals			
2				
3	Observed Frequencies			
4		CPA?		
5	Gender	No	Yes	Total
6	Female	6	8	14
7	Male	7	6	13
8	Total	13	14	27
9				
10	Expected Frequencies			
11		CPA?		
12	Gender	No	Yes	Total
13	Female	6.740741	7.259259	14
14	Male	6.259259	6.740741	13
15	Total	13	14	27
16				
17	Data			
18	Level of Significance	0.05		
19	Number of Rows	2		
20	Number of Columns	2		
21	Degrees of Freedom	1		
22				
23	Results			
24	Critical Value	3.84146		
25	Chi-Square Test Statistic	0.32605		
26	*p*-Value	0.568		
27	Do not reject the null hypothesis			
28				
29	*Expected frequency assumption*			
30	*is met.*			

FIGURE 4.31 *PHStat* Chi-Square Test Results

Two Excel functions provide related information. The function CHIDIST(*statistic, degrees_freedom*) with the calculated test statistic = 0.32605 and 1 degree of freedom yields the *p*-value 0.568. Excel also includes the function CHITEST(*actual_range, expected_range*) which will also return the *p*-value for the test.

NONPARAMETRIC HYPOTHESIS TESTS

The hypothesis tests that we have discussed depend on the assumption that the populations from which the samples are drawn are normally distributed. When this assumption cannot be made or is clearly violated, the conclusions from such tests may be suspect. As an alternative, statisticians have developed a variety of **nonparametric tests** that do not require such assumptions. Among these are the Wilcoxon rank sum test for testing the difference between two medians and the Kruskal–Wallis rank test for determining whether multiple populations have equal medians. These tests are supported by *PHStat,* and we refer you to more comprehensive texts on statistics for further information and examples.

DISTRIBUTION FITTING: AN APPLICATION OF HYPOTHESIS TESTING

In many decision models, empirical data may be available, either in historical records or collected through special efforts. For example, maintenance records might provide data on machine failure rates and repair times, or observers might collect data on service times in a bank or post office. Consider, for example, the sample data in Table 4.7. We might take these data and create an empirical distribution by developing a histogram, as shown in Figure 4.32. If these data represent an important variable in a decision model, we might wish to attempt to fit a theoretical distribution to the data and to verify goodness-of-fit statistically. We would then use this theoretical distribution in our model analysis.

To select an appropriate theoretical distribution, we might begin by examining the histogram to look for the distinctive shapes of particular distributions. This is why we studied different distributions in Chapter 3. For example, normal data are symmetric, with a peak in the middle. Exponential data are very positively skewed, with no negative values. Various forms of the gamma, Weibull, or beta distributions could be used for distributions that do not seem to fit one of the other common forms. This approach is not, of course, always accurate or valid, and sometimes it can be difficult to apply, especially if sample sizes are small. However, it may narrow the search down to a few potential distributions. For example, we might suspect that the histogram in Figure 4.32

TABLE 4.7	A Sample of 50 Observations			
1.81	2.43	4.20	2.75	3.38
4.11	3.24	2.69	2.37	2.80
2.27	2.72	3.90	3.10	2.25
4.67	3.14	2.10	2.17	4.18
3.58	4.31	2.79	3.26	2.00
2.54	4.21	3.74	2.12	2.86
3.59	3.23	3.25	2.07	3.30
2.22	2.80	2.67	1.68	4.67
2.96	2.83	3.18	3.03	3.20
2.17	3.38	2.69	1.75	3.16

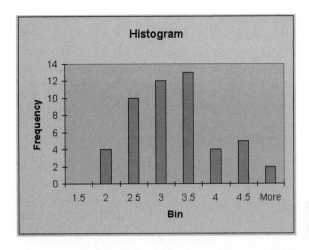

FIGURE 4.32 Histogram of Data in Table 4.7

might derive from a normal distribution, but the lack of symmetry makes it difficult to draw this conclusion. However, we can easily be fooled by the variation that arises from small sample sizes. Thus, we should gather more information.

Summary statistics can provide additional clues about the nature of a distribution. The mean, median, standard deviation, and coefficient of variation often provide clues about the nature of the distribution. For instance, normally distributed data tend to have a fairly low coefficient of variation; however, this may not be true if the mean is small. For normally distributed data, we would also expect the median and mean to be approximately the same. For exponentially distributed data, however, the median will be less than the mean. Also, we would expect the mean to be about equal to the standard deviation. We could also look at the coefficient of skewness. Normal data are not skewed, while lognormal and exponential data are positively skewed.

Figure 4.33 shows some summary statistics for the sample data. The coefficient of variation is 0.76/2.99 = 0.25 and is rather low. The coefficient of skewness, 0.40, likewise is quite low, indicating that the distribution is basically symmetric. The mean and median are very close. All this suggests that the sample might have been drawn from a normal distribution, despite the fact that the histogram does not look very "normal."

Another visual way to attempt to verify whether a set of data fits a particular distribution is to construct a **probability plot.** A probability plot transforms the cumulative probability scale (vertical axis) so that the graph of the cumulative distribution will be a straight line. This is illustrated in Figure 4.34 for a standard normal

Mean	2.9904
Standard Error	0.107683194
Median	2.91
Mode	4.67
Standard Deviation	0.761435165
Sample Variance	0.57978351
Kurtosis	-0.413581592
Skewness	0.402716822
Range	2.99
Minimum	1.68
Maximum	4.67
Sum	149.52
Count	50

FIGURE 4.33 Summary Statistics for Sample Data

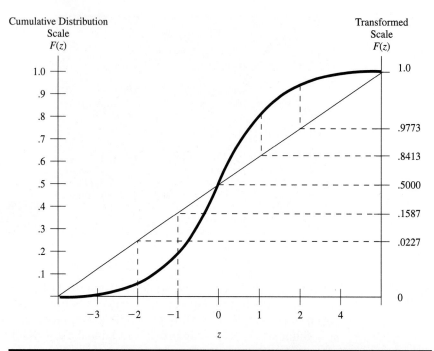

FIGURE 4.34   Constructing a Normal Probability Plot Scale

distribution. A probability plot allows us to check the validity of the assumed distribution. The closer the points are to a straight line, the better the fit to the assumed distribution. A normal probability plot of the sample data in Table 4.7 generated by *PHStat* (see *PHStat Note: Normal Probability Plot*) is shown in Figure 4.35. Although the data appear to follow a relatively straight line, there is some systematic nonlinearity to the data, making it difficult to draw a definitive conclusion.

The examination of histograms and summary statistics might provide some tentative hypotheses; however, these should be verified in a more formal manner. **Goodness-of-fit tests** provide statistical evidence to test hypotheses about the *nature* of the distribution. The most commonly used goodness-of-fit test is the chi-square (χ^2) test. The chi-square goodness-of-fit test tests the hypothesis

H_0: *the sample data come from a specified distribution (e.g., normal)*
H_1: *the sample data do not come from the specified distribution*

PHSTAT NOTE

NORMAL PROBABILITY PLOT

From the *PHStat* menu, select *Probability Distributions* and then *Normal Probability Plot*. In the dialog box, you need to specify the range of the data. The tool creates the plot on a new worksheet as well as an additional worksheet with the calculations used to construct the chart.

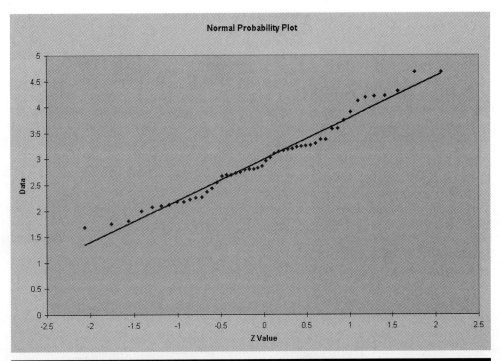

FIGURE 4.35   Normal Probability Plot from *PHStat*

As with any hypothesis test, you can disprove the null hypothesis but cannot statistically *prove* that data come from the specified distribution. The hypothesized distribution is partitioned into cells like a frequency distribution, and we need to compute the expected number of observations that would fall into each cell, if indeed the null hypothesis is true. The test statistic is computed in the same fashion as in the test for independence in contingency tables, by summing the squares of the differences between the observed and expected frequencies divided by the expected frequency. Finding the expected frequencies often requires some advanced knowledge of working with probability distributions, so we will not show the detailed calculations, especially because these can be performed within *Crystal Ball*. Other tests are available, such as the Kolmogorov–Smirnov test, and the Anderson–Darling test, which is similar to the Kolmogorov–Smirnov test, except that it places more weight on the tail observations. The *Crystal Ball* Help function provides some technical details of these tests.

Distribution Fitting with *Crystal Ball*

Crystal Ball provides a very useful and powerful data-fitting capability. We will illustrate this capability using the data given in Table 4.7. Figure 4.36 shows the Excel screen after *Crystal Ball* has been loaded. Three new menu items appear on the main menu bar: *Cell, Run,* and *CB Tools.* (The third line of buttons also provides shortcuts to invoke *Crystal Ball* menu commands.)

To apply the distribution fitting capability, first click on any data value, and then click on *Cell* from the main menu, and select *Define Assumption . . . .* The *Crystal Ball* distribution gallery (see Figure 4.37) is displayed. Click on *Fit.* The first of two dialog boxes, shown in Figure 4.38, is displayed. If the data are in the frontmost spreadsheet, select *Active Worksheet* (*Crystal Ball* also allows fitting data from a separate text file), and enter the range of the data in the box to the right. Clicking on *Next* displays the

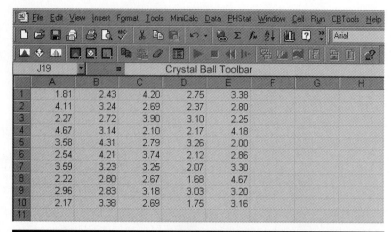

FIGURE 4.36   *Crystal Ball* Menus and Toolbar

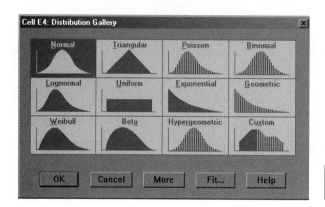

FIGURE 4.37   *Crystal Ball* Distribution Gallery

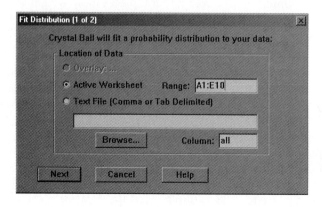

FIGURE 4.38   First *Crystal Ball* Dialog Box for Distribution Fitting

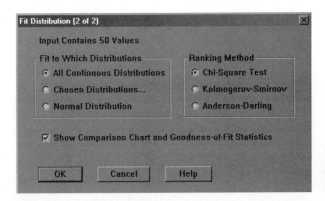

FIGURE 4.39 Second *Crystal Ball* Dialog Box for Distribution Fitting

second dialog box, shown in Figure 4.39. You may select all continuous distributions in the distribution gallery, any subset, or just the normal distribution. You must also select the type of test; in this example, we select the chi-square test. Check the box *Show Comparison Chart and Goodness-of-Fit Statistics* to display comparative results. *Crystal Ball* then fits each of the 11 continuous distributions available in the distribution gallery to the data set. It then rank orders them by the chi-square *p*-values (largest first). The best-fitting distribution is then displayed in a Comparison Chart window with distribution parameters and goodness-of-fit scores, shown in Figure 4.40. You may select the Prefs button to customize the chart display type; in Figure 4.40, we used a cumulative distribution instead of the frequency distribution because of the small sample size and irregular shape of the data. A large *p*-value indicates that we cannot reject the null hypothesis. The best-fitting distribution is an Extreme Value distribution. By clicking the *Next Distribution* button, the comparison charts for other distributions can be displayed in descending order of *p*-values. The *p*-value for a normal distribution is 0.0082, leading us to reject the hypothesis that the data come from a normal distribution. What may be surprising is that the data set was actually generated in Excel from a normal distribution! With small sample sizes, it may be difficult to obtain a good fit because of high sampling error, as this example shows. Thus, for practical decision models, it is important to try to obtain a large, representative sample of data.

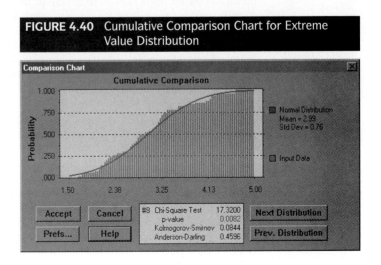

FIGURE 4.40 Cumulative Comparison Chart for Extreme Value Distribution

Questions and Problems

1. Define a sampling plan. What is the purpose of using a sampling plan?
2. Why might a frame differ from the target population?
3. Explain the common types of sampling methods and when each might be useful.
4. Your college wishes to obtain reliable information about student perceptions of administrative communication. Describe an appropriate sampling plan to implement for this situation.
5. How does nonsampling error differ from sampling error?
6. Explain the difference between point and interval estimates. What is a confidence interval?
7. For the *TV Viewing.xls* data, we developed a 99 percent confidence interval for the 18–24 age group. Construct 99 percent confidence intervals for the means of the remaining age groups using the formula in the text. Verify your calculations using the appropriate *PHStat* tool. For sample sizes 30 or more, use both the standard normal and *t*-distributions to compute the confidence intervals and compare them.
8. A manufacturer conducted a survey among 400 randomly selected target market households in the test market for its new disposable diapers. The objective of the survey was to determine the market share for its new brand. If the sample estimate for market share is 20 percent, develop a 95 percent confidence interval.
9. If a manufacturer conducted a survey among randomly selected target market households and wanted to be 95 percent confident that the difference between the sample estimate and the actual market share for its new product was no more than 4 percent, what sample size would be needed?
10. If, based on a sample size of 500, a political candidate finds that 245 people would vote for him in a two-person race, what is the 90 percent confidence interval for his expected proportion of the vote?
11. If, based on a sample size of 100, a political candidate found that 59 people would vote for her in a two-person race, what is the 95 percent confidence interval for her expected proportion of the vote?
12. Trade associations such as the United Dairy Farmers Association frequently conduct surveys to identify characteristics of their membership. If this organization conducted a survey to estimate the annual per-capita consumption of milk, and wanted to be 95 percent confident that the estimate was no more than 0.5 gallons away from the actual average, what sample size is needed? Past data have indicated that the standard deviation is approximately four gallons.
13. How many samples would be needed to ensure an error of no more than $E = 1$ hours in estimating the number of TV viewing hours/week in each of the age groups in *TV Viewing.xls*?
14. An auditor of a small business has sampled 50 of 700 accounts. The sample mean total receivables is $435, and the sample standard deviation is $86. Find a 95 percent CI for the total amount of receivables.
15. Examine the data in *Energy Production & Consumption.xls* to determine whether the time series are stationary.
16. Discuss the different forms of hypotheses that one may test. How should the null hypothesis be stated relative to the alternative hypothesis?
17. The Excel file *Baseball Attendance.xls* shows the attendance in thousands at San Francisco Giants' baseball games for the 10 years before the Oakland A's moved to the Bay Area in 1968, as well as the combined attendance for both teams for the next 11 years.
   a. Do the data appear to be stationary?

b. Develop a 98 percent confidence interval for the difference in mean attendance of the two groups.

c. Is there a statistical reason to believe that overall attendance has changed after the A's move?

18. Find a 95 percent confidence interval for the variance of each age group (except for 18–24) in *TV Viewing.xls*.

19. A study of nonfatal occupational injuries in the United States found that about 31% of all injuries in the service sector involved the back. The National Institute for Occupational Safety and Health (NIOSH) recommended conducting a comprehensive ergonomics assessment of jobs and workstations. In response to this information, Mark Glassmeyer developed a unique ergonomic handcart to help field service engineers be more productive and also to reduce back injuries from lifting parts and equipment during service calls. Using a sample of 382 field service engineers who were provided with these carts, Mark collected the following data:

	Year 1 (without cart)	Year 2 (with cart)
Average call time	8.05 hours	7.84 hours
Standard deviation call time	1.39 hours	1.34 hours
Proportion of back injuries	0.018	0.010

a. Develop a 95 percent confidence interval on the average call time for each year.

b. Determine if there is statistical evidence that average call time has decreased as a result of using the cart. What other factors might account for any changes?

c. Determine if there is statistical evidence that the proportion of back injuries has decreased as a result of using the cart.

20. A marketing study found that the mean spending in 15 categories of consumer items for 297 respondents in the 18–34 age group was $71.86 with a standard deviation of $70.90. For 736 respondents in the 35+ age group, the mean and standard deviation were $61.53 and $45.29, respectively.

a. Develop 95 percent confidence intervals for the population mean spending amounts for each age group.

b. Test the hypothesis that there is no difference in the mean spending between these two groups.

21. The Excel file *Accounting Professionals.xls* provides the results of a survey of 27 employees in a tax division of a Fortune 100 company.

a. Test the hypothesis that the average number of years of service is the same for males and females.

b. Test the hypothesis that the average years of undergraduate study is the same for males and females.

c. Perform a chi-square test of independence to determine if age group is independent of having a graduate degree.

22. The U.S. Census Bureau *1998 Current Population Reports* P20-513 provides data on the educational status of persons 25 years and older (see the Excel file *Census Education Data.xls*).

a. Conduct a chi-square test of independence to determine if educational level is independent of age group.

b. Conduct a chi-square test of independence to determine if educational level is independent of sex.

c. Conduct a chi-square test of independence to determine if educational level is independent of race.

    d. Conduct a chi-square test of independence to determine if educational level is independent of marital status.

    e. Conduct a chi-square test of independence to determine if educational level is independent of employment status.

23. Call centers have high turnover rates because of the stressful environment. The national average is approximately 50 percent. The director of human resources for a large bank has compiled data about 70 former employees at one of the bank's call centers (see the Excel file *Call Center Data.xls*). For each of the following, assume equal variances of the two populations.

    a. Test the hypothesis that the average length of service for males is the same as for females.

    b. Test the hypothesis that the average length of service for individuals without prior call center experience is the same as those with experience.

    c. Test the hypothesis that the average length of service for individuals with a college degree is the same as for individuals without a college degree.

    d. Now conduct tests of hypotheses for equality of variances. Were your assumptions of equal variances valid? If not, repeat the test(s) for means using the unequal variance test.

24. A producer of computer-aided design software for the aerospace industry receives numerous calls for technical support. Tracking software is used to monitor response and resolution times. In addition, the company surveys customers who request support using the following scale:

    0—Did not exceed expectations
    1—Marginally met expectations
    2—Met expectations
    3—Exceeded expectations
    4—Greatly exceeded expectations

The questions are

    Q1: Did the support representative explain the process for resolving your problem?
    Q2: Did the support representative keep you informed about the status of progress in resolving your problem?
    Q3: Was the support representative courteous and professional?
    Q4: Was your problem resolved?
    Q5: Was your problem resolved in an acceptable amount of time?
    Q6: Overall, how did you find the service provided by our technical support department?

A final question asks the customer to rate the overall quality of the product using a scale of

    0—Very poor
    1—Poor
    2—Good
    3—Very good
    4—Excellent

A sample of survey responses and associated resolution and response data are provided in the Excel file *Customer Support Survey Data.xls*.

    a. Develop a 95 percent confidence interval for mean resolution time.

    b. The company has set a service standard of one day for the mean resolution time. Test the hypothesis that the response time is no greater than one day at a 0.05 level of significance. How do the outliers in the data affect your result? What should you do about them?

    c. Test the hypothesis that the average service index is equal to the average engineer index.

25. The file *1999 Baseball Data.xls* contains data for professional baseball teams for 1999, including their total payroll, winning percentage, batting averages, home runs, runs, runs batted in, earned run average, and pitching saves. Test the hypothesis that the average winning percentage of the 10 teams with the highest payroll is equal to that of the 10 teams with the lowest payroll.

26. The State of Ohio Department of Education has a mandated ninth-grade proficiency test that covers writing, reading, mathematics, citizenship (social studies), and science. The Excel file *Ohio Education Performance.xls* provides data on success rates (defined as the percent of students passing) in school districts in the Greater Cincinnati metropolitan area along with state averages.
    a. Find 50 and 90 percent probability intervals for each of the variables in the *Ohio Education Performance.xls* data.
    b. Test the hypothesis that the average score in the Cincinnati area is equal to the state average in each test and for the composite score.
    c. Test the hypotheses that the mean difference in writing and reading scores is zero. Use the paired sample procedure.
    d. Test the hypotheses that the mean difference in math and science scores is zero. Use the paired sample procedure.
    e. Apply analysis of variance to test the hypothesis that the mean success rate in each subject is equal. If the null hypothesis is rejected, apply the Tukey–Kramer multiple comparison procedure to identify significant differences.

27. The Excel file *TV Viewing.xls* provides sample data on the number of hours of TV viewing per week for six age groups. Conduct an ANOVA to determine if the mean number of hours of TV viewing per week is the same for all age groups. If the null hypothesis is rejected, apply the Tukey–Kramer multiple comparison procedure to identify significant differences.

28. The Excel file *Salary Data.xls* provides information on current salary, beginning salary, previous experience in months when hired, and total years of education for a sample of 100 employees in a firm. Develop 95 percent confidence intervals for each of the variables in the data set.

29. An engineer measured the surface finish of 35 parts produced on a lathe, noting the revolutions per minute of the spindle and the type of tool used (see the Excel file *Surface Finish.xls*).
    a. Develop 95 percent confidence intervals for the surface finish for each type of tool.
    b. Use analysis of variance to test the hypothesis that the mean surface finish is the same for each tool.

30. The Excel file *Infant Mortality.xls* provides data on infant mortality rate (deaths per 1000 births), female literacy (percent who read), and population density (people per square kilometer) for 85 countries. Develop a 90 percent confidence interval for infant mortality.

31. The Excel file *Economic Indexes.xls* provides data on the annual percent change in the Dow Jones Industrial average, Consumer Price Index, Standard & Poor's 500, and average yield for one-year Treasury bills from 1960 through 1999. Test the hypothesis that the variance of the change in the DJIA is the same as the variance of the change in the S&P 500 indexes. What do the results mean about the relative risk of investing in index funds tied to these measures?

32. The Excel file *Weather.xls* contains mean temperatures for January and July and average annual precipitation for selected cities across the United States. Construct 90 percent confidence intervals for the mean temperatures and precipitation.

33. A mental health agency measured the self-esteem score for randomly selected individuals with disabilities who were involved in some work activity within the past year. The Excel file *Self-Esteem.xls* provides the data, including the individuals' marital status, length of work, type of support received (direct support includes job-related services such as job coaching and counseling), education, and age.
    a. Apply ANOVA to determine if self-esteem is the same for all marital status levels. If the null hypothesis is rejected, apply the Tukey–Kramer multiple comparison procedure to identify significant differences.
    b. Use the chi-square test to determine if marital status is independent of support level.

34. The Excel file *Washington DC Weather.xls* provides a variety of data on statistical averages of weather parameters by month. Conduct hypothesis tests to determine if
    a. The proportion of cloudy days in June is significantly different from that in December
    b. The proportion of partly cloudy days in January is significantly different from that in March
    c. The proportion of clear days in January is significantly different from that in September

35. The Excel file *Blood Pressure.xls* shows the monthly blood pressure (diastolic) readings for a patient before and after medication.
    a. Test the hypothesis that the variances of monthly blood pressure readings before and after medication are the same.
    b. Conduct an appropriate hypothesis test to determine if there is evidence that the medication has lowered the patient's blood pressure.

36. The Excel file *Unions and Labor Law Data.xls* reports the percent of public- and private-sector employees in unions in 1982 for each state, along with indicators whether the states had a bargaining law that covered public employees or right-to-work laws.
    a. Test the hypothesis that the percent of employees in unions for both the public sector and private sector is the same for states having bargaining laws as for those who do not.
    b. Test the hypothesis that the percent of employees in unions for both the public sector and private sector is the same for states having right-to-work laws as for those who do not.

37. Jim Aspenwall, a NASCAR enthusiast, has compiled some key statistics for NASCAR Winston Cup racing tracks across the United States. These tracks range in shape, length, and amount of banking on the turns and straightaways (see the Excel file *NASCAR Track Statistics.xls*). Test the hypothesis that there is no difference in qualifying record speed between oval and other shapes of tracks.

38. Use *Crystal Ball* to fit a distribution to each of the variables in the *Infant Mortality.xls* data.

39. Use *Crystal Ball* to fit a distribution to the reading, writing, and math scores in the *Ohio Education Performance.xls* data.

40. Use *Crystal Ball* to fit a distribution to each of the variables in the *Smoking and Cancer.xls* data.

CASE

STATISTICAL INFERENCE FOR TRACWAY

Henry Hudson has reviewed the information in the Tracway database. As he was looking at the data, several questions came to mind:

1. For the current year (2002), are there significant differences in the proportion of top box survey responses (which he defines as scale levels 4 and 5) among different marketing regions for Dealer Satisfaction and End-User Satisfaction?

2. Are there significant differences in ratings of specific product/service attributes in the 2002 Customer Survey?

3. Has the proportion of on-time deliveries in 2002 significantly improved since 1998?

4. Has Defects After Delivery changed significantly over the past five years?

5. What estimates can we give customers for response times to customer service calls with reasonable assurance?

6. Although engineering has collected data on alternative process costs for building transmissions in the worksheet *S2 Transmission Costs,* why didn't they reach a conclusion as to whether one of the proposed processes is better than the current process?

7. What do the data in *S4 Mower Test* tell me?

8. Are there differences in employee retention due to gender, college graduation status, or whether the employee is from the local area in the data in the worksheet *S6 Employee Retention?*

Conduct appropriate statistical analyses and hypothesis tests to answer these questions and summarize your results in a formal report to Mr. Hudson. ∎

CHAPTER

5

REGRESSION ANALYSIS

INTRODUCTION

In Chapter 2 we discussed statistical relationships and introduced correlation as a measure of the strength of a linear relationship between two numerical variables. Decision makers are often interested in predicting the value of a dependent variable from the value of one or more independent, or explanatory, variables. For example, many colleges try to predict the success of their students as measured by their college GPA (the dependent variable) from various independent variables such as SAT scores, high school rank, high school GPA, type of school (public, private, college prep), and other variables. Such a model might be used for admission decisions. Another example is predicting the demand for a product (the dependent variable) as a function of price and advertising (the independent variables). This model might be used to help determine optimal values of price and advertising. **Regression analysis** is a tool for building statistical models that characterize relationships between a dependent variable and one or more independent variables, all of which are numerical.

Two broad categories of regression models are used often in business settings: (1) regression models of cross-sectional data, such as those just described, and (2) regression models of time series data, in which the independent variables are time or some function of time and the focus is on predicting the future. Time series regression is an important tool in *forecasting,* which is the subject of Chapter 6.

TABLE 5.1 Tools and Functions for Regression Analysis in Excel	
Excel Function	*Description*
INTERCEPT(*known_y's, known_x's*)	Calculates the intercept by using a best-fit regression line
LINEST(*known_y's, known_x's, const, stats*)	Returns an array that describes a best-fitting straight line calculated using least squares
SLOPE(*known_y's, known_x's*)	Calculates the slope of a linear regression line
Analysis Toolpak Tools	*Description*
Regression	Performs linear regression using least squares
Prentice-Hall Statistics Add-In	*Description*
Simple Linear Regression	Generates a simple linear regression analysis
Multiple Regression	Generates a multiple linear regression analysis
Best Subsets	Generates a best-subsets regression analysis
Stepwise Regression	Generates a stepwise regression analysis

A regression model that involves a single independent variable is called *simple regression*. For example, we might wish to develop a simple regression model for predicting Points Scored as a function of Yards Gained in the *2000 NFL Data.xls* worksheet. Points Scored would be the dependent variable, and Yards Gained would be the independent variable. A regression model that involves several independent variables is called *multiple regression*. In the NFL data, a multiple regression model might predict Games Won (the dependent variable) as a function of the other (independent) variables (Yards Gained, Takeaways, Giveaways, Yards Allowed, and Points Scored).

In this chapter we describe how to develop and analyze both single and multiple regression models. Our principal focus is to gain a basic understanding of the assumptions of regression models, statistical issues associated with interpreting regression results, and practical issues in using regression as a tool for making and evaluating decisions. We will investigate

- Simple linear regression, focusing on the development of the model, understanding the significance of regression and the use of hypothesis tests, and interpreting key statistics such as the coefficient of determination and standard error of the estimate
- Multiple linear regression, including understanding how to select variables in models and evaluate goodness of fit and incorporating ordinal and nominal variables in the models
- Developing regression models to capture nonlinearities in data

Table 5.1 summarizes Excel support for regression analysis.

SIMPLE LINEAR REGRESSION

We first discuss the case of a single independent variable. The relationship between two variables can assume many forms, as illustrated in Figure 5.1. The relationship may be linear or one of many types of nonlinear forms, or there may be no relationship at all.

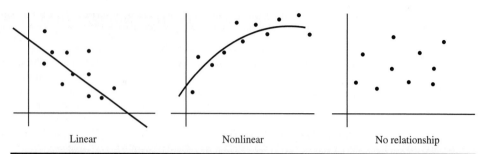

| Linear | Nonlinear | No relationship |

FIGURE 5.1   Examples of Functional Forms for Regression Models

To develop a regression model, you first must specify the type of function that best describes the data. This is important, because using a linear model for data that are clearly nonlinear, for instance, would probably lead to poor business decisions and results. The type of relationship can usually be seen in a scatter diagram, and we always recommend that you create one first to gain some understanding of the nature of any potential relationship.

The simplest type of regression model is a linear relationship involving one independent variable, X, and one dependent variable, Y, as illustrated in Figure 5.2(a). We assume that for any given value of X, we have a distribution of values of Y—a population whose distribution is $f(Y|X)$ and whose mean is $E(Y|X) = \beta_0 + \beta_1 X$. Therefore, $E(Y|X) = \beta_0 + \beta_1 X$ represents the equation of a straight line (the **regression line**) through the means of these populations. Here, β_0 is the intercept of the line, that is, the

FIGURE 5.2   Illustration of a Regression Model

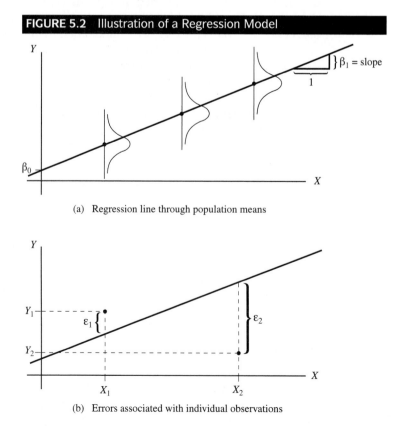

(a) Regression line through population means

(b) Errors associated with individual observations

value of Y when $X = 0$; and β_1 is the slope, which measures the change in Y as X is increased by 1. However, individual data points—samples from the distributions $f(Y|X)$—will not lie on this line; therefore, we must include an error term to characterize the individual data points in the regression model. The mathematical form of this model is

$$Y = \beta_0 + \beta_1 X + \varepsilon$$

where ε is an error term. This is illustrated in Figure 5.2(b). For example, suppose that one observation of the ith dependent variable is Y_i when the value of the independent variable is X_i. Then the error associated with this data point is

$$\varepsilon_i = Y_i - \beta_0 - \beta_1 X_i$$

The error is positive if the data point lies above the line, and negative if it is below. Another way of looking at this is that the error term ε_i represents the difference between the mean value of the dependent variable $(\beta_0 + \beta_1 X_i)$ and the actual value, Y_i, for a given value of X.

Least-Squares Estimation

Because we will only have sample data available, we must estimate the values of β_0 and β_1. Let us call these estimates b_0 and b_1, respectively. Then $\hat{Y} = b_0 + b_1 X$ represents the estimate of the population mean for any value of X within the range of the sample data. The best estimates of the population parameters are typically determined by choosing estimates b_0 and b_1 to minimize some function of the errors associated with all the data. The most common approach for doing this is called **least-squares regression,** which minimizes the sum of squares of the observed errors e_i:

$$\sum_{i=1}^{n} e_i^2 = \sum_{i=1}^{n}(Y_i - [b_0 + b_1 X_i])^2$$

Note that X_i and Y_i are the known observations and that b_0 and b_1 are unknowns. Using calculus, we can show that the solution that minimizes this function is

$$b_1 = \frac{\sum_{i=1}^{n} X_i Y_i - n\overline{X}\,\overline{Y}}{\sum_{i=1}^{n} X_i^2 - n\overline{X}^2}$$

$$b_0 = \overline{Y} - b_1 \overline{X}$$

Although these calculations appear to be somewhat complicated, they can easily be performed on an Excel spreadsheet. Fortunately, Excel has built-in capabilities to do this.

To illustrate simple linear regression, we will use the data in the worksheet *2000 NFL Data.xls*. We first create a scatter diagram for the data using the Excel *Chart Wizard* as described in Chapter 2 (see Figure 5.5). The data appear to have a linear relationship; therefore, simple linear regression would be appropriate. After the chart has been created and is selected (so that the *Chart* menu appears on the Excel menu bar), we apply the *Add Trendline* option (see the *Excel Note: Using the Add Trendline* option). This results in the least-squares regression line shown in Figure 5.6. The regression model is $\hat{Y} = 0.0854X - 108.59$ (Excel expresses the model as $Y = b_1 X + b_0$). Thus, the intercept, b_0, is -108.59 and the slope, b_1, is 0.0854. The slope tells us that for

EXCEL NOTE

USING THE ADD TRENDLINE OPTION

The *Add Trendline* option is selected from the *Chart* menu. The dialog box in Figure 5.3 is displayed, and you may choose among a linear and a variety of nonlinear functional forms to fit the data. Selecting an appropriate nonlinear form requires some advanced knowledge of functions and mathematics, so we will restrict our discussion to the linear case at this time. From the *Options* tab (see Figure 5.4), you may customize the name of the trendline, forecast forward or backward, set the intercept at a fixed value, and display the regression equation and *R*-squared value on the chart. The *R*-squared value will be described later in this chapter. Once Excel displays these results, you may move the equation and *R*-squared value for better readability by dragging them with a mouse. For the linear trendline option only, you may simply click on the data series in the chart to select the series, and then add a trendline by clicking on the right mouse button (try it!).

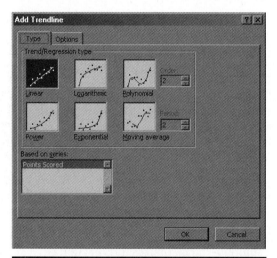

FIGURE 5.3 Add Trendline Dialog Box

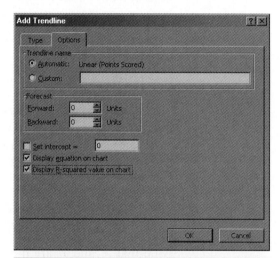

FIGURE 5.4 Options Tab in Add Trendline Dialog Box

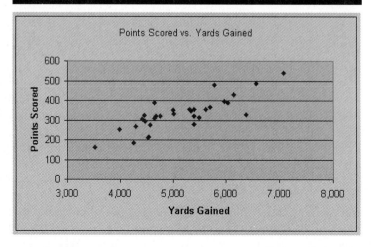

FIGURE 5.5 Scatter Plot of Points Scored Versus Yards Gained

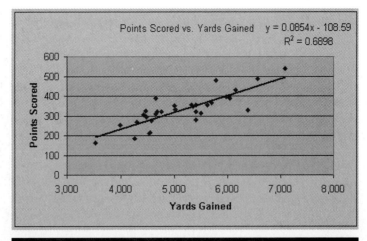

FIGURE 5.6   Scatter Plot with Added Trendline

every extra yard gained, the number of points scored increases by 0.0854. Thus, the model suggests that scoring an additional 10 points during the season would require $10/0.0854 = 117.1$ additional yards gained. The model can also be used to predict the number of points scored over the season. For example, if a team gains 6000 yards, the model predicts $\hat{Y}_{6000} = 0.0854(6000) - 108.59 = 403.81$ points scored. This can also be found by using the Excel function TREND(*known_Y's, known_X's, new_X's*). Thus, using the *2000 NFL Data.xls* worksheet, we would estimate $\hat{Y}_{6000} = $ TREND(F2:F32,B2:B32,6000) = 403.94 (difference due to rounding).

One point we should make is that it is dangerous to extrapolate a regression model outside the ranges covered by the observations. For instance, if you wanted to predict the number of points scored by a team that gains 8000 yards, the model would predict $\hat{Y}_{8000} = 0.0854(8000) - 108.59 = 574.61$. That may or may not be accurate, but because the regression model does not have any observations with approximately 8000 yards gained, you cannot be sure that a linear extrapolation will hold and should not use the model to make such predictions.

MEASURING VARIATION ABOUT THE REGRESSION LINE

The objective of regression analysis is to explain the variation of the dependent variable around its mean value as the independent variable changes. Figure 5.7 helps to understand this. In Figure 5.7(a), the independent variable has no effect; thus β_1 would be zero and the model would reduce to $Y = \beta_0 + \varepsilon$. In this case, the best estimate of the intercept β_0 would be the mean, $\overline{Y}$, and the variation between the observations and the estimate of the mean, $(Y - \overline{Y})$, is pure error. In Figure 5.7(b), we have the other extreme case in which all points lie on the regression line; that is, all of the variation in the data around the mean is explained by the independent variable. In this case, the error term is zero, and the value of each observation is equal to its predicted value: $\hat{Y} = b_0 + b_1 X$. Thus, the variation around the mean, $(Y - \overline{Y})$, is simply the variation from the regression line to the mean, $(\hat{Y} - \overline{Y})$. Finally, Figure 5.7(c) shows the typical case in which some of the variation is explained by the independent variable, while some is also due to error. The total variation from the mean, $(Y - \overline{Y})$, can be expressed as $(\hat{Y} - \overline{Y}) + (Y - \hat{Y})$. The first term represents the variation explained by regression, while the second represents the variation due to error.

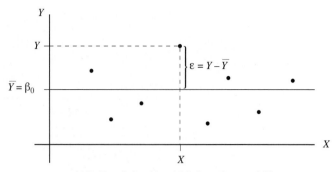

(a) No relationship with independent varriable

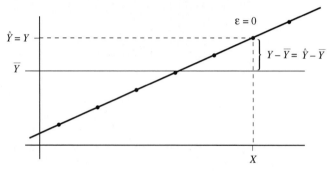

(b) Perfect relationship

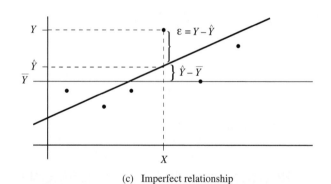

(c) Imperfect relationship

FIGURE 5.7 Illustrations of Variation in Regression

Because some points lie above the mean and others below it, we need to square the deviations from the mean to obtain a useful measure of the total variation in all the data; otherwise, they will sum to zero. The sums of squares of the deviations of individual observations from the mean, $\Sigma(Y_i - \overline{Y})^2$, is called the total sum of squares, or **SST.** Mathematically, this can be shown to equal $\Sigma(\hat{Y} - \overline{Y})^2 + \Sigma(Y - \hat{Y})^2$, which is simply the sums of squares of the variation explained by regression, called **SSR,** and the sum of squares of the errors, or unexplained variation, **SSE.** (Another term often used for errors is **residuals.**) In other words,

$$SST = SSR + SSE$$

| | (X) | (Y) | 0.0854(X)-108.59 | Sum of Squares Calculations for | | |
Team	Yards Gained	Points Scored	Estimate	SST	SSR	SSE
Tennessee	5,350	346	348.30	231.83	307.15	5.29
Baltimore	5,014	333	319.61	4.95	124.74	179.41
New York Giants	6,376	328	435.92	7.70	11055.72	11646.81
Oakland	5,776	479	384.68	21970.89	2905.88	8896.19
Minnesota	5,961	397	400.48	4385.86	4858.82	12.11
Philadelphia	5,006	351	318.92	409.08	140.47	1028.97
Denver	6,567	485	452.23	23785.60	14751.95	1073.75
Miami	4,461	323	272.38	60.44	3409.95	2562.45
Indianapolis	6,141	429	415.85	9648.31	7238.13	172.89
Tampa Bay	4,649	388	288.43	3274.79	1792.64	9913.27
St. Louis	7,075	540	495.62	43775.44	27172.49	1970.03
New Orleans	5,397	354	352.31	539.44	463.95	2.84
New York Jets	5,395	321	352.14	95.53	456.63	969.89
Pittsburgh	4,766	321	298.43	95.53	1046.38	509.57
Green Bay	5,321	353	345.82	493.99	226.48	51.50
Detroit	4,422	307	269.05	565.21	3810.02	1440.29
Washington	5,396	281	352.23	2477.47	460.28	5073.48
Buffalo	5,498	315	360.94	248.83	909.93	2110.41
Carolina	4,654	310	288.86	431.57	1756.67	446.83
Jacksonville	5,690	367	377.34	1312.31	2168.00	106.83
Kansas City	5,614	355	370.85	586.89	1605.72	251.08
Seattle	4,680	320	291.08	116.08	1575.47	836.25
San Francisco	6,040	388	407.23	3274.79	5844.88	369.64
Dallas	4,475	294	273.58	1352.34	3271.75	417.18
Chicago	4,541	216	279.21	13173.12	2658.72	3995.68
New England	4,571	276	281.77	3000.21	2401.08	33.33
Atlanta	3,994	252	232.50	6205.37	9658.29	380.34
Cincinnati	4,260	185	255.21	21250.12	5709.34	4930.01
Cleveland	3,530	161	192.87	28823.28	19017.01	1015.82
Arizona	4,528	210	278.10	14586.41	2774.44	4637.77
San Diego	4,300	269	258.63	3816.05	5204.78	107.54
	Average	330.7741935		209999.42	144777.77	65147.47
				SST	SSR	SSE

FIGURE 5.8   Sums of Squares Calculations

Figure 5.8 shows the calculations of these sums of squares on an Excel worksheet. You can see that this relationship holds, within errors due to rounding the coefficients of the regression model. Sums of squares are useful in explaining the strength of regression relationships, obtaining variance estimates, and performing hypothesis tests.

Coefficient of Determination and Correlation Coefficient

These sums of squares provide information about the strength of the regression relationship. Specifically, the ratio SSR/SST gives the proportion of variation that is explained by the independent variable of the regression model, and is called the **coefficient of determination, R^2.** The value of R^2 will be between 0 and 1. A value of 1.0 indicates a perfect fit, while a value of 0 indicates that no relationship exists. For the NFL data in Figure 5.6, we see that $R^2 = 0.6898$ (calculating SSR/SST from Figure 5.8 yields $144{,}777.77/209{,}999.42 = 0.6894$, with the difference due to rounding). The value of R^2 means that approximately 69 percent of the variation in the dependent variable, Points Scored, is explained by regression (i.e., the independent variable, Yards Gained). The remaining variation is due to other factors that were not included in the model. Although we would like high values of R^2, it is difficult to specify a "good" value that signifies a strong relationship, as this depends on the application. For example, in marketing research studies, an R^2 of 0.6 or more is considered very good, whereas in many social science applications even smaller values in the neighborhood of 0.3 are considered acceptable.

The square root of the coefficient of determination is the **sample correlation coefficient, R.** Values of R range from -1 to 1, where the sign is determined by the sign of the slope of the regression line. A correlation coefficient of $R = 1$ indicates perfect positive correlation; that is, as the independent variable increases, the dependent variable does also; $R = -1$ indicates perfect negative correlation — as X increases, Y decreases. As with R^2, a value of $R = 0$ indicates no correlation. Because R^2 measures the actual *proportion* of the variation explained by regression, it is generally easier to interpret than R.

Standard Error of the Estimate and Confidence Bands

In Chapter 4 we saw that sums of squares divided by their appropriate degrees of freedom provide estimates of variances, which we called mean squares. The sum of squares (SSE) has 2 degrees of freedom because we estimated two parameters of the regression line, the slope and intercept. Thus, MSE = SSE$/(n - 2)$ is the variance of the errors about the regression line. The square root of MSE is called **standard error of the estimate, S_{YX},** and is simply the standard deviation of the errors about the regression line. This is computed as

$$S_{YX} = \sqrt{\frac{\text{SSE}}{n - 2}}$$

Intuitively, S_{YX} measures the spread of the data about the regression line. If the data are clustered close to the regression line, then the standard error will be small. For the NFL data, MSE = 65,147.47/29 = 2246.46. Thus, $S_{YX} = 47.4$.

The standard error can be used to develop **confidence bands** around the regression line that are analogous to confidence intervals for point estimates. You might think of a confidence band as a collection of confidence intervals, one for each mean of the dependent variable. A $100(1 - \alpha)$ percent confidence band around the regression line is

$$\hat{Y} \pm t_{\alpha/2, n-2} S_{YX} \sqrt{h_i}$$

where $\hat{Y} = b_0 + b_1 X_i$ is the predicted mean of Y for a given value, X_i, of the independent variable, and

$$h_i = \frac{1}{n} + \frac{(X_i - \overline{X})^2}{\sum_{i=1}^{n} (X_i - \overline{X})^2}$$

From this formula you can see that h_i varies with the value of X; in particular, h_i will be larger for values of X farther away from its mean, implying that the confidence intervals will be wider and that more uncertainty exists about the true population mean. Figure 5.9 shows the confidence bands for the NFL data that illustrates this. The mean number of Yards Gained is 5143.5; values close to this correspond to the narrowest confidence intervals.

REGRESSION AS ANALYSIS OF VARIANCE

In Chapter 4 we introduced the concept of analysis of variance (ANOVA), which determines whether the variation due to a particular factor is significantly larger than that due to error. You may recall that ANOVA is based on computing sums of squares and associated mean square values and then conducting an *F*-test. ANOVA is commonly applied to regression to test for the significance of regression.

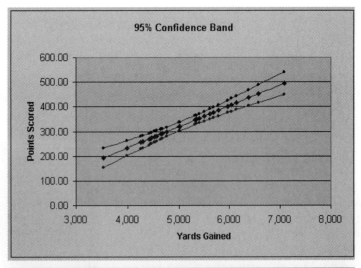

95% Confidence Band

FIGURE 5.9 Confidence Bands About the Regression Line

Significance of regression is simply a hypothesis test of whether the regression coefficient β_1 is zero:

H$_0$: $\beta_1 = 0$
H$_1$: $\beta_1 \neq 0$

As we discussed earlier, if $\beta_1 = 0$, then any variation about the mean is due to other factors that are not explained by the independent variable chosen for the model (in the NFL example, Yards Gained).

In examining the sums of squares for a simple linear regression model with one explanatory variable, we see that since we estimate the mean, the total sum of squares, SST, has $n - 1$ degrees of freedom. Because SSE has $n - 2$ degrees of freedom, the regression sum of squares, SSR, has $(n - 1) - (n - 2) = 1$ degree of freedom. Thus, MSR = SSR/1 represents the variance between observations explained by regression, while MSE = SSE/$(n - 2)$ represents the remaining variance. By dividing MSR by MSE, we obtain an *F*-statistic. For the NFL data, we have

$$F = \frac{\text{MSR}}{\text{MSE}} = \frac{144,777.77/1}{65,147.47/29} = 64.47$$

If this number is higher than the critical value from the *F*-distribution for a chosen level of significance, then we would reject the null hypothesis. Logically, if the null hypothesis is true, then SST = SSE, and SSR (and MSR) would be zero. Therefore, the smaller the *F*-ratio, the greater is the likelihood that H$_0$ is true. Likewise, the larger the *F*-ratio, the greater the likelihood is that $\beta_1 \neq 0$ and that the independent variable explains more of the variation in the data about the mean.

An alternative to using the *F*-test for testing for significance of regression is to use a *t*-test. Actually, this test allows you to test a hypothesis that the population slope is equal to any specified value, β_1, including zero. The *t*-statistic is

$$t = \frac{b_1 - \beta_1}{S_{YX}/\sqrt{\sum_{i=1}^{n}(X_i - \overline{X})^2}}$$

EXCEL NOTE

USING THE REGRESSION TOOL

From the *Tools* menu, select *Data Analysis* and the *Regression* tool. The dialog box shown in Figure 5.10 is displayed. In the box for the *Input Y Range,* specify the range of the dependent variable values. In the box for the *Input X Range,* specify the range for the independent variable values. Check *Labels* if your data range contains a descriptive label. You have the option of forcing the intercept to zero by checking *Constant is Zero;* however, you will usually not check this box, as adding an intercept term allows a better fit to the data. You also can set a *Confidence Level* (the default of 95 percent is commonly used) to provide confidence intervals for the intercept and slope parameters. In the *Residuals* section, you have the option of including a residuals output table by checking *Residuals, Standardized Residuals, Residual Plots,* and *Line Fit Plots.* The *Residual Plots* generates a chart for each independent variable versus the residual, and the *Line Fit Plots* generates a chart for

predicted versus observed values. Finally, you may also choose to have Excel construct a normal probability plot (see Chapter 4) for the dependent variable.

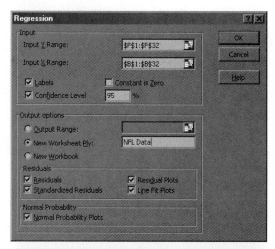

FIGURE 5.10 Excel Dialog Box for Regression Tool

The denominator is simply the standard error of the slope. This statistic has $n - 2$ degrees of freedom. To test for significance of regression, set β_1 to zero. In our example, $b_1 = 0.0854$, $S_{YX} = 47.4$, and $\sum_{i=1}^{n}(X_i - \overline{X})^2 = 19{,}851{,}119.74$. Then the t-statistic is

$$t = \frac{0.0854}{47.4/\sqrt{19{,}851{,}119.74}} = \frac{0.0854}{0.0106} = 8.03$$

Using a 5 percent significance level, the critical value for t with $n - 2 = 29$ degrees of freedom is 2.0452; therefore, we reject the null hypothesis that $\beta_1 = 0$.

The *Data Analysis Regression* tool provides all the information to perform these tests (see the *Excel Note: Using the Regression Tool*). The summary output from the *Regression* tool is shown in Figure 5.11. In the *Regression Statistics* section are the correlation coefficient (called *Multiple R*), R^2, Adjusted R^2, standard error, and the sample size. The **Adjusted R^2** is a statistic that incorporates the sample size and the number of explanatory variables in the model and is computed as

$$R_{\text{adj}}^2 = 1 - \left[(1 - R^2)\frac{n - 1}{n - 2}\right]$$

While it does not give the actual percent of variation explained by the model as R^2 does, it is useful when comparing this model with other models that include additional

	A	B	C	D	E	F	G
1	SUMMARY OUTPUT						
2							
3	*Regression Statistics*						
4	Multiple R	0.8305					
5	R Square	0.6898					
6	Adjusted R Square	0.6791					
7	Standard Error	47.3967					
8	Observations	31					
9							
10	ANOVA						
11		*df*	*SS*	*MS*	*F*	*Significance F*	
12	Regression	1	144852.3426	144852.3426	64.4805	0.0000	
13	Residual	29	65147.0768	2246.4509			
14	Total	30	209999.4194				
15							
16		*Coefficients*	*Standard Error*	*t Stat*	*P-value*	*Lower 95%*	*Upper 95%*
17	Intercept	-108.5930	55.3741	-1.9611	0.0595	-221.8459	4.6598
18	Yards Gained	0.0854	0.0106	8.0300	0.0000	0.0637	0.1072

FIGURE 5.11 Regression Output for NFL Data

explanatory variables. We will discuss it more fully in the context of multiple linear regression later in this chapter.

The *ANOVA* section presents the results of the analysis of variance. The sum of squares, mean squares, and *F*-statistic are computed. The *Significance F* measure is the *p*-value for the *F*-test and represents the probability of wrongfully concluding that the independent variable does significantly explain the variation in the dependent variable about the mean. In this example, the *p*-value is zero (to within 4 decimal places) and would lead us to conclude that Yards Gained does indeed explain a significant amount of the variation in Points Scored.

Finally, the last section presents the estimated regression coefficients of the model, their standard errors, a *t*-statistic, the *p*-value, and confidence interval limits for the coefficients. Thus, from the Coefficients column, we read the regression model as $\hat{Y} = 0.0854X - 108.593$. The standard errors are associated with the intercept and independent variable. The *t*-statistics are associated with hypothesis tests of the individual regression coefficients, specifically to test the null hypothesis that the parameters are zero. Usually, it makes little sense to test or interpret the hypothesis that $\beta_0 = 0$, unless the intercept has a significant physical meaning in the context of the application. The result for Yards Gained confirms the *t*-test for β_1 that we conducted earlier. Note that the standard error of $b_1 = 0.0106$ and is the same as the denominator in the *t*-statistic computed earlier. Again, the small *p*-value leads us to reject the null hypotheses that the slope is zero. Note that the *p*-value associated with the slope is equal to the *Significance F* value. This will always be true for a regression model with one independent variable, because it is the only explanatory variable.

The residual output is shown in Figure 5.12. The residuals are simply the deviations between the model's prediction and the actual value for each observation, $e_i = Y_i - \hat{Y}_i$. These are shown graphically in the *Residual Plot* (Figure 5.13). Standardized residuals are residuals divided by the standard error S_{YX} (in this example, 47.3967) and describe how far each residual is from its mean in units of standard deviations (similar to a *z*-value for a standard normal distribution). Standardized residuals are useful in checking assumptions underlying regression analysis, which we will address in the next section.

The regression tool also provides a *Line Fit Plot* (Figure 5.14), which is essentially a scatter diagram with the values predicted by the regression model included (no

	A	B	C	D
22	RESIDUAL OUTPUT			
23				
24	*Observation*	*Predicted Points Scored*	*Residuals*	*Standard Residuals*
25	1.0000	348.4152	-2.4152	-0.0518
26	2.0000	319.7134	13.2866	0.2851
27	3.0000	436.0583	-108.0583	-2.3188
28	4.0000	384.8051	94.1949	2.0213
29	5.0000	400.6081	-3.6081	-0.0774
30	6.0000	319.0300	31.9700	0.6860
31	7.0000	452.3739	32.6261	0.7001
32	8.0000	272.4750	50.5250	1.0842
33	9.0000	415.9841	13.0159	0.2793
34	10.0000	288.5343	99.4657	2.1345
35	11.0000	495.7684	44.2316	0.9492
36	12.0000	352.4301	1.5699	0.0337
37	13.0000	352.2592	-31.2592	-0.6708
38	14.0000	298.5287	22.4713	0.4822
39	15.0000	345.9380	7.0620	0.1515
40	16.0000	269.1435	37.8565	0.8124
41	17.0000	352.3447	-71.3447	-1.5310
42	18.0000	361.0577	-46.0577	-0.9884
43	19.0000	288.9615	21.0385	0.4515
44	20.0000	377.4588	-10.4588	-0.2244
45	21.0000	370.9667	-15.9667	-0.3426
46	22.0000	291.1824	28.8176	0.6184
47	23.0000	407.3565	-19.3565	-0.4154
48	24.0000	273.6709	20.3291	0.4362
49	25.0000	279.3088	-63.3088	-1.3586
50	26.0000	281.8714	-5.8714	-0.1260
51	27.0000	232.5829	19.4171	0.4167
52	28.0000	255.3051	-70.3051	-1.5087
53	29.0000	192.9470	-31.9470	-0.6856
54	30.0000	278.1983	-68.1983	-1.4635
55	31.0000	258.7220	10.2780	0.2206

FIGURE 5.12 Residual Output from Regression Tool

FIGURE 5.13 Residual Plot

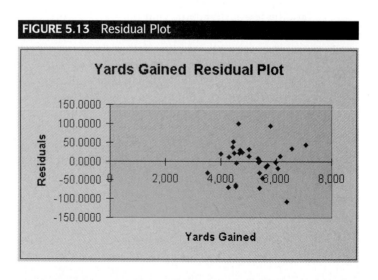

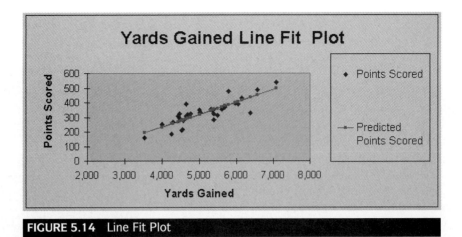

FIGURE 5.14   Line Fit Plot

different from the chart obtained using the *Add Trendline* option) and a normal probability plot (Figure 5.15) for the dependent variable.

PHStat also provides a tool for simple linear regression that provides output similar to the Excel regression tool (see the *PHStat Note: Simple Linear Regression*). The basic output is identical to that produced by the Excel *Regression* tool. In addition, *PHStat* provides confidence and prediction intervals for a specified value of X. This is shown in Figure 5.17 for $X = 6000$ in the NFL example. The confidence interval for the mean of Y when $X = 6000$ is [378.437, 429.442], and represents a "slice" of the confidence band shown in Figure 5.9. The prediction interval is a probability interval for an individual value of Y (not a population parameter) when X is specified. Thus, when $X = 6000$, a 95 percent prediction interval is [303.704, 504.175]. Note that the prediction interval is wider than the confidence interval, because the confidence interval is based on the sampling distribution of the mean, which has a smaller variance (standard error).

FIGURE 5.15   Normal Probability Plot

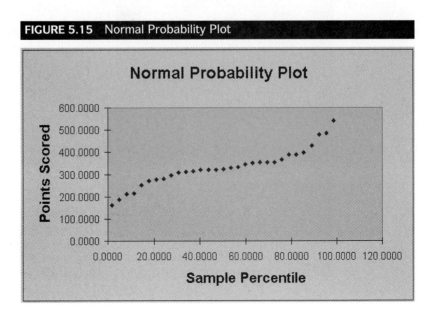

PHSTAT NOTE

SIMPLE LINEAR REGRESSION

From the *PHStat* menu, select *Regression* and then *Simple Linear Regression*. Figure 5.16 shows the dialog box. In the *Data* section, you provide the ranges of the dependent and independent variables. Output options include regression statistics and ANOVA calculations, a residuals table (however, this tool does not compute standardized residuals), and a residuals plot (similar to Figures 5.11–5.13). *PHStat* also provides a scatter diagram of the data, the Durbin–Watson statistic (discussed in the next section), and confidence and prediction intervals for a specified value of the independent variable.

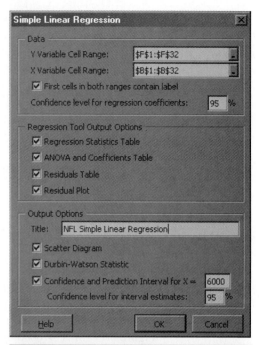

FIGURE 5.16   *PHStat* Dialog Box for Regression

	A	B
1	**Confidence Interval Estimate**	
2		
3	**Data**	
4	**X Value**	**6000**
5	**Confidence Level**	**95%**
6		
7	Intermediate Calculations	
8	Sample Size	31
9	Degrees of Freedom	29
10	t Value	2.045231
11	Sample Mean	5143.484
12	Sum of Squared Difference	19851120
13	Standard Error of the Estimate	47.39674
14	h Statistic	0.069214
15	Average Predicted Y (YHat)	403.9396
16		
17	**For Average Predicted Y (YHat)**	
18	Interval Half Width	25.50282
19	**Confidence Interval Lower Limit**	**378.437**
20	**Confidence Interval Upper Limit**	**429.442**
21		
22	**For Individual Response Y**	
23	Interval Half Width	100.2359
24	**Prediction Interval Lower Limit**	**303.704**
25	**Prediction Interval Upper Limit**	**504.175**

FIGURE 5.17   *PHStat* Output for Confidence and Prediction Interval Estimation

ASSUMPTIONS OF REGRESSION ANALYSIS

Regression analysis is predicated on some key assumptions about the data. Clearly, the first assumption is linearity. This is usually checked by examining a scatter diagram of the data or examining the residual plot. If the model is appropriate, then the residuals should appear to be randomly scattered about zero, with no apparent pattern. If the residuals exhibit some well-defined pattern, such as a linear trend, a U-shape, and so on, then there is good evidence that some other functional form might better fit the data. We saw that a scatter diagram of the NFL data appeared to be linear; looking at the residual plot in Figure 5.13 also confirms no pattern in the residuals.

The next key assumption is that the errors for each individual value of X are normally distributed, with a mean of zero and a constant variance. This can be verified by examining a histogram of the residuals associated with each value of the independent variable and inspecting for a bell-shaped distribution or using more formal goodness-of-fit tests as described in Chapter 4. Figure 5.18 shows a histogram of the residuals for the NFL data, which appear to satisfy this assumption.

The third assumption is **homoscedasticity,** which means that the variation about the regression line is constant for all values of the independent variable. This can also be evaluated by examining the residual plot and looking for large differences in the variances at different values of the independent variable. In Figure 5.13, we see no serious differences in the spread of the data for different values of Yards Gained, so this assumption is verified.

Finally, residuals should be independent for each value of the independent variable. For cross-sectional data, this assumption is usually not a problem. However, when time is the independent variable, this is an important assumption. If successive observations appear to be correlated—for example, by becoming larger over time or exhibiting a cyclical type of pattern—then this assumption is violated. Correlation among successive observations over time is called **autocorrelation** and can be identified by residual plots having clusters of residuals with the same sign. Autocorrelation

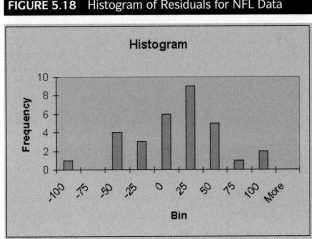

FIGURE 5.18   Histogram of Residuals for NFL Data

can be evaluated more formally using a statistical test based on the **Durbin–Watson statistic.** The Durbin–Watson statistic is

$$D = \frac{\sum\limits_{i=2}^{n}(e_i - e_{i-1})^2}{\sum\limits_{i=1}^{n}e_i^2}$$

This is a ratio of the squared differences in successive residuals to the sum of the squares of all residuals. D will range from 0 to 4. When successive residuals are positively auto-correlated, D will approach 0. Critical values of the statistic have been tabulated based on the sample size and number of independent variables that allow you to conclude that there is either evidence of autocorrelation, no evidence of autocorrelation, or the test is inconclusive. *PHStat* computes the Durbin–Watson statistic, and for most practical purposes, values below 1 suggest autocorrelation; values above 1.5 and below 2.5 suggest no autocorrelation; and values above 2.5 suggest negative autocorrelation.

When assumptions of regression are violated, then statistical inferences drawn from ANOVA may not be valid. Thus, before drawing inferences about regression models and performing hypothesis tests, these assumptions should be checked.

APPLICATION OF REGRESSION ANALYSIS TO INVESTMENT RISK

Investing in the stock market is highly attractive to everyone. However, stock investments do carry an element of risk. Risk associated with an individual stock can be measured in two ways. The first is **systematic risk,** which is the variation in stock price explained by the market—as the market moves up or down, the stock tends to move in the same direction. The Standard & Poor's 500 index is most commonly used as a measure of the market. For example, we generally see that stocks of consumer products companies are highly correlated with the S&P index, while utility stocks generally show less correlation with the market. The second type of risk is called **specific risk** and is the variation that is due to other factors, such as the earnings potential of the firm, acquisition strategies, and so on. Specific risk is measured by the standard error of the estimate.

Systematic risk is characterized by a measure called *beta*. A beta value equal to 1.0 means that the specific stock will match market movements, a beta less than 1.0 indicates that the stock is less volatile than the market, and a beta greater than 1.0 indicates that the stock has greater variance than the market. Thus, stocks with large betas are riskier than those with lower beta values. Beta values can be calculated by developing a regression model of a particular stock's returns (the dependent variable) against the average market returns (the independent variable). The slope of the regression line is the beta risk. This can be explained through the graph in Figure 5.19. If we plot the market returns against the returns of the individual stock and find the regression line, we would observe that if the slope equals 1, the stock changes at the same rate as the market. However, if the stock price changes are less than the market changes, the slope of the regression line would be less than 1, while the slope would be greater than 1 when the stock price changes exceed that of the market. A negative slope would indicate a stock that moves in the opposite direction to the market (e.g., if the market goes up, the stock price goes down).

Table 5.2 shows hypothetical daily stock prices and S&P 500 indexes over a six-month period. Figure 5.20 shows a scatter diagram of the S&P 500 performance and the stock performance. You can see that a correlation appears to exist.

The percentage change from one day to the next for both the S&P 500 index and stock price provides the data for the regression model. For example, the percentage

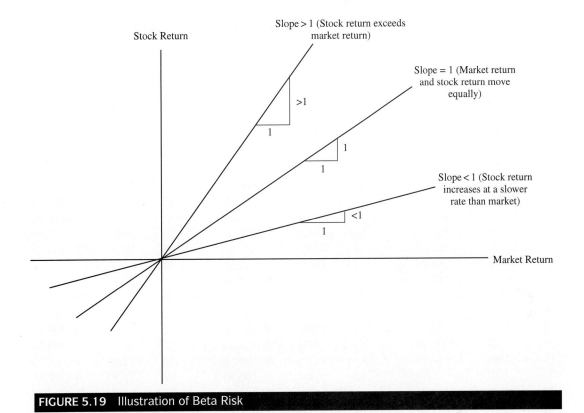

FIGURE 5.19   Illustration of Beta Risk

FIGURE 5.20   Scatter Diagram of Stock Price and S&P 500 Index

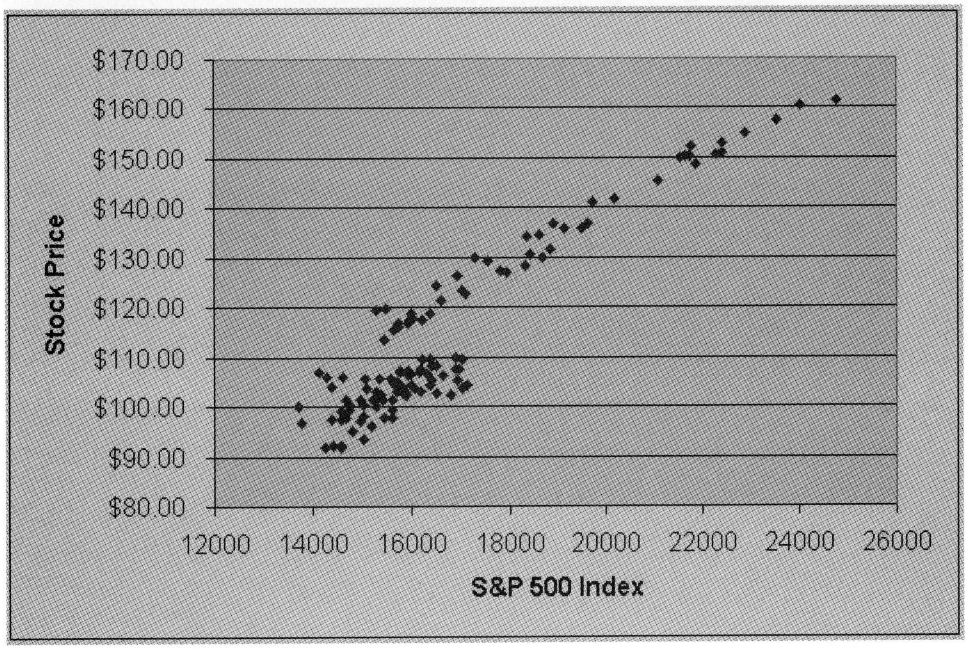

TABLE 5.2 Hypothetical Stock and S&P 500 Prices

Day	S&P500	Stock Price	Day	S&P500	Stock Price	Day	S&P500	Stock Price
1	15300	$ 100.00	43	14686	$ 101.40	85	16006	$ 118.80
2	15438	$ 101.50	44	16518	$ 108.20	86	16013	$ 118.70
3	15867	$ 102.50	45	16158	$ 107.00	87	15967	$ 117.30
4	14984	$ 97.10	46	15727	$ 104.90	88	16629	$ 121.30
5	15468	$ 97.70	47	13783	$ 96.60	89	17945	$ 127.10
6	15608	$ 99.50	48	16219	$ 107.70	90	17042	$ 123.20
7	16218	$ 103.10	49	15598	$ 105.60	91	15750	$ 116.90
8	16386	$ 104.40	50	15939	$ 106.30	92	16042	$ 117.70
9	16949	$ 105.20	51	15811	$ 103.20	93	16397	$ 118.60
10	16805	$ 102.50	52	14742	$ 99.50	94	17102	$ 122.80
11	17037	$ 103.70	53	15890	$ 102.90	95	17829	$ 127.40
12	17154	$ 104.40	54	15634	$ 101.50	96	19502	$ 135.80
13	17143	$ 104.20	55	15225	$ 101.30	97	19155	$ 136.00
14	16528	$ 102.70	56	15906	$ 102.50	98	20184	$ 141.80
15	15631	$ 97.80	57	14394	$ 97.30	99	21084	$ 145.50
16	14413	$ 92.00	58	14681	$ 97.80	100	21863	$ 148.80
17	15053	$ 93.60	59	15293	$ 103.00	101	21627	$ 150.40
18	14585	$ 92.20	60	14971	$ 101.20	102	21744	$ 150.40
19	14599	$ 91.70	61	14576	$ 99.20	103	22295	$ 150.50
20	14259	$ 91.90	62	15028	$ 100.30	104	24767	$ 161.40
21	14805	$ 95.00	63	15716	$ 102.90	105	24041	$ 160.40
22	15214	$ 96.00	64	16437	$ 108.20	106	22401	$ 153.00
23	15207	$ 96.10	65	15797	$ 104.40	107	22395	$ 150.90
24	15048	$ 98.10	66	16318	$ 106.70	108	22888	$ 154.90
25	14599	$ 97.30	67	16909	$ 110.00	109	23556	$ 157.60
26	15803	$ 102.90	68	15998	$ 106.60	110	21772	$ 152.40
27	15382	$ 102.40	69	15957	$ 107.10	111	21539	$ 150.00
28	14747	$ 100.30	70	15374	$ 105.70	112	19741	$ 141.10
29	16009	$ 104.20	71	15788	$ 106.90	113	18385	$ 134.10
30	16903	$ 107.60	72	15797	$ 107.30	114	18918	$ 136.70
31	16433	$ 105.40	73	16223	$ 109.70	115	18637	$ 134.60
32	15259	$ 101.40	74	15085	$ 105.50	116	19628	$ 136.70
33	15398	$ 101.70	75	14390	$ 104.00	117	18329	$ 128.40
34	16966	$ 107.60	76	13717	$ 100.00	118	18843	$ 131.70
35	16070	$ 103.60	77	14607	$ 105.80	119	18678	$ 130.00
36	16656	$ 106.30	78	14286	$ 105.90	120	18428	$ 130.70
37	15823	$ 104.00	79	14137	$ 107.00	121	17567	$ 129.20
38	17050	$ 109.60	80	15450	$ 113.60	122	16941	$ 126.30
39	15646	$ 104.60	81	15746	$ 116.10	123	15292	$ 119.50
40	16391	$ 109.50	82	16228	$ 117.50	124	15491	$ 119.70
41	15768	$ 107.30	83	15665	$ 115.40	125	16514	$ 124.20
42	15102	$ 103.60	84	15938	$ 116.90	126	17318	$ 130.00

	A	B	C	D	E	F	G
1	SUMMARY OUTPUT						
2							
3	*Regression Statistics*						
4	Multiple R	0.950684862					
5	R Square	0.903801707					
6	Adjusted R Square	0.903019607					
7	Standard Error	0.010344035					
8	Observations	125					
9							
10	ANOVA						
11		*df*	*SS*	*MS*	*F*	*Significance F*	
12	Regression	1	0.123649065	0.123649065	1155.608964	2.20035E-64	
13	Residual	123	0.013160884	0.000106999			
14	Total	124	0.136809949				
15							
16		*Coefficients*	*Standard Error*	*t Stat*	*P-value*	*Lower 95%*	*Upper 95%*
17	Intercept	0.001239606	0.000926122	1.338490995	0.183205299	-0.000593595	0.003072807
18	X Variable 1	0.621240016	0.018274856	33.99424899	2.20035E-64	0.585066073	0.65741396

FIGURE 5.21   Regression Results for Evaluating Beta Risk

change in the S&P 500 index from day 1 to day 2 is $(15{,}438 - 15{,}300)/15{,}300 = 0.90$ percent. After calculating these daily changes, Figure 5.21 shows the results of applying the *Regression* tool from Excel to the model

$$\text{Daily Change in Stock Price} = \beta_0 + \beta_1 \text{ S\&P Change}$$

The resulting model is

$$\text{Daily Change in Stock Price} = 0.00124 + 0.62124 \text{ S\&P Change}$$

The R^2 value of 0.90 shows that a large percentage of the variation is explained by the model.

The slope of the regression line, β_1—the beta risk of the stock—is 0.62. This indicates that the stock is less risky than the average S&P 500 stock.

MULTIPLE LINEAR REGRESSION

In the 2000 NFL data, it would be logical to suspect that the number of Games Won would depend not only on Yards Gained but also on the other variables—Takeaways, Giveaways, Yards Allowed, and Points Scored. Thus, we might be interested in determining a statistical relationship between the number of Games Won and the other variables to determine which of these are significant factors in winning. A regression model with more than one independent variable is called a **multiple regression** model. If all terms in the model are linear, we have a **multiple linear regression** model. Simple linear regression is just a special case of multiple linear regression.

Multiple regression has been effectively used in many business applications. Kimes and Fitzsimmons[1] developed a model for La Quinta Motor Inns to evaluate proposed sites for new motels. This model had 35 variables that included 6 variables about competition, 18 variables about demand, 3 demographic variables,

---

[1] S. E. Kimes and J. A. Fitzsimmons, "Selecting Profitable Hotel Sites at La Quinta Motor Inns," *Interfaces*, Vol. 19, No. 6, 1990, pp. 83–94.

4 market-related variables, and 4 physical variables. The characteristics of each proposed site could be entered into a spreadsheet containing the regression model and evaluated immediately.

A multiple linear regression model has the form

$$Y = \beta_0 + \beta_1 X_1 + \beta_2 X_2 + \cdots + \beta_k X_k + \varepsilon$$

where

Y is the dependent variable
$X_1 \ldots X_k$ are the independent (explanatory) variables
β_0 is the intercept term
$\beta_1 \ldots \beta_k$ are the regression coefficients for the independent variables
ε is the error term

For the NFL example, we would have five independent variables, so the model is

$$\text{Games Won} = \beta_0 + \beta_1 \text{ Yards Gained} + \beta_2 \text{ Takeaways} + \beta_3 \text{ Giveaways} + \beta_4 \text{ Yards Allowed} + \beta_5 \text{ Points Scored} + \varepsilon$$

Similar to the simple linear regression case, we estimate the regression coefficients—called **partial regression coefficients**—as $b_0, b_1, b_2, \ldots, b_k$, and then use them to predict the value of the dependent variable using the model

$$\hat{Y} = b_0 + b_1 X_1 + b_2 X_2 + \cdots + b_k X_k$$

The partial regression coefficients represent the expected change in the dependent variable when the associated independent variable is increased by one unit *while the values of all other independent variables are held constant.* Thus, b_2 would represent an estimate of the change in Games Won for a unit increase in Takeaways while holding all other variables constant.

As with simple linear regression, multiple linear regression uses least squares to estimate the intercept and slope coefficients that minimize the sum of squared error terms over all observations. The principal assumptions discussed for simple linear regression also hold here. The *Data Analysis Regression* tool in Excel or the *PHStat Multiple Regression* tool provide the ability to perform multiple linear regression; you need only specify the full range for the independent variable data.

The output for the NFL model is shown in Figure 5.22. From Figure 5.22, we see that the model is

$$\text{Games Won} = 8.29 + 0.00074 \text{ Yards Gained} + 0.1001 \text{ Takeaways} - 0.0839 \text{ Giveaways} - 0.0018 \text{ Yards Allowed} + 0.0138 \text{ Points Scored}$$

The signs of the coefficients make sense; increasing the Giveaways and Yards Allowed should result in fewer Games Won. The model might be used to estimate performance based on estimates of the variables midway through the season. For instance, a team that is estimated to gain 5200 yards, have 25 Takeaways, give up the ball 30 times, allow 5400 yards, and score 310 points would be predicted to win

$$8.29 + 0.00074 (5200) + 0.1001 (25) - 0.0839 (30) - 0.0018 (5400) + 0.0138 (310) = 6.68$$

or approximately 6–7 games. As with simple linear regression, the model should only be used for values of the independent variables within the range of the data.

	A	B	C	D	E	F	G
1	SUMMARY OUTPUT						
2							
3	*Regression Statistics*						
4	Multiple R	0.882527379					
5	R Square	0.778854575					
6	Adjusted R Square	0.734625491					
7	Standard Error	1.623592763					
8	Observations	31					
9							
10	ANOVA						
11		*df*	*SS*	*MS*	*F*	*Significance F*	
12	Regression	5	232.0986635	46.4197327	17.60955664	1.74951E-07	
13	Residual	25	65.9013365	2.63605346			
14	Total	30	298				
15							
16		*Coefficients*	*Standard Error*	*t Stat*	*P-value*	*Lower 95%*	*Upper 95%*
17	Intercept	8.292400914	5.555722027	1.492587439	0.148058568	-3.149814772	19.7346166
18	Yards Gained	0.00074124	0.00075398	0.983103134	0.33497591	-0.000811609	0.002294089
19	Takeaways	0.100133243	0.050895822	1.967415771	0.060324999	-0.004688591	0.204955078
20	Giveaways	-0.083653196	0.047123903	-1.779419572	0.087332715	-0.180906624	0.013200232
21	Yards Allowed	-0.001794503	0.000649291	-2.763789193	0.010568613	-0.003131741	-0.000457264
22	Points Scored	0.013836179	0.007671661	1.803544216	0.083368302	-0.001963891	0.029636249

FIGURE 5.22   Multiple Linear Regression Results for NFL Data

Interpreting Results from Multiple Linear Regression

The results from the *Regression* tool are in the same format as we saw for simple linear regression. *Multiple R,* the **multiple correlation coefficient,** and *R Square,* the **coefficient of multiple determination,** indicate the strength of association between the dependent and independent variables. The relatively high value of R^2 (0.78) indicates that a large percentage of the variation in the dependent variable is explained by these independent variables.

The ANOVA section in Figure 5.22 tests for significance of the entire model. That is, it computes an *F*-statistic for testing the hypotheses

$$H_0: \beta_1 = \beta_2 = \cdots = \beta_k = 0$$
$$H_1: \text{at least one } \beta_j \text{ is not 0}$$

The null hypothesis states that no linear relationship exists between the dependent and any of the independent variables, while the alternative hypothesis states that the dependent variable has a linear relationship with at least one independent variable. It cannot conclude that a relationship exists with every independent variable individually. The test is identical to the simple linear regression case. The *F*-statistic is computed as MSR/MSE, except that it has k and $n - k - 1$ degrees of freedom. At a 5 percent significance level, we reject the null hypothesis because *Significance F* is essentially zero. The residual plots in Figure 5.23 do not exhibit any serious abnormalities, considering the relatively small sample size, suggesting that the assumptions of regression hold.

The last section in Figure 5.22 provides information to test hypotheses on individual regression coefficients, which define the marginal contributions of each independent variable in the model. For example, to test the hypothesis that the population slope β_1 (associated with Yards Gained) is zero, we compute a *t*-statistic by dividing b_1 (0.00074124) by its standard error (0.00075398), which equals 0.9831, as shown in column D. This statistic has $n - k - 1$ degrees of freedom, or in this case, $31 - 5 - 1 = 25$. From the *t*-table in Appendix A.3, we find $t_{25, 0.025} = 2.0595$. Therefore, we cannot reject the null hypothesis at the 0.05 significance level. This conclusion may also be drawn by examining the *p*-value in the next column of the results, which is 0.33 and is larger than

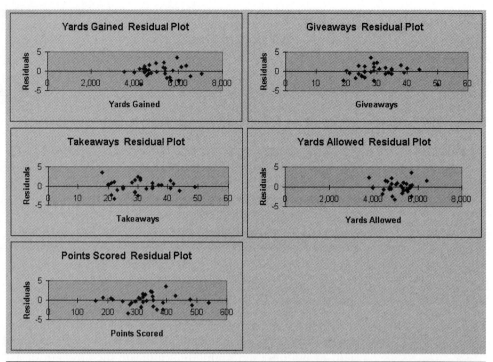

FIGURE 5.23 Residual Plots for Multiple Regression

0.05. We may also use this information to compute confidence intervals for slope coefficients. A confidence interval for β_j would be:

$$b_j \pm t_{n-k-1} \text{ s.e.}$$

where s.e. is the standard error. You may also observe that the 95 percent confidence interval for β_1 includes zero. Thus, it would appear that Yards Gained is not a significant factor in predicting the number of Games Won.

From the p-values, we also see that at a 0.05 significance level, only the coefficient for Yards Allowed is statistically different from zero. This leads to the question of how to build good regression models that include the "right" set of variables.

BUILDING GOOD REGRESSION MODELS

A good regression model should include only significant independent variables. A simple approach is to simply experiment with different models. For example, suppose we drop Yards Gained from the model. The multiple regression model and results are shown in Figure 5.24. We see that R^2 has dropped only slightly and that the overall model is significant. However, we also see now from the p-values that both Yards Allowed and Points Scored are significant variables in this model. Therefore, it is not always clear exactly what will happen when we add or remove variables from a model; variables that are (or are not) significant in one model may (or may not) be significant in another. This suggests that a more structured approach is necessary in building useful multiple regression models.

	A	B	C	D	E	F	G
1	SUMMARY OUTPUT						
2							
3	*Regression Statistics*						
4	Multiple R	0.877670306					
5	R Square	0.770305166					
6	Adjusted R Square	0.734967499					
7	Standard Error	1.6225462					
8	Observations	31					
9							
10	ANOVA						
11		*df*	*SS*	*MS*	*F*	*Significance F*	
12	Regression	4	229.5509395	57.38773488	21.79841617	5.45644E-08	
13	Residual	26	68.44906048	2.632656172			
14	Total	30	298				
15							
16		*Coefficients*	*Standard Error*	*t Stat*	*P-value*	*Lower 95%*	*Upper 95%*
17	Intercept	11.93568795	4.13645186	2.885489388	0.007757264	3.433083806	20.43829209
18	Takeaways	0.075789982	0.044437562	1.705538716	0.100014949	-0.015552794	0.167132759
19	Giveaways	-0.089006445	0.046801272	-1.901795423	0.068332866	-0.185207901	0.007195011
20	Yards Allowed	-0.00200648	0.000612048	-3.27830442	0.00296506	-0.003264564	-0.000748396
21	Points Scored	0.020310181	0.003933014	5.16402509	2.18069E-05	0.012225751	0.028394612

FIGURE 5.24   Multiple Regression Results After Dropping Yards Gained

Using Adjusted R^2 to Evaluate Fit

A useful way of examining the relative fit of different models is through the Adjusted R^2. Adding an independent variable to a regression model will always result in R^2 equal to or greater than the R^2 of the original model. This is true even when the new independent variable has little true relationship with the dependent variable. Adjusted R^2, which we introduced earlier in the context of simple linear regression, reflects both the number of independent variables and the sample size. This helps to better understand the value of adding independent variables to the model. Adjusted R^2 for a multiple linear regression model is computed as

$$\text{Adjusted } R^2 = 1 - \frac{\text{SSE}}{\text{SST}}\left(\frac{n-1}{n-k-1}\right)$$

where

SSE = sum of squared errors (residuals)
SST = total sum of squares
  n = number of observations
  k = number of independent variables

Essentially, the adjustment term $(n - 1)/(n - k - 1)$ represents the ratio of the degrees of freedom of SSE and SST. For the NFL data with all five independent variables, we have

$$\text{Adjusted } R^2 = 1 - \frac{65.901}{298}\left(\frac{30}{25}\right) = 0.7346$$

For the regression model after dropping Yards Gained (Figure 5.24), the Adjusted R^2 is 0.7350. Note that while *R Square* decreased from 0.7789 to 0.7703 by dropping Yards Gained from the model, the *Adjusted R^2* actually increased very slightly, to 0.7350, indicating a better model. Thus, the Adjusted R^2 provides a way to evaluate the effect of adding or removing variables to or from a model.

From a practical perspective, the independent variables selected should make some sense in attempting to explain the dependent variable (i.e., you should have some reason to believe that changes in the independent variable will cause changes in the dependent variable even though causation cannot be proven statistically). From a statistical viewpoint, it is best to have as simple a model as possible — an age-old principle known as **parsimony** — with the fewest number of explanatory variables that will provide an adequate interpretation of the dependent variable. One approach to constructing a good model is to collect data on as many candidate independent variables as possible (plus, of course, the dependent variable) and then try to eliminate those that have little effect on the dependent variable. This can be viewed as an effort to obtain *model efficiency*. The modern use of statistics, however, makes model efficiency much less important. Two common approaches to building useful regression models are *best subsets* and *stepwise regression*.

Best-Subsets Regression

Best-subsets regression evaluates either all possible regression models for a set of independent variables or the best subsets of models for a fixed number of independent variables. *PHStat* includes a useful tool for performing best-subsets regression (see the *PHStat Note: Best-Subsets Regression*). Figure 5.25 shows the *PHStat* output for the *2000 NFL Data* example. The Adjusted R^2 is typically used to compare models. We

FIGURE 5.25   *PHStat* Best-Subsets Regression Results

	A	B	C	D	E	F	G
1	Best Subsets for 2000 NFL Data						
2							
3	Intermediate Calculations						
4	$R2T$	0.778855					
5	1 - $R2T$	0.221145					
6	n	31					
7	T	6					
8	n - T	25					
9							Consider
10	Model	Cp	k	R Square	Adj. R Square	Std. Error	This Model?
11	X1	45.14908	2	0.361782	0.339774983	2.560905	No
12	X1X2	12.87506	3	0.664964	0.641033049	1.888316	No
13	X1X2X3	10.3705	4	0.704811	0.672011868	1.804997	No
14	X1X2X3X4	7.252772	5	0.750081	0.711632098	1.69247	No
15	X1X2X3X4X5	6	6	0.778855	0.734625491	1.623593	Yes
16	X1X2X3X5	11.63853	5	0.711286	0.66686792	1.819096	No
17	X1X2X4	8.853006	4	0.718234	0.686926823	1.76348	No
18	X1X2X4X5	7.166334	5	0.750846	0.712514343	1.689879	No
19	X1X2X5	14.0518	4	0.672247	0.635829471	1.901954	No
20	X1X3	32.17448	3	0.494245	0.458119668	2.32006	No
21	X1X3X4	17.22237	4	· 0.6442	0.604667016	1.981659	No
22	X1X3X4X5	7.870725	5	0.744615	0.705324829	1.710879	No
23	X1X3X5	25.92876	4	0.567185	0.51909461	2.185633	No
24	X1X4	23.25373	3	0.573156	0.542667517	2.131393	No
25	X1X4X5	10.51024	4	0.703575	0.670638377	1.808773	No
26	X1X5	35.10451	3	0.468326	0.430349803	2.378765	No
27	X2	47.67713	2	0.33942	0.316641185	2.605385	No
28	X2X3	33.67356	3	0.480984	0.44391186	2.350278	No
29	X2X3X4	29.59928	4	0.534716	0.483018229	2.266132	No
30	X2X3X4X5	4.966492	5	0.770305	0.734967499	1.622546	Yes
31	X2X3X5	13.69992	4	0.675359	0.639288019	1.892901	No
32	X2X4	41.22832	3	0.414156	0.372310452	2.497008	No
33	X2X4X5	6.578656	4	0.738353	0.709280689	1.699356	No
34	X2X5	17.70443	3	0.622244	0.595261879	2.005093	No
35	X3	52.89491	2	0.293264	0.26889402	2.694869	No
36	X3X4	37.42076	3	0.447837	0.408397207	2.424167	No
37	X3X4X5	5.871605	4	0.744607	0.716230072	1.678923	No
38	X3X5	24.16462	3	0.565099	0.534034416	2.151416	No
39	X4	56.25721	2	0.263522	0.238126154	2.75099	No
40	X4X5	8.519573	3	0.703492	0.682312848	1.776427	No
41	X5	33.56641	2	0.464241	0.445766197	2.346357	No

see that the maximum Adjusted R^2 value occurs for the model that includes all variables except X1 (Yards Gained). Another criterion is based on a statistic called *Cp*, which measures the difference of a fitted regression model from a *true* model, along with random error. When a regression model with *p* independent variables contains only random differences from a true model, the average value of *Cp* is *p* + 1. Thus, good models are those for which *Cp* is close to or below *p* + 1. From Figure 5.25, *PHStat* suggests that we consider only one other model that meets this criterion—the one with all independent variables. The tool also provides worksheets with ANOVA output for each of the combinations for further analysis.

Stepwise Regression

Because best-subsets regression depends on exhaustive enumeration of all possible models, it is not always practical. **Stepwise regression** is a search procedure that attempts to find the best regression model without examining all possible regression models. In stepwise regression, variables are either added to or deleted from the current regression model at each step of the process. The process continues until no addition or removal of variables can improve the model.

Figure 5.27 shows the results of applying the *PHStat Stepwise Regression* tool to the NFL data (see *PHStat Note: Stepwise Regression*). Note that using *p*-value thresholds of 0.05 results in the inclusion of only Points Scored, Yards Allowed, and Giveaways in the final model. Each of these variables is significant at the 0.05 level. However, note that this procedure does not provide the R^2 or Adjusted R^2 values, so comparisons with other models is not as easy as in best-subsets regression. In this example, best subsets did identify better models than the stepwise procedure based on these criteria.

Correlation and Multicollinearity

As discussed in Chapter 2, correlation, a numerical value between -1 and $+1$, measures the linear relationship between pairs of variables. The higher the absolute value of the correlation, the greater the strength of the relationship. The sign simply indicates whether variables tend to increase together (positive) or not (negative). Therefore, examining correlations between the dependent and independent variables can be useful in selecting variables to include in a multiple regression model because a strong correlation indicates a strong linear relationship. The Excel *Data Analysis Correlation* tool computes the correlation between all pairs of variables (see the *Excel Note: Using the Correlation Tool*). While strong correlations between the independent and dependent

---

PHSTAT NOTE

STEPWISE REGRESSION

From the *PHStat* menu, select *Regression,* then *Stepwise Regression.* The dialog box that appears (Figure 5.26) prompts you to enter the range for the dependent variable and the independent variables, as well as the confidence level for the regression. One of two criteria may be chosen to guide the stepwise selection: *p*-values or *t*-values. Choosing *p*-values, for example, would result in the procedure selecting the variable with the smallest *p*-value below a threshold to include in the model or a variable with a *p*-value greater than a threshold to be removed. Other options include *General Stepwise, Forward Selection,* and *Backward Elimination. General Stepwise* considers including or deleting variables that meet the criteria, as appropriate. *Forward Selection* begins with a model having no independent variables and successively adds one at a time until no additional variable makes a significant contribution. *Backward Elimination* begins with all independent variables in the model and deletes one at a time until the best model is identified. The procedure produces two worksheets: one that contains the multiple regression model that includes all independent variables, and another with a table of stepwise results.

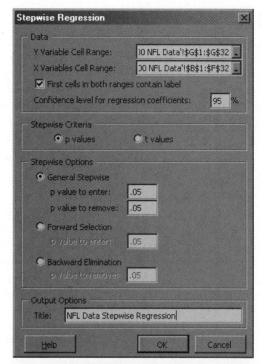

FIGURE 5.26   *PHStat* Stepwise Regression Dialog Box

---

variables are desirable, strong correlations *among the independent variables* can be problematic.

Figure 5.29 shows the correlation matrix for the variables in the *2000 NFL Data* worksheet. You can see that all independent variables have a moderate correlation with the dependent variable, Games Won. However, the strongest correlation is between Points Scored and Yards Gained. This is called **multicollinearity,** a condition occurring when two or more independent variables in the same regression model contain high levels of the same information and consequently are strongly correlated with one another. In this situation, they can predict each other better than the dependent variable, making it difficult to interpret regression coefficients and often leading to poor statistical conclusions.

When multicollinearity is present, the β coefficients of the independent variables can be unstable, and even the signs of these β coefficients may change when different variables are included. Also, *p*-values can be inflated, resulting in the conclusion not to reject the null hypothesis for significance of regression when it should be rejected. Although a full discussion of multicollinearity is beyond the introductory scope of this book, it is important that you are aware of the problems that it may cause and seek

	A	B	C	D	E	F	G	H
1	NFL Data Stepwise Regression							
2	Table of Results for General Stepwise							
3								
4	Points Scored entered.							
5								
6			df	SS	MS	F	Significance F	
7		Regression	1	138.3437159	138.3437159	25.12878075	2.44754E-05	
8		Residual	29	159.6562841	5.505389109			
9		Total	30	298				
10								
11			Coefficients	Standard Error	t Stat	P-value	Lower 95%	Upper 95%
12		Intercept	-0.489894442	1.745265005	-0.280699172	0.780934038	-4.059364111	3.079575227
13		Points Scored	0.025666738	0.005120177	5.012861533	2.44754E-05	0.015194794	0.036138681
14								
15								
16	Yards Allowed entered.							
17								
18			df	SS	MS	F	Significance F	
19		Regression	2	209.6406134	104.8203067	33.21626261	4.05985E-08	
20		Residual	28	88.35938656	3.155692377			
21		Total	30	298				
22								
23			Coefficients	Standard Error	t Stat	P-value	Lower 95%	Upper 95%
24		Intercept	13.85559325	3.294632596	4.205504816	0.000241635	7.106836731	20.60434977
25		Points Scored	0.025003006	0.003879001	6.445733639	5.5633E-07	0.017057224	0.032948788
26		Yards Allowed	-0.002763709	0.000581439	-4.753220766	5.44505E-05	-0.003954735	-0.001572684
27								
28								
29	Giveaways entered.							
30								
31			df	SS	MS	F	Significance F	
32		Regression	3	221.8929052	73.96430173	26.23981578	3.69599E-08	
33		Residual	27	76.1070948	2.818781289			
34		Total	30	298				
35								
36			Coefficients	Standard Error	t Stat	P-value	Lower 95%	Upper 95%
37		Intercept	16.35459497	3.336535751	4.901669334	3.96684E-05	9.508593685	23.20059626
38		Points Scored	0.022031787	0.003933349	5.601278926	6.08661E-06	0.013961226	0.030102348
39		Yards Allowed	-0.00247087	0.000567192	-4.356319061	0.000171453	-0.003634652	-0.001307089
40		Giveaways	-0.100002092	0.047965736	-2.084865175	0.046668196	-0.198419586	-0.001584598
41								
42								
43	No other variables could be entered into the model. Stepwise ends.							

FIGURE 5.27 *PHStat* Stepwise Regression Results

EXCEL NOTE

USING THE CORRELATION TOOL

From the *Tools* menu, select *Data Analysis* and the *Correlation* tool. The dialog box shown in Figure 5.28 is displayed. In the box for the *Input Range,* you specify the range of the data for which you want correlations. As with other tools, check *Labels* if your data range contains a descriptive label.

FIGURE 5.28 Excel Correlation Tool Dialog Box

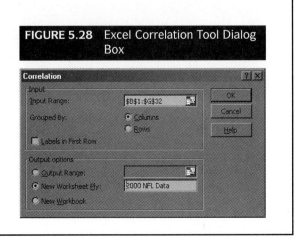

	A	B	C	D	E	F	G
1		Yards Gained	Takeaways	Giveaways	Yards Allowed	Points Scored	Games Won
2	Yards Gained	1					
3	Takeaways	0.054527278	1				
4	Giveaways	-0.328911463	-0.31702097	1			
5	Yards Allowed	-0.092363341	-0.46593399	0.243849975	1		
6	Points Scored	0.830526921	0.298211056	-0.359934561	-0.035998535	1	
7	Games Won	0.601483569	0.58259747	-0.541538751	-0.513343889	0.68135208	1

FIGURE 5.29 Correlation Matrix for NFL Data

expert advice when appropriate. In the NFL example, notice that dropping Yards Gained from the full model eliminates this multicollinearity and results in an improved Adjusted R^2.

Multicollinearity may be measured using the variance inflation factor (VIF) for each independent variable. $\text{VIF}_j = 1/1 - r_j^2$, where r_j^2 is the coefficient of multiple determination of X_j with all other independent variables. If the independent variables are not correlated, then $\text{VIF}_j = 1$. Conservative guidelines suggest that a maximum VIF of 5 or more suggests too much multicollinearity. The variance inflation factor can be computed in the *PHStat Multiple Regression* tool by checking the appropriate box in the dialog. For the NFL data, we find that Points Scored has the largest VIF, 4.69. Although not greater than 5, it is sufficiently large to consider dropping from the model and would eliminate multicollinearity between Points Scored and Yards Gained.

Best subsets, stepwise approaches, and correlation analysis are all heuristic methods that help you to identify potentially good models. In considering alternative models, you should consider whether the regression assumptions can be validated, issues of interpreting the model in its application context, and the significance of regression. None of the recommendations should be construed to be an "optimal" model.

REGRESSION WITH CATEGORICAL INDEPENDENT VARIABLES

Some data of interest in a regression study may be ordinal or nominal. For instance, the Excel file *Surface Finish.xls* provides measurements of the surface finish of 35 parts produced on a lathe, along with the revolutions per minute (RPM) of the spindle and one of four types of cutting tools used. The engineer who collected the data is interested in predicting the surface finish as a function of RPM and type of tool using a regression model of the form

$$Y = \beta_0 + \beta_1 X_1 + \beta_2 X_2 + \varepsilon$$

where

Y = surface finish
X_1 = RPM
X_2 = tool type

The types of tools, however, are nominal data. Since regression analysis requires numerical data, we could include them by *coding* the variables. For example, we might define $X_2 = 0$ if tool A is used, $X_2 = 1$ if tool B is used, $X_2 = 2$ if tool C is used, and $X_2 = 3$ if tool D is used. Such variables are often called *dummy variables*.

We might begin by running a regression on the entire data set, yielding the output shown in Figure 5.30. The resulting model is

$$\hat{Y} = 21.68 + 0.102 \text{ RPM} - 8.926 \text{ TOOL}$$

	A	B	C	D	E	F	G
1	SUMMARY OUTPUT						
2							
3	*Regression Statistics*						
4	Multiple R	0.972622739					
5	R Square	0.945994992					
6	Adjusted R Square	0.942619679					
7	Standard Error	2.328748401					
8	Observations	35					
9							
10	ANOVA						
11		*df*	*SS*	*MS*	*F*	*Significance F*	
12	Regression	2	3039.834348	1519.917174	280.2688186	5.23534E-21	
13	Residual	32	173.5382117	5.423069115			
14	Total	34	3213.37256				
15							
16		*Coefficients*	*Standard Error*	*t Stat*	*P-value*	*Lower 95%*	*Upper 95%*
17	Intercept	21.68436237	5.258705803	4.123516923	0.000247227	10.97273825	32.3959865
18	RPM	0.101626543	0.02222237	4.573164114	6.83944E-05	0.056361096	0.146891991
19	Cutting Tool	-8.92630076	0.382263516	-23.35117106	1.14251E-21	-9.704945403	-8.147656117

FIGURE 5.30 Surface Finish Regression Model Results

Thus, if the RPM is 230 and cutting tool type C ($X_2 = 2$) is used, this regression model would predict surface finish:

$$\hat{Y} = 21.68 + 0.102(230) - 8.926(2) = 27.288$$

This model has an R^2 of 0.946, indicating that the independent variables explain a high percentage of the variance in the surface finish and all *p*-values are significant.

Because X_2 is a categorical variable, the estimate b_2 does not represent a slope, but rather is an indicator of the effect of the type of cutting tool. Thus, by substituting each value of X_2, we derive four different models:

TOOL A: $\hat{Y} = 21.68 + 0.102 \text{ RPM} - 8.926(0) = 21.68 + 0.102 \text{ RPM}$
TOOL B: $\hat{Y} = 21.68 + 0.102 \text{ RPM} - 8.926(1) = 12.754 + 0.102 \text{ RPM}$
TOOL C: $\hat{Y} = 21.68 + 0.102 \text{ RPM} - 8.926(2) = 3.828 + 0.102 \text{ RPM}$
TOOL D: $\hat{Y} = 21.68 + 0.102 \text{ RPM} - 8.926(3) = -5.098 + 0.102 \text{ RPM}$

Note that the only differences among these models are the intercepts; the slopes associated with RPM are the same. This may not be true, as the slope of X_1 may depend on the value of X_2. Such a dependence is called an **interaction.** We can test for interactions by defining a new variable, $X_3 = X_1 \times X_2$ and testing whether this variable is significant. If so, then the original model should not be used.

With the interaction term, the new model is

$$Y = \beta_0 + \beta_1 X_1 + \beta_2 X_2 + \beta_3 X_3 + \varepsilon$$

In the worksheet, we need to create a new column (called Interaction) by multiplying RPM by the cutting tool indicator for each part (see Figure 5.31). The regression results are shown in Figure 5.32. We see the *p*-value for the interaction term is 0.047. At a 0.05 significance level, we would reject the null hypothesis that $\beta_3 = 0$ and conclude that the interaction term is significant. Note also that the *p*-value for Cutting Tool is large, suggesting that this variable is not significant in this model. Dropping it results in a slightly higher Adjusted R^2 and highly significant *p*-values, as shown in Figure 5.33. The final model is

$$\hat{Y} = 10.36 + 0.15 \text{ RPM} - 0.0378 \text{ RPM} \times \text{TOOL}$$

	A	B	C	D	E
1	Part	Surface Finish	RPM	Cutting Tool	Interaction
2	1	45.44	225	0	0
3	2	42.03	200	0	0
4	3	50.10	250	0	0
5	4	48.75	245	0	0
6	5	47.92	235	0	0
7	6	47.79	237	0	0
8	7	52.26	265	0	0
9	8	50.52	259	0	0
10	9	45.58	221	0	0
11	10	44.78	218	0	0
12	11	33.50	224	1	224
13	12	31.23	212	1	212
14	13	37.52	248	1	248
15	14	37.13	260	1	260
16	15	34.70	243	1	243
17	16	33.92	238	1	238
18	17	32.13	224	1	224
19	18	35.47	251	1	251
20	19	33.49	232	1	232
21	20	32.29	216	1	216
22	21	27.44	225	2	450
23	22	24.03	200	2	400
24	23	27.33	250	2	500
25	24	27.20	245	2	490
26	25	27.10	235	2	470
27	26	27.30	237	2	474
28	27	28.30	265	2	530
29	28	28.40	259	2	518
30	29	26.80	221	2	442
31	30	26.40	218	2	436
32	31	21.40	224	3	672
33	32	20.50	212	3	636
34	33	21.90	248	3	744
35	34	22.13	260	3	780
36	35	22.40	243	3	729

FIGURE 5.31 Modified Surface Finish Data with Interaction Term

FIGURE 5.32 Regression Results for Interaction Model

	A	B	C	D	E	F	G
1	SUMMARY OUTPUT						
2							
3	*Regression Statistics*						
4	Multiple R	0.975981018					
5	R Square	0.952538947					
6	Adjusted R Square	0.947945942					
7	Standard Error	2.218034919					
8	Observations	35					
9							
10	ANOVA						
11		*df*	*SS*	*MS*	*F*	*Significance F*	
12	Regression	3	3060.862514	1020.287505	207.3890442	1.3528E-20	
13	Residual	31	152.5100459	4.9196789			
14	Total	34	3213.37256				
15							
16		*Coefficients*	*Standard Error*	*t Stat*	*P-value*	*Lower 95%*	*Upper 95%*
17	Intercept	9.323519528	7.799575187	1.195388121	0.241000171	-6.583827814	25.23086687
18	RPM	0.154038493	0.033025384	4.664245399	5.60989E-05	0.086682742	0.221394245
19	Cutting Tool	0.81484983	4.725749677	0.172427633	0.864222161	-8.823385557	10.45308522
20	Interaction	-0.041233525	0.01994427	-2.067437156	0.047127581	-0.081910155	-0.000556895

	A	B	C	D	E	F	G
1	SUMMARY OUTPUT						
2							
3	*Regression Statistics*						
4	Multiple R	0.975957698					
5	R Square	0.952493428					
6	Adjusted R Square	0.949524267					
7	Standard Error	2.184149679					
8	Observations	35					
9							
10	ANOVA						
11		*df*	*SS*	*MS*	*F*	*Significance F*	
12	Regression	2	3060.716246	1530.358123	320.7955082	6.73068E-22	
13	Residual	32	152.6563143	4.770509822			
14	Total	34	3213.37256				
15							
16		*Coefficients*	*Standard Error*	*t Stat*	*P-value*	*Lower 95%*	*Upper 95%*
17	Intercept	10.3556928	4.923583469	2.103283688	0.043392669	0.32668995	20.38469564
18	Interaction	-0.037804803	0.001513109	-24.98485719	1.46399E-22	-0.040886902	-0.034722705
19	RPM	0.149688291	0.020985598	7.132905782	4.28112E-08	0.106942064	0.192434519

FIGURE 5.33   Regression Results for Final Model

Substituting the indicator variables for TOOL yields the following four models:

TOOL A: $\hat{Y} = 10.36 + 0.15$ RPM $- 0.0378$ RPM $\times (0) = 10.36 + 0.15$ RPM
TOOL B: $\hat{Y} = 10.36 + 0.15$ RPM $- 0.0378$ RPM $\times (1) = 10.36 + 0.1122$ RPM
TOOL C: $\hat{Y} = 10.36 + 0.15$ RPM $- 0.0378$ RPM $\times (2) = 10.36 + 0.0744$ RPM
TOOL D: $\hat{Y} = 10.36 + 0.15$ RPM $- 0.0378$ RPM $\times (3) = 10.36 + 0.0366$ RPM

Because of the interaction effect, we have a unique model for each tool with a different slope associated with RPM.

REGRESSION MODELS WITH NONLINEAR TERMS

Linear regression models are not appropriate for every situation. If there is a reason to suspect a nonlinear relationship between the dependent variable and one or more independent variables, we might propose a nonlinear regression model to explain the relationships. One basis for selecting an appropriate model is to plot the dependent variable against the independent variable. If the relationship is clearly nonlinear, different forms of nonlinear models will probably fit the data better than a straight line. In the *Add Trendline* dialog box in Figure 5.3, you can see a variety of nonlinear forms of regression models involving a single variable. For instance, a second-order polynomial model would be

$$Y = \beta_0 + \beta_1 X + \beta_2 X^2 + \varepsilon$$

Multiple regression models might involve interaction terms as we saw in the last section:

$$Y = \beta_0 + \beta_1 X_1 + \beta_2 X_2 + \beta_{12} X_1 X_2 + \varepsilon$$

In this model, we are assuming that the relationship between X_1 and Y changes when the value of X_2 changes and vice versa.

While these models appear to be quite different from ordinary linear regression models, they both have the property that they are *linear in the parameters* (the betas). In other words, all terms are a product of a beta coefficient and some function of the data. In such cases, we can apply least squares to estimate the regression coefficients just as we did in the interaction model.

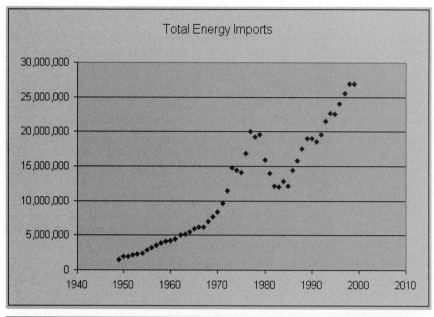

FIGURE 5.34 Energy Imports

To illustrate a nonlinear model, we will use the Excel worksheet *Energy Production & Consumption.xls*. Figure 5.34 shows a plot of total energy imports against time. Even without the aberration in the 1970s, the data appear to have an increasing nonlinear trend, so simple linear regression would not be appropriate.

Because the oil embargo of the 1970s explains the aberration in the chart, we deleted the data for the years 1972 through 1981 in order to develop a model that better describes the long-term trend of energy imports. As a basis for comparison, we will first fit a simple linear regression model to the data with time being the dependent variable. The model is

$$\text{Total Imports} = -938{,}764{,}498.6 \pm 481{,}246.5728 \text{ Year}$$

The fit of this model is quite good, with an Adjusted R^2 of 0.944 and a high level of significance. However, in viewing the residual plot in Figure 5.35, the errors appear to have somewhat of a U-shape, an indication of an inappropriate model.

FIGURE 5.35 Residual Plot

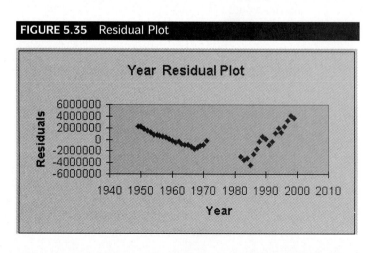

As an alternative, we might try a second-order polynomial model:

$$Y = \beta_0 + \beta_1 X + \beta_2 X^2 + \varepsilon$$

This requires adding another column of data to the worksheet that represents the square of the unit number. The resulting regression model is

$$\text{Total Imports} = 3{,}292{,}116{,}394 - 33{,}822{,}316.2\,\text{Year} + 8687.66\,\text{Year}^2$$

The results of this model improve the Adjusted R^2 to 0.985. The residual plots also are more stable.

An alternative model that has a similar nonlinear shape is the exponential model

$$Y = ae^{bX}$$

where e is the base of natural logarithms, 2.71828 . . . . This model is no longer linear in the regression coefficients (statisticians often call such a model *intrinsically nonlinear*). This means that least-squares regression cannot be applied because the assumptions will be violated. Fortunately, it is easy to transform this model to one that is linear in the coefficients by taking the natural logarithm of both sides of the equation. This yields the model

$$\ln Y = \ln a + bX$$

In Excel, the natural logarithm of a number is obtained by the function: =LN(*cell reference*). By performing this transformation on both the dependent and independent variable data values, and applying the regression tool, we obtain the model

$$\ln Y = -87.14 + 0.052\,\text{Year}$$

FIGURE 5.36 Exponential Model for Energy Imports

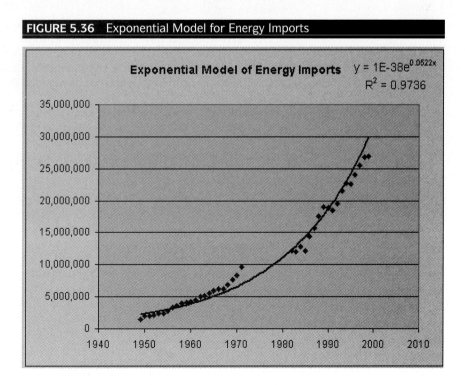

The fit of this model is almost as good as the quadratic model, with Adjusted R^2 = 0.973 (although when using logarithmic transformations, you need to keep in mind that the scale has been changed). However, the residual plot shows some pattern, suggesting that this model is inferior to the quadratic model. To transform this back into the original data units, we find $e^{-87.14} = 1.43E - 38$, obtaining $Y = 1.43E - 38\ e^{0.052X}$. This, in fact, is the model you would find by using the *Add Trendline* option in Excel on the data series in Figure 5.34 after removing the data for the years 1972–1981 (see Figure 5.36).

You can see that dealing with nonlinear models is not easy. Good model building is more of an art than a science. You need to have a good understanding of the mathematics of different functional forms.

Questions and Problems

1. Explain the difference between the model $Y = \beta_0 + \beta_1 X + \varepsilon$ and the model $\hat{Y} = b_0 + b_1 X$.
2. What is least-squares estimation? Illustrate how least-squares regression defines the best-fitting regression line.
3. Explain the coefficient of determination, R^2. How does it differ from the sample correlation coefficient?
4. Explain the assumptions of linear regression. How can you determine if each of these assumptions holds?
5. Explain how Adjusted R^2 is used in evaluating the fit of multiple regression models.
6. Describe the differences, and advantages/disadvantages, of using best-subsets regression, stepwise regression, and examination of correlations in developing multiple regression models.
7. Find real data on daily changes in the S&P 500 (or the Dow Jones Industrial Average) and a stock of your interest. Use regression analysis to estimate the beta risk of the stock.
8. Construct a scatter diagram for Takeaways and Yards Allowed in the *2000 NFL Data.xls* worksheet. Does there appear to be a linear relationship? Develop a regression model for predicting Yards Allowed as a function of Takeaways. Explain the statistical significance of the model.
9. Construct a 95 percent confidence band chart for the model developed in Problem 8.
10. Develop simple linear regression models for predicting Games Won as a function of each of the independent variables in the *2000 NFL Data.xls* worksheet individually. Do the assumptions of linear regression hold for your models? How do these models compare to the multiple regression model developed in the chapter?
11. Data obtained from a county auditor (see the file *Market Value.xls*) provides information about the age, square footage, and current market value of houses along one street in a particular subdivision.
    a. Construct a scatter diagram showing the relationship between market value as a function of the age and size of the house, and add trendlines using the *Add Trendline* option in Excel.
    b. Develop simple linear regression models for estimating the market value as a function of the age of the house and size of the house separately.
    c. Develop a multiple linear regression model for estimating the market value as a function of both the age and size of the house.
    d. How do the models developed in parts (b) and (c) compare?
12. Excel file *TV Viewing.xls* provides sample data on the number of hours of TV viewing per week for six age groups.

a. Using all the data, develop a simple linear regression model for estimating TV viewing time as a function of age.

b. Is a linear model appropriate? If not, propose an alternative model.

13. A deep foundation engineering contractor has bid on a foundation system for a new world headquarters building for a Fortune 500 company. A part of the project consists of installing 311 augercast piles. The contractor was given bid information for cost estimating purposes, which consisted of the estimated depth of each pile; however, actual drill footage of each pile could not be determined exactly until construction was performed. The Excel file *Pile Foundation.xls* contains the estimates and actual pile lengths after the project was completed.

a. Develop a linear regression model to estimate the actual pile length as a function of the estimated pile lengths. What do you conclude?

14. The file *1999 Baseball Data.xls* contains data for professional baseball teams for 1999, including their total payroll, winning percentage, batting average, home runs, runs, runs batted in, earned run average, and pitching saves.

a. Develop a multiple regression equation for predicting the winning percentage as a function of all the other variables. How good is your model? Is multicollinearity a problem?

b. Find the best set of independent variables that predict the winning percentage by examining the correlation matrix.

c. Find the best set of independent variables that predict the winning percentage using best subsets regression.

d. Find the best set of independent variables that predict the winning percentage using stepwise regression.

15. The State of Ohio Department of Education has a mandated ninth-grade proficiency test that covers writing, reading, mathematics, citizenship (social studies), and science. The Excel file *Ohio Education Performance.xls* provides data on success rates (defined as the percent of students passing) in school districts in the Greater Cincinnati metropolitan area along with state averages.

a. Develop a multiple regression model to predict math success as a function of success in all other subjects. Is multicollinearity a problem?

b. Develop the best regression model to predict math success as a function of success in the other subjects by examining the correlation matrix.

c. Develop the best regression model to predict math success as a function of success in the other subjects using best-subsets regression.

d. Develop the best regression model to predict math success as a function of success in the other subjects using stepwise regression.

16. A national homebuilder builds single-family homes and condominium-style townhouses. The Excel file *House Sales Data.xls* provides information on the selling price, lot cost, type of home, and region of the country (M = Midwest, S = South) for closings during one month.

a. Develop a multiple regression model for sales price as a function of lot cost, region of country, and type of home.

b. Determine if any interactions exist between lot cost, region, and type of home.

17. The Excel file *Salary Data.xls* provides information on current salary, beginning salary, previous experience in months when hired, and total years of education for a sample of 100 employees in a firm.

a. Develop a multiple regression model for predicting current salary as a function of the other variables.

b. Find the best model for predicting current salary.

18. The Excel file *Cereal Data.xls* provides a variety of nutritional information about 67 cereals and their shelf location in a supermarket. Use regression

analysis to determine if a relationship exists between calories and the other variables. Investigate the model assumptions and clearly explain your conclusions.

19. The Excel file *Infant Mortality.xls* provides data on infant mortality rate (deaths per 1000 births), female literacy (percent who read), and population density (people per square kilometer) for 85 countries. Develop simple and multiple regression models for the relationship between mortality, population density, and literacy. Explain all statistical output.

20. A mental health agency measured the self-esteem score for randomly selected individuals with disabilities who were involved in some work activity within the past year. The Excel file *Self Esteem.xls* provides the data, including the individuals' marital status, length of work, type of support received (direct support includes job-related services such as job coaching and counseling), education, and age.
    a. Use simple linear regression to determine if there is a relationship between self-esteem and length of work.
    b. Use multiple linear regression for predicting self-esteem as a function of the other variables. Investigate possible interaction effects and determine the best model.

21. Data collected in 1960 from the National Cancer Institute provides the per-capita numbers of cigarettes sold along with death rates for various forms of cancer (see the Excel file *Smoking and Cancer.xls*). Use simple linear regression to determine if a significant relationship exists between the number of cigarettes sold and each form of cancer.

Questions 22–30 relate to the following data.

The Excel file *HATCO.xls* (adopted from Hair, Anderson, Tatham, and Black in *Multivariate Analysis,* 5th ed., Prentice-Hall, 1998) consists of data related to predicting the level of business (Usage Level) obtained from a survey of purchasing managers of customers of an industrial supplier, HATCO. The independent variables are
    1. *Delivery speed*—amount of time it takes to deliver the product once an order is confirmed
    2. *Price level*—perceived level of price charged by product suppliers
    3. *Price flexibility*—perceived willingness of HATCO representatives to negotiate price on all types of purchases
    4. *Manufacturing image*—overall image of the manufacturer or supplier
    5. *Overall service*—overall level of service necessary for maintaining a satisfactory relationship between supplier and purchaser
    6. *Salesforce image*—overall image of the manufacturer's salesforce
    7. *Product quality*—perceived level of quality of a particular product
    8. *Size of firm* relative to others in this market (0 = small; 1 = large)

Responses to the first seven variables were obtained using a graphic rating scale, where a 10 centimeter line was drawn between endpoints labeled "poor" and "excellent." Respondents indicated their perceptions using a mark on the line, which was measured from the left endpoint. The result was a scale from 0 to 10 rounded to one decimal place.

22. Develop a correlation matrix, and interpret the ability of each independent variable to explain Usage Level.
23. Construct a simple linear regression model of Usage Level as a function of Overall Service and interpret the results.
24. Construct a simple linear regression model of Usage Level as a function of Delivery Speed and interpret the results.

25. Construct a multiple regression model with Usage Level as the dependent variable, and Delivery speed and Overall Service as independent variables. Interpret the results.
26. Compare the models developed in Problems 23–25.
27. Develop a multiple regression model of Usage Level as a function of the first seven independent variables and interpret the results.
28. Use best-subsets and stepwise regression to find good models for Usage Level using the first seven independent variables. What is your recommendation?
29. Include the categorical variable Size of Firm (coded as 0 for small firms, and 1 for large firms) in identifying the best model for predicting Usage Level. Be sure to investigate possible interactions.
30. Segregate the HATCO data by firm size. Run separate regressions on the data for small firms and the data for large firms. Compare your results with Problem 29.
31. (From Horngren, Foster, and Datar, *Cost Accounting: A Managerial Emphasis,* 9th ed., Prentice Hall, 1997, p. 371.) The managing director of a consulting group has the following monthly data on total overhead costs and professional labor hours to bill to clients.

TOTAL OVERHEAD COSTS	BILLABLE HOURS
$340,000	3000
$400,000	4000
$435,000	5000
$477,000	6000
$529,000	7000
$587,000	8000

Generate a regression model to identify the fixed overhead costs to the consulting group.
a. What is the constant component of the consultant group's overhead?
b. If a special job requiring 1000 billable hours that would contribute a margin of $38,000 before overhead was available, would the job be attractive?

32. (From Horngren, Foster, and Datar, *Cost Accounting: A Managerial Emphasis,* 9th ed., Prentice Hall, 1997, p. 349.) Cost functions are often non-linear with volume, as production facilities are often able to produce larger quantities at lower rates than smaller quantities. Using the following data, plot the data and use the Excel *Add Trendline* feature. Compare a linear trendline with a logarithmic trendline.

UNITS PRODUCED	COSTS
500	$12,500
1000	$25,000
1500	$32,500
2000	$40,000
2500	$45,000
3000	$50,000

33. (From Horngren, Foster, and Datar, *Cost Accounting: A Managerial Emphasis,* 9th ed., Prentice Hall, 1997, p. 349.) The Helicopter Division of Aerospatiale is studying assembly costs at its Marseilles plant. Past data indicates the following costs per helicopter. Use linear regression, and

compare the results with a second-order polynomial regression model. Using the model with the best fit, predict the hours required for a ninth helicopter. (*Hint:* A model often used in such situation is $Y = aX^b$).

HELICOPTER NUMBER	LABOR HOURS
1	2000
2	1400
3	1238
4	1142
5	1075
6	1029
7	985
8	957

34. For the data in Problem 33, use an exponential regression model, and estimate the hours required for the ninth helicopter.

35. (From Crask, Fox, and Stout, *Marketing Research: Principles & Applications,* Prentice Hall, 1995, p. 252.) A real estate company hired a small market research firm to develop a model to calculate a ballpark price for a home based only on square footage. The real estate company felt that this model would be useful in helping customers set the list prices of their homes. The market research firm wants a linear regression relating price as a function of square footage based on the following sample data:

LIST PRICE	SQUARE FOOTAGE
$75,900	1750
$61,000	1590
$110,000	2100
$83,500	1800
$94,600	1890
$54,500	1360
$96,000	2050
$70,700	1760
$50,800	1500
$69,400	1650
$87,500	1700
$105,000	1920
$76,500	1800
$103,200	2150
$59,000	1600

CASE

REGRESSION ANALYSIS FOR TRACWAY

In reviewing the Tracway data, Henry Hudson notices that defects received from suppliers has decreased (worksheet *Defects After Delivery*). Upon investigation, he learned that in 1998, Tracway experienced some quality problems due to an increasing number of defects in materials received from suppliers. The company instituted an initiative in August 1999 to work with suppliers to reduce these defects, to more closely coordinate deliveries, and to improve materials quality through reengineering supplier production policies. To assess the impact of this program, Tracway measured the number of defects in supplier deliveries each month. Henry noted that the program appeared to reverse an increasing trend in defects; he would like to predict what might have happened had the supplier initiative not been implemented and how the number of defects might further be reduced in the near future.

In meeting with Tracway's human resources director, Henry also discovered a concern about the high rate of turnover in its field service staff. Senior managers have suggested that the department look closer at its recruiting policies, particularly to try to identify the characteristics of individuals that lead to greater retention. However, in a recent staff meeting, HR managers could not agree on these characteristics. Some argued that years of education and grade point averages were good predictors. Others argued that hiring more mature applicants would lead to greater retention. To study these factors, the staff agreed to conduct a statistical study to determine the effect that years of education, college grade point average, and

age when hired have on retention. A sample of 40 field service engineers hired 10 years ago was selected to determine the influence of these variables on how long each individual stayed with the company. Data are compiled in the *Employee Retention* worksheet.

Finally, as part of its efforts to remain competitive, Tracway tries to keep up with the latest in production technology. This is especially important in the highly competitive lawn mower line, where competitors can gain a real advantage if they develop more cost-effective means of production. The Tracway lawn mower division therefore spends a great deal of effort in testing new technology. When new production technology is introduced, firms often experience learning, resulting in a gradual decrease in the time required to produce successive units. Generally, the rate of improvement declines until the production time levels off. One example is the production of a new design for lawn mower engines. To determine the time required to produce these engines, Tracway produced 50 units on its production line; test results are given on the worksheet *Engines* in the Tracway database. Because Tracway is continually developing new technology, understanding the rate of learning can be useful in estimating future production costs without having to run extensive prototype trials, and Henry would like a better handle on this.

Use techniques of regression analysis to assist Henry in evaluating the data in these three worksheets and reaching useful conclusions. Summarize your work in a formal report with all appropriate results and analyses. ∎

References

Evans, J. R., *Operations Management: Quality Performance and Value,* 5th ed. (St. Paul, MN: West Publishing Company, 1996).

Harnett, D. L., and J. F. Horrell, *Data, Statistics, and Decision Models with Excel* (New York: John Wiley & Sons, 1998).

Kime, S. E., and J. A. Fitzsimmons, "Selecting Profitable Hotel Sites at La Quinta Motor Inns," *Interfaces,* Vol. 20, No. 2, 1990, 12–20.

Lentner, M., and T. Bishop, *Experimental Design and Analysis,* 2nd ed. (Blacksburg, VA: Valley Book Company, 1993).

Levine, D. M., M. L. Berenson, and D. Stephan, *Statistics for Managers Using Microsoft Excel* (Upper Saddle River, NJ: Prentice-Hall, Inc., 1997).

Pindyck, R. S., and D. L. Rubinfeld, *Econometric Models and Economic Forecasts* (New York: McGraw-Hill, 1976).

Ragsdale, C. T., *Spreadsheet Modeling and Decision Analysis,* 2nd ed. (Cincinnati, OH: Southwestern Publishing, 1998).

CHAPTER

6

FORECASTING

INTRODUCTION

One of the major problems that managers face is forecasting future events in order to make good decisions. For example, forecasts of interest rates, energy prices, and other economic indicators are needed for financial planning; sales forecasts are needed to plan production and workforce capacity; and forecasts of trends in demographics, consumer behavior, and technological innovation are needed for long-term strategic planning. The government also invests significant resources on predicting short-run U.S. business performance using the Index of Leading Indicators. This index focuses on the performance of individual businesses, which often is highly correlated with the performance of the overall economy, and is used to forecast economic trends for the nation as a whole. In this chapter we introduce some common methods and approaches to forecasting, including both qualitative and quantitative techniques.

Managers may choose from a wide range of forecasting techniques. Selecting the appropriate method depends on the characteristics of the forecasting problem, such as the time horizon of the variable being forecast, as well as available information on which the forecast will be based. Three major categories of forecasting approaches are *qualitative and judgmental techniques, statistical time series models,* and *explanatory/causal methods*. Qualitative and judgmental techniques rely on experience and intuition; they are necessary when historical data are not available or when the decision maker needs to forecast far into the future. For example, a forecast of when the next generation of a microprocessor will be available and what capabilities it might have will depend greatly on the opinions and expertise of individuals who understand the technology.

Statistical time series models find greater applicability for short-range forecasting problems. A **time series** is a stream of historical data, such as weekly sales. Time series models assume that whatever forces have influenced sales in the recent past will continue into the near future; thus, forecasts are developed by extrapolating these data into the future.

Explanatory/causal models seek to identify factors that explain statistically the patterns observed in the variable being forecast, usually with regression analysis. While time series models only use time as the independent variable, explanatory/causal models generally include other factors. For example, forecasting the price of oil might incorporate independent variables such as the demand for oil measured in barrels, the proportion of oil stock generated by OPEC countries, and tax rates. Although we can never prove that changes in these variables actually cause changes in the price of oil, we often have evidence that a strong influence exists.

Surveys of forecasting practices (see Sanders and Manrodt, 1994) have shown that both judgmental and quantitative methods are used for forecasting sales of product lines or product families, as well as for broad company and industry forecasts. Simple time series models are used for short- and medium-range forecasts, while regression analysis is the most popular method for long-range forecasting. However, many companies rely on judgmental methods far more than quantitative methods, and almost half judgmentally adjust quantitative forecasts.

In this chapter we focus on these three approaches to forecasting. Specifically, we will discuss

- Historical analogy and the Delphi method as approaches to judgmental forecasting
- Moving average, exponential smoothing, and Holt–Winters models of time series forecasting, with a discussion of evaluating the quality of forecasts
- The use of regression models for explanatory/causal forecasting, and
- Some insights into the practical issues associated with forecasting

QUALITATIVE AND JUDGMENTAL METHODS

Qualitative, or judgmental, forecasting methods are valuable in situations for which no historical data are available or for those that specifically require human expertise and knowledge. One example might be identifying future opportunities and threats as part of a SWOT (Strengths, Weaknesses, Opportunities, and Threats) analysis within a strategic planning exercise. Another use of judgmental methods is to incorporate nonquantitative information, such as the impact of government regulations or competitor behavior, in a quantitative forecast. Judgmental techniques range from such simple methods as a manager's opinion or a group-based jury of executive opinion to more structured approaches like historical analogy and the Delphi method.

Historical Analogy

One judgmental approach is **historical analogy,** in which a forecast is obtained through a comparative analysis with a previous situation. For example, if a new product is being introduced, the response of similar previous products to marketing campaigns can be used as a basis to predict how the new marketing campaign might fare. Of course, temporal changes or other unique factors might not be fully considered in such an approach. However, a great deal of insight can often be gained through an analysis of past experiences. For example, in early 1998 the price of oil was over $22 a barrel. However, in mid-1998, the price of a barrel of oil dropped to around $11. The reasons for this price drop included an oversupply of oil from new production in the Caspian Sea region, high production in non-OPEC regions, and lower-than-normal demand. In similar circumstances in the past, OPEC would meet and take action to raise the price of oil. Thus, from historical analogy, we might forecast a rise in the price of oil. OPEC members did in fact meet in mid-1998 and agreed to cut their production, but nobody believed that they would actually cooperate effectively, and the price continued to drop for a time. Subsequently, in 2000 the price of oil rose dramatically, falling again in late 2001. Analogies often provide good forecasts, but you need to be careful to recognize new or different circumstances. Another analogy is international conflict relative to the price of oil. Should war break out, the price would be expected to rise, analogous to what it has done in the past.

The Delphi Method

A popular judgmental forecasting approach is called the **Delphi method.** The Delphi method uses a panel of experts, whose identities are typically kept confidential from one another, to respond to a sequence of questionnaires. After each round of responses, individual opinions, edited to ensure anonymity, are shared, allowing each to see what the other experts think. Seeing other experts' opinions helps to reinforce those in agreement and to influence those who did not agree to possibly consider other factors. In the next round, the experts revise their estimates, and the process is repeated, usually for no more than two or three rounds. The Delphi method promotes unbiased exchanges of ideas and discussion and usually results in some convergence of opinion. It is one of the better approaches to forecasting long-range trends and impacts. The following example shows how the Delphi method might be applied to a situation at Tracway, Inc. (see the Case Problem in Chapter 1 for background on this fictitious company).

Applying the Delphi Method

Sales data in the *Tracway.xls* database show that the mower business is relatively flat, while tractor sales have experienced significant growth, increasing from about 10 percent to nearly 17 percent in the past five years. This growth is not the same in all sales regions; for example, it appears that growth in North America, South America, and China is strong, but that sales in the European and Pacific regions are either steady or declining. With continued global expansion and increasing demand, Tracway faces a need to expand production capacity. However, before deciding on new locations of plants and their specific capacities, which involve substantial capital investment, management needs to better understand the growth that might be expected in the global market. Thus, Mike Mortensen, Tracway's CEO, needs to address the question: Where will significant changes in regional markets occur in the future?

Mike hired three industry experts to provide their opinions of expected changes to Tracway market share in each key region. In order to obtain forecasts with the least amount of bias, Mike decided to use the Delphi method. To keep the experts anonymous, they were identified only as A, B, and C. To begin, each expert was asked to provide his or her estimates of the market for mowers and tractors by region over the next ten years, which were then shared among the group. For the money budgeted, Mike was able to obtain the commitment of the three experts for two rounds of reports.

Delphi First Round

In the first round, Expert A forecast that worldwide mower sales would decline slightly, with decreases in the North American and European regions and some compensating increases in South America, the Pacific, and China. Because these last three regions had a much lower sales base, Expert A expected mower sales in total to be slightly lower. This expert saw much brighter prospects for the small tractor market, especially in North America. The South American region was forecasted to have stronger proportional increases but lower absolute increases because they currently had a much lower sales level than in North America. In addition, the Chinese market for small tractors was forecasted to boom, and European demand for small tractors was expected to grow slightly. However, due to economic problems, demand in the Pacific region was highly uncertain.

Expert B had a strong reputation for his knowledge of the European region. He forecasted regional strong growth in demand for small tractors over the next five years and steady demand for mowers. However, he also felt that the European Economic Union was expected to make it quite difficult for outside companies (such as Tracway) to compete.

Expert C was known for her expertise about Pacific Rim economies, China, and South America. She forecast that demand for small tractors would increase substantially in South America and China. Pacific region demand for small tractors should increase, but a great deal of uncertainty would exist, especially in the first five years of the forecast period. Demand for mowers was expected to increase in South America to a small degree and to be quite small in the Pacific region. After five years, she believed that the Pacific region would have a strong economic recovery.

Mike read the first round of reports and shared them with the team of experts. For the second round, Mike requested that each expert provide numerical forecasts for expected changes by region over a five-year horizon, along with assessments of market risks.

Delphi Second Round

Table 6.1 shows the percent changes that each expert forecast. Expert A considered the North American and European markets to be very predictable and steady,

TABLE 6.1 Results of First Round of Delphi Method			
	Expert A	*Expert B*	*Expert C*
Tractors—NA region	+20% to +25%		
Tractors—SA region	+50% to +70%		+30% to +60%
Tractors—European region	+10% to +20%	+20% to +30%	
Tractors—Pacific region	−20% to +30%		+20% to +100%
Tractors—Chinese region	+200% to +300%		+50% to +150%
Mowers—NA region	−10% to −5%		
Mowers—SA region	+30% to +50%		+10% to +20%
Mowers—European region	−10% to −5%	No change to +10%	
Mowers—Pacific region	No change to +10%		No change to +20%

with little risk but low growth. The South American region was expected to promise the greatest opportunities for growth, but there was a risk that rampant inflation could return and disrupt economies, leading to the real possibility of market declines. The Pacific region was viewed as the most turbulent, already suffering some economic hardship that could easily lead to political unrest, further deteriorating that market. Expert A considered the China region to be safe and a promising new market for small tractors. Expert B was very optimistic about the growth potential for the European region. However, regulatory conditions could make the market increase potential for Tracway quite low. Expert C was optimistic about the South American region. This expert did not expect inflation to get out of control, because the governments in that region had seen what damage inflation could do and were experienced in dealing with it. Expert C felt that the Pacific region would also be able to deal with its economic problems, given time. There was more concern about political factors in China, which could change the current strong growth in demand for small tractors.

Delphi Conclusions

The Delphi process ideally yields agreement among all of the participating experts, although this does not always occur. The value of Delphi is the learning that takes place because of the exchanges among the experts and, most important of all, the learning experienced by the decision maker. The process can stop when the decision maker is confident of the expected outcomes.

In this case, after the second round, Mike Mortensen felt confident that tractor sales growth would be strong, with the bulk of the increase being in the North American region (25 percent increase) and the South American region (50 percent increase). Sales were expected to be the same as last year in the European region (despite the more optimistic impressions of Expert A and Expert B) and the Pacific region. Extremely high rates of growth were expected from the China region, although the volumes involved were expected to be inconsequential for a few more years given the much higher volumes in North and South America.

The expectation for mower sales was much less optimistic. The vast majority of sales from mowers occurred in the North American region, and a slight decrease in sales (about 5 percent) was expected over the next year. The same was true for the European region, the only other region with significant mower sales volume. Sales in South America and the Pacific regions might provide pleasant surprises, but Mike was not counting on significant growth in mower demand and was planning on holding mower production capacity to no more than its current level, and in fact slight decreases in capacity were planned. We will return to Tracway in the case problem at the end of this chapter.

INDICATORS AND INDEXES

Indicators and indexes generally play an important role in developing judgmental forecasts. **Indicators** are measures that are believed to influence the behavior of a variable we wish to forecast. By monitoring changes in indicators, we expect to gain insight about the future behavior of the variable to help forecast the future. For example, one variable that is important to the nation's economy is the Gross Domestic Product (GDP), which is a measure of the value of all goods and services produced in the United States. Despite its shortcomings (for instance, unpaid work such as housekeeping and child care is not measured; production of poor-quality output inflates the measure, as does work expended on corrective action), it is a practical and useful measure of economic performance. Like most time series, the GDP rises and falls in a cyclical fashion. Predicting future trends in the GDP is often done by analyzing *leading indicators*—series that tend to rise and fall some predictable length of time prior to the peaks and valleys of the GDP. One example of a leading indicator is the formation of business enterprises; as the rate of new businesses grows, one would expect the GDP to increase in the future. Other examples of leading indicators are the percent change in the money supply (M1) and net change in business loans. Other indicators, called *lagging indicators,* tend to have peaks and valleys that follow those of the GDP. Some lagging indicators are the Consumer Price Index, prime rate, business investment expenditures, or inventories on hand. The GDP can be used to predict future trends in these indicators.

Indicators are often combined quantitatively into an **index.** The direction of movement of all the selected indicators are weighted and combined, providing an index of overall expectation. For example, financial analysts use the Dow Jones Industrial Average as an index of general stock market performance. Indexes do not provide a complete forecast, but rather a better picture of direction of change, and thus play an important role in judgmental forecasting.

The Department of Commerce began an Index of Leading Indicators to help predict future economic performance. Components of the index include

- Average weekly hours, manufacturing
- Average weekly initial claims, unemployment insurance
- New orders, consumers goods and materials
- Vendor performance—slower deliveries
- New orders, nondefense capital goods
- Building permits, private housing
- Stock prices, 500 common stocks (S&P)
- Money supply
- Interest rate spread
- Index of consumer expectations (University of Michigan)

Business Conditions Digest included over 100 time series in seven economic areas. This publication was discontinued in March 1990, but information related to the Index of Leading Indicators was continued in *Survey of Current Business.* In December 1995 the U.S. Department of Commerce sold this data source to The Conference Board, which now markets the information under the title *Business Cycle Indicators;* information can be obtained at its Web site [http://www.conference-board.org/products/bcinfo.cfm]. The site includes excellent current information about the calculation of the index, as well as its current components.

STATISTICAL FORECASTING MODELS

Many forecasts are based on analysis of historical time series data and are predicated on the assumption that the future is an extrapolation of the past. We will assume that a time series consists of T periods of data, $A_t, t = 1, 2, \ldots, T$. A naive approach is to eyeball a **trend**—a gradual shift in the value of the time series—by visually examining a plot of the data. For instance, Figure 6.1 shows a graph of total energy production from the data in *Energy Production & Consumption.xls.* We see that energy production was rising quite rapidly during the 1960s; however, the slope appears to have decreased after 1970. It appears that production is increasing by about 500,000 each year and that this can provide a reasonable forecast provided that the trend continues.

Time series may also exhibit short-term *seasonal effects* (over a year, month, week, or even a day) as well as longer-term *cyclical effects* or nonlinear trends. At a

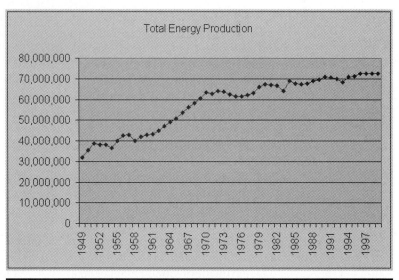

FIGURE 6.1   Chart of Total Energy Production

neighborhood grocery store, for instance, short-term seasonal patterns may occur over a week, with the heaviest volume of customers on weekends, and even during the course of a day. Cycles relate to much longer-term behavior, such as periods of inflation and recession or bull and bear stock market behavior. Figure 6.2 shows a chart of the percent change in the Consumer Price Index from the Excel worksheet *Economic Indexes.xls*. We see some evidence of a potential long-term cycle in which the time series will eventually rise. Of course, with the economic volatility that the world has experienced in recent years, it may not be appropriate to reach this conclusion solely from examination of the time series.

Of course, such unscientific approaches may be a bit unsettling to a manager making important decisions. Subtle effects and interactions of seasonal and cyclical factors may not be evident from simple visual extrapolation of data. Statistical methods, which

FIGURE 6.2   Chart of Percent Change in Consumer Price Index

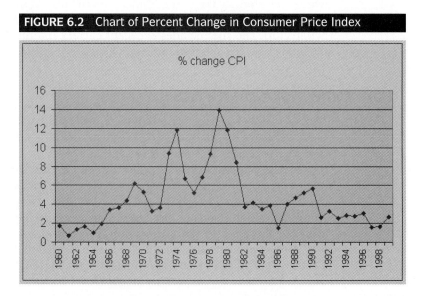

TABLE 6.2 Excel Support for Forecasting

Excel Functions	*Description*
TREND(*known_y's, known_x's, new_x's, constant*)	Returns values along a linear trend line
GROWTH(*known_y's, known_x's, new_x's, constant*)	Calculates predicted exponential growth
LINEST(*known_y's, known_x's, new_x's, constant, stats*)	Returns an array that describes a straight line that best fits the data
FORECAST(*x, known_y's, known_x's*)	Calculates a future value along a linear trend
Analysis Toolpak	*Description*
Moving average	Projects forecast values based on the average value of the variable over a specific number of preceding periods
Exponential smoothing	Predicts a value based on the forecast for the prior period, adjusted for the error in that prior forecast
Regression	Used to develop a model relating time series data to a set of variables assumed to influence the data

involve more formal analyses of time series, are invaluable in developing good forecasts. A variety of statistically based forecasting methods for time series are commonly used. Among the most popular are *moving average methods, exponential smoothing,* and *regression analysis.* These can be implemented very easily on a spreadsheet using basic functions available in Microsoft Excel and its *Data Analysis* tools; these are summarized in Table 6.2. Moving average and exponential smoothing models work best for stationary time series. For time series that involve trends and/or seasonal factors, other techniques have been developed. These include double moving average and exponential smoothing models, seasonal additive and multiplicative models, and Holt–Winters additive and multiplicative models. We will review each of these types of models. The CD-ROM accompanying this book contains an Excel add-in, *CB Predictor,* that applies these methods and incorporates some intelligent technology. We will describe *CB Predictor* later in this chapter.

FORECASTING MODELS FOR STATIONARY TIME SERIES

Two simple approaches that are useful over short time periods when trend, seasonal, or cyclical effects are not significant are moving average and exponential smoothing models.

Moving Average Models

The **simple moving average** method is based on the idea of averaging random fluctuations in the time series to identify the underlying direction in which the time series is changing. Because the moving average method assumes that future observations will be similar to the recent past, it is most useful as a short-range forecasting method. Although this method is very simple, it has proven to be quite useful in stable environments, such as inventory management, in which it is necessary to develop forecasts for a large number of items.

Specifically, the simple moving average forecast for the next period is computed as the average of the most recent k observations. The value of k is somewhat arbitrary, although its choice affects the accuracy of the forecast. The larger the value of k, the more the current forecast is dependent on older data; the smaller the value of k, the quicker the forecast responds to changes in the time series. (In the next section we discuss how to select k by examining errors associated with different values.)

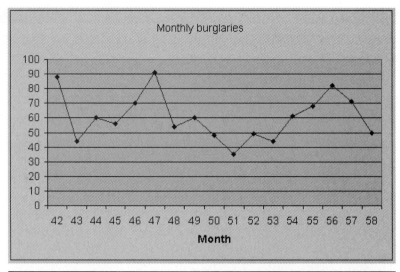

FIGURE 6.3 Chart of Burglaries

For instance, suppose that we want to forecast monthly burglaries from the work-sheet *Burglaries.xls* since the citizen–police program began. Figure 6.3 shows a graph of these data. The time series appears to be relatively stable, without trend, seasonal, or cyclical effects; thus, a moving average model would be appropriate. Setting $k = 3$, the three-period moving average forecast for month 59 is

$$\text{Month 59 forecast} = \frac{82 + 71 + 50}{3} = 67.67$$

Moving average forecasts can be generated easily on a spreadsheet. Figure 6.4 shows the computations for a three-period moving average forecast of burglaries.

FIGURE 6.4 Moving Average Forecasts for Burglaries

	C	D	E	F
1	After Citizen-Police Program			
2	Month	Monthly burglaries	Moving Average Forecast	
3	42	88		
4	43	44		=AVERAGE(D3:D5)
5	44	60		
6	45	56	64.00	Forecast for Month 45
7	46	70	53.33	
8	47	91	62.00	
9	48	54	72.33	
10	49	60	71.67	
11	50	48	68.33	
12	51	35	54.00	
13	52	49	47.67	
14	53	44	44.00	
15	54	61	42.67	
16	55	68	51.33	
17	56	82	57.67	
18	57	71	70.33	
19	58	50	73.67	
20	59		67.67	Forecast for Month 59
21				

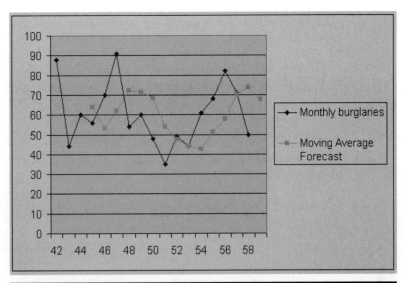

FIGURE 6.5   Chart of Burglaries and Moving Average Forecasts

Figure 6.5 shows a graph that contrasts the data with the forecasted values. Moving average forecasts can also be obtained from Excel's *Data Analysis* options (see the *Excel Note: Forecasting with Moving Averages*).

Weighted Moving Averages

In the simple moving average approach, the data are weighted equally. This may not be desirable, as we might wish to put more weight on recent observations than on older observations, particularly if the time series is changing rapidly. For example, you might assign a 60 percent weight to the most recent observation, 30 percent to the observation two periods prior, and the remaining 10 percent of the weight to the observation three periods prior. In this case, the three-period weighted moving average forecast for month 59 would be

$$\text{Month 59 Forecast} = \frac{0.1 \times 82 + 0.3 \times 71 + 0.6 \times 50}{0.1 + 0.3 + 0.6} = \frac{59.5}{1} = 59.5$$

Different weights can easily be incorporated into Excel formulas. This leads us to the questions of how to measure forecast accuracy and also how to select the best parameters for a forecasting model.

Error Metrics and Forecast Accuracy

The quality of a forecast depends on how accurate it is in predicting future values of a time series. The error in a forecast is the difference between the forecast and the actual value of the time series (once it is known!). In Figure 6.5, the forecast error is simply the vertical distance between the forecast and the data for the same time period. In the simple moving average model, different values for k will produce different forecasts. How do we know, for example, if a two-, three-period moving average forecast or a three-period weighted moving average model (or others) would be the best predictor for burglaries? We might first generate different forecasts using each of these models, as shown in Figure 6.8, and compute the errors associated with each model.

To analyze the accuracy of these models, we can define *error metrics,* which compare quantitatively the forecast with the actual observations. Three metrics that are

EXCEL NOTE

FORECASTING WITH MOVING AVERAGES

From the *Tools* menu, select *Data Analysis,* and then *Moving Average.* Excel displays the dialog box shown in Figure 6.6. You need to enter the *Input Range* of the data, the *Interval* (the value of k), and the first cell of the *Output Range.* To align the actual data with the forecasted values in the worksheet, select the first cell of the *Output Range* to be one row below the first value. You may also obtain a chart of the data and the moving averages, as well as a column of standard errors, by checking the appropriate boxes. However, we do not recommend using the chart or error options because the forecasts are not properly aligned with the data (the forecast value aligned with a particular data point represents the forecast for the *next* month) and thus can be misleading. Rather, we recommend that you generate your own chart as we did in Figure 6.5. Figure 6.7 shows the results produced by the *Moving*

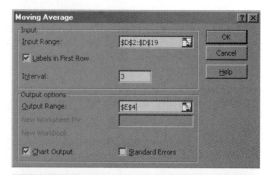

FIGURE 6.6   Excel Dialog Box for Moving Average Tool

Average tool (with some customization of the chart to show the months on the *x* axis). Note that the forecast for month 59 is aligned with the actual value for month 58 on the chart. Compare this to Figure 6.5 and you can see the difference.

FIGURE 6.7   Results of Excel Moving Average Tool (note misalignment of forecasts with actual data)

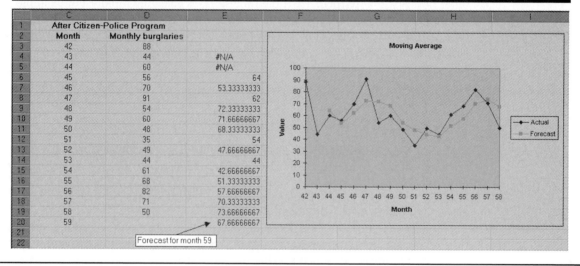

commonly used are the *mean absolute deviation, mean square error,* and *mean absolute percentage error.* The **mean absolute deviation (MAD)** is the average difference between the actual value and the forecast, averaged over a range of forecasted values:

$$\text{MAD} = \frac{\sum_{i=1}^{n} |A_t - F_t|}{n}$$

	C	D	E	F	G	H	I	J
1	After Citizen-Police Program						3 period	
2	Month	Monthly burglaries	k = 2	Error	k = 3	Error	weighted	Error
3	42	88						
4	43	44						
5	44	60	66.00	-6.00				
6	45	56	52.00	4.00	64.00	-8.00	58.00	-2.00
7	46	70	58.00	12.00	53.33	16.67	56.00	14.00
8	47	91	63.00	28.00	62.00	29.00	64.80	26.20
9	48	54	80.50	-26.50	72.33	-18.33	81.20	-27.20
10	49	60	72.50	-12.50	71.67	-11.67	66.70	-6.70
11	50	48	57.00	-9.00	68.33	-20.33	61.30	-13.30
12	51	35	54.00	-19.00	54.00	-19.00	52.20	-17.20
13	52	49	41.50	7.50	47.67	1.33	41.40	7.60
14	53	44	42.00	2.00	44.00	0.00	44.70	-0.70
15	54	61	46.50	14.50	42.67	18.33	44.60	16.40
16	55	68	52.50	15.50	51.33	16.67	54.70	13.30
17	56	82	64.50	17.50	57.67	24.33	63.50	18.50
18	57	71	75.00	-4.00	70.33	0.67	75.70	-4.70
19	58	50	76.50	-26.50	73.67	-23.67	74.00	-24.00
20	59		60.50		67.67		59.50	

FIGURE 6.8   Alternative Moving Average Forecasting Models

where A_t is the actual value of the time series at time t, F_t is the forecast value for time t, and n is the number of forecast values (*not* the number of data points since we do not have a forecast value associated with the first k data points). MAD provides a robust measure of error and is less affected by extreme observations.

Mean square error (MSE) is probably the most commonly used error metric. It penalizes larger errors because squaring larger numbers has a greater impact than squaring smaller numbers. The formula for MSE is

$$\text{MSE} = \frac{\sum_{i=1}^{n}(A_t - F_t)^2}{n}$$

Again, n represents the number of forecast values used in computing the average. Sometimes the square root of MSE, called the **root mean square error (RMSE),** is used.

A third commonly used metric is **mean absolute percentage error (MAPE).** MAPE is the average of absolute errors divided by actual observation values.

$$\text{MAPE} = \frac{\sum_{i=1}^{n}\left|\dfrac{A_t - F_t}{A_t}\right|}{n} \times 100$$

The values of MAD and MSE depend on the measurement scale of the time series data. For example, forecasting profit in the range of millions of dollars would result in very large MAD and MSE values, even for very accurate forecasting models. On the other hand, market share is measured in proportions, and therefore even bad forecasting models will have small values of MAD and MSE. Thus, these measures have no meaning except in comparison with other models used to forecast the same data. Generally, MAD is less affected by extreme observations and is preferable to MSE if such extreme observations are considered rare events with no special meaning. MAPE is different in that the measurement scale is eliminated by dividing the absolute error by the time series data value. This allows a better relative comparison. Although these

TABLE 6.3 Error Metrics for Moving Average Models of Burglary Data			
	k = 2	*k = 3*	*3-period weighted*
MAD	13.63	14.86	13.70
MSE	254.38	299.84	256.31
MAPE	23.63%	26.53%	24.46%

comments provide some guidelines, there is no universal agreement on which measure is best.

These measures can be used to compare the moving average forecasts in Figure 6.8. The results, shown in Table 6.3, verifies that the two-period moving average model provides the best forecast among these alternatives.

Exponential Smoothing Models

A versatile, yet highly effective approach for short-range forecasting is **simple exponential smoothing.** The basic simple exponential smoothing model is

$$F_{t+1} = (1 - \alpha)F_t + \alpha A_t$$
$$= F_t + \alpha(A_t - F_t)$$

where F_{t+1} is the forecast for time period $t + 1$, F_t is the forecast for period t, A_t is the observed value in period t, and α is a constant between 0 and 1, called the **smoothing constant.** To begin, the forecast for period 2 is set equal to the actual observation for period 1.

Using the two forms of the forecast equation just given, we can interpret the simple exponential smoothing model in two ways. In the first model, the forecast for the next period, F_{t+1}, is a weighted average of the forecast made for period t, F_t, and the actual observation in period t, A_t. The second form of the model, obtained by simply rearranging terms, states that the forecast for the next period, F_{t+1}, equals the forecast for the last period, F_t, plus a fraction α of the forecast error made in period t, $A_t - F_t$. Thus, to make a forecast once we have selected the smoothing constant, we need only know the previous forecast and the actual value. By repeated substitution for F_t in the equation, it is easy to demonstrate that F_{t+1} is a decreasingly weighted average of all past time series data. Thus, the forecast actually reflects *all* the data, provided that α is strictly between 0 and 1.

For the burglary data, the forecast for month 43 is 88, the actual observation for month 42. Suppose we choose $\alpha = 0.7$, then the forecast for month 44 would be

$$\text{Month 44 Forecast} = (1 - 0.7)(88) + (0.7)(44) = 57.2$$

The actual observation for month 44 is 60; thus, the forecast for month 45 would be

$$\text{Month 45 Forecast} = (1 - 0.7)(57.2) + (0.7)(60) = 59.16$$

Since the simple exponential smoothing model requires only the previous forecast and the current time series value, it is very easy to calculate; thus, it is highly suitable for environments such as inventory systems where many forecasts must be made. The smoothing constant α is usually chosen by experimentation in the same manner as choosing the number of periods to use in the moving average model. Different values of α affect how quickly the model responds to changes in the time series. For instance, a value of $\alpha = 0$ would simply repeat last period's forecast, while $\alpha = 1$ would forecast

	C	D	E	F	G	H	I	J	K	L	M
1	After Citizen-Police Program										
2	Month	Monthly burglaries	0.1	0.2	0.3	0.4	0.5	0.6	0.7	0.8	0.9
3	42	88	88.00	88.00	88.00	88.00	88.00	88.00	88.00	88.00	88.00
4	43	44	88.00	88.00	88.00	88.00	88.00	88.00	88.00	88.00	88.00
5	44	60	83.60	79.20	74.80	70.40	66.00	61.60	57.20	52.80	48.40
6	45	56	81.24	75.36	70.36	66.24	63.00	60.64	59.16	58.56	58.84
7	46	70	78.72	71.49	66.05	62.14	59.50	57.86	56.95	56.51	56.28
8	47	91	77.84	71.19	67.24	65.29	64.75	65.14	66.08	67.30	68.63
9	48	54	79.16	75.15	74.37	75.57	77.88	80.66	83.53	86.26	88.76
10	49	60	76.64	70.92	68.26	66.94	65.94	64.66	62.86	60.45	57.48
11	50	48	74.98	68.74	65.78	64.17	62.97	61.87	60.86	60.09	59.75
12	51	35	72.28	64.59	60.45	57.70	55.48	53.55	51.86	50.42	49.17
13	52	49	68.55	58.67	52.81	48.62	45.24	42.42	40.06	38.08	36.42
14	53	44	66.60	56.74	51.67	48.77	47.12	46.37	46.32	46.82	47.74
15	54	61	64.34	54.19	49.37	46.86	45.56	44.95	44.70	44.56	44.37
16	55	68	64.00	55.55	52.86	52.52	53.28	54.58	56.11	57.71	59.34
17	56	82	64.40	58.04	57.40	58.71	60.64	62.63	64.43	65.94	67.13
18	57	71	66.16	62.83	64.78	68.03	71.32	74.25	76.73	78.79	80.51
19	58	50	66.65	64.47	66.65	69.22	71.16	72.30	72.72	72.56	71.95
20	59		64.98	61.57	61.65	61.53	60.58	58.92	56.82	54.51	52.20
21		MAD	19.33	17.16	16.15	15.36	14.93	14.71	14.72	14.88	15.36
22		MSE	496.07	390.84	359.18	346.56	340.77	338.41	339.03	343.32	352.38
23		MAPE	38.28%	32.71%	30.12%	28.36%	27.54%	27.09%	27.09%	27.38%	28.23%

FIGURE 6.9   Exponential Smoothing Forecasts for Burglary Data

last period's actual demand. The closer α is to 1, the quicker the model responds to changes in the time series because it puts more weight on the actual current observation than on the forecast. Likewise, the closer α is to 0, the more weight is put on the prior forecast, so the model would respond to changes more slowly.

An Excel spreadsheet for evaluating exponential smoothing models for the burglary data using values of α between 0.1 and 0.9 is shown in Figure 6.9. A smoothing constant of $\alpha = 0.6$ provides the least error for all three metrics. Excel has a *Data Analysis* tool for exponential smoothing (see the *Excel Note: Forecasting with Exponential Smoothing*).

FORECASTING MODELS WITH LINEAR TRENDS

Double moving average and **double exponential smoothing** models are more appropriate for time series with a linear trend but no significant cyclical or seasonal components. Both methods are based on the linear trend equation

$$F_{t+k} = a_t + b_t k$$

This may look familiar from simple linear regression. That is, the forecast for k periods into the future from period t is a function of a base value a_t, also known as the *level*, and a *trend* or slope b_t. Double moving average and double exponential smoothing differ in how the data are used to arrive at appropriate values for a_t and b_t.

Double Moving Average

Double moving average involves taking averages of averages. Let M_t be the simple moving average for the last k periods (including period t):

$$M_t = [A_{t-k+1} + A_{t-k+2} + \cdots + A_t]/k$$

The double moving average, D_t, for the last k periods (including period t) is the average of the simple moving averages:

EXCEL NOTE

FORECASTING WITH EXPONENTIAL SMOOTHING

From the *Tools* menu, select *Data Analysis,* and then *Exponential Smoothing.* As in the *Moving Average* dialog box, you must enter the *Input Range* of the time series data, the *Damping Factor* $(1 - \alpha)$—*not* the smoothing constant as we have defined it (!)—and the first cell of the *Output Range* (see Figure 6.10). You also have options for labels, to chart output, and to obtain standard errors. As opposed to the *Moving Average* tool, the chart generated by this tool does correctly align the forecasts with the actual data, as shown in Figure 6.11. You can see that the exponential smoothing model follows the pattern of the data quite closely, although it tends to lag with an increasing trend in the data.

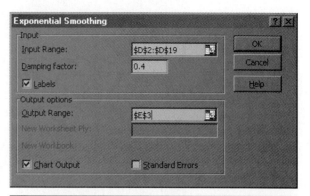

FIGURE 6.10 Exponential Smoothing Dialog Box

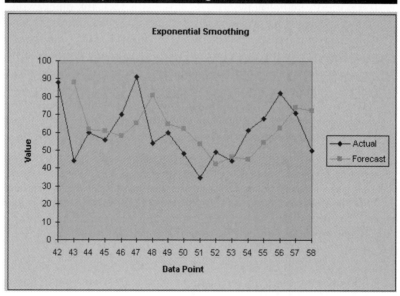

FIGURE 6.11 Exponential Smoothing Forecasts for $\alpha = 0.6$

$$D_t = [M_{t-k+1} + M_{t-k+2} + \cdots + M_t]/k$$

Using these values, the double moving average method estimates the values of a_t and b_t in the linear trend model as

$$a_t = 2M_t - D_t$$
$$b_t = (2/(k - 1))[M_t - D_t]$$

These equations are derived essentially by minimizing the sum of squared errors using the last k periods of data. Once these parameters are determined, forecasts beyond the

	A	B	C	D	E	F	G
1	Double Moving Average						
2	k=	3					
3		Total Energy					
4	Year	Consumption	M(t)	D(t)	Level	Trend	Forecast
5	1949	31,999,960					
6	1950	34,634,733					
7	1951	36,996,399	34543697.33				
8	1952	36,770,393	36133841.67				
9	1953	37,683,501	37150097.67	35942545.56	38357649.78	1207552.11	
10	1954	36,659,898	37037930.67	36773956.67	37301904.67	263974.00	39565201.89
11	1955	40,241,679	38195026.00	37461018.11	38929033.89	734007.89	37565878.67
12	1956	41,790,841	39564139.33	38265698.67	40862580.00	1298440.67	39663041.78
48	1992	85,512,231	84586828.67	84272470.44	84901186.89	314358.22	85732972.56
49	1993	87,309,434	85628067.67	84831820.89	86424314.44	796246.78	85215545.11
50	1994	89,233,821	87351828.67	85855575.00	88848082.33	1496253.67	87220561.22
51	1995	90,939,626	89160960.33	87380285.56	90941635.11	1780674.78	90344336.00
52	1996	93,910,936	91361461.00	89291416.67	93431505.33	2070044.33	92722309.89
53	1997	94,315,875	93055479.00	91192633.44	94918324.56	1862845.56	95501549.67
54	1998	94,569,997	94265602.67	92894180.89	95637024.44	1371421.78	96781170.11
55	1999	96,595,737	95160536.33	94160539.33	96160533.33	999997.00	97008446.22
56							97160530.33

FIGURE 6.12 Portion of Double Moving Average Forecasting Calculations

end of the observed data (time period T) are calculated using the linear trend model with values of a_T and b_T. That is, for k periods beyond period T, the forecast is $F_{T+k} = a_T + b_T k$. The forecast for the next period would be $F_{T+1} = a_T + b_T(1)$.

To illustrate the double moving average, we use Total Energy Consumption in the worksheet *Energy Production & Consumption.xls*. This time series has a general linear trend. Figure 6.12 shows a portion of a worksheet for calculating the forecasts. The intermediate calculations for the first forecast (year 1954) are as follows:

$$M_{1951} = (31{,}999{,}960 + 34{,}634{,}733 + 36{,}996{,}399)/3 = 34{,}543{,}697.33$$
$$M_{1952} = (34{,}634{,}733 + 36{,}996{,}399 + 36{,}770{,}393)/3 = 36{,}133{,}841.67$$
$$M_{1953} = (36{,}996{,}399 + 36{,}770{,}393 + 37{,}683{,}501)/3 = 37{,}150{,}097.67$$
$$D_{1953} = (M_{1951} + M_{1952} + M_{1953})/3 = (34{,}543{,}697.33 + 36{,}133{,}841.67$$
$$+ 37{,}150{,}097.67)/3 = 35{,}942{,}545.56$$

$$a_{1953} = 2M_{1953} - D_{1953} = 2(37{,}150{,}097.67) - 35{,}942{,}545.56 = 38{,}357{,}649.78$$
$$b_{1953} = (2/(3-1))[M_{1953} - D_{1953}] = 37{,}150{,}097.67 - 35{,}942{,}545.56 = 1{,}207{,}552.11$$

The forecast for year 1954 is

$$F_{1954} = a_{1953} + b_{1953} = 38{,}357{,}649.78 + 1{,}207{,}552.11 = 39{,}565{,}201.89$$

Other forecasts are calculated in a similar manner. The model for predicting future energy consumption for year 2000 and beyond is

$$F_{1999+k} = 96{,}160{,}533.33 + 999{,}997k$$

Figure 6.13 shows a chart of the actual values and forecasts.

Double Exponential Smoothing

Like double moving average, double exponential smoothing is also based on the linear trend equation, $F_{t+k} = a_t + b_t k$, but the estimates of a_t and b_t are obtained from the following equations:

$$a_t = \alpha y_t + (1 - \alpha)(a_{t-1} + b_{t-1})$$
$$b_t = \beta(a_t - a_{t-1}) + (1 - \beta)b_{t-1}$$

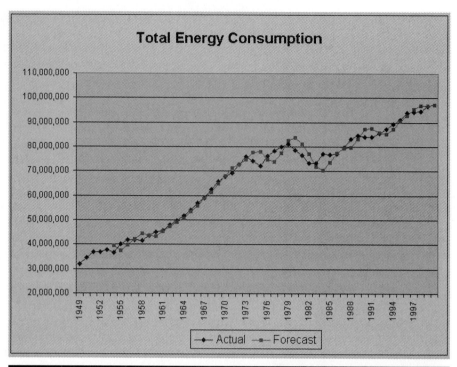

FIGURE 6.13 Double Moving Average Forecasts

In essence, we are smoothing both parameters of the linear trend model. From the first equation, the estimate of the level in period t is a weighted average of the observed value at time t and the predicted value at time t, $a_{t-1} + b_{t-1}(1)$ based on single exponential smoothing. For large values of α, more weight is placed on the observed value. Lower values of α put more weight on the smoothed predicted value. Similarly, from the second equation, the estimate of the trend in period t is a weighted average of the differences in the estimated levels in periods t and $t - 1$ and the estimate of the level in period $t - 1$. Larger values of β place more weight on the differences in the levels, while lower values of β put more emphasis on the previous estimate of the trend.

To initialize the double exponential smoothing process, we need values for a_1 and b_1. One approach is to let $a_1 = A_1$ and $b_1 = A_2 - A_1$; that is, estimate the initial level with the first observation and the initial trend with the difference in the first two observations. As with single exponential smoothing we are free to choose the values of α and β. MAD, MSE, or MAPE may be used to find good values for these smoothing parameters. We leave it to you as an exercise to implement this model on a spreadsheet for the total energy consumption data.

FORECASTING MODELS WITH SEASONALITY

Seasonal factors (with no trend) can be incorporated in one of two ways, as an additive factor using the model

$$F_{t+k} = a_t + S_{t-s+k}$$

or as a multiplicative factor using the model

$$F_{t+k} = a_t S_{t-s+k}$$

In both models, S_j is the seasonal factor for period j and s is the number of periods in a season. A "season" can be a year, quarter, month, or even a week, depending on the application. In any case, the forecast for period $t + k$ is adjusted up or down from a level (a_t) by the seasonal factor. The multiplicative model is perhaps more appropriate when the seasonal factors are increasing or decreasing over time.

Additive Seasonality

The level and seasonal factors are estimated in the additive model using the following equations:

$$a_t = \alpha(A_t - S_{t-s}) + (1 - \alpha)a_{t-1}$$
$$S_t = \gamma(A_t - a_t) + (1 - \gamma)S_{t-s}$$

where α and γ are smoothing constants. The first equation estimates the level for period t as a weighted average of the deseasonalized data for period t, $(A_t - S_{t-s})$, and the previous period's level. The seasonal factors are updated as well using the second equation. The seasonal factor is a weighted average of the estimated seasonal component for period t $(A_t - a_t)$ and the seasonal factor for the last period of that season type. Then the forecast for the next period is $F_{t+1} = a_t + S_{t-s+1}$. For k periods out from the final observed period T, the forecast is

$$F_{T+k} = a_T + S_{T-s+k}$$

To initialize the model, we need to estimate the level and seasonal factors for the first s periods (e.g., for an annual season with quarterly data this would be the first 4 periods, for monthly data it would be the first 12 periods, etc.). We will use the following approach:

$$a_s = \sum_{t=1}^{s} A_t/s$$
$$a_t = a_s \qquad t = 1, 2, \ldots s$$

and

$$S_t = A_t - a_t \qquad t = 1, 2, \ldots s$$

That is, we initialize the level for the first s periods to the average of the observed values over these periods and the seasonal factors to the difference between the observed data and the estimated levels. Once these have been initialized, the smoothing equations can be implemented for updating.

To illustrate this model, we will use the data in the worksheet *Gas & Electric.xls*, which provides two year's data on natural gas and electricity usage for a family residence, as shown in Figure 6.14. The data are clearly seasonal, with gas usage being high during the winter heating season and low in the summer. Electric usage is the opposite, with heavier usage during the summer months because of air conditioning.

To forecast gas usage, we will choose $\alpha = 0.7$ and $\gamma = 0.7$. The initial level for the first 12 periods is

$$a_s = \sum_{t=1}^{12} A_t/12 = 105.75$$

and the seasonal factors are computed by subtracting this value from the actual observations. Using the first seasonal factor for January, the forecast for the following January is

$$F_{13} = a_{12} + S_1 = 105.75 + 138.25 = 244.00$$

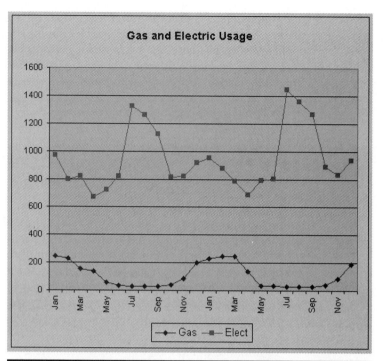

FIGURE 6.14   Chart of Natural Gas and Electric Usage

Once the actual value for January (period 13) is known, we may update the parameters using the smoothing equations:

$$a_{13} = \alpha(A_{13} - S_1) + (1 - \alpha)a_{12} = 0.7(230 - 138.25) + 0.3(105.75) = 95.95$$
$$S_{13} = \gamma(A_{13} - a_{13}) + (1 - \gamma)S_1 = 0.7(230 - 95.95) + 0.3(138.25) = 135.31$$

The forecasted value for February is then

$$F_{14} = a_{13} + S_2 = 95.95 + 122.25 = 218.20$$

Other forecasts are calculated in a similar manner. These are summarized in the worksheet in Figure 6.15. The forecast appears to track the data quite well, although we might consider experimenting with other smoothing constants.

Multiplicative Seasonality

The multiplicative seasonal model has the same basic smoothing structure as the additive seasonal model but is more appropriate for seasonal time series that increase in amplitude over time. The smoothing equations are

$$a_t = \alpha(A_t/S_{t-s}) + (1 - \alpha)a_{t-1}$$
$$S_t = \gamma(A_t/a_t) + (1 - \gamma)S_{t-s}$$

where α and γ are again the smoothing constants. Here, A_t/S_{t-s} is the deseasonalized estimate for period t. Large values of α put more emphasis on this term in estimating the level for period t. The term A_t/a_t is an estimate of the seasonal factor for period t. Large values of γ put more emphasis on this in the estimate of the seasonal factor.

The forecast for the next period is $F_{t+1} = a_t S_{t-s+1}$. For k periods out from the final observed period T, the forecast is

$$F_{T+k} = a_T S_{T-s+k}$$

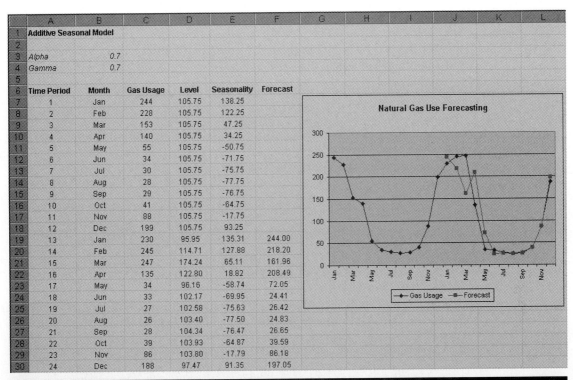

	A	B	C	D	E	F
1	Additive Seasonal Model					
2						
3	Alpha	0.7				
4	Gamma	0.7				
5						
6	Time Period	Month	Gas Usage	Level	Seasonality	Forecast
7	1	Jan	244	105.75	138.25	
8	2	Feb	228	105.75	122.25	
9	3	Mar	153	105.75	47.25	
10	4	Apr	140	105.75	34.25	
11	5	May	55	105.75	-50.75	
12	6	Jun	34	105.75	-71.75	
13	7	Jul	30	105.75	-75.75	
14	8	Aug	28	105.75	-77.75	
15	9	Sep	29	105.75	-76.75	
16	10	Oct	41	105.75	-64.75	
17	11	Nov	88	105.75	-17.75	
18	12	Dec	199	105.75	93.25	
19	13	Jan	230	95.95	135.31	244.00
20	14	Feb	245	114.71	127.88	218.20
21	15	Mar	247	174.24	65.11	161.96
22	16	Apr	135	122.80	18.82	208.49
23	17	May	34	96.16	-58.74	72.05
24	18	Jun	33	102.17	-69.95	24.41
25	19	Jul	27	102.58	-75.63	26.42
26	20	Aug	26	103.40	-77.50	24.83
27	21	Sep	28	104.34	-76.47	26.65
28	22	Oct	39	103.93	-64.87	39.59
29	23	Nov	86	103.80	-17.79	86.18
30	24	Dec	188	97.47	91.35	197.05

FIGURE 6.15   Additive Seasonal Model for Natural Gas Use Forecasting

As in the additive model, we need initial values for the level and seasonal factors. We do this as follows:

$$a_s = \sum_{t=1}^{s} A_t/s$$
$$a_t = a_s \qquad t = 1, 2, \ldots s$$

and

$$S_t = A_t/a_t \qquad t = 1, 2, \ldots s$$

Once these have been initialized, the smoothing equations can be implemented for updating.

MODELS FOR TIME SERIES WITH TREND AND SEASONAL COMPONENTS

Many time series exhibit both trend and seasonality. Such might be the case for growing sales of a seasonal product. The methods we describe are based on the work of two researchers, C. C. Holt, who developed the basic approach, and P. R. Winters, who extended Holt's work. Hence, this approach is commonly referred to as Holt–Winters models. The additive model applies to time series with relatively stable seasonality, while the multiplicative model applies to time series whose amplitude increases over time.

Holt–Winters Additive Model

The Holt–Winters additive model is similar to the additive model incorporating seasonality that we described in the last section, but it also includes a trend component. The smoothing equations are

$$a_t = \alpha(A_t - S_{t-s}) + (1 - \alpha)(a_{t-1} + b_{t-1})$$
$$b_t = \beta(a_t - a_{t-1}) + (1 - \beta)b_{t-1}$$
$$S_t = \gamma(A_t - a_t) + (1 - \gamma)S_{t-s}$$

Here, α, β, and γ are the smoothing parameters for level, trend, and seasonal components, respectively. The forecast for period $t + 1$ is

$$F_{t+1} = a_t + b_t + S_{t-s+1}$$

The forecast for k periods beyond the last period of observed data (period T) is

$$F_{T+k} = a_T + b_T k + S_{T-s+k}$$

The initial values of level and trend are estimated in the same fashion as in the additive model for seasonality. The initial values for the trend are $b_t = b_s$, for $t = 1, 2, \ldots s$, where

$$b_s = [(A_{s+1} - A_1)/s + (A_{s+2} - A_s)/s + \cdots + (A_{s+s} - A_s)/s]/s$$

Note that each term inside the brackets is an estimate of the trend over one season. We average these over the first $2s$ periods.

Holt–Winters Multiplicative Model

The Holt–Winters multiplicative model parallels the additive model:

$$a_t = \alpha(A_t/S_{t-s}) + (1 - \alpha)(a_{t-1} + b_{t-1})$$
$$b_t = \beta(a_t - a_{t-1}) + (1 - \beta)b_{t-1}$$
$$S_t = \gamma(A_t/a_t) + (1 - \gamma)S_{t-s}$$

The forecast for period $t + 1$ is

$$F_{t+1} = (a_t + b_t)S_{t-s+1}$$

The forecast for k periods beyond the last period of observed data (period T) is

$$F_{T+k} = (a_T + b_T k)S_{T-s+k}$$

The initial values of level and trend are estimated in the same fashion as in the multiplicative model for seasonality, and the trend component as in the Holt–Winters additive model.

As Holt–Winters models are somewhat more complicated than the others, we will not provide numerical examples. In addition, having three smoothing constants makes it more difficult to optimize the forecasting method. Fortunately, specialized software makes using all the models we have described quite easy. In the next section, we describe an Excel add-in, *CB Predictor*, for easily identifying the best forecasting models.

CB PREDICTOR

CB Predictor is an Excel add-in that was developed by Decisioneering, Inc., the makers of *Crystal Ball.* The student version of *CB Predictor,* provided with this text, includes the time series forecasting approaches we have discussed. We will illustrate the use of *CB Predictor* first for the data in the worksheet *Burglaries.xls* (see the *Excel Note: Using CB Predictor* for basic information on using the add-in). Both the single moving average and single exponential methods were chosen for this example. *CB Predictor* found the best fit to be a 2-period moving average based on RMSE, as shown in Figure 6.18. This method was also the best for the MAD and MAPE error metrics. The Durbin–Watson statistic checks for autocorrelation (see Chapter 5), with values of 2 indicating no auto-correlation. Theil's *U*-statistic is a relative error measure that compares the results with

---

EXCEL NOTE

USING *CB PREDICTOR*

After *CB Predictor* has been installed, it may be accessed in Excel from the *CB Tools* menu; if the menu is not present in Excel, make sure that the *Crystal Ball* box is checked in the *Tools . . . Add-Ins* window. When *CB Predictor* is started, the dialog box shown in Figure 6.16 appears. The dialog box contains four tabs that query you for information one step at a time. *Input Data* allows you to specify the data range on which to base your forecast; *Data Attributes* allows you to specify the type of data and whether or not seasonality is present (for the natural gas data, the data are expressed in months with a seasonality of 12); *Method Gallery* allows you to select one of eight time series methods—single moving average, double moving average, single exponential smoothing, double exponential smoothing, seasonal additive, seasonal multiplicative, Holt–Winters additive, or Holt–Winters multiplicative (see Figure 6.17). The graphs shown in the *Method Gallery* suggest the method that is best suited for the data. For example, single moving average and exponential smoothing best apply to nonseasonal data with no trend; double moving average and double exponential smoothing are best for nonseasonal data with a trend. However, *CB Predictor* will run each method you select and will recommend the one that best forecasts your data. The final tab, *Results,* allows you to specify a variety of reporting options.

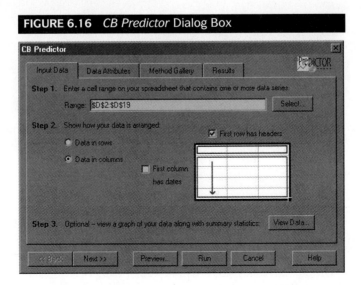

FIGURE 6.16   *CB Predictor* Dialog Box

(Continued)

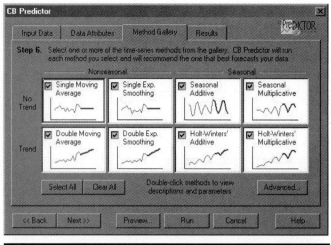

FIGURE 6.17 *CB Predictor* Method Gallery

FIGURE 6.18 *CB Predictor* Results—Methods Table

	A	B	C	D	E	F	G	H	I
1	**Methods Table for Burglary Data**								
2	Created: 11/4/2001 at 6:47:33 PM								
3									
19	Series	Monthly burglaries							
20									
21		Table Items							
22	Methods	Rank	RMSE	MAD	MAPE	Durbin-Watson	Theil's U	Periods	Alpha
23	Single Exponential Smoothing	2	17.843	13.753	25.333	1.806	0.93		0.631
24	**Single Moving Average**	1	15.949	13.633	23.626	1.457	1.015	2	

FIGURE 6.19 *CB Predictor* Results—Results Table

	A	B	C	D	E	F
1	**Results Table for Burglary Data**					
2	Created: 11/4/2001 at 6:47:32 PM					
3						
23	Series	Monthly burglaries				
24						
25		Data				
26	Date	Historical Data	Lower: 5%	Fit & Forecast	Upper: 95%	Residuals
27	Period 1	88				88
28	Period 2	44				44
29	Period 3	60		66		-6
30	Period 4	56		52		4
31	Period 5	70		58		12
32	Period 6	91		63		28
33	Period 7	54		80.5		-26.5
34	Period 8	60		72.5		-12.5
35	Period 9	48		57		-9
36	Period 10	35		54		-19
37	Period 11	49		41.5		7.5
38	Period 12	44		42		2
39	Period 13	61		46.5		14.5
40	Period 14	68		52.5		15.5
41	Period 15	82		64.5		17.5
42	Period 16	71		75		-4
43	Period 17	50		76.5		-26.5
44	Period 18		32.62344079	60.5	88.37655921	

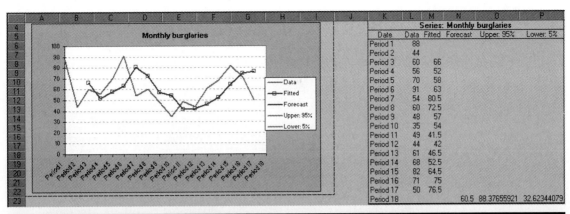

FIGURE 6.20   *CB Predictor* Results—Chart and Forecast Values

a naïve forecast. A value less than 1 means that the forecasting technique is better than guessing, a value equal to 1 means that the technique is about as good as guessing, and a value greater than 1 means that the forecasting technique is worse than guessing. Note that *CB Predictor* identifies the best number of periods for the moving average or the best smoothing constants as appropriate. For instance, in Figure 6.18, we see that the best-fitting single exponential smoothing model has alpha = 0.631. Figures 6.19 and 6.20 show other portions of the *CB Predictor* output.

For the gas usage data in *Gas & Electric.xls,* we selected all methods in the *Method Gallery.* Figure 6.21 shows the results. In this example, the Holt–Winters' method had the best value based on RMSE, but that the Seasonal Multiplicative method was slightly better on the MAD and MAPE error metrics. Figures 6.22 and 6.23 show the results table and chart and forecast values.

REGRESSION MODELS

We introduced regression in the previous chapter as a means of developing relationships between dependent and independent variables. Simple linear regression using time as the independent variable is one approach to forecasting; however, it requires the assumption of linearity, which severely limits its applicability. For example, Figure 6.24 shows a linear trend line fitted to the last nine years of data for total energy consumption in the worksheet *Energy Production & Consumption.xls* using the *Add*

FIGURE 6.21   *CB Predictor* Results for Gas Use Forecasting—Methods Table

	Methods	Rank	RMSE	MAD	MAPE	Durbin-Watson	Theil's U	Periods	Alpha	Beta	Gamma
71	Methods	Rank	RMSE	MAD	MAPE	Durbin-Watson	Theil's U	Periods	Alpha	Beta	Gamma
72	Double Exponential Smoothing	5	48.063	37.225	52.88	1.889	1.367		0.999	0.795	
73	Double Moving Average	8	57.467	44.655	76.398	1.237	1.795	2			
74	Holt-Winters' Additive	4	31.545	16.581	12.689	1.377	0.214		0.982	0.001	0.001
75	**Holt-Winters' Multiplicative**	**1**	**13.495**	**8.4323**	**8.967**	**2.101**	**0.147**		**0.021**	**0.999**	**0.001**
76	Seasonal Additive	3	31.481	16.577	12.686	1.378	0.215		0.981		0.001
77	Seasonal Multiplicative	2	13.958	7.3199	6.546	2.024	0.116		0.116		0.001
78	Single Exponential Smoothing	6	52.116	34.113	42.459	0.874	1		0.999		
79	Single Moving Average	7	53.211	35.565	44.252	0.871	1	1			

	A	B	C	D	E	F
30	Series	Gas Use ▼				
31						
32		Data ▼				
33	Date ▼	Historical Data	Lower: 5%	Fit & Forecast	Upper: 95%	Residuals
34	Period 1	244		231.9877737		12.01222633
35	Period 2	228		231.7271492		-3.727149216
36	Period 3	153		195.3057729		-42.30577289
37	Period 4	140		133.7946425		6.205357499
38	Period 5	55		43.400919		11.599081
39	Period 6	34		32.81340696		1.186593036
40	Period 7	30		28.05697291		1.943027085
41	Period 8	28		26.74426997		1.255730032
42	Period 9	29		28.41500403		0.584995973
43	Period 10	41		40.15420871		0.845791294
44	Period 11	88		87.93254586		0.067454139
45	Period 12	199		196.9247166		2.075283398
46	Period 13	230		252.2601518		-22.26015185
47	Period 14	245		252.0891453		-7.089145309
48	Period 15	247		213.0518383		33.94816169
49	Period 16	135		148.8029184		-13.80291843
50	Period 17	34		48.52628461		-14.52628461
51	Period 18	33		36.09732802		-3.097328024
52	Period 19	27		30.58614297		-3.586142969
53	Period 20	26		28.7381628		-2.738162796
54	Period 21	28		30.03598853		-2.035988534
55	Period 22	39		41.72616514		-2.726165136
56	Period 23	86		89.66867048		-3.668670476
57	Period 24	188		197.0871515		-9.087151516
58	Period 25		224.2201094	247.383836	270.5475627	

FIGURE 6.22   *CB Predictor* Results—Results Table

Trendline option in Excel. In the short-term, such a model might be appropriate, whereas a linear fit to the complete set of data (see Figure 6.25) would not be as accurate. Although regression models do not reflect changes as accurately as short-range forecasting models, they do have an advantage in that they can forecast out as far into the future as you wish. You must realize, however, that forecast errors are larger the further into the future forecasts are made.

FIGURE 6.23   *CB Predictor* Results—Chart and Forecast Values

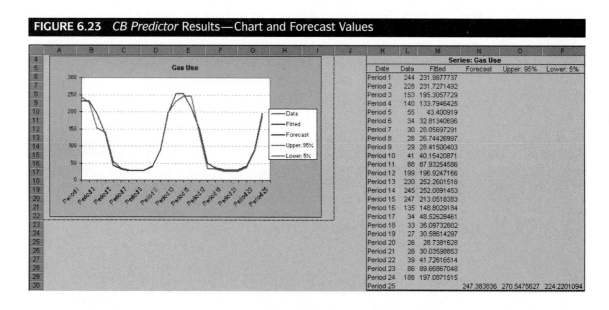

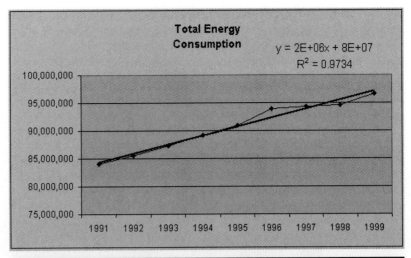

FIGURE 6.24 Linear Trend Line for Short-Term Energy Consumption

Even if the time series is not linear, we can use the *Add Trendline* option in Excel to fit a nonlinear function. Excel provides a variety of functional forms (see Figure 6.26). Figure 6.27 shows a fourth-degree polynomial trend line for females in Ohio prisons from the worksheet *Ohio Prison Population.xls*. You can see that this function captures the general trend in the data quite well, with an R^2 of 0.9937. Selecting the appropriate function requires some knowledge of the mathematical properties of functions and some experimentation. The Excel functions TREND, GROWTH, LINEST, and FORECAST, summarized in Table 6.2, also provide limited forecasting ability for linear or exponential time series.

Incorporating Seasonality in Regression Models

Quite often, time series data exhibit seasonality, especially on an annual basis, as we saw in the *Gas & Electric.xls* data. Regression models can be used for time series with

FIGURE 6.25 Linear Trend Line for Long-Term Energy Consumption

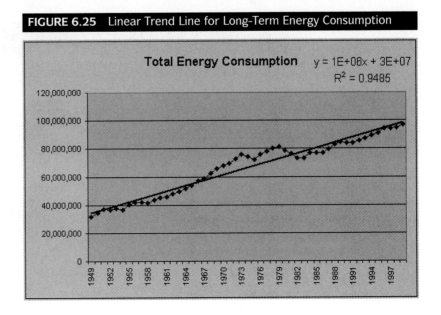

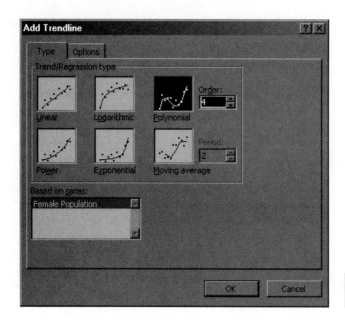

FIGURE 6.26 Excel Dialog Box for *Add Trendline*

seasonality. To do this, we use ordinal variables for the seasonal components, creating a multiple regression model as described in the previous chapter. With monthly data, as we have for natural gas usage, we have 12 seasonal components. Thus, we define 12 ordinal variables. Each month's variable will have an observed value of 0, except for the month corresponding to the actual observation, which is assigned a value of 1. This model picks up trends from the regression coefficient for time, and seasonality from the ordinal variables for each month.

If we included all 12 seasonality variables in the regression model, we would encounter a problem of dependence among the independent variables, because the time column could be expressed as a weighted sum of the remaining columns of

FIGURE 6.27 Fourth-Degree Polynomial Trend Line and Regression Equation

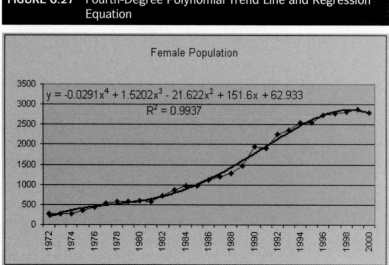

independent variables, violating an important theoretical assumption for using regression. Therefore, we will use only the first 11 ordinal variables, and the model is

$$\text{Gas Usage} = \beta_0 + \beta_1 \text{ Time} + \beta_2 \text{ January} + \beta_3 \text{ February} + \beta_4 \text{ March} + \beta_5 \text{ April}$$
$$+ \beta_6 \text{ May} + \beta_7 \text{ June} + \beta_8 \text{ July} + \beta_9 \text{ August} + \beta_{10} \text{ September}$$
$$+ \beta_{11} \text{ October} + \beta_{12} \text{ November}$$

The data matrix for the regression analysis is given below:

Month	Gas Use	Time	Jan	Feb	Mar	Apr	May	Jun	Jul	Aug	Sep	Oct	Nov
Jan	244	1	1	0	0	0	0	0	0	0	0	0	0
Feb	228	2	0	1	0	0	0	0	0	0	0	0	0
Mar	153	3	0	0	1	0	0	0	0	0	0	0	0
Apr	140	4	0	0	0	1	0	0	0	0	0	0	0
May	55	5	0	0	0	0	1	0	0	0	0	0	0
Jun	34	6	0	0	0	0	0	1	0	0	0	0	0
Jul	30	7	0	0	0	0	0	0	1	0	0	0	0
Aug	28	8	0	0	0	0	0	0	0	1	0	0	0
Sep	29	9	0	0	0	0	0	0	0	0	1	0	0
Oct	41	10	0	0	0	0	0	0	0	0	0	1	0
Nov	88	11	0	0	0	0	0	0	0	0	0	0	1
Dec	199	12	0	0	0	0	0	0	0	0	0	0	0
Jan	230	13	1	0	0	0	0	0	0	0	0	0	0
Feb	245	14	0	1	0	0	0	0	0	0	0	0	0
Mar	247	15	0	0	1	0	0	0	0	0	0	0	0
Apr	135	16	0	0	0	1	0	0	0	0	0	0	0
May	34	17	0	0	0	0	1	0	0	0	0	0	0
Jun	33	18	0	0	0	0	0	1	0	0	0	0	0
Jul	27	19	0	0	0	0	0	0	1	0	0	0	0
Aug	26	20	0	0	0	0	0	0	0	1	0	0	0
Sep	28	21	0	0	0	0	0	0	0	0	1	0	0
Oct	39	22	0	0	0	0	0	0	0	0	0	1	0
Nov	86	23	0	0	0	0	0	0	0	0	0	0	1
Dec	188	24	0	0	0	0	0	0	0	0	0	0	0

The forecast for December of the first year will be $\beta_0 + \beta_1(12)$. The variable coefficients (betas) for each of the other 11 months will show the adjustment relative to December. For example, the January forecast (Time = 1) would be $\beta_0 + \beta_1(1) + \beta_2(1)$. The forecast for the *following* January (Time = 13) would be $\beta_0 + \beta_1(13) + \beta_2(1)$.

Figure 6.28 shows the results of using the *Regression* tool in Excel. The R^2 for this model is 0.972, which is very good. The regression model obtained from the two years' of data is

$$\text{Gas Usage} = 187.375 + 0.340 \text{ Time} + 47.234 \text{ January} + 46.403 \text{ February}$$
$$+ 9.563 \text{ March} - 53.278 \text{ April} - 146.618 \text{ May} - 157.958 \text{ June}$$
$$- 163.299 \text{ July} - 165.139 \text{ August} - 163.979 \text{ September}$$
$$- 152.819 \text{ October} - 106.160 \text{ November}$$

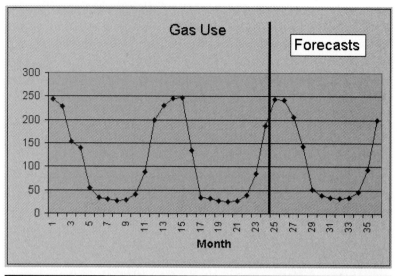

FIGURE 6.28 Regression-Based Forecasts

From the *p*-values, we see that Time and March are not significant. Because the data are relatively stable with no trend, it is not surprising that Time is not significant. March is not significant because there is considerable difference in the March data values for the two years, and with only two data points, the sample size is too small to obtain a good estimate of the seasonal factor. Figure 6.28 shows the forecasts for the next year generated by the model.

THE PRACTICE OF FORECASTING

In practice, managers use a variety of judgmental and quantitative forecasting techniques. Statistical methods alone cannot account for such factors as sales promotions, unusual environmental disturbances, new product introductions, large one-time orders, and so on. Many managers begin with a statistical forecast and adjust it to account for intangible factors. Others may develop independent judgmental and statistical forecasts, and then combine them, either objectively by averaging or in a subjective manner. It is impossible to provide universal guidance as to which approaches are best, for they depend on a variety of factors, including the presence or absence of trends and seasonality, the number of data points available, length of the forecast time horizon, and the experience and knowledge of the forecaster. Often, quantitative approaches will miss significant changes in the data, such as reversal of trends, while qualitative forecasts may catch them, particularly when using indicators as discussed earlier in this chapter.

Here we briefly highlight two practical examples of forecasting and encourage you to read the full articles cited for better insight into the practice of forecasting.

• Allied-Signal's Albuquerque Microelectronics Operation (AMO) produced radiation-hardened microchips for the U.S. Department of Energy (DOE). In 1989, a decision was made to close a plant, but operations at AMO had to be phased out over several years because of long-term contractual obligations. AMO experienced fairly erratic yields in the production of some of its complex microchips, and accurate forecasts of yields were critical. Overestimating yields could lead to an inability to meet contractual obligations in a timely manner, requiring the plant to remain open longer. Underestimates would cause AMO to produce more chips than actually needed. AMO's yield forecasts had previously been made by simply averaging all historical data. More sophisticated forecasting techniques were implemented, resulting in improved forecasts of wafer fabrication. Using more accurate yield forecasts and optimization models, AMO was able to close the plant sooner, resulting in significant cost savings.[1]

• Over 70 percent of the total sales volume at L.L. Bean is generated through orders to its call center. Calls to the L.L. Bean call center are classified into two types: telemarketing (TM), which involve placing an order, and telephone-inquiry (TI), which involve customer inquiries such as order status or order problems. Accurately forecasting TM and TI calls helps the company better plan the number of agents to have on hand at any point in time. Analytical forecasting models for both types of calls take into account historical trends, seasonal factors, and external explanatory variables such as holidays and catalog mailings. The estimated benefit from better precision from the two forecasting models is approximately $300,000 per year.[2]

• DIRECTV was founded in 1991 to provide subscription satellite television. Prior to launching this product, it was vital to forecast how many homes in the United States would subscribe to satellite television, and when. A forecast was developed using the Bass diffusion model, which describes the adoption pattern of new products and technologies. The model is based on the proposition that the conditional probability of adoption by potential consumers of a new product at a given time will be a linear-increasing function of the number of previous adopters. The model was supported by forecasting analogies with cable TV. The 1992 forecast proved to be quite good in comparison with actual data over the five-year period from 1994 through 1999.[3]

Questions and Problems

1. Explain the difference between time series and explanatory/causal forecasting models.
2. Summarize the common approaches used for qualitative (judgmental) forecasting.
3. Are judgmental or quantitative forecasts more commonly used for forecasting product sales? Why?
4. Apply the concept of historical analogy to forecast the success of a specific candidate in the next presidential election.
5. Find the last report of the Index of Leading Indicators. These occur at the beginning of every month and are reported in the news (print and broadcast). What did the indicators predict this month?
6. Obtain the daily or weekly Dow Jones Industrial Average for the past year (from the Internet, from the business pages of a newspaper, or from a business magazine). The business pages of newspapers just after the close of

[1] D. W. Clements and R. A. Reid, "Analytical MS/OR Tools Applied to a Plant Closure," *Interfaces,* Vol. 24, No. 2, pp. 1–12, March–April, 1994.
[2] B. H. Andrews and S. M. Cunningham, "L.L. Bean Improves Call-Center Forecasting," *Interfaces,* Vol. 25, No. 6, pp. 1–13, November–December, 1995.
[3] Frank M. Bass, Kent Gordon, and Teresa L. Ferguson, "DIRECTV: Forecasting Diffusion of a New Technology Prior to Product Launch," *Interfaces,* Vol. 31, No. 3, Part 2 of 2, May–June 2001, S82–S93.

business December 31 will generally publish a graph of these data. These graphs typically show a lot of variance over short periods, as well as interesting shapes over the year. What factors do you expect to be the reason for these changes? What implications do these factors have for the ability to forecast the future?

7. Obtain data on the price of a barrel of oil (from the Internet, from the business pages of a newspaper, or from a business magazine). Most of these sources will provide you with a graph, typically showing a lot of variance over short periods. What factors do you expect to be the reason for these changes? What implications do these factors have for the ability to forecast the future?

8. Discuss the types of forecasts for which simple time series models and regression models are applicable.

9. Discuss the difference between trends, cycles, and seasonal effects.

10. The Excel file *Economic Indexes.xls* provides data on the annual percent change in the Dow Jones Industrial Average, Consumer Price Index, Standard & Poor's 500, and average yield for one-year Treasury bills from 1960 through 1999.
    a. Develop spreadsheet models for forecasting each of the variables using single moving average and single exponential smoothing.
    b. Using MAD, MSE, and MAPE as guidance, find the best number of moving average periods and best smoothing constant for exponential smoothing. (You might consider using data tables to facilitate your search.)
    c. Try to develop a good four-period weighted moving average model.
    d. Compare your results to the best moving average and exponential smoothing models found by *CB Predictor*.

11. For the data in the Excel file *Baseball Attendance.xls:*
    a. Develop spreadsheet models for forecasting attendance using single moving average and single exponential smoothing.
    b. Using MAD, MSE, and MAPE as guidance, find the best number of moving average periods and best smoothing constant for exponential smoothing.
    c. Compare your results to the best moving average and exponential smoothing models found by *CB Predictor*.

12. For the data in the Excel file *Ohio Prison Population.xls:*
    a. Develop spreadsheet models for forecasting both male and female populations using single moving average and single exponential smoothing.
    b. Using MAD, MSE, and MAPE as guidance, find the best number of moving average periods and best smoothing constant for exponential smoothing.
    c. Find good double moving average and double exponential smoothing models. Why would these be more appropriate?
    d. Compare your results to the best moving average and exponential smoothing models found by *CB Predictor*.

13. For the data in the Excel file *Blood Pressure.xls:*
    a. Develop spreadsheet models for forecasting blood pressure after medication using single moving average and single exponential smoothing.
    b. Using MAD, MSE, and MAPE as guidance, find the best number of moving average periods and best smoothing constant for exponential smoothing.
    c. Compare your results to the best moving average and exponential smoothing models found by *CB Predictor*.

14. For the data in the Excel file *US Average Temperature.xls:*
    a. Develop the best models for forecasting January and July temperatures using single moving average and single exponential smoothing.
    b. Find the best double moving average and double exponential smoothing models, and compare the results with part (a).
    c. Find the best models using *CB Predictor* and compare them with your answers to parts (a) and (b).
15. Construct a line chart for each of the variables in the data file *Energy Production & Consumption.xls,* and suggest the best forecasting technique. Then apply *CB Predictor* to find the best forecasting models for these variables.
16. Examine the chart of the data in *Arizona Population.xls*.
    a. Suggest the best-fitting functional form for forecasting these data.
    b. Use the *Add Trendline* option in Excel to find the best-fitting model.
    c. Compare these results to the linear trend model for the last 10 years of data.
17. Examine the chart of the data in *California Disposable Income.xls*.
    a. Suggest the best-fitting functional form for forecasting these data.
    b. Use the *Add Trendline* option in Excel to find the best-fitting model.
    c. Compare these results to the linear trend model for the last 10 years of data.
18. For each of the variables in the data file *Energy Production & Consumption.xls,* find a good fitting regression model based on R^2 using the *Add Trendline* option in Excel.
19. Develop a good additive seasonal model to forecast electric usage for the data in the Excel worksheet *Gas & Electric.xls*. How do your results compare with the model found by *CB Predictor*?
20. Develop a spreadsheet for the multiplicative seasonal model, and apply it to forecast both gas and electric usage in the worksheet *Gas & Electric.xls*. How do your results compare with the model found by *CB Predictor*?
21. Use *CB Predictor* to find the best Holt–Winters forecasting model for the data in the worksheets
    a. *New Car Sales.xls*
    b. *Housing Starts.xls*
    c. *Computer and Software Sales.xls*
    d. *Coal Consumption.xls*
    How would your results differ if you used only the last five years of the data?
22. Use *CB Predictor* to find the best forecasting model for predicting temperature in the worksheet *Washington DC Weather.xls*.
23. Develop multiple regression models with ordinal variables for forecasting both gas and electric usage in the worksheet *Gas & Electric.xls*.
24. Develop a multiple regression model with ordinal variables for forecasting temperature in the worksheet *Washington DC Weather.xls*.
25. Develop a multiple regression model with ordinal variables for forecasting sales in the worksheet *Computer and Software Sales.xls*.
26. Develop a multiple regression model with ordinal variables for forecasting sales in the worksheet *New Car Sales.xls*.
27. The Excel file *Olympic Track and Field Data.xls* provides the gold medal winning distances for the high jump, discus, and long jump for the modern Olympic Games through 1984. Develop forecasting models for each of the events. What does the model predict for the years 1988, 1992, 1996, and 2000? Find out the winning distances for these years, compare your results, and update your models for the 2004 games in Athens.

28. Examine the chart of the data in *30 Year Mortgage Rates.xls*. What type of forecasting model would be appropriate? Confirm your hypothesis with *CB Predictor*.
29. Examine the chart of the data in *Prime Rate.xls*. What type of forecasting model would be appropriate? Confirm your hypothesis with *CB Predictor*.
30. Examine the chart of the data in *Consumer Price Index.xls*. What type of forecasting model would be appropriate? Confirm your hypothesis with *CB Predictor*.

C A S E

FORECASTING FOR TRACWAY

An important input to planning manufacturing capacity is a good forecast of sales. In reviewing the Tracway database, Henry Hudson is interested in forecasting sales for mowers and tractors in each marketing region. Although Henry has obtained expert opinions on sales forecasts using the Delphi process, he would like to generate time series forecasts for the next year for each product by region and incorporate the judgmental forecasts. One of his staff analysts has suggested using regression. Develop regression models for each product by region, and forecast sales for the next year. Then use the Delphi results discussed in this chapter to suggest modifications to the time series forecasts, assuming that Henry puts a 70 percent weight on the judgmental forecasts and a 30 percent weight on the regression forecasts.

In addition, Henry's boss would like forecasts for total industry sales and Tracway market share. Develop appropriate time series or regression models for these data, and prepare a report of your results. ■

References

Cryer, J. D., *Time Series Analysis* (Boston: PWS Publishers, 1986).

Goodwin, P., and G. Wright, "Improving Judgmental Time Series Forecasting: A Review of the Guidance Provided by Research," *International Journal of Forecasting*, Vol. 9, pp. 147–161, 1993.

Newbold, P., and T. Bos, *Introductory Business Forecasting* (Cincinnati: South-Western Publishing Co., 1990).

Sanders, Nada R., and Karl B. Manrodt, "Forecasting Practices in U.S. Corporations: Survey Results," *Interfaces*, Vol. 24, No. 2, March–April 1994.

CHAPTER

7

STATISTICAL QUALITY CONTROL

INTRODUCTION

An important application of statistics and data analysis in both manufacturing and service operations is in the area of *quality control*. Quality control methods help employees monitor production operations to ensure that output conforms to specifications. This is important in manufactured goods since product performance depends on achieving design tolerances. It is also vital to service operations to ensure that customers receive error-free, consistent, service.

Why is quality control necessary? The principal reason is that no two outputs from any production process are exactly alike. If you measure any quality characteristic—such as the diameters of machined parts, the amount of soft drink in a bottle, or the number of errors in processing orders at a distribution center—you will discover some variation. Variation is the result of many small differences in those factors that comprise a process: people, machines, materials, methods, and measurement systems. Taken together, they are called **common causes of variation.**

Other causes of variation occur sporadically and can be identified and either eliminated or at least explained. For example, when a tool wears down it can be replaced; when a machine falls out of adjustment, it can be reset; or when a bad lot of material is discovered, it can be returned to the supplier. Such examples are called **special causes of variation.** Special causes of variation cause the distribution of process output to change over time. Using statistical tools, we can identify when they occur and take appropriate action, thus preventing unnecessary quality problems. Equally important is knowing when to leave the process alone and not react to common causes over which we have no control.

In this chapter we introduce basic ideas of *statistical process control* and *process capability analysis*—two important tools in helping to achieve quality. The key concepts that we will describe are

- The statistical basis and the application of control charts for monitoring both attributes and variables data
- Rules for determining when data signal the need for change
- The use of statistics for measuring the capability of a process to meet specifications

The applications of statistics to quality control are far more extensive than we can present; much additional information may be found in the references.

THE ROLE OF STATISTICS AND DATA ANALYSIS IN QUALITY CONTROL

We can learn a lot about the common causes of variation in a process and their effect on quality by studying process output. For example, suppose that a company like General Electric Aircraft Engines produces a critical machined part. Key questions might be: What is the average dimension? How much variability occurs in the output of the process? What does the distribution of part dimensions look like? What proportion of output, if any, does not conform to design specifications? These are fundamental questions that can be addressed with statistics.

The role of statistics is to provide tools to analyze data collected from a process and enable employees to make informed decisions when the process needs short-term corrective action or long-term improvements. Statistical methods have been used for quality control since the 1920s when they were pioneered at the Western Electric Company. They became a mainstay of Japanese manufacturing in the early 1950s; however, they did not become widely used in the United States until the quality management movement of the 1980s, led by pioneers such as W. Edwards Deming and Joseph M. Juran, both of whom were instrumental in the adoption of these methods in Japan. Since then, statistical quality control has been shown to be a proven means of improving customer satisfaction and reducing costs in many industries.

To illustrate the applications of statistics to quality control, we will use the Excel file *Syringe Data.xls,* which provides data from a Midwest pharmaceutical company that manufactures individual syringes with a self-contained, single dose of an injectable drug.[1] In the manufacturing process, sterile liquid drug is filled into glass syringes and sealed with a rubber stopper. The remaining stage involves insertion of the cartridge into plastic syringes and the electrical "tacking" of the containment cap at a precisely determined length of the syringe. A cap that is "tacked" at a shorter than desired length (less than 4.920 inches) leads to pressure on the cartridge stopper and, hence, partial or complete activation of the syringe. Such syringes must then be scrapped. If the cap is "tacked" at a longer than desired length (4.980 inches or longer), the tacking is incomplete or inadequate, which can lead to cap loss and potentially a cartridge loss in shipment and handling. Such syringes can be reworked manually to attach the cap at a lower position. However, this process requires a 100 percent inspection of the tacked syringes and results in increased cost for the items. This final production step seemed to be producing more and more scrap and reworked syringes over successive weeks. At this point, statistical consultants became involved in an attempt to solve this problem and recommended statistical process control for the purpose of improving the tacking operation.

---

[1] Adapted from LeRoy A. Franklin and Samar N. Mukherjee, "An SPC Case Study on Stabilizing Syringe Lengths," *Quality Engineering,* Vol. 12, No. 1, 1999–2000, 65–71.

STATISTICAL PROCESS CONTROL

In Chapter 1 we defined two types of data: attributes and variables. Data that come from counting are called *attributes data*. Examples of attributes data are the number of defective pieces in a shipment of components, the number of errors on an invoice, and the percent of customers rating service a 6 or 7 on a seven-point satisfaction scale. Data that come from measurements along a continuous scale are called *variables data*. Examples of variables data are the inside diameter of a drilled hole, the weight of a carton, and the time between order and delivery. This distinction is important because different statistical process control tools must be used for each type of data.

When a process operates under ideal conditions, variation in the distribution of output is due to common causes. When only common causes are present, the process is said to be **in control.** A controlled process is stable and predictable to the extent that we can predict the likelihood that future output will fall within some range once we know the probability distribution of outcomes. Special causes, however, cause the distribution to change. The change may be a shift in the mean, and increase or decrease in the variance, or a change in shape. Clearly, if we cannot predict how the distribution may change, then we cannot compute the probability that future output will fall within some range. When special causes are present, the process is said to be **out of control** and needs to be corrected to bring it back to a stable state. **Statistical process control— SPC—**provides a means of identifying special causes as well as telling us when the process is in control and should be left alone. Control charts were first used by Dr. Walter Shewhart at Bell Laboratories in the 1920s (they are sometimes called Shewhart charts). Dr. Shewhart was the first to make a distinction between common causes of variation and special causes of variation.

SPC consists of the following:

1. Selecting a sample of observations from a production or service process
2. Measuring one or more quality characteristics
3. Recording the data
4. Making a few calculations
5. Plotting key statistics on a *control chart*
6. Examining the chart to determine if any unusual patterns, called **out-of-control conditions,** can be identified
7. Determining the cause of out-of-control conditions and taking corrective action

When data are collected, it is important to clearly record the data, the time the data were collected, the measuring instruments that were used, who collected the data, and any other important information such as lot numbers, machine numbers, and the like. By having a record of such information, we can trace the source of quality problems more easily.

Control Charts

A **run chart** is a line chart in which the independent variable is time and the dependent variable is the value of some sample statistic, such as the mean, range, or proportion. A **control chart** is a run chart that has two additional horizontal lines, called **control limits,** as illustrated in Figure 7.1. Control limits are chosen statistically so that there is a high probability (usually greater than 0.99) that sample statistics will fall randomly within the limits *if the process is in control.*

To understand the statistical basis for control charts, let us assume that we are dealing with a variables measurement that is normally distributed with a mean μ and standard deviation σ. If the process is stable, or in control, then each individual measurement will stem from this distribution. In high-volume production processes, it is

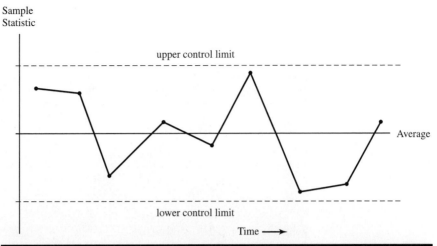

Sample
Statistic

upper control limit

Average

lower control limit

Time ⟶

FIGURE 7.1   Structure of a Control Chart

generally difficult, if not impossible, to measure each individual output, so we take samples at periodic intervals. For samples of a fixed size, n, we know from Chapter 3 that the sampling distribution will be normal with mean μ and standard deviation (standard error) $\sigma_{\bar{x}} = \sigma/\sqrt{n}$. We would expect that about 99.7 percent of sample means will lie within three standard errors of the mean, or between $\mu - 3\sigma_{\bar{x}}$ and $\mu + 3\sigma_{\bar{x}}$, provided the process remains in control. These values become the theoretical control limits for a control chart to monitor the centering of a process using the sample mean. Of course, we do not know the true population parameters, so we estimate them by the sample mean and sample standard deviation. Thus, the actual control limits would be

$$\text{Lower control limit:} \bar{x} - 3s_{\bar{x}}$$
$$\text{Upper control limit:} \bar{x} + 3s_{\bar{x}}$$

In general, control limits are established as plus or minus 3 standard errors from the mean of the sampling distribution of the statistic we plot on the chart. Statisticians have devised various formulas for computing these limits in a practical manner that is easy for shop floor workers to understand and use. However, the theory is based on understanding the sampling distribution of the statistic we measure.

There are many different types of control charts. We will introduce two types of control charts in this chapter: $\bar{x}$- and R-charts for variables data and p-charts for attributes data. Discussions of other types of charts may be found in the references.

$\bar{x}$- and R-charts

The **$\bar{x}$-chart** monitors the centering of process output for variables data over time by plotting the mean of each sample. In manufacturing, for example, the permissible variation in a dimension is usually stated by a **nominal specification** (target value) and some **tolerance.** For example, the specifications on the syringe length are 4.950 ± 0.030 inches. The nominal is 4.950 and the tolerance is ± 0.030. Therefore, the lengths should be between 4.920 to 4.980 inches. The $\bar{x}$-chart is used to monitor the centering of a process. The **R-chart,** or range-chart, monitors the variability in the data as measured by the range of each sample. Thus, the R-chart monitors the uniformity or consistency of the process. The smaller the value of R, the more uniform is the process. Any increase in the average range is undesirable; this would mean that the variation is getting larger. However, decreases in variability signify improvement. We could use the

	A	B	C	D	E	F	G	H
1	First Shift Data							
2	Sample		Sample Observations				Average	Range
3	1	4.9600	4.9460	4.9500	4.9560	4.9580	4.9540	0.0140
4	2	4.9580	4.9270	4.9350	4.9400	4.9500	4.9420	0.0310
5	3	4.9710	4.9290	4.9650	4.9520	4.9380	4.9510	0.0420
6	4	4.9400	4.9820	4.9700	4.9530	4.9600	4.9610	0.0420
7	5	4.9640	4.9500	4.9530	4.9620	4.9560	4.9570	0.0140
8	6	4.9690	4.9510	4.9550	4.9660	4.9540	4.9590	0.0180
9	7	4.9600	4.9440	4.9570	4.9480	4.9510	4.9520	0.0160
10	8	4.9690	4.9490	4.9630	4.9520	4.9620	4.9590	0.0200
11	9	4.9840	4.9280	4.9600	4.9430	4.9550	4.9540	0.0560
12	10	4.9700	4.9340	4.9610	4.9400	4.9650	4.9540	0.0360
13	11	4.9750	4.9590	4.9620	4.9710	4.9680	4.9670	0.0160
14	12	4.9450	4.9770	4.9500	4.9690	4.9540	4.9590	0.0320
15	13	4.9760	4.9640	4.9700	4.9680	4.9720	4.9700	0.0120
16	14	4.9700	4.9540	4.9640	4.9590	4.9680	4.9630	0.0160
17	15	4.9820	4.9620	4.9680	4.9750	4.9630	4.9700	0.0200

FIGURE 7.2 Portion of the Excel File *Syringe Data.xls*

standard deviation of each sample instead of the range to provide a more accurate characterization of variability; however, for small samples (around 8 or less), little differences will be apparent, and if the calculations are done manually by a worker on the shop floor, *R*-charts are much easier to apply.

The basic procedure for constructing and using any control chart is first to gather at least 25–30 samples of data with a fixed sample size *n* from a production process, measure the quality characteristic of interest, and record the data. We will illustrate the construction of a control chart using the worksheet *Syringe Data.xls* (see Figure 7.2). This worksheet shows 47 samples that were taken every 15 minutes from the syringe manufacturing process over three shifts. Each sample consists of 5 individual observations. In column G we calculate the mean of each sample, and in column H, the range.

We will work with the first 15 samples (typically, it is recommended that at least 25–30 samples be used to construct a control chart, but we will assume that only the first 15 samples are available). After we have calculated the mean and range for each sample, we compute the average mean, $\bar{x} = 4.9581$, and the average range, $\bar{R} = 0.0257$. Figures 7.3 and 7.4 show plots of the sample means and ranges. Although the chart for

FIGURE 7.3 Chart of Sample Means for Syringe Data

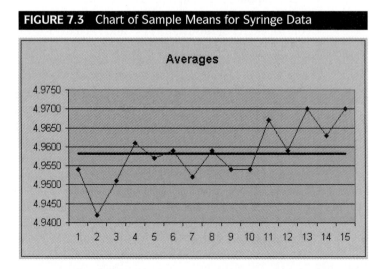

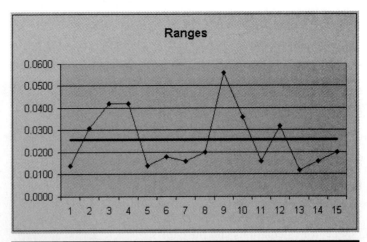

FIGURE 7.4 Chart of Sample Ranges for Syringe Data

sample ranges shows some variation, we cannot yet determine statistically whether this variation might be due to some assignable cause or is simply due to chance. The chart for sample means appears to show an increasing trend.

The final step to complete the control charts is to compute control limits. As we explained earlier, control limits are boundaries within which the process is operating in statistical control. Control limits are based on past performance and tell us what values we can expect for $\bar{x}$ or R as long as the process remains stable. If a point falls outside the control limits or if some unusual pattern occurs, then we should be suspicious of a special cause. The upper control limit for the R-chart is given by the formula

$$\text{UCL}_R = D_4\bar{R}$$

and the lower control limit for the R-chart is given by the formula

$$\text{LCL}_R = D_3\bar{R}$$

D_3 and D_4 are constants that depend on the sample size and are found in Table 7.1. The theory is a bit complicated, but suffice it to say that these constants have been

TABLE 7.1	Control Chart Factors		
Sample Size	A_2	D_3	D_4
2	1.880	0	3.267
3	1.023	0	2.574
4	0.729	0	2.282
5	0.577	0	2.114
6	0.483	0	2.004
7	0.419	0.076	1.924
8	0.373	0.136	1.864
9	0.337	0.184	1.816
10	0.308	0.223	1.777
11	0.285	0.256	1.744
12	0.266	0.283	1.717
13	0.249	0.307	1.693
14	0.235	0.328	1.672
15	0.223	0.347	1.653

$\bar{x}$- AND *R*-CHARTS

From the *PHStat* menu, select *Control Charts*, followed by *R & Xbar Charts*. The dialog box that appears is shown in Figure 7.5. Your worksheet must have already calculated the sample means and ranges. The cell ranges for these data are entered in the appropriate boxes. You must also provide the sample size in the Data section and have the option of selecting only the *R*-chart or both the $\bar{x}$- and *R*-charts. *PHStat* will create several worksheets for calculations and the charts.

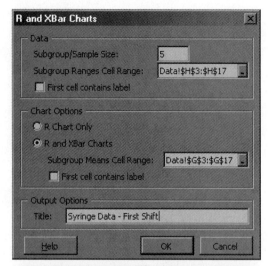

FIGURE 7.5 *PHStat* Dialog Box for *R*- and $\bar{x}$-Charts

determined from the sampling distribution of *R* so that, for example, $D_4\bar{R} = \bar{R} + 3s_R$, as we had described earlier.

Since the sample size is 5, $D_4 = 2.114$. Therefore, the upper control limit for the example is $2.114(0.0257) = 0.0543$. In this example, D_3 for a sample size of 5 is 0, so therefore the lower control limit is 0. We then draw and label these control limits on the chart.

For the $\bar{x}$-chart, the control limits are given by the formulas:

$$\text{UCL}_{\bar{x}} = \bar{\bar{x}} + A_2\bar{R}$$
$$\text{LCL}_{\bar{x}} = \bar{\bar{x}} - A_2\bar{R}$$

Again, the constant A_2 is determined so that $A_2\bar{R}$ is equivalent to 3 standard errors in the sampling distribution of the mean. For a sample of size 5, $A_2 = 0.577$. Therefore, the control limits are

$$\text{UCL}_{\bar{x}} = 4.9581 + (0.577)(0.0257) = 4.973$$
$$\text{LCL}_{\bar{x}} = 4.9581 - (0.577)(0.0257) = 4.943$$

We could draw these control limits on the charts to complete the process. *PHStat* includes a routine for constructing $\bar{x}$- and *R*-charts (see the *PHStat Note: $\bar{x}$- and R-Charts*). The charts generated by this routine are shown in Figures 7.6 and 7.7. The next step is to analyze the charts to determine the state of statistical control.

ANALYZING CONTROL CHARTS

When a process is in statistical control, the points on a control chart should fluctuate at random between the control limits, and no recognizable patterns should exist. The following checklist provides a set of general rules for examining a control chart to see if a process is in control. These rules are based on the assumption that the

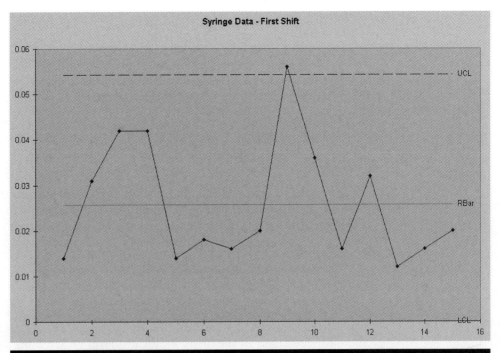

FIGURE 7.6 *PHStat R-Chart for Syringe Data*

FIGURE 7.7 *PHStat x̄-Chart for Syringe Data*

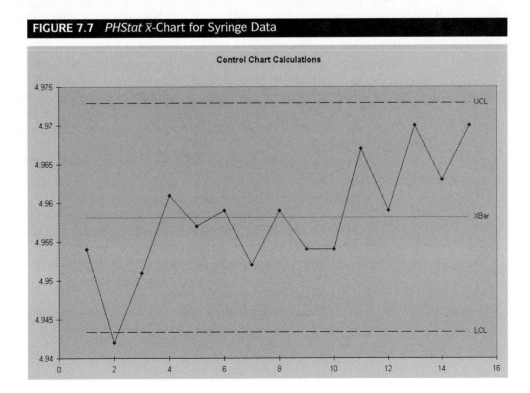

underlying distribution of process output — and therefore the sampling distribution — is normal.

1. ***No points are outside the control limits.***   Since the control limits are set at 3 standard errors from the mean, the probability of a point falling outside the control limits when the process is in control is only 0.0027, under the normality assumption.

2. ***The number of points above and below the center line is about the same.***   If the distribution is symmetric, as a normal distribution is, we would expect this to occur. If the distribution is highly skewed, we might find a disproportionate amount on one side.

3. ***The points seem to fall randomly above and below the center line.***   If the distribution is stable, we would expect the same chances of getting a sample above the mean as below. However, if the distribution has shifted during the data collection process, we would expect a nonrandom distribution of sample statistics.

4. ***There are no steady upward or downward trends of points moving toward either control limit.***   These would indicate a gradual movement of the distribution mean.

5. ***Most points, but not all, are near the center line; only a few are close to the control limits.***   For a normal distribution, about 68 percent of observations fall within 1 standard deviations of the mean. If, for instance, we see a high proportion of points near the limits, we might suspect that the data came from two distinct distributions (visualize an inverted normal distribution).

For the syringe data, the R-chart has one point above the upper control limit. In the $\bar{x}$-chart, not only is one point below the lower control limit but we see a clear upward trend. Thus, we would conclude that the process is not in control, particularly in the ability to maintain a stable average of the syringe length. It is important to keep good records of data — the time at which each sample was taken and the process conditions at that time (who was running the process, where the material came from, etc.). Most of the time, it is easy to identify a logical cause. A common reason for a point falling outside a control limit is an error in the calculation of the sample values of $\bar{x}$ or R. Other possible causes are a sudden power surge, a broken tool, measurement error, or an incomplete or omitted operation in the process. Once in a while, however, they are a normal part of the process and occur simply by chance. When assignable causes are identified, these data should be deleted from the analysis, and new control limits should be computed.

The most common types of other out-of-control conditions are summarized next.

Sudden Shift in the Process Average

When an unusual number of consecutive points fall on one side of the center line (see Figure 7.8), it usually indicates that the process average has suddenly shifted. Typically, this is the result of an external influence that has affected the process; this would be a special cause. In both the $\bar{x}$- and R-charts, possible causes might be a new operator, a new inspector, a new machine setting, or a change in the setup or method.

In the R-chart, if the shift is up, the process has become less uniform. Typical causes are carelessness of operators, poor or inadequate maintenance, or possibly a fixture in need of repair. If the shift is down in the R-chart, uniformity of the process has improved. This might be the result of improved workmanship or better machines or materials.

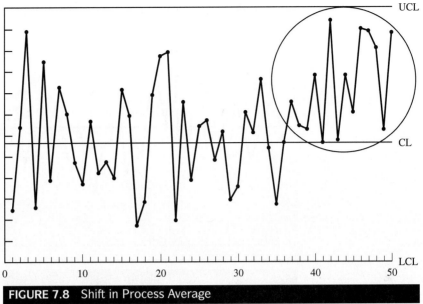

FIGURE 7.8 Shift in Process Average

Cycles

Cycles are short, repeated patterns in the chart, having alternative high peaks and low valleys (see Figure 7.9). These are the result of causes that come and go on a regular basis. In the $\bar{x}$-chart, cycles may be the result of operator rotation or fatigue at the end of a shift, different gauges used by different inspectors, seasonal effects such as temperature or humidity, or differences between day and night shifts. In the R-chart, cycles can occur from maintenance schedules, rotation of fixtures or gauges, differences between shifts, or operator fatigue.

FIGURE 7.9 Cycles

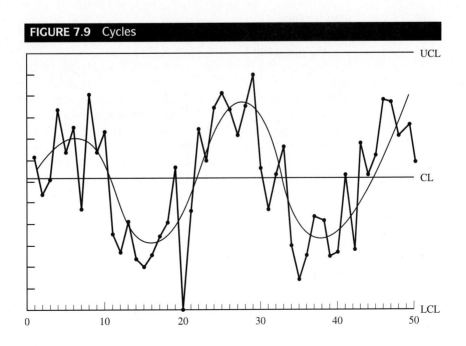

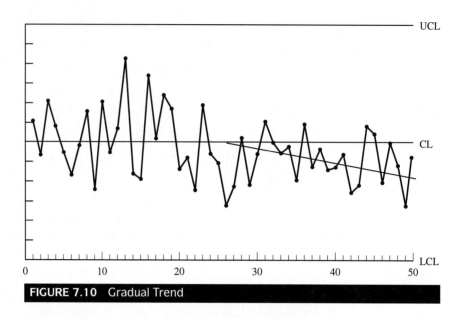

FIGURE 7.10 Gradual Trend

Trends

A trend is the result of some cause that gradually affects the quality characteristics of the product and causes the points on a control chart to gradually move up or down from the center line (see Figure 7.10). As a new group of operators gain experience on the job, for example, or as maintenance of equipment improves over time, a trend may occur. In the $\bar{x}$-chart, trends may be the result of improving operator skills, dirt or chip buildup in fixtures, tool wear, changes in temperature or humidity, or aging of equipment. In the R-chart, an increasing trend may be due to a gradual decline in material quality, operator fatigue, gradual loosening of a fixture or a tool, or dulling of a tool. A decreasing trend often is the result of improved operator skill, improved work methods, better purchased materials, or improved or more frequent maintenance.

Hugging the Center Line

Hugging the center line occurs when nearly all the points fall close to the center line (see Figure 7.11). In the control chart, it appears that the control limits are too wide. A common cause of this occurrence is the sample being taken by selecting one item systematically from each of several machines, spindles, operators, and so on. A simple example will serve to illustrate this. Suppose that one machine produces parts whose diameters average 7.508 with variation of only a few thousandths; and a second machine produces parts whose diameters average 7.502, again with only a small variation. Taken together, you can see that the range of variation would probably be between 7.500 and 7.510 and average about 7.505. Now suppose that we sample one part from each machine and compute a sample average to plot on an $\bar{x}$-chart. The sample averages will consistently be around 7.505, since one will always be high and the second will always be low. Even though there is a large variation in the parts taken as whole, the sample averages will not reflect this. In such a case, it would be more appropriate to construct a control chart for each machine, spindle, operator, and so on.

An often overlooked cause for this pattern is miscalculation of the control limits, perhaps by using the wrong factor from the table or misplacing the decimal point in the computations.

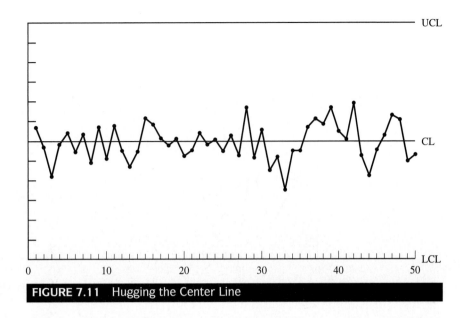

FIGURE 7.11   Hugging the Center Line

Hugging the Control Limits

This pattern shows up when many points are near the control limits with very few in between (see Figure 7.12). It is often called a *mixture* and is actually a combination of two different patterns on the same chart. A mixture can be split into two separate patterns, as Figure 7.13 illustrates. A mixture pattern can result when different lots of material are used in one process or when parts are produced by different machines but fed into a common inspection group.

Quality control practitioners advocate simple rules, based on sound statistical principles, for operationalizing these concepts. For example, if 8 consecutive points fall on one side of the center line, then you can conclude that the mean has shifted. Why? If the distribution is symmetric, then the probability that the next sample falls above or

FIGURE 7.12   Hugging Control Limits

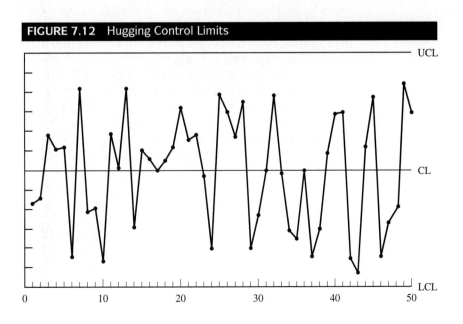

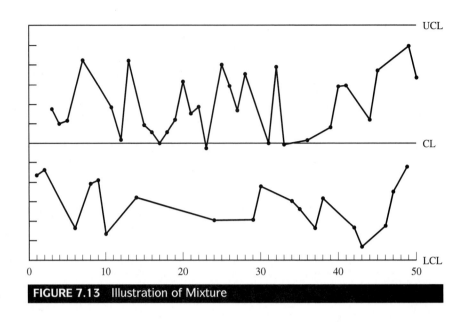

FIGURE 7.13 Illustration of Mixture

below the mean is 0.5. Because samples are independent, the probability that 8 consecutive samples will fall on one side of the mean is $(0.5)^8 = 0.0039$—a highly unlikely occurrence. Another rule often used to detect a shift is finding 10 of 11 consecutive points on one side of the center line. The probability of this occurring can be found using the binomial distribution:

$$p(10) = \binom{11}{10}(0.5)^{10}(0.5)^1 = 0.00537$$

These examples show the value of statistics and data analysis in common production operations.

Let us return to the syringe data. After examining the first set of charts, a technician was called to adjust the machine prior to the second shift, and 17 more samples were taken. Figure 7.14 shows one of the calculation worksheets created by *PHStat* for developing the control charts. We see that the average range is now 0.0129 (versus 0.0257 in the first set of data) and the average mean is 4.9736 (versus 4.9581). Although the average dispersion appears to have been reduced, the centering of the process has gotten worse, since the target dimension is 4.950. The charts in Figures 7.15 and 7.16 also suggest that the variation has gotten out of control and that the process mean continues to drift upward.

After another adjustment by a technician, the third shift collected another 15 samples. We leave it to you as an exercise to develop the control charts and verify that the *R*-chart appears to be in control, that the variability has stabilized, and that the $\bar{x}$-chart is also in control, although the average length of the syringes is 4.963, slightly above target. In reviewing the process, the maintenance technician discovered that as he tried to move the height adjustment stop down on its threaded shaft, it was difficult to tighten the locknut because of worn threads. As a result, the vibration from the machine loosened the locknut and adjustment cap, resulting in drifts off-center of the lengths. When he set the adjustment cap a bit higher (resulting in a slightly higher average length), the threads were good enough to hold the locknut in place, reducing the variation and bringing the process into control. This example shows the value of using control charts to help monitor a process and diagnose quality problems.

	A	B
1	**Second Shift Data**	
2		
3	**Data**	
4	**Sample/Subgroup Size**	5
5		
6	R Chart Intermediate Calculations	
7	RBar	0.012882353
8	D3 Factor	0
9	D4 Factor	2.114
10		
11	**R Chart Control Limits**	
12	**Lower Control Limit**	0
13	**Center**	0.012882353
14	**Upper Control Limit**	0.027233294
15		
16	XBar Chart Intermediate Calculations	
17	Average of Subgroup Averages	4.973647059
18	A2 Factor	0.577
19	A2 Factor * RBar	0.007433118
20		
21	**XBar Chart Control Limits**	
22	**Lower Control Limit**	4.966213941
23	**Center**	4.973647059
24	**Upper Control Limit**	4.981080176

FIGURE 7.14 Calculations for Second Shift Control Charts

FIGURE 7.15 Second Shift *R*-Chart

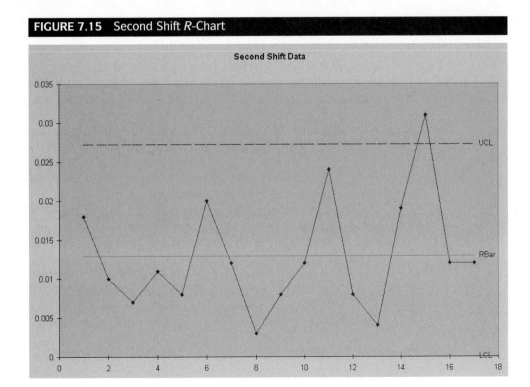

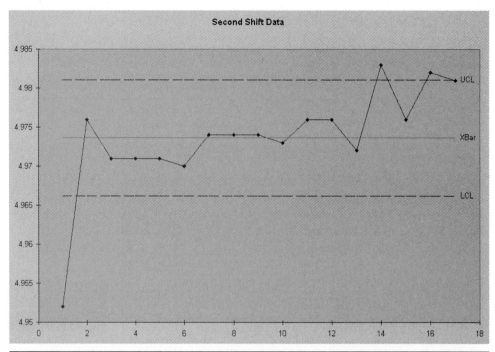

FIGURE 7.16   Second Shift $\bar{x}$-Chart

CONTROL CHARTS FOR ATTRIBUTES

Attributes data assume only two values, such as good or bad, present or absent, acceptable or not acceptable, and so on. Attributes data cannot be measured, only counted. The most common control chart for attributes data is the *p*-chart. A **p-chart** monitors the proportion of nonconforming items. Sometimes it is called a *fraction nonconforming* or *fraction defective* chart. For example, a *p*-chart might be used to monitor the proportion of checking account statements that are sent out with errors, FedEx packages delivered late, hotel rooms not cleaned properly, or surgical infections in a hospital.

As with variables data, a *p*-chart is constructed by first gathering 25 to 30 samples of the attribute being measured. For attributes data, it is recommended that each sample size be at least 100; otherwise, it is difficult to obtain good statistical results. The size of each sample may vary. It is usually recommended that a constant sample size be used, as this makes interpreting patterns in the *p*-chart easier; however, for many applications this may not be practical or desirable.

The steps in constructing a *p*-chart are similar to those used for $\bar{x}$- and *R*-charts. We will first consider the case of a fixed sample size, *n*. Assume we have *k* samples, each of size *n*. For each sample, we compute the fraction nonconforming, *p*, that is, the number of nonconforming items divided by the number in the sample. The average fraction nonconforming, $\bar{p}$, is computed by summing the total number of nonconforming items in all samples and dividing by the total number of items ($= nk$ if the sample size is constant) in all samples combined. Because the number of nonconforming items in each sample follows a binomial distribution, the standard deviation is

$$s = \sqrt{\frac{\bar{p}(1 - \bar{p})}{n}}$$

Using the principles we described earlier in this chapter, upper and lower control limits are given by

$$UCL_p = \bar{p} + 3s$$
$$LCL_p = \bar{p} - 3s$$

Whenever LCL_p turns out negative, we use zero as the lower control limit, since the fraction nonconforming can never be negative. We may now plot the fraction nonconforming on a control chart just as we did for the averages and ranges and use the same procedures to analyze patterns in a *p*-chart as we did for *x*- and *R*-charts. That is, we check that no points fall outside of the upper and lower control limits and that no peculiar patterns (runs, trends, cycles, and so on) exist in the chart.

To illustrate a *p*-chart, suppose that housekeeping supervisors at a hotel inspect 100 rooms selected randomly each day to determine if they are cleaned properly. Any nonconformance, such as a failure to replace used soap or shampoo or empty the wastebasket results in the room being listed as improperly cleaned. The worksheet *Room Inspection.xls* (shown in Figure 7.17) provides data for 25 days. The total number of nonconforming rooms is 55. Therefore, the average fraction nonconforming, $\bar{p}$, is $55/2500 = 0.022$. This leads to the standard deviation

$$s = \sqrt{\frac{0.022(1 - 0.022)}{100}} = 0.01467$$

The control limits are computed as

$$UCL_p = \bar{p} + 3s = 0.022 + 3(0.01467) = 0.066$$
$$LCL_p = \bar{p} - 3s = 0.022 - 3(0.01467) = -0.022$$

Because the lower control limit is negative, we use 0.

FIGURE 7.17 *Room Inspection.xls* Worksheet

	A	B	C	D
1	Sample	Rooms Inspected	Nonconforming Rooms	Fraction Nonconforming
2	1	100	3	0.03
3	2	100	1	0.01
4	3	100	0	0.00
5	4	100	0	0.00
6	5	100	2	0.02
7	6	100	5	0.05
8	7	100	3	0.03
9	8	100	6	0.06
10	9	100	1	0.01
11	10	100	4	0.04
12	11	100	0	0.00
13	12	100	2	0.02
14	13	100	1	0.01
15	14	100	3	0.03
16	15	100	4	0.04
17	16	100	1	0.01
18	17	100	1	0.01
19	18	100	2	0.02
20	19	100	5	0.05
21	20	100	2	0.02
22	21	100	3	0.03
23	22	100	4	0.04
24	23	100	1	0.01
25	24	100	0	0.00
26	25	100	1	0.01

PHSTAT NOTE

p-CHARTS

From the *PHStat* menu, select *Control Charts*, followed by *p-Chart*. The dialog box, shown in Figure 7.18, prompts you for the cell range for the number of nonconformances and the sample size. This procedure also allows you to have nonconstant sample sizes; if so, you need to enter the cell range of the sample size data. *PHStat* creates several new worksheets for the calculations and the actual chart.

FIGURE 7.18 *PHStat* Dialog Box for *p*-Charts

PHStat has a procedure for constructing *p*-charts (see the *PHStat Note: p-Charts*). Figure 7.19 shows the *Calculations* worksheet created by the tool and the resulting control chart. Although there is some variation in the proportion of rooms not cleaned properly, the chart appears to be in control, suggesting that this variation is due to common causes within the system (perhaps insufficient training of the housekeeping staff).

Variable Sample Size

In many applications, it is desirable to use all data available rather than a sample. For example, hospitals collect monthly data on the number of infections after surgeries. To monitor the infection rate, a sample would not provide complete information. The

	A	B
1	**Room Inspection Control Chart**	
2		
3	Intermediate Calculations	
4	Sum of Subgroup Sizes	2500
5	Number of Subgroups Taken	25
6	Average Sample/Subgroup Size	100
7	Average Proportion of Nonconforming Items	0.022
8	Three Standard Deviations	0.044005
9		
10	p Chart Control Limits	
11	**Lower Control Limit**	-0.022005
12	**Center**	0.022
13	**Upper Control Limit**	0.066005

FIGURE 7.19 *p*-Chart Calculations and Control Chart

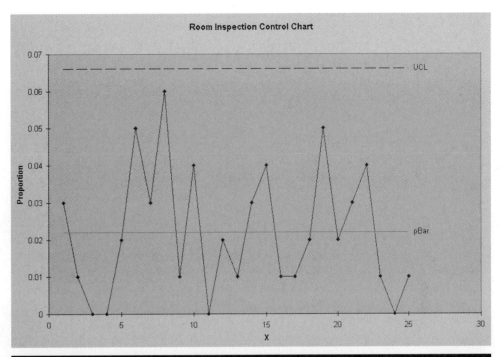

FIGURE 7.19   (Continued)

worksheet *Surgeries.xls* provides monthly data over a three-year period, a portion of which is shown in Figure 7.20. Because the sample size varies, we must modify the calculation of the standard deviation and control limits. One approach (used by *PHStat*) is to compute the average sample size, $\bar{n}$, and use this value in the calculation of the standard deviation:

$$s = \sqrt{\frac{\bar{p}(1 - \bar{p})}{\bar{n}}}$$

Generally, this is acceptable as long as the sample sizes fall within 25 percent of the average. If sample sizes vary by a larger amount, then other approaches, which are

	A	B	C	D
1	Month	Surgeries	Infections	Infection Rate
2	1	208	1	0.0048
3	2	225	3	0.0133
4	3	201	3	0.0149
5	4	236	1	0.0042
6	5	220	3	0.0136
7	6	244	1	0.0041
8	7	247	1	0.0040
9	8	245	1	0.0041
10	9	250	1	0.0040
11	10	227	0	0.0000
12	11	234	2	0.0085
13	12	227	6	0.0264
14	13	213	2	0.0094
15	14	212	1	0.0047
16	15	193	2	0.0104

FIGURE 7.20   Portion of *Surgeries.xls*

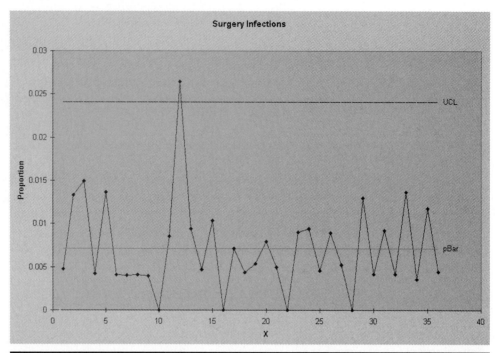

FIGURE 7.21   Control Chart for Surgery Infection Rate

beyond the scope of this book, should be used. When using this approach, note that because control limits are approximated using the average sample size, points that are actually out of control may not appear so on the chart and nonrandom patterns may be difficult to interpret; thus, some caution should be used. Figure 7.21 shows the control chart constructed using *PHStat*. The chart shows that the infection rate exceeds the upper control limit in month 12, indicating that perhaps some unusual circumstances occurred at the hospital.

STATISTICAL ISSUES IN THE DESIGN OF CONTROL CHARTS

In designing control charts, we must consider three issues:

1. The selection of the sample data
2. The sample size
3. The frequency of sampling

Sampling is useful only if the sample data are representative of the entire population at the time they are taken. Each sample should reflect the system of common causes or special causes that may be present at that point in time. If special causes are present, then the sample should have a good chance of reflecting those special causes.

Consecutive measurement over a short period of time generally provides good samples for control charts, and this is the method that is most often used. (Such samples are called **rational subgroups.**) It is also important to select samples from a single process. A process is a specific combination of equipment, people, materials, tools, and methods. We saw that selecting samples from each of several machines can lead to hugging the control limits. Separate control charts should be set up for multiple machines or processes.

The sample size is also important. We suggested using samples of size 5 for variables data; this is probably the most common in practice. Small samples, however, do not allow you to detect small changes in the mean value of the quality characteristic that is being monitored. For example, samples of size 5 only allow you to detect a shift in the mean of 2 standard deviations or more in the next sample with a probability of at least 0.95. To detect smaller shifts in the process mean, say only 1 standard deviation, a sample of about 20 must be used. Of course, you must also consider the cost of sampling. If it is expensive or very time-consuming to take a measurement, then smaller samples may be desirable.

The third issue is the frequency of sampling. It may not be economical to sample too often. There are no hard-and-fast rules for sampling frequency. Samples should be close enough so that special causes can be detected before a large amount of nonconforming product is made. This decision should take into account how often special causes are observed and the volume of production.

This discussion suggests that many statistical issues exist in implementing SPC; this is why users need to have a good understanding of statistical principles!

PROCESS CAPABILITY ANALYSIS

The purpose of SPC is to monitor a process over time to maintain a state of statistical control. However, just because a process is in control does not mean that it is capable of meeting specifications on the quality characteristic that is being measured. In the game of golf, for example, you might consistently shoot between 85 and 90; however, this is far from meeting the "specification" — par! **Process capability analysis** involves comparing the distribution of process output to specifications when only common causes (natural variations in materials, machines and tools, methods, operators, and the environment) determine the variation. As such, process capability is meaningless if special causes occur in the process. Therefore, before conducting a process capability analysis, control charts should be used to ensure that all special causes have been eliminated and that the process is in control.

Process capability is measured by the proportion of output that can be produced within design specifications. By collecting data, constructing frequency distributions and histograms, and computing basic descriptive statistics such as the mean and variance, we can better understand the nature of process variation and its ability to meet quality standards.

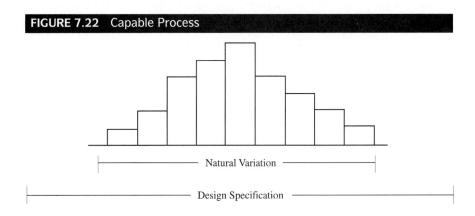

FIGURE 7.22   Capable Process

Natural Variation

Design Specification

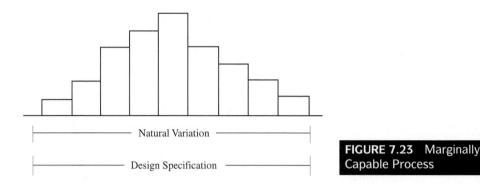

FIGURE 7.23 Marginally Capable Process

There are three important elements of process capability: the design specifications, the centering of the process, and the range of variation. Let us examine three possible situations:

1.   The natural variation in the output is smaller than the tolerance specified in the design (Figure 7.22). The probability of exceeding the specification limits is essentially zero; you would expect that the process will almost always produce output that conforms to the specifications, as long as the process remains centered. Even slight changes in the centering or spread of the process will not affect its ability to meet specifications.

2.   The natural variation and the design specification are about the same (Figure 7.23). A very small percentage of output might fall outside the specifications. The process should probably be closely monitored to make sure that the centering of the process does not drift and that the spread of variation does not increase.

3.   The range of process variation is larger than the design specifications (Figure 7.24). The probability of falling in the tails of the distribution outside the specification limits is significant. The only way to improve product quality is to change the process.

To illustrate process capability analysis, we will use the third shift data in the worksheet *Syringe Data.xls*. Recall that the specifications of syringe lengths are 4.950 ± 0.030 inches. Figure 7.25 shows the output of Excel's *Descriptive Statistics* and *Histogram* tools applied to these data. The process mean is 4.963667, which is higher than the target specification for reasons described earlier. We would expect nearly all

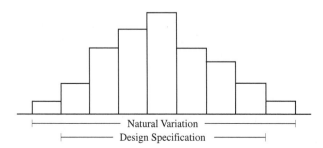

FIGURE 7.24 Incapable Process

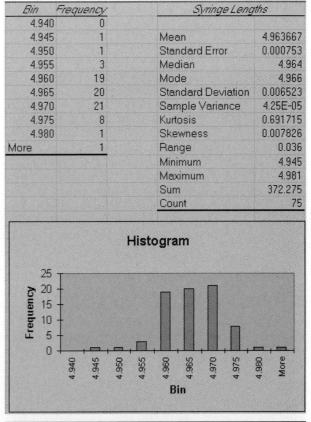

Bin	Frequency		Syringe Lengths	
4.940	0			
4.945	1		Mean	4.963667
4.950	1		Standard Error	0.000753
4.955	3		Median	4.964
4.960	19		Mode	4.966
4.965	20		Standard Deviation	0.006523
4.970	21		Sample Variance	4.25E-05
4.975	8		Kurtosis	0.691715
4.980	1		Skewness	0.007826
More	1		Range	0.036
			Minimum	4.945
			Maximum	4.981
			Sum	372.275
			Count	75

FIGURE 7.25   Summary Statistics and Histogram for Process Capability Analysis

process output to fall within ±3 standard deviations of the mean. With a standard deviation of 0.006523, this is 4.963667 ± 3(0.006523), or between 4.944 and 4.983. This 6-standard deviation spread represents the capability of the process. As long as the process remains in control, we would expect the syringe lengths to fall within this range. Thus, we expect a small percentage of syringes to exceed the upper specification of 4.980. As you can see, one of the data points in this sample does exceed this specification.

The relationship between the process capability and the design specifications is often quantified by a measure called the **process capability index,** denoted by C_p. C_p is simply the ratio of the specification width to the process capability:

$$C_p = \frac{\text{USL} - \text{LSL}}{6s}$$

For the syringe example, $C_p = (4.98 - 4.92)/(0.039) = 1.54$. A C_p value greater than 1.0 means that the process is capable of meeting specifications; values lower than 1.0 mean that some nonconforming output will always be produced unless the process technology is improved. However, despite the fact that the capability is good, the process is not centered properly on the target value and some nonconforming output will occur.

Questions and Problems

1. Define the terms *process capability* and *statistical process control,* and explain their importance in manufacturing and service.
2. What are some reasons that production output varies?
3. Explain the difference between common causes of variation and special causes of variation.
4. What is the difference between variables data and attributes data?
5. Describe the meaning of the term *in control.*
6. Describe the steps involved in applying statistical process control.
7. Describe the difference between an $\bar{x}$- and an R-chart.
8. Find the upper and lower control limits for $\bar{x}$- and R-charts for the width of a chair seat when the sample grand mean (based on 30 samples of 6 observations each) is 27.104 inches, and the average range is 0.316 inches.
9. Suppose that the sample grand mean (based on 25 samples of 10 observations each) for the weight of a satellite component is 0.806 grams and the average range for each batch is 0.013 grams. Find the upper and lower control limits for $\bar{x}$- and R-charts.
10. The sample grand mean (based on 30 samples of 8 observations each) for the weight of a pouch of stuffed crab is 0.503 pounds and the average range is 0.068 pounds. Find the upper and lower control limits for $\bar{x}$- and R-charts.
11. Why would you not expect all observations to fall within control chart limits?
12. If 30 batches of 100 items are tested for nonconformity and on average 96.0 of the samples contain no defects, find the upper and lower control limits for a *p*-chart.
13. If 25 batches of 200 samples are run through a battery of tests and on average 98.6 of the samples contain no defects, calculate the upper and lower control limits for a *p*-chart.
14. If 50 batches of 100 items are tested for nonconformity and on average 98.6 of the samples contain no defects, identify the upper and lower control limits for a *p*-chart.
15. If an operation produces output with a standard deviation of 0.35 pounds, and the upper control limit is 8 pounds and the lower control limit is 6 pounds, what is the process capability index?
16. If an operation produces output with a standard deviation of 0.12 inch, and the upper control limit is 3.60 inches and the lower control limit is 2.00 inches, what is the process capability index?
17. Compute control limits for $\bar{x}$- and R-charts for the following data. Draw and interpret the charts.

Sample					
1	105	100	99	96	103
2	102	100	99	100	100
3	98	104	98	106	97
4	99	101	99	99	99
5	95	97	104	102	97
6	102	107	100	101	100
7	97	98	105	96	101
8	102	101	102	100	105
9	101	98	103	99	100
10	96	97	100	96	104
11	97	97	100	99	96
12	105	103	102	100	96

13	96	103	102	99	105
14	97	99	99	100	99
15	102	103	99	95	102
16	100	104	96	100	99
17	92	104	105	97	96
18	97	98	96	99	99
19	100	101	104	95	103
20	104	98	96	104	97
21	103	97	97	98	100
22	101	97	96	104	98
23	102	100	98	104	99
24	96	97	105	102	97
25	98	99	97	98	100

18. Compute control limits for $\bar{x}$- and R-charts for the following 50 samples. Draw and interpret the charts.

Sample						
1	33	48	33	36	37	10
2	35	49	16	41	14	34
3	24	24	20	20	17	49
4	19	45	20	23	28	34
5	25	37	26	30	15	30
6	29	25	49	17	35	35
7	27	39	38	28	45	26
8	23	29	27	19	42	16
9	33	19	15	33	44	25
10	42	34	30	13	11	42
11	15	13	32	44	21	39
12	21	49	24	42	11	27
13	23	12	45	17	42	19
14	11	43	19	48	42	25
15	14	31	39	17	40	32
16	33	21	10	18	36	15
17	26	21	44	13	40	37
18	28	34	38	22	20	30
19	18	26	13	13	48	48
20	13	46	29	35	48	33
21	40	21	33	29	16	42
22	22	11	14	39	42	39
23	20	34	29	38	16	13
24	11	43	41	31	41	41
25	29	23	11	20	43	23
26	41	49	14	41	41	33
27	28	33	33	26	12	21
28	39	25	48	34	22	27
29	38	29	10	12	12	20
30	31	40	27	26	44	13
31	28	10	19	36	21	45

Continued

32	49	19	16	11	22	16
33	44	28	28	46	24	29
34	39	32	22	49	15	34
35	11	47	30	48	25	41
36	45	34	11	46	48	45
37	36	36	20	35	46	26
38	46	17	10	10	45	41
39	22	42	20	46	40	21
40	31	28	10	39	28	20
41	40	27	36	31	35	49
42	20	49	33	27	39	30
43	40	41	29	29	44	49
44	13	10	14	10	10	21
45	44	25	25	14	43	33
46	41	37	45	31	42	14
47	40	49	14	22	18	44
48	41	14	19	48	41	49
49	40	39	24	12	29	17
50	42	33	20	33	17	32

19. Hunter Nut Company produces cans of mixed nuts, advertised as containing no more than 20 percent peanuts. Hunter Nut Company wants to establish control limits for their process to ensure meeting this requirement. They have taken 30 samples of 144 cans of nuts from the production process at periodic intervals, inspected each can, and identified the proportion of cans that did not meet the peanut requirement. Compute the average proportion nonconforming and the upper and lower control limits for this process. Draw the p-chart and interpret the results.

Sample	Proportion Nonconforming
1	0.230
2	0.214
3	0.215
4	0.209
5	0.235
6	0.218
7	0.203
8	0.214
9	0.216
10	0.225
11	0.211
12	0.197
13	0.208
14	0.223
15	0.198
16	0.191
17	0.232
18	0.185
19	0.219
20	0.210

21	0.199
22	0.216
23	0.181
24	0.223
25	0.216
26	0.193
27	0.195
28	0.213
29	0.195
30	0.219

20. Doctor and Ramble produces high quality medicinal soap, advertised as 99 and 44/100 percent free of medically offensive pollutants. Twenty-five samples of 100 bars of soap were gathered at the beginning of each hour of production; the numbers of bars not meeting this requirement follows. Develop a *p*-chart for these data and interpret the results.

Sample	Number Nonconforming
1	0
2	1
3	1
4	0
5	2
6	5
7	1
8	2
9	1
10	0
11	0
12	1
13	0
14	2
15	0
16	1
17	3
18	2
19	3
20	5
21	4
22	7
23	3
24	5
25	8

C A S E

QUALITY CONTROL AT TRACWAY

In reviewing the Tracway data, Henry Hudson found several data sources that provide information about the quality of Tracway's products and processes but is uncertain how best to analyze them. In particular, he is interested in the data in the worksheets *Blade Weight,* which provides sample data from the manufacturing process of mower blades; *Mower Test,* which gives samples of functional performance test results; and *Process Capability,* which contains additional sample data of mower blade weights. Use appropriate control charts and statistical analyses to provide a complete report to Henry about quality issues he should understand or be concerned with. ■

References

Evans, James R., *Statistical Process Control for Quality Improvement* (Englewood Cliffs, NJ: Prentice-Hall, 1991).

Evans, James R., and William M. Lindsay, *The Management and Control of Quality,* 5th ed. (Cincinnati, OH: South-Western, 2002).

General Motors Statistical Process Control Manual (Milwaukee, WI: American Society for Quality, 1986).

Statistical Quality Control Handbook, AT&T Technologies, Commercial Sales Clerk, Select Code 700-444, P.O. Box 19901, Indianapolis, IN 46219.

DECISION MODELING AND ANALYSIS

8

RISK ANALYSIS AND MONTE CARLO SIMULATION

INTRODUCTION

Risk is the probability of occurrence of an undesirable outcome. Thus, risk is related to the uncertainty associated with things that one cannot control and the results of this uncertainty. In fact, it is difficult to find any decision—business or personal—that has no risk associated with it. The pharmaceutical industry, for example, operates in a high-risk environment.[1] It costs hundreds of millions of dollars and as much as 10 years to bring a drug to market. Once there, seven of ten products fail to return the cost of the company's capital. With interest rate and currency rate fluctuations, financial risk becomes even more of a concern. In consumer goods industries, manufacturers maintain "safety stock" inventories of goods to protect against the risk of running out of stock due to uncertain demand. On a personal level, individuals insure their homes, automobiles, vacation packages, and lives because of risk. Investing in the stock market is fraught with risk, as the ups and downs of technology stocks have demonstrated over the past several years. To measure risk in evaluating mutual funds, *Fortune* magazine introduced the standard deviation in 1997, as it explains how much of a fund's short-term results vary from its

---

[1] Nancy A. Nichols, "Scientific Management at Merck: An Interview with CFO Judy Lewent," *Harvard Business Review,* January–February 1994, 89–99.

long-term average, noting that the "standard deviation can be an important tool for investors—one that can offer some insight not only into how risky a fund is but even into how it might perform in a given market environment in the future."[2]

The importance of risk in business has long been recognized. The renowned management writer, Peter Drucker, observed in 1974:

> To try to eliminate risk in business enterprise is futile. Risk is inherent in the commitment of present resources to future expectations. Indeed, economic progress can be defined as the ability to take greater risks. The attempt to eliminate risks, even the attempt to minimize them, can only make them irrational and unbearable. It can only result in the greatest risk of all: rigidity.[3]

In recent years, managers have taken a renewed interest in the subject, spawned to a large extent by the ability to analyze risk using spreadsheet models and powerful personal computer software. In this chapter we provide the details on how to conduct risk analysis using Monte Carlo simulation with the Excel add-in, *Crystal Ball*.[4]

RISK ANALYSIS

Risk analysis is an approach for developing "a comprehensive understanding and awareness of the risk associated with a particular variable of interest (be it a payoff measure, a cash flow profile, or a macroeconomic forecast)."[5] Hertz and Thomas present a simple scenario to illustrate the concept of risk analysis:

> The executives of a food company must decide whether to launch a new packaged cereal. They have come to the conclusion that five factors are the determining variables: advertising and promotion expense, total cereal market, share of market for this product, operating costs, and new capital investment. On the basis of the "most likely" estimate for each of these variables the picture looks very bright—a healthy 30 percent return indicating a significantly positive expected net present value. This future, however, depends on each of the "most likely" estimates coming true in the actual case. If each of these "educated guesses" has, for example, a 60 percent chance of being correct, there is only an 8 percent chance that all five will be correct (0.60 × 0.60 × 0.60 × 0.60 × 0.60) if the factors are assumed to be independent. So the "expected" return or present value measure is actually dependent on a rather unlikely coincidence. The decision-maker needs to know a great deal more about the other values used to make each of the five estimates and about what he stands to gain or lose from various combinations of these values.[6]

---

[2] David Whitford, "Why Risk Matters," *Fortune*, December 29, 1997, 147–152.
[3] P. F. Drucker, *The Manager and the Management Sciences in Management: Tasks, Responsibilities, Practices* (London: Harper and Row, 1974).
[4] Much of this chapter has been adopted from *Crystal Ball 2000 User Manual*, © 1988–2000 Decisioneering, Inc. The *User Manual* provides many other details about *Crystal Ball* that cannot be described here. Copies of the *User Manual* can be purchased from the Technical Support or Sales Department of Decisioneering at (303) 534–1515; Toll-free sales: 1-800-289-2550. The Decisioneering Web site is [http://www.decisioneering.com].
[5] David B. Hertz and Howard Thomas, *Risk Analysis and Its Applications* (Chichester, UK: John Wiley & Sons, Ltd., 1983), p. 1.
[6] *Ibid.*, p. 24.

Thus, risk analysis seeks to examine the impacts of uncertainty in the estimates and their potential interaction with one another on the output variable of interest.

Hertz and Thomas also note that the challenge to risk analysts is to frame the output of risk analysis procedures in a manner that makes sense to the manager and provides clear insight into the problem, suggesting that simulation has many advantages. We laid the foundation for risk analysis when we introduced Monte Carlo simulation in Chapter 3—this might be a good time to review that material. The process of applying Monte Carlo simulation to risk analysis consists of the following steps:

1. Building a model that describes the key factors associated with a decision problem.
2. Recognizing and identifying the uncertainty associated with the variables in the model.
3. Generating a probability distribution for the outcome variables we wish to better understand.
4. Analyzing the effects of uncertainty in the outcome variables on the decision. For example, we could answer such questions as: What is the probability that we will incur a financial loss? What is the probability that we will run out of inventory? and What are the chances that a project will be completed on time?

We will use the financial spreadsheet model (*New Store Financial Model.xls*) we introduced in Chapter 1 (and shown again in Figure 8.1) as the basis for much of our discussion of risk analysis and the use of *Crystal Ball* in this chapter. To set the context behind such a model, think of any retailer that operates many stores throughout the country, such as Old Navy, Hallmark Cards, or Radio Shack, to name just a few. The

FIGURE 8.1   Financial Analysis Model

	A	B	C	D	E	F	G
1	**New Store Financial Analysis Model**						
2							
3	**Model Assumptions**		Year 1	Year 2	Year 3	Year 4	Year 5
4	Annual Growth Rate			20%	12%	9%	5%
5	Sales Revenue		$ 800,000				
6							
7	Cost of Merchandise (% of sales)	30%					
8	Operating Expenses						
9	Labor Cost	$ 200,000					
10	Rent Per Square Foot	$ 28					
11	Other Expenses	$ 325,000					
12							
13	Inflation Rate	2%					
14	Store Size (square feet)	$ 5,000					
15	Total Fixed Assets	$ 300,000					
16	Depreciation period (straight line)	5					
17	Discount Rate	10%					
18	Tax Rate	34%					
19							
20	**Model Outputs**	Year	1	2	3	4	5
21	Sales Revenue		$ 800,000	$ 960,000	$ 1,075,200	$ 1,171,968	$ 1,230,566
22	Cost of Merchandise		$ 240,000	$ 288,000	$ 322,560	$ 351,590	$ 369,170
23	Operating Expenses						
24	Labor Cost		$ 200,000	$ 204,000	$ 208,080	$ 212,242	$ 216,486
25	Rent Per Square Foot		$ 140,000	$ 142,800	$ 145,656	$ 148,569	$ 151,541
26	Other Expenses		$ 325,000	$ 331,500	$ 338,130	$ 344,893	$ 351,790
27	Net Operating Income		$ (105,000)	$ (6,300)	$ 60,774	$ 114,674	$ 141,579
28	Depreciation Expense		$ 60,000	$ 60,000	$ 60,000	$ 60,000	$ 60,000
29	Net Income Before Tax		$ (165,000)	$ (66,300)	$ 774	$ 54,674	$ 81,579
30	Income Tax		$ (56,100)	$ (22,542)	$ 263	$ 18,589	$ 27,737
31	Net After Tax Income		$ (108,900)	$ (43,758)	$ 511	$ 36,085	$ 53,842
32	Plus Depreciation Expense		$ 60,000	$ 60,000	$ 60,000	$ 60,000	$ 60,000
33	Annual Cash Flow		$ (48,900)	$ 16,242	$ 60,511	$ 96,085	$ 113,842
34	Discounted Cash Flow		(44,454.55)	13,423.14	45,462.69	65,627.36	70,687.05
35	Cumulative Discounted Cash Flow		(44,454.55)	(31,031.40)	14,431.28	80,058.65	150,745.70

retailer is often seeking to open new stores and has developed the model to evaluate the profitability of a new site of a certain size that would be leased for five years. If you examine the model closely, you will see that the key assumptions in the model might be based on historical data (e.g., cost of merchandise as a percent of sales and operating expenses), current economic forecasts (e.g., inflation rate), or judgmental estimates based on preliminary market research (e.g., first-year sales revenue and annual growth rates). These assumptions represent the "most likely" estimates, and as a deterministic model, the spreadsheet shows that the new store will appear to be quite profitable by the end of five years. However, the model does not provide any information about what might happen if these variables do not attain these most likely values, and considerable uncertainty exists about their true values.

To characterize the uncertainty, we first have to ask some questions about the uncertainty of each assumption. For example,

- What are the chances that first-year sales revenue will exceed $900,000?
- Is there any possibility that first-year sales revenue will exceed $1 million?
- What are the chances that first-year sales revenue will be as low as $500,000?

Answers to such questions can help us to select an appropriate probability distribution to characterize the uncertainty associated with each model assumption. Once we have done this, we can perform Monte Carlo simulation to generate a distribution of the cumulative discounted cash flow in each year. Then we can address questions about risk, such as

- What are the chances that the store would not be profitable by the third year?
- How likely is it that cumulative profits over five years would not exceed $100,000?
- What profit are we likely to realize with a probability of at least 0.70?

MONTE CARLO SIMULATION WITH *CRYSTAL BALL*

During installation, *Crystal Ball* may be set up to run automatically whenever Excel is loaded (however, this causes Excel to take more time to load), or it can be run from the Windows *Start* menu. You may also start *Crystal Ball* after Excel is running by going to *Tools . . . Add-Ins* and checking the box for *Crystal Ball*. Three new menu items appear on the main menu bar: *Cell, Run,* and *CBTools.* A new button bar also provides shortcut ways to invoke *Crystal Ball* menu commands.

To use *Crystal Ball,* we must perform the following steps:

1. Develop the spreadsheet model
2. Define *assumptions* for probabilistic variables, that is, the probability distributions that describe the uncertainty
3. Define the *forecast cells,* that is, the output variables of interest
4. Set the number of trials and other run preferences
5. Run the simulation
6. Interpret the results

To illustrate this process, we will use the financial analysis model in Figure 8.1.

A Financial Analysis Risk Simulation

In Figure 8.1, the **assumption cells** are shaded in the Model Assumptions section of the spreadsheet. These represent the uncertainty variables for which we must define a probability distribution. In the Model Outputs section, the output variables in which we are interested—*Crystal Ball* calls these **forecast cells**—are also shaded. You may control the shading and formatting of the assumption and forecast cells by selecting *Cell . . . Cell Preferences* in the *Crystal Ball* menu.

Specifying Input Information

The first step in using *Crystal Ball* is to define the probability distributions for assumption cells. Suppose that the new business development manager for the firm has identified the following distributions and parameters for these variables:

> First year sales revenue: normal, mean = $800,000, standard deviation = $70,000, minimum = $650,000
>
> Annual growth rate, year 2: lognormal, mean = 20 percent, standard deviation = 8 percent
>
> Annual growth rate, year 3: lognormal, mean = 12 percent, standard deviation = 4 percent
>
> Annual growth rate, year 4: lognormal, mean = 9 percent, standard deviation = 2 percent
>
> Annual growth rate, year 5: lognormal, mean = 5 percent, standard deviation = 1 percent
>
> Cost of merchandise: uniform between 27 percent and 33 percent
>
> Labor cost: triangular, minimum = $175,000, most likely = $200,000, maximum = $225,000
>
> Rent per square foot: uniform between $26 and $30
>
> Other expenses: triangular, minimum = $310,000, most likely = $325,000, maximum = $350,000
>
> Inflation rate: triangular, minimum = 1 percent, most likely = 2 percent, maximum = 5 percent

To define them in *Crystal Ball,* first select a cell or range of cells. Assumption cells must contain a value; they cannot be defined for formula, nonnumeric, or blank cells. From the *Cell* menu, select *Define Assumption. Crystal Ball* displays a gallery of probability distributions from which to choose and prompts you for the parameters. For example, let us define the distribution for the first-year sales revenue. First click on cell C5. Then select *Cell . . . Define Assumption. Crystal Ball* displays the distribution gallery shown in Figure 8.2. Since we assume that this variable has a normal distribution, we click on the normal distribution and then the OK button (or simply double

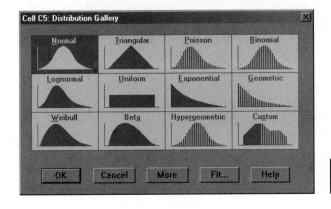

FIGURE 8.2   *Crystal Ball* Distribution Gallery

click the distribution). A dialog box is then displayed prompting you for the parameters associated with this distribution.

We suggest that you first enter a clear, descriptive name for your assumptions in the top box. *Crystal Ball* will automatically use text in cells next to or above assumption cells, but these may not be the correct ones for your application. For most continuous distributions, you have several options on how to specify the distribution using percentiles. For example, with the normal distribution, the default is to enter the mean and standard deviation; however, you can also define the distribution by its 10th and 90th percentiles, the mean and the 90th percentile, and several other ways. This option is useful when only percentile information is available or when specific parameters such as the mean and standard deviation are unknown. As a practical illustration, suppose that you are interviewing a construction manager to identify the distribution of the time it takes to complete a task. Although a beta distribution is often appropriate in such applications, it would be very difficult to define the beta distribution parameters from judgmental information. However, it would be easy for the manager to estimate the 10th and 90th percentiles for task times. In *Crystal Ball,* these input options can be found in a pop-up box by clicking on the Parms button in the dialog box. We suggest you check this when using a new distribution.

Crystal Ball anticipates the default parameters based on the current values in the spreadsheet model. For example, with a normal distribution, the default mean is the assumption cell value, and the standard deviation is assumed to be 10 percent of the mean. Therefore, in our example, we need to change the standard deviation to $70,000. Clicking on Enter fixes these values and rescales the picture to allow you to see what the distribution looks like (this feature is quite useful for flexible families of distributions such as the triangular, gamma, or beta). The result for the example is shown in Figure 8.3. However, the manager believes that first-year sales will never be less than $650,000. Therefore, we must truncate the distribution to reflect this. This can be done by entering the minimum value in the box above the mean (which currently reads "-Infinity") or by clicking and holding and then moving the small triangular "grabber" under the left tail of the distribution (when you do this, you will notice the value in the minimum box automatically change). The result of this change is shown in Figure 8.4. However, truncating distributions changes the true values of the mean and standard deviation. In this case, for example, the mean of the resulting distribution is no longer $800,000. To view the mean value of the assumption,

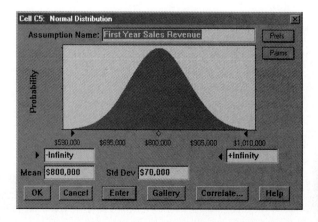

FIGURE 8.3 Normal Distribution Assumption Dialog Box

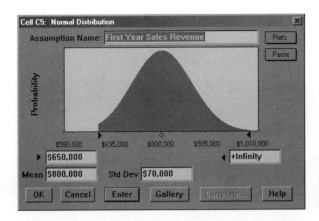

FIGURE 8.4 Truncated Normal Distribution Assumption

click on *Prefs . . . Show Mean*. Clicking on OK accepts your choice and returns to the main screen.

We repeat this process for each of the probabilistic assumptions in the model. Figure 8.5, for example, shows the lognormal distribution for the annual growth rate in year 2. For the lognormal distribution, the default parameters are the mean and standard deviation of the normal random variable; however, you can enter the log mean and log standard deviation and other options from the Parms button. Figures 8.6 and 8.7 show the dialog boxes for the uniform distribution assumption for cost of merchandise and triangular assumption for inflation rate, respectively. In Figure 8.7 you may notice three "grabbers"—two small black triangles and one open diamond just below the horizontal axis. The end grabbers truncate the distribution, while the center grabber allows you to adjust the shape and skewness of the distribution. Many other distributions in the gallery have similar grabbers.

After all assumptions are defined, you must define one or more forecast cells that define the output variables of interest. In our example, these are cells C35:G35. Instead of choosing them individually, highlight the entire range, and then select *Define Forecast* from the *Cell* menu. The *Define Forecast* dialog box is shown in Figure 8.8. You may enter a name and unit of measure for each forecast. When you click OK, *Crystal Ball* will automatically bring up the dialog box for the next cell in the range. If *Display Window Automatically* is checked, you will see the output distribution being built as *Crystal Ball* runs each trial of the simulation.

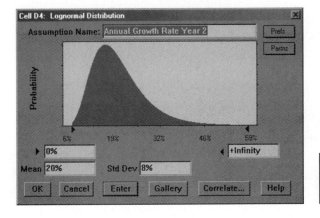

FIGURE 8.5 Lognormal Distribution Assumption Dialog Box

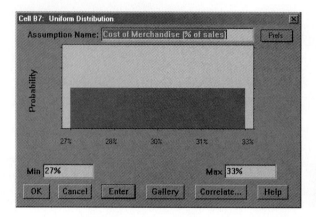

FIGURE 8.6 Uniform Distribution Assumption Dialog Box

The Excel Cut, Copy, and Paste commands only address cell values and attributes and *do not* copy *Crystal Ball* data. *Crystal Ball* provides edit commands to let you copy, paste, or clear assumptions or forecasts from cells. These are useful, for example, when you have several assumptions with the same properties. These commands are found under the *Cell* menu as *Copy Data, Paste Data,* and *Clear Data.* The *Cell* menu options *Select All Assumptions* and *Select All Forecasts* allow you to select all relevant cells to clear.

Prior to running a simulation, you need to define some specifications. To do this, select the *Run Preferences* item from the *Run* menu. The *Trials* dialog box, shown in Figure 8.9, allows you to choose the number of trials. If you check the *Stop if Specified Precision is Reached* box (and set the precision control parameters when you define the forecast by clicking the *More* button in Figure 8.9), the simulation will stop if confidence intervals for all forecast statistics meet the specified level of precision or the maximum number of trials is reached. We recommend you leave this box unchecked until you become an experienced user.

The *Sampling Preferences* dialog box (Figure 8.10) allows you to use the same sequence of random numbers for generating random variates; this allows you to repeat the simulation results at other times. This is controlled by the *Initial Seed Value. Crystal Ball* has two types of sampling methods: Monte Carlo and Latin Hypercube. Monte Carlo sampling selects random variates independently over the entire range of possible values. With Latin Hypercube sampling, *Crystal Ball* divides

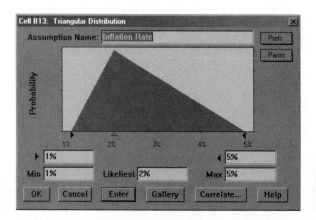

FIGURE 8.7 Triangular Distribution Assumption Dialog Box

FIGURE 8.8 *Define Forecast* Dialog Box

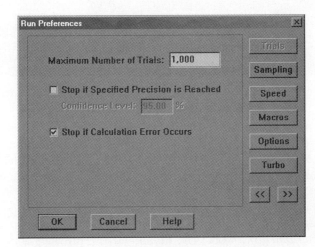

FIGURE 8.9 *Run Preferences* Dialog Box (Trials)

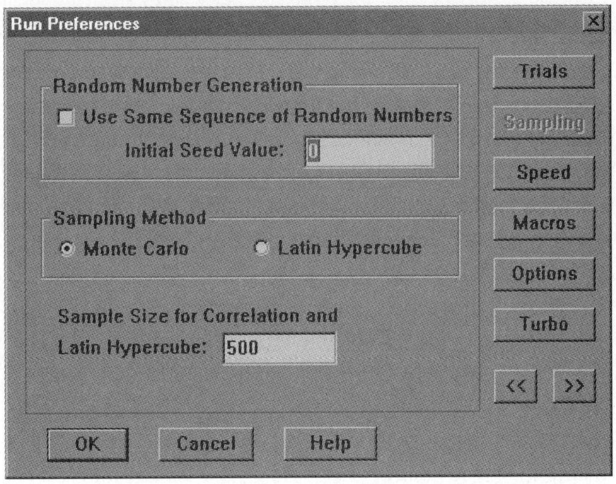

FIGURE 8.10 *Run Preferences* Dialog Box (Sampling)

each assumption's probability distribution into intervals of equal probability and generates an assumption value randomly within each interval. Latin Hypercube sampling is more precise because it samples the entire range of the distribution in a more even and consistent manner, thus achieving the same accuracy as a larger number of Monte Carlo trials. However, it requires additional memory requirements, which typically is not a problem.

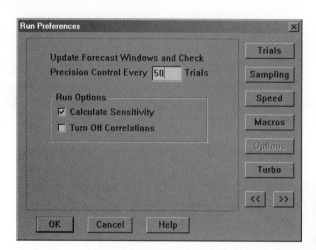

FIGURE 8.11 *Run Preferences* Dialog Box (Options)

The *Options* dialog box (Figure 8.11) controls how often *Crystal Ball* redraws forecast charts during a simulation (we recommend the default value of 50 trials) and allows you to generate sensitivity information and turn off correlations. We will discuss these options later in this chapter. We recommend leaving the *Speed, Macros,* and *Turbo* (which applies only to network servers) options at their default values unless you are an advanced user.

The last step in running a simulation is to select *Run* from the *Run* menu and watch *Crystal Ball* go to work! The *Run* menu also provides options to stop a simulation in progress, continue, and reset values (i.e., clear statistics and results). It is important to clear statistics if you need to rerun a simulation.

Crystal Ball Output

The principal output reports provided by *Crystal Ball* are the *forecast chart, percentiles summary,* and *statistics summary.* Figure 8.12 shows the forecast chart for the five-year cumulative discounted cash flow after 1000 trials. The forecast chart is simply a histogram of the outcome variable that includes all values within 2.6 standard deviations of the mean, which represents approximately 99 percent of the data. (This may be changed in the *Preferences/Display Range* menu.) The number of outliers is shown in the upper-right corner of the chart. For this example, we have 17 data points outside 2.6 standard deviations of the mean. Just below the horizontal axis at the extremes of the distribution are two *endpoint grabbers.* The range values of the variable at these positions are given in the boxes at the bottom left and right corners of the chart. The percent of data values between the grabbers is displayed in the Certainty box at the lower center of the chart. A certainty level is a probability interval that states the probability of falling within a specified range.

Questions involving risk can be answered by manipulating the endpoint grabbers or by changing the range and certainty values in the boxes. Several options exist.

1. *You may move an endpoint grabber by clicking and holding the left mouse button on the grabber and moving it.* As you do, the distribution outside of the middle range changes color, the range value corresponding to the grabber changes to reflect its current position, and the certainty level changes to reflect the new percentage between the grabbers. Figure 8.13 shows the result of moving the left grabber to the value $100,420.71. The dark portion of the histogram represents 52.60 percent of

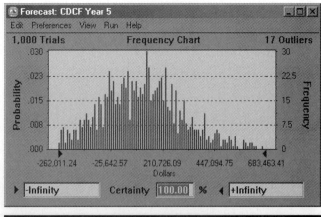

FIGURE 8.12   Forecast Chart (Cumulative Discounted
Cash Flow, Year 5)

the distribution (as given in the Certainty box). This represents the likelihood that the cumulative discounted cash flow will exceed $100,420.71.

2.   *You may type in specific values in the range boxes.*   When you do, the grabbers automatically move to the appropriate positions and the certainty level changes to reflect the new percentage of values between the range values. For example, suppose you wanted to determine the percentage of values greater than $0. If you enter this in the left range box, the grabber will automatically move to that position, the portion of the histogram to the right of 0 will lighten, and the certainty level will change to reflect the percentage of the distribution between the grabbers. This is illustrated in Figure 8.14, which shows a 72.10 percent chance of a positive cash flow in year 5.

3.   *You may specify a certainty level.*   If the endpoint grabbers are free (as indicated by a black color), the certainty range will be centered around the mean (or median as specified in the *Preferences/Statistics* menu option). For example, Figure 8.15 shows the

FIGURE 8.13   Probability That CDCF Exceeds
$100,420.71

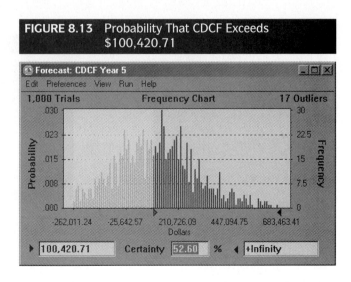

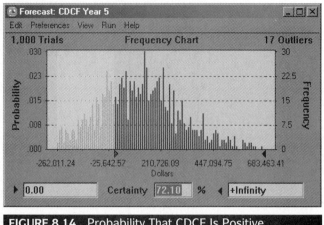

FIGURE 8.14   Probability That CDCF Is Positive

result of changing the certainty level to 90 percent. The range centered about the mean is from −$181,699 to $460,404. You may anchor an endpoint grabber by clicking on it. When anchored, the grabber will be a lighter color. (To free an anchored grabber, click anywhere in the chart area.) If a grabber is anchored and you specify a certainty level, the free grabber moves to a position corresponding to this level. Finally, you may cross over the grabbers and move them to opposite ends to determine certainty levels for the tails of the distribution.

We caution you that a certainty level is *not* a confidence interval. It is simply a probability interval. Confidence intervals, as you should remember from Chapter 4, depend on the sample size.

The forecast chart may be customized to change its appearance through the *Preferences/Chart Preferences* dialog box. The chart may be displayed as an area, outline, or column (bar) chart and may be displayed as a frequency distribution (the default), cumulative distribution, or reverse cumulative distribution. The number of groups determines the granularity of the chart—a smaller number of groups provides less detail. The number format may be changed in the *Preferences/Format Preferences*

FIGURE 8.15   90 Percent Probability Interval for CDCF

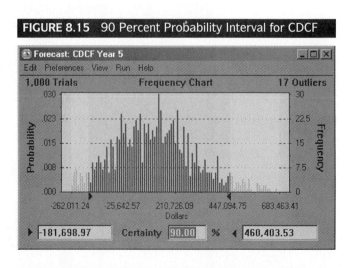

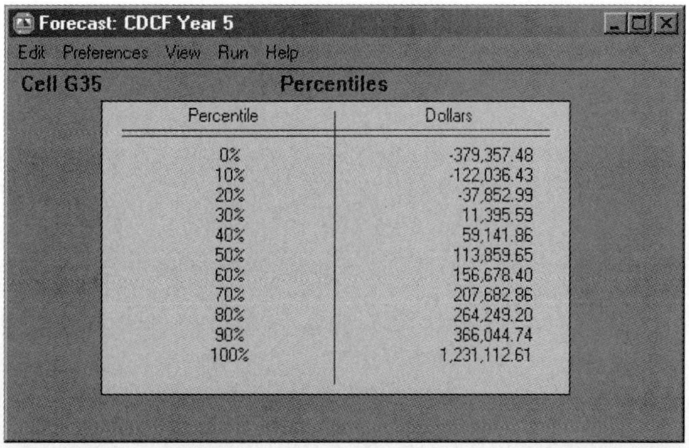

Percentile	Dollars
0%	-379,357.48
10%	-122,036.43
20%	-37,852.99
30%	11,395.59
40%	59,141.86
50%	113,859.65
60%	156,678.40
70%	207,682.86
80%	264,249.20
90%	366,044.74
100%	1,231,112.61

FIGURE 8.16 Forecast Chart—Percentiles View

dialog box. You may also improve the appearance of the forecast chart by checking the box *Round Axis Values* from the *Preferences/Display Range* dialog.

The percentiles chart can be displayed from the *View* menu. An example is shown in Figure 8.16. For example, we see that the chance that the total profit will be less than \$207,683 is about 70 percent. From the *View* menu you may also select a statistics report. This report, shown in Figure 8.17, provides a summary of key descriptive statistical measures. The mean standard error, $\sigma/\sqrt{n}$,is reported on the last line of the statistics report and defines the standard deviation for the sampling distribution of the mean. We may use this to construct a confidence interval for the mean using the formula given in Chapter 4:

$$\bar{x} \pm z_{\alpha/2}(\sigma/\sqrt{n})$$

Because a *Crystal Ball* simulation will generally have a large number of trials, we may use the standard normal value $z_{\alpha/2}$ instead of the *t*-distribution. Thus, for the year 5 CDCF results, a 95 percent confidence interval would be

$$\$120{,}010.29 \pm 1.96(\$6152.25) \quad \text{or} \quad [\$107{,}951.88, \$132{,}068.70]$$

FIGURE 8.17 Forecast Chart—Statistics View

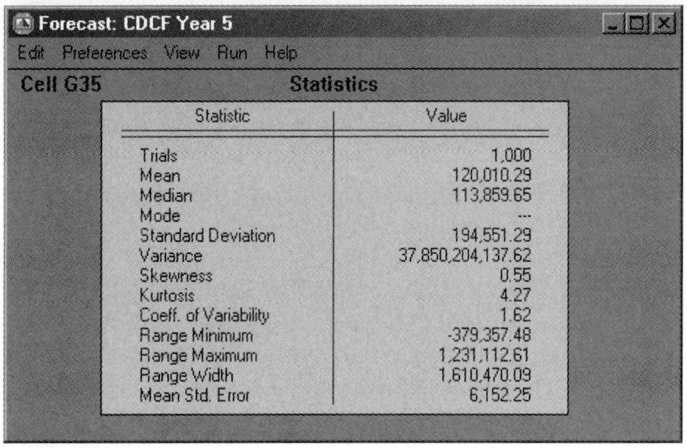

Statistic	Value
Trials	1,000
Mean	120,010.29
Median	113,859.65
Mode	---
Standard Deviation	194,551.29
Variance	37,850,204,137.62
Skewness	0.55
Kurtosis	4.27
Coeff. of Variability	1.62
Range Minimum	-379,357.48
Range Maximum	1,231,112.61
Range Width	1,610,470.09
Mean Std. Error	6,152.25

To reduce the size of the confidence interval, we would need to run the simulation for a higher number of trials, as discussed in Chapter 4.

To close *Crystal Ball* without closing Excel, select *Close Crystal Ball* from the *Run* menu. *Crystal Ball* also closes automatically when you exit Excel. When you save your spreadsheet in Excel, any assumptions and forecasts that you defined for *Crystal Ball* are also saved. However, this does not save the results of a *Crystal Ball* simulation. To save a *Crystal Ball* simulation, select *Run . . . Save Run*. Doing so allows you to save any customized chart settings and other simulation results and recall them without rerunning the simulation. To retrieve a *Crystal Ball* simulation, choose *Restore* from the *Run* menu. You may also copy a saved simulation to other computers where *Crystal Ball* is installed.

Creating *Crystal Ball* Reports

Customized reports may be created from the *Run* menu by choosing *Create Report*. This option allows you to select a summary of assumptions and output information that we described. These are created in a separate Excel worksheet and may be printed or customized for reporting purposes. In addition, *Crystal Ball* allows you to extract selected data to a new Excel workbook for further analysis. From the *Run* menu, select *Extract Data*. In the dialog box that appears, you may select various types of data to extract

- Forecast values—each of the forecast values generated from each simulation trial
- Statistics—the data in the *Statistics View* of the forecast chart
- Percentiles
- Frequency counts—a tabular frequency distribution of the forecast chart histogram
- Cumulative counts—a cumulative tabular frequency distribution
- Sensitivity data (which will be described later in this chapter)

Finally, you may access *Crystal Ball* data directly in Excel using CB functions. A complete list may be found by invoking the function wizard button $[f_x]$ on the Excel menu bar and going to the *Crystal Ball* category. Some of the more useful functions for customizing reports are

- *CB.GetForeStatFN(forecast_cell_reference, index).* The first argument is a valid forecast cell; *index* is a number from 1 to 13 that refers to a forecast statistic, as shown in Figure 8.17. Index = 1 refers to the number of trials; index = 2 refers to the mean, etc. Thus, to get the standard deviation for year 5 CDCF, you would use the function =CB.GetForeStatFN(G35, 5).

- *CB.GetCertaintyFN(forecast_cell_reference, value).* The first argument is a valid forecast cell; value refers to the threshold value for which you want to calculate the certainty level—the probability of achieving a forecast value at or below the threshold. For example, to find the probability that year 5 CDCF is $100,000 or less, use the function =CB.GetCertaintyFN(G35, 100000).

- *CB.GetForePercentFN(forecast_cell_reference, percent).* Returns a percentile for a forecast cell. The first argument is a valid forecast cell; *percent* is a number from 0 to 100 that specifies the desired percentile. Thus, to find the 75th percentile for year 5 CDCF, use the function =CB.GetForePercentFN(G35, 75).

Using these techniques allows you to create a useful, customized, managerial report for interpreting statistical results.

ADDITIONAL *CRYSTAL BALL* MODELING AND ANALYSIS OPTIONS

Crystal Ball contains a variety of additional options that facilitate risk analysis modeling and interpretation of results. In this section we review these capabilities.

Correlated Assumptions

In *Crystal Ball* each random input variable is assumed to be independent of the others by default. In many situations we might wish to explicitly model dependencies between variables. Although this may be done using cell formulas directly in Excel, *Crystal Ball* allows you to specify correlation coefficients to define dependencies between assumptions. *Crystal Ball* uses the correlation coefficients to rearrange the generated random variates to produce the desired correlations. This can be done only after assumptions have been defined. For example, in the new store financial analysis model, suppose that we wish to correlate the annual growth rates. For instance, if the annual growth rate in year 2 is high, then it would make sense that the annual growth rate in year 3 would be high also. You probably would not expect the growth rate in one year to be high if the growth rate in the previous year is low. Thus, we might expect a positive correlation between these variables.

To define correlations in *Crystal Ball,* select one of these cells, for instance, the annual growth rate in year 2 (D4), then select *Define Assumption* from the *Cell* menu. When the distribution dialog box appears, click on the *Correlate . . .* button. The *Correlation Dialog* box, shown in Figure 8.18, appears. The *Select Assumption* button provides a list of the assumptions that you have defined. We then select the other assumption to correlate, for instance, the annual growth rate in year 3, and then enter a correlation coefficient.

You may enter a correlation coefficient in one of three ways. First, you can enter a value between −1 and 1 in the *Coefficient Value* box. Second, you may drag the slider control along the Correlation Coefficient scale; the specific value you select is displayed in the box to the left of the scale. Third, you may click on *Calc . . .* and enter ranges of cells in the spreadsheet that contain empirical values that should be used to

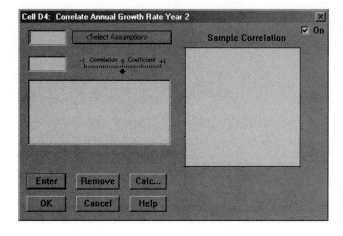

FIGURE 8.18 *Correlation Dialog* Box

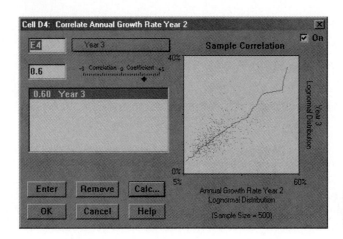

FIGURE 8.19 Correlation Chart

calculate a correlation coefficient. After the correlation coefficient is specified, *Crystal Ball* displays a sample correlation chart, as shown in Figure 8.19. The solid line indicates where values of a perfect correlation would fall; the points represent the actual pairing of assumption values that would occur during the simulation. When using this option, you must be cautious if you have a large number of correlations, since it is possible that some correlations might conflict with others, preventing *Crystal Ball* from running. If *Crystal Ball* detects a conflict, it will try to reset the correlation coefficients by asking the user to update them.

Instead of manually entering the correlations between several variables one at a time, *Crystal Ball* has a tool that allows you to define a matrix or correlations between assumptions in one step. Under the *CBTools* menu, select *Correlation Matrix*. In the dialog box that appears, include all the assumptions you want to define in the correlation matrix by moving them from the *Available Assumptions* field to the *Selected Assumptions* field by either double clicking on each assumption to move or selecting it and clicking on the >> button. When you click *Next,* the *Specify Options* dialog box appears. Select your options (e.g., create a temporary matrix on a new worksheet) and click *Start.* You may enter the correlation coefficients into the matrix and click on *Load* to put them into your model (the *Load* button only appears if a temporary matrix has been selected).

Overlay Charts

If a simulation has multiple, related forecasts, the overlay chart feature allows you to superimpose the frequency data from selected forecasts on one chart in order to compare differences and similarities that might not be apparent. You may also use the overlay chart to fit a standard distribution to any single forecast, similar to the distribution fitting feature described in Chapter 3. This option is invoked from the *Run* menu by selecting *Open Overlay Chart.* In the *Overlay Chart* dialog box that appears, click on *Add Forecast* to select the forecasts to include. You may select them individually or click on *Choose All* to include all of them. You may customize the appearance of the chart in many ways by clicking on the *Chart Prefs* button. This allows you to choose the type of chart and the distribution type. Figure 8.20 shows an outline-type overlay chart for the cumulative distribution of each of the five years' CDCF values. You can easily see that the probability of cumulative discounted cash flow values increases each year.

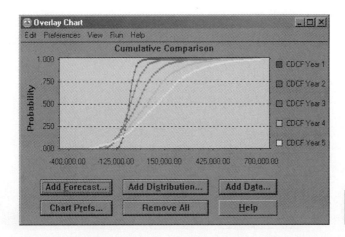

FIGURE 8.20   Overlay Chart Example

From the overlay chart, you may also fit a distribution to a forecast. (See Chapter 3 for an explanation of *Crystal Ball's* distribution fitting capability. The difference here is that you are fitting the distribution to the forecast values, not historical data for identifying input distributions.) Figure 8.21 shows a fit of the year 5 CDCF forecast to the best distribution, a gamma distribution. The *p*-value of approximately 0.59 suggests a reasonable fit. This would allow you to use the gamma distribution with the specified parameters in other simulation analyses.

Trend Charts

If a simulation has multiple forecasts that are related to one another (such as over time), you can view the certainty ranges of all forecasts on a single chart, called a *trend chart*. Figure 8.22 shows a trend chart for the five-year cumulative discounted cash flows in our example. The trend chart displays certainty ranges in a series of patterned bands centered on the medians. For example, the band representing the 90 percent certainty range shows the range of values into which a forecast has a 90 percent chance of falling. From the trend chart in Figure 8.22, we see that although the median cash flow increases over time, so does the variation, indicating that the uncertainty also increases with time. Trend charts are opened from the *Run* menu by selecting *Open Trend Chart*. Clicking on *Trend Preferences . . .* displays a dialog box that allows

FIGURE 8.21   Gamma Distribution Fit with Overlay Chart

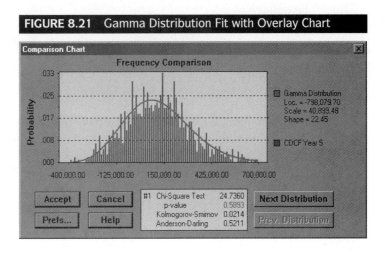

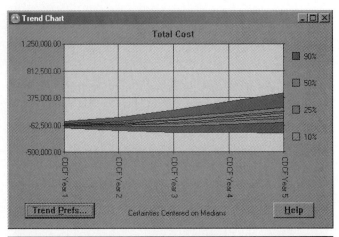

FIGURE 8.22   Trend Chart for Cumulative Discounted Cash Flows

you to customize the trend chart by selecting the number and type of certainty bands as well as the chart type.

Sensitivity Analysis

An important reason for using simulation for risk analysis is the ability to conduct sensitivity analyses to understand the impacts of individual variables or their distributional assumptions on forecasts. A somewhat naïve way to investigate the impact of assumptions on forecast cells is to freeze, or hold, certain assumptions constant in the model and compare the results with a base case simulation. The *Freeze Assumptions . . .* option under the *Cell* menu allows you to temporarily exclude certain assumptions from a simulation and conduct this type of sensitivity analysis. While this might be necessary to do in certain situations, freezing assumptions is somewhat tedious.

The uncertainty in a forecast is the result of the combined effect of the uncertainties of all assumptions as well as the formulas used in the model. An assumption might have a high degree of uncertainty yet have little effect on the forecast because it is not weighted heavily in the model formulas. For instance, a forecast might be defined as

$$0.9(\text{Assumption 1}) + 0.1(\text{Assumption 2})$$

In the model the forecast is nine times as sensitive to changes in the value of Assumption 1 as it is to changes in the value of Assumption 2. Thus, even if Assumption 2 has a much higher degree of uncertainty, as specified by the variance of its probability distribution, it would have a relatively minor effect on the uncertainty of the forecast. The *Sensitivity Chart* feature of *Crystal Ball* allows you to determine the influence that each assumption cell has individually on a forecast cell. The sensitivity chart displays the rankings of each assumption according to their impact on a forecast cell as a bar chart. This provides three benefits:

1. It tells which assumptions are influencing forecasts the most and which need better estimates.

2. It tells which assumptions are influencing forecasts the least and can be ignored or discarded altogether.
3. By understanding how assumptions affect your model, you can develop more realistic spreadsheet models and improve the accuracy of your results.

To create a sensitivity chart, you must ensure that the *Calculate Sensitivity* box is checked in the *Run Preferences Options* dialog box before running the simulation. After the simulation is completed, select *Open Sensitivity Chart* from the *Run* menu. The assumptions (and possibly other forecasts) are listed on the left, beginning with the assumption having the highest sensitivity. Sensitivity charts for the cash flow example are shown in Figures 8.23 and 8.24. The sensitivities in Figure 8.23 are measured by **rank correlation coefficients.** Correlation coefficients provide a measure of the degree to which assumptions and forecasts change together. Rank correlation is a method whereby *Crystal Ball* replaces assumption values with their ranking from lowest to highest and uses the rankings to compute a correlation coefficient. Positive coefficients indicate that an increase in the assumption is associated with an increase in the forecast; negative coefficients imply the reverse. The larger the absolute value of the correlation coefficient, the stronger is the relationship. Thus, the cash flow in year 1 changes more strongly with changes in the first-year sales revenue.

Figure 8.24 shows the sensitivities as a percent of the contribution to the variance of the forecast. This addresses the question, What percentage of the variance or uncertainty in the target forecast is due to a specific assumption? However, it is important to note that this method is only an approximation and not precisely a variance decomposition in a statistical sense. The option can by changed by clicking on the *Sensitivity Prefs . . .* button on the sensitivity chart. This also allows you to select forecasts to include in the sensitivity chart. However, if assumptions are correlated or assumptions are nonmonotonic with the target forecast (meaning an increase or decrease in the assumption does not necessarily lead to an increase or decrease in the forecast, respectively), the sensitivity results may not be accurate.

Crystal Ball has another means of providing a priori sensitivity analysis information—the *Tornado Chart* tool. This tool tests the range of each variable at specified percentiles and then calculates the value of the forecast at each point. It illustrates the range between the minimum and maximum forecast values for each variable and arranges them from largest to smallest in a "funnel" shape of a tornado, called a **tornado chart.** This differs from the sensitivity chart in that it tests each assumption independently, while

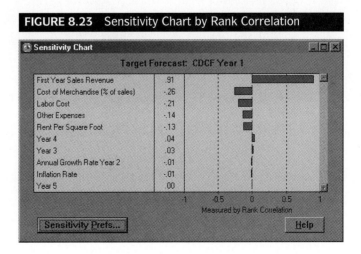

FIGURE 8.23   Sensitivity Chart by Rank Correlation

Sensitivity Chart		Target Forecast: CDCF Year 1
First Year Sales Revenue	.91	
Cost of Merchandise (% of sales)	-.26	
Labor Cost	-.21	
Other Expenses	-.14	
Rent Per Square Foot	-.13	
Year 4	.04	
Year 3	.03	
Annual Growth Rate Year 2	-.01	
Inflation Rate	-.01	
Year 5	.00	

Measured by Rank Correlation

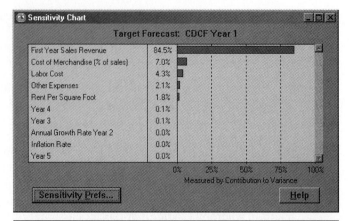

FIGURE 8.24 Sensitivity Chart by Contribution to Variance

freezing the other variables at their base values. Thus, it measures the effect of each variable on the forecast cell while removing the effects of the other variables. Its usefulness lies in quickly prescreening the variables in a model to determine which are good candidates to define as assumptions prior to building a *Crystal Ball* simulation model. Those variables having little effect on a forecast might not need to be defined as assumptions and can be kept as constants in the model, thus simplifying it. Figure 8.25 shows a tornado

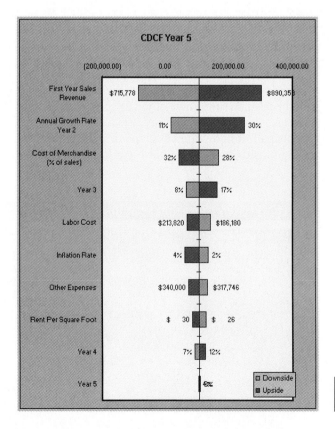

FIGURE 8.25 *Crystal Ball* Tornado Chart

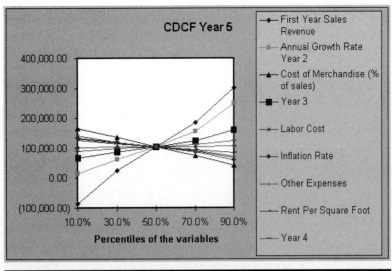

FIGURE 8.26   *Crystal Ball* Spider Chart

chart for year 5 CDCF. This shows that the first-year sales revenue and annual growth rate in year 2 have the most effect on the forecast, while the rent per square foot and annual growth rates for years 4 and 5 have comparatively little effect.

The *Tornado Chart* tool also creates a **spider chart,** as shown in Figure 8.26. A spider chart provides information similar to a tornado chart and illustrates the differences between the minimum and maximum forecast values by graphing a curve through all the variable values tested. Curves with steep slopes indicate that those variables have a large effect on the forecast, while curves that are almost horizontal have little or no effect on the forecast. The slopes also indicate whether a positive or negative change in the variable has a positive or negative effect on the forecast.

While tornado and spider charts are useful, they do not consider correlations defined between variables and depend significantly on the base case used for the variables. To confirm the accuracy of the results, you should run the tool multiple times with different base cases. The sensitivity chart is somewhat preferable, since it computes sensitivity by sampling the variables all together while a simulation is running.

Other *Crystal Ball* Tools

This classical approach for confidence intervals assumes that the sampling distribution of the mean is normal. However, if the sampling distribution is not normally distributed, such a confidence interval is not valid. Also, if we wanted to develop a confidence interval for the median, standard deviation, or maximum forecast value, for example, we may not know the sampling distribution of these statistics. A statistical technique called **bootstrapping** analyzes sample statistics empirically by repeatedly sampling the data and creating distributions of the statistics. This approach allows you to estimate the sampling distribution of any statistic, even an unconventional one such as the minimum or maximum endpoint of a forecast.

The *Crystal Ball Bootstrap* tool does this. The tool has two alternative methods:

1. One-simulation method, which simulates the model data once and then repeatedly samples with replacement.
2. Multiple-simulation method, which repeatedly simulates the model and then creates a sampling distribution from each simulation. This method is more accurate but might take a prohibitive amount of time.

The *Bootstrap* tool constructs sampling distributions for the following statistics:

- Mean
- Median
- Standard deviation
- Variance
- Skewness
- Kurtosis
- Coefficient of variability
- Range minimum (multiple-simulation method only)
- Range maximum (multiple-simulation method only)
- Range width (multiple-simulation method only)

The forecast chart constructed for each statistic visually conveys the accuracy of the statistic: A narrow and symmetric distribution is better than a wide and skewed distribution. A small standard error of the statistic and coefficient of variability are quantitative indicators of reliable statistical estimates.

To apply the tool, select *Bootstrap* from the *CBTools* menu, and follow the dialog box instructions to select the forecast you wish to analyze, choose the method of analysis (you must choose multiple-simulation method to obtain statistics on the maximum, minimum, and range), and set the number of samples. Figure 8.27 shows the results for bootstrapping the CDCF year 5 forecast. We used 200 bootstrap samples with 500 trials per sample. Row 2 in the spreadsheet shows the statistics of the sampling distribution of the cash flow; the sampling distribution of the mean is displayed in the forecast chart in Figure 8.28. The results spreadsheet also displays a correlation matrix showing the correlations between the various statistics. High correlation between certain statistics, such as between the mean and the standard deviation, usually indicates a highly skewed distribution. Figure 8.29 shows the statistics associated with the forecast chart in Figure 8.28. Because this is an approximation of the sampling distribution, the

FIGURE 8.27 *Bootstrap* Results and Correlation Matrix

	A	B Mean	C Median	D Standard Deviation	E Variance	F Skewness	G Kurtosis	H Minimum	I Maximum	J Range
2	CDCF Year 5	127,778.85	115,323.20	194,405.68	37,847,449,631.12	0.40	3.30	-350350.33	856,369.44	1,206,719.77
3										
4	Correlations:									
5	Mean	1.000	0.820	0.148	0.148	-0.047	-0.029	0.094	0.071	0.061
6	Median		1.000	0.005	0.005	-0.307	-0.078	0.066	0.022	0.016
7	Standard Deviation			1.000	1.000	0.385	0.241	-0.241	0.437	0.491
8	Variance				1.000	0.385	0.241	-0.241	0.437	0.491
9	Skewness					1.000	0.745	0.031	0.609	0.554
10	Kurtosis						1.000	-0.099	0.819	0.785
11	Minimum							1.000	-0.030	-0.352
12	Maximum								1.000	0.925
13	Range									1.000

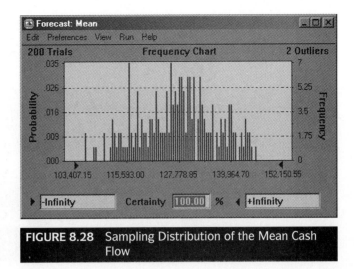

FIGURE 8.28 Sampling Distribution of the Mean Cash Flow

standard deviation in this chart represents the standard error of a single 200-trial *Crystal Ball* simulation. Thus, a confidence interval for the mean is found by adding and subtracting the appropriate z-value times the standard deviation—not the standard error—from the mean.

Figures 8.30 and 8.31 show the sampling distribution and associated statistics for the maximum cash flow. We see that the maximum cash flow can range from $652,526 to $1,295,143, and that a 95 percent confidence interval is $856,369.44 ± 1.96($130,384.54) or [$600,816, $1,111,923].

Crystal Ball has three other tools in the *CBTools* menu: *Batch Fit, Two-Dimensional Simulation,* and *Decision Table.* The *Batch Fit* tool fits probability distributions to multiple data series in the same fashion that we discussed in Chapter 3 for fitting distributions to data. The advantage of this tool is that it eliminates the necessity to fit each distribution individually. The only requirement is that the data must be in adjacent rows or columns. The *Two-Dimensional Simulation* tool allows you to distinguish between uncertainty in assumptions due to limited information or data and variability—assumptions that change because they describe a population with different values. Theoretically, you can eliminate uncertainty by gathering more information;

FIGURE 8.29 Sampling Distribution of the Mean Cash Flow, Statistics View

Forecast: Mean

Edit Preferences View Run Help

Cell B2   **Statistics**

Statistic	Value
Trials	200
Mean	127,778.85
Median	128,161.01
Mode	---
Standard Deviation	9,373.73
Variance	87,866,803.89
Skewness	-0.08
Kurtosis	2.73
Coeff. of Variability	0.07
Range Minimum	101,722.56
Range Maximum	155,419.13
Range Width	53,696.57
Mean Std. Error	662.82

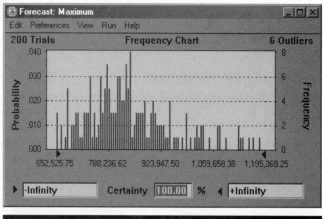

FIGURE 8.30 Sampling Distribution of the Maximum Cash Flow

practically, it is usually impossible or cost-prohibitive. Variability is inherent in the system, and you cannot eliminate it by gathering more information. Separating these two types of assumptions lets you more accurately characterize risk. The *Two-Dimensional Simulation* tool runs an outer loop to simulate the uncertainty values and then freezes them while it runs an inner loop to simulate variability. The process repeats for some small number of outer simulations, providing a portrait of how the forecast distribution varies due to the uncertainty. The *Decision Table* tool will be discussed in the next chapter.

APPLICATIONS OF MONTE CARLO SIMULATION

In this section we present some additional examples of Monte Carlo simulation using *Crystal Ball*. These serve to illustrate the wide range of applications to which the approach may be applied.

Project Management

Project management is concerned with scheduling the activities of a project involving interrelated activities. An important aspect of project management is identifying the

FIGURE 8.31 Sampling Distribution of the Maximum Cash Flow, Statistics View

Forecast: Maximum

Edit Preferences View Run Help

Cell i2   **Statistics**

Statistic	Value
Trials	200
Mean	856,369.44
Median	829,969.85
Mode	---
Standard Deviation	130,384.54
Variance	17,000,129,000.24
Skewness	1.07
Kurtosis	3.98
Coeff. of Variability	0.15
Range Minimum	652,525.75
Range Maximum	1,295,142.53
Range Width	642,616.78
Mean Std. Error	9,219.58

TABLE 8.1   Activity and Time Estimate List

	Activity	Predecessors	10th Percentile	Most Likely	90th Percentile
A	Select steering committee	—	15	15	15
B	Develop requirements list	—	40	45	60
C	Develop system size estimates	—	10	14	30
D	Determine prospective vendors	—	2	3	5
E	Form evaluation team	A	5	7	9
F	Issue request for proposal	B,C,D,E	4	5	8
G	Bidders conference	F	1	1	1
H	Review submissions	G	25	30	50
I	Select vendor short list	H	3	5	10
J	Check vendor references	I	3	7	10
K	Vendor demonstrations	I	20	30	45
L	User site visit	I	3	4	5
M	Select vendor	J,K,L	3	3	3
N	Volume sensitive test	M	10	13	20
O	Negotiate contracts	M	10	14	28
P	Cost–benefit analysis	N,O	2	2	2
Q	Obtain board of directors approval	P	5	5	5

expected completion time of the project. Activity times can be deterministic or probabilistic. We often assume that probabilistic activity times have a beta or triangular distribution, especially when times are estimated judgmentally. Analytical methods such as PERT allow us to determine probabilities of project completion times by assuming that the expected activity times define the critical path and invoking the central limit theorem to make an assumption of normality of the distribution of project completion time. However, this assumption may not always be valid, and we will explore this later. Simulation can provide a more realistic characterization of the project completion time and the associated risks. We will illustrate risk analysis in project management through the following example.

A consulting firm has been hired to assist in the evaluation of new software. The manager of the IS department is responsible for coordinating all of the activities involving consultants and the company's resources. The activities shown in Table 8.1 have been defined for this project, which is depicted graphically in Figure 8.32. The target project completion date is 150 working days. Because this is a new application, no historical data on activity times are available and must be estimated judgmentally. The IS manager has determined the most likely time for each activity but recognizing the uncertainty in the times to complete each task, has estimated the 10th and 90th percentiles. Setting the parameters in this way is a common approach for estimating

FIGURE 8.32   Project Network Corresponding to Table 8.1

the distribution, since managers typically cannot estimate the absolute minimum or maximum times but can reasonably determine a time that might be met or exceeded 10 percent of the time. With only these estimates, a triangular distribution is an appropriate assumption.

Figure 8.33 shows a spreadsheet designed to simulate the project completion time. For those activity times that are not constant, we define the cell for the activity time as a *Crystal Ball* assumption. After selecting the triangular distribution in the *Crystal Ball* gallery, click on the *Parms* button in the top right of the dialog box. This provides a list of alternative ways to input the data. We select the 10th percentile, most likely, and 90th percentile option. To facilitate data input, we may use cell references in the input boxes, as shown for the time for activity B (cell E6) in Figure 8.34. Then we may use the *Copy* and *Paste Data* commands under the *Cell* menu to copy the *Crystal Ball* assumptions to the other appropriate cells (remember not to use the Excel *Copy* and *Paste* commands). Note that *Crystal Ball* determines the appropriate minimum (*a*) and maximum (*b*) values for the triangular distribution based on the percentile information.

The project completion time depends on the specific time for each activity. To find this, we compute the activity schedule and slack for each activity. Activities A, B, C, and D have no immediate predecessors, and therefore have early start times of 0. The early start time for each other activity is the maximum of the early finish times for the activity's immediate predecessor. Early finish times are computed as the early start time plus the activity time. The early finish time for the last activity, Q, represents the earliest time the project can be completed, that is, the minimum project completion time. This is defined as the forecast cell for the *Crystal Ball* simulation.

To compute late start and late finish times, we set the late finish time of the terminal activity equal to the project completion time. The late start time is computed by subtracting the activity time from the late finish time. The late finish time for any other activity, say X, is defined as the minimum late start of all activities to which activity X is an immediate predecessor. Slack is computed as the difference between the late finish and early finish. The critical path consists of activities with zero slack. Based on the

FIGURE 8.33 Project Management Simulation Model

	Activity	10th Percentile	Most Likely	90th Percentile	Activity Time	Early Start	Early Finish	Latest Start	Latest Finish	Slack	On Critical Path?
1	Project Management Model										
5	A	15	15	15	15.00	0.00	15.00	27.32	42.32	27.32	0
6	B	40	45	60	49.32	0.00	49.32	0.00	49.32	0.00	1
7	C	10	14	30	19.19	0.00	19.19	30.12	49.32	30.12	0
8	D	2	3	5	3.43	0.00	3.43	45.88	49.32	45.88	0
9	E	5	7	9	7.00	15.00	22.00	42.32	49.32	27.32	0
10	F	4	5	8	5.86	49.32	55.18	49.32	55.18	0.00	1
11	G	1	1	1	1.00	55.18	56.18	55.18	56.18	0.00	1
12	H	25	30	50	36.49	56.18	92.67	56.18	92.67	0.00	1
13	I	3	5	10	6.29	92.67	98.96	92.67	98.96	0.00	1
14	J	3	7	10	6.57	98.96	105.53	124.54	131.11	25.58	0
15	K	20	30	45	32.15	98.96	131.11	98.96	131.11	0.00	1
16	L	3	4	5	4.00	98.96	102.96	127.11	131.11	28.15	0
17	M	3	3	3	3.00	131.11	134.11	131.11	134.11	0.00	1
18	N	10	13	20	14.72	134.11	148.83	137.71	152.43	3.60	0
19	O	10	14	28	18.32	134.11	152.43	134.11	152.43	0.00	1
20	P	2	2	2	2.00	152.43	154.43	152.43	154.43	0.00	1
21	Q	5	5	5	5.00	154.43	159.43	154.43	159.43	0.00	1
23				Project completion time	159.43						

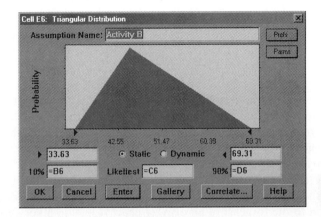

FIGURE 8.34 Triangular Distribution for Activity B

expected activity times, the critical path consists of activities B-F-G-H-I-K-M-O-P-Q and has an expected duration of 159.43 days.

In the analytical approach found in most textbooks, probabilities of completing the project within a certain time are computed assuming that

1. The distribution of project completion times is normal (by appealing to the central limit theorem).
2. The expected project completion time is the sum of the expected activity times along the critical path, which is found using the expected activity times.
3. The variance of the distribution is the sum of the variances of those activities along the critical path, which is found using the expected activity times. If more than one critical path exists, use the path with the largest variance.

Using the minimum and maximum values for the triangular distribution computed by *Crystal Ball* from the percentile data input, we may use the formula presented in Chapter 3 to compute the variance for each activity, as shown in Figure 8.35. Thus, for this example, the variance of the critical path is 281.88 (found by adding the variances

M	N	O	P	Q
a	m	b	mean	variance
15	15	15	15	0
33.63	45	69.31	49.3133	55.369872
4.07	14	39.51	19.1933	55.704406
0.95	3	6.34	3.43	1.2336167
3.38	7	10.62	7	2.1840667
2.73	5	9.89	5.87333	2.2314056
1	1	1	1	0
17.58	30	61.89	36.49	87.07235
0.67	5	13.21	6.29333	6.7612389
0.03	7	12.68	6.57	6.6907167
10.66	30	55.79	32.15	85.441017
2.19	4	5.81	4	0.5460167
3	3	3	3	0
6.62	13	24.55	14.7233	13.766439
4.48	14	36.48	18.32	44.999467
2	2	2	2	0
5	5	5	5	0
On critical path:			159.44	281.87535
standard deviation				16.789144

FIGURE 8.35 Triangular Distribution Parameters and Activity Means and Variances

of those activities with zero slack). With the normality assumption, the probability that the project will be completed within 150 days is found by computing the z-value:

$$z = \frac{150 - 159.43}{16.789} = -0.562$$

From Table A.1, this corresponds to a probability of approximately 0.29.

Variations in actual activity times may yield different critical paths than the one resulting from expected times. This may change both the mean and variance of the actual project completion time, resulting in an inaccurate assessment of risk. Simulation can easily address these issues.

Figure 8.36 shows the *Crystal Ball* forecast and statistics charts for 5000 trials. The mean and variance are quite close to those predicted; in fact, fitting the normal distribution to the forecast in an overlay chart results in a very good fit. Whereas the analytical approach computed the probability of completing the project within 150 days as 0.29, analysis of the forecast chart shows this to be somewhat smaller, about 0.25. Note, however, that the structure of the project network in Figure 8.32 is quite "linear," resulting in few options for critical paths. For projects that have many more parallel paths, the results of the simulation and analytical models may differ significantly more.

Retirement Planning

Forecasting income streams and rates of return of investments forms the basis for retirement planning. We will demonstrate an example of using simulation to evaluate a retirement plan for a thirty-year-old individual. We will assume that the employee's current income is $30,000 per year, and that 7 percent is contributed into a retirement fund that is matched equally by the employer. Two key inputs in determining a future retirement fund balance are the individual's future income as determined by annual raises and the rate of return of the investment portfolio. We will assume that the individual's annual raise is estimated to be 4 percent and that investment returns are indexed to changes in the Standard & Poor's 500. Figure 8.37 shows a histogram for the historical annual returns of the S&P 500 over the time period 1960–1999 (drawn from the data in *Economic Indexes.xls*). If we smooth these 40 data points to form a continuous distribution by assuming a uniform distribution within each cell interval, we find an average annual return of 9.13 percent. (We note that the actual average annual return for the 40 data points is 9.3 percent; the difference is due to the fact that the

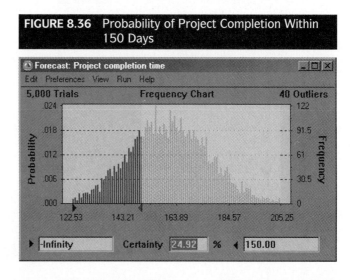

FIGURE 8.36 Probability of Project Completion Within 150 Days

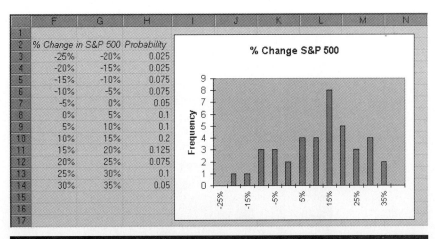

FIGURE 8.37   40-Year Historical Returns for S&P 500

actual data are not truly uniformly distributed within each cell interval.) As an alternative, we may sample from the actual distribution or fit a theoretical distribution to the data, as discussed in Chapter 3. We leave it as an exercise for you to investigate the sensitivity of the results to the distributional assumptions. Assuming an annual return of 9.13 percent, we may construct a spreadsheet and estimate a mean retirement fund of about $1.6 million at age 65, as shown in Figure 8.38. However, with the high volatility in market returns as seen over the past 40 years, the timing of the actual returns and influence of compounding can yield a significantly different result.

To simulate uncertainty in the annual returns, we define each year's annual return as a *Crystal Ball* assumption using the frequency distribution in the range F3:H14 and the *Crystal Ball Custom* distribution. To facilitate data input for the *Custom* distribution, you may click the Data button in the *Custom* distribution dialog box and simply enter the cell reference of the data range (see Chapter 3 for a discussion of the input options for the *Custom* distribution). In this case, the range is F3:H14, as shown in Figure 8.37. The result is shown in Figure 8.39. You need only do this once for the first-year return (cell D8), and then use the *Copy* and *Paste Data* commands under the *Cell* menu to copy these assumptions to the other cells (do not use the Excel *Copy* command as it does not copy *Crystal Ball* data!). The fund balance at age 65, cell E43, is defined as the forecast cell.

Figure 8.40 shows some of the *Crystal Ball* results for this example. Although the mean fund balance is $1.565 million, the percentiles chart shows that there is about a 30 percent chance that it will be less than $1 million. Knowing this risk might help the individual to consider other investment strategies.

Cash Budgeting[7]

Cash budgeting is the process of projecting and summarizing a company's cash inflows and outflows expected during a planning horizon, usually 6 to 12 months. The cash budget also shows the monthly cash balances and any short-term borrowing used to cover cash shortfalls. Positive cash flows can increase cash, reduce outstanding loans, or be used elsewhere in the business; negative cash flows can reduce cash available or be offset with additional borrowing. Most cash budgets are based on sales forecasts.

---

[7] Adapted from Douglas R. Emery, John D. Finnerty, and John D. Stowe, *Principles of Financial Management* (Upper Saddle River, NJ: Prentice-Hall, 1998), pp. 652–654.

	A	B	C	D	E
1	**Retirement Planning**				
2					
3	*Contribution rate (indiv. & matching)*			7%	
4	*Expected annual raise*			4%	
5					
6				Annual	
7	Age	Income	Contribution	Return	Fund Value
8	30	$30,000	$2,100	9.13%	$4,583
9	31	$31,200	$2,184	9.13%	$9,369
10	32	$32,448	$2,271	9.13%	$14,767
11	33	$33,746	$2,362	9.13%	$20,839
12	34	$35,096	$2,457	9.13%	$27,654
13	35	$36,500	$2,555	9.13%	$35,287
14	36	$37,960	$2,657	9.13%	$43,822
15	37	$39,478	$2,763	9.13%	$53,347
16	38	$41,057	$2,874	9.13%	$63,963
17	39	$42,699	$2,989	9.13%	$75,778
18	40	$44,407	$3,109	9.13%	$88,910
19	41	$46,184	$3,233	9.13%	$103,488
20	42	$48,031	$3,362	9.13%	$119,656
21	43	$49,952	$3,497	9.13%	$137,568
22	44	$51,950	$3,637	9.13%	$157,394
23	45	$54,028	$3,782	9.13%	$179,320
24	46	$56,189	$3,933	9.13%	$203,550
25	47	$58,437	$4,091	9.13%	$230,305
26	48	$60,774	$4,254	9.13%	$259,829
27	49	$63,205	$4,424	9.13%	$292,387
28	50	$65,734	$4,601	9.13%	$328,270
29	51	$68,363	$4,785	9.13%	$367,795
30	52	$71,098	$4,977	9.13%	$411,310
31	53	$73,941	$5,176	9.13%	$459,194
32	54	$76,899	$5,383	9.13%	$511,861
33	55	$79,975	$5,598	9.13%	$569,765
34	56	$83,174	$5,822	9.13%	$633,401
35	57	$86,501	$6,055	9.13%	$703,309
36	58	$89,961	$6,297	9.13%	$780,080
37	59	$93,560	$6,549	9.13%	$864,361
38	60	$97,302	$6,811	9.13%	$956,856
39	61	$101,194	$7,084	9.13%	$1,058,336
40	62	$105,242	$7,367	9.13%	$1,169,643
41	63	$109,451	$7,662	9.13%	$1,291,696
42	64	$113,829	$7,968	9.13%	$1,425,500
43	65	$118,383	$8,287	9.13%	$1,572,150

FIGURE 8.38 Retirement Planning Spreadsheet Model

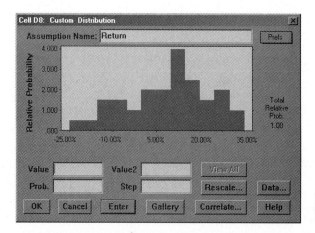

FIGURE 8.39 *Crystal Ball* Custom Distribution

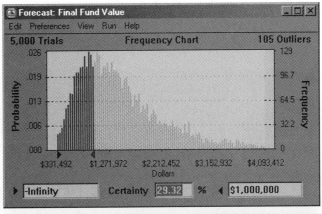

FIGURE 8.40   Retirement Planning Simulation Results

With the inherent uncertainty in such forecasts, Monte Carlo simulation is an appropriate tool to analyze cash budgets.

Figure 8.41 shows an example of a cash budget spreadsheet (*Cash Budget.xls*). The budget begins in April (thus, sales for April and subsequent months are uncertain). These are assumed to be normally distributed with a standard deviation of 10 percent of the mean. In addition, we assume that sales in adjacent months are correlated with one another, with a correlation coefficient of 0.6. On average, 20 percent of sales is collected in the month of sale, 50 percent in the month following the sale, and 30 percent in the second month following the sale. However, these figures are uncertain, so a uniform distribution is used to model the first two values (15 percent–20 percent and 40 percent–50 percent, respectively) with the assumption that all remaining revenues are collected in the second month following the sale. Purchases are 60 percent of sales and are paid for one month prior to the sale. Wages and salaries are 12 percent of sales and are paid in the same month as the sale. Rent of $10,000 is paid each month. Additional cash operating expenses of $30,000 per month will be incurred for April through July, decreasing to $25,000 for August and September. Tax payments of $20,000 and $30,000

FIGURE 8.41   Cash Budgeting Model

	A	B	C	D	E	F	G	H	I	J	K
1	Cash Budgeting										
2	Desired Minimum Balance	$ 100,000									
3				February	March	April	May	June	July	August	September October
4		Sales		$400,000	$500,000	$600,000	$700,000	$800,000	$800,000	$700,000	$600,000 $500,000
5	Cash Receipts										
6	Collections (current)	20%				$120,000	$140,000	$160,000	$160,000	$140,000	$120,000
7	Collections (previous month)	50%				$250,000	$300,000	$350,000	$400,000	$400,000	$350,000
8	Collections (2nd month previous)	30%				$120,000	$150,000	$180,000	$210,000	$240,000	$240,000
9	Total Cash Receipts					$490,000	$590,000	$690,000	$770,000	$780,000	$710,000
10											
11	Cash Disbursements										
12	Purchases					$420,000	$480,000	$480,000	$420,000	$360,000	$300,000
13	Wages and Salaries					$ 72,000	$ 84,000	$ 96,000	$ 96,000	$ 84,000	$ 72,000
14	Rent					$ 10,000	$ 10,000	$ 10,000	$ 10,000	$ 10,000	$ 10,000
15	Cash Operating Expenses					$ 30,000	$ 30,000	$ 30,000	$ 30,000	$ 25,000	$ 25,000
16	Tax Installments					$ 20,000			$ 30,000		
17	Capital Expenditure							$150,000			
18	Mortgage Payment					$ 60,000					
19	Total Cash Disbursements					$552,000	$664,000	$766,000	$586,000	$479,000	$ 407,000
20											
21	Ending Cash Balance										
22	Net Cash Flow					$ (62,000)	$ (74,000)	$ (76,000)	$184,000	$301,000	$ 303,000
23	Beginning Cash Balance					$150,000	$100,000	$100,000	$100,000	$122,000	$ 423,000
24	Available Balance					$ 88,000	$ 26,000	$ 24,000	$284,000	$423,000	$ 726,000
25	Monthly Borrowing					$ 12,000	$ 74,000	$ 76,000	$ -	$ -	$ -
26	Monthly Repayment					$ -	$ -	$ -	$162,000	$ -	$ -
27	Ending Cash Balance			$150,000	$100,000	$100,000	$100,000	$122,000	$423,000	$ 726,000	
28	Cumulative Loan Balance			$ -	$ 12,000	$ 86,000	$162,000	$ -	$ -	$ -	

B	Sales April	Sales May	Sales June	Sales July	Sales August	Sales September	October
31 Correlation Matrix							
32 Sales April	1.000	0.600					
33 Sales May		1.000	0.600				
34 Sales June			1.000	0.600			
35 Sales July				1.000	0.600		
36 Sales August					1.000	0.600	
37 Sales September						1.000	0.600
38 October							1.000

FIGURE 8.42 Correlation Matrix for Cash Budgeting Model

are expected in April and July, respectively. A capital expenditure of $150,000 will occur in June, and the company has a mortgage payment of $60,000 in May. The cash balance at the end of March is $150,000, and managers want to maintain a minimum balance of $100,000 at all times. The company will borrow the amounts necessary to ensure that the minimum balance is achieved. Any cash above the minimum will be used to pay off any loan balance until it is eliminated. The available cash balances in row 24 of the spreadsheet are the *Crystal Ball* forecast cells.

The *Crystal Ball Correlation Matrix* tool is used to specify the correlations between sales assumptions. Selecting this tool from the *CBTools* menu brings up a series of dialog boxes that allow you to specify what assumptions to correlate and how to input the data. For this example, we chose to include a correlation matrix in the spreadsheet that is linked to the assumptions, shown in Figure 8.42. This allows you to change the correlations to investigate different scenarios. Figure 8.43 shows the trend chart for the monthly cash balances. We see that there is a high likelihood that cash balances will be negative for the first three months before increasing. Viewing the forecast chart and statistics for individual months will provide the details on the distribution of cash balances and the likelihood of requiring loans. For example, the forecast chart for April shows that the probability that the balance will not exceed the minimum of $100,000 and require an additional loan is about 0.40. For June, however, this probability decreases to about 0.14 and is virtually zero by September.

FIGURE 8.43 Trend Chart for Monthly Cash Balances

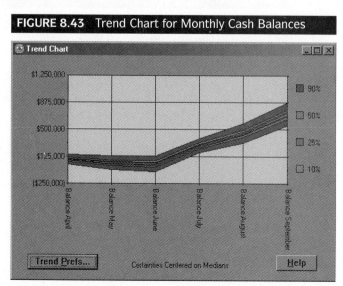

Questions and Problems

1. Open the workbook *New Store Financial Model.xls.* Define the *Crystal Ball* assumptions and forecasts as described in the chapter (save the model under a new name). Run your model for 1000 trials. From the *Run* menu, select *Forecast Windows,* then *Open All Forecasts.* What is the probability that the cumulative discounted cash flow will be positive in each of the first four years? What is the mean and range for each year?

2. With the *Crystal Ball* model you developed in Problem 1, use the *Correlation Matrix* tool to define the following correlations. Run the *Crystal Ball* model. How have the results changed?

	Year 2	Year 3	Year 4	Year 5
Year 2	1.00	0.60		
Year 3		1.00	0.70	
Year 4			1.00	0.80
Year 5				1.00

3. Open the workbook *Project Management.xls.* Replace the assumption cells with triangular distributions using the parameters $a, m,$ and b, shown in Figure 8.35, which were determined based on the original estimates of percentiles. Rerun the simulation. Would you expect to see nearly identical results?

4. Open the workbook *Retirement Planning.xls.* Modify the spreadsheet to include the assumption that the annual raise is uncertain. Assume a triangular distribution with a minimum of 1 percent, most likely value of 4 percent, and maximum value of 5 percent, and use *Crystal Ball* to find the distribution of the ending retirement fund balance under this assumption. How do the results compare with the base case?

5. Open the workbook *Cash Budget.xls.* In the *Run Preferences Options* dialog box, check the box to turn off correlations, and rerun the model. What effect does not correlating the sales data have on the forecasts?

6. A garage band wants to hold a concert. The expected crowd is normally distributed with mean of 3000 and standard deviation 500 (minimum of 0). The average expenditure on concessions is also normally distributed with mean $5, standard deviation $2, and minimum 0. Tickets sell for $10 each, and the band's profit is 80 percent of the gate, along with concession sales, minus a fixed cost of $10,000. Develop a spreadsheet model and simulate 100 trials using *Crystal Ball* to identify the mean profit, the minimum observed profit, maximum observed profit, and the probability of achieving a positive profit. Repeat for 1000 trials, and compute and compare confidence intervals for the mean profit for both cases.

7. A warehouse manager currently has one truck for local deliveries and is considering the purchase of an additional one to handle occasional high volumes. Currently, she rents additional trucks as needed for $300 per day. The truck that the company currently owns is charged off at a rate of $200 per day whether it is used or not. A new one would have a charge-off rate of $250 per day. Historical records show that the number of trucks needed each day has the distribution:

NUMBER NEEDED	PROBABILITY
0	0.20
1	0.30
2	0.40
3	0.10

Develop a spreadsheet model to evaluate both policies (using the same demand for each) and simulate it for 2000 trials with *Crystal Ball,* using the *Custom* distribution for the number of trucks needed each day. Identify the average, minimum, and maximum profit for both policies. In your spreadsheet, identify when the new policy is inferior to the current one, and use the simulation to estimate the percent of trials for which the current policy is better. Create an overlay chart to compare the mean profits.

8. A firm produces guava juice in distinctive 1 gallon jugs. The profit function is

$$\text{Profit} = (\$10 - \text{variable cost})*\text{gallons sold} - \text{fixed cost}$$

The current plant capacity is 5 million gallons per year. The firm can expand the plant by an additional 1 million or 2 million gallons per year, with the following cost impacts:

	Plant Capacity (gallons/year)	Fixed Cost	Variable Cost
Current	5 million	$5 million	$5/gallon
Add 1 million	6 million	$6 million	$4.90/gallon
Add 2 million	7 million	$7 million	$4.80/gallon

Annual demand follows the normal distribution with a mean of 5 million and a standard deviation of 1 million. Build a *Crystal Ball* model, and based on 500 simulation trials, identify the average profit for each option, as well as the percentile report for profit for each option.

9. Develop a *Crystal Ball* model for a three-year financial analysis of total profit based on the following data and information. Sales volume in the first year is estimated to be 100,000 units and is projected to grow at a rate that is normally distributed with a mean of 7 percent per year, and a standard deviation of 4 percent. The selling price is $10 and the amount of sales increase is normally distributed with a mean increase of $0.50 (and standard deviation of $0.05) each year. Per-unit variable costs are $3, and annual fixed costs are $200,000. Per-unit costs are expected to increase by an amount normally distributed with a mean of 5 percent per year (standard deviation 2 percent). Fixed costs are expected to increase following a normal distribution with a mean of 10 percent per year (standard deviation 3 percent). Based on 1000 simulation trials, identify the average three-year cumulative profit, as well as the percentile report for profit. Identify the number of times a negative cumulative profit was experienced, and generate a trend chart showing net profit by year.

10. A hotel wants to analyze its room pricing structure prior to a major remodeling effort. Currently, rates and average number of rooms sold are as follows:

Room Type	Rate	Average Sold/Day
Standard	$ 85	250
Gold	$ 98	100
Platinum	$139	50

Each market segment has its own elasticity of demand to price. The elasticity values are: standard, − 1.5; gold, − 2; platinum, − 1. These mean, for example, if the price of a standard room is reduced by 1 percent, the number of rooms sold each day is expected to increase by 1.5 percent. The projected number of rooms sold can be determined using the following formula: Projected Number Sold = Elasticity*(Price Change in $)*(Average Daily Sales/Room Rate), where the average daily sales and room rates are those in the preceding table. Develop a *Crystal Ball* model to compute the projected revenue for each market segment and the total projected revenue for any set of price changes. Develop a 90 percent confidence interval for revenues for the policy of room rates of $78, $90, and $145 for standard, gold, and platinum rooms, respectively.

11. An auto parts store stocks special halogen bulbs. These bulbs are high quality, and the demand averages 12 per day, which the manager's son (who is getting an MBA) tells him is Poisson distributed. The manager currently has a stocking policy of reordering 12 bulbs whenever current stock drops to 12 or below. Bulbs are delivered overnight at a cost of $1 per delivery. Holding one bulb one day costs the store $0.01. Build a *Crystal Ball* model to simulate 14 days of operations using 1000 trials, and calculate holding costs, ordering costs, and shortage costs. Compute a 95 percent confidence interval for the total of these three costs for policies of ordering 12, 24, or 36 bulbs whenever an order is placed. Examine the skewness and kurtosis of the distribution of the holding, order, and shortage costs. What can you conclude?

12. The manager of an apartment complex has observed that the number of units rented during any given month varies between 30 and 40 (use a triangular distribution with minimum 30, most likely 34, maximum 40). Rent is $500 per month. Operating costs average $15,000 per month but vary following a normal distribution with mean $15,000. Operating costs are assumed to be normal with a standard deviation of $300. Use *Crystal Ball* to estimate the 80 percent, 90 percent, and 95 percent confidence interval for the profitability of this business.
    a. What is the probability that monthly profit will be positive?
    b. What is the probability that monthly profit will exceed $4000?
    c. Compare the 80 percent, 90 percent, and 95 percent certainty ranges.
    d. What is the probability that profit will be between $1000 and $3000?

13. A trucking company deals with many flat tires every year. The number of tires that needed repairing last year was 20,000. This growth rate has been normally distributed with a mean of 10 percent and a standard deviation of 3 percent. Currently the company has truckers get their flats fixed on the open market, which last year cost an average of $50 per tire. Inflation in tire repair cost has been $5 per year (normally distributed, mean $5, standard deviation $2). The company is considering an opportunity to sign a contract with a tire firm. Under this contract, the tire company

would provide patrolling vehicles that would repair tires in about the same time as the current system at a fixed cost of $60 per tire. This price would be constant over the three-year contract period. Management wants a comparison of net present costs for repairing tires under both options, assuming a 12 percent discount rate. Use 1000 trials and Monte Carlo sampling.

a. Find the mean and maximum net present cost for each option.

b. Compute a 90 percent confidence interval for each option.

c. Find the probability for each system of having a net present cost greater than $3.5 million, greater than $3.7 million, greater than $3.9 million

d. Construct a tornado and a spider chart for both net present costs.

14. An entrepreneur has agreed to provide software to a distributor on demand. Over the next year, the demand is highly variable, following the exponential distribution with a mean of 1000 sales per year. The contract price is $500 per copy, and variable cost to produce this product (including packaging and manuals) is $400. There is a fixed cost per year of $50,000. The entrepreneur wants to estimate expected profit for this operation.

Compare the following statistics for Monte Carlo and Latin Hypercube sampling for 1000 trials:

a. Average expected profit

b. The decile report

c. The distribution of the output (based on visual inspection)

15. A software development project consists of six activities, each with time estimates expressed in terms of minimum, most likely, and maximum durations. Assume a triangular distribution for the durations of activities A, B, E, and F. Predecessor relationships are given in the following table. Assume that activity start time is zero if there are no predecessor activities.

	Activity	Min Duration	Likely Duration	Max Duration	Predecessors
A	Requirements analysis	2 months	3 months	4 months	None
B	Programming	6 months	7 months	9 months	A
C	Hardware	Constant	3 months		A
D	User training	Constant	12 months		A
E	Implementation	3 months	5 months	7 months	B,C
F	Testing	1 month	1 month	2 months	E

Find:

a. Mean project completion time

b. Minimum and maximum project completion times

c. Skewness of the completion time distribution

d. Probability of completing the project in 140, 150, 160, or 170 months

16. A firm needs to install a new software system. Activities and data (in weeks) are given in the following table:

	Activity	Predecessors	Min	Most Likely	Max
A	Requirements analysis	None	2	3	3
B	Programming	A	6	7	7
C	Hardware acquisition	A	3	3	3
D	Train users	B	12	12	12
E	Implement	B,C	3	5	5
F	Test	E	1	1	1

Distributions are triangularly distributed with the given parameters. Due to the need to coordinate across departments, all simulated times are to be rounded up. Compute expected project completion time, mean project completion time, minimum and maximum project completion times, percentiles of project completion time, and the frequency distribution of the project completion time.

17. For the *Retirement Planning.xls* model, assume that the average raise after age 40 is triangularly distributed with minimum 0, most likely 2 percent, and maximum 4 percent; and that the average raise after age 50 is also triangularly distributed with minimum 0, most likely 0, and maximum 3 percent. Use common random number seeds, and compare results against the original distribution of minimum 1 percent, most likely 4 percent, and maximum 5 percent for all ages. Find the mean 90 percent certainty ranges for final pay and fund value at age 65, and hypothesize the distribution of final fund value based on visual inspection.

18. Using the *Cash Budget.xls* model, create a new cell to find the worst case of borrowing. (This will be the maximum of cells E28:J28.) Make this an assumption cell, and based on 1000 trials, find the mean maximum borrowing amount, a 95 percent confidence interval for the mean, the worst maximum borrowing amount, and the probability of having to borrow.

19. A toy company has a teddy bear stuffed with Styrofoam that they want to release in conjunction with a new movie. The proposed price of the toy is $8.00, and marketing expects to sell 900,000 units, following a normal distribution with a mean of 900,000 and the relatively high standard deviation of 300,000 (and a minimum of 0). Fixed production costs are estimated to be normally distributed with mean $700,000 and standard deviation $50,000. Per-unit variable costs are normally distributed with mean $3 and standard deviation $0.25. Selling expenses are lognormally distributed with mean $900,000 and standard deviation $50,000. General and administrative costs are fixed at $300,000. Identify the mean, standard deviation, and range for profit. Also find the 60 percent, 80 percent, and 90 percent probability intervals for expected profit. Find the probabilities of attaining profits greater than or equal to 0, $1 million, $2 million, $3 million, $4 million, and $5 million. Finally, examine the tornado chart to explain the relative impact of the assumption variables.

CASE

DETERMINING A MACHINE MAINTENANCE STRATEGY AT TRACWAY

In one of Tracway's plants, a large milling machine has three different bearings that often fail because of the stresses in the manufacturing process. The time to failure is uncertain, and is characterized by a probability distribution obtained from historical data:

Bearing life	Probability
950–1050 hours	0.10
1050–1150	0.13
1150–1250	0.25
1250–1350	0.13
1350–1450	0.09
1450–1550	0.12
1550–1650	0.02
1650–1750	0.06
1750–1850	0.05
1850–1950	0.05

Assume that within each interval, the lifetime is uniformly distributed. Also, the life of each bearing is identical. When a bearing fails, the mill stops, a repairperson is called, and a new bearing is installed.

However, there may be a delay until the repairperson arrives at the machine; this is also a random variable. On average, a 5-minute delay occurs 60 percent of the time, a 10-minute delay 30 percent of the time, and a 15-minute delay 10 percent of the time.

Downtime for the mill is estimated to be $10 per minute, and the direct on-site cost of the repairperson is $24 per hour. It takes 20 minutes to change one bearing, 30 minutes to change two bearings, and 40 minutes to change all three. Each bearing costs $30. A proposal has been made to re-place all three bearings whenever a bearing fails instead of replacing them individually. Tracway wishes to determine if this proposal is worthwhile.

Develop spreadsheet simulation models for the policies of replacing each bearing individually and for replacing all three whenever any one fails and computing the total cost associated with each policy. Because of the uncertainty in the assumptions, simulate your models using *Crystal Ball* and make a recommendation to Tracway management in the form of a memo with a complete description of your analyses and results. ■

CHAPTER

9

SYSTEM SIMULATION MODELING AND ANALYSIS

INTRODUCTION

Production or service operations usually involve the flow of some type of **entity** through a system over time. The entity might be a physical object, such as a job being processed in a factory or inventory being transferred from a warehouse to a customer. An entity might be a piece of information, such as a message sent through a communication system or a job awaiting processing at a computer center. Often, the model involves the simultaneous flow of many entities within the system. Decisions regarding such operations often involve determining the best design configuration or operating policies of the system. Modeling such systems generally is more complicated than other types of decision models. **System simulation** is an approach for reproducing the activities that control the flow of entities and the logic by which events occur over time.

In this chapter we focus on simple types of system simulation models that can be implemented on spreadsheets in order to develop the basic concepts; more complex models require sophisticated commercial software to implement. The key concepts that we will discuss are

- Different approaches for building systems simulation models: activity scanning, process modeling, and event-driven approaches

- Basic concepts of inventory systems and simulation of inventory systems using activity scanning approaches
- Analytical and process-driven simulation models of waiting line problems
- The logic for using event-driven simulation for both inventory and waiting line problems
- An introduction to system dynamics and continuous simulation models

SYSTEM SIMULATION MODELING APPROACHES

System simulation models can be implemented in several ways. First, we could describe the activities that occur during fixed intervals of time, such as a week, day, or hour. This is called **activity scanning.** For example, to model the operation of an inventory system, we could describe the sequence of events that occur during a specific time period: fulfilling customer demand, ordering new stock, and receiving stock that was ordered at an earlier time. Then we advance time to the next period and repeat. A second approach— **process-driven simulation**—describes the process through which entities in the system flow. For example, in a service system, customers arrive, wait in line if the server is busy, receive service, and then leave the system. A process-driven simulation models the logical sequence of events for each customer as he or she arrives to the system. A third approach is called **event-driven simulation.** With this approach, we describe the changes that occur in the system at the instant of time that each event occurs. Events are sequenced in chronological order and may not correspond to a natural flow of entities. In the service system example, for instance, the key events are the arrival of customers, the start of service, and the end of service. The arrival of the second customer might precede the starting time of service for the first customer. The simulation logic would describe what happens when customer 1 arrives first, the arrival of customer 2 second, the start of service for customer 1 third, and so on. Finally, for special situations in which variables change continuously over time, **continuous simulation** techniques are used.

Activity-scanning simulation models are generally easy to develop. We increment time by some fixed interval and describe what happens during the time interval. For example, in modeling a mail-order operation in which daily orders are aggregated, picked, and packaged in the evening, we might increment time by daily intervals and simulate the entire day's demand and order-processing activities, looking only at the aggregate changes in inventory levels from one day to the next. However, this approach might not be appropriate for a simulation model of a retail store that fulfills customer's orders immediately upon arrival at different times of the day. Thus, selecting the appropriate method depends on the purpose of the simulation model and the level of detail and accuracy needed in the analysis.

An important issue in activity-scanning models is selecting the size of the time interval. If it is too large, we may lose information due to the fact that many different activities occur during the time interval (this is particularly important if we are interested in statistical information about *when* things happen). If it is too small, then nothing may happen for a large number of intervals, causing the simulation model to be somewhat inefficient. In the next section we illustrate a more complex example of activity-scanning simulation for inventory problems.

SIMULATING INVENTORY SYSTEMS USING ACTIVITY SCANNING

Inventory is any resource that is set aside for future use. Inventory is necessary because the demand and supply of goods usually are not perfectly matched at any given time or place. Many different types of inventories exist. Examples include raw materials (such as coal, crude oil, cotton), semifinished products (aluminum ingots, plastic sheets, lumber), and finished products (cans of food, computer terminals, shirts). Inventories can also be human resources (standby crews and trainees), financial resources (cash on hand, accounts receivable), and other resources, such as airplane seats.

Inventories represent a considerable investment for many organizations; thus, it is important that they be managed well. Excess inventories can cause a business to fail. On the other hand, not having inventory when it is needed can also result in business failure. Although many analytic models for managing inventories exist, the complexity of many practical situations often requires simulation. Before we study applications of simulation to inventory decisions, we will review some basic concepts and terminology.

Basic Concepts of Inventory Modeling

The two basic inventory decisions that managers face are *how much* additional inventory to order or produce and *when* to order or produce it. Although it is possible to consider these two decisions separately, they are so closely related that a simultaneous solution is usually necessary. Typically, the objective is to minimize total inventory costs.

Total inventory costs can include four components: holding costs, ordering costs, shortage costs, and purchasing costs. **Holding costs,** or *carrying costs,* represent costs associated with maintaining inventory. These costs include interest incurred or the opportunity cost of having capital tied up in inventories; storage costs such as insurance, taxes, rental fees, utilities, and other maintenance costs of storage space; warehousing or storage operation costs, including handling, record keeping, information processing, and actual physical inventory expenses; and costs associated with deterioration, shrinkage, obsolescence, and damage. Total holding costs are dependent on how many items are stored and for how long they are stored. Therefore, holding costs are expressed in terms of *dollars associated with carrying one unit of inventory for a unit of time.*

Ordering costs represent costs associated with replenishing inventories. These costs are not dependent on how many items are ordered at a time, but on the number of orders that are prepared. Ordering costs include overhead, clerical work, data processing, and other expenses that are incurred in searching for supply sources, as well as costs associated with purchasing, expediting, transporting, receiving, and inspecting. In manufacturing operations, **setup cost** is the equivalent to ordering cost. Setup costs are incurred when a factory production line has to be shut down in order to reorganize machinery and tools for a new production run. Setup costs include the cost of labor and other time-related costs required to prepare for the new product run. We usually assume that the ordering or setup cost is constant, and it is expressed in terms of *dollars per order.*

Shortage costs, or *stock-out costs,* are those costs that occur when demand exceeds available inventory in stock. A shortage may be handled as a *back order,* in which a customer waits until the item is available, or as a *lost sale.* In either case, a shortage represents lost profit and possible loss of future sales. Shortage costs depend on how much shortage has occurred and sometimes for how long. Shortage costs are expressed in terms of *dollar cost per unit of short item.*

Purchasing costs are what firms pay for the material or goods. In most inventory models, the price of materials is the same regardless of the quantity purchased; in this case, purchasing costs can be ignored. However, when price varies by quantity purchased, called the *quantity discount* case, inventory analysis must be adjusted to account for this difference.

The **Economic Order Quantity (EOQ)** model is the simplest and most elementary inventory model. Although its assumptions often do not hold in practice, it is a good starting point for developing more realistic inventory models. The objective of the EOQ model is to determine the optimal order quantity that will minimize total inventory cost. The EOQ model assumes

1. The demand for inventory is known with certainty. For example, inventory demand might be three units per day and is assumed to be three units per day, every day.
2. Inventory replenishment is instantaneous (orders are received all at once) and occurs only when the inventory level reaches zero.
3. **Lead time**—the time between placement and receipt of an order—is constant.
4. A fixed order quantity, Q, is always ordered.
5. No shortages are incurred.
6. The holding cost per unit and ordering cost per order are constant.

The EOQ model applies to a *continuous review* inventory system. In a continuous review system, the inventory position is continuously monitored. **Inventory position** is defined as the amount of inventory on hand plus any amount on order but not received, less any back orders (which, under assumption 5 must be zero). Whenever the inventory position falls at or below a level *r*, called the **reorder point,** an order is placed for Q units. (Note that the reorder decision is based on the inventory position and *not* the inventory level. If we used the inventory level, orders would be placed continuously as the inventory level falls below *r* until the order is received.) When the order is received after the lead time, the inventory level jumps from zero to Q, and the cycle repeats. This is illustrated in Figure 9.1.

Using these assumptions and defining

Q = order quantity
OC = ordering cost per order
D = annual demand for items in inventory
HC = holding cost per unit per year

the total annual cost is given by

$$TC = Q(HC)/2 + D(OC)/Q$$

FIGURE 9.1 EOQ Inventory Process

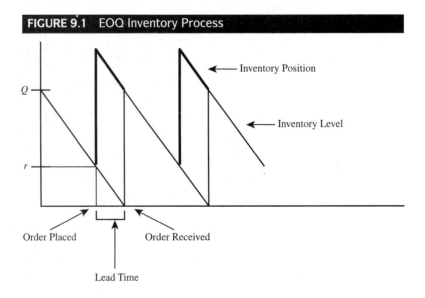

Here, Q(HC)/2 represents the annual holding cost and D(OC)/Q is the annual order-ing cost. We can easily show that the optimal order quantity (Q*) minimizing total inventory cost is

$$Q^* = \sqrt{\frac{2(D)(OC)}{HC}}$$

The EOQ model, as well as other classic analytical models, makes rather unreal-istic assumptions about the constancy of demand rates and lead times. In real life, demand is usually uncertain, and the lead time can be variable as well. To protect against incurring shortages because of these uncertainties, safety stock is often main-tained. **Safety stock** is an additional quantity kept in inventory above planned usage rates. Setting the safety stock level requires knowing the distribution of expected demand and the desired probability of not running out of stock. For instance, if demand during lead time is normal and has a mean of 200 units and a variance of 100 units, and management wants to have a 0.90 assurance of not incurring a shortage, then we must order a quantity x for which the area under the normal curve to the right is 0.10. This corresponds to $z = 1.282$. Thus, $1.282 = (x - 200)/10$, or $x = 212.82$. Of this quantity, 200 units are expected to be used to cover demand. The extra 12.82 units (13) would be required to cover demand greater than average 90 percent of the time. The safety stock would thus be 13. The reorder point is defined as the expected demand during lead time plus safety stock. Thus, in this example, when inventory falls to 213 units, an order for Q units would be placed.

Continuous Review Model with Lost Sales

In probabilistic situations, it is not clear what order quantities and reorder points should be used to minimize expected total inventory cost. In this section we present a simulation model for addressing this question. We will assume that demand is Poisson distributed with a mean of 100 units per week; thus, the expected annual demand is 5200 units.[1] It costs $0.20 to hold one unit for one week (HC = $10.40), and each order costs $50. Every unfilled demand is lost and is charged a penalty of $100 in estimated lost profit. The lead time between placing an order and the time the order is received is assumed to be constant and equal to two weeks. Therefore, the expected demand dur-ing lead time is 200 units. Orders are placed at the end of the week and received at the beginning of the week.

The EOQ model suggests an order quantity:

$$Q^* = \sqrt{\frac{2(5200)(50)}{10.4}} = 224$$

For the EOQ policy, the reorder point should be equal to the lead time demand; that is, we place an order when the inventory position falls to 200 units. If the lead time demand is *exactly* 200 units, the order will arrive when the inventory level reaches zero, as illustrated in Figure 9.1. However, if demand fluctuates about a mean of 200 units, we would expect shortages to occur approximately half the time. Because of the high shortage costs, we would probably want to use either a larger reorder point or a larger order quantity. In either case, we will carry more inventory on average, which should

---

[1] For large values of λ, the Poisson distribution is approximately normal. Thus, this assumption is tantamount to saying that the demand is normally distributed with a mean of 100 and standard deviation of √100 = 10. The Poisson is discrete, thus eliminating the need to round off normally distributed random variates.

result in a lower total shortage cost but a higher total holding cost. With a higher order quantity, we would order less frequently, thus incurring lower total ordering costs. However, the appropriate choice is not clear. We can use simulation to test various reorder point/order quantity policies.

Inventory models lend themselves well to activity-scanning approaches. To develop a simulation model, we need to step through the logic of how this inventory system operates. This is shown in Figure 9.2. Let us assume that no orders are

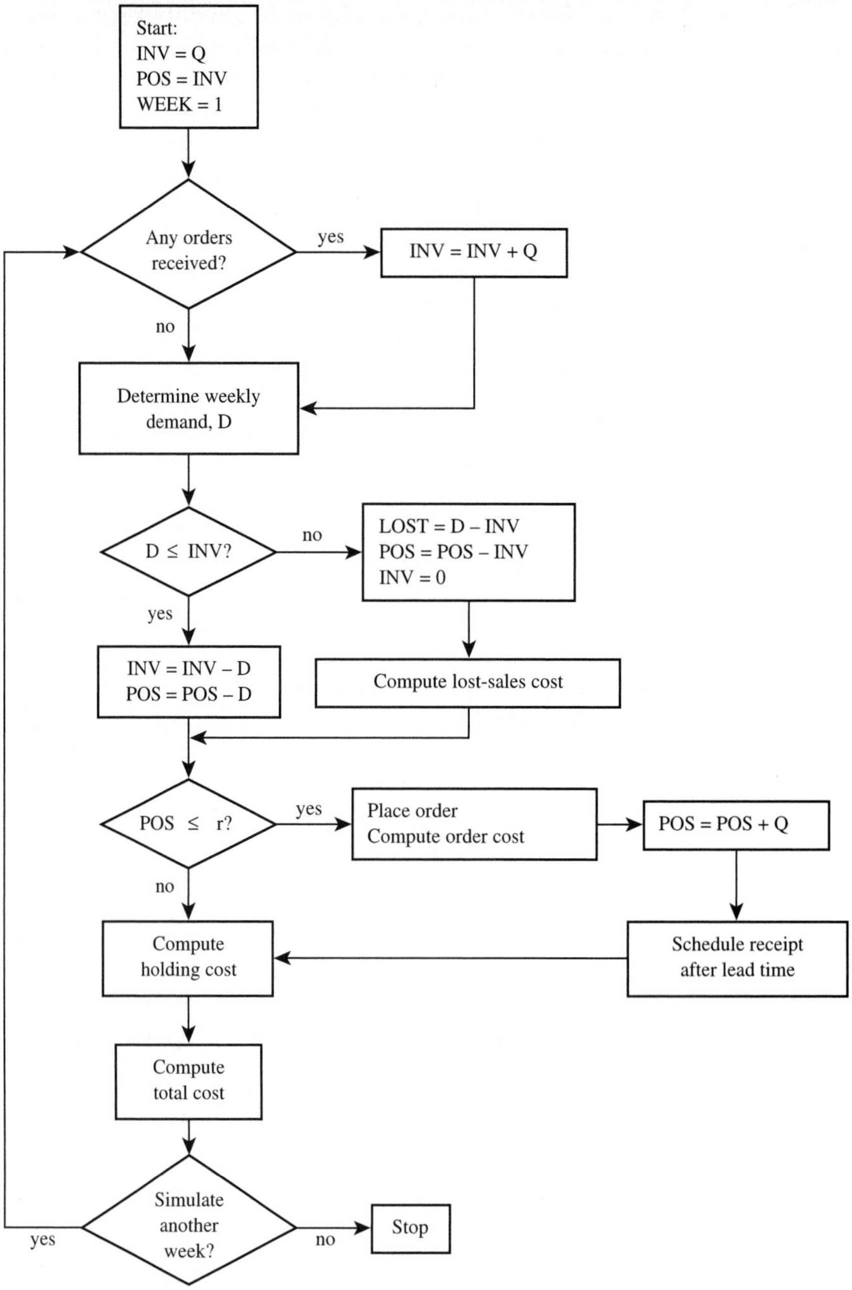

FIGURE 9.2 Logic for a Continuous Review Inventory System with Lost Sales

outstanding initially and that the initial inventory level (INV) is equal to the order quantity (Q). Therefore, the beginning inventory position (POS) will be the same as the inventory level. We will use a one-week time interval for the activity-scanning approach. As we noted, this approach does not capture detailed information about the timing of individual demands, for example, and forces us to make an assumption that orders are received at the beginning of the week. We could make the time interval one day, but this would require a larger spreadsheet and more computation.

At the beginning of the week, we check to see if any outstanding orders have arrived. If so, we add the order quantity Q to the current inventory level. Next, we determine the weekly demand, D, by generating an appropriate random variate, and check if sufficient inventory is on hand to meet this demand (is D ≤ INV?). If not, then the number of lost sales is D − INV. We subtract the current inventory level from the inventory position, set INV to zero, and compute the lost sales cost. If sufficient inventory is available, we satisfy all demand from stock and reduce both the inventory level and inventory position by D.

The next step is to check if the inventory position is at or below the reorder point. If so, we place an order for Q units and compute the order cost. The inventory position is increased by Q, but the inventory level remains the same. We then schedule a receipt of Q units to arrive after the lead time.

Finally, we compute the holding cost based on the inventory level at the end of the week (after demand is satisfied) and the total cost. If we wish to simulate another week, we return to the start of the week; otherwise, stop.

A portion of the spreadsheet model for this simulation is shown in Figure 9.3 (*Lost Sales Inventory Model.xls*). The model follows the logic of the flowchart in Figure 9.2; however, it is necessary to use some logical functions in Excel in order to implement it correctly. This requires some explanation. (We strongly encourage you to view the formulas in the cells of the spreadsheet to understand the logic of the Excel implementation.) The basic problem data are shown in the upper-left corner. The spreadsheet is designed so that lead times of 1 to 5 weeks can be specified. The beginning inventory position and inventory level for each week are equal to the ending levels for the previous week, except for the first week, which is specified in the problem data. The demands in column F were obtained using the Poisson distribution with a mean of 100 and implemented using the CB.Poisson( ) function; this is easier than defining an assumption cell for each week within the *Crystal Ball* environment. Since all shortages

FIGURE 9.3 Inventory Simulation Model—Lost Sales Case

Week	Beg Inv Pos	Beg Inv	Order Rec'd	Units Rec'd	Dmd	End Inv	Lost Sales	Order Placed?	Ending Inv Pos	Lead time	Hold Cost	Order Cost	Short Cost	Total Cost
Inventory Simulation With Lost Sales														

Order Quantity 224 | Order Cost $ 50
Reorder Point 200 | Holding Cost $ 0.20
Initial Inventory 224 | Lost Sales Cost $ 100
Lead time(1-5) 2

Note: Crystal Ball must be running

Total Annual Costs
$ 770 $ 1,050 $56,300 $58,120

Week	Beg Inv Pos	Beg Inv	Order Rec'd	Units Rec'd	Dmd	End Inv	Lost Sales	Order Placed?	Ending Inv Pos	Lead time	Hold Cost	Order Cost	Short Cost	Total Cost
1	224	224		0	94	130	0	YES	354	2	$ 26.00	$ 50	$ -	$ 76
2	354	130		0	87	43	0	NO	267		$ 8.60	$ -	$ -	$ 9
3	267	43		0	107	0	64	YES	448	2	$ -	$ 50	$ 6,400	$ 6,450
4	448	0	YES	224	96	128	0	NO	352		$ 25.60	$ -	$ -	$ 26
5	352	128		0	109	19	0	NO	243		$ 3.80	$ -	$ -	$ 4
6	243	19	YES	224	97	146	0	YES	370	2	$ 29.20	$ 50	$ -	$ 79
7	370	146		0	103	43	0	NO	267		$ 8.60	$ -	$ -	$ 9
8	267	43		0	93	0	50	YES	448	2	$ -	$ 50	$ 5,000	$ 5,050
9	448	0	YES	224	92	132	0	NO	356		$ 26.40	$ -	$ -	$ 26
10	356	132		0	92	40	0	NO	264		$ 8.00	$ -	$ -	$ 8

are lost sales, the inventory level cannot be negative. Thus, the ending inventory each week is computed as the maximum of zero and the beginning inventory level less demand plus any orders received. Lost sales are computed by checking if demand exceeds available stock and computing the difference.

In column I we determine if an order should be placed by checking if the beginning inventory position less the weekly demand is at or below the reorder point. Ending inventory position is computed as beginning inventory position less weekly demand plus lost sales plus any orders that may have been placed that week. This formula might not appear to be obvious. However, it essentially incorporates both cases in Figure 9.2. Clearly, if there are no lost sales, the ending inventory position is simply the beginning position less the demand plus any order that may have been placed. If lost sales have occurred, computing the ending inventory position in this way would also have reduced it by the unfulfilled demand, which would be incorrect. Thus, we add back the number of lost sales to account for this. To see this better, examine row 12 in the spreadsheet. We have POS = 267, INV = 43, D = 107, and LS = 64. The ending inventory position should be $267 - 43 + 224 = 448$. The formula in cell J12 computes this as $267 - 107 + 64 + 224 = 448$. Observe that the negative demand plus lost sales $(-107 + 64)$ is equal to the negative of the available inventory.

The most complicated part of this spreadsheet is determining if an order is received and the amount received in columns D and E. First note that orders are placed at the end of the week and received at the beginning of the week and that lead times of 1 to 5 weeks are allowed. Thus, in Figure 9.3, the order placed at the *end* of the first week with a lead time of 2 will arrive at the *beginning* of the fourth week. The spreadsheet is designed to allow lead times to vary; thus the formula in cell D13, for example, must check if any order was placed either at the end of week 1 or week 2. Similarly, the formula for cells D16 and lower must step back to determine if an order was placed anywhere from one to five weeks before.

Consider the formula in cell D13, corresponding to the beginning of week 4:

=IF(OR(AND(I11="YES",K11=1),AND(I10="YES",K10=2)),"YES"," ")

This formula consists of nested IF, OR, and AND logic functions. The AND function is true if all its arguments are true. Thus, if the content of cell I11 is "YES" and K11 is 1, an order was placed in week 2 with a lead time of 1 and will arrive at the beginning of week 4. But an order can also arrive if it were ordered in week 1 and had a lead time of 2. This is captured by the function AND(I10="YES",K10=2). If either of these are true, then the contents of cell D13 should be YES. This logic is captured by the OR function, which is true if any of its arguments are true. The IF function simply checks if any of these conditions hold and puts "YES" or a blank in the cell. In cell D16, for example, we use the same logic, only going back five periods. In column E, the logic is similar. If lead times vary, it may occur that more than one order might arrive at the same time. We check if orders were placed in prior weeks and add the order quantities.

The total annual cost, cell O6, is defined as a forecast cell for *Crystal Ball* simulation. Figure 9.4 shows the forecast chart for 1000 trials. You can see a large amount of variability in the total annual cost for one simulation, with a range of over $30,000.

Analyzing Decision Alternatives

Often, the purpose of simulation is to help make a choice among several decisions or to find the best configuration or policy. For example, in the inventory simulation described in the previous section, we would be interested in finding the best values of Q and *r* that minimize total cost. To do this, we might experiment with different combinations using the spreadsheet and use *Crystal Ball* to run a new simulation for

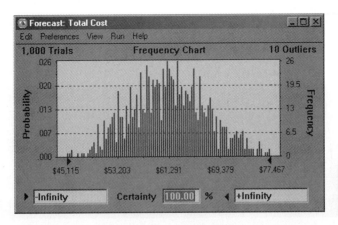

FIGURE 9.4 *Crystal Ball*
Total Cost Forecast Chart
for Inventory Simulation

each decision variable. This can be tedious; fortunately, *Crystal Ball* includes a *Decision Table* tool that runs multiple simulations to test different values for one or two *decision variables*—which represent quantities that a decision maker can control in a model. The results are displayed in a table that you can analyze using *Crystal Ball* forecast, trend, or overlay charts (see the *Crystal Ball Note: Using the Decision Table Tool*).

For the inventory problem, we defined the range of order quantity decisions to be discrete between 200 and 400 in steps of 25. We set the reorder point between 200 and

---

CRYSTAL BALL NOTE

USING THE DECISION TABLE TOOL

First define the decision variables in your model. To do this, click on the cell, then select *Define Decision Variable* from the *Cell* menu. The dialog box is shown in Figure 9.5. Enter the lower and upper limits over which you wish to search, and define whether the search values are continuous

FIGURE 9.5 *Define Decision Variable* Dialog Box

Cell E2: Define Decision Variable

Name: Order Quantity

Variable Bounds

Lower: 200

Upper: 400

Variable Type

○ Continuous

◉ Discrete

Step: 25

OK   Cancel   Help

or discrete by clicking the appropriate radio button. If discrete, enter a step size for changing the value of this variable. We also recommend setting the *Sampling* options in the *Run Preferences* dialog box to use the same sequence of random numbers and set an initial seed value (e.g., 999) and selecting Monte Carlo simulation. Next, select the *Decision Table* tool from the *CBTools* menu. *Crystal Ball* will display three dialog boxes in which you specify the target cell (forecast) to evaluate, select the decision variables, and specify the number of trials for each simulation. These options make the resulting simulations comparable. *Crystal Ball* constructs a new Excel workbook showing the simulation results for each level of a single decision variable. If you have two decision variables, the results would be displayed in a table. After selecting one or more forecast cells in the table, you may click on the buttons in cell A1 of the table to view trend, overlay, or forecast charts.

	A	B	C	D	E	F	G	H	I	J	K
1	Trend Chart / Overlay Chart / Forecast Charts	Order Quantity (200)	Order Quantity (225)	Order Quantity (250)	Order Quantity (275)	Order Quantity (300)	Order Quantity (325)	Order Quantity (350)	Order Quantity (375)	Order Quantity (400)	
2	Reorder Point (200)	$84,653	$61,204	$62,729	$45,667	$70,522	$97,830	$66,774	$38,529	$59,260	1
3	Reorder Point (250)	$24,300	$35,388	$25,600	$25,859	$11,403	$19,866	$28,231	$33,739	$10,774	2
4	Reorder Point (300)	$15,335	$11,217	$8,794	$6,152	$4,638	$3,496	$3,626	$3,542	$4,038	3
5	Reorder Point (350)	$12,874	$10,365	$7,893	$5,475	$3,643	$3,051	$3,068	$3,159	$3,265	4
6	Reorder Point (400)	$13,314	$10,889	$8,375	$5,966	$4,111	$3,563	$3,566	$3,642	$3,755	5
7		1	2	3	4	5	6	7	8	9	

FIGURE 9.6 *Crystal Ball Decision Table* Results

400 in steps of 50. Figure 9.6 shows the simulation results of the mean total annual cost for each of these combinations. We see that the total annual cost has a minimum around Q = 325 and *r* = 350.

Continuous Review Model with Back Orders

Another common type of stock-out situation occurs when customers are willing to wait for an item that is temporarily out of stock; this is called a **back order** situation. The principal difference between this and the lost sales case is that the inventory level—from an accounting standpoint—can be negative. A negative inventory level represents accumulated back orders. When an order arrives, it goes first to satisfy any back orders. For example, suppose the inventory level is −14 when an order of 20 units arrives. This means that 14 items are on back-order status. When the firm receives the order for 20 units, 14 of them will go to satisfy the current back orders, resulting in a net inventory level of 6.

Figure 9.7 shows the simulation logic for the back-order case. The only differences from Figure 9.2 occur when the demand is greater than the available inventory. If so, we compute the number of back orders as D − INV and the back-order cost. Then, instead of a separate computation to adjust the inventory position and stock level, we branch to the same box as if there were sufficient inventory to satisfy demand and compute INV = INV − D and POS = POS − D. Everything else is the same. Figure 9.8 shows a spreadsheet that implements this logic for a situation in which demand is Poisson-distributed with a mean of 1.8 units (*Back Order Inventory Model.xls*).

In this model, we have allowed the lead time to vary probabilistically using a *Crystal Ball* custom distribution and the data in the range K4:L8. The other principal differences from the lost-sales case are that we allow the ending inventory level to be negative to reflect accumulated back orders, and the back-order computation is changed to account for a negative inventory level and ensure the correct number of back orders.

SIMULATING WAITING LINE SYSTEMS USING PROCESS-DRIVEN MODELS

Waiting lines occur in many important business operations. Most service systems, such as fast-food restaurants, banks, gasoline stations, and technical support telephone hot lines involve customer waiting. Arrivals to the system and the service times vary probabilistically. The important issue in designing such systems involves the trade-off

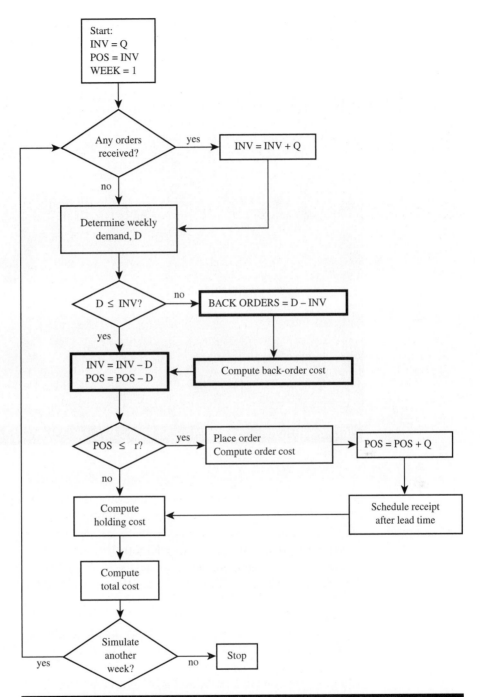

FIGURE 9.7 Logic for a Continuous Review Inventory System with Back Orders

between customer waiting and system cost, usually determined by the number of servers. A design that balances the average demand with the average service rate will cause unacceptable delays. The decision is difficult because the marginal return for increasing service capacity declines. For example, a system that can handle 99 percent of expected demand will cost much more than a system designed to handle 90 percent

	A	B	C	D	E	F	G	H	I	J	K	L	M	N	O
1	Inventory Simulation With Back Orders										Lead Time Distribution				
2		Order Quantity		5		Order Cost	$	50		Lead					
3		Reorder Point		3		Holding Cost	$	4.00		Time	Prob.				
4		Initial Inventory		5	Back Order Cost		$	20		1	0.2				
5										2	0.3				
6	Note: Crystal Ball must be running									3	0.2				
7										4	0.2				
8										5	0.1				
9															
10												Total Annual Costs			
11												$ 264	$ 950	$ 780	$ 1,994
12		Beg								End					
13		Inv	Beg	Order	Units		End	Back	Order	Inv	Lead	Hold	Order	Short	Total
14	Week	Pos	Inv	Rec'd	Rec'd	Dmd	Inv	Orders	Placed?	Pos	time	Cost	Cost	Cost	Cost
15	1	5	5		0	0	5	0	NO	5		$ 20.00	$ -	$ -	$ 20
16	2	5	5		0	2	3	0	YES	8	2	$ 12.00	$ 50	$ -	$ 62
17	3	8	3		0	0	3	0	NO	8		$ 12.00	$ -	$ -	$ 12
18	4	8	3		0	2	1	0	NO	6		$ 4.00	$ -	$ -	$ 4
19	5	6	1	YES	5	2	4	0	NO	4		$ 16.00	$ -	$ -	$ 16
20	6	4	4		0	3	1	0	YES	8	5	$ 4.00	$ 50	$ -	$ 54
21	7	6	1		0	1	0	0	NO	5		$ -	$ -	$ -	$ -
22	8	5	0		0	0	0	0	NO	5		$ -	$ -	$ -	$ -
23	9	5	0		0	3	-3	3	YES	7	3	$ -	$ 50	$ 60	$ 110
24	10	7	-3		0	2	-5	2	NO	5		$ -	$ -	$ 40	$ 40
25	11	5	-5		0	1	-6	1	NO	4		$ -	$ -	$ 20	$ 20
26	12	4	-6	YES	5	1	-2	1	YES	8	1	$ -	$ 50	$ 20	$ 70
27	13	8	-2	YES	5	2	1	0	NO	6		$ 4.00	$ -	$ -	$ 4
28	14	6	1	YES	5	0	6	0	NO	6		$ 24.00	$ -	$ -	$ 24
29	15	6	6		0	2	4	0	NO	4		$ 16.00	$ -	$ -	$ 16

FIGURE 9.8   Simulation Model for an Inventory System with Back Orders

of expected demand. In this section we discuss the basic components of waiting line models and illustrate a process-driven simulation model for a simple case.

Basic Concepts of Queueing Models

A **waiting line** (or **queueing**) **system** has three basic components: arrivals of entities to the system, waiting lines (or queues), and the service facility.

Arrivals

Arrivals to a queueing system can occur in a number of different ways. Arrivals can be constant, as with an assembly line fed by a machine operating at a constant rate. Usually, however, arrivals occur randomly and are described by some probability distribution. The Poisson distribution is often used to describe the number of arrivals in a fixed time period. An important fact in waiting line applications is if the *number of arrivals* in an interval of time is Poisson, then the *time between arrivals* has an exponential distribution.

Queues

If the service facility is busy when an entity arrives, the entity will wait in a line, or queue. Entities wait in the queue according to a decision rule that prescribes how they are to be served. This rule is referred to as the *queue discipline*. The most common queue discipline is *first-come, first-served (FCFS)*. Other decision rules found in real-world applications include last-come, first-served; random service; or some sort of priority decision rule.

Service Facility

The **service facility** consists of the servers that provide service. Many different configurations exist, for example, a single server (an ATM), multiple servers (several bank tellers), or sequential servers (gasoline pumping followed by a car wash). Service rates typically vary according to some probability distribution. A common assumption in analytical models is that service times are exponential. Of course, assumptions about the arrival and service time distributions should be validated with empirical data. The distribution-fitting capability of *Crystal Ball* can be used to identify appropriate distributions.

The total system cost consists of *service costs* and *waiting costs*. A key objective of waiting line studies is to minimize the total expected cost of the waiting line system. As the level of service increases (e.g., as the number of checkout counters in a grocery store increases), the cost of service increases. Simultaneously, customer waiting time will decrease, and consequently, expected waiting cost will decrease. Waiting costs are difficult to measure because they depend on customers' perceptions of waiting. It is difficult to quantify how much revenue is lost because of long lines. However, managerial judgment, tempered by experience, can provide estimates of waiting costs. If waiting occurs in a work situation, such as workers waiting in line at a copy machine, the cost of waiting should reflect the cost of productive resources lost while waiting. Although we usually cannot eliminate customer waiting completely without prohibitively high costs, we can minimize the total expected system cost by balancing service and waiting costs.

Analytical Models

Many analytical models have been developed for predicting the characteristics of waiting line systems. The ability to obtain analytical results depends on the assumptions made about the arrival distribution, service distribution, number of servers, queue discipline, system capacity, and population of customers. These models can be found in general textbooks on management science. The outputs of these models that are of interest to managers, called **operating characteristics,** include

1. The mean (expected) waiting time for each customer, W_q
2. The mean (expected) length of the waiting line, L_q
3. The mean time in the system for each customer (waiting plus being served), W
4. The mean number of customers in the system (including those waiting and those receiving service), L
5. The probability that the service facility will be idle (i.e., zero units are in the system), P_0
6. The average utilization of the system (i.e., the percent of time that servers are busy), ρ

Single-Server Model

The most basic queueing model assumes Poisson arrivals, exponential service times, a single server, and a FCFS queue discipline. If we define

λ = mean arrival rate, expressed in customer arrivals per time period ($1/\lambda$ = mean time between arrivals)

μ = mean service rate, expressed as customers served per time period ($1/\mu$ = mean service time)

then the operating characteristics are

Average waiting time: $W_q = \dfrac{\lambda}{\mu(\mu - \lambda)}$

Average number in queue: $L_q = \dfrac{\lambda^2}{\mu(\mu - \lambda)}$

Average time in system: $W = \dfrac{1}{\mu - \lambda}$

Average number in system: $L = \dfrac{\lambda}{\mu - \lambda}$

Probability server is idle: $P_0 = 1 - \dfrac{\lambda}{\mu}$

Percent busy: $\rho = \dfrac{\lambda}{\mu}$

Note that the arrival rate, λ, must be less than the service rate, μ, or these formulas do not make sense. If λ is greater than or equal to μ, the queue will grow forever.

These analytical formulas provide long-term expected values for the operating characteristics; they do not describe short-term dynamic behavior of system performance. In a real waiting line system, we typically see large fluctuations around the averages, and in systems in which the system begins empty, it may take a very long time to reach these expected performance levels. Simulation provides information about the dynamic behavior of waiting lines that analytical models cannot. In addition, simulation is not constrained by the restrictive assumptions necessary to obtain a mathematical solution. Thus, simulation has some important advantages over analytical approaches.

Single-Server Queueing Model

Dan O'Callahan operates a car wash. Dan is in charge of finance, accounting, marketing, and analysis; his son is in charge of production. During the "lunch hour," which Dan defines as the period from 11 A.M. to 1 P.M., customers arrive randomly at an average of 15 cars per hour (or one car every 4 minutes). A car takes an average of 3 minutes to wash (or 20 cars per hour), but this fluctuates quite a bit due to variations in hand-prepping. Dan doesn't understand how a line could possibly pile up when his son can work faster than the rate at which cars arrive. While customers complain a bit, they do not leave if they have to wait. Dan is particularly interested in understanding the waiting time, the number waiting, and how long his son is actually busy before considering improving his facility.

Because customers arrive randomly, a Poisson distribution is a good assumption to model the number of customers arriving each hour using a mean rate $\lambda = 15$. Recall from Chapter 3 that this implies that the time between arrivals is exponentially distributed. We will also assume that the service time has an exponential distribution with $\mu = 20$ cars per hour. Since there is only one server and customers are processed on a FCFS basis, this problem meets the assumptions for the analytical model presented in the previous section.

The operating characteristics in which Dan is interested and their expected values are

Average waiting time: $W_q = \dfrac{\lambda}{\mu(\mu - \lambda)} = \dfrac{15}{20(20 - 15)} = 0.15$

Average number in queue: $L_q = \dfrac{\lambda^2}{\mu(\mu - \lambda)} = \dfrac{15^2}{20(20 - 15)} = 2.25$

Probability server is idle: $P_0 = 1 - \dfrac{\lambda}{\mu} = 1 - \dfrac{15}{20} = 0.25$

However, these expected values apply in the long run; they may not be representative of what to expect during the short lunchtime interval. We will compare these results with simulated results.

To develop a process-driven simulation model, consider the sequence of activities that each customer undergoes:

1. Customer arrives.
2. Customer waits for service if the server is busy.
3. Customer receives service.
4. Customer leaves the system.

In order to compute the waiting time, we need to know the time a customer arrived and the time service began; the waiting time is the difference. Similarly, to compute the server idle time, we need to know if the arrival time of the next customer is greater than the time at which the current customer completes service. If so, the idle time is the difference. To find the number in the queue, we note that when a customer arrives, then all prior customers who have not completed service by that time must still be waiting. We can make three other observations:

a. If a customer arrives and the server is idle, then service can begin immediately upon arrival.
b. If the server is busy when a customer arrives, then the customer cannot begin service until the previous customer has completed service.
c. The time that a customer completes service equals the time service begins plus the actual service time.

These observations provide all the information we need to run the simulation.

The logic of the simulation is shown in Figure 9.9. The definitions of the variables are

ARRIVAL.TIME(I) = arrival time of customer I

START.TIME(I) = time service for customer I is begun

COMPLETION.TIME(I) = time service for customer I is completed

WAIT.TIME(I) = waiting time for customer I

IDLETIME(I) = idle time incurred by server between customer I-1 and customer I

NUMBER.IN.QUEUE = number of customers waiting

TBA(I) = time between arrival from customer I-1 to customer I

ST(I) = service time for customer I

The simulation is initialized by setting the arrival and completion times of a fictitious "customer 0" to zero. As each new customer arrives, we generate the time since the last arrival, TBA(I), using the arrival time distribution. The arrival time for customer I is set to TBA(I) minutes after the previous customer arrival.

Next, we check if the completion time of customer I-1 is greater than the arrival time of customer I. If it is, then customer I begins service when customer I-1 completes service; if not, customer I can go immediately into service. In either case, we generate a service time, ST(I). Next, we compute the waiting time and service completion time for

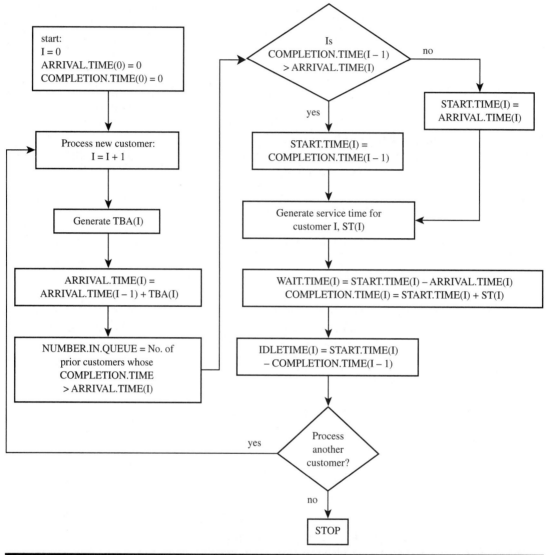

FIGURE 9.9 Simulation Logic for Single-Server Waiting Line Model

customer I and compute any idle time the server may have incurred. Finally, we make a decision whether to repeat the process.

Finding the length of the queue when a customer arrives is a bit tricky. We use the Excel function MATCH to determine the last customer, say X, whose completion time is less than or equal to the arrival time of the current customer, say Y. Then all customers who arrived after customer X are still in the system (including, now, customer Y). Therefore, the system has Y − X customers, one of whom is in service, leaving Y − X − 1 customers in the queue. This is the same as Y minus the value of the MATCH function.

Figure 9.10 shows a portion of the spreadsheet (*Queueing Simulation.xls*) designed to simulate this problem (the entire simulation is for 500 customers). To generate the time between arrivals and service times, we use the *Crystal Ball* CB.Exponential function. We encourage you to examine the formulas for the arrival time, start time,

Dan's Car Wash

Mean arrival rate	15	
Mean service rate	20	
Expected No. in Queue	2.250	
Expected Waiting Time	0.150	
Expected % idle time	25%	
Simulation Results		
No. in Queue	2.2124	
Waiting Time	0.1544	
% idle time	26%	
Note: Crystal Ball must be running		

Customer	TBA	Arrival Time	No. in Queue	Start Time	Service Time	Completion Time	Wait Time	Idle Time	Cum. No. in Queue	Avg. No. in Queue	Cum. Wait Time	Avg. Wait Time	Cum. Idle Time	Avg. % Idle Time
						0.00								
1	0.0031	0.0031	0	0.0031	0.0515	0.0545	0.0000	0.0031	0.0000	0.0000	0.0000	0.0000	0.0031	6%
2	0.0615	0.0646	0	0.0646	0.0884	0.1530	0.0000	0.0101	0.0000	0.0000	0.0000	0.0000	0.0132	9%
3	0.1002	0.1648	0	0.1648	0.0541	0.2189	0.0000	0.0118	0.0000	0.0000	0.0000	0.0000	0.0249	11%
4	0.1283	0.2931	0	0.2931	0.1340	0.4271	0.0000	0.0742	0.0000	0.0000	0.0000	0.0000	0.0992	23%
5	0.0307	0.3238	1	0.4271	0.0468	0.4739	0.1033	0.0000	0.0307	0.0947	0.1033	0.0207	0.0992	21%
6	0.1036	0.4273	1	0.4739	0.0847	0.5586	0.0465	0.0000	0.1342	0.3141	0.1499	0.0250	0.0992	18%
7	0.0107	0.4381	2	0.5586	0.0240	0.5826	0.1205	0.0000	0.1557	0.3554	0.2704	0.0386	0.0992	17%
8	0.0355	0.4736	3	0.5826	0.1343	0.7169	0.1091	0.0000	0.2622	0.5536	0.3795	0.0474	0.0992	14%
9	0.1286	0.6021	1	0.7169	0.0287	0.7456	0.1148	0.0000	0.3908	0.6489	0.4942	0.0549	0.0992	13%
10	0.0268	0.6290	2	0.7456	0.0194	0.7650	0.1167	0.0000	0.4444	0.7066	0.6109	0.0611	0.0992	13%
11	0.1367	0.7657	0	0.7657	0.0307	0.7964	0.0000	0.0007	0.4444	0.5804	0.6109	0.0555	0.0999	13%
12	0.0504	0.8161	0	0.8161	0.0037	0.8197	0.0000	0.0196	0.4444	0.5446	0.6109	0.0509	0.1195	15%
13	0.0706	0.8867	0	0.8867	0.0501	0.9368	0.0000	0.0670	0.4444	0.5012	0.6109	0.0470	0.1865	20%
14	0.0634	0.9501	0	0.9501	0.0035	0.9535	0.0000	0.0132	0.4444	0.4678	0.6109	0.0436	0.1997	21%
15	0.0504	1.0005	0	1.0005	0.0164	1.0168	0.0000	0.0469	0.4444	0.4442	0.6109	0.0407	0.2467	24%
16	0.0236	1.0241	0	1.0241	0.0084	1.0325	0.0000	0.0072	0.4444	0.4340	0.6109	0.0382	0.2539	25%
17	0.0770	1.1011	0	1.1011	0.0247	1.1257	0.0000	0.0685	0.4444	0.4036	0.6109	0.0359	0.3224	29%
18	0.0321	1.1331	0	1.1331	0.0060	1.1392	0.0000	0.0074	0.4444	0.3922	0.6109	0.0339	0.3298	29%
19	0.2802	1.4133	0	1.4133	0.0043	1.4176	0.0000	0.2741	0.4444	0.3144	0.6109	0.0322	0.6040	43%
20	0.0502	1.4635	0	1.4635	0.0007	1.4642	0.0000	0.0459	0.4444	0.3037	0.6109	0.0305	0.6499	44%

FIGURE 9.10 Simulation Model for Single-Server Waiting Line

completion time, wait time, and idle time and compare them to the logic in Figure 9.9. Columns L through Q compute and maintain updated statistics of the average number in the queue, average wait time, and average percent idle time as each customer is processed. The final values in columns M, O, and Q, which represent the averages for the 500 customers, are shown in the *Simulation Results* section in cells B12:B14.

Using the Excel *Chart* tool, we may construct graphs of these performance measures to provide better insight into the dynamics of the queueing system. These are shown in Figures 9.11 through 9.14. Figure 9.11 shows that the number in the queue fluctuates significantly over time. During the simulation, Dan had as few as zero and as many as 14 customers waiting. However, if we look at the *average* number in the queue at any point in the simulation (Figure 9.12), we see that the average eventually converges to the expected value calculated by the analytical model (the solid black line on the chart). This can be better understood if we realize that each simulation began with an *empty system.* Early arrivals to the system would not expect to wait very long, but when a short-term random surge of customers arrives, the queue begins to build up

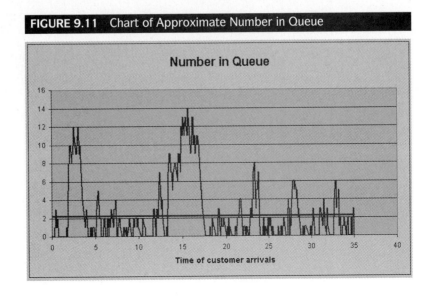

FIGURE 9.11 Chart of Approximate Number in Queue

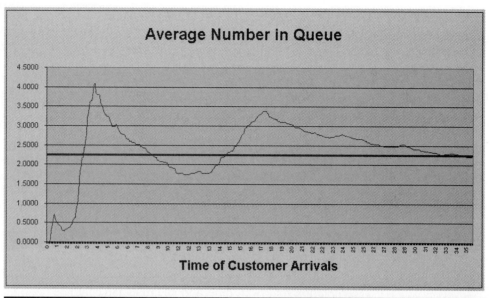

FIGURE 9.12 Chart of Average Number in Queue

(we call this the "warm up" or "transient" period, which will be discussed further in the next chapter). As the number of customers increases, the number in the queue averaged over all customers begins to level off, reaching what is termed *steady state*. This is what the analytical results provide. However, during the lunch period, the car wash would probably not run long enough to reach steady state; therefore, the analytical results will never present an accurate picture of the system behavior. We see similar phenomena for the average waiting time and percent idle time in Figures 9.13 and 9.14.

FIGURE 9.13 Chart of Average Waiting Time/Customer

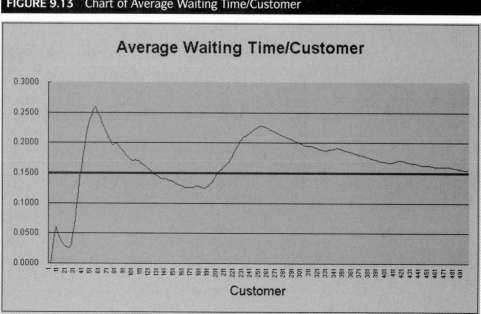

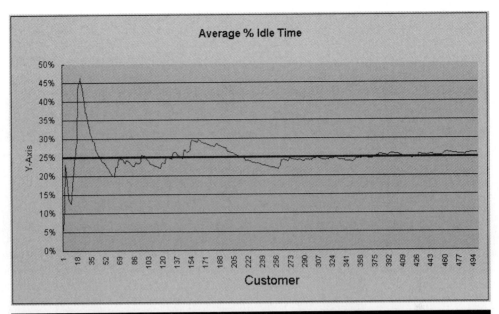

FIGURE 9.14   Chart of Average Percent Idle Time

Figure 9.11, which shows the number in the queue when each customer arrives, deserves further explanation. It is important to realize that this chart is an approximation because we compute it only when a new customer arrives and do not update it when a customer leaves (this is a characteristic of the process-driven simulation approach; we will rectify this when discussing event-driven models later in this chapter). We can see this more clearly by plotting the actual number in the queue for the first several minutes of operation based on the data in the spreadsheet. This is shown by the shaded area in Figure 9.15. Customer 1 arrives at time 0.0034 and goes immediately into service and completes service at time 0.0201. Customer 2 arrives at 0.1208 and completes service at 0.1886. However, customer 3 arrives at 0.1268 and must wait until customer 2 is finished, and so on. The chart in Figure 9.11 displays only the points shown by the solid dots. This results in only an approximation of the average number in the queue in Figure 9.12. The true average number in the queue at the time that

FIGURE 9.15   Graph of Number in Queue (Actual versus Approximate)

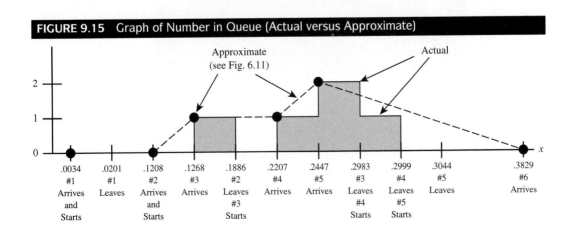

customer 6 arrives (0.3829) is calculated by taking the shaded area and dividing by the length of time, or

$$[(0.1896 - 0.1268)*1 + (0.2447 - 0.2207)*1 + (0.2983 - 0.2447)*2$$
$$+ (0.2999 - 0.2983)*1]/0.3829 = 0.5108$$

The spreadsheet, however, approximates this as 0.3864 (cell M9). Nevertheless, this does provide a means of understanding the dynamic behavior of the queue.

The results shown in Figure 9.10 represent a single trial. Figure 9.16 shows the results for 1000 trials using *Crystal Ball*. The first thing we notice is that the distributions

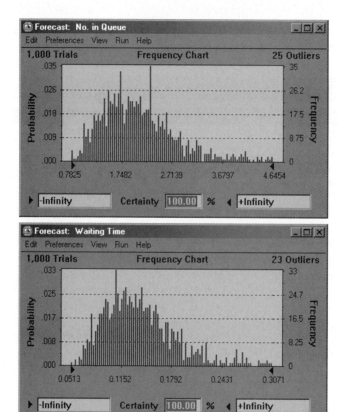

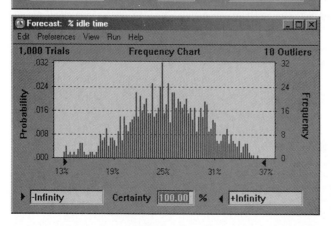

FIGURE 9.16 *Crystal Ball* Forecast Charts for Queueing Simulation Results

	A	B	C	D	E	F	G	H	I	J	K	L	M	N
1	Dan's Car Wash - Two Server Model				Note: Crystal Ball must be running									
2														
3	Mean arrival rate	2												
4	Mean service rate	3												
5					Arrival		Start	Service		Completion Time			Wait	Cum. Wait	Avg. Wait
6	Simulation Results		Customer	TBA	Time	Server	Time	Time	Customer	Server 1	Server 2	Time	Time	Time
7	Waiting Time	0.054	1	1.225	1.225	1	1.225	0.313	1.539	1.539	0.000	0.000	0.000	0.000
8			2	0.154	1.379	2	1.379	0.150	1.529	1.539	1.529	0.000	0.000	0.000
9			3	0.143	1.522	2	1.529	0.005	1.534	1.539	1.534	0.008	0.008	0.003
10			4	0.277	1.798	2	1.798	0.092	1.890	1.539	1.890	0.000	0.008	0.002
11			5	0.492	2.290	1	2.290	0.440	2.730	2.730	1.890	0.000	0.008	0.002
12			6	0.920	3.209	2	3.209	0.895	4.104	2.730	4.104	0.000	0.008	0.001
13			7	0.214	3.423	1	3.423	0.569	3.993	3.993	4.104	0.000	0.008	0.001
14			8	0.092	3.515	1	3.993	0.053	4.045	4.045	4.104	0.477	0.485	0.061
15			9	1.329	4.845	1	4.845	1.113	5.958	5.958	4.104	0.000	0.485	0.054
16			10	0.028	4.873	2	4.873	0.243	5.116	5.958	5.116	0.000	0.485	0.048

FIGURE 9.17   Two-Server Queueing Simulation Model

for the forecasts have considerable variability; that is, single trials of the simulation show dramatically different results. This is not unusual for system simulation models and shows the necessity of replicating a model many times to obtain good estimates of the unknown population parameters we wish to estimate.

Multiple-Server Models

Many queueing systems have more than one server. You have undoubtedly experienced these in banks or perhaps when calling computer technical support functions. Customers form a single line (usually behind a "Wait Here for the Next Available Server" sign) and are processed in order by the next server who is free. It is not difficult to extend the spreadsheet model in the last section to the multiple-server case.

To illustrate this, suppose that Dan's Carwash is considering adding a second server to reduce customer waiting. When a customer arrives, a check must be made to see if any server is idle. If so, then the free server (or server 1 when both are idle) can process the customer immediately. If both servers are busy, the customer waits in the queue. The necessary changes in the logic of Figure 9.9 are rather straightforward, and a question at the end of this chapter addresses this.

Figure 9.17 shows an implementation of a two-server model on Excel (*Queueing Simulation—Two Server.xls*). The spreadsheet is quite similar to the single-server model. An extra column, F, identifies which of the two servers is assigned to the customer. This is selected using an IF statement, selecting for each server the smallest of the finish times of the prior customer. The only other difference is that we need to identify the completion times for each server. This is done in columns H and I in a similar manner as was done in the single-server case. For this example, we have not included the percent idle time for each server; this is left as an exercise.

Figure 9.18 shows the *Crystal Ball* forecast chart for the waiting time. You can see that the average waiting time has dropped significantly by adding a second server. As a practical matter, however, Dan must consider the trade-off between this improvement in customer service and the additional cost of the extra server. In this way, simulation can help answer the "what if?" questions that form the basis for the best decision.

EVENT-DRIVEN SIMULATION MODELS

Although activity-scanning and process-driven approaches to simulation work well for certain types of problems, they do not provide the flexibility required to model many practical problems. For example, in a manufacturing system, many different

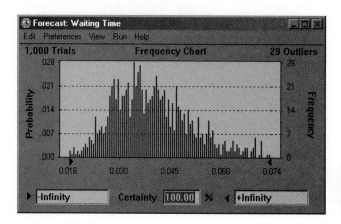

FIGURE 9.18 *Crystal Ball* Forecast Chart for Waiting Time (Two-Server Model)

types of events occur. Jobs arrive for processing, materials must be moved from one work center to another, jobs begin and end at individual work centers, and machines break down and must be repaired. With an activity-scanning approach, so many things can occur within a time interval that crucial information may be lost because the exact times of their occurrence are not known. For instance, in the inventory example, we assumed that all demand occurred at the end of the week and did not record the times at which individual demands occurred. In addition, every possible activity must be scanned in each time period, even if it does not occur (as in the case of reordering). For complex problems, this can waste a significant amount of computing time. Similarly, a process orientation may not be applicable; for instance, the breakdown of a machine is a random occurrence that is not associated with the flow of a job through a factory.

In this section we introduce event-driven simulation. An **event** is an occurrence in a system at which changes to a system occur. Events take place at an instance of time. For example, in an inventory model, an event might be the time at which a demand occurs or the time when an order is received. In a queueing model, the system changes when a customer arrives and when a customer departs the system. With event-driven simulation, a system is modeled by defining the events that occur in the system and describing the logic that takes place at these times. Events are processed in chronological order, and simulated time is advanced from one event to the next. This is a very efficient approach from a computational point of view. Most popular commercial simulation languages are based on event-driven simulation. We will also describe some of these languages in this chapter.

An Event-Driven Simulation for a Single-Server Queue

In a single-server queueing situation, the only occurrences that change the system are the arrival of a customer and the end of a service. When a customer arrives, the system changes because the number of customers in the system has increased. Similarly, when service is completed, the customer departs, and the number of customers in the system decreases. Thus, arrivals and departures represent the two events that drive the system.

In an event-driven simulation, we must describe the logical sequence of activities that happen when each event occurs. Figure 9.19 shows the logic for an arrival event. When an arrival occurs, we first schedule the next arrival by generating a random variate from the interarrival time distribution and adding it to the current time. This

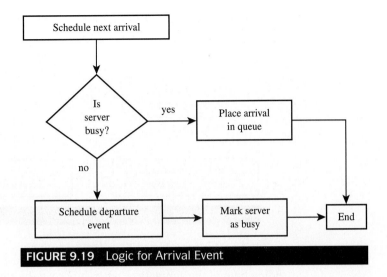

FIGURE 9.19   Logic for Arrival Event

ensures that we have an event scheduled to occur in the future to keep the simulation going. (Shortly, we will describe how we handle these "future" events.) When a customer arrives, we check to see if the server is currently busy. If not, the customer can immediately go into service, and we schedule a departure event by generating a random variate from the service time distribution and adding it to the current time. We then mark the server as busy so that we can collect statistics on server utilization. If the server is busy when the customer arrives, the customer is placed in the queue. This logic follows exactly what you would encounter if you arrived at a drive-up window, for instance.

Figure 9.20 shows the logic for a departure event. In this case, put yourself in the place of the server. After a service is completed, we check to see if any customers are waiting. If there are none, the server is idle and awaits the arrival of the next customer. If the queue is not empty, the first customer waiting in the queue goes into service.

Earlier we stated that events are processed in chronological order. To keep track of future events and control the simulation, we use a control routine, shown in Figure 9.21. Future events and their times of occurrence are placed in a calendar file, which stores them in chronological order. As each event is completed, the control routine removes the next event from the calendar file, advances the simulated time to the event time, and calls the appropriate event routine. To stop the simulation, we can place an

FIGURE 9.20   Logic for Department Event

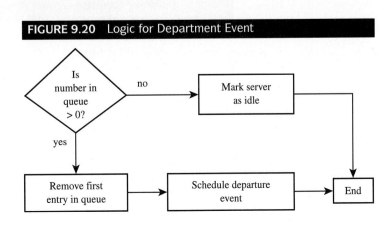

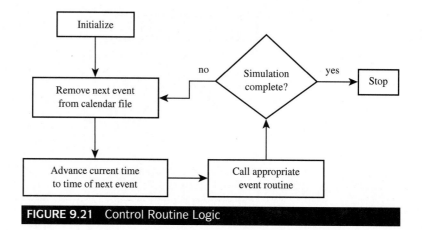

FIGURE 9.21 Control Routine Logic

end-of-simulation event in the control routine at the start of the simulation. This stores the ending time of the simulation; when it occurs, the simulation is terminated.

To illustrate this approach, we will use the data from the spreadsheet simulation for Dan's Car Wash shown in Figure 9.10. We actually set the foundation for an event-driven simulation when we discussed the calculation of the number in the queue in Figure 9.15. Table 9.1 shows the time between arrivals and service time for each customer. We will assume that these are the random variates generated whenever the simulation logic requires us to do so.

We will arbitrarily initialize the control routine with an end-of-simulation event at time 30 (or whatever length of simulated time we wish) and the first arrival at time 0.0031. Thus, at time 0, the calendar file would be

EVENT	**TIME**	**CURRENT TIME = 0**
arrival	0.0031	
endsim	30.000	

The control routine removes the first event, an arrival at time 0.0031, advances the simulation clock to 0.0031, and calls the arrival event routine. We schedule the next arrival at the current time plus the time between arrivals from Table 9.1: $0.0031 + 0.0615 = 0.0646$ and place this event in the calendar file. Since the server is idle, the customer can

TABLE 9.1 Arrival and Service Time Data for Dan's Car Wash Example

Customer	Time Between Arrivals	Service Time
1	0.0031	0.0515
2	0.0615	0.0884
3	0.1002	0.0541
4	0.1283	0.1340
5	0.0307	0.0468
6	0.1036	0.0847
7	0.0107	0.0240
8	0.0355	0.1343
9	0.1286	0.0287
10	0.0268	0.0194

go immediately into service. We schedule a departure event at the current time plus the service time: $0.0031 + 0.0515 = 0.0546$ (differences with Figure 9.10 are due to rounding). Because we maintain the calendar file sorted in chronological order, it looks like

EVENT	TIME	CURRENT TIME = 0.0031
departure	0.0546	
arrival	0.0646	
endsim	30.000	

The server is marked as busy, and we return to the control routine.

The next event is the departure of the first customer at time 0.0546. Because no other customers are waiting, the server becomes idle. The calendar file is

EVENT	TIME	CURRENT TIME = 0.0546
arrival	0.0646	
endsim	30.000	

The next event is an arrival at time 0.0646. We generate the next arrival at time $0.0646 + 0.1002 = 0.1648$. Because the server is idle, we schedule a departure at time $0.0646 + 0.0884 = 0.1530$ and mark the server as busy. The calendar file is

EVENT	TIME	CURRENT TIME = 0.0646
departure	0.1530	
arrival	0.1648	
endsim	30.000	

The next event removed from the calendar file is the departure at time 0.1530. The calendar file is

EVENT	TIME	CURRENT TIME = 0.1530
arrival	0.1648	
endsim	30.000	

We would continue this process until we reach the end-of-simulation event. If an arrival occurs while the server is still busy, the arrival would be placed in the queue to wait; such is the case with customer 5 in Figure 9.10.

Table 9.2 summarizes the sequence of events for the portion of the simulation we have described as well as the number in the system and queue, server status, and idle time. Note that whenever an arrival event occurs, the number in the system is increased

TABLE 9.2   Summary of Events for Dan's Car Wash Simulation Example

Event	Event Type	Clock Time	Number in System	Number in Queue	Server Status	Idle Time
1	arrival	0.0031	1	0	busy	0.0031
2	departure	0.0546	0	0	idle	
3	arrival	0.0646	1	0	busy	0.0100
4	departure	0.1530	0	0	idle	
5	arrival	0.1648	1	0	busy	0.0118

	A	B	C	D	E	F	G	H	I	J	K	L	M
1	Dan's Car Wash Event-Driven Simulation					Note: Crystal Ball must be running							
2													
3	Mean arrival rate	2											
4	Mean service rate	3											
5												Temporary data	
6	*Simulation Results*		Event	Type	Clock	No. in	No. in	Server	Idle	Next	Next	used to compute	
7	Avg. No. in System	1.444			Time	System	Queue	Status	Time	Arrival	Departure	simulation results	
8	Avg. No. in Queue	0.847	1	arrival	0.79	1	0	busy	0.00	1.37	0.90		
9	% Idle Time	0.397	2	depart	0.90	0	0	idle	0.00	1.37	99999.00	0.108	0.000
10			3	arrival	1.37	1	0	busy	0.47	1.44	1.83	0.000	0.000
11			4	arrival	1.44	2	1	busy	0.00	2.78	1.83	0.065	0.000
12			5	depart	1.83	1	0	busy	0.00	2.78	2.06	0.785	0.393
13			6	depart	2.06	0	0	idle	0.00	2.78	99999.00	0.229	0.000
14			7	arrival	2.78	1	0	busy	0.73	4.43	2.93	0.000	0.000
15			8	depart	2.93	0	0	idle	0.00	4.43	99999.00	0.141	0.000
16			9	arrival	4.43	1	0	busy	1.51	4.58	4.46	0.000	0.000
17			10	depart	4.46	0	0	idle	0.00	4.58	99999.00	0.031	0.000

FIGURE 9.22   Event-Driven Queueing Simulation Model

by 1; when there is a departure, the number decreases by 1. Server status refers to the status immediately after the event occurs. Thus, if the server is idle and an arrival occurs, the status changes to busy. If the number in the system drops to zero, the server becomes idle. Idle time is computed whenever the server status changes from idle to busy. You should work through the remainder of this table using the data in Table 9.1 to verify your understanding of the event-driven approach. From this table, you can easily see how a graph of the number in the queue or system, such as the one in Figure 9.15, can be derived.

Using the principles we have described, it is relatively easy to construct an event-driven spreadsheet simulation model for the single-server waiting line simulation, shown in Figure 9.22 (*Queueing Simulation—Event Driven.xls*). Columns C through I are identical to Table 9.2. To initialize the simulation, we schedule an arrival as the first event. As the simulation progresses, we use the following logic. In column D, we check whether the time of the next scheduled departure is less than the time of the next scheduled arrival (from columns J and K in the previous row) and list the appropriate event. In column E, the clock time is updated to the appropriate time. This logic follows the control routine in Figure 9.21. In column F, if the event is a departure, we decrease the number in the system by 1; otherwise, we increase it by 1. The number in the queue (column G) is one less than the number in the system or zero, whichever is greater. If the number in the system is zero, the server is marked as idle in column F; otherwise, busy. Whenever the server status changes from idle to busy, we compute the idle time from the last departure until the current arrival in column I. Columns J and K essentially mimic the calendar file. In column J, we schedule a new arrival if the current event is an arrival; otherwise, we simply copy the next arrival time from the previous row. When the server is idle, no departure is scheduled, and a large number (99999) is used in column K to designate this. Columns L and M are used to compute data needed for calculating the average number in the system and in the queue along the same lines as in our discussion of Figure 9.15. Figure 9.23 shows a chart of the number in the system (a chart for number in queue is also available in the Excel workbook) that is correct, as opposed to the approximation we used in Figure 9.11.

The only complicated logic in this spreadsheet is in column K for determining the next departure time. The formula for cell K9 follows, broken down into its three nested IF statements:

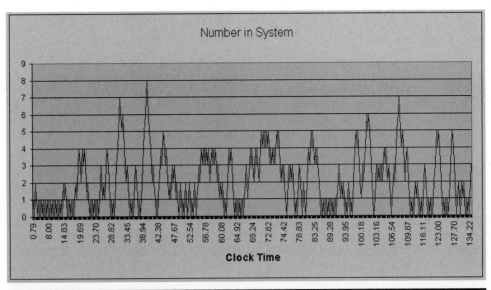

FIGURE 9.23   Chart of Number in System

(part 1): =IF(AND(D9="depart",F9>0),E9+CB.Exponential($B$4),

(part 2): IF(AND(D9="depart",F9=0),99999,

(part 3): IF(AND(D9="arrival",H8="idle"),E9+CB.Exponential
($B$4),K8)))

In part 1, if the current event is a departure and cell F9 is greater than 0, indicating that a customer is still waiting, we schedule the next departure at the current time plus an exponential random variate. In part 2, if the current event is a departure and the system is empty, the next departure time is set to an arbitrarily high number (this corresponds to a calendar file with no scheduled departures). Finally, in part 3, if the current event is an arrival and the server is idle, we schedule the next departure. If both conditions of the AND function are not true, which can only be the case if the current event is an arrival and the server is busy, we copy the already-scheduled next departure time from the previous row. Studying this logic is a good way to better understand the procedures associated with event-driven simulation models.

AN EVENT-DRIVEN INVENTORY SIMULATION MODEL

In the previous section we presented a simulation model for simulating a continuous-review inventory system with lost sales using an activity-scanning approach. In this section we show how to simulate this problem using an event-driven approach. The major difference is that instead of scanning each week to determine the value of the weekly demand and if any orders are received, we let events correspond to (1) the demand for an individual item, and (2) the receipt of an order. This requires that the demand be characterized by a probability distribution representing the time between individual demands, not the number of items demanded during a time period. This approach is particularly useful for high-value, low-demand items and infrequent ordering situations, particularly when it is important to capture the exact amount of time that items remain in inventory in order to compute accurate holding costs.

In the logic that we will discuss, we will also include the calculation of average inventory and the average level of safety stock (the stock level just before an order

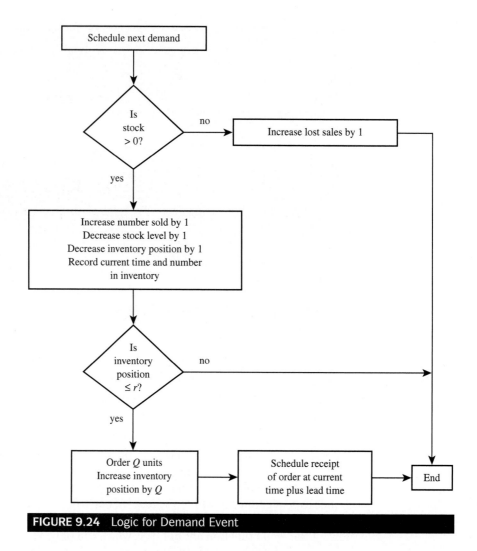

FIGURE 9.24 Logic for Demand Event

arrives). Figures 9.24 and 9.25 show the logic for the demand and receipt-of-order events. When a demand occurs, we schedule the next demand at the current time plus a random variate drawn from the time-between-demand distribution. Next, we check if any stock is available. If no stock is available, we increase lost sales by 1 and quit. Otherwise, we increase the number sold by 1, and decrease both the stock level and inventory position by 1. We also record the current time and number in inventory. This allows us to compute the average number of units in inventory in a manner similar to the way we computed the average number in the queue for the Dan's Carwash simulation. Next, we check if the inventory position has reached the reorder point. If so, we order Q units and increase the inventory position by the order quantity. Then we schedule a receipt-of-order event at the current time plus the lead time (which may be a random variate).

The receipt-of-order event is simple. Prior to "receiving" the order, we record the current time and number of units in inventory and the amount of safety stock. Then we increase the stock level by Q. The simulation is driven by the same control routine shown in Figure 9.21.

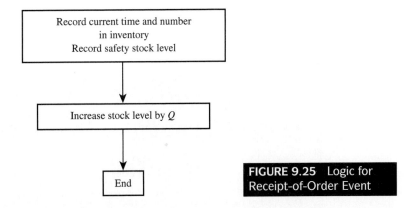

FIGURE 9.25   Logic for Receipt-of-Order Event

Figure 9.26 shows a spreadsheet implementation for this approach (*Inventory Simulation—Event Driven.xls*). In this model, we assume that the demand is Poisson distributed with a mean of 10 units per week; equivalently, the time between individual demands is exponential with a mean of 1/10 weeks. We also assume that the lead time is uniformly distributed between 0.2 and 0.5 weeks, the order quantity is Q = 8, and the reorder point is *r* = 4. This implementation also assumes that at most one order will be outstanding at any one time. Therefore, if the lead time is too long, the results may be in error.

Columns K and L list the times of the next demand and next order receipt as would be recorded in the calendar file; the smaller of these two determines the next event in column E and the current clock time in column F. In column G, if the event is a demand and the stock level is positive, the total sold is incremented by 1. If the stock level is 0 and a demand occurs, the total lost sales is incremented by 1 in column H.

Column I records the current stock level, either decreasing it by 1 when a demand occurs or increasing it by Q when an order receipt occurs. Figure 9.27 shows the stock level as a function of time. In column J, the inventory position is increased by Q whenever an order was placed as the previous event, decreased by 1 if a simple demand occurred, or left the same if the current event is a receipt or if stock is zero. In column K, the next demand is determined by adding an exponential random variate to the current clock time, in a manner similar to that used in the Dan's Carwash example. Finally,

FIGURE 9.26   Event-Driven Inventory Simulation Model

A	B	C	D	E	F	G	H	I	J	K	L	M	N
Event-Driven Inventory Simulation				Note: Crystal Ball must be running									
Mean Demand Rate	10 units/week												
Order Quantity	8				Clock	Total	Total	Stock	Inventory	Next	Next order	Used for computing	
Reorder Point	4		Event	Type	Time	sold	lost	level	position	demand	receipt	average stock level	
Initial Inventory	8		1	demand	0.108	1	0	7	7	0.138	99999.000	0.8604	
			2	demand	0.138	2	0	6	6	0.343	99999.000	0.2160	
Simulation Results			3	demand	0.343	3	0	5	5	0.366	99999.000	1.2283	
Lost Sales/Week	0.818		4	demand	0.366	4	0	4	4	0.736	0.782	0.1133	
Average Stock Level	5.001		5	demand	0.736	5	0	3	11	0.744	0.782	1.4808	
			6	demand	0.744	6	0	2	10	0.758	0.782	0.0232	
			7	demand	0.758	7	0	1	9	0.764	0.782	0.0279	
			8	demand	0.764	8	0	0	8	0.772	0.782	0.0061	
			9	demand	0.772	8	1	0	8	0.804	0.782	0.0000	
			10	receipt	0.782	8	1	8	8	0.804	99999.000	0.0000	
			11	demand	0.804	9	1	7	7	0.812	99999.000	0.1710	

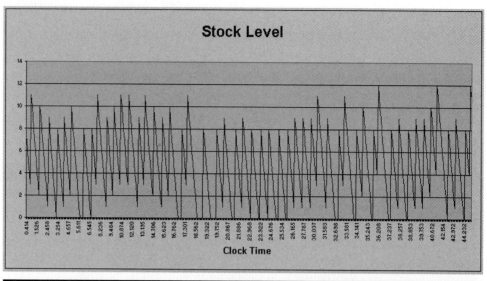

FIGURE 9.27 Chart of Stock Level

in column L, we record the time of the next order receipt. This is set to 99999 if no order is currently scheduled in the calendar file or the current time plus the lead time if an order is pending. Three nested IF statements are used. In the first part, we check if the inventory position has been reached. If so, we schedule the next order receipt by adding a uniform random variate to the current clock time. In the second part, we check if the current clock time is less than the time of the next order receipt from the previous event; if so, we know that the time of the next order receipt will not change. If neither of these conditions is true and the current event is a receipt, we copy the time from the previous row. We could use *Crystal Ball* to find the distribution of the average number of lost sales or stock level, as shown in the forecast charts in Figure 9.28.

You can see that the logic necessary to handle an event-driven simulation on a spreadsheet is more complex and requires more ingenuity than that of the activity-scanning or process-driven approaches. Next, we discuss some of the features of more complicated event-driven simulations that are usually incorporated into commercial simulation languages.

ENTITIES AND ATTRIBUTES

Often, the information we need to compute an important output statistic is a characteristic of the entities that move through the system. We saw this in the process-driven simulation for Dan's Carwash. Each customer has an associated waiting time. We may compute the waiting time of a customer whenever the customer begins service, as long as we know the time that the customer arrived. In the event-driven simulation described in the previous section, it is not clear how to compute waiting times because the simulation does not keep track of this information. To see how to do this, let us return to the logic for the arrival and departure events in Figures 9.19 and 9.20.

In Figure 9.19, we see that if the server is not busy, the waiting time of the arriving customer is zero. However, if the server is busy, we need to record the arrival time of the customer in order to compute the waiting time when the customer eventually begins service. The arrival time is unique to each customer; that is, it is an attribute of the customer. In general, an **attribute** is a characteristic associated with an entity.

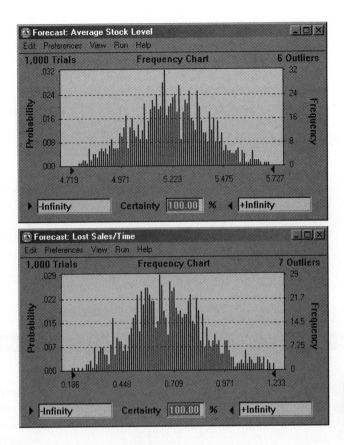

FIGURE 9.28   *Crystal Ball Results for Event-Driven Inventory Simulation*

(Other examples of attributes are the quantity ordered of an order entity in an inventory system, the priority of a job entity arriving at a manufacturing department, or the number of items purchased by a shopper entity in a supermarket.) Attributes are necessary when we must access information associated with different entities at different points of the simulation process. Figures 9.29 and 9.30 show the modifications to Figures 9.19 and 9.20 required to incorporate waiting time computations into the simulation logic. The boxes with heavy lines represent the changes in the logic.

Because attributes are associated with entities, they can easily be incorporated into process-driven spreadsheet simulations, as we saw in the previous section, since each row corresponds to an entity. For an event-driven simulation, this is more difficult to do using a spreadsheet; however, commercial simulation software generally captures both process and event-oriented approaches together.

CONTINUOUS SIMULATION MODELING

Many models contain variables that change continuously over time. One example would be a model of an oil refinery. The amount of oil moving between various stages of production is clearly a continuous variable. In other models, changes in variables occur gradually (though discretely) over an extended time period; however, for all intents and purposes, they may be treated as continuous. An example would be the amount of inventory at a warehouse in a production-distribution system over several years. As customer demand is fulfilled, inventory is depleted, leading to factory orders to

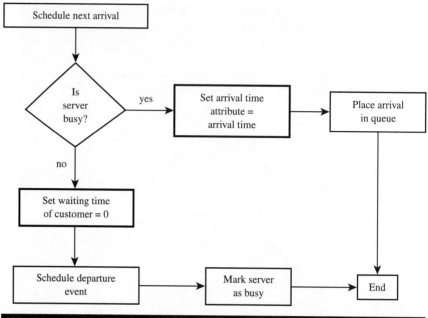

FIGURE 9.29 Logic for Arrival Event with Waiting-Time Computation

replenish the stock. As orders are received from suppliers, the inventory increases. Over time, particularly if orders are relatively small and frequent, as we see in just-in-time environments, the inventory level can be represented by a smooth, continuous, function.

Continuous variables are often called *state variables.* **A continuous simulation model** defines equations for relationships among state variables so that the dynamic behavior of the system over time can be studied. To simulate continuous systems, we use an activity-scanning approach whereby time is decomposed into small increments. The defining equations are used to determine how the state variables change during an increment of time. A specific type of continuous simulation is called *system dynamics,* which dates back to the early 1960s and a classic work by Jay Forrester of MIT (see the chapter references). System dynamics focuses on the structure and behavior of systems that are composed of interactions among variables and feedback loops. A system dynamics model usually takes the form of an influence diagram that shows the relationships and interactions among a set of variables.

FIGURE 9.30 Logic for Departure Event with Waiting-Time Computation

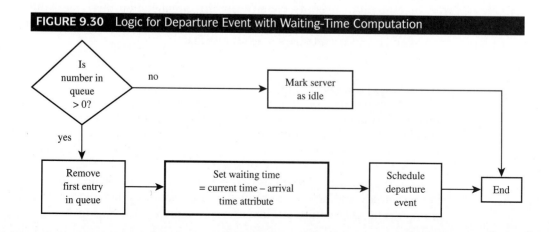

To gain an understanding of system dynamics and how continuous simulation models work, let us develop a model for the cost of medical care. Doctors and hospitals charge more for services, citing the rising cost of research, equipment, and insurance rates. Insurance companies cite rising court awards in malpractice suits as the basis for increasing their rates. Lawyers stress the need to force professionals to provide their patients with the best care possible and use the courts as a means to enforce patient rights. The medical cost system has received focused attention from those paying for medical care and from government officials.

Let us suppose that we are interested in how medical rates (MEDRATE) are influenced by other factors, specifically:

1. The demand for medical service (DEMAND)
2. Insurance rates (INSRATE)
3. Population levels (POPLVL)
4. Medical-related lawsuits (MEDSUIT)
5. Avoidance of risk by doctors (RISK)

Figure 9.31 shows an influence diagram of how these factors might relate to one another. For example, rates rise as the demand for medical service increases and as insurance rates rise. The demand is influenced by the population level and its growth rate. Also, increasing rates have a negative influence on demand, meaning that as rates rise, the demand will decrease. Insurance rates increase as medical lawsuits increase and drop as doctors avoid taking risks. At the same time, lawsuits increase as medical rates increase but also decline with risk avoidance. Some of these influences do not occur immediately, as noted by the "delay" factors in the figure. It might take about one year before some variables actually influence others.

We may express these relationships quantitatively through a set of equations that describes how each variable changes from one year to the next (that is, year $t-1$ to year t). At time $t=0$, we index all variables to 1.0. We will assume that the population

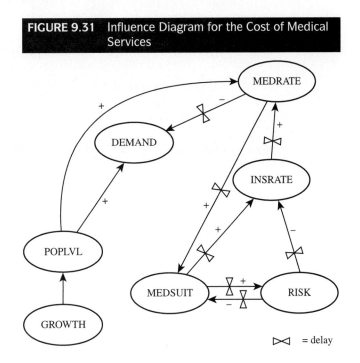

FIGURE 9.31   Influence Diagram for the Cost of Medical Services

level grows each year by a value, GROWTH(t), that is normally distributed with a mean of 0.05 and a standard deviation of 0.03. This is expressed by the equation:

$$POPLVL(t) = POPLVL(t - 1) + GROWTH(t)$$

The demand for medical services increases with the population and decreases with the rate of increase in the cost of medical service, lagged by one year. Thus, demand is computed by the formula:

$$DEMAND(t) = POPLVL(t) - [MEDRATE(t - 1) - MEDRATE(t - 2)]$$

The cost of medical services increases with the change in population level and a portion (80 percent) of the increase in insurance rates, lagged by one year:

$$MEDRATE(t) = MEDRATE(t - 1) + POPLVL(t) - POPLVL(t - 1) \\ + .8*[INSRATE(t - 1) - INSRATE(t - 2)]$$

Insurance rates increase by a fraction (10 percent) of the previous year's level of lawsuits and decrease with any increases in doctor's adoption of safer practices to avoid risk:

$$INSRATE(t) = INSRATE(t - 1) + .10*MEDSUIT(t - 1) \\ - [RISK(t - 1) - RISK(t - 2)]$$

Increase in lawsuits is proportional to the increased costs of medical service and inversely proportional to risk avoidance, both lagged by one year:

$$MEDSUIT(t) = MEDSUIT(t - 1) + [MEDRATE(t - 1) - 1]/RISK(t - 1)$$

Finally, the avoidance of risk increases as a proportion (10 percent) of the increase in the level of lawsuits, based on the previous year:

$$RISK(t) = RISK(t - 1) + .10*[MEDSUIT(t - 1) - 1]$$

Figure 9.32 presents a spreadsheet model for simulating this system (*Continuous Simulation Model.xls*). This simulation model is deterministic, as none of the variables are assumed to be uncertain. Figure 9.33 shows a graph of each of the variables over the 30-year period of the simulation. Based on our assumptions, the population has increased by almost 350 percent. However, the demand for medical services has not quite reached that level, dampened by a 5-fold increase in the cost of medical services. Insurance rates have increased 5 times, and lawsuits have increased 13 times (a compounded rate of 9 percent per year) while risk avoidance practices have increased an average of over 10 percent per year.

System dynamics has been applied to the analysis of material and information flows in logistics systems, sales and marketing problems, social organizations, ecology, and many other fields. System dynamics was quite popular among researchers and practitioners until the early 1970s. The concept was brought back to the attention of business in the 1990s by Peter Senge through his book *The Fifth Discipline* (see the chapter references), which explores the role and importance of systems thinking in modern organizations, and has formed the basis for many contemporary concepts in supply chain management.

	A	B	C	D	E	F	G	H
1	Time	Population	Population	Med. Service	Medical	Insurance	Medical	Risk
2	period	growth	level	demand	rate	rate	lawsuits	avoidance
3	0		1	1	1	1	1	1
4	1	0.053	1.053	1.053	1.053	1	1	1
5	2	0.054	1.107	1.054	1.107	1.1	1.053	1
6	3	0.076	1.183	1.129	1.263	1.205	1.160	1.005
7	4	0.038	1.221	1.066	1.385	1.316	1.422	1.021
8	5	0.052	1.273	1.151	1.526	1.442	1.799	1.064
9	6	0.078	1.351	1.211	1.705	1.580	2.294	1.143
10	7	0.035	1.386	1.207	1.850	1.729	2.910	1.273
11	8	0.124	1.510	1.365	2.094	1.891	3.578	1.464
12	9	0.046	1.556	1.312	2.269	2.058	4.326	1.722
13	10	0.042	1.599	1.423	2.445	2.233	5.063	2.054
14	11	0.121	1.719	1.543	2.705	2.406	5.766	2.461
15	12	0.066	1.785	1.525	2.910	2.577	6.459	2.937
16	13	0.069	1.854	1.649	3.116	2.746	7.109	3.483
17	14	0.082	1.937	1.731	3.333	2.911	7.717	4.094
18	15	-0.007	1.929	1.711	3.458	3.072	8.287	4.768
19	16	0.034	1.963	1.839	3.621	3.229	8.802	5.494
20	17	0.039	2.003	1.840	3.786	3.380	9.279	6.275
21	18	0.036	2.039	1.874	3.943	3.528	9.723	7.102
22	19	0.070	2.109	1.951	4.131	3.672	10.138	7.975
23	20	0.070	2.179	1.991	4.317	3.814	10.530	8.889
24	21	0.062	2.241	2.055	4.492	3.953	10.904	9.842
25	22	0.013	2.254	2.079	4.616	4.090	11.258	10.832
26	23	0.037	2.291	2.167	4.764	4.226	11.592	11.858
27	24	0.106	2.397	2.250	4.978	4.359	11.910	12.917
28	25	0.046	2.443	2.229	5.131	4.491	12.218	14.008
29	26	0.055	2.498	2.346	5.291	4.622	12.513	15.130
30	27	0.067	2.565	2.405	5.463	4.751	12.796	16.281
31	28	0.027	2.593	2.421	5.594	4.880	13.070	17.461
32	29	0.046	2.638	2.508	5.742	5.007	13.333	18.668
33	30	0.079	2.717	2.569	5.923	5.133	13.587	19.901

FIGURE 9.32   Spreadsheet Model for Continuous Simulation Example

FIGURE 9.33   Dynamic Behavior of Variables in Medical Rate Simulation

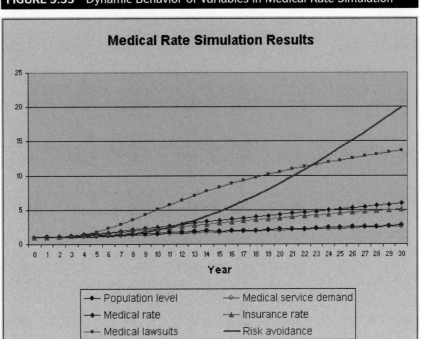

Questions and Problems

1. Explain how systems simulation models differ from Monte Carlo simulation models.
2. Describe the differences among activity-scanning, process-driven, and event-driven approaches to simulation.
3. Consider the following scenario. An airport having a single runway and a three-gate terminal is being proposed for a small city. Actual arrival and departure times will vary from their scheduled times anywhere from 10 minutes early to 60 minutes late due to a variety of factors such as weather, air traffic control, etc. On the runway, arriving aircraft have priority over departures. The time to taxi from the runway to the terminal after landing or from the terminal to the runway before a departure is 5 minutes. Landings and/or takeoffs must have a minimum separation of 2 minutes. Thus, a plane cannot depart if an arrival is scheduled within 2 minutes. Each arriving airplane waits for its assigned gate if it is currently occupied. Discuss how a simulation model might be developed using an activity-scanning, process-driven, or event-driven approach. What advantages and disadvantages would each approach have for this problem?
4. For the inventory model with lost sales, determine the best order quantity–reorder point combination to minimize average annual cost given the lead time distribution:

LEAD TIME	PROBABILITY
1	0.2
2	0.5
3	0.3

You will need to modify the worksheet formulas to incorporate this.
5. Using the *Lost Sales Inventory Model.xls* model, make cells E2 (order quantity) and E3 (reorder point) decision cells. Set the order quantity to range between 200 to 400 in increments of 25, and the reorder point from 200 to 400 in increments of 50. Find the optimal combination of order quantity and reorder point.
6. Using the back-order simulation model (*Back Order Inventory Model.xls*), determine the best order quantity–reorder point combination to minimize expected total annual costs.
7. Use the *Back Order Inventory Model.xls* model and set the annual holding cost, annual order cost, and annual shortage cost as forecast variables. Then create an overlay chart to examine the relative importance of these three costs to total annual inventory cost.
8. Modify the spreadsheet *Back Order Inventory Model.xls* to allow a fixed number, k, of back orders, at which point the remaining sales are lost.
9. Modify the spreadsheet *Back Order Inventory Model.xls* to reflect the situation in which 80 percent of the shortages are back orders and the rest are lost sales (where each is chosen randomly).
10. Describe the basic elements of waiting line systems and how they affect simulation models.
11. An airport ticket counter has a service rate of 180 per hour, exponentially distributed, with Poisson arrivals at the rate of 120 per hour.
    a. Find the operating characteristics of this system using the analytical formulas presented in this chapter.
    b. Determine the average number in queue, average waiting time, and percent idle time using the spreadsheet model. Use *Crystal Ball* to quantify

the variability in the simulation results and compute 90 percent confidence intervals for these statistics.

c. Compare the results from parts (a) and (b) and explain any differences.

12. Suppose that the arrival rate to a waiting line system is 10 customers per hour (exponentially distributed). Using simulation, analyze how the average waiting time changes as the service rate varies from 2 to 10 customers per hour (exponentially distributed) in increments of 2. (You can use *Queueing Simulation.xls.*)

13. A machine shop has a large number of machines that fail regularly. One repairperson is available to fix them. Each machine fails on average every 3 hours, with time between failures being exponential. Repair time has the distribution

TIME	PROBABILITY
15 min.	0.1
30 min.	0.2
45 min.	0.3
50 min.	0.4

Simulate the system to determine the average time that machines spend waiting for repair and the average percent of time the repairperson is busy. Obtain averages and 90 percent certainty ranges based on 1000 trials.

14. A trash collection company uses 15-ton trucks. The trucks leave the landfill at 5:00 A.M. and travel to their collection routes, pick up garbage until the truck is full, return to the landfill to dump the load, and repeat this process until 2:00 P.M. At 2:00 P.M. they return to the landfill, empty their load, and wait until the next morning. The amount of trash collected each hour varies according to the distribution:

TONS/QUARTER HOUR	PROBABILITY
0.25	0.05
0.50	0.25
0.75	0.30
1.00	0.25
1.25	0.15

Similarly, the time to travel to or from the landfill to the routes has the distribution

TIME (MIN.)	PROBABILITY
15	0.10
30	0.45
45	0.30
60	0.15

Develop a process-driven simulation model (both in flowchart and spreadsheet form). The model should simulate a full day's work. Replicate the simulation using *Crystal Ball,* and determine the productivity of the trucks (i.e., the amount of trash collected per day).

15. A small factory has two workstations: mold/trim and assemble/package. Jobs to the factory arrive at an exponentially distributed rate of 1 every 10 hours. Time at the mold/trim station is exponential, with a mean of 7 hours. Each job proceeds next to the assemble/package station and requires an average of 5 hours, again exponentially distributed. Based on 20 jobs and 1000 trials, estimate the average time in system, average waiting time at mold and trim, and average waiting time at assembly and packaging (along with 90 percent confidence intervals for each of the three statistics).

16. Modify the factory simulation in Problem 15 to include two molding/trim servers (both with the original time distribution).

17. Modify the *Queueing Simulation—Two-Server Model.xls* spreadsheet to include the calculation of the percent idle time for each server.

18. Donna Sweigart, an independent tax preparer, is getting ready for the oncoming season. She works in 5- or 6-hour blocks during which an average of 30 customers arrive. Arrivals are distributed exponentially, with an arrival rate of 5 per hour. Each tax season consists of 78 such sessions, beginning with 5 per week in mid-January and finishing with 7 per week in April. Revenue averages $50 per customer whose tax is prepared. Donna was swamped last year and feels that some good profit potential was lost. Customers who waited 15 minutes left and went to other tax preparers. As a result, she is considering other options:

> Option 1: She works alone, completing an average of 6 tax returns per hour, exponentially distributed.
> Option 2: She hires a partner, who would split the work as well as the revenue. This partner would have the same service rate of 6 returns per hour, again exponentially distributed.
> Option 3: Donna attends a class to make her more efficient and expects to be able to service 8 customers per hour. The cost of this course is $500.
> Option 4: Buy an expert system tax preparation package that takes 10 minutes to prepare each return (constant). The cost of this software is $1000.

The single-server system has the capacity of serving 6 customers per hour, exponentially distributed.

19. Define an *event*. How are events used to drive simulation models?

20. Explain the function of a calendar file and a control routine in event-driven simulations.

21. Arrival and processing times in a waiting line system are as follows:

ARRIVAL TIME	SERVICE TIME
116	20
202	25
214	51
235	3
329	24
336	4
442	58
553	80
580	10
696	29

Simulate the system manually using an event-driven approach. Show the status of the calendar file when the next event is to be selected, and summarize your results in a table.

22. A manufacturing department has three machines and one repair person. Machines fail after running approximately 3 hours, exponentially distributed. Repair times have the following distribution:

REPAIR TIME	PROBABILITY
15 min.	0.1
30 min.	0.2
45 min.	0.3
60 min.	0.3
75 min.	0.1

Simulate this situation using an event-driven approach to determine the average waiting time of machines awaiting repair.

23. Explain how continuous simulation and system dynamics models are constructed.

24. A fast-food restaurant has two parallel drive-through windows. Customers have a preference for window 1 if neither is occupied or if the waiting lines are equal. At all other times, the customer chooses the shortest line. After a customer has entered the system, he or she remains there until receiving service. However, the customer may change lines if he or she is the last customer in the line and the other line has two fewer cars. Because of the physical configuration of the system, only three cars may wait in each line. If the system is full, any arriving customers simply leave.
    a. Using only arrival, end-of-service, and end-of-simulation events, construct logical flowcharts for simulating this system using an event-driven approach.
    b. Modify this logic to have the model compute statistics on percent of time windows are occupied, average number of customers in the system, time between departures from each window, and average time the customer is in the system.

25. A small manufacturing facility produces custom-molded plastic parts. The process consists of two sequential operations: mold/trim and assemble/package. Jobs arrive at a mean rate of five jobs every 2 hours. For any job, the mold/trim process is exponential, with a mean of 15 minutes, and the assemble/package operation is also exponential, with a mean of 30 minutes. The mold/trim workstation has room to store only four jobs awaiting processing. The assemble/package station has room to store only two waiting jobs. Jobs are transported from the first to the second workstation in 10 minutes. If the mold/trim workstation is full when a job arrives, the job is subcontracted. If the assemble/package workstation is full when a job is completed at the mold/trim operation, the mold/trim operation cannot process any further jobs until space is freed up in the assemble/package area.
    a. Using events defined as arrivals at the facility, end-of-services at each workstation, and an end-of-simulation event, construct logical flowcharts for simulating this system using the event-driven approach.
    b. Generate arrival and service times on a spreadsheet, and manually conduct a simulation for 20 jobs. Assume that at the start of the simulation, both workstations are busy with end-of-services scheduled at time 1; 3 units are in the queue of the mold/trim area; and no units are waiting in the assemble/package area.

26. The time between demands for an item has a mean of 1/5th week, exponentially distributed. Ordering lead time is constant at 3 weeks. A periodic review policy has been suggested by which the inventory position is checked at 2-week intervals and an order is placed so that the inventory position at the time of ordering is increased to 36 if the inventory position is 18 or less. Any stockouts are lost sales.
    a. Define events and construct logical flowcharts for an event-driven simulation.
    b. Generate demands and manually simulate to determine average number of lost sales per week and average safety stock.
27. Consider the continuous system dynamics model of medical rates in Figure 9.31. A proposal has been made to improve the system by limiting medical rate and/or insurance rate increases to a maximum of 5 percent per year. Modify the spreadsheet to simulate each of the following scenarios and discuss the results:
    a. Limit medical rate increases to 5 percent per year only
    b. Limit insurance rate increases to 5 percent per year only
    c. Limit both medical rate and insurance rate increases to 5 percent per year
28. The "cobweb" model in economics assumes that the quantity demanded of a particular product in a specified time period depends on the price in that period. The quantity supplied depends on the price in the preceding period. Also, the market is assumed to be cleared at the end of each period. These assumptions can be expressed in the following equations:

$$S(t) = c + dP(t - 1) + v(t)$$
$$D(t) = a - bP(t - 1) + w(t)$$
$$P(t) = \frac{a - c - dP(t - 1) - v(t) + w(t)}{b} + u(t)$$

where $P(t)$ is the price in period t, $D(t)$ is the demand in period t, and $S(t)$ is the quantity supplied in period t. The variables $u(t)$, $v(t)$, and $w(t)$ are random variables with mean zero and some variance.
    a. Draw an influence diagram.
    b. Suppose that $a = 10{,}000$, $b = 2$, $c = 0$, $d = 0.1$, $u(t)$ is normal with variance 1, $v(t)$ is normal with variance 0.5, $w(t)$ is normal with variance 0.2, and $P(0) = 4738$. Simulate this model for 50 time periods. (Note that prices are not allowed to be less than zero.)
    c. Examine the effect on $P(t)$ of increasing the variance of $v(t)$ from 0.5 to 10 and from 10 to 15.
    d. Compare the results from part (b) with the assumptions that u, v, and w are fixed at zero.

C A S E

TRACWAY PRODUCTION/INVENTORY PLANNING

One of Tracway's manufacturing plants supplies various engine components to manufacturers of motorcycles on a just-in-time basis. Planned production capacity for one component is 100 units per shift. Because of fluctuations in customers' assembly operations, demand fluctuates and is historically between 80 and 130 units per day. To maintain sufficient inventory to meet its just-in-time commitments, Tracway's management is considering a policy to run a second shift if inventory falls to 50 or below. For the annual budget planning process, managers need to know how many additional shifts will be needed.

The fundamental equation that governs this process each day is

Ending inventory = Beginning inventory + Production − Demand

Develop a spreadsheet model to simulate 260 working days (one year), and count the number of additional shifts that are required. Use this variable as a forecast cell for a *Crystal Ball* simulation of the model to find a distribution of the number of shifts required over the next year. Then use the *Crystal Ball Bootstrap* tool to find the sampling distribution of the maximum number of additional shifts required, and compute a 95 percent confidence interval for this statistic. Summarize your findings in a report to the plant manager. ■

References

Brennan, J. E., B. L. Golden, and H. K. Rappoport, "Go with the Flow: Improving Red Cross Bloodmobiles Using Simulation Analysis," *Interfaces,* Vol. 22, No. 5, 1992, 1–13.

Johnson, L. C., and D. C. Montgomery, *Operations Research in Production Planning, Scheduling, and Inventory Control* (New York: John Wiley & Sons, 1974).

Orlicky, J., *Material Requirements Planning* (New York: McGraw-Hill, 1975).

Peterson, R., and E. A. Silver, *Decision Systems for Inventory Management and Production Planning,* 2nd ed. (New York: John Wiley & Sons, 1985).

Senge, P. M. *The Fifth Discipline: The Art and Practice of the Learning Organization* (New York: Doubleday Currency, 1990).

CHAPTER

10

SELECTION MODELS AND DECISION ANALYSIS

INTRODUCTION

Up to this point, we have discussed many different statistical approaches for gathering data, analyzing data, and converting it into useful information. This chapter focuses on using data and information to *make decisions,* particularly those that involve an element of risk. Managers make many kinds of decisions. Some of these decisions are repetitive, perhaps on an annual or quarterly basis. These might include selecting new employees from a pool of applicants or selecting specific business improvement projects from a pool of proposals. These types of decisions have little financial impact and would not be considered very risky. Other decisions, such as deciding where to locate a plant or warehouse or determining whether to pursue a major investment opportunity commit the firm to spending large sums of money. These usually are one-time decisions and generally involve a higher level of risk because of uncertain data and imperfect information.

For example, suppose that a company is considering a proposal to develop an Internet-based sales system. This system will involve substantial money for development, as well as for daily operations. Although projections suggest that the revenue impact can be substantial, this venture entails a considerable amount of risk, as the future revenues are highly uncertain. Some issues the firm must consider include what criteria should be used to evaluate this project, how risk can be quantified and assessed, and how a decision should be chosen.

Business decisions usually fall into one of four categories:

1. Decisions involving the acceptance or rejection of a proposal or project, for instance, a new marketing campaign, acquisition of another company, or the purchase of a new machine. These decisions are usually based on whether or not the proposal or project meets some acceptance criteria such as return on investment or some measure of value added.
2. Decisions among a set of non–mutually exclusive alternatives (i.e., of which more than one may be chosen), for example, selecting research and development projects or choosing stocks or other investment instruments to create a portfolio. These decisions are usually made by ranking the alternatives and selecting those that meet threshold criteria or budgetary limitations.
3. Decisions involving the selection of the best decision among a set of mutually exclusive alternatives, for example, the choice of one marketing campaign among four competing proposals, selecting a new hire from a pool of candidates, or selecting a location to build a new plant. These decisions are often made by ranking the alternatives according to some criteria and selecting the best.
4. Decisions involving uncertainty — those involving a sequence of choices and chance events in which the objective is to choose the best strategy; that is, a set of choices that are contingent upon the occurrence of chance events. These decisions are usually made by computing the expected value associated with each choice.

In this chapter we present various approaches for evaluating and making decisions using simple "what if?" analysis and more complex simulation models and decision analysis techniques. Specifically, we will discuss

- Common types of decisions: acceptance/rejection of a single proposal, selecting from a set of mutually exclusive alternatives, selecting non–mutually exclusive alternatives, and decisions involving probabilistic events
- Decision criteria used to evaluate these decisions, including net present value, internal rate of return, expected value, risk to return ratio, and opportunity loss
- Single and multistage decision trees for modeling decision problems

DECISIONS INVOLVING A SINGLE ALTERNATIVE

Most business ventures are evaluated on the basis of financial criteria. Two common criteria for evaluating decisions for which financial impacts are the most important are *net present value* (*NPV*) and *internal rate of return* (*IRR*). We will review the basic concepts of net present value to provide a foundation for our discussion of decision analysis approaches; more complete discussions can be found in basic finance texts, for example, Gallagher and Andrew (1997).

Net present value measures the worth of a stream of cash flows, taking into account the time value of money. That is, a cash flow of F dollars t time periods in the future is worth $F/(1 + i)^t$ dollars today, where i is the **discount rate,** or required rate of return from an investment. The discount rate reflects the opportunity costs of spending funds now versus achieving a return through another investment, as well as the risks associated with not receiving returns until a later time. The sum of the present values of all cash flows over a stated time horizon is the net present value:

$$NPV = \sum_{t=0}^{n} \frac{F_t}{(1 + i)^t}$$

where F_t = cash flow in period t. A positive NPV means that the investment will provide added value since the projected return exceeds the discount rate. Projects with a negative NPV should be rejected.

The **internal rate of return (IRR)** is the estimated rate of return for a project. It is the discount rate that makes the total present value of all cash flows sum to zero:

$$\sum_{t=0}^{n} \frac{F_t}{(1 + IRR)^t} = 0$$

IRR is often used to compare a project against a predetermined *hurdle rate,* a rate of return required by management to accept a project. If IRR is greater than the hurdle rate, the project is accepted; otherwise, it is rejected. Net present value and internal rate of return can be computed in Excel using standard functions (see the *Excel Note: Using the NPV and IRR Functions*).

We assume that expenditures and operating expenses will be incurred at the end of every month and that revenues are collected at the end of every month. The company's discount rate is 7 percent per year. Figure 10.1 shows a spreadsheet model for cash flows expected from the project. The formula in cell E20, the net present value of the net profit, is =NPV($B$3,E7:E11)+E6. Note that the initial investment is not included in the NPV calculation because it is not a future cash flow value. While the proposal appears to be highly profitable by the fourth year, the net present value is only $11,628.23 when the time value of money is factored in. However, the IRR is 11.72%, indicating a good return on the investment.

Sensitivity Analysis

One of the limitations of any spreadsheet model is that it is based on a fixed set of assumptions. In fact, these assumptions are what a decision model consists of—relationships between inputs that describe the modeler's opinion. For example, the discount rate is most likely only an estimate, since the company's true cost of capital may

---

EXCEL NOTE

USING THE NPV AND IRR FUNCTIONS

The Excel function *NPV(rate,value1,value2, . . .)* calculates the net present value of an investment by using a discount rate and a series of future payments (negative values) and income (positive values). *Rate* is the rate of discount over the length of one period (i), and *value1, value2, . . .* are 1 to 29 arguments representing the payments and income. The values must be equally spaced in time and are assumed to occur at the end of each period. The NPV investment begins one period before the date of the *value1* cash flow and ends with the last cash flow in the list. The NPV calculation is based on *future* cash flows. If the first cash flow (such as an initial investment) occurs at the beginning of the first period, then it must be added to the NPV result and *not* included in the function arguments.

The Excel function for internal rate of return is *IRR(values, guess)*. *Values* represents the series of cash flows (at least one of which must be positive and one of which must be negative). *Guess* is a number believed close to the value of IRR that is used to facilitate the mathematical algorithm used to find the solution. Occasionally, the function might not converge to a solution; in those cases, you should try a different value for *guess*. In most cases, the value of *guess* can be omitted from the function.

	A	B	C	D	E
1	Internet Project Proposal				
2					
3	Discount rate	7%			
4		Development	Operating		
5	Month	Expense	Expense	Revenue	Net Profit
6	Initial investment	$ 50,000.00	$ -	$ -	$ (50,000.00)
7	Year 1	$ 10,000.00	$ 10,000.00	$ 5,000.00	$ (15,000.00)
8	Year 2	$ -	$ 10,000.00	$ 15,000.00	$ 5,000.00
9	Year 3	$ -	$ 10,000.00	$ 25,000.00	$ 15,000.00
10	Year 4	$ -	$ 10,000.00	$ 50,000.00	$ 40,000.00
11	Year 5	$ -	$ 10,000.00	$ 50,000.00	$ 40,000.00
12					
13	Net Present Values	$59,345.79	$41,001.97	$111,975.99	$11,628.23
14					
15	IRR	11.72%			

FIGURE 10.1   Spreadsheet for Evaluating Internet Project Proposal

change in the future, and we might like to know what would happen if this assumption were changed. **Sensitivity analysis** involves changing key input values and examining critical outputs, with the purpose of identifying how much change from assumed inputs would matter with respect to the outputs of interest. Of course, one approach would be to change the rate in cell B3 and recalculate the spreadsheet. However, this would have to be done for each value. A better approach is to use an Excel data table, which we introduced in Chapter 1.

Figure 10.2 shows a one-way data table for examining the sensitivity of the discount rate to NPV for the Internet project proposal. We see that a change in the discount rate by a quarter percent changes the NPV by approximately $700 (the change is not quite linear). Should it increase substantially (for example, because of increases in the discount rate by the Federal Reserve), the company might want to rethink this decision.

Two-way data tables allow you to investigate simultaneous impacts of two key input data values in decision models. Figure 10.3 shows a two-way data table for simultaneously changing the initial investment and discount rate assumptions. This analysis shows that the company can tolerate higher values of the discount rate if it

Discount Rate	$11,628.23
5.00%	$17,456.14
5.25%	$16,694.43
5.50%	$15,942.50
5.75%	$15,200.21
6.00%	$14,467.40
6.25%	$13,743.94
6.50%	$13,029.68
6.75%	$12,324.49
7.00%	$11,628.23
7.25%	$10,940.76
7.50%	$10,261.95
7.75%	$9,591.68
8.00%	$8,929.81
8.25%	$8,276.23
8.50%	$7,630.80
8.75%	$6,993.41
9.00%	$6,363.95

FIGURE 10.2 One-Way Data Table for Evaluating Discount Rate Scenarios

			Discount Rate			
$11,628.23		5%	6%	7%	8%	9%
Initial	$40,000.00	$27,456.14	$24,467.40	$21,628.23	$18,929.81	$16,363.95
Investment	$45,000.00	$22,456.14	$19,467.40	$16,628.23	$13,929.81	$11,363.95
	$50,000.00	$17,456.14	$14,467.40	$11,628.23	$8,929.81	$6,363.95
	$55,000.00	$12,456.14	$9,467.40	$6,628.23	$3,929.81	$1,363.95
	$60,000.00	$7,456.14	$4,467.40	$1,628.23	-$1,070.19	-$3,636.05

FIGURE 10.3 Two-Way Data Table for Initial Investment and Discount Rate

could reduce the initial investment in the project. Such analyses provide useful information to consider in making alternative decisions. In reality, however, not only are the initial investment and the discount rate uncertain but so are all the cash flows in the model. Such assumptions can be analyzed using Monte Carlo simulation, as discussed in Chapter 8.

DECISIONS INVOLVING NON–MUTUALLY EXCLUSIVE ALTERNATIVES

If several non–mutually exclusive alternatives are being considered, various ranking criteria, such as return on investment (ROI) or more general benefit/cost ratios, provide a basis for evaluation and selection. ROI is computed as

$$ROI = \frac{\text{Annual Revenue} - \text{Annual Costs}}{\text{Initial Investment}}$$

Proposals are typically ranked in order of highest ROI first and are selected until total initial investment exceeds a budget. Benefit/cost analysis is based on examining the ratios of expected benefits to expected costs. In business applications, benefits can usually be quantified as revenues or cost savings. Both benefits and costs should be converted to present values in order to account for the time value of money. Ratios greater than 1.0 indicate that a proposal should be adopted if sufficient resources exist to support it.

To illustrate the application of benefit/cost analysis, we will consider the evaluation of potential technology projects to improve operations in an information systems department. In the current period, 13 projects have come before the finance committee, which allocates the project development budget. The proposals are shown in Figure 10.4, with estimated benefits consisting of added revenue and cost reduction as well as estimated costs, all computed as net present values.

	A	B	C	D	E
1	Information System Project Proposals				
2	Project	Cost	Revenue Impact	Cost Reduction	ROI
3	A1	$175,600.00	$ -	$ 200,358.00	1.14
4	A2	$126,512.00	$ 422,580.00	$ (103,420.00)	2.52
5	A3	$198,326.00	$ 415,625.00	$ (226,413.00)	0.95
6	B4	$421,618.00	$ -	$ 486,312.00	1.15
7	B5	$322,863.00	$ -	$ 456,116.00	1.41
8	B6	$398,810.00	$ -	$ 508,213.00	1.27
9	B7	$212,506.00	$ -	$ 356,067.00	1.68
10	C8	$813,620.00	$ 416,283.00	$ 386,229.00	0.99
11	C9	$850,418.00	$ 583,260.00	$ 398,014.00	1.15
12	D10	$522,615.00	$ 916,426.00	$ (155,106.00)	1.46
13	D11	$486,283.00	$ 816,420.00	$ (103,210.00)	1.47
14	D12	$683,407.00	$ 758,420.00	$ (75,896.00)	1.00
15	D13	$722,813.00	$ 950,128.00	$ (120,063.00)	1.15

FIGURE 10.4 Information System Project Proposals

Projects are coded by the submitting department. The A-series projects involve application of technology in marketing products. The B-series projects are in the production area, with no expected impact on increased revenues, but substantial reductions in operating expenses. C-series projects combine revenue increases with cost reductions, but involve heavy expenses in project implementation. D-series projects are expected to have strong impact on increased revenue, but also increased operating expenses.

Benefit/cost ratios provide a way to evaluate these diverse projects. First, those projects with negative net present values—projects A3, C8, and D12—do not pay for their implementation costs, and therefore can be eliminated. Thus, benefit/cost ratios less than 1 correspond to negative NPVs. Suppose that the company sets a benefit/cost threshold of 1.2, meaning that project benefits must be at least 20 percent higher than costs. The following projects meet this criterion:

Rank	Project	Benefit/Cost Ratio	Implementation Cost
1	A2	2.52	$126,512
2	B7	1.68	$212,506
3	D11	1.47	$486,283
4	D10	1.46	$522,615
5	B5	1.41	$322,863
6	B6	1.27	$398,810

This ranking can be used a number of ways. If sufficient budget is available to cover the implementation costs, all projects could be adopted, as they all satisfy management's threshold criteria. If a budget is limited, the projects could be funded in order of benefit/cost ratio until the budget ran out. Using this approach, any residual budget might be used to fund another project that ranks lower. Benefit/cost analysis is often used in evaluating social projects where benefits generally cannot be quantified (such as improved police protection). Even in business, such intangible benefits as customer goodwill, obtaining market share, or having added flexibility in production may be important factors in a decision. Nevertheless, as a quantitative technique, benefits need to be converted into some numerical measure. When this is viable, this approach can be useful when comparing multiple alternatives.

DECISIONS INVOLVING MUTUALLY EXCLUSIVE ALTERNATIVES

Many decisions involve a choice among several mutually exclusive alternatives. Some examples would be decisions about purchasing automobiles, choosing colleges, selecting mortgage instruments, investing money, introducing new product, locating plants, and choosing suppliers, to name just a few. When only one alternative can be selected from among many, the best choice can usually be identified by evaluating each alternative according to some criterion.

Decision alternatives represent the choices that a decision maker can make, for instance, locating a factory from five potential sites or choosing one of three corporate health plan options. Generating viable alternatives might involve some prescreening (perhaps using optimization models that we discuss in the final two chapters of this book). Managers must ensure that they have considered all possible options so that the "best" one will be included in the list. This often requires a good deal of creativity to define unusual options that might not normally be considered.

Decision makers also must have well-defined criteria on which to evaluate potential options. Decision criteria might be to maximize discounted net profits or social benefits, or to minimize costs or some measure of loss. Net present value and internal rate of return are popular criteria for capital budgeting decisions. To choose among competing projects, simply compute the NPV or IRR for each project and select the best.

Scoring Models

For decisions involving multiple criteria, simple scoring models are often used. A **scoring model** is a quantitative assessment of a decision alternative's value based on a set of attributes. Usually, each attribute is characterized by several levels, and a score is assigned to each level that reflects the relative benefits of that level. For example, in evaluating new product ideas, some attributes might include

1. Product development time

LEVEL	SCORE
a. Less than 6 months	+5
b. 6 months to 1 year	+3
c. 1–2 years	0
d. 2–3 years	−3
e. more than 2 years	−5

2. Competitive environment

a. None	+5
b. Few minor competitors	+3
c. Many minor competitors	0
d. Few major competitors	−3
e. Many major competitors	−5

3. Return on investment

a. 30% or more	+5
b. 25–30%	+3
c. 15–25%	0
d. 10–15%	−3
e. below 15%	−5

A score would be assigned to each attribute (which might be weighted), and the overall score would be used as a basis for selection.

A more formal approach to evaluating decisions involving multiple criteria is called the *analytic hierarchy process*, which we discuss next.

The Analytic Hierarchy Process

The **analytic hierarchy process (AHP)** is a technique developed by Thomas L. Saaty for incorporating multiple criteria into decision making. AHP consists of four major steps:

1. Modeling the decision problem by breaking it down into a hierarchy of interrelated decision elements: decision criteria and decision alternatives
2. Developing judgmental preferences for the decision alternatives for each criterion and judgmental importance of the decision criteria by pairwise comparisons

3. Computing relative priorities for each of the decision elements through a set of numerical calculations
4. Aggregating the relative priorities to arrive at a priority ranking of the decision alternatives

We will discuss each of these steps and illustrate them using an example.

AHP requires breaking down a complex multicriteria decision problem into a hierarchy of levels. The top level corresponds to the overall objective of the decision process. The second level represents the major criteria (which may be further broken down into subcriteria at the next level). The last level corresponds to the decision alternatives. This is illustrated in Figure 10.5.

To better illustrate this process and the subsequent calculations, we introduce a simple example involving the selection of a supplier from among three competing alternatives. This becomes the top level in the decision hierarchy in Figure 10.5. For most companies, suppliers are often selected on the basis of three criteria: quality, price, and service. In this example, we will assume that there are no subcriteria. Finally, at the third level, we list the decision alternatives, namely, the suppliers. Because each criterion will affect the overall objective, and each supplier is evaluated on each criterion, we connect the elements between successive levels to indicate this. The hierarchical model of this decision problem is shown in Figure 10.6.

After the decision problem is modeled in this hierarchical fashion, the decision maker must develop a set of comparison matrices that numerically define the relative preference of each decision alternative with respect to each criterion and also the relative importance of each criterion. This is done by comparing the elements in a pairwise fashion and assigning a numerical score that expresses preference between every two elements. Usually, the following scale is used:

PREFERENCE SCORE	DEFINITION
1	Equally important or preferred
3	Moderately important or preferred
5	Strongly important or preferred
7	Very strongly important or preferred
9	Extremely important or preferred

FIGURE 10.5   Hierarchical Representation of a Decision Problem

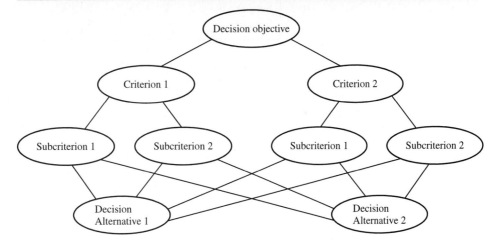

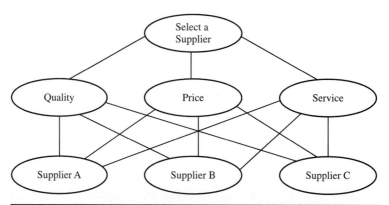

FIGURE 10.6 Decision Hierarchy for Supplier Selection Problem

Intermediate values between each category may be used when the decision maker feels that a comparison falls between two categories. For example, if a decision maker feels that one element is more than strongly preferred but not quite very strongly preferred, then a value of 6 would be used.

In the supplier selection decision problem, we first compare each supplier on each of the three criteria. Consider the criterion of quality. Since there are three suppliers, we must compare A with B, B with C, and A with C. When queried as to relative preferences for supplier A and supplier B with respect to quality, suppose the purchasing manager states that supplier B is somewhere between equally and moderately preferred to A, corresponding to a numerical value of 2. Comparing supplier C to A results in a score of 6, with C being between strongly and very strongly preferred to A. In comparing B with C, the manager indicates that supplier C is strongly preferred to supplier B (a score of 5).

We express these data in a matrix called a **comparison matrix,** in which the value in row i and column j is the preference score of the element of row i when compared with the element in column j. Since each element should be equally preferred to itself, we assign a 1 along the diagonal, as shown below.

Quality	Supplier A	Supplier B	Supplier C
Supplier A	1	—	—
Supplier B	2	1	—
Supplier C	6	5	1

We may complete this matrix by making the following assumption: If decision element i is n times preferred to or as important as j, then j is $1/n$ times preferred to or as important as i. Thus, if the preference value of B is 2 when compared to A, the preference value of A is 1/2 when compared to B. The complete preference matrix is shown here.

Quality	Supplier A	Supplier B	Supplier C
Supplier A	1	1/2	1/6
Supplier B	2	1	1/5
Supplier C	6	5	1

Therefore, it is only necessary to complete either the lower triangular or upper triangular portion of the matrix. Using the same principles, the purchasing manager would develop preference matrices for price and service, as follows:

Price	Supplier A	Supplier B	Supplier C
Supplier A	1	4	5
Supplier B	1/4	1	3
Supplier C	1/5	1/3	1

Service	Supplier A	Supplier B	Supplier C
Supplier A	1	2	4
Supplier B	1/2	1	5
Supplier C	1/4	1/5	1

Finally, the manager must rate the importance of each criterion with respect to the others. The matrix is shown next; it shows that quality is moderately more important than price, quality is strongly more important than service, and price is moderately more important than service.

Criteria	Quality	Price	Service
Quality	1	3	5
Price	1/3	1	3
Service	1/5	1/3	1

The next step in the AHP analysis is to perform various calculations to determine the priority of each of the decision elements using the pairwise comparison information. The mathematical basis for this approach is beyond the scope of this book; however, a simplified approximation yields very good results. This procedure is explained as follows:

1. Sum each column of the pairwise comparison matrix. Then divide each element of that column by the column sum. The result is the *normalized comparison matrix*.
2. Compute the average of each row of the normalized comparison matrix. These averages provide the relative priority of the decision elements corresponding to the rows of the matrix.

The pairwise comparison matrix for quality (converted to decimal representation) and column sums are

Quality	Supplier A	Supplier B	Supplier C
Supplier A	1	0.5	0.167
Supplier B	2	1	0.2
Supplier C	6	5	1
Sum	9	6.5	1.367

If we divide each element in the matrix by the column sum, we obtain the normalized comparison matrix:

Quality	Supplier A	Supplier B	Supplier C
Supplier A	0.111	0.077	0.122
Supplier B	0.222	0.154	0.146
Supplier C	0.667	0.769	0.732

Averaging the rows yields the priorities for each supplier:

SUPPLIER	ROW AVERAGE
A	0.103
B	0.174
C	0.723

We see that the most preferred supplier on the basis of quality is supplier C; supplier B is second, and supplier A is third. This is not surprising as you examine the original quality comparison matrix. We may record these numbers on the links of the hierarchy network as shown in Figure 10.7. This will be useful in developing the final ranking of the decision alternatives.

A critical issue with AHP is the consistency of judgments specified in the pairwise comparison matrices. For example, if you know that A is strongly preferred to B (5), and B is moderately preferred to C (3), then you would expect that A would be at least strongly preferred to C (7 or higher). By considering only one pair at a time, it is easy for the decision maker to specify preference scores that are not consistent with such a chain of relationships, particularly as the number of decision elements increases. Fortunately, AHP provides a measure of the consistency of pairwise comparative judgments. This measure, called the *consistency ratio,* indicates when it might be desirable to reconsider and revise the original judgments in the comparison matrices. The consistency ratio is computed in the following manner:

1. Multiply each column of the original pairwise comparison matrix by the relative priority of the decision element corresponding to that column, and sum these "weighted columns."
2. Divide each element of the weighted column by the corresponding priority value of that decision element.
3. Average the values computed in step 2; this is denoted as λ_{max}.

FIGURE 10.7 Recording Priorities on the Decision Hierarchy

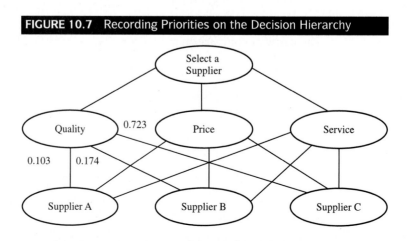

TABLE 10.1
Random Index
Values

n	RI
3	0.58
4	0.90
5	1.12
6	1.24
7	1.32
8	1.41

4. The consistency index (CI) is defined as

$$CI = \frac{\lambda_{max} - n}{n - 1}$$

where n is the number of decision elements in the comparison.

5. Compute the consistency ratio (CR) by dividing CI by a random index, RI, found in Table 10.1:

$$CR = CI/RI$$

A consistency ratio of 0.10 or less is considered acceptable and indicates good consistency of the pairwise comparative judgments. If the consistency ratio is greater than 0.10, then the decision maker should reexamine the pairwise comparisons.

We will compute the consistency ratio for the quality comparison matrix. We first multiply each column by the relative priority of the decision element corresponding to that column and sum the results:

$$\begin{pmatrix} 1 \\ 2 \\ 6 \end{pmatrix}(0.103) + \begin{pmatrix} 0.5 \\ 1 \\ 5 \end{pmatrix}(0.174) + \begin{pmatrix} 0.167 \\ 0.2 \\ 1 \end{pmatrix}(0.723) = \begin{pmatrix} 0.311 \\ 0.525 \\ 2.213 \end{pmatrix}$$

Since 0.311 corresponds to supplier A, 0.525 to supplier B, and 2.213 to supplier C, we divide these numbers by the priority values corresponding to these suppliers:

Supplier A: 0.311/0.103 = 3.008
Supplier B: 0.525/0.174 = 3.017
Supplier C: 2.213/0.7317 = 3.063

The average of these values is called λ_{max}:

$$\lambda_{max} = (3.008 + 3.017 + 3.063)/3 = 3.029$$

Then

$$CI = \frac{3.029 - 3}{3 - 1} = 0.015$$

With $n = 3$, RI = 0.58, we have

$$CR = 0.0146/0.58 = 0.025$$

Since CR is less than 0.10, we have a very good consistency among the pairwise comparisons.

The final step in the AHP is ranking the decision alternatives, taking into account all the decision elements of the hierarchy. This is computed by multiplying the importance of each decision criterion by the priority of each alternative with respect to that criterion and summing across all criteria. Figure 10.8 shows an Excel worksheet designed to perform all the AHP computations for the supplier selection problem. The relative priorities and importance values are found in column J of the spreadsheet. We see that for price, supplier A is preferred (0.665), followed by suppliers B (0.231) and C (0.104), respectively. For service, supplier A is preferred (0.532), followed by suppliers B (0.366) and C (0.101). When comparing the criteria with each other, we see that quality is the most important (0.633), followed by price (0.260) and service (0.106).

	A	B	C	D	E	F	G	H	I	J	K	L	M	N	O
1	Supplier Selection Decision Model														
2	Analytic Hierarchy Process														
3															
4	n =	3													
5	Quality Comparison Matrix					Normalized Matrices				Priorities		Consistency Ratio Calculations			
6		A	B	C			A	B	C			Weighted Sum			
7	A	1.000	0.500	0.167		A	0.111	0.077	0.122	0.103		0.311	3.009		
8	B	2.000	1.000	0.200		B	0.222	0.154	0.146	0.174		0.525	3.017		
9	C	6.000	5.000	1.000		C	0.667	0.769	0.732	0.722		2.213	3.064		
10	SUM	9.000	6.500	1.367								Lambda max	3.030	CI	0.015
11														CR	0.026
12	Comparison Matrix														
13		A	B	C			A	B	C						
14	A	1.000	4.000	5.000		A	0.690	0.750	0.556	0.665		2.109	3.170		
15	B	0.250	1.000	3.000		B	0.172	0.188	0.333	0.231		0.709	3.067		
16	C	0.200	0.333	1.000		C	0.138	0.062	0.111	0.104		0.314	3.022		
17	Sum	1.450	5.333	9.000								Lambda max	3.087	CI	0.043
18														CR	0.075
19	Comparison Matrix														
20		A	B	C			A	B	C						
21	A	1.000	2.000	4.000		A	0.571	0.625	0.400	0.532		1.671	3.141		
22	B	0.500	1.000	5.000		B	0.286	0.313	0.500	0.366		1.141	3.117		
23	C	0.250	0.200	1.000		C	0.143	0.063	0.100	0.102		0.308	3.026		
24	Sum	1.750	3.200	10.000								Lambda max	3.095	CI	0.047
25														CR	0.082
26	Comparison Matrix														
27		Quality	Price	Service			Quality	Price	Service						
28	Quality	1.000	3.000	5.000		Quality	0.652	0.692	0.556	0.633		1.945	3.071		
29	Price	0.333	1.000	3.000		Price	0.217	0.231	0.333	0.260		0.790	3.032		
30	Service	0.200	0.333	1.000		Service	0.130	0.077	0.111	0.106		0.320	3.011		
31	Sum	1.533	4.333	9.000								Lambda max	3.038	CI	0.019
32														CR	0.033
33										Priority Ranking					
34									A	0.295					
35									B	0.209					
36									C	0.495					

FIGURE 10.8   AHP Excel Model

To compute the priorities of the decision alternatives, we multiply the criterion importance value by the relative priority for that criterion and add:

Supplier	Quality Weighting		Price Weighting		Service Weighting		
A	(0.633)(0.103)	+	(0.260)(0.665)	+	(0.106)(0.532)	=	0.295
B	(0.633)(0.174)	+	(0.260)(0.231)	+	(0.106)(0.366)	=	0.209
C	(0.633)(0.723)	+	(0.260)(0.104)	+	(0.106)(0.102)	=	0.495

FIGURE 10.9   Ranking Decision Alternatives Using AHP

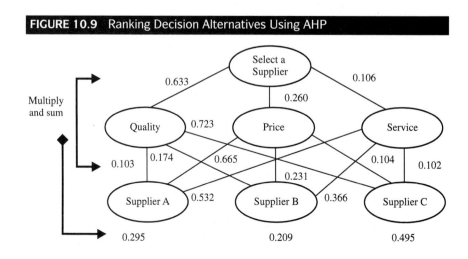

We see that supplier C is the preferred supplier. Figure 10.9 shows how these calculations follow from the decision hierarchy diagram.

DECISIONS INVOLVING UNCERTAINTY

Many decisions involve selection from a small set of mutually exclusive alternatives with uncertain consequences. For example, an investor might have three types of investments from which to choose, but only wants to select one:

1. Aggressive stock fund
2. Balanced stock and bond fund
3. Pure bond fund

Once a decision is made, one of a set of possible outcomes, or chance events, occurs. These events provide the basis for evaluating risks associated with decisions and may be quantitative or qualitative. For instance, in selecting the size of a new factory, a company needs to consider the future demand for the product. The demand might be expressed quantitatively in sales units or dollars. If you are planning a spring break vacation to Florida in January, you might define uncertain weather-related outcomes qualitatively: sunny and warm, sunny and cold, rainy and warm, or rainy and cold. For our investor, the outcomes, or events, that might result are

- Market rises
- Market falls
- Market remains stable

Considerable uncertainty usually exists about the events, and this uncertainty can be expressed as a probability of occurrence. For instance, the investor might also estimate that based on current economic conditions, the probability that the market will rise is 0.5, the probability that it will fall is 0.2, and the probability that it will remain stable is 0.3.

Finally, to provide the basis for making a decision, a decision maker needs to estimate the return or loss—generally called a **payoff**—associated with making a particular decision and having a particular event occur. Our investor might determine that, over a specified period of time, the payoffs associated with each decision and event are

Decision \ Event	Market Rises	Market Falls	Market Stable
Aggressive	$1000	−$1500	$0
Balanced	$600	−$500	$200
Bond	$200	$300	$100

Decisions, events, probabilities of occurrence of events, and payoffs provide a complete characterization of a decision problem.

Expected Monetary Value and Risk

A decision criterion used in these types of problems is **expected monetary value (EMV)**, that is, we compute the expected payoff for each decision based on the probabilities that the chance events will occur, and select the alternative with the best expected value. *PHStat* provides tools for computing EMV and other decision information (see the *PHStat Note: Using the Expected Monetary Value Tool*). From the results in Figure 10.11, we see that choosing the balanced fund has the best expected monetary value, $260, given the assumptions made about the probabilities of the events.

PHSTAT NOTE

USING THE EXPECTED MONETARY VALUE TOOL

From the *PHStat* menu, select *Decision Making* and then *Expected Monetary Value*. The dialog box is shown in Figure 10.10; you need only specify the number of actions (alternatives) and events. *PHStat* creates a worksheet in which you must enter your data (see Figure 10.11). You may customize the worksheet to change the row and column labels in the Probabilities & Payoffs Table for your specific problem (this is similar to the chi-square application discussed in Chapter 4). After you enter the data, the expected values and other statistical information are automatically computed. The *Expected Opportunity Loss* option in the dialog box will be discussed shortly.

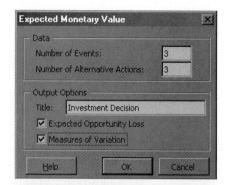

FIGURE 10.10 *PHStat* Dialog Box for *Expected Monetary Value*

FIGURE 10.11 Completed *PHStat* Worksheet for *Expected Monetary Value*

	A	B	C	D	E	F
1	Investment Decision					
2						
3	Probabilities & Payoffs Table:					
4		P	Aggressive	Balanced	Bond	
5	Market rises	0.5	$1,000	$600	$200	
6	Market falls	0.2	-$1,500	-$500	$300	
7	Market stable	0.3	$0	$200	$100	
8						
9		Statistics for:	Aggressive	Balanced	Bond	
10	Expected Monetary Value		200	260	190	
11		Variance	910000	174400	4900	
12	Standard Deviation		953.939201	417.61226	70	
13	Coefficient of Variation		4.76969601	1.606201	0.368421	
14	Return to Risk Ratio		0.20965697	0.62258709	2.714286	
15						
16	Opportunity Loss Table:					
17		Optimum	Optimum		Alternatives	
18		Action	Profit	Aggressive	Balanced	Bond
19	Market rises	Aggressive	1000	0	400	800
20	Market falls	Bond	300	1800	800	0
21	Market stable	Balanced	200	200	0	100
22				Aggressive	Balanced	Bond
23	Expected Opportunity Loss			420	360	430
24					EVPI	

One of the problems with expected value decision making is that it is predicated on the assumption of a long-run average; that is, the expected value is the result of many repeated decisions. For example, a pharmaceutical manufacturer can afford to base a product development decision on expected values even though perhaps only a small percentage will be commercially successful because it develops hundreds of new

TABLE 10.2 Illustration of Risk Differences

Potential Returns

Project A	Project B
$4,000	
$5,000	
$6,000	$6,000
$7,000	$7,000
$8,000	$8,000
$9,000	$9,000
$10,000	$10,000

(a)

Potential Returns and Probabilities

Project A	Probability	Project B	Probability
$4,000	0.02		
$5,000	0.03		
$6,000	0.05	$6,000	0.20
$7,000	0.10	$7,000	0.20
$8,000	0.70	$8,000	0.20
$9,000	0.08	$9,000	0.20
$10,000	0.02	$10,000	0.20

(b)

drugs every year. For an individual who is considering starting his or her own business, the decision is a one-time choice, so risk must be considered.

Risk analysis focuses on understanding the degree of uncertainty in a situation; the higher the uncertainty, the greater the risk. As a simple example, suppose we know the possible returns of two projects as given in Table 10.2(a). Can you tell which is riskier? You might think that since Project A has a wider range of possible returns, particularly on the low side, it must be riskier than Project B. Project A has an expected value of only $7750 as compared to Project B's expected value of $8000.

However, suppose you know the probability distribution of the returns for each project, as shown in Table 10.2(b). There is much less likelihood of achieving a return below $8000 for Project A than for Project B. On this basis, we might conclude that Project B is riskier than Project A because we would be more uncertain of the outcome—in fact, there is an 80 percent chance of realizing a return of $8000 or more from Project A but only a 60 percent chance for Project B. Using the formula for the variance of a random variable we presented in Chapter 3, we can compute the standard deviation of returns to be $993.7 for Project A and $1414.2 for Project B. When the expected values are roughly comparable, standard deviation is an important measure of risk. The higher the standard deviation, the greater will be the chances that the actual outcome will differ from the expected value, leading to outcomes that might not be acceptable. In Figure 10.11, we see that the aggressive stock fund has the highest standard deviation, and therefore, is the riskiest from this perspective.

Another key measure of risk is the **coefficient of variation,** defined in Chapter 2 as the ratio of the standard deviation to the mean. This is particularly useful when comparing alternatives that have different expected values. For the two projects we are considering, the respective coefficients of variation are

$$\text{Project A: CV} = 993.7/7750 = 0.1282$$
$$\text{Project B: CV} = 1414.2/8000 = 0.1768$$

Although Project B has a higher expected return, it is also relatively more risky since the coefficient of variation is larger.

The **return-to-risk ratio** is simply the reciprocal of the coefficient of variation, that is, the expected value divided by the standard deviation. While it provides the same information as the coefficient of variation, it is easier to understand because its measure is similar to the decision maker's objective. That is, if the objective is to maximize return, a higher return-to-risk ratio is often considered better. In the preceding example, the return-to-risk ratio for Project A is 7.80, while the ratio for Project B is 5.656. On a risk-adjusted basis, Project A provides a higher return.

Applying these ideas to the example in Figure 10.11, the return-to-risk ratio of the balanced fund is 0.623. Although the pure bond fund has a smaller expected value, its return-to-risk ratio is much higher, 2.71, indicating that this decision is relatively less risky. We can understand this by examining the payoffs. For the pure bond fund, the investor cannot lose any money. However, with the balanced fund, if the market falls, the investor stands to lose $500. Even more risk exists with the aggressive stock fund—a chance of losing $1500—and is verified by the low return-to-risk ratio. An investor who has a low tolerance for risk might wish to forego a higher expected return for the comfort of a lower risk.

Analysis of Portfolio Risk

Concepts of expected value decisions and risk may be applied to the analysis of portfolios. A **portfolio** is simply a collection of assets, such as stocks, bonds, or other investments, that are managed as a group. In constructing a portfolio, one usually seeks to maximize expected return while minimizing risk. The expected return of a two–asset portfolio is computed as

$$E[P] = wE[X] + (1 - w)E[Y]$$

where

w = fraction of portfolio for asset X
and $(1 - w)$ = fraction of portfolio for asset Y.

Risk depends on the correlation among assets in a portfolio. This can be seen by examining the formula for the standard deviation of a two-asset portfolio:

$$\sigma_P = \sqrt{w\sigma_X^2 + (1 - w)\sigma_Y^2 + 2w(1 - w)\sigma_{XY}}$$

Here, σ_{XY} = covariance between X and Y. Note that if the covariance is zero, the variance of the portfolio is simply a weighted sum of the individual variances. If the covariance is negative, the standard deviation of the portfolio is smaller, while if the covariance is positive, the standard deviation of the portfolio is larger. Thus, if two investments (such as two technology stocks) are positively correlated, the overall risk increases, for if the stock price of one falls, the other would generally fall also. However, if two investments are negatively correlated, when one increases, the other decreases, reducing the overall risk. This is why financial experts advise diversification. The *PHStat* tool *Covariance and Portfolio Analysis,* found under *Decision Making* in the menu, can be used to perform these calculations for a two-asset portfolio. Figure 10.12 shows the output for equal proportions of balanced and aggressive funds in the investment example we have considered. Note that the expected return is $230, the covariance

	A	B	C	D
1	Investment Decision			
2				
3	Probabilities & Outcomes:	P	Balanced	Aggressive
4		0.5	$600	$1,000
5		0.2	-$500	-$1,500
6		0.3	$200	$0
7				
8	Weight Assigned to X	0.5		
9				
10	Statistics			
11	E(X)	260		
12	E(Y)	200		
13	Variance(X)	174400		
14	Standard Deviation(X)	417.6123		
15	Variance(Y)	910000		
16	Standard Deviation(Y)	953.9392		
17	Covariance(XY)	398000		
18	Variance(X+Y)	1880400		
19	Standard Deviation(X+Y)	1371.277		
20				
21	Portfolio Management			
22	Weight Assigned to X	0.5		
23	Weight Assigned to Y	0.5		
24	Portfolio Expected Return	230		
25	Portfolio Risk	685.6384		

FIGURE 10.12   *PHStat* Output for Computing Portfolio Risk

is positive, and the portfolio risk is $685.64. In contrast, a portfolio consisting of equal proportions of the balanced and bond funds has a negative covariance and a smaller portfolio risk of $195.26 while yielding an expected return of $225.

Opportunity Loss and Expected Value of Perfect Information

The **expected opportunity loss** in row 23 of Figure 10.11 represents the average additional amount the investor would have achieved by making the right decision instead of a wrong one. To find the expected opportunity loss, we first create an **opportunity loss table,** as shown in Figure 10.13. This can be done using the *PHStat* tool *Opportunity Loss* from the *Decision Making* options. We ask the question: What is the best decision if a particular event would occur? For example, if the event "market rises" occurs, then the best decision would have been to select the aggressive stock fund, and realize a return of $1000. Thus, no opportunity is lost. However, if the investor selects the balanced fund, then he or she achieves a return of only $600, losing the opportunity of an extra $400. Likewise, the opportunity loss associated with

	A	B	C	D	E	F
1	Investment Decision					
2						
3	Payoff Table:					
4		Aggressive	Balanced	Bond		
5	Market rises	$1,000	$600	$200		
6	Market falls	-$1,500	-$500	$300		
7	Market stable	$0	$200	$100		
8						
9						
10	Opportunity Loss Table:					
11		Optimum	Optimum	Alternatives		
12		Action	Profit	Aggressive	Balanced	Bond
13	Market rises	Aggressive	1000	0	400	800
14	Market falls	Bond	300	1800	800	0
15	Market stable	Balanced	200	200	0	100

FIGURE 10.13   *PHStat-* Generated Opportunity Loss Table

choosing the bond fund is $1000 − $200 = $800. In general, the opportunity loss is the difference between the payoff for a particular decision and the best decision, given the occurrence of each event. Once the opportunity loss table is constructed, the expected opportunity loss for each action is found by weighting the values by the event probabilities. This is given in row 23 in Figure 10.11. We see that the balanced fund has the smallest expected opportunity loss. *It will always be true that the decision having the best expected value will also have the minimum expected opportunity loss.*

The minimum expected opportunity loss is called the **expected value of perfect information (EVPI).** EVPI represents the maximum improvement in the expected return that can be achieved if the decision maker is able to acquire—before making a decision—perfect information about the future event that will take place. For example, if we know with certainty that the market will rise, then the optimal decision is to choose the aggressive stock fund and get a return of $1000. Likewise, if we know that the market will fall, we should choose the bond fund with a return of $300. Finally, if the market is stable, we should choose the balanced fund with a return of $200. By weighting these outcomes by the probabilities of occurrence, we find that the expected return will now be

$$\text{Expected Return with Perfect Information} = 0.5(\$1000) + 0.2(\$300) + 0.3(\$200)$$
$$= \$620$$

Since the expected value without having the perfect information is only $260, we would have increased our average return by $620 − $260 = $360. This is the expected value of perfect information. EVPI is often used to assess the value of acquiring less-than-perfect information; one would never want to pay more than the EVPI for any information about the future event, no matter how good.

Decision Trees

Another approach to structuring a decision problem involving uncertainty is to use a graphical model called a **decision tree.** Decision trees consist of a set of **nodes** and **branches.** Nodes are points in time at which events take place. The event can be a selection of a decision from among several alternatives, represented by a **decision node,** or an outcome over which the decision maker has no control, an **event node.** Event nodes are conventionally depicted by circles, while choice nodes are expressed by squares (see Figure 10.14). Many decision makers find decision trees are more useful than the tabular form because *sequences* of decisions and outcomes over time can be modeled easily.

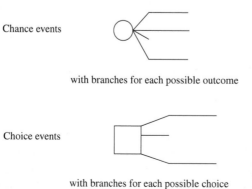

Chance events

with branches for each possible outcome

Choice events

with branches for each possible choice

FIGURE 10.14 Decision Tree Symbols

To illustrate the application of decision analysis techniques using decision trees, we will consider one of the projects from Figure 10.4. Project A1 involves developing a group support system to enable employees to conduct meetings electronically. The proposed system involves development expenses of $50,000 to purchase software, $10,000 to hire a consultant to help with installing the system, and four information systems personnel for a six-week development period, with a labor cost of $30,000. Fringe benefits are 20 percent of labor, adding another $6000. Eight personal computers would be required for the system, at an estimated cost of $2000 each, for a hardware cost of $16,000. These estimated costs total $112,000 for the project. To operate the project, two people would be needed on a full-time basis at an estimated cost of $68,000. With fringes, this amounts to $81,600, growing in years 2 and 3 at the rate of 5 percent inflation per year. However, uncertainty exists as to whether the system can be installed successfully using internal expertise. The review team has estimated a 70 percent chance of successful installation with an 84 percent availability (accounting for expected downtime).

The main benefit to the company is expected to be reduction of travel expenses, which are estimated at about $500 per person per meeting. An average of five people travel to each meeting, and it is expected that the system will serve 50 meetings per year (low-usage scenario), resulting in a savings of $125,000, to as high as 100 meetings per year (high-usage scenario), resulting in a $250,000 savings. However, with the system availability of 0.84, these savings can only be estimated as $105,000 and $210,000, respectively. The project is to be evaluated on a three-year basis, using a discount rate of 12 percent per year.

The proposal could be made more reliable by hiring consultants to do most of the installation (thereby increasing the probability of a successful implementation to 0.9). This second decision alternative, called the *buy-up proposal,* is expected to increase the availability of the system to 95 percent. The costs would be the same except for an increase to $100,000 for the consultants and a reduction in labor development costs for information systems personnel. The benefits increase because of the higher system reliability increase to $118,750 for the low-usage scenario, and $237,500 for the high-usage case.

Finally, a less expensive version of the system can be obtained by buying a turnkey software package that requires no consulting expertise to install. This is a riskier proposition, and the information systems group is only willing to estimate a 0.5 probability of full successful system installation. This alternative reduces the total project development expenses to $77,414. However, this system is expected to be more unreliable and available only 60 percent of the time. Figure 10.15 shows a spreadsheet model for computing the net present value of these proposals under both usage scenarios.

The CD-ROM accompanying this book contains an Excel add-in called *TreePlan,* which allows you to construct decision trees and perform calculations within an Excel worksheet (see the *TreePlan Note: Constructing Decision Trees in Excel*). The disk contains further documentation and examples of how to use *TreePlan,* and we encourage you to take advantage of it for many of the problems in this chapter.

A decision tree for the information systems project decision constructed in *TreePlan* is shown in Figure 10.19. This is an example of a **single-stage decision tree,** one having a single set of decisions (one decision node) followed by a set of chance events. In *TreePlan,* there are two ways of specifying the terminal values (payoffs). First, a value for the terminal value at the end of a path can simply be entered in the appropriate cell. Because the values for this example were computed from a separate worksheet, we choose this approach. A second method is to enter values or formulas

	A	B	C	D	E	F	G
1		**Original proposal**		**Buy-up proposal**		**Buy-down proposal**	
2							
3	Development expenses						
4	Software	$ 50,000		$ 50,000		$ 20,000	
5	Consultant	$ 10,000		$ 100,000			
6	Labor	$ 30,000		$ 8,000		$ 40,000	
7	Fringes (20%)	$ 6,000		$ 1,600		$ 8,000	
8	Hardware	$ 16,000		$ 16,000		$ 9,414	
9							
10	Total	$ (112,000)		$ (175,600)		$ (77,414)	
11							
12	Operating expenses						
13	Year 1	$ 81,600		$ 81,600		$ 81,600	
14	Year 2	$ 85,680		$ 85,680		$ 85,680	
15	Year 3	$ 89,964		$ 89,964		$ 89,964	
16							
17	System availability	0.84		0.95		0.6	
18		Low usage	High usage	Low usage	High usage	Low usage	High usage
19	Savings benefits	$ 125,000	$ 250,000	$ 125,000	$ 250,000	$ 125,000	$ 250,000
20	Year 1	$ 105,000	$ 210,000	$ 118,750	$ 237,500	$ 75,000	$ 150,000
21	Year 2	$ 105,000	$ 210,000	$ 118,750	$ 237,500	$ 75,000	$ 150,000
22	Year 3	$ 105,000	$ 210,000	$ 118,750	$ 237,500	$ 75,000	$ 150,000
23							
24	Net benefits						
25	Year 1	$ 23,400	$ 128,400	$ 37,150	$ 155,900	$ (6,600)	$ 68,400
26	Year 2	$ 19,320	$ 124,320	$ 33,070	$ 151,820	$ (10,680)	$ 64,320
27	Year 3	$ 15,036	$ 120,036	$ 28,786	$ 147,536	$ (14,964)	$ 60,036
28							
29	Net present values	($65,003.03)	$187,189.25	($95,577.85)	$189,639.61	($102,471.97)	$77,665.38

FIGURE 10.15   Financial Analysis of Information System Proposals

TREEPLAN NOTE

CONSTRUCTING DECISION TREES IN EXCEL

To use *TreePlan* within Excel, double click the file *Treeplan.xla,* and allow Excel to enable macros. First select the upper-left corner of the worksheet where you wish to draw the tree. Note that *TreePlan* writes over existing values in the spreadsheet; therefore, begin your tree to the *right* of the area where your data is stored, and do not subsequently add or delete rows or columns in the tree-diagram area. You can start a new tree in *TreePlan* either by pressing Ctrl-t or by selecting *Tools . . . Decision Tree* from the menu bar. *TreePlan* then prompts you with a dialog box with three options; choose *New* to begin a new tree. *TreePlan* will then draw a default initial decision tree with its upper-left corner at the selected cell. Figure 10.16 shows the initial tree when B2 is selected.

Expand a tree by adding or modifying branches or nodes in the default tree. To change

FIGURE 10.16   *TreePlan* Initial Decision Tree

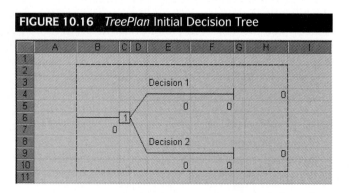

the branch labels or probabilities, click on the cell containing the label or probability and type the new label or probability. To modify the structure of the tree (e.g., add or delete branches or nodes in the tree), select the node or branch in the tree to modify and select *Tools . . . Decision Tree* or hit Ctrl-t. *TreePlan* will then present a dialog box showing the available commands. For example, to add an event node to the top branch of the tree in Figure 10.16, select the terminal node at the end of that branch (G4) and hit Ctrl-t. *TreePlan* then presents the dialog box shown in Figure 10.17. To add an event node to the branch, change the selected terminal node to an event node by selecting *Change to event node* in the dialog box, select the number of branches (two), and press Enter. *TreePlan* then redraws the tree with a chance node in place of the terminal node, as shown in Figure 10.18. The dialog boxes presented by *TreePlan* vary depending on what is selected. For instance, if you select an event node, a different dialog box appears, allowing you options to add a branch, insert another event, change it to a decision, and so on. When

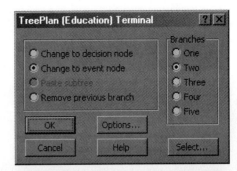

FIGURE 10.17   *TreePlan* Dialog Box

building large trees, the *Copy subtree* option allows you to copy a selected node and everything to the right of it. You can then select a terminal node and choose *Paste subtree*.

The *Options* button in a *TreePlan* dialog box allows you to use expected values (default) or an exponential utility function and to select whether the objective is to maximize (default) or minimize. Exponential utility functions convert cash flows into "utilities," or scaled payoffs for individuals with risk-averse attitudes.

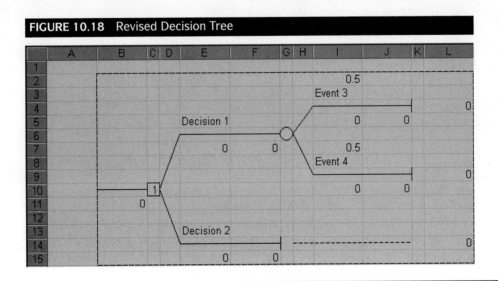

FIGURE 10.18   Revised Decision Tree

for partial cash flows associated with each branch. This approach is particularly useful when we wish to examine the sensitivity of the decision to specific values associated with decisions or events.

A decision tree is evaluated by "rolling back" the tree from right to left. When we encounter an event node, we compute the expected value of all events that emanate from the node, since each branch will have an associated probability. For example,

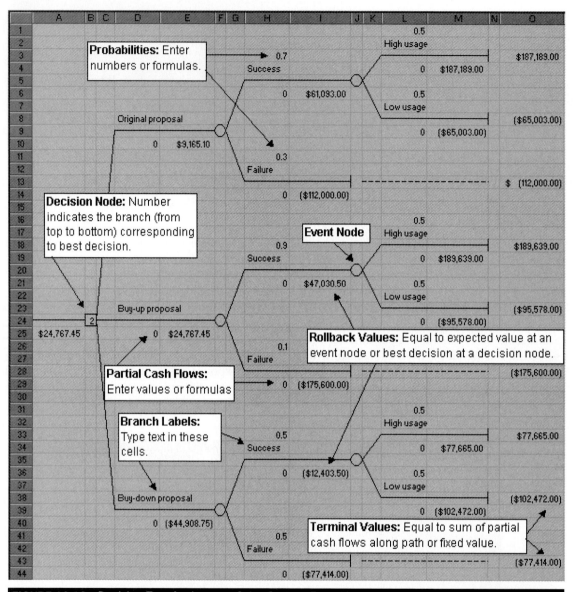

FIGURE 10.19 Decision Tree for Internet Sales System Example

the rollback value of the top-right event node in Figure 10.19 is found by taking the expected value of the payoffs associated with high and low usage (note that payoffs in parentheses are negative values):

$$\$187,189 \times 0.50 + (\$65,003) \times 0.50 = \$61,093$$

Likewise, the expected value corresponding to the branch "Original proposal" is computed as

$$\$61,093 \times 0.7 + (\$112,000) \times 0.3 = \$9,165.10$$

When we encounter a decision node (in this case, the only decision node is the first node in the tree), we take the best of the expected values of all nodes that follow. Since we are dealing with net present values of benefits less costs, the best decision is to

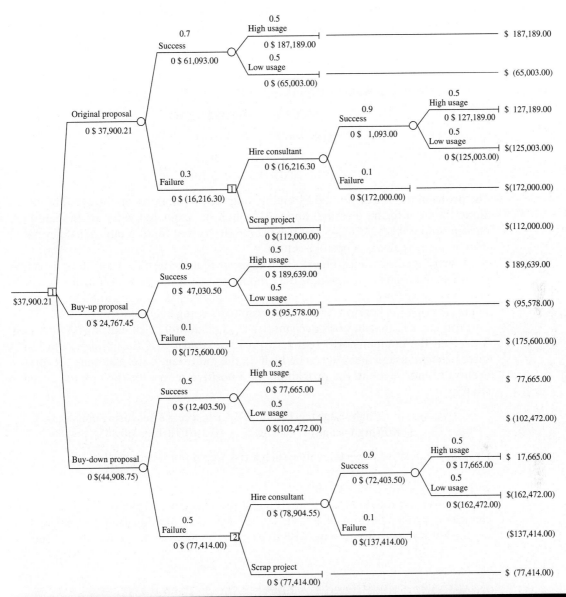

FIGURE 10.20 Multistage Decision Tree for Internet Sales System Decision

pursue the buy-up proposal having an expected value of $24,768. *TreePlan* designates the best choice by entering the number of the branch in the decision node square.

Multistage decision trees involve a sequence of interrelated decisions and chance events. Suppose, for instance, that if either the original or buy-down proposals failed, the company might consider hiring a consultant to salvage the project. Because some of the work would have already been performed, the consultant fees would be $60,000, but there is still a 10 percent chance of failure. The other alternative is to scrap the project entirely. Figure 10.20 shows a decision tree for this situation. Note that the payoffs now include the additional cost of the consultant along those paths that have been added to the original decision tree. A **decision strategy** is a specification of an initial decision and subsequent decisions to make after knowing what events occur. For example, one strategy is to select the original proposal and if it fails, to scrap the project. Another strategy would be to choose the buy-up proposal and await its outcome (no further decisions would be made). Each strategy has an associated payoff distribution, called a **risk profile.** Risk profiles show the possible payoff values that can occur and their probabilities. For example, consider the strategy of selecting the buy-up proposal. The only possible outcomes that can occur are

OUTCOME	PROBABILITY
$189,639	0.45
($95,578)	0.45
($175,600)	0.10

The probabilities are computed by multiplying the probabilities on the event branches along the path to the terminal node. Although the expected value of choosing the buy-up proposal is $24,767.45, the risk profile shows that there is only a 0.45 probability of actually realizing a positive return.

Using expected values, Figure 10.20 suggests that the best decision strategy is first to pursue the original proposal. If the original proposal succeeds, no further decisions need be made. However, if the original proposal fails, the company should hire the consultant (having the best expected value, despite its being negative).

You can see that in both decision trees, considerable risk exists. The only case for which the company will realize a positive return is if the implementation is successful *and* usage turns out to be high. In the multistage case, assuming the chance events are independent, the probability of a positive return for the optimal decision strategy is

$$P(\text{success}) \times P(\text{high usage}) + P(\text{failure}) \times P(\text{success after hiring consultant})$$
$$\times P(\text{high usage}) = (0.7)(0.5) + (0.3)(0.9)(0.5) = 0.485$$

Despite the positive expected value, such a risk might not be acceptable.

Sensitivity Analysis in Decision Trees

We may use Excel data tables to investigate the sensitivity of the optimal decision to changes in probabilities or payoff values. We will illustrate this using the single-stage model. For instance, suppose we wish to examine changes in the probability of success

Buy-up Proposal P(Success)	Expected Value	Best Decision
	$24,767.45	2
0.80	$9,165.10	1
0.81	$9,165.10	1
0.82	$9,165.10	1
0.83	$9,183.31	2
0.84	$11,409.62	2
0.85	$13,635.93	2
0.86	$15,862.23	2
0.87	$18,088.54	2
0.88	$20,314.84	2
0.89	$22,541.15	2
0.90	$24,767.45	2
0.91	$26,993.76	2
0.92	$29,220.06	2
0.93	$31,446.37	2
0.94	$33,672.67	2
0.95	$35,898.98	2

FIGURE 10.21 Data Table for Sensitivity of the Optimal Decision

for the buy-up proposal. In Figure 10.19, the input cell for a data table is H18. However, we must first modify the worksheet so that probabilities will always sum to 1. To do this, enter the formula =1− H18 in cell H26 corresponding to the probability of failure. Figure 10.21 shows a data table for varying the probability of success with two output columns, one providing the expected value and the second the best decision. We see that if *P*(Success) is greater than 0.83, the buy-up proposal #2 is optimal, while for smaller values the original proposal is best. Because the current estimate is 0.9, further information might be needed to ensure that this estimate is indeed accurate. Two-way data tables may also be used to study simultaneous changes in model parameters.

Questions and Problems

1. Explain the concepts of net present value and internal rate of return. Why are they important for business decision making? Why might you use one criterion over the other?
2. Discuss how a reasonable value for the discount rate can be established in a personal context as well as in a business context.
3. Suppose that an investment costs $5000 on January 1 of this year and returns $1000 at the end of this year and each of the five following years.
   a. Calculate the net present value (as of January 1 this year) of these cash flows using a discount rate of 10 percent per year.
   b. Calculate the internal rate of return, ignoring the discount rate assumption.
4. An investment requires an initial cash outlay of $100,000 and additional outlays of $50,000 at the end of each of the first three years. This investment is expected to result in incomes of $40,000 at the end of the first year, $70,000 at the end of the second year, $90,000 at the end of the third year, and $120,000 at the end of the fourth year.
   a. Calculate the net present value using a discount rate of 15 percent per year.
   b. Calculate the internal rate of return for these cash flows, ignoring the discount rate assumption.
5. A prospective product is expected to have sales of $100,000 in its first year. The rate of sales growth is debatable but is expected to be somewhere between 5 percent and 15 percent per year. Cost of sales are expected to be $45,000 in the first year, growing by $5000 each year thereafter. Indirect costs assigned to this product include the following:

Salaries:	$40,000 first year, increasing $1000 per year
Benefits:	10 percent of salaries
Administrative expense:	$5000 first year, increasing 4 percent per year
Depreciation	$8000 every year
Interest	$2000 for years 1 through 3, $3000 year 4

   a. Develop a spreadsheet and analyze earnings before tax for each year, assuming sales growth rates of 5 percent, 7 percent, 9 percent, 10 percent, 11 percent, 13 percent, and 15 percent.
   b. Compare the net present values for the rates of growth, using a discount rate of 12 percent per year.
6. An MBA student nearing graduation has been offered a job package that includes a retirement plan that will involve first-year investment (coming from her paycheck as well as company matching funds) of 15 percent of her annual pay, which initially would be $70,000. She can select a retirement option that has averaged 15 percent growth on the year's beginning balance

each year. This growth rate could, however, be as low as 5 percent or as high as 25 percent. The MBA's average annual raise could range from 3 percent to 20 percent per year, with the most likely value 7 percent per year. The MBA plans on working 20 years before retiring to study her first love of philosophy.

    a. Calculate the expected value of her retirement plan after 20 years, as well as the value using the minimum and maximum rates for all assumptions.

    b. How realistic is such an analysis? What is the principal problem in using such an approach? What might be a better approach?

7. Oil field exploration involves high levels of risk. Geological exploration often provides prospective investors with estimates of the thickness of the hydrocarbon deposit (the oil), estimates of the oil field area, saltwater saturation, and porosity of the oil-bearing material. A model for estimating the original oil in place (OOIP) in barrels is

$$OOIP = 7758 hA(1 - Sw)\phi$$

where h is hydrocarbon thickness in feet, A is the productive area in acres, Sw is saltwater saturation, and ϕ is the porosity. The worst, most likely, and best estimated values for each parameter are

	Worst	Most Likely	Best
h	15	30	100
A	100	200	700
Sw	0.9	0.6	0.1
ϕ	0.08	0.2	0.47

Given a development cost of $20 million, a value per barrel of $12, and a cost of production of $6 per barrel, calculate profit based on the worst, most likely, and best scenarios.

8. Compare the money spent on buying a house for $100,000 versus renting an apartment over a 15-year period. Assume that a loan for $95,000 can be obtained at the rate of 7 percent per year (payable monthly). The value of the house increases at the rate of 5 percent per year. House taxes cost the owner 12 percent of the value of the house each year. House insurance is $150 the first year, growing at the rate of 5 percent per year. Utilities cost $2400 per year, growing at the rate of 3 percent per year. Calculate the amortized payment with the Excel function =PMT(0.07/12,180,95000), reflecting a 7 percent annual rate of interest with 15 years of monthly payments for a loan of $95,000. Compare the net present value of these expenses with that of renting a house for $9600 per year the first year, growing at a rate of 5 percent per year. Utilities for the rental are $1200 per year the first year, growing at the rate of 3 percent per year.

9. In the housing situation in Problem 8, assume that $10,000 was required for down payment and closing costs. In the rental option, this $10,000 would be placed in savings (with a rate of interest of 3 percent per year on a positive beginning balance, paying 7 percent interest if the beginning balance is negative). The difference between the housing payment + house taxes + house insurance − rent is added savings (this value might go negative later in the analysis). Calculate the value of the house versus the value of the savings account after 15 years.

10. Use a data table to calculate the net present value of the money expended for buying or renting, as well as the value of the asset in each case, assuming

real estate growth rates of 3 percent, 4 percent, 5 percent, 6 percent, and 7 percent per year.

11. The cost accountant of a large truck fleet is evaluating options for dealing with a large volume of flat tires. Currently, the company repairs tires on the open market by having the driver take the flat tire to the nearest tire dealer. Last year this cost an average of $30 per flat tire. The volume of flat tires experienced per year was 10,000 last year, and the expected rate of growth in flat tires is 10 percent per year. However, some feel that flat tire growth will be as low as 5 percent; others as high as 15 percent. A complicating factor is that the cost to repair a tire grows an average of 3 percent per year.

    The company has two alternatives. A tire dealer has offered to fix all the company's flat tires for a fixed rate of $36 per tire over a three-year period. The other alternative is for the company to go into the tire repair business for themselves. This option is expected to require an investment in equipment of $200,000, with a salvage value of $50,000 after three years. It would require an overhead expense of $40,000 per year in the first year, $45,000 the second year, and $50,000 the third year. The variable cost for fixing a flat tire is $12 per tire for the three-year period of analysis. Compare the net present costs over three years for each of these three options under conditions of tire growth ranging from 5 percent to 15 percent per year in increments of 1 percent.

12. A company has surplus cash available to invest at the end of each quarter. The chief financial officer has requested a report that will display the options available, ranked by internal rate of return. These are to be short-term investments, no longer than nine months before payment is due. The CFO's policy is that a maximum of $100,000 can be invested in any one option. Expected cash flows for six alternatives are given here. Develop the list showing IRR.

		Cash Flows		
Alternative	Now	End of 1st Quarter	End of 2nd Quarter	End of 3rd Quarter
ABC Corp	−$40,000		$20,000	$25,000
1st Bank	−$100,000	$101,000		
5th Bank	−$100,000		$102,500	
FBN Air	−$50,000			$53,500
OM Farms	−$100,000		$30,000	$75,000
OTB	−$80,000	$82,500		

13. A firm's information systems department receives many requests for proposed projects to improve the system. Each project proposal is processed, using the proposing department's estimate of benefits and the information systems department's estimate of project costs. The costs are incurred within three months of project adoption (and are treated as occurring at the present). Estimated benefits are calculated as of the end of 12 months, 24 months, and 36 months after project completion. Company policy is to disregard any benefits beyond 36 months, as technology will probably outdate systems by that time. The company discount rate is 18 percent per year. Calculate net present values of the following eight proposed projects:

Department	Cost	Benefits@12 mo.	Benefits@24 mo.	Benefits@36 mo.
Production	$300,000	$100,000	$120,000	$150,000
Production	260,000	150,000	200,000	0
Marketing	220,000	150,000	200,000	300,000
Marketing	520,000	250,000	240,000	220,000
Marketing	360,000	200,000	180,000	150,000
Transport	360,000	200,000	200,000	200,000
Admin.	580,000	0	500,000	400,000

14. The information systems group has received nine proposed projects with positive net present values as given here. These projects also have resource requirements in the form of systems analysis and programming. Assume that this period 200 hours of systems analysis time and 300 hours of programmer time are available. Recommend projects to adopt, seeking to maximize net present value to the firm.

Project	Net Present Value	Systems Analysis Hours	Programmer Hours
Mkt4	$512,862	100	120
Mkt7	103,841	50	60
Prod8	90,439	20	30
Admin	86,521	40	80
Mkt6	42,106	50	70
Prod9	12,655	30	100
Trans3	− 8,312	40	50
Mkt8	− 36,783	20	80
Mkt5	− 89,112	50	80

15. A company is considering two investments. The expected outcomes have been estimated in net present value terms with probabilities as shown here. Calculate the expected outcome for each investment. Identify the decision by a very pessimistic decision maker, a risk-neutral decision maker, and a very optimistic decision maker.

Investment A		Investment B	
+1 million	0.3 probability	−100,000	0.1 probability
+2 million	0.6 probability	0	0.1 probability
+3 million	0.1 probability	+1 million	0.2 probability
		+2 million	0.3 probability
		+3 million	0.2 probability
		+4 million	0.1 probability

16. The manager of a toy store is faced with the opportunity to buy this year's fad toy at ridiculous prices. He can buy cartons of 100 of these insane monstrosities at various quantity discounts. If he buys 100, they cost him $50 each. If he buys 200, 300, or 400, they cost him $45 each. If he buys 500 or more, they cost him $40 each. Demand is expected to be at least 100. The manager estimates that there is a 10 percent chance that it will be no more than 100, a 20 percent chance it will be 200, a 40 percent chance demand will be 300, a 20 percent chance demand will be 400, and a 10 percent chance demand will reach 500. The store retails these to their customers at $60

each. If any are left over, they are worthless. Calculate the expected monetary value and expected opportunity loss for the options of buying 100, 200, 300, 400, or 500 of these toys.

17. An investor can invest in three highly speculative opportunities. The returns and standard deviations are given here.

	Expected Return	Standard Deviation
Investment A	50,000	25,000
Investment B	40,000	24,000
Investment C	30,000	10,000

Based on the coefficient of variation, which of these is the least risky investment?

18. An information system consultant is bidding on a project that involves some uncertainty. Based on past experience, if all went well (probability 0.1), the project would cost $1.2 million to complete. If moderate debugging were required (probability 0.7), the project would probably cost $1.4 million. If major debugging problems were encountered (probability 0.2), the project could cost $1.8 million. Assume that the firm is bidding competitively, and the expectation of successfully gaining the job at a bid of $2.2 million is 0, at $2.1 million is 0.1, at $2.0 million is 0.2, at $1.9 million is 0.3, at $1.8 million is 0.5, at $1.7 million is 0.8, and at $1.6 million is practically certain.
   a. Calculate the expected monetary value for the given bids.
   b. Calculate the expected value of perfect information.

19. Jim Bridger developed a new ski slope in the wilds of Montana. This operation holds great promise for success, but business depends on the snowfall. Too little snowfall would drive business way down, while too much snow would make it hard for customers to get to the resort. Jim faced the decision of how much to advertise. A massive advertising campaign has been drawn together by a local ad agency with a nominal price tag of $10 million. Jim asked for a more economical alternative, which the ad agency grudgingly put together with a price tag of $1 million. The following table shows the expected profit including the cost of the ad campaigns for various levels of snow:

	Too Little Snow	Great Snow	Too Much Snow
Probabilities	0.2	0.5	0.3
Major ad campaign	−$7 million	+$40 million	+$15 million
Minor ad campaign	0	+$24 million	+$6 million

Find the expected monetary value of each option, as well as the expected value of perfect information.

20. A newly married couple is looking for a new home. They have three principal decision criteria: size, neighborhood, and style. They have narrowed down their search to two houses: a turn-of-the-century colonial (C) and a new transitional (T) in a better neighborhood. Using pairwise comparisons, they developed the following preference and importance matrixes:

Size	C	T
C	1	3
T	1/3	1

Neighborhood	C	T
C	1	1/5
T	5	1

Style	C	T
C	1	2
T	1/2	1

Criteria	Size	Neighborhood	Style
Size	1	3	1/4
Neighborhood	1/3	1	1/5
Style	4	5	1

    a. Develop a decision hierarchy diagram for their problem of choosing a home.

    b. Determine the relative priorities for each criterion and the relative importance of the criteria, and compute the priorities for the two houses.

    c. Compute the consistency ratio for each matrix. How might these results influence the answer in part (b)?

21. A marketing research firm is seeking to hire a new statistical analyst. Among the many applicants, they have selected three finalists: Rachel, Andrew, and Mike. The firm evaluates their analysts on three criteria: technical ability, writing skills, and maturity. Based on interviews and other application materials, the recruiting team constructed the following preference matrixes. Conduct an analysis using the analytic hierarchy process to recommend a new hire.

Technical Ability	Rachel	Andrew	Mike
Rachel	1	7	5
Andrew	1/7	1	3
Mike	1/5	1/3	1

Writing Skills	Rachel	Andrew	Mike
Rachel	1	2	1/4
Andrew	1/2	1	1/6
Mike	4	6	1

Maturity	Rachel	Andrew	Mike
Rachel	1	1/3	1
Andrew	3	1	2
Mike	1	1/2	1

22. An investor is considering a two-asset portfolio. Stock A has an expected return of $4.50 per share with a standard deviation of $1.00, while stock B has an expected return of $3.75 with a standard deviation of $0.75. The correlation between the two stocks is -0.35. Find the portfolio risk if

    a. The stocks are weighted equally in the portfolio.

    b. The amount of stock A is one-fourth as much as stock B.

    c. The amount of stock B is one-fourth as much as stock A.

23. Find daily stock prices for two of your favorite stocks, and compute the covariance using whatever data you collect. What is the portfolio risk of an equally weighted portfolio of these two stocks? Use a data table to examine how the risk varies with different weights.

24. Gulf Exploration is considering making a bid for oil drilling rights off the Mexican coast. The company has decided to bid $520 million for these rights. At this bid, experts have told Gulf Exploration that they have about a 60 percent probability of winning the job. If the firm should win the contract, it can drill on its own, it can join a joint venture, or it can sell its rights.

Should the firm drill, costs of drilling are expected to be $80 million. These expenses in the joint venture would be only $45 million. The negotiation process involved in selling the rights is expected to cost $2 million.

The outcomes for the two drilling options are

	Big Find	Average Find	Dry (Wet) Hole
Drill on their own	$900 million	$600 million	$250 million
Probabilities	0.6	0.2	0.2
Joint venture	$750 million	$500 million	$200 million
Probabilities	0.6	0.3	0.1
Sale of rights	$600 million		

Note that the costs have not been deducted from these values. Develop a decision tree to analyze this problem, and conduct sensitivity analysis on the probability of winning the job.

25. Farben Chemical is faced with a serious lawsuit over contentions of damage from pollution generation. The CEO has gathered much of the corporate legal staff as well as other top decision makers to discuss their options. The outcome of this discussion is

OPTION	RESULT
(1) Settle completely	Loss of $6 billion
(2) Negotiate	50% chance of settling for $2 billion
	50% chance of the choice:
	settle for $5 billion
	fight in court with:
	40% chance win, legal cost $200 million
	60% chance lose, $8 billion
(3) Fight in court	40% chance win, legal cost $100 million
	60% chance lose, $10 billion

a. Draw a decision tree and identify the expected value of each of the initial options.
b. What rationale might lead to a different decision than that of minimizing expected monetary loss?
c. What would be the value of perfect knowledge of a trial's outcome?

26. A national restaurant chain has developed a new specialty sandwich. Initially, it faces two possible decisions: introduce the sandwich nationally at a cost of $200,000, or evaluate it in a regional test market at a cost of $30,000. If it introduces the sandwich nationally, the chain might find either a high or low response to the idea. Probabilities of these events are estimated to be 0.6 and 0.4, respectively. With a high response, gross revenues of $700,000 (at net present value) are expected; with a low response, the figure is $150,000. If it starts with a regional marketing strategy, it might find a low response or a high response at the regional level with probabilities 0.7 and 0.3, respectively. This may or may not reflect the national market potential. In any case, the chain needs next to decide whether to remain regional, market nationally, or drop the product. If the regional response is high and it remains regional, the expected revenue is $200,000. If it markets nationally (at an additional cost of $200,000), the probability of a high national response is 0.9 with revenues of $700,000 ($150,000 if the national response is low). If the regional response is low and it remains regional, the expected

revenue is $100,000. If it markets nationally (at an additional cost of $200,000), the probability of a high national response is 0.05 with revenues of $700,000 ($150,000 if the national response is low). Construct a decision tree and determine the optimal strategy.

27. Many automobile dealers advertise lease options for new cars. Suppose that you are considering three alternatives:
    a. Purchase the car outright with cash
    b. Purchase the car with 20 percent down and a 48-month loan
    c. Lease the car

    Select an automobile whose leasing contract is advertised in a local paper. Using current interest rates and advertised leasing arrangements, perform a decision analysis of these options. Make, but clearly define, any assumptions that may be required.

C A S E

A TRACWAY DECISION PROBLEM

Tracway engineers have proposed a change in metal processing that should result in reduced costs for Tracway mower and tractor production. There are three options to fuel this system: natural gas (NG), bunker oil (BO), and wood (W). Each of the three fuels involves different investment costs, operating expense rates, and material cost rates.

Operating expenses are functions of the quantity processed, which is expected to be 1 million tons during the first year, growing at the rate of 10 percent per year. Material cost is also calculated on the basis of a ton of metal processed. Material costs for BO and NG depend on the price of a barrel of oil, P. Specific cost parameters (all in millions of dollars) are given in the table below.

There are two major sources of uncertainty. The first is demand growth. The expected rate of growth in metal processed is 10 percent, but it could easily range from 5 percent to 15 percent. Second, the future price of a barrel of oil (P) is highly uncertain. In 1972, it was about $3 per barrel. In the early 1980s, the price rose to about $35 per barrel. Currently, it varies around $15–$20. Construct a spreadsheet model for this decision, and find the best option on a net present value basis. To examine the impact of changes in the two key parameters on the model, construct two-way data tables for each alternative using the key variables *growth rate* and the *price of a barrel of oil*. Explain your results and its implications for what Tracway should do next. ∎

		NG	BO	W
Investment	*Year 1*	$6	$6	$4
	Year 2	0	0	$2
Operating expense rate/ton		$0.50	$0.60	$1.00
Material expense/ton		$(0.30 + 0.01P)$	$0.02P$	$0.10

References

Gallagher, T. J., and J. D. Andrew, Jr., *Financial Management* (Upper Saddle River, NJ: Prentice-Hall, 1997).

Keeney, R. L., *Value-Focused Thinking: A Path to Creative Decisionmaking* (Cambridge, MA: Harvard University Press, 1992).

Nas, T. F., *Cost-Benefit Analysis: Theory and Application* (Newbury Park, CA: Sage, 1996).

Saaty, T. L., *The Analytic Hierarchy Process,* 2nd ed. (New York: McGraw-Hill, 1988).

Sharpe, P., and T. Keelin, "How SmithKline Beecham Makes Better Resource-Allocation Decisions," *Harvard Business Review,* March–April 1998, 45–57.

CHAPTER

11

OPTIMIZATION MODELING

INTRODUCTION

Throughout this book we have explored the role of data in managerial decisions. While many decisions involve only a limited number of alternatives and can be addressed using statistical analysis, simple decision models, or simulation, others have a very large or even an infinite number of possibilities. To identify the best decision in these situations, we often use techniques of **optimization**—the process of selecting values of decision variables that *minimize* or *maximize* some quantity of interest—usually with constraints that limit the choices. This quantity we seek to minimize or maximize is called the **objective function,** and the set of decision variable values that maximize or minimize the objective function is called the **optimal solution.**

To illustrate an optimization model, suppose that a firm wishes to determine the best pricing for one of its products to maximize revenue over the next fiscal year. A market research study has collected data that estimate the expected annual sales for different levels of pricing as shown in Figure 11.1. Plotting these data on a scatter chart

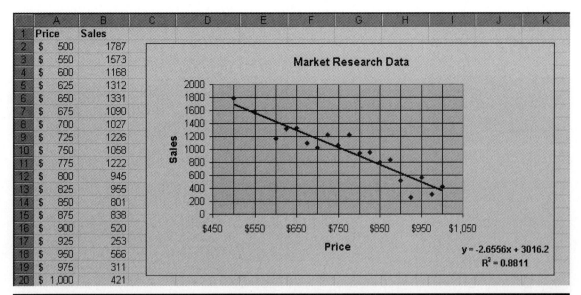

FIGURE 11.1 Price/Sales Data and Regression Trendline

suggests that sales and price have a linear relationship; adding a trendline and regression equation confirms a high correlation between price and sales, as shown in the accompanying chart. Thus, the regression equation Sales $= -2.6556$ Price $+ 3016.2$ is a good predictor of expected sales for any pricing decision within the relevant range of the data.

Since revenue = price multiplied by sales, an equation for revenue is

$$\text{Revenue} = \text{Price} (-2.6556 \text{ Price} + 3016.2)$$
$$= -2.6556(\text{Price})^2 + 3016.2 \text{ Price}$$

The problem is to determine the best value of price to maximize the revenue. Figure 11.2 shows a tabulation of revenue for various levels of price. We see that as the price increases from $500, the revenue increases and then falls off. The maximum revenue appears to be at a price somewhere between $500 and $600.

Optimization is a very broad and complex topic; our principal focus in this chapter is to introduce you to basic concepts of optimization to provide some idea of its applications in business and important issues involved in developing and modeling optimization problems. The key concepts we will discuss are

- Developing mathematical models for linear, integer, and nonlinear optimization problems and
- Implementing optimization models on spreadsheets

In the next chapter we will focus on solving and interpreting solutions to optimization problems.

CONSTRAINED OPTIMIZATION

In the example we posed in the introduction to this chapter, we could estimate the optimal price rather easily by developing a simple data table in a spreadsheet that evaluates the objective function for various values of the decision variables. Most practical

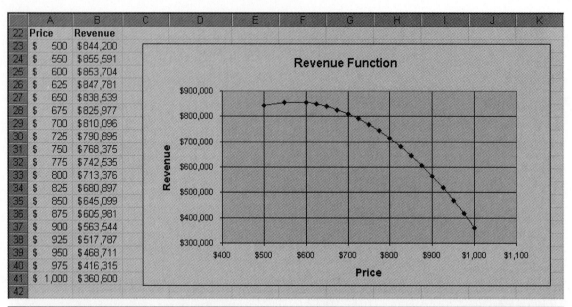

	A	B
22	Price	Revenue
23	$ 500	$844,200
24	$ 550	$855,591
25	$ 600	$853,704
26	$ 625	$847,781
27	$ 650	$838,539
28	$ 675	$825,977
29	$ 700	$810,096
30	$ 725	$790,895
31	$ 750	$768,375
32	$ 775	$742,535
33	$ 800	$713,376
34	$ 825	$680,897
35	$ 850	$645,099
36	$ 875	$605,981
37	$ 900	$563,544
38	$ 925	$517,787
39	$ 950	$468,711
40	$ 975	$416,315
41	$ 1,000	$360,600
42		

FIGURE 11.2 Tabulation and Plot of Revenue as a Function of Price

optimization problems have **constraints**—limitations or requirements that decision variables must satisfy. The presence of constraints usually makes identifying an optimal solution considerably more difficult. Some examples of constraints are

- The amount of material used to produce a set of products cannot exceed the available amount of 850 square feet.
- The amount of money spent on research and development projects cannot exceed the assigned budget of $300,000.
- Contractual requirements specify that at least 500 units of product must be produced.
- A mixture of fertilizer must contain exactly 30 percent nitrogen.
- We cannot produce a negative amount of product (*nonnegativity*).

Constraints are generally expressed mathematically as equations or inequalities. For the examples above, we might write:

- Amount of material used ≤ 850 square feet
- Amount spent on research and development ≤ $300,000
- Number of units of product produced ≥ 500
- Amount of nitrogen in mixture/total amount in mixture = 0.30
- Amount of product produced ≥ 0

The left-hand side of each of these expressions is called a **constraint function.** When represented mathematically, a constraint function is a function of the decision variables. For example, suppose that in the first case, the material requirements of three products are 3.0, 3.5, and 2.3 square feet per unit. If A, B, and C represent the number of units of each product to produce, then $3.0A$ represents the amount of material used to produce A units of product A, $3.5B$ represents the amount of material used to produce B units of product B, and so on. Note that dimensions of these terms are (square feet/unit)(units) = square feet. Therefore, the constraint that limits the amount of material that can be used can be expressed as

$$3.0A + 3.5B + 2.3C \leq 850$$

As another example, if two ingredients contain 20 percent and 33 percent nitrogen, respectively, then the fraction of nitrogen in a mixture of x lb of the first ingredient and y lb of the second ingredient is expressed by the constraint function

$$(0.20x + 0.33y)/(x + y)$$

If the fraction of nitrogen in the mixture must be 0.30, then we would have

$$(0.20x + 0.33y)/(x + y) = 0.3$$

This can be rewritten as

$$(0.20x + 0.33y) = 0.3(x + y)$$

or

$$-0.1x + 0.03y = 0$$

Any solution that satisfies all constraints of a problem is called a **feasible solution.** An optimization problem that has no feasible solutions is called **infeasible.** The presence of constraints makes finding optimal solutions more difficult than for unconstrained problems. In fact, it may be very difficult to even identify a feasible solution, much less an optimal one. Thus, to solve constrained optimization problems, we generally rely on special solution procedures.

Types of Optimization Problems

In addition to classifying optimization problems by whether or not they have constraints, we may also classify them by their mathematical structure. The most common types of optimization problems are *linear, integer,* and *nonlinear.* A **linear optimization problem** (often called a **linear program**) has two basic properties. First, the objective function and all constraints are *linear functions* of the decision variables. This means that each function is simply a sum of terms, each of which is some constant multiplied by a decision variable, for example:

$$2x + 3y - 12z$$

Second, all variables are *continuous,* meaning that they may assume any real value (typically, nonnegative).

In an **integer linear optimization problem,** some or all of the variables are restricted to being whole numbers. If only a subset of variables is restricted to being integers while others are continuous, we call this a **mixed integer linear optimization problem.** A special type of integer problem is one in which variables can only be 0 or 1. These *binary variables* help us to model logical, "yes or no" decisions. Integer linear optimization models are generally more difficult to solve than pure linear models.

Finally, in a **nonlinear optimization problem,** the objective function and/or constraint functions are *nonlinear functions* of the decision variables; that is, terms cannot be written as a constant times a variable. An example is

$$3x^2 + \frac{4}{y} - 6xy$$

Note that the example involving the mixture of ingredients to meet a nitrogen requirement that we discussed earlier was formulated originally as a nonlinear constraint. However, through simple algebra we were able to convert it to a linear form. Nonlinear optimization models are considerably more difficult to solve than either linear or integer models.

Developing an optimization model consists of defining the decision variables, an objective function, and any appropriate constraints. However, building optimization models is more of an art than a science, as there often are several ways of formulating a particular problem. Learning how to build optimization models requires logical thought but can be facilitated by studying examples of different models and observing their characteristics. In the remainder of this chapter we will guide you through the development of models for linear, integer, and nonlinear optimization and spreadsheet implementation.

LINEAR OPTIMIZATION MODELS

Linear optimization models, often called *linear programs* or *linear programming models,* have the characteristic that all constraints are linear functions of the decision variables and that the decision variables may assume any continuous value (i.e., they are not restricted to being whole numbers, for example). Table 11.1 summarizes many common types of generic linear optimization models. We usually represent decision

TABLE 11.1 Generic Examples of Linear Optimization Models

Type of Model	*Decision Variables*	*Objective Function*	*Typical Constraints*
Product mix	Quantities of product to produce and sell	Maximize contribution to profit	Resource limitations (e.g., production time, labor, material); maximum sales potential; contractual requirements
Media selection	Number of advertisements in different media	Minimize cost	Budget limitation; requirements on number of customers reached; media requirements and restrictions
Process selection	Quantities of product to make using alternative processes	Minimize cost	Demand requirements; resource limitations
Blending	Quantity of materials to mix to produce one unit of product	Minimize cost	Specifications on acceptable mixture
Production planning	Quantities of product to produce in each of several periods; amount of inventory to hold between successive periods	Minimize production and inventory costs	Limited production rates; material balance equations (production + available inventory − inventory held to next period = demand)
Portfolio selection	Amounts to invest in different financial instruments	Maximize future expected return	Limit on available funds; sector requirements and restrictions (minimum and maximum amounts in different types of instruments)
Multiperiod investment planning	Amounts to invest in various instruments each year	Maximize return	Limit on available funds; cash balance equations between periods
Transportation planning	Amount to ship between origins and destinations	Minimize total transportation cost	Limited availability at origins; requirement to meet demands at destinations

variables by short, descriptive acronyms or subscripted letters. For example, we might define the amount of money invested in General Electric stock as GE, STOCK1, or x_1. For purposes of mathematical formulations, subscripted letters are usually best; however, in spreadsheet models we recommend using more descriptive names.

The most challenging aspect of model formulation is identifying constraints. Constraints generally fall into one of the following categories:

- *Simple Bounds.* Simple bounds constrain the value of a single variable. You can recognize simple bounds in problem statements like "no more than $10,000 may be invested in any single stock" or "we must produce at least 350 units of product Y to meet customer commitments this month." The mathematical forms for these examples are

$$\text{STOCK} \leq 10,000$$
$$\text{Y} \geq 350$$

- *Limitations.* Limitations usually involve the allocation of scarce resources. Problem statements such as "the amount of material used in production cannot exceed the amount available in inventory," "production should not exceed the market potential of the product," or "the amount shipped from the Austin plant in July cannot exceed the plant's capacity" are typical of these types of constraints. Limitations generally have the form:

Constraint Function ≤ Value (or Another Constraint Function)

- *Requirements.* Requirements involve the specification of minimum levels of performance. Such statements as "enough cash must be available in February to meet financial obligations," "production must be sufficient to meet promised customer orders," or "the marketing plan should ensure that at least 400 customers are contacted each month" are some examples. Requirements generally have the form:

Constraint Function ≥ Value (or Another Constraint Function)

- *Proportional Relationships.* Proportional relationships are often found in problems involving mixtures or blends of materials or strategies. Examples include "the amount invested in aggressive growth stocks cannot be more than twice the amount invested in equity-income funds," or "the octane rating of gasoline obtained from mixing different crude blends must be at least 89."

- *Balance Constraints.* Balance constraints essentially state that "input = output" and ensure that the flow of material or money is accounted for at locations or between time periods. Examples include "production in June plus any available inventory must equal June's demand plus inventory held to July," "the total amount shipped to a distribution center from all plants must equal the amount shipped from the distribution center to all customers," or "the total amount of money invested or saved in March must equal the amount of money available at the end of February."

Most constraints in linear programming models are some combination of constraints from these categories. Problem data or verbal clues in a problem statement often help you identify the appropriate constraint. In some situations, all constraints may not be explicitly stated, but are required for the model to represent the real problem accurately. A simple example of implicit constraints is nonnegativity of the decision variables. Nonnegativity means that the values of decision variables cannot be negative, which generally is true for most applications.

In the following sections we present examples of each type of linear programming application described in Table 11.1. These are a representative sample of the wide variety of problems that can be modeled using linear programming. Each of these models has different characteristics, and by studying how they are developed, you will improve your ability to model other types of problems.

Product Mix

A manufacturer of MP3 players assembles two models: Gold Player and Platinum Player. Both models use many of the same electronic components. Because of the proprietary design, two of these components can only be obtained from a small manufacturer. For the next quarter, the supplier can provide only 3000 of component A and 1750 of component B. Table 11.2 shows the number of each component required for each product and the profit per unit of product sold. How many of each product should be assembled during the next month to maximize the manufacturer's profit? Assume that the firm can sell all it produces.

To develop an optimization model for this problem, we first define the decision variables. Define G to be the number of units of Gold Player to assemble and P the number of units of Platinum Player to make. Because the profit per unit is known, the total profit is simply the quantity sold times the profit/unit, summed over both products. Therefore, the objective function is

$$\text{Maximize Profit} = 48G + 70P$$

The limited quantities of the two components specify constraints. Each product requires 6 of component A; thus, a total of $6G + 6P$ units of component A will be needed to make G Gold Players and P Platinum Players. Because the number of component A is limited to 3000 units, we have the constraint

$$6G + 6P \leq 3000$$

Similarly, the quantity of component B used ($3G + 5P$) cannot exceed the amount available:

$$3G + 5P \leq 1750$$

Finally, it is logical to ensure that the number of units produced is not less than zero. These are defined by the nonnegativity constraints

$$G \geq 0 \quad \text{and} \quad P \geq 0$$

Therefore, the complete model is

$$\text{Maximize Profit} = 48G + 70P$$

subject to the constraints

$$
\begin{aligned}
6G + 6P &\leq 3000 && \text{(Component A limitation)} \\
3G + 5P &\leq 1750 && \text{(Component B limitation)} \\
G \geq 0, P &\geq 0 && \text{(Nonnegativity)}
\end{aligned}
$$

TABLE 11.2 Component Requirements and Profit Data

| | *Components Required/Unit* | | |
	Component A	*Component B*	*Profit/Unit*
Gold Player	6	3	$48
Platinum Player	6	5	$70

Media Selection

Marketing managers have various media alternatives, such as radio, TV, magazines, etc., in which to advertise and must determine which to use, the number of insertions in each, and the timing of insertions to maximize advertising effectiveness within a limited budget. Suppose that three media options are available: radio, TV, and magazine. Let R, T, and M be the number of ads placed in each of these media, respectively. Table 11.3 provides some information about costs, exposure values, and bounds on the permissible number of ads in each medium desired by a client firm. The exposure value is a measure of the number of people exposed to the advertisement and is derived from market research studies, and the client's objective is to maximize the total exposure value. A total budget of $50,000 is available for purchasing the ads.

To develop an LP model, let

R = number of radio ads purchased
T = number of TV ads purchased
M = number of magazine ads purchased

By multiplying the exposure value per ad by the number of ads purchased and summing over all media, we obtain the objective function

$$\text{Maximize } 2000R + 3500T + 2700M$$

The constraints arise from the budget limitation and the specified minimum and maximum media units. By multiplying the cost/ad by the number of ads purchased, we obtain the total amount spent. This must not exceed the budget, resulting in the constraint

$$500R + 2000T + 200M \le 50,000$$

Finally, the specifications on the minimum and maximum number of media units purchased are modeled by simple bounds on the variables:

$$R \ge 0$$
$$T \ge 12$$
$$M \ge 6$$
$$R \le 15$$
$$M \le 30$$

Note that nonnegativity constraints are not required here because each variable has a lower bound. The complete model can be written as

$$\text{Maximize } 2000R + 3500T + 2700M$$

$$500R + 2000T + 200M \le 50,000$$
$$0 \le R \le 15$$
$$T \ge 12$$
$$6 \le M \le 30$$

TABLE 11.3 Media Selection Data

Medium	Cost/Ad	Exposure Value/Ad	Minimum Units	Maximum Units
Radio	$500	2000	0	15
TV	$2000	3500	12	—
Magazine	$200	2700	6	30

Process Selection

A textile mill produces three types of fabrics on a make-to-order basis. The mill operates on a 24/7 basis. The key decision facing the plant manager is on what type of loom to process each fabric during the coming quarter (13 weeks). Two types of looms are used: dobbie and regular. Dobbie looms can be used to make all fabrics and are the only looms that can weave certain fabrics, such as plaids. Demands, variable costs for each fabric, and production rates on the looms are given in Table 11.4. The mill has 15 regular looms and 3 dobbie looms. After weaving, fabrics are sent to the finishing department and then sold. Any fabrics that cannot be woven in the mill because of limited capacity will be purchased from an external supplier, finished at the mill, and sold at the selling price. In addition to determining which looms to process the fabrics, the manager also needs to determine which fabrics to buy externally.

To formulate a linear programming model, define

D_i = number of yards of fabric i to produce on dobbie looms, $i = 1, \ldots, 3$
R_i = number of yards of fabric i to produce on regular looms, $i = 1, \ldots, 3$
P_i = number of yards of fabric i to purchase from an outside supplier, $i = 1, \ldots, 3$

Note that we are using *subscripted variables* to simplify their definition, rather than defining nine individual variables with unique names. The objective function is to minimize total cost:

$$\text{Min } 0.65D_1 + 0.61D_2 + 0.50D_3 + 0.61R_2 + 0.50R_3 + 0.85P_1 + 0.75P_2 + 0.65P_3$$

Constraints to ensure meeting production requirements are

$$D_1 + P_1 = 45{,}000$$
$$D_2 + R_2 + P_2 = 76{,}500$$
$$D_3 + R_3 + P_3 = 10{,}000$$

To specify the constraints on loom capacity, we must convert yards per hour into hours per yard. For example, for fabric 1 on a dobbie loom, 4.7 yards/hour = 1.428 hours/yard. Therefore, the term $0.213D_1$ represents the total time required to produce D_1 yards of fabric 1 on a dobbie loom. The total capacity for dobbie looms is (24 hours/day)(7 days/week)(13 weeks)(3 looms) = 6552 hours. Thus, the constraint on available production time on dobbie looms is

$$0.213D_1 + 0.192D_2 + 0.227D_3 \leq 6552$$

For regular looms we have

$$0.192R_2 + 0.227R_3 \leq 32{,}760$$

Finally, all variables must be nonnegative.

TABLE 11.4 Textile Production Data

Fabric	Demand (yards)	Dobbie Loom Capacity (yards/hour)	Regular Loom Capacity (yards/hour)	Mill Cost ($/yard)	Outsourcing Cost ($/yard)
1	45,000	4.7	0.00	$0.65	$0.85
2	76,500	5.2	5.2	$0.61	$0.75
3	10,000	4.4	4.4	$0.50	$0.65

Blending

The BG Seed Company specializes in food products for birds and other household pets. In developing a new birdseed mix, company nutritionists have specified that the mixture must contain at least 13 percent protein and 15 percent fat and no more than 14 percent fiber. The percentages of each of these nutrients in eight types of ingredients that can be used in the mix are given in Table 11.5 along with the wholesale cost per pound. What is the minimum cost mixture that meets the stated nutritional requirements?

In this example, the decisions are the amount of each ingredient to include in a given quantity—for example, one pound—of mix. Define X_i = number of pounds of ingredient i to include in one pound of the mix, for $i = 1, \ldots, 8$. The objective is to minimize total cost:

Minimize $0.22X_1 + 0.19X_2 + 0.10X_3 + 0.10X_4 + 0.07X_5 + 0.05X_6 + 0.26X_7 + 0.11X_8$

To ensure that the mix contains the appropriate proportion of ingredients, observe that multiplying the number of pounds of each ingredient by the percentage of nutrient in that ingredient (a dimensionless quantity) specifies the number of pounds of nutrient provided. For example, $0.169X_1$ represents the number of pounds of protein in sunflower seeds. Therefore, the total number of pounds of protein provided by all ingredients is

$$0.169X_1 + 0.12X_2 + 0.085X_3 + 0.154X_4 + 0.085X_5 + 0.12X_6 + 0.18X_7 + 0.119X_8$$

Because the total number of pounds of ingredients that are mixed together equals $X_1 + X_2 + X_3 + X_4 + X_5 + X_6 + X_7 + X_8$, the proportion of protein in the mix is

$$(0.169X_1 + 0.12X_2 + 0.085X_3 + 0.154X_4 + 0.085X_5 + 0.12X_6 + 0.18X_7 \\ + 0.119X_8)/(X_1 + X_2 + X_3 + X_4 + X_5 + X_6 + X_7 + X_8)$$

This proportion must be at least 0.13. However, we wish to determine the best amount of ingredients to include in *one pound* of mix; therefore, we add the constraint

$$X_1 + X_2 + X_3 + X_4 + X_5 + X_6 + X_7 + X_8 = 1$$

Now we can substitute 1 for the denominator in the proportion of protein, yielding the constraint

$$0.169X_1 + 0.12X_2 + 0.085X_3 + 0.154X_4 + 0.085X_5 \\ + 0.12X_6 + 0.18X_7 + 0.119X_8 \geq 0.13$$

This ensures that at least 13 percent of the mixture will be protein. In a similar fashion, the constraints for the fat and fiber requirements are

TABLE 11.5 Birdseed Nutrition Data

Ingredient	Protein %	Fat %	Fiber %	Cost/lb
Sunflower seeds	16.9	26	29	$0.22
White millet	12	4.1	8.3	$0.19
Kibble corn	8.5	3.8	2.7	$0.10
Oats	15.4	6.3	2.4	$0.10
Cracked corn	8.5	3.8	2.7	$0.07
Wheat	12	1.7	2.3	$0.05
Safflower	18	17.9	28.8	$0.26
Canary grass seed	11.9	4	10.9	$0.11

$$0.26X_1 + 0.041X_2 + 0.038X_3 + 0.063X_4 + 0.038X_5 + 0.017X_6$$
$$+ 0.179 X_7 + 0.04X_8 \geq 0.15$$

$$0.29X_1 + 0.083X_2 + 0.027X_3 + 0.024X_4 + 0.027X_5 + 0.023X_6$$
$$+ 0.288X_7 + 0.109X_8 \leq 0.14$$

Finally, we have nonnegative constraints:

$$X_i \geq 0, \quad \text{for } i = 1, 2, \ldots, 8$$

The complete model is

Minimize $0.22X_1 + 0.19X_2 + 0.10X_3 + 0.10X_4 + 0.07X_5 + 0.05X_6 + 0.26X_7 + 0.11X_8$

$$X_1 + X_2 + X_3 + X_4 + X_5 + X_6 + X_7 + X_8 = 1$$

$$0.169X_1 + 0.12X_2 + 0.085X_3 + 0.154X_4 + 0.085X_5 + 0.12X_6$$
$$+ 0.18X_7 + 0.119X_8 \geq 0.13$$

$$0.26X_1 + 0.041X_2 + 0.038X_3 + 0.063X_4 + 0.038X_5 + 0.017X_6$$
$$+ 0.179X_7 + 0.04X_8 \geq 0.15$$

$$0.29X_1 + 0.083X_2 + 0.027X_3 + 0.024X_4 + 0.027X_5 + 0.023X_6$$
$$+ 0.288X_7 + 0.109X_8 \leq 0.14$$

$$X_i \geq 0, \quad \text{for } i = 1, 2, \ldots, 8$$

Production Planning

Contemporary Fashions is a home-based company that makes hand-painted sweat-shirts for children. Forecasts of sales for the next year are 150 in the autumn, 400 in the winter, and 50 in the spring. Plain sweatshirts are purchased for $20. The cost of capital is 24 percent per year (or 6 percent per quarter); thus, the holding cost per shirt is $0.06(20) = \$1.20$ per quarter. The owner hires students part-time to craft the clothing during the autumn, and they earn $5.50 per hour. Because of the high demand for part-time help during the winter holiday season, labor rates are higher in the winter, and workers earn $7.00 per hour. In the spring, labor is more difficult to keep, and the owner must pay $6.25 per hour to retain qualified help. Each sweatshirt takes two hours to complete. How should production be planned over the three quarters to mini-mize the combined production and inventory holding costs?

The principal decision variables are the number of sweatshirts to produce during each of the three quarters. However, it may be advantageous to produce in excess of demand during some quarter and carry the shirts in inventory, thereby letting lower labor rates offset the carrying costs. Therefore, we must also define decision variables for the number of units to hold in inventory at the end of each quarter. The decision variables are

P_A = amount to produce in quarter 1
P_W = amount to produce in quarter 2
P_S = amount to produce in quarter 3
I_A = inventory held at the end of autumn
I_W = inventory held at the end of winter
I_S = inventory held at the end of spring

The production cost per sweatshirt is computed by multiplying the labor rate by the number of hours required to produce one. Thus, the unit cost in the autumn is ($5.50)(2) = \$11.00$; in the winter, ($7.00)(2) = \$14.00$; and in the spring, ($6.25)(2) = \$12.50$. The objective function is to minimize the total cost of production and inventory. (Since the cost of the sweatshirts themselves is constant, it is not relevant to the prob-lem we are addressing.) The objective function is therefore

Minimize $11P_A + 14P_W + 12.50P_S + 1.20I_A + 1.20I_W + 1.20I_S$

The only explicit constraint is that demand must be satisfied. Note that both the production in a quarter as well as the inventory held from the *previous* time quarter can be used to satisfy demand. In addition, any amount in excess of the demand is held to the next quarter. Therefore, the constraints take the form of *inventory balance equations* that essentially say "what is available in any time period must be accounted for somewhere." More formally,

Production + Inventory from the Previous Quarter

= Demand + Inventory Held to the Next Quarter

This can be represented visually using the diagram in Figure 11.3. For each quarter, the sum of the variables coming in must equal the sum of the variables going out. Drawing such a figure is very useful for any type of multitime period planning model. This results in the constraint set

$$P_A + 0 = 150 + I_A$$
$$P_W + I_A = 400 + I_W$$
$$P_S + I_W = 50 + I_S$$

Moving all variables to the left side (a common practice in formulating linear programs) results in the model

$$\text{Minimize } 11P_A + 14P_W + 12.50P_S + 1.20I_A + 1.20I_W + 1.20I_S$$

Subject to

$$P_A - I_A = 150$$
$$P_W + I_A - I_W = 400$$
$$P_S + I_W - I_S = 50$$
$$P_i \geq 0, \quad \text{for all } i$$
$$I_i \geq 0, \quad \text{for all } i$$

As we have noted, developing models is more of an art than a science; consequently, there is often more than one way to model a particular problem. Using the ideas presented in this example, we may construct an alternative model involving only the production variables. We simply have to make sure that demand is satisfied. We can do this by ensuring that the cumulative production in each quarter is at least as great as the cumulative demand. This is expressed by the following constraints:

$$P_A \geq 150$$
$$P_A + P_W \geq 550$$
$$P_A + P_W + P_S \geq 600$$
$$P_A, P_W, P_S \geq 0$$

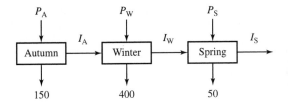

FIGURE 11.3 Material Balance Constraint Structure

The differences between the left and right hand sides of these constraints are the ending inventories for each period (and we need to keep track of these amounts because inventory has a cost associated with it). Thus, we use the following objective function:

$$\text{Minimize } 11P_A + 14P_W + 12.50P_S + 1.20(P_A - 150) + 1.20(P_A + P_W - 550)$$
$$+ 1.20(P_A + P_W + P_S - 600)$$

Of course, this function can be simplified algebraically by combining like terms. While these two models look very different, they are equivalent and will produce the same solution.

Cash Management

A financial manager must ensure that funds are available to pay company expenditures but would also like to maximize interest income. Three short-term investment options are available over the next six months: A, a one-month CD that pays 0.5 percent, available each month; B, a three-month CD that pays 1.75 percent, available at the beginning of the first four months; and C, a six-month CD that pays 2.3 percent, available in the first month. The net expenditures for the next six months are forecast as $50,000, ($12,000), $23,000, ($20,000), $41,000, ($13,000). Amounts in parentheses indicate a net inflow of cash. The company must maintain a cash balance of at least $100,000 at the end of each month. The company currently has $200,000 in cash.

This is another multitime period problem. At the beginning of each month, the manager must decide how much to invest in each alternative that may be available. Define

A_i = amount ($) to invest in a one-month CD at the start of month i
B_i = amount ($) to invest in a three-month CD at the start of month i
C_i = amount ($) to invest in a six-month CD at the start of month i

Because the time horizons on these alternatives vary, it is helpful to draw a picture to represent the investments and returns for each year as shown in Figure 11.4. Each circle represents the beginning of a month. Arrows represent the investments and cash flows. For example, investing in a three-month CD at the start of month 1 (B_1) matures at the beginning of month 4. It is reasonable to assume that all funds available would be invested.

From Figure 11.4, we see that investments A_6, B_4, and C_1 will mature at the end of month 6. To maximize the amount of cash on hand at the end of the planning period,

$$\text{Maximize } 1.005A_6 + 1.0175B_4 + 1.023C_1$$

The only constraints necessary are minimum cash balance equations. For each month, the net cash available, which is equal to the cash in less cash out, must be at least

FIGURE 11.4 Cash Balance Constraint Structure

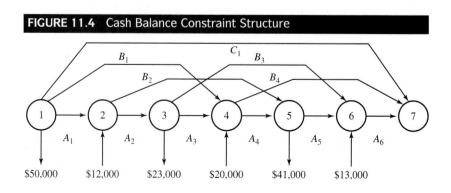

$100,000. These follow directly from Figure 11.4. The complete model is

$$\text{Maximize } 1.005A_6 + 1.0175B_4 + 1.023C_1$$

Subject to

$$200{,}000 - (A_1 + B_1 + C_1 + 50{,}000) \geq 100{,}000 \qquad \text{(Month 1)}$$
$$1.005A_1 + 12{,}000 - (A_2 + B_2) \geq 100{,}000 \qquad \text{(Month 2)}$$
$$1.005A_2 - (A_3 + B_3 + 23{,}000) \geq 100{,}000 \qquad \text{(Month 3)}$$
$$1.005A_3 + 1.0175B_1 + 20{,}000 - (A_4 + B_4) \geq 100{,}000 \qquad \text{(Month 4)}$$
$$1.005A_4 + 1.0175B_2 - (A_5 + 41{,}000) \geq 100{,}000 \qquad \text{(Month 5)}$$
$$1.005A_5 + 1.0175B_3 + 13{,}000 - A_6 \geq 100{,}000 \qquad \text{(Month 6)}$$
$$A_i, B_i, C_i \geq 0, \quad \text{for all } i$$

Transportation Problem

General Appliance Corporation produces refrigerators at two plants: Marietta, Georgia, and Minneapolis, Minnesota. They ship them to major distribution centers in Cleveland, Baltimore, Chicago, and Phoenix. The Accounting, Production, and Marketing departments have provided the information in Table 11.6, which shows the unit cost of shipping between any plant and distribution center, plant capacities over the next planning period, and distribution center demands. GAC's logistics manager faces the problem of determining how much to ship between each plant and distribution center to minimize the total transportation cost, not exceed available capacity, and meet customer demand.

To develop a linear optimization model, we first define the decision variables as the amount to ship between each plant and distribution center. In this model, we will use *double-subscripted variables* to simplify the formulation. Define X_{ij} = amount shipped from plant i to distribution center j, where $i = 1$ represents Marietta, $i = 2$ represents Minneapolis, $j = 1$ represents Cleveland, and so on. Using the unit cost data in Table 11.6, the total cost of shipping is equal to the unit cost times amount shipped, summed over all combinations of plants and distribution centers. Therefore, the objective function is to minimize total cost:

$$\text{Minimize } 12.60X_{11} + 14.35X_{12} + 11.52X_{13} + 17.58X_{14} + 9.75X_{21}$$
$$+ 12.63X_{22} + 8.11X_{23} + 15.88X_{24}$$

Because capacity is limited, the amount shipped from each plant cannot exceed its capacity. The total amount shipped from Marietta, for example, is $X_{11} + X_{12} + X_{13} + X_{14}$. Therefore, we have the constraint:

$$X_{11} + X_{12} + X_{13} + X_{14} \leq 1200$$

Similarly, the capacity limitation at Minneapolis leads to the constraint

$$X_{21} + X_{22} + X_{23} + X_{24} \leq 800$$

TABLE 11.6 Cost, Capacity, and Demand Data					
Plant/D.C.	*Cleveland*	*Baltimore*	*Chicago*	*Phoenix*	*Capacity*
Marietta	$12.60	$14.35	$11.52	$17.58	1200
Minneapolis	$9.75	$12.63	$8.11	$15.88	800
Demand	150	350	500	1000	

Next, we must ensure that the demand at each distribution center is met. This means that the total amount shipped to any distribution center from both plants must equal the demand. For instance, at Cleveland, we must have

$$X_{11} + X_{21} = 150$$

For the remaining three distribution centers, the constraints are:

$$X_{12} + X_{22} = 350$$
$$X_{13} + X_{23} = 500$$
$$X_{14} + X_{24} = 1000$$

Last, we need nonnegativity, $X_{ij} \geq 0$, for all i and j. The complete model is

Minimize $12.60X_{11} + 14.35X_{12} + 11.52X_{13} + 17.58X_{14} + 9.75X_{21}$
$$+ 12.63X_{22} + 8.11X_{23} + 15.88X_{24}$$

$$X_{11} + X_{12} + X_{13} + X_{14} \leq 1200$$
$$X_{21} + X_{22} + X_{23} + X_{24} \leq 800$$
$$X_{11} + X_{21} = 150$$
$$X_{12} + X_{22} = 350$$
$$X_{13} + X_{23} = 500$$
$$X_{14} + X_{24} = 1000$$
$$X_{ij} \geq 0, \quad \text{for all } i \text{ and } j$$

SPREADSHEET IMPLEMENTATION OF LINEAR PROGRAMMING MODELS

In the next chapter we will learn how to solve optimization models using an Excel tool called *Solver.* To facilitate the use of *Solver,* we suggest the following guidelines for designing spreadsheet models for optimization problems:

• Put the objective function coefficients, constraint coefficients, and right-hand-side values in a logical format in the spreadsheet. For example, you might assign the decision variables to columns and the constraints to rows, much like the mathematical formulation of the model, and input the model parameters in a matrix. If you have many more variables than constraints, it might make sense to use rows for the variables and columns for the constraints.

• Define a set of cells (either rows or columns) for the values of the decision variables. In some models, it may be necessary to define a matrix to represent the decision variables. The names of the decision variables should be listed directly above or immediately to the left of the decision variable cells.

• Define separate cells for the objective function and each constraint function (the left-hand side of a constraint). Use descriptive labels either immediately to the left or directly above these cells.

We will illustrate Excel models for two of the examples presented earlier in this chapter, the product mix model and the transportation problem.

Product Mix Spreadsheet Model
Figure 11.5 shows a spreadsheet model for the product mix example (*Product Mix Model.xls*). The *Data* portion of the spreadsheet provides the objective function coefficients, constraint coefficients, and right-hand sides of the model. Such data should be

	A	B	C	D
1	Product Mix Model			
2				
3	Data			
4		Gold	Platinum	Limitation
5	Component A	6	6	3000
6	Component B	3	5	1750
7	Profit/unit	$ 48.00	$ 70.00	
8				
9	Model			
10		Gold	Platinum	
11	Quantity Produced	100	200	Components Used
12	Component A Used	600	1200	1800
13	Component B Used	300	1000	1300
14				Total Profit
15	Profit Contribution	$ 4,800.00	$ 14,000.00	$ 18,800.00

FIGURE 11.5 Product Mix Model Spreadsheet Implementation

kept separate from the actual model so that if any data are changed, the model will automatically be updated. In the *Model* section, the number of each product to make is given in cells B11 and C11. Also in the *Model* section are calculations for the objective function, $48G + 70P$, in cell D15, and the constraint functions:

$6G$ (units of A used in production of Gold Players, cell B12)
$6P$ (units of A used in production of Platinum Players, cell C12)
$3G$ (units of B used in production of Gold Players, cell B13)
$5P$ (units of A used in production of Platinum Players, cell C13)
$6G + 6P$ (total units of component A used, cell D12)
$3G + 5P$ (total units of component B used, cell D13)

To show the correspondence between the mathematical model and the spreadsheet model more clearly, we will write the model in terms of the spreadsheet:

$$\text{Maximize Profit} = \text{D15} = \text{B7} \times \text{B11} + \text{C7} \times \text{C11}$$

subject to the constraints

$$\text{B5} \times \text{B11} + \text{C5} \times \text{C11} \leq \text{D5} \qquad \text{(component A limitation)}$$
$$\text{B6} \times \text{B11} + \text{C6} \times \text{C11} \leq \text{D6} \qquad \text{(component B limitation)}$$
$$\text{B11} \geq 0, \text{C11} \geq 0 \qquad \text{(nonnegativity)}$$

The solution shown in Figure 11.5 is to produce 100 Gold Players and 200 Platinum Players for a total profit of $20,800. This solution is feasible because the number of components used does not exceed the limitations. However, we do not know whether or not this solution is optimal.

Transportation Problem Spreadsheet Model

Figure 11.6 shows a spreadsheet implementation for the GAC transportation problem (*Transportation Model.xls*). In the *Model* section, the decision variables are stored in the plant-distribution center matrix. The objective function is computed in cell A18 as

$$\text{Total Cost} = \text{B6} \times \text{B13} + \text{C6} \times \text{C13} + \text{D6} \times \text{D13} + \text{E6} \times \text{E13} + \text{B7} \times \text{B14}$$
$$+ \text{C7} \times \text{C14} + \text{D7} \times \text{D14} + \text{E7} \times \text{E14}$$

To simplify this expression, you could also use the SUMPRODUCT function in Excel, and write this as

	A	B	C	D	E	F
1	**Transportation Model**					
2						
3	**Data**					
4			**Distribution Center**				
5	**Plant**	Cleveland	Baltimore	Chicago	Phoenix	**Capacity**
6	Marietta	$ 12.60	$ 14.35	$ 11.52	$ 17.58	1200
7	Minneapolis	$ 9.75	$ 12.63	$ 8.11	$ 15.88	800
8	**Demand**	150	350	500	1000	
9						
10	**Model**					
11			**Distribution Center**			**Total**
12	**Plant**	Cleveland	Baltimore	Chicago	Phoenix	**shipped**
13	Marietta	0	0	0	0	0
14	Minneapolis	0	0	0	0	0
15	**Demand met**	0	0	0	0	
16						
17	**Total cost**					
18	$ -					

FIGURE 11.6 Transportation Model Spreadsheet

Total Cost = SUMPRODUCT(B6:E6;B13:E13) + SUMPRODUCT(B7:E7;B14:E14)
$$= SUMPRODUCT(B6:E7;B13:E14)$$

To ensure that we do not exceed the capacity of any plant, the total shipped from each plant (cells F13:F14) cannot be greater than the plant capacities (cells F6:F7). For example,

Total Shipped from Marietta (cell F13) = B13 + C13 + D13 + E13
$$= SUM(B13:E13) \leq 1200 \text{ (cell F6)}$$

The constraint for Minneapolis is similar. Can you write it?

To ensure that demands are met, the total shipped to each distribution center (cells B15:E15) must equal or exceed the demands (cells B8:E8). Thus, for Cleveland,

Total Shipped to Cleveland (cell B15) = B13 + B14
$$= SUM(B13:B14) = 150 \text{ (cell B8)}$$

As you become more proficient in using spreadsheets, you should consider creating range names for the decision variables and constraint functions. This allows you to locate and manipulate elements of the model more easily. For example, in the product mix model, you might define the range B11:C11 as *Decisions* and the range B7:C7 as *Profit*. The total profit can then be computed easily as SUMPRODUCT (Decisions, Profit). In this book, however, we will stick with using cell references in all formulas.

Excel Functions to Avoid in Modeling Linear Programs

Several common functions in Excel can cause difficulties when attempting to solve linear programs using *Solver* because they are discontinuous at some point and introduce nonlinearities into what might appear to be a linear model. For instance, in the formula IF(A12<45, 0, 1), the cell value jumps from 0 to 1 when the value of cell A12 crosses 45. In such situations, the correct solution may not be identified. Common Excel functions to avoid are

- ABS
- MIN
- MAX

- INT
- ROUND
- IF
- COUNT

While these are useful in general modeling tasks with spreadsheets, you should avoid them in optimization models.

INTEGER OPTIMIZATION MODELS

An *integer programming (IP) model* is a linear program in which some or all of the decision variables are restricted to integer (whole-number) values. For many practical applications, we need not worry about forcing the decision variables to be integers. For example, in deciding on the optimal number of cases of diapers to produce next month, we could use an LP model, since rounding a value like 5621.63 would have little impact on the results. However, in a production planning decision involving low-volume, high-cost items such as airplanes, an optimal value of 10.42 would make little sense, and a difference of one unit could have significant economic consequences. Decision variables that we force to be integers are called *general integer variables.*

Many useful models require *binary variables,* which are variables that are restricted to being either 0 or 1. Mathematically, a binary variable x is simply a general integer variable that is restricted to being between 0 and 1:

$$0 \le x \le 1 \text{ and integer}$$

However, we usually just write this as

$$x = 0 \text{ or } 1$$

Binary variables enable us to model logical decisions in optimization models. For example, binary variables can be used to model decisions such as whether ($x = 1$) or not ($x = 0$) to place a facility at a certain location, whether or not to run a production line, or whether or not to invest in a certain stock.

Project Selection
A company's research and development group has identified five potential new engineering and development projects; however, the firm is constrained by its available budget and human resources. Each project is expected to generate a return (given by the net present value) but requires a fixed amount of cash and personnel. Because the resources are limited, all projects cannot be selected. Projects cannot be partially completed; thus, either the project must be undertaken completely or not at all. The data are given in Table 11.7. If a project is selected, it generates the full value of the expected return and requires the full amount of cash and personnel shown in Table 11.7. For example, if we select projects 1 and 3, the total return is $180,000 + $150,000 = $330,000, and these projects require cash totaling $55,000 + $24,000 = $79,000 and 5 + 2 = 7 personnel.

To model this situation, we define the decision variables to be binary, corresponding to either not selecting or selecting each project, respectively. Define $x_i = 1$ if project i is selected, and 0 otherwise. By multiplying these binary variables by the expected returns, the objective function is

$$\text{Maximize } \$180{,}000x_1 + \$220{,}000x_2 + \$150{,}000x_3 + \$140{,}000x_4 + \$200{,}000x_5$$

Because cash and personnel are limited, we have the constraints

TABLE 11.7 Project Selection Data

	Project 1	Project 2	Project 3	Project 4	Project 5	Available Resources
Expected return (NPV)	$180,000	$220,000	$150,000	$140,000	$200,000	
Cash requirements	$55,000	$83,000	$24,000	$49,000	$61,000	$150,000
Personnel requirements	5	3	2	5	3	12

$$\$55,000x_1 + \$83,000x_2 + \$24,000x_3 + \$49,000x_4$$
$$+ \$61,000x_5 \leq \$150,000 \quad \text{(cash limitation)}$$
$$5x_1 + 3x_2 + 2x_3 + 5x_4 + 3x_5 \leq 12 \quad \text{(personnel limitation)}$$

Note that if projects 1 and 3 are selected, then $x_1 = 1$ and $x_3 = 1$ and the objective and constraint functions equal

$$\text{Return} = \$180,000(1) + \$220,000(0) + \$150,000(1) + \$140,000(0)$$
$$+ \$200,000(0) = \$330,000$$
$$\text{Cash Required} = \$55,000(1) + \$83,000(0) + \$24,000(1) + \$49,000(0)$$
$$+ \$61,000(0) = \$79,000$$
$$\text{Personnel Required} = 5(1) + 3(0) + 2(1) + 5(0) + 3(0) = 7$$

The complete model is

$$\text{Maximize } \$180,000x_1 + \$220,000x_2 + \$150,000x_3 + \$140,000x_4 + \$200,000x_5$$
$$\$55,000x_1 + \$83,000x_2 + \$24,000x_3 + \$49,000x_4 + \$61,000x_5 \leq \$150,000$$
$$5x_1 + 3x_2 + 2x_3 + 5x_4 + 3x_5 \leq 12$$
$$x_i = 0, 1 \quad \text{for all } i$$

This model is easy to implement on a spreadsheet, as shown in Figure 11.7 (*Project Selection Model.xls*). The decision variables are defined in cells B11:F11. The objective function, computed in cell G14, is the total return, which can be expressed as the sum of the product of the return from each project and the binary decision variable:

Total Return = B5 × B11 + C5 × C11 + D5 × D11 + E5 × E11 + F5 × F11

These constraints can be written as

Cash Used = B6 × B11 + C6 × C11 + D6 × D11 + E6 × E11 + F6 × F11 ≤ G6
Personnel Used = B7 × B11 + C7 × C11 + D7 × D11 + E7 × E11 + F7 × F11 ≤ G7

The left-hand sides of these functions can be found in cells G12 and G13.

FIGURE 11.7 Project Selection Model Spreadsheet

	A	B	C	D	E	F	G
1	Project Selection Model						
2							
3	Data						Available
4		Project 1	Project 2	Project 3	Project 4	Project 5	Resources
5	Expected Return (NPV)	$ 180,000	$ 220,000	$ 150,000	$ 140,000	$ 200,000	
6	Cash requirements	$ 55,000	$ 83,000	$ 24,000	$ 49,000	$ 61,000	$ 150,000
7	Personnel requirements	5	3	2	5	3	12
8							
9	Model						
10							
11	Project selection decisions	1	0	0	1	0	Total
12	Cash Used	$ 55,000	$ -	$ -	$ 49,000	$ -	$ 104,000
13	Personnel Used	5	0	0	5	0	10
14	Return	$ 180,000	$ -	$ -	$ 140,000	$ -	$ 320,000

Constraint functions of binary variables can be used to model many different logical conditions. For instance, suppose that the R&D group has determined that at most one of projects 1 and 2 should be pursued. This can be modeled as

$$x_1 + x_2 \leq 1$$

Similarly, the constraint "If project 4 is chosen, then project 2 must also be chosen" can be modeled as

$$x_2 \geq x_4$$

or equivalently,

$$x_2 - x_4 \geq 0$$

Note that if project 4 is chosen ($x_4 = 1$), then x_2 must be at least 1 (i.e., project 2 must be chosen). On the other hand, if project 4 is not chosen ($x_4 = 0$), then the constraint reduces to $x_2 \geq 0$, and project 2 can either be selected or not.

Distribution Center Location

Binary variables can be combined with continuous variable models to include more complex decisions. Suppose that in the transportation model example discussed earlier, demand forecasts exceed the existing capacity and the company is considering adding a new plant from among two choices: Fayetteville, Arkansas, or Chico, California. Both plants would have a capacity of 1500 units but only one would be built. Table 11.8 shows the revised data.

The company now faces two decisions. It must decide which plant to build, and then how to best ship the product from the plant to the distribution centers. Of course, one approach would be to solve two separate transportation models, one that includes the Fayetteville plant, and the other that includes the Chico plant. However, we will demonstrate how to answer both questions simultaneously, as this provides the most efficient approach, especially if the number of alternatives and combinations is larger than for this example.

Define a binary variable for the decision of which plant to build: $Y_1 = 1$ if the Fayetteville plant is built, and $Y_2 = 1$ if the Chico plant is built. The objective function now includes terms for the proposed plant locations:

$$\text{Minimize } 12.60X_{11} + 14.35X_{12} + 11.52X_{13} + 17.58X_{14} + 9.75X_{21} + 12.63X_{22}$$
$$+ 8.11X_{23} + 15.88X_{24} + 10.41X_{31} + 11.54X_{32} + 9.87X_{33}$$
$$+ 8.32X_{34} + 13.88X_{41} + 16.95X_{42} + 12.51X_{43} + 11.64X_{44}$$

Capacity constraints for the Marietta and Minneapolis plants remain as before. However, for Fayetteville and Chico, we can only allow shipping from those locations if a plant is built there. To do this, we multiply the capacity by the binary variable corresponding to the location:

TABLE 11.8 Distribution Center Location Data

Plant/D.C.	Cleveland	Baltimore	Chicago	Phoenix	Capacity
Marietta	$12.60	$14.35	$11.52	$17.58	1200
Minneapolis	$ 9.75	$12.63	$ 8.11	$15.88	800
Fayetteville	$10.41	$11.54	$ 9.87	$ 8.32	1500
Chico	$13.88	$16.95	$12.51	$11.64	1500
Demand	300	500	700	1800	

$$X_{11} + X_{12} + X_{13} + X_{14} \leq 1200$$
$$X_{21} + X_{22} + X_{23} + X_{24} \leq 800$$
$$X_{31} + X_{32} + X_{33} + X_{34} \leq 1500Y_1$$
$$X_{41} + X_{42} + X_{43} + X_{44} \leq 1500Y_2$$

Note that if the binary variable is zero, then the right-hand side of the constraint is zero, forcing all shipment variables to be zero also. If, however, a particular Y variable is 1, then shipping up to the plant capacity is allowed. The demand constraints are the same as before, except that additional variables corresponding to the possible plant locations are added and new demand values are used:

$$X_{11} + X_{21} + X_{31} + X_{41} = 300$$
$$X_{12} + X_{22} + X_{32} + X_{42} = 500$$
$$X_{13} + X_{23} + X_{33} + X_{43} = 700$$
$$X_{14} + X_{24} + X_{34} + X_{44} = 1800$$

To guarantee that only one new plant is built, we must have

$$Y_1 + Y_2 = 1$$

Finally, we have nonnegativity for the continuous variables.

$$X_{ij} \geq 0, \quad \text{for all } i \text{ and } j$$

The complete model is

Minimize $12.60X_{11} + 14.35X_{12} + 11.52X_{13} + 17.58X_{14} + 9.75X_{21} + 12.63X_{22}$
$+ 8.11X_{23} + 15.88X_{24} + 10.41X_{31} + 11.54X_{32} + 9.87X_{33}$
$+ 8.32X_{34} + 13.88X_{41} + 16.95X_{42} + 12.51X_{43} + 11.64X_{44}$

$$X_{11} + X_{12} + X_{13} + X_{14} \leq 1200$$
$$X_{21} + X_{22} + X_{23} + X_{24} \leq 800$$
$$X_{31} + X_{32} + X_{33} + X_{34} \leq 1500Y_1$$
$$X_{41} + X_{42} + X_{43} + X_{44} \leq 1500Y_2$$
$$X_{11} + X_{21} + X_{31} + X_{41} = 300$$
$$X_{12} + X_{22} + X_{32} + X_{42} = 500$$
$$X_{13} + X_{23} + X_{33} + X_{43} = 700$$
$$X_{14} + X_{24} + X_{34} + X_{44} = 1800$$
$$Y_1 + Y_2 = 1$$
$$X_{ij} \geq 0, \quad \text{for all } i \text{ and } j$$
$$Y_1, Y_2 = 0, 1$$

Direct Marketing

For many years, R. Hahn Ski Outfitters has published a Christmas catalog that is sent to current customers on file. This strategy has been shown to generate additional mail-order business while also attracting more customers to the stores. Barb Hahn, vice president of marketing, is thinking about purchasing mailing lists of magazine subscribers through a list broker. The assumption behind this strategy is that subscribers to magazines having a high proportion of current customers would be viable targets for future purchases at company stores. To get a handle on which magazines might be more appropriate, 500 customers were selected randomly and asked which of 10 ski and outdoor activity magazines they read. So far, only 53 surveys have been returned, with results shown in Table 11.9 that are also available in the Excel worksheet *Direct*

TABLE 11.9 Survey Results			
Customer	*Magazines*	*Customer*	*Magazines*
1	10	28	4,7
2	1,4	29	6
3	1	30	3,4,5,10
4	5,6	31	4
5	5	32	8
6	10	33	1,3,10
7	2,9	34	4,5
8	5,8	35	1,5,6
9	1,5,10	36	1,3
10	4,6,8,10	37	3,5,8
11	6	38	3
12	3	39	2,7
13	5	40	2,7
14	2,6	41	7
15	8	42	4,5,6
16	6	43	NONE
17	4,5	44	5,10
18	7	45	1,2
19	5,6	46	7
20	2,8	47	1,5,10
21	7,9	48	3
22	6	49	1,3,4
23	3,6,10	50	NONE
24	NONE	51	2,6
25	5,8	52	NONE
26	3,10	53	2,5,8,9,10
27	2,8		

Marketing Data.xls. The costs of lists from these 10 magazines follow, and a budget of $2500 has been established. What magazines should be chosen to maximize overall exposure?

List	1	2	3	4	5	6	7	8	9	10
Cost	$900	$1000	$1100	$1500	$1500	$1500	$1000	$1200	$500	$1100

The decision variables are binary and represent whether or not to purchase a magazine list. Define $x_j = 1$ if list j is purchased, and 0 if not. From the survey results, we know which customers read each magazine. Let $a_{ij} = 1$ if customer i reads magazine j. Suppose we buy the list for magazine 1. Then $\sum_i a_{i1}$ is the number of customers who would be reached. Now suppose we buy the lists for both magazines 1 and 2. Summing a_{i1} plus a_{i2} over all customers, however, would *not* be the number of customers who would be reached if some of them read both magazines (i.e., the readership of the magazines is not mutually exclusive). We would have to subtract the number of customers who read both. This makes it difficult to relate the decision variables to our objective, which is to maximize exposure. Fortunately, we may use binary variables in a clever fashion.

Note that $\sum_j a_{ij} x_j$ will be at least 1 if customer i reads any magazines that are selected (i.e., magazines for which $x_j = 1$). Define a new variable $y_i = 1$ if customer i reads any magazine selected. Now consider the constraint

$$y_i \leq \sum_j a_{ij} x_j$$

If the right-hand side is 0 (customer i does not read any selected magazines), then y_i is forced to be 0. However, if the right-hand side is 1 or more, then y_i is allowed to be 1, which means that customer i reads at least one of the selected magazines. To maximize exposure, we simply have to maximize the objective function $\sum_i y_i$. In addition, we have the budget constraint

$$\$900x_1 + \$1000x_2 + \$1100x_3 + \$1500x_4 + \$1500x_5 + \$1500x_6 + \$1000x_7$$
$$+ \$1200x_8 + \$500x_9 + \$1100x_{10} \leq \$2500$$

The final model is

$$\text{Maximize} \sum_i y_i$$
$$y_i \leq \sum_j a_{ij} x_j$$

$$900x_1 + \$1000x_2 + \$1100x_3 + \$1500x_4 + \$1500x_5 + \$1500x_6 + \$1000x_7$$
$$+ \$1200x_8 + \$500x_9 + \$1100x_{10} \leq \$2500$$
$$x_i, y_j = 0, 1$$

NONLINEAR OPTIMIZATION

In many situations, the relationship among variables in a model is not linear. Whenever either the objective function or a constraint is not linear, the model becomes a *nonlinear optimization problem*, requiring different solution techniques. Nonlinear models do not have a common structure as do linear models, making it more difficult to develop appropriate models. We present two examples of nonlinear optimization models in business.

Hotel Pricing

The Marquis Hotel is considering a major remodeling effort and needs to determine the best combination of rates and room sizes to maximize revenues. Currently, the hotel has 450 rooms with the following history:

Room Type	Rate	Daily Avg. No. Sold	Revenue
Standard	$ 85	250	$21,250
Gold	$ 98	100	$ 9,800
Platinum	$139	50	$ 6,950
		Total Revenue	$38,000

Each market segment has its own price/demand elasticity. Estimates are

Room Type	Price Elasticity of Demand
Standard	−1.5
Gold	−2.0
Platinum	−1.0

This means, for example, that a *1 percent decrease* in the price of a standard room will *increase* the number of rooms sold by *1.5 percent.* Similarly, a 1 percent increase in the price will decrease the number of rooms sold by 1.5 percent. For any pricing structure (in $), the projected number of rooms of a given type sold (we will allow continuous values for this example) can be found using the formula:

(Historical Average Number of Rooms Sold) + (Elasticity)(New Price − Current Price)(Historical Average Number of Rooms Sold)/(Current Price)

The hotel owners want to keep the price of a standard room between $70 and $90; a gold room between $90 and $110; and a platinum room between $120 and $149. Define S = price of a standard room, G = price of a gold room, and P = price of a platinum room. Thus, for standard rooms, the projected number of rooms sold is $250 - 1.5(S - 85)(250/85) = 625 - 4.41176S$. The objective is to set the room prices to maximize total revenue. Total revenue would equal the price times the projected number of rooms sold, summed over all three types of rooms. Therefore, total revenue would be

$$\text{Total Revenue} = S(625 - 4.41176S) + G(300 - 2.04082G) + P(100 - 0.35971P)$$
$$= 625S + 300G + 100P - 4.41176S^2 - 2.04082G^2 - 0.35971P^2$$

To keep prices within the stated ranges, we need constraints:

$$70 \leq S \leq 90$$
$$90 \leq G \leq 110$$
$$120 \leq P \leq 149$$

Finally, although the rooms may be renovated, there are no plans to expand beyond the current 450-room capacity. Thus, the projected number of total rooms sold cannot exceed 450:

$$(625 - 4.41176S) + (300 - 2.04082G) + (100 - 0.35971P) \leq 450$$

or

$$1025 - 4.41176S - 2.04082G - 0.35971P \leq 450$$

The full model is

$$\text{Maximize } 625S + 300G + 100P - 4.41176S^2 - 2.04082G^2 - 0.35971P^2$$

$$70 \leq S \leq 90$$
$$90 \leq G \leq 110$$
$$120 \leq P \leq 149$$
$$1025 - 4.41176S - 2.04082G - 0.35971P \leq 450$$

Figure 11.8 shows a spreadsheet model for this situation (*Hotel Pricing.xls*). The decision variables, the new prices to charge, are given in cells B13:B15. The projected numbers of rooms sold are computed in cells E13:E15 using the preceding formula. By multiplying the number of rooms sold by the new price for each room type, the projected revenue is calculated, as given in cells F13:F15. The total revenue in cell F16 represents the objective function. Note that it is easier to formulate this model more as a financial spreadsheet than to enter the analytical formulas as they were developed above.

The constraints—(1) the new price must fall within the allowable price range and (2) the total projected number of rooms sold must not exceed 450—can be expressed within the spreadsheet model as

$$\text{B13:B15} \geq \text{C13:C15}$$
$$\text{B13:B15} \leq \text{D13:D15}$$

and

$$\text{E16} \leq \text{E6}$$

	A	B	C	D	E	F
1	Marquis Hotel					
2						
3	Data					
4		Current	Average		Total Room	
5	Room type	Rate	Daily Sold	Elasticity	Capacity	
6	Standard	$ 85.00	250	-1.5	450	
7	Gold	$ 98.00	100	-2		
8	Platinum	$ 139.00	50	-1		
9						
10	Model				Projected	
11					Rooms	Projected
12	Room type	New Price	Price Range		Sold	Revenue
13	Standard	$ 70.00	$ 70.00	$ 90.00	316	$22,132.35
14	Gold	$ 110.00	$ 90.00	$ 110.00	76	$ 8,306.12
15	Platinum	$ 120.00	$ 120.00	$ 149.00	57	$ 6,820.14
16					Totals 448.521207	$37,258.62

FIGURE 11.8 Spreadsheet Model for Hotel Pricing Problem

Markowitz Portfolio Model[1]

The Markowitz portfolio model seeks to minimize the risk of a portfolio of stocks subject to a constraint on the portfolio's expected return. For example, suppose an investor is considering three stocks. The expected return for stock 1 is 10 percent; for stock 2, 12 percent; and for stock 3, 7 percent; and she would like an expected return of at least 10 percent. Clearly one option is to invest everything in stock 1; however, this may not be a good idea as the risk might be too high. Recall from Chapter 8 that risk is measured by the variance. Research has found the variance–covariance matrix of the individual stocks to be:

	Stock 1	Stock 2	Stock 3
Stock 1	0.025	0.015	−0.002
Stock 2		0.030	0.005
Stock 3			0.004

Thus, the decision variables are the percent of each stock to allocate to the portfolio. (You might be familiar with the term "asset allocation model" that many financial investment companies suggest to their clients; for example, "maintain 60 percent equities, 30 percent bonds, and 10 percent cash.") Define x_j = fraction of the portfolio to invest in stock j.

The objective function is to minimize the risk of the portfolio as measured by its variance. Because stock prices are correlated with one another, the variance of the portfolio must reflect not only variances of the stocks in the portfolio but also the covariance between stocks. The variance of a portfolio is the weighted sum of the variances and covariances:

$$\text{Variance of Portfolio} = \sum_{i=1}^{k} s_i^2 x_i^2 + \sum_{i=1}^{k} \sum_{j>1}^{k} 2 s_{ij} x_i x_j$$

where

s_i^2 = the sample variance in the return of stock i
s_{ij} = the sample covariance between stocks i and j

[1] H. M. Markowitz, *Portfolio Selection, Efficient Diversification of Investments* (New York: John Wiley & Sons, 1959).

Using the preceding data, the objective function is

$$\text{Minimize Variance} = 0.025x_1^2 + 0.030x_2^2 + 0.004x_3^2 + 2(0.015)x_1x_2$$
$$+ 2(-0.002)x_1x_3 + 2(0.005)x_2x_3$$

The constraints must first ensure that we invest 100 percent of our budget. Since the variables are defined as fractions, we must have

$$x_1 + x_2 + x_3 = 1$$

Second, the portfolio must have an expected return of at least 10 percent. The expected return on a portfolio is simply the weighted sum of the expected returns of the stocks in the portfolio.

$$10x_1 + 12x_2 + 7x_3 \geq 10$$

Finally, we cannot invest negative amounts:

$$x_1, x_2, x_3 \geq 0$$

The complete model is

$$\text{Minimize Variance} = 0.025x_1^2 + 0.030x_2^2 + 0.004x_3^2 + 0.03x_1x_2$$
$$- 0.004x_1x_3 + 0.010x_2x_3$$

$$x_1 + x_2 + x_3 = 1$$
$$10x_1 + 12x_2 + 7x_3 \geq 10$$
$$x_1, x_2, x_3 \geq 0$$

Figure 11.9 shows a spreadsheet model for this example (*Markowitz Model.xls*). The decision variables (fraction of each stock in the portfolio) are entered in cells B14:B16. The expected return and variance of the portfolio are computed in cells B18 and B19. The solution shown is feasible in that it meets the target return. The variance of the portfolio is 0.017.

FIGURE 11.9   Spreadsheet for Markowitz Portfolio Model

	A	B	C	D	E	F	G
1	Markowitz Model						
2							
3	Data						
4		Expected			Variance-Covariance Matrix		
5		Return			Stock 1	Stock 2	Stock 3
6	Stock 1	10%		Stock 1	0.025	0.015	-0.002
7	Stock 2	12%		Stock 2		0.03	0.005
8	Stock 3	7%		Stock 3			0.004
9	Target Return	10%					
10							
11	Model						
12				Variance Calculations			
13		Allocation		Squared Terms	Cross-Products		
14	Stock 1	0.20		0.001	0.0036		
15	Stock 2	0.60		0.0108	-0.00016		
16	Stock 3	0.20		0.00016	0.0012		
17	Total	1					
18	Expected Return	10.6%					
19	Variance	0.017					

An alternative approach would be to maximize the return subject to a constraint on risk. For example, suppose the investor wants to maximize expected return subject to a risk (variance) no greater than 1 percent? This form of the model would be

$$\text{Maximize } 10x_1 + 12x_2 + 7x_3$$

$$x_1 + x_2 + x_3 = 1$$
$$0.025x_1^2 + 0.030x_2^2 + 0.004x_3^2 + 0.03x_1x_2 - 0.004x_1x_3 + 0.010x_2x_3 \leq 0.01$$
$$x_1, x_2, x_3 \geq 0$$

In this case, we would have a linear objective function and a mixture of linear and non-linear constraints.

Questions and Problems

1. For each of the examples in this chapter, classify the constraints into the following categories. Are there any other types of constraints that do not fall into these categories?
   a. Simple bounds
   b. Limitations
   c. Requirements
   d. Proportional relationships
   e. Balance constraints

2. A manufacturer of office equipment produces two types of desks, standard and deluxe. Deluxe desks have oak tops and more expensive hardware and require additional time for finishing and polishing. Standard desks require 80 square feet of pine wood and 12 hours of labor, while deluxe desks require 62 square feet of pine, 18 square feet of oak, and 18 hours of labor. For the next week, the company has 5000 square feet of pine, 700 square feet of oak, and 400 hours of labor available. Standard desks net a profit of $75, while deluxe desks net a profit of $160. All desks can be sold to national chains such as Staples or Office Depot. Develop a model to determine how many of each the company should make next week to maximize profit contribution.

3. The International Chef, Inc. markets three blends of oriental tea: premium, Duke Grey, and breakfast. The firm uses tea leaves from India, China, and new domestic California sources.

Quality	Tea Leaves (percent)		
	Indian	Chinese	California
Premium	40	20	40
Duke Grey	20	30	40
Breakfast	20	40	40

Net profit per pound for each blend is $0.50 for premium, $0.30 for Duke Grey, and $0.20 for breakfast. The firm's regular weekly supplies are 20,000 pounds of Indian tea leaves and 22,000 pounds of Chinese tea leaves. Because it is new, and until it proves itself, no more than 16,000 pounds of California tea is to be used in a week. The Marketing Research Department reports that there is an almost unlimited market for premium and fine blends. However, the maximum expected sale for breakfast blend is 2000 pounds. Develop a linear optimization model to determine the optimal mix to maximize profit.

4. Metropolitan Airport Services, Inc. is considering purchasing cars for transportation service between the municipal airport and hotels in the downtown area. They are considering station wagons, minibuses, and large buses. Purchase prices are $45,000 for each station wagon, $90,000 for each minibus, and $200,000 for each large bus. The board of directors has authorized a maximum budget of $5,000,000 for purchases. Because of the heavy air travel in the area, these vehicles would be utilized at maximum capacity regardless of the type of vehicle purchased. Expected net annual profit would be $1500 per station wagon, $3500 per minibus, and $5000 per large bus. The company has hired 30 new drivers for these vehicles, each qualified to drive any one of the three vehicle types. The Maintenance Department has the capacity to handle an additional 80 station wagons. A minibus is equivalent to $1\frac{2}{3}$ station wagons for maintenance purposes, and a large bus is equivalent to 2 station wagons for maintenance purposes. Develop a linear optimization model to determine the optimal number of each type of vehicle to purchase in order to maximize profit.

5. A company in Victoria, Texas produces bottles of aspirin products. Sales prices are

PRODUCT	SALES PRICE
Super Seltzer	$3.00
Capsules	$3.50
Cheap Seltzer	$2.00
Tablets	$2.50

The company ships these products to two distributors, located at Hearne, Texas and Cuero, Texas. There is unlimited demand at each distributor. Shipping costs per bottle and contracted minimum quantities for each distributor are

	Hearne	Cuero
Shipping cost/bottle	$0.21	$0.22
Minimum demand		
Super Seltzer	700	1000
Capsules	800	1500
Cheap Seltzer	1000	800
Tablets	1800	5000

Raw material costs and maximum available quantities are given below:

	Cost/Ounce	Maximum Ounces
Acetylsalicylic acid	$0.60	50,000
Sodium	$0.30	25,000

The production costs per bottle and raw materials required per bottle are

	Production Cost/Bottle	Ounces Acet. Acid	Ounces Sodium
Super Seltzer	$0.25	2	3
Capsules	0.35	4	0
Cheap Seltzer	0.15	2	2
Tablets	0.10	3	0

Because capsules have become an insurance problem, the total number of bottles of capsules produced is to be no more than 20 percent of the total number of bottles produced. Develop a linear optimization model.

6. You have been given $1 million by a deceased relative. You plan to invest this money (in varying amounts) in up to four long-term investment instruments (stocks, bonds, savings, and real estate). You evaluate investments in stocks and bonds at the beginning of each of the next six years. Each dollar invested in stocks at the beginning of the year is expected to return an average of $1.15 in time for immediate reinvestment one year later. Each dollar invested in bonds at the beginning of each year is expected to return $1.30 three years later (a profit of 30 percent in three years). Credit Union Savings returns $1.05 one year later, and each dollar invested in real estate is expected to return $1.30 four years later. A maximum of $200,000 can be invested in real estate in any one year.

    You want to diversify your investments to minimize risk. The total invested in stocks in a given year should not exceed 30 percent of the total investment in the other alternatives for that year. At least 25 percent of the total investment should be in Credit Union Savings certificates. You also want to have $150,000 available in cash (which can be immediately reinvested) at the end of the third year as leverage in negotiating with your relatives. Develop a model to maximize the cash on hand at the end of the sixth year.

7. JDC Inc. is planning the purchase of a component needed for its new product soon to be released. The anticipated demands for the next 12 months are given here. The cost to hold the component in inventory is $2.75 per component per month. The price of the component is expected to be constant at $10 per unit. Develop a model to determine when to purchase the component to minimize the cost of satisfying demand.

Period	1	2	3	4	5	6	7	8	9	10	11	12
Demand	15	20	30	40	150	360	400	600	450	80	30	20

8. A city council is reviewing housing proposals for a new development area. There is some dispute among various interest groups as to what the goals are. The zoning committee has recommended three types of housing: single-family houses, deluxe condominiums, and apartments, and has also provided the following data:

	Family	Condos	Apartment
Land usage, acres/unit	0.25	0.40	0.125
Families housed/unit	1	4	6
Tax base generated/unit	$50,000	$100,000	$25,000
Utility installation expense/unit	$ 4,000	$ 8,000	$ 6,000

Twenty acres are available for zoning. Utility installation expense is to be held to no more than $1 million.

A public opinion survey has been conducted, and the city council has reviewed this survey. Important issues are to provide housing to families, generate tax base, and minimize installation costs. Develop linear optimization models to maximize families housed and also for maximizing the tax base added.

9. Larry Doyle was recently named by Governor McGraw as campaign director for his upcoming reelection campaign. Governor McGraw thinks that if he can get his message to 2 million people in the state, he has a good chance to win a large chunk of votes at the state Libertarian Party convention. Larry has obtained the following information about advertising media availability and cost:

Medium	Voter Exposure per $1,000 Spent	Cost per Insertion	Maximum Units
Prime-time TV	10,000	$5,000	60
Non-prime-time TV	4,000	$4,000	60
Radio	3,500	$3,000	100
Newspaper	1,500	$2,000	120
Billboards	750	$1,000	150

Governor McGraw has a campaign fund of $6 million available, which according to state election law, cannot be exceeded. As a traditionalist, Governor McGraw has specified that he wants to place at least one ad in each of the 50 largest newspapers in the state (just before it is time for them to make their editorial recommendations to voters). Formulate a linear model to maximize voter exposure.

10. A small canning company specializes in gourmet canned foods. They can five combinations of ham, lima beans, and jalapeno peppers.

Product (16 oz. Cans)	Maximum Demand (Includes Signed Contracts)	Signed Contracts/Day (Minimum Demands)
Ham & Beans	10,000 cans/day	5,000 cans/day
Jalapeno Ham & Beans	4,000	1,000
Lima Beans	6,000	1,000
Jalapeno Lima Beans	4,000	2,000
Jalapeno Peppers	1,000	0 (new product)

The Production Department obtains input materials and fills 16 oz. cans. All quantities are in ounces, and all costs and sales prices/can are in $. There is a maximum production limit of 24,000 cans/day. Canning costs are constant.

Product	Ham	Lima Beans	Jalapenos	Water	Can Cost	Price ($)
Ham & Beans	4	9	0	3	0.05	2.31
Jalapeno Ham & Beans	3	9	1	3	0.05	2.00
Lima Beans	0	14	0	2	0.05	0.85
Jalapeno Lima Beans	0	12	1	3	0.05	0.90
Jalapeno Peppers	0	0	12	4	0.05	1.35
Cost of Materials	$0.40/oz	$0.05/oz	$0.10/oz	free		

The company has a contract with a ham supplier for daily delivery of up to 30,000 oz. of ham at $.30/oz. They also have a contract with a lima bean supplier for up to 100,000 oz. of lima beans per day at $.05/oz. They do not have to pay for materials they do not use. They grow their own jalapenos, which cost $.10/oz to pick, as shown in the preceding table, with no limitations on the supply. Formulate an appropriate optimization model.

11. You are in the business of producing and selling 100 pound bags of health food for pet pigs. You plan to advertise that each bag will provide a pet pig its minimum weekly requirements of protein (200 grams), calcium (300 grams), and fiber (100 grams) and will contain no more than 500 calories. You have found supplies at reasonable cost for three possible ingredients.

	Cost	Protein	Calcium	Fiber	Calories
Corn	$.03/lb	100 g/lb	2 g/lb	1 g/lb	50/lb
Fishbones	$.005/lb	1 g/lb	50 g/lb	none	2/lb
Sawdust	$.001/lb	none	none	200 g/lb	1/lb

You plan to sell the bag for $1. Develop an optimization model for this problem.

12. A department store chain is planning opening a new store. It needs to decide how to allocate the 100,000 square feet of available floor space among seven departments. Data on expected performance of each department per month, in terms of square feet (sf), are

Department	Investment/ sf	Risk as a % of $ Invested	Minimum sf	Maximum sf	Expected Profit per sf
Electronics	$100	24	6000	30000	$12.00
Furniture	50	12	10000	30000	6.00
Men's Clothing	30	5	2000	5000	2.00
Clothing	600	10	3000	40000	30.00
Jewelry	900	14	1000	10000	20.00
Books	50	2	1000	5000	1.00
Appliances	400	3	12000	40000	13.00

The company has gathered $20 million to invest in floor stock. The risk element is a measure of risk associated with investment in floor stock. The idea is that electronics loses $10/$100 invested per month, based on past records at other places for outdated inventory, pilferage, breakage, etc. Electronics is the highest-risk item. Expected profit is after covering risk. Develop a linear optimization model to maximize profit that includes a constraint to measure total investment, as well as a constraint to measure dollars at risk.

13. Gulf Coast Oil Company is a petroleum refining company headquartered in Cut-and-Shoot, Texas. The company does not operate its own oil wells. Instead, it purchases crude oil from a number of drilling companies on a long-term contract basis. The company has refineries located in Houston, Corpus Christi, and Fort Worth and has three distribution depots located in San Antonio, Texarkana, and El Paso.

The transportation problem faced by Gulf Coast Oil is to supply the required quantity of gasoline to each of the distribution depots. Each depot has specific demands, and each refinery has specific capacities. These parameters and the costs of moving one load of fuel from each refinery to each depot are

	Capacity			Demand	
Source:	Houston	150	Depot:	San Antonio	200
	Corpus Christi	100		Texarkana	120
	Fort Worth	250		El Paso	180

From	To	Unit Cost
Houston	San Antonio	20
	Texarkana	9
	El Paso	5
Corpus Christi	San Antonio	6
	Texarkana	10
	El Paso	18
Fort Worth	San Antonio	2
	Texarkana	15
	El Paso	12

Develop a linear optimization model to minimize the cost of transportation.

14. Liquid Gold, Inc. transports radioactive waste from nuclear power plants to disposal sites around and about the country. Each plant has an amount of material that must be moved each period. Each site has a limited capacity per period. The cost of transporting between sites is given here (some combinations of plants and storage sites are not to be used, and no figure is given).

Plant	Material	Cost to Site				Site	Capacity
		S51	S62	S73	S87		
P1	20,876	105	86	—	23	S51	285,922
P2	50,870	86	58	41	—	S62	308,578
P3	38,652	93	46	65	38	S73	111,955
P4	28,951	116	27	94	—	S87	208,555
P5	87,423	88	56	82	89		
P6	76,190	111	36	72	—		
P7	58,237	169	65	48	—		

Develop a transportation model for this problem.

15. The personnel director of a company that recently absorbed another firm and is now downsizing must relocate five information systems analysts from recently closed locations. Unfortunately, there are only three positions available for five people. Salaries are fairly uniform among this group (those with higher pay were already given the opportunity to begin anew). Moving expenses will be used as the means of determining who will be sent where. Estimated moving expenses are

Analyst	Moving Cost to		
	Gary	Salt Lake City	Fresno
Arlene	$8,000	$7,000	$5,000
Bobby	$5,000	$8,000	$12,000
Charlene	$9,000	$15,000	$16,000
Douglas	$4,000	$8,000	$13,000
Emory	$7,000	$3,000	$4,000

Model this as an integer optimization model to minimize cost and determine which analysts to relocate to the three locations.

16. You have the responsibility of providing analytic support to a company committee in charge of administering new computer projects. This committee has a budget of $2,500,000 to fund projects. There are four company departments (A, B, C, and D) that have submitted project proposals. Each proposal includes estimates of total cost, number of systems analysts required, number of special programmers required, and estimated cash flow for the next year, estimated after-tax profit for the next year, and net present value. There are 12 systems analysts available, and 6 special programmers who could be devoted to these projects. The board of directors has given minimum required limits for next year's cash flow and after-tax profits. Cash flow from these projects is to be at least $300,000. After-tax profits from these projects is to be at least $200,000. The board would like to maximize the net present value of the selected projects, subject to the preceding limits and the restriction that projects must be either adopted or not adopted. (You cannot recommend partial project funding.)

	Project Cost ($1,000)	Estimated Analysts (People)	Systems Programmers (People)	Cash Flow	Net Present After-Tax	
					Profit ($1,000)	Value ($1,000)
A01	230	3	0	50	20	100
A02	370	4	1	75	30	190
A03	180	2	0	40	20	80
A04	90	1	2	10	10	30
A05	570	4	1	160	70	220
B06	750	3	0	240	110	390
B07	370	3	1	100	40	180
B08	250	3	0	55	20	140
B09	190	2	0	30	10	90
B10	200	1	2	0	10	90
C11	310	2	0	50	20	70
C12	430	3	1	125	10	10
C13	680	3	0	205	100	170
C14	550	1	3	0	50	100
D15	290	1	1	100	40	140
D16	200	1	1	50	20	90
D17	150	1	2	0	10	110

The letter in the project name indicates the department that submitted the project. An additional limit, for political purposes, is that each of these four departments receives funding for at least one project. Model this problem to find a solution yielding the maximum net present value.

17. Many high technology products such as crystals and alloys can be manufactured more efficiently in the weightless environment of earth orbit. You are planning production operations for a space flight. Five products are being considered. There are unit profits, volumes, weights, labor hours per unit, and maximum demands. Model this problem as an integer optimization problem.

Products	Alloy 1	Alloy 2	Crystal 1	Crystal 2	Interferon
Profit ($/unit)	10	1.7	3.5	1.6	2.6
Volume (CF/unit)	9	3	10	7	13
Weight (lb/unit)	59	18	26	26	10
Labor (/unit)	2.2	0.5	0.7	0.2	1.1
Demand ($\leq$)	22	69	90	40	85

Volume available: 600 CF
Weight allowable: 2100 lb
Labor available: 40 hr

18. The producers of cassette tapes (for those who still buy them!) are faced with the problem of placing songs on either side of the tape so that the total time on each side is as close as possible to being equal in length (they sometimes fail in this endeavor, as evidenced by those blank portions we must endure on certain tapes). Formulate this problem as a linear integer program for the following example:

SONG	RUN TIME (MINUTES:SECONDS)
1	2:56
2	3:37
3	3:44
4	3:50
5	4:00
6	4:05
7	4:06
8	4:08
9	4:16
10	4:20

19. Larsen E. Whipsnade is a young entrepreneur. His latest invention is an air-adjustable basketball shoe with pump, similar to those advertised widely by more expensive brand names. Larsen contacted a supplier of Victor basketball shoes, a little-known brand with low advertising. This supplier would provide shoes at the nominal price of $6 per pair of shoes. Larsen needed to know the best price at which to sell these shoes.

    As a business student with strong economics training, Larsen remembered that the volume sold is affected by the product's price—the higher the price, the lower the volume. He asked his friends and acquaintances what they would pay for a premium pair of basketball shoes that were a "little off-brand." Based on this data, he developed the formula:

$$\text{Volume} = 1000 - 20 \times \text{Price}$$

There are some minor expenses involved, including a $50 fee for selling shoes in the neighborhood (a fixed cost), as well as his purchase price of $6 per shoe. Develop an appropriate objective function to find the optimal price level.

20. Larsen (Problem 19) did very well selling Victor shoes. His shoe supplier told him of a new product, Abibas, that was entering the market. This shoe would be a product substitute for Victors, so that the higher the price of either shoe, the greater the demand for the other. Larsen interviewed more

potential clients to determine price response and cross elasticities. This yielded the following relationships:

$$\text{Volume of Victors} = 1000 - 20P_v + 1P_a$$
$$\text{Volume of Abibas} = 800 + 2P_v - 18P_a$$

where P_v = price of Victors and P_a = price of Abibas. Develop a new profit function to include this information.

21. Kern's Meats has developed a sausage that consists of a blend of the finest meats available locally, along with hot peppers for flavor, okra for fiber, and club soda for additional sodium. Sausages are to each weigh exactly one pound. The meat purchased is not uniform; the variance in the content of meat is shown in the following table along with other important data.

	Pork	Hamburger	Goat	Peppers	Okra	Soda
Cost	$1.5/lb	$2.0/lb	$0.6/lb	$0.25/lb	$0.2/lb	$0.01/lb
Fiber	0.05 cc/lb	0.1 cc/lb	0.2 cc/lb	0.03 cc/lb	0.8 cc/lb	0
Sodium	0.05 cc/lb	0.02 cc/lb	0.03 cc/lb	0	0	0.01 cc/lb
Variance in meat content	0.1	0.1	0.3			

The mixture is to contain at least 50 percent meat (pork, hamburger, and goat) by weight and should contain at least 0.35 cc of fiber and no more than 0.02 cc of salt. Soda should be no more than 10 percent of the sausage by weight. Define decision variables as the number of pounds of each material per sausage. The meat requirement constraint that incorporates the variance of meat content is

Pork + Hamburger + Goat − z(SQRT[0.1 Pork + 0.1 Hamburger
+ 0.3 Goat]) ≥ 0.5(Pork + Hamburger + Goat
+ Peppers + Okra + Soda)

where z is the value of the standard normal distribution corresponding to a probability of actually achieving the meat requirement. Develop an optimization model for this problem.

22. The Hal Chase Investment Planning Agency is in business to help investors optimize their return from investment, including consideration of risk. Hal deals with three investment mediums: a stock fund, a bond fund, and his own Sports and Casino Investment Plan (SCIP). The stock fund is a mutual fund investing in openly traded stocks. The bond fund focuses on the bond market, which has a much stabler but lower expected return. SCIP is a high-risk scheme, often resulting in heavy losses but occasionally coming through with spectacular gains. Average returns, their variances, and covariances are

	Stock	Bond	SCIP
Average return	0.148	0.060	0.152
Variance	0.014697	0.000155	0.160791
Covariance with stock		0.000468	−0.002222
Covariance with bond			−0.000227

Negative covariance indicates that SCIP tends to move in the opposite direction to stocks or bonds. Develop a portfolio optimization model for this situation.

23. Develop a spreadsheet model for the media selection problem described in this chapter.
24. Develop a spreadsheet model for the process selection problem described in this chapter.
25. Develop a spreadsheet model for the blending problem described in this chapter.
26. Develop a spreadsheet model for the production planning problem described in this chapter.
27. Develop a spreadsheet model for the cash management problem described in this chapter.
28. Develop a spreadsheet model for the distribution center location problem described in this chapter.
29. Develop a spreadsheet model for the direct marketing problem described in this chapter.

C A S E

DISTRIBUTION CENTER LOCATION FOR TRACWAY

Tracway produces its most popular model of lawn tractor in its St. Louis, Greenwood, and Camarillo plants and ships these units to major distribution centers in Atlanta, Chicago, and San Diego. To support its growing presence in the Pacific Rim, Tracway is considering adding two distribution centers. Locations being considered are Taiwan; Singapore; Sydney, Australia; and Auckland, New Zealand. Tracway anticipates locating distribution centers in two of these new locations. Data acquired from accounting, marketing, and production are shown in Figure 11.10. Total demand in the Pacific Rim is expected to be 5000 units. Develop an appropriate optimization model to identify the best location for the new DCs and transportation allocations to meet demand. Experiment with your spreadsheet model to find the least-cost solution you can. Describe the model you developed and the logic you used in finding a solution in a memo to the VP of Distribution. ■

FIGURE 11.10 Tracway Distribution Data

Plant				Distribution Center				
	Atlanta	Chicago	San Diego	Taiwan	Singapore	Sydney	Auckland	Capacity
St. Louis	$ 35	$ 40	$ 60	$ 130	$ 120	$ 148	$ 145	12000
Greenwood	$ 30	$ 30	$ 45	$ 136	$ 130	$ 160	$ 170	8000
Camarillo	$ 60	$ 65	$ 50	$ 115	$ 100	$ 120	$ 170	7500
Demand	9000	3000	9500					

CHAPTER

12

SOLVING AND ANALYZING OPTIMIZATION MODELS

INTRODUCTION

In Chapter 11 we focused on the development of linear, integer, and nonlinear optimization models. Microsoft Excel contains an add-in called *Solver* that allows you to find optimal solutions to constrained optimization problems formulated as spreadsheet models. (Check the list of available add-ins under *Tools/Add-Ins*. If *Solver* is not listed, you will have to re-install Excel, using a custom installation.) *Solver* was developed and is maintained by Frontline Systems, Inc. [www.frontsys.com]. Frontline Systems also supports a more powerful version of *Solver, Premium Solver,* an educational version of which is also packaged with this book. We suggest that you install it and use it, as it avoids certain errors that Microsoft has yet to correct in the Excel-supplied version. Although we will describe how to use *Solver,* we encourage you to visit Frontline Systems' Web site for additional examples, tutorials, updates, and other information about the software.

In this chapter we will discuss

- Solving optimization problems on spreadsheets
- How to use *Solver* to find optimal solutions to spreadsheet optimization models
- How to interpret solution reports, with an emphasis on the managerial information contained in the output
- Exploring the use of simulation and risk analysis to better understand the implications of solutions to optimization models

431

USING SPREADSHEET MODELS FOR OPTIMIZATION

One of the significant advantages of spreadsheets is their ability to update formulas as data are changed. Thus, it is easy to seek good solutions to optimization problems by manipulating the values of decision variables on the spreadsheet model. Often, we may use our intuition to change the values of decision variables and improve the objective function. For example, consider the product mix model from the previous chapter (we suggest that you experiment with the spreadsheet model as you follow this discussion). Suppose we increase the production of each product by 1 unit from the current solution. We find the following:

Gold	Platinum	Component A Used	Component B Used	Profit
100	200	1800	1300	$18,800.00
101	200	1806	1303	$18,848.00
100	201	1806	1305	$18,870.00

Although the profit increases at a faster rate for higher production of Platinum Players, we see that we also use more units of component B, a limited resource. We can produce up to 290 Platinum Players (while still producing 100 Gold Players) until all 1750 units of component B are used. This will result in a profit of $25,100. On the other hand, we could produce up to 250 Gold Players (while still producing 200 Platinum Players) until all units of component B are used, with a profit of $26,000. This suggests that we might want to produce as many Gold Players as possible without producing any Platinum Players. With a little experimentation, you would find that the maximum number of Gold Players you can produce without producing any Platinum Players is 500. At this level, all units of component A are used, while some units of component B are left over. The profit, however, is only $24,000. How many Platinum Players can you produce if no Gold Players are made? You should find that the best profit is only $24,500. Therefore, it appears that the optimal solution consists of some mixture of both products. With a little experimentation and perhaps a bit of luck, you can probably zero in on the optimal solution, which is to produce 375 Gold and 125 Platinum Players for a profit of $26,750.

Finding optimal solutions using spreadsheet models and intuition alone is not an easy task, particularly as the models become more complex. In some cases, it might be very difficult to even identify a feasible solution. Clearly, some type of mathematical solution procedure is necessary. Fortunately, such a procedure is provided by the Excel *Solver* tool, which we discuss next.

SOLVING LINEAR OPTIMIZATION MODELS

To use *Solver,* you should follow the design guidelines for building optimization models on spreadsheets that we described in the previous chapter, particularly defining a cell for each of the constraint functions in your model. In *Solver,* decision variables are called *adjustable cells* or *changing cells;* and the objective function cell is called the *target cell. Solver* identifies values of the changing cells that minimize or maximize the target cell value. Constraints are entered by referencing constraint functions and data using a special dialog box.

	A	B	C	D
1	**Product Mix Model**			
2				
3	**Data**			
4		Gold	Platinum	Limitation
5	Component A	6	6	3000
6	Component B	3	5	1750
7	Profit/unit	$ 48.00	$ 70.00	
8				
9	**Model**			
10		Gold	Platinum	
11	Quantity Produced	100	200	Components Used
12	Component A Used	600	1200	1800
13	Component B Used	300	1000	1300
14				Total Profit
15	Profit Contribution	$ 4,800.00	$ 14,000.00	$ 18,800.00

FIGURE 12.1   Product Mix Model

Solving the Product Mix Model

Figure 12.1 shows the spreadsheet model of the product problem developed in the previous chapter. *Solver* is started by selecting *Tools/Solver* from the menu bar in Excel. The *Solver Parameters* dialog box shown in Figure 12.2 will then be displayed. Note the button on the right side entitled *Premium*. This button will be displayed if *Premium Solver* is installed. We will use *Premium Solver* in this chapter. Clicking on the Premium button displays the dialog box in Figure 12.3. First, select *Standard Simplex LP* from the drop-down box on the right. This specifies the mathematical solution procedure to use for solving a linear optimization model. The other options, *Standard GRG Nonlinear* and *Standard Evolutionary* will be discussed later in this chapter.

Start by setting the target cell in the *Set Cell* field by either typing in D15 or clicking on cell D15 in the spreadsheet. Next, select the type of optimization option (*Max* or *Min*) by choosing the appropriate radio button; *Max* is the default. Finally, define the changing cells by either entering B11:C11 in the *By Changing Variable Cells* field, or by clicking in the field and then highlighting the changing cell range in the spreadsheet.

To add constraints, click the Add button. The *Add Constraint* dialog box (Figure 12.4) will appear. "Cell Reference:" refers to the left-hand side of a constraint; "Constraint:" refers to the right-hand side. In either case, you may enter a single cell reference or a range of cells. The drop-down menu in the center of the dialog box allows you to choose the type of constraint: <=, = , >=, int, or binary. "Int" restricts

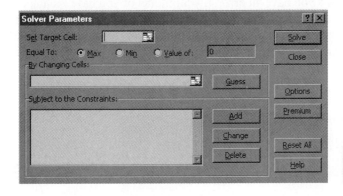

FIGURE 12.2 *Solver* Parameters Dialog Box

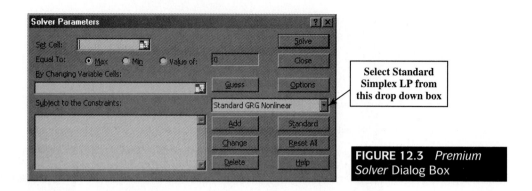

FIGURE 12.3 *Premium Solver* Dialog Box

the cell reference range to integers, and "binary" restricts it to 0 or 1. For example, the component limitation constraints are expressed as

Amount of Component Used (cells D12:D13) ≤ Amount Available (cells D5:D6)

In the *Cell Reference* field, you may either enter the range D12:D13 directly or highlight the range in the spreadsheet using your mouse (which is generally easier). Then click in the *Constraint:* field, and enter the right-hand-side range, D5:D6, or highlight this range using the mouse. If you then click the Enter button, the *Add Constraint* dialog box will remain, allowing you to enter other constraints. For this example, we have no other constraints to add.

When all constraints are entered, click the OK button to return to the *Solver Parameters* dialog box. The constraints will be displayed as shown in Figure 12.5. You may add, change, or delete these as necessary by clicking the appropriate buttons.

For linear models with the nonpremium version of *Solver,* you must select the Options button and check the boxes for *Assume Linear Model* and *Assume Non-Negative* when these are conditions of the problem. (You do not have to enter nonnegativity constraints explicitly in the model.) If you do not check *Assume Linear Model, Solver* will treat your model as nonlinear, and the output reports will not be in the proper form to interpret. Generally, you may leave the other options at their default values for linear models. Return to the *Solver Parameters* dialog box by clicking OK. With the premium version, however, the *Standard Simplex LP* assumes linearity and nonnegativity by default (although you can remove the nonnegativity assumption in the *Options* dialog box).

To find the optimal solution, click the Solve button. The *Solver Results* dialog box will appear, as shown in Figure 12.6, with the message "Solver found a solution." If a solution could not be found, *Solver* will notify you with a message to this effect. This generally means that you have an error in your model or you have included conflicting constraints that no single solution can satisfy. In such cases, you need to reexamine your model.

Solving a linear programming model can result in four possible outcomes:

1. Unique optimal solution
2. Alternate optimal solutions

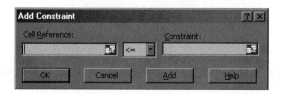

FIGURE 12.4 *Add Constraint* Dialog Box

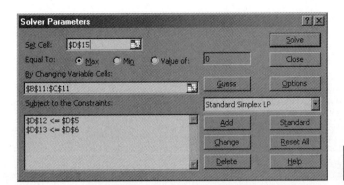

FIGURE 12.5 Completed *Solver* Model Definition

3. Unboundedness
4. Infeasibilty

When an LP has a *unique optimal solution,* it means that there is exactly one solution that will result in the maximum (or minimum) objective. If an LP has *alternate optimal solutions,* the objective is maximized (or minimized) by more than one combination of decision variables, all of which have the same objective function value. *Solver* does not tell you when alternate solutions exist (although this can be identified by examining the output reports) and only reports one of the many possible alternate optimal solutions. A problem is *unbounded* if the objective can be increased or decreased without bound (i.e., to infinity or negative infinity) while the solution remains feasible. This generally indicates an incorrect model, usually when some constraint or set of constraints has been left out. A model is unbounded if *Solver* reports "The Set Cells do not converge." Finally, an *infeasible* LP is one for which no feasible solution exists. Infeasible problems *can* occur in practice, for example, when demand is higher than available capacity. In the infeasible case, *Solver* will report "Solver could not find a feasible solution."

Solver generates three reports: Answer, Sensitivity, and Limits. To add them to your Excel workbook, click on each of them, and then click OK. The optimal solution is shown in Figure 12.7. The maximum profit is $26,750, obtained by producing 375 Gold Players and 125 Platinum Players.

Interpreting *Solver* Reports
The Answer Report (Figure 12.8) provides basic information about the solution, including the values of the optimal objective function and decision variables. The *Status* column in the *Constraints* section tells whether each constraint is binding or not binding. A **binding constraint** is one that is satisfied as an equality. For example, we see that the constraints for both component limitations are binding. This means

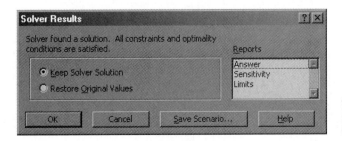

FIGURE 12.6 *Solver Results* Dialog Box

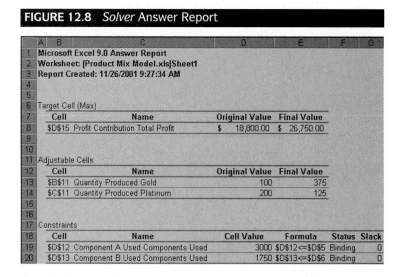

	A	B	C	D
1	**Product Mix Model**			
2				
3	**Data**			
4		Gold	Platinum	Limitation
5	Component A	6	6	3000
6	Component B	3	5	1750
7	Profit/unit	$ 48.00	$ 70.00	
8				
9	**Model**			
10		Gold	Platinum	
11	Quantity Produced	375	125	Components Used
12	Component A Used	2250	750	3000
13	Component B Used	1125	625	1750
14				Total Profit
15	Profit Contribution	$ 18,000.00	$ 8,750.00	$ 26,750.00

FIGURE 12.7 Optimal Product Mix Solution

that all available components are used in producing the products. If the number of components used was actually less than the number available, the difference would be shown in the *Slack* column. In general, the slack is the difference between the left- and right-hand sides of a constraint. For example, the component A limitation is

$$6G + 6P \leq 3000$$

We interpret this as

Amount of Component A Used ≤ Amount Available

Note that if the amount used is strictly less than the availability, we have slack, which represents the amount unused; thus,

Amount of Component A Used + Amount of Component A Unused
= Amount Available

or

Slack = Amount of Component A Unused
= Amount Available − Amount of Component A Used
= 3000 − (6G + 6P)

FIGURE 12.8 *Solver* Answer Report

	A	B	C	D	E	F	G
1		Microsoft Excel 9.0 Answer Report					
2		Worksheet: [Product Mix Model.xls]Sheet1					
3		Report Created: 11/26/2001 9:27:34 AM					
4							
5							
6		Target Cell (Max)					
7		Cell	Name	Original Value	Final Value		
8		$D$15	Profit Contribution Total Profit	$ 18,800.00	$ 26,750.00		
9							
10							
11		Adjustable Cells					
12		Cell	Name	Original Value	Final Value		
13		$B$11	Quantity Produced Gold	100	375		
14		$C$11	Quantity Produced Platinum	200	125		
15							
16							
17		Constraints					
18		Cell	Name	Cell Value	Formula	Status	Slack
19		$D$12	Component A Used Components Used	3000	$D$12<=$D$5	Binding	0
20		$D$13	Component B Used Components Used	1750	$D$13<=$D$6	Binding	0

	A	B	C	D	E	F	G	H
1	Microsoft Excel 9.0 Sensitivity Report							
2	Worksheet: [Product Mix Model.xls]Sheet1							
3	Report Created: 11/24/2001 11:11:56 AM							
4								
5								
6	Adjustable Cells							
7				Final	Reduced	Objective	Allowable	Allowable
8		Cell	Name	Value	Cost	Coefficient	Increase	Decrease
9		$B$11	Quantity Produced Gold	375	0	48	22	6
10		$C$11	Quantity Produced Platinum	125	0	70	10	22
11								
12	Constraints							
13				Final	Shadow	Constraint	Allowable	Allowable
14		Cell	Name	Value	Price	R.H. Side	Increase	Decrease
15		$D$12	Component A Used Components Used	3000	2.5	3000	500	900
16		$D$13	Component B Used Components Used	1750	11	1750	750	250

FIGURE 12.9 *Solver* Sensitivity Report

Slack variables are always nonnegative, so for ≥ constraints, slack represents the difference between the left-hand-side constraint function and the right-hand-side requirement. The slack on a binding constraint will always be zero.

The Sensitivity Report (Figure 12.9) provides a variety of useful information for managers. In the *Adjustable Cells* section, the final value for each decision variable is given, along with its reduced cost, objective coefficient, and allowable increase and decrease. The **reduced cost** tells how much the objective coefficient needs to change in order for a variable to become positive in an optimal solution. If a variable is currently positive in the solution, as it is for both variables in this example, its reduced cost is always zero.

The Allowable Increase and Allowable Decrease values tell how much an individual objective coefficient can change before the optimal values of the decision variables will change (a value listed as "1E+30" is interpreted as infinity.) For example, if the unit profit for Gold Players either increases by more than 22 or decreases by more than 6, then the optimal values of the decision variables will change. Note that if the objective coefficient of any one variable that has positive value in the current solution changes but stays within the range specified by the Allowable Increase and Allowable Decrease, the optimal decision variables will stay the same, but the objective function value will change. For example, if the unit profit of Gold Players were changed to 50 (an increase of 2, within the allowable range), each of the 375 units produced and sold would realize $2 more profit—a total increase of 375($2) = $750. If an objective coefficient changes beyond the Allowable Increase or Allowable Decrease, we must re-solve the problem with the new value.

The range within which the objective function will not change provides a manager with some confidence about the stability of the solution in the face of uncertainty. If the allowable ranges are large, then reasonable errors in estimating the coefficients will have no effect on the optimal policy (although they will affect the value of the objective function). Tight ranges suggest that more effort might be spent in ensuring that accurate data or estimates are used in the model.

The *Constraints* section of the Sensitivity Report lists the final value of the constraint function (the left-hand side), the shadow price, the constraint right-hand side, and an Allowable Increase and Allowable Decrease. The **shadow price** tells *how much the value of the objective function will change as the right-hand side of a constraint is increased by 1*. Whenever a constraint has positive slack, the shadow price is zero. However, if a constraint is binding, then any change in the right-hand side will cause the optimal values of the decision variables as well as the objective function value to change. For example, all 3000 units of component A are used in the optimal solution.

The shadow price of 2.5 states that if an additional unit of component A is available, profit will change by $2.50. To see this, change the limitation of component A to 3001 and re-solve the problem. The new solution is to produce 375.4166667 Gold Players and 124.75 Platinum Players, yielding a profit of $26,752.50 (remember that a linear program assumes continuity of the decision variables so fractional solutions are allowed). We see that the total profit increases by $2.50. The shadow price is a valid predictor of the change in the objective function value for each unit of increase in the constraint right-hand side up to the value of the Allowable Increase. Thus, if up to 3500 units of component A were available, profit would increase by $2.50 for each additional unit (but we would have to re-solve the problem to actually find the optimal values of the decision variables). Similarly, the negative of the shadow price predicts the change in the objective function value for each unit the constraint right-hand side is decreased, up to the value of the Allowable Decrease. Beyond these ranges, the shadow price does not predict what will happen, and the problem must be re-solved. Changes in the availability of component B will change the total profit by $11 as long as the number of units of component B remains between 1500 and 2500 as determined by the Allowable Increase and Allowable Decrease.

To better understand what is going on, let us increase the component A limitation to 3012 so that the new optimal solution is integer. The solution, shown in Figure 12.10, is to produce 380 Gold and 122 Platinum Players for a total profit of $26,780. How are the additional 12 units used? We produce five additional Gold Players, which require 15 additional units of component B. Since we have not increased the availability of component B, we must produce three fewer Platinum Players to free up 15 units of component B, so that the total number used is still 1750. This also provides an additional 18 units of component A that are needed to produce the five extra Gold Players. The five additional Gold Players yield a profit of 5($48) = $240, but we lose 3($70) = $210 for the three fewer Platinum Players. The net increase in profit is $30. Thus, the change in profit per additional unit of component A is $30/12 = $2.50.

Why are shadow prices useful to a manager? They provide guidance on how to reallocate resources or change values over which the manager may have control. In LP models, the parameters of some constraints cannot be controlled. For instance, the amount of time available for production or physical limitations on machine capacities would clearly be uncontrollable. Other constraints represent policy decisions, which, in essence, are arbitrary. Although it is correct to state that having an additional unit

	A	B	C	D
1	Product Mix Model			
2				
3	Data			
4		Gold	Platinum	Limitation
5	Component A	6	6	3012
6	Component B	3	5	1750
7	Profit/unit	$ 48.00	$ 70.00	
8				
9	Model			
10		Gold	Platinum	
11	Quantity Produced	380	122	Components Used
12	Component A Used	2280	732	3012
13	Component B Used	1140	610	1750
14				Total Profit
15	Profit Contribution	$ 18,240.00	$ 8,540.00	$ 26,780.00

FIGURE 12.10 Optimal Product Mix When Component A Limitation = 3012

A B	C	D	E F	G H I	J
Microsoft Excel 9.0 Limits Report					
Worksheet: [Product Mix Model.xls]Sheet1					
Report Created: 11/24/2001 11:11:56 AM					

	Target			Lower Target	Upper Target
Cell	Name	Value		Limit Result	Limit Result
$D$15	Profit Contribution Total Profit	$26,750.00			

	Adjustable			Lower Target	Upper Target
Cell	Name	Value		Limit Result	Limit Result
$B$11	Quantity Produced Gold	375		0 8750	375 26750
$C$11	Quantity Produced Platinum	125		0 18000	125 26750

FIGURE 12.11 *Solver* Limits Report

of component A will improve profit by $2.50, does this necessarily mean that the company should spend up to this amount for additional units? This depends on whether the relevant costs have been included in the objective function coefficients. If the costs of the components *have not* been included in the objective function unit profit coefficients, then the company will benefit by paying up to $2.50 for additional components. However, if the component costs *have* been included in the profit calculations, the company should be willing to pay up to an *additional* $2.50 over and above the component costs that have already been included in the unit profit calculations.

The Limits Report (Figure 12.11) shows the lower limit and upper limit that each variable can assume while satisfying all constraints and holding all of the other variables constant. Generally, this report provides little useful information for decision making and can be effectively ignored.

Solver Reports for Problems with Lower or Upper Bounds

The version of *Solver* included in Microsoft Office 97 and later releases handles simple lower bounds (e.g., $x \geq 10$) and upper bounds (e.g., $x \leq 150$) quite differently from ordinary constraints in the Sensitivity Report. To see this, consider a modified version of the product mix problem to which we have added a lower bound constraint on the number of Gold Players that must be produced (G $\geq$ 400). The Sensitivity Report is shown in Figure 12.12. The solution is to produce 400 Gold and 100 Platinum Players for a profit of $26,200, which is $550 less than the base case.

FIGURE 12.12 Sensitivity Report for Modified Product Mix Problem

A B	C	D	E	F	G	H
Microsoft Excel 9.0 Sensitivity Report						
Worksheet: [Product Mix Model.xls]Sheet1						
Report Created: 11/24/2001 3:14:39 PM						

Adjustable Cells

Cell	Name	Final Value	Reduced Cost	Objective Coefficient	Allowable Increase	Allowable Decrease
$B$13	Quantity Produced Gold	400	-22	48	22	1E+30
$C$13	Quantity Produced Platinum	100	0	70	1E+30	22

Constraints

Cell	Name	Final Value	Shadow Price	Constraint R.H. Side	Allowable Increase	Allowable Decrease
$D$14	Component A Used Components Used	3000	11.66666667	3000	60	600
$D$15	Component B Used Components Used	1700	0	1750	1E+30	50

In *Solver,* lower or upper bounds are treated in a manner similar to nonnegativity constraints, which do not appear explicitly as constraints in the model. Recall that the reduced cost tells how much the objective coefficient needs to change in order for a variable to become positive in an optimal solution. We can think of reduced costs as essentially being shadow prices of nonnegativity constraints. If we increase the right-hand side of a nonnegativity constraint by 1, we are essentially forcing the variable to become positive. If we change the objective coefficient by the reduced cost for a variable not currently in the optimal solution, then it would be profitable to force the variable into the solution. Thus, a variable at its lower bound is similar to one being zero in a typical LP model.

In the *Solver* output, only the structural model constraints are listed with shadow prices in the *Constraints* section of the sensitivity report. Any variable that is at its lower or upper bound in the final solution will appear in the *Adjustable Cells* section and have a nonzero reduced cost. In this case, the reduced cost may be interpreted as the shadow price of the bound constraint. In Figure 12.12, we see that the reduced cost for Gold Players is −$22. This means that profit decreases for every additional unit of Gold Players we would have to produce. In fact, notice that by adding the constraint, we forced an additional 25 Gold Players to be made from the base case. At a shadow price of −$22, the total profit decreased by 25(−$22) = $550.

Difficulties with *Solver*

A poorly scaled model—one in which the parameters of the objective and constraint functions differ by several orders of magnitude (as we have in the transportation example where costs are in tens and supplies/demands in thousands)—may cause roundoff errors in internal computations or error messages such as "The conditions for Assume Linear Model are not satisfied." This does not happen often (but may in older versions of *Solver*); if it does, you should consult the Frontline Systems' Web site for additional information. Usually, all you need to do is to keep the solution that *Solver* found and run *Solver* again starting from that solution.

SOLVING INTEGER OPTIMIZATION MODELS

Integer optimization models are set up in the same manner as linear models in *Solver,* except that any integer variables must be defined as such in the *Add Constraint* dialog box by using the *int* or *bin* options. For example, to define all the variables for the Project Selection model (*Project Selection.xls*) developed in Chapter 11 as binary, we would select *bin* for the range of these variables in the drop-down menu in the *Add Constraint* dialog box, as shown in Figure 12.13. Figure 12.14 shows the constraints after they are entered in the *Solver Parameters* dialog box. (In the standard version of *Solver,* you should still choose *Assume Linear Model* in the *Solver Options* dialog box.) For integer models you also need to ensure that *the value of Tolerance in the Solver Options dialog box is set to zero* to ensure finding an optimal solution. In *Premium Solver,* this is found by clicking on the button Integer Options in the *Solver Options* dialog box, as shown in Figure 12.15. The solution for this example is shown in

FIGURE 12.13 Specifying Changing Cells as Binary Variables

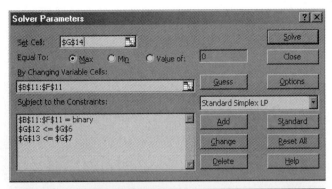

FIGURE 12.14 *Solver* Model for Project Selection

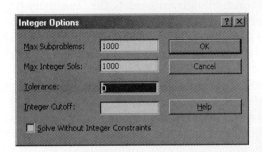

FIGURE 12.15 Setting *Tolerance* for Integer Optimization in *Solver*

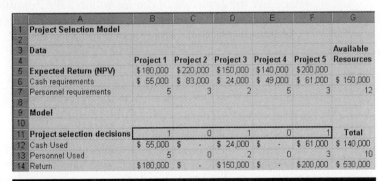

FIGURE 12.16 Project Selection Model Solution

Figure 12.16. However, because integer models are discontinuous by their very nature, the Sensitivity Analysis report cannot be interpreted in the same manner as for linear programs and thus is ignored by *Solver;* only the Answer Report is available.

SOLVING NONLINEAR OPTIMIZATION MODELS

Nonlinear optimization models are formulated with *Solver* in the same fashion as linear or integer models, except that in the standard version of *Solver* you should *not* choose *Assume Linear Model* in the *Options* box. In *Premium Solver,* you should select *Standard GRG Nonlinear* as the solution procedure. Figure 12.17 shows the *Solver Parameters* dialog box for the hotel pricing model (*Hotel Pricing.xls*) formulated in Chapter 11. The optimal solution is shown in Figure 12.18. The optimal prices predict a demand for all 450 rooms with a total revenue of $39,380.65.

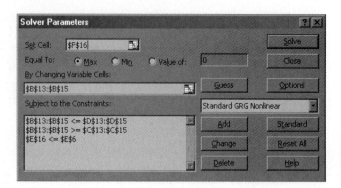

FIGURE 12.17   *Solver Parameters* Dialog Box for Hotel Pricing Example

The information contained in the Answer Report (Figure 12.19) is the same as for linear models. However, for nonlinear models, the Sensitivity Report (Figure 12.20) is quite different. In the *Adjustable Cells* section, the *Reduced Gradient* is analogous to the *Reduced Cost* in linear models. For this problem, however, the objective function coefficient of each price depends on many parameters, and therefore the reduced gradient is more difficult to interpret in relation to the problem data. *Lagrange Multipliers* in the *Constraints* section are similar to shadow prices for linear models. For nonlinear models, the Lagrange multipliers give the *approximate* rate of change in the objective function as the right-hand side of a binding constraint is increased by one unit. Thus, for the hotel pricing problem, if the number of available rooms in increased by 1 to 451, the total revenue would increase by approximately $12.08. For linear models, shadow prices give the *exact* rate of change within the Allowable Increase and Decrease limits. Thus, you should be somewhat cautious when interpreting these values and will need to re-solve the models to find the true effect of changes to constraints.

Metaheuristics for Nonlinear Optimization

Solver is not guaranteed to find an optimal solution for every nonlinear optimization problem. Whether or not it does converge to an optimal solution depends on the mathematical properties of the objective function and constraints. To overcome the limitations of nonlinear optimization procedures, new approaches called *metaheuristics* have been proposed. These approaches include genetic algorithms, neural networks, tabu search, and other heuristic methods. The *Premium Solver* "Standard Evolutionary" algorithm is based on a heuristic that remembers the best solution it finds, then modifies

FIGURE 12.18   Solution to Hotel Pricing Problem

	A	B	C	D	E	F
1	Marquis Hotel					
2						
3	Data					
4		Current	Average		Total Room	
5	Room type	Rate	Daily Sold	Elasticity	Capacity	
6	Standard	$ 85.00	250	-1.5	450	
7	Gold	$ 98.00	100	-2		
8	Platinum	$ 139.00	50	-1		
9						
10	Model				Projected	
11					Rooms	Projected
12	Room type	New Price	Price Range		Sold	Revenue
13	Standard	$ 76.87	$ 70.00	$ 90.00	286	$ 21,974.39
14	Gold	$ 90.00	$ 90.00	$ 110.00	116	$ 10,469.39
15	Platinum	$ 145.04	$ 120.00	$ 149.00	48	$ 6,936.87
16					Totals 449.999836	$ 39,380.65

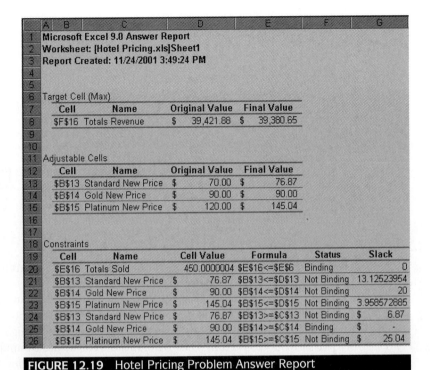

FIGURE 12.19 Hotel Pricing Problem Answer Report

Microsoft Excel 9.0 Answer Report
Worksheet: [Hotel Pricing.xls]Sheet1
Report Created: 11/24/2001 3:49:24 PM

Target Cell (Max)

Cell	Name	Original Value	Final Value
$F$16	Totals Revenue	$ 39,421.88	$ 39,380.65

Adjustable Cells

Cell	Name	Original Value	Final Value
$B$13	Standard New Price	$ 70.00	$ 76.87
$B$14	Gold New Price	$ 90.00	$ 90.00
$B$15	Platinum New Price	$ 120.00	$ 145.04

Constraints

Cell	Name	Cell Value	Formula	Status	Slack
$E$16	Totals Sold	450.0000004	$E$16<=$E$6	Binding	0
$B$13	Standard New Price	$ 76.87	$B$13<=$D$13	Not Binding	13.12523954
$B$14	Gold New Price	$ 90.00	$B$14<=$D$14	Not Binding	20
$B$15	Platinum New Price	$ 145.04	$B$15<=$D$15	Not Binding	3.958572885
$B$13	Standard New Price	$ 76.87	$B$13>=$C$13	Not Binding	$ 6.87
$B$14	Gold New Price	$ 90.00	$B$14>=$C$14	Binding	$ -
$B$15	Platinum New Price	$ 145.04	$B$15>=$C$15	Not Binding	$ 25.04

Microsoft Excel 9.0 Sensitivity Report
Worksheet: [Hotel Pricing.xls]Sheet1
Report Created: 11/24/2001 3:49:24 PM

Adjustable Cells

Cell	Name	Final Value	Reduced Gradient
$B$13	Standard New Price	$ 76.87	$ -
$B$14	Gold New Price	$ 90.00	$ (42.69)
$B$15	Platinum New Price	$ 145.04	$ -

Constraints

Cell	Name	Final Value	Lagrange Multiplier
$E$16	Totals Sold	450.0000004	12.08293216

FIGURE 12.20 Hotel Pricing Problem Sensitivity Report

and combines these solutions in attempting to find better solutions. We encourage you to try it if you encounter a difficult nonlinear problem, but we will not illustrate it here.

OptQuest, which is part of the *Crystal Ball* software packaged with this text, also falls into this category. *OptQuest* is designed to be used in conjunction with simulation, but it can be used alone to find solutions to difficult deterministic optimization problems. We will discuss *OptQuest* later in this chapter.

RISK ANALYSIS OF OPTIMIZATION RESULTS

It is rare that any optimization model is completely deterministic; in most cases, some of the data will be uncertain. This implies that inherent risk exists in using the optimal solution obtained from a model. Using the capabilities of risk analysis software such as

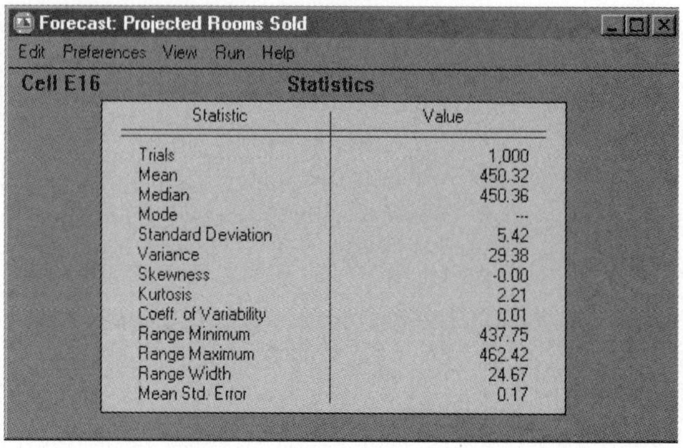

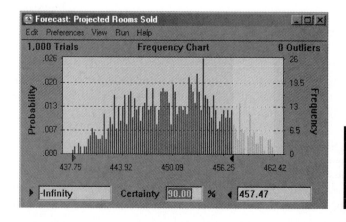

FIGURE 12.21 *Crystal Ball* Statistics Report for Hotel Pricing Problem

Crystal Ball, these risks can be better understood and mitigated. To illustrate this, we will use the hotel pricing problem.

In this problem, the price–demand elasticities of demand are only estimates and most likely are quite uncertain. Because we probably will not know anything about their distributions, let us conservatively assume that the true values might vary from the estimates by plus or minus 25 percent. Thus, we model the elasticities by uniform distributions. Using the optimal prices identified by *Solver* earlier in this chapter, let us see what happens to the forecast of the number of rooms sold under this assumption using *Crystal Ball*.

In the spreadsheet model, select cells D6:D8 as assumption cells with uniform distributions having minimum and maximum values equal to 75 percent and 125 percent of the estimated values, respectively. The total rooms sold (E16) is defined as a forecast cell. The model was replicated 1000 times, creating the report in Figure 12.21. We see that the mean number of rooms sold under these prices is 450, which should be expected, since the mean values of the elasticities were used to derive the optimal prices. However, because of the uncertainty associated with the elasticities, the probability that *more* than 450 rooms will be sold (demanded) is approximately 0.5! This suggests that if the assumptions of the uncertain elasticities are true, the hotel might anticipate that demand will exceed its room capacity about half the time, resulting in many unhappy customers.

We could use these results, however, to identify the appropriate hotel capacity to ensure, for example, only a 10 percent chance exists that demand will exceed capacity. Figure 12.22 shows the forecast chart when the certainty level is set at 90 percent and

FIGURE 12.22 Forecast Chart to Identify Capacity Needed for a 10 Percent Risk That Demand Exceeds Capacity

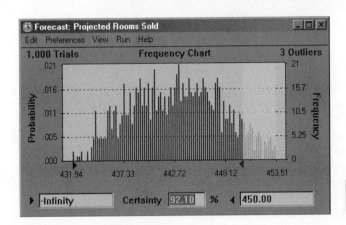

	A	B	C	D	E	F
1	Marquis Hotel					
2						
3	Data					
4		Current	Average		Total Room	
5	Room type	Rate	Daily Sold	Elasticity	Capacity	
6	Standard	$ 85.00	250	-1.5	443	
7	Gold	$ 98.00	100	-2		
8	Platinum	$ 139.00	50	-1		
9						
10	Model				Projected	
11					Rooms	Projected
12	Room type	New Price	Price Range		Sold	Revenue
13	Standard	$ 78.34	$ 70.00	$ 90.00	279	$ 21,886.69
14	Gold	$ 90.00	$ 90.00	$ 110.00	116	$ 10,469.39
15	Platinum	$ 146.51	$ 120.00	$ 149.00	47	$ 6,929.72
16				Totals	443	$ 39,285.80

FIGURE 12.23 *Solver* Solution for 443-Room Capacity

FIGURE 12.24 Forecast Chart for Confirmation Run

the left grabber is anchored. We could interpret this as stating that if the hotel capacity were about 457 or 458 rooms, then demand will exceed capacity at most 10 percent of the time. So if we shift the capacity constraint down by 7 rooms to 443 and find the optimal prices associated with this constraint, we would expect demand to exceed 450 at most 10 percent of the time. Figure 12.23 shows the *Solver* results for this case, and Figure 12.24 shows the results of a *Crystal Ball* run confirming that with these prices, demand will exceed 450 less than 10 percent of the time.

COMBINING OPTIMIZATION AND SIMULATION

OptQuest, also a product of Decisioneering, Inc., enhances the analysis capabilities of *Crystal Ball* by allowing you to search for optimal solutions within spreadsheet simulation models. To find an optimal set of decision variables for any simulation-based model, you generally need to search in a heuristic or ad hoc fashion. This usually involves running a simulation for an initial set of variables, analyzing the results, changing one or more variables, rerunning the simulation, and repeating this process until a satisfactory solution is obtained. This process can be very tedious and time-consuming, and often how to adjust the variables from one iteration to the next is not clear.

OptQuest overcomes this limitation by automatically searching for optimal solutions within *Crystal Ball* simulation model spreadsheets. Within *OptQuest,* you describe your optimization problem and search for values of decision variables that maximize or minimize a predefined objective. Additionally, *OptQuest* is designed to find solutions that satisfy a wide variety of constraints or a set of goals that you may define.

A Portfolio Allocation Model

We will use a portfolio allocation model to illustrate the steps of setting up and running an optimization problem using *Crystal Ball* and *OptQuest*. An investor has $100,000 to invest in four assets. The expected annual returns and minimum and maximum amounts with which the investor will be comfortable allocating to each investment follow:

Investment	Annual Return	Minimum	Maximum
1. Life insurance	5%	$ 2,500	$5,000
2. Bond mutual funds	7%	$30,000	none
3. Stock mutual funds	11%	$15,000	none
4. Savings account	4%	none	none

The major source of uncertainty in this problem is the annual return of each asset. In addition, the decision maker faces other risks, for example, unanticipated changes in inflation or industrial production, the spread between high- and low-grade bonds, and the spread between long- and short-term interest rates. One approach to incorporating such risk factors in a decision model is arbitrate pricing theory (APT).[1] APT provides estimates of the sensitivity of a particular asset to these types of risk factors. Let us assume that the risk factors per dollar allocated to each asset have been determined as follows:

Asset	Risk Factor/Dollar Invested
1. Life insurance	−0.5
2. Bond mutual funds	1.8
3. Stock mutual funds	2.1
4. Savings account	−0.3

The investor may specify a target level for the weighted risk factor, leading to a constraint that limits the risk to the desired level. For example, suppose that our investor will tolerate a weighted risk per dollar invested of at most 1.0. Thus, the weighted risk for a $100,000 total investment will be limited to 100,000. If our investor allocates $5,000 in life insurance, $50,000 in bond mutual funds, $15,000 in stock mutual funds, and $30,000 in a savings account (which fall within the minimum and maximum amounts specified), the total expected annual return would be

---

[1]See Schniederjans, M., T. Zorn, and R. Johnson, "Allocating Total Wealth: A Goal Programming Approach," *Computers and Operations Research*, 20, 7, 1993, 679–685.

$$0.06(\$5,000) + 0.07(\$50,000) + 0.11(\$15,000) + 0.04(\$30,000) = \$6,650.$$

However, the total weighted risk associated with this solution is

$$-0.5(5,000) + 1.8(50,000) + 2.1(15,000) - 0.3(30,000) = 110,000$$

Because this is greater than the limit of 100,000, this solution could not be chosen.

The decision problem, then, is to determine how much to invest in each asset to maximize the total expected annual return, remain within the minimum and maximum limits for each investment, and meet the limitation on the weighted risk.

Using *OptQuest*

The basic process for using *OptQuest* is described as follows:

1. Create a *Crystal Ball* model of the decision problem.
2. Define the decision variables within *Crystal Ball*.
3. Invoke *OptQuest* from the *Crystal Ball* toolbar or the corresponding menu.
4. Create a new optimization file.
5. Select decision variables.
6. Specify constraints.
7. Select the forecast.
8. Modify *OptQuest* options.
9. Solve the optimization problem.
10. Save the optimization files.
11. Exit *OptQuest*.

Creating the *Crystal Ball* Spreadsheet Model

An important task in using *OptQuest* is to create a useful spreadsheet model. A spreadsheet for this problem is shown in Figure 12.25 (*Portfolio Allocation Model.xls*). Problem data are specified in rows 4 through 8. On the bottom half of the spreadsheet, we specify the model outputs, namely, the values of the decision variables, objective function, and constraints (the total weighted risk and total amount invested). You can see that this particular solution is not feasible because the total weighted risk exceeds the limit of 100,000.

FIGURE 12.25 Portfolio Allocation Model

	A	B	C	D	E
1	Portfolio Allocation Model				
2		Annual			Risk factor
3	Investment	return	Minimum	Maximum	per dollar
4	Life Insurance	5.0%	$ 2,500.00	$ 5,000.00	-0.5
5	Bond mutual funds	7.0%	$ 30,000.00	none	1.8
6	Stock mutual funds	11.0%	$ 15,000.00	none	2.1
7	Savings Account	4.0%	none	none	-0.3
8	Total amount available	$100,000		Limit	100,000
9					
10		Amount			Total weighted
11	Decision variables	invested			risk
12	Life Insurance	$ 5,000.00			146,000.00
13	Bond mutual funds	$ 50,000.00			
14	Stock mutual funds	$ 30,000.00			Total expected
15	Savings Account	$ 15,000.00			return
16	Total amount invested	$ 100,000.00			$ 7,650.00

Now that the basic model is developed, we define the assumptions and forecast cells in *Crystal Ball*. We will assume that the annual returns for life insurance and mutual funds are uncertain, but that the rate for the savings account is constant. We will make the following assumptions in the *Crystal Ball* model:

- Cell B4: uniform distribution with minimum 4 percent and maximum 6 percent
- Cell B5: normal distribution with mean 7 percent and standard deviation 1 percent
- Cell B6: lognormal distribution with mean 11 percent and standard deviation 4 percent

We define the forecast cell to be the total expected return, cell B16. As would be the case with any *Crystal Ball* application, you would select *Run Preferences* from the *Run* menu and choose appropriate settings. Set the number of trials per simulation to 500.

Define Decision Variables

The next step is to identify the decision variables in the model. This is something that is not done in a regular *Crystal Ball* application; however, it is required in order to use *OptQuest*. This is accomplished using the *Define Decision Variables* option in the *Cell* menu. Position the cursor on cell B12. From the *Cell* menu, choose *Define Decision Variables*. Set the minimum and maximum values according to the problem data (i.e., columns C and D in the spreadsheet), as shown in Figure 12.26.

Next, we repeat the process of defining decision variables for cells B13, B14, and B15. When the maximum limit is "none," you may use a value of $100,000 because this is the total amount available. You are now in a position to call *OptQuest* by clicking on the *OptQuest* button on the *Crystal Ball* toolbar or selecting it from the corresponding menu.

Creating a New Optimization File

Select *OptQuest* from the *CBTools* menu. From the opening screen in *OptQuest*, select *New* from the *File* menu. This option allows you to create different optimization files for the same simulation. This brings up the wizard tool that will step you through the process of setting up your optimization model. You will then see the screen shown in Figure 12.27. You will need to select the subset of decision variables from your *Crystal Ball* model that will be used for optimization, the forecast cell and corresponding statistic that will be used as the objective to minimize or maximize, any forecast cells and corresponding statistics that will be used as goals, and any additional restrictions or constraints that you may wish to specify.

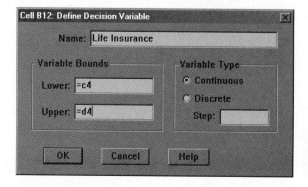

FIGURE 12.26 *Define Decision Variable* Dialog Box

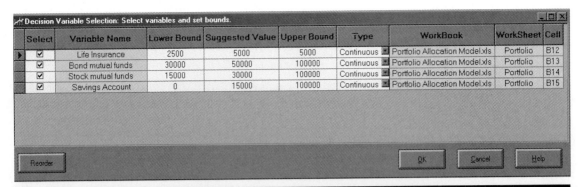

FIGURE 12.27   *OptQuest Decision Variable Selection* Screen

Select Decision Variables

In the *Decision Variable Selection* screen, all decision variables defined in the *Crystal Ball* model appear and are initially selected in the *Select* column. You may unselect any of them as appropriate. For each selected variable, a lower and an upper bound must be given in the appropriate columns. If you would like to include a starting solution that *OptQuest* will improve upon, you can suggest the values of the selected variables in the *Suggested Value* column. The suggested value by default is the value that appears in the corresponding cell in your *Crystal Ball* model. If the suggested values are out of range or do not meet the problem constraints, these values are ignored. The *Type* column indicates whether a variable is discrete or continuous. The variable type can be changed in this window or in the *Define Decision Variable* window of *Crystal Ball*. A step size is associated with discrete variables. A variable of the type Discrete_2, for example, has a step size of 2. Therefore, if the lower and upper bounds for this variable are 0 and 7, respectively, the only feasible values are 0, 2, 4, and 6. To change the step size, you must click on the *Discrete* item of the drop-down menu and enter the new step size in the dialog box. In Figure 12.27, we see that all decision variables are selected for the optimization model.

Specify Constraints

The next screen displayed allows you to specify any constraints (see Figure 12.28). A *constraint* is any limitation or requirement that restricts the possible solutions to the problem. In our example, we have two constraints. The first constraint limits the total weighted risk to 100,000, and the second ensures that we do not allocate more than $100,000 in total to all assets. In the *OptQuest* screen, a listing of all previously selected decision variables is displayed. Constraints may only use these variables. You then type the constraints one-by-one, placing a single constraint on each line. (To facilitate the process, you may click on the decision variable names in the right-hand column to move the name to where the cursor is.) Constraints should be one in each line. An asterisk must be used to indicate the product of a constant and a variable (e.g., 3*X).

Thus, in our example, the risk constraint is:

$$-0.5*\text{Life insurance} + 1.8*\text{Bond mutual funds} + 2.1*\text{Stock mutual funds}$$
$$-0.3*\text{Savings account} <= 100000$$

and the total investment constraint is:

$$\text{Life insurance} + \text{Bond mutual funds} + \text{Stock mutual funds}$$
$$+ \text{Savings account} <= 100000$$

The newly entered constraints are saved by clicking the OK button.

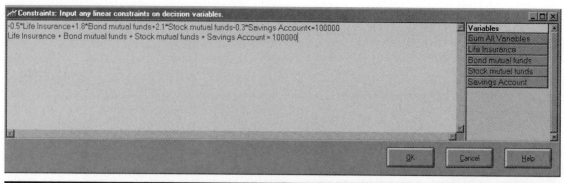

FIGURE 12.28 *OptQuest Constraints* Window

Select the Forecast

Every *OptQuest* run requires the selection of a statistic of at least one forecast cell to act as the objective function to be minimized or maximized. You can select a forecast to be a *Maximize Objective* or a *Minimize Objective* from the drop-down menu in the *Select Objective/Requirements* column.

In addition to an objective, you may choose to set optimization *requirements*. Requirements are used to constrain forecast statistics to fall within specified lower and upper target values. This is done by choosing the *Requirement* option from the drop-down menu in the *Select Objective/Requirements* column and will be illustrated in other examples. In the *Crystal Ball* model, we have only defined one forecast, whose mean value we wish to maximize as shown in Figure 12.29.

Modify *OptQuest* Options

Next, a window with the following three tabs appears:

- *Time*
- *Settings*
- *Preferences*

The *Time* tab allows you to specify the total time that the system is allowed to search for the best values for the optimization variables. You may either enter the total number of minutes or a date and time when the process must stop. Performance will depend on the speed of your microprocessor. The default optimization time is 10 minutes; however, you are able to choose any time limit you desire. Selecting a very long time limit does not present a problem, because you are always able to terminate the search by selecting *Stop* in

FIGURE 12.29 *OptQuest Forecast Selection* Window

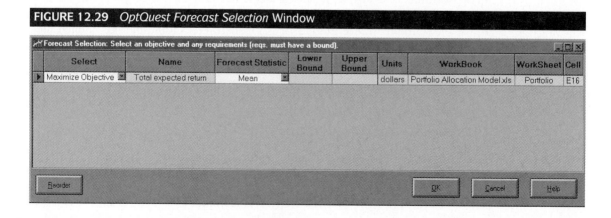

Select	Name	Forecast Statistic	Lower Bound	Upper Bound	Units	WorkBook	WorkSheet	Cell
Maximize Objective	Total expected return	Mean			dollars	Portfolio Allocation Model.xls	Portfolio	E16

the *Run* menu or pressing the Esc key. Additionally, you will be given the option to extend the search and carry the optimization process farther once the selected time has expired.

In the *Preferences* tab screen you can select which *Crystal Ball* runs to save (default is *Only Best*) and other cosmetic options. Finally, in the *Advanced* tab, you can set the optimization type as stochastic—that is, with *Crystal Ball* assumptions or deterministic without assumptions.

Solve the Optimization Problem

The optimization process is initiated from the next dialog box or from the *Run* menu. As the simulation is running, you may also select three additional options from the *View* menu: *Performance Graph, Bar Graph,* or *Log*. The *Performance Graph* shows a plot of the value of the objective as a function of the number of simulations evaluated. The *Bar Graph* shows how the value of each decision variable changes during the optimization search procedure. Finally, the *Optimization Log* provides details of the sequence of best solutions generated during the search.

As the optimization progresses, the sequence of best solutions identified during the search is displayed on the *Status and Solutions* screen. Each time a better solution is identified, a new line is added to the screen, showing the new objective value and values of the decision variables. In the upper-left corner of the *Status and Solutions* screen, you can monitor the time remaining and the simulation trial number currently under evaluation. (This information disappears when the time limit is reached.)

Figure 12.30 shows the *Status and Solutions* screen upon completion of the optimization using a 1.7 GHz desktop computer. Note that the first solution does *not* correspond to the solution in the spreadsheet in Figure 12.25, because that solution is not feasible. *OptQuest* identifies an initial feasible solution to begin the search process.

Saving an Optimization File

The *Save* and *Save As . . .* options in the *File* menu allow you to save the current optimization model for future use. Note that the file that you save refers to the optimization problem and the *OptQuest* options only, and not to the *Crystal Ball* simulation model (which is saved in the Excel file). The optimization files are

FIGURE 12.30 *OptQuest Status and Solutions* Window

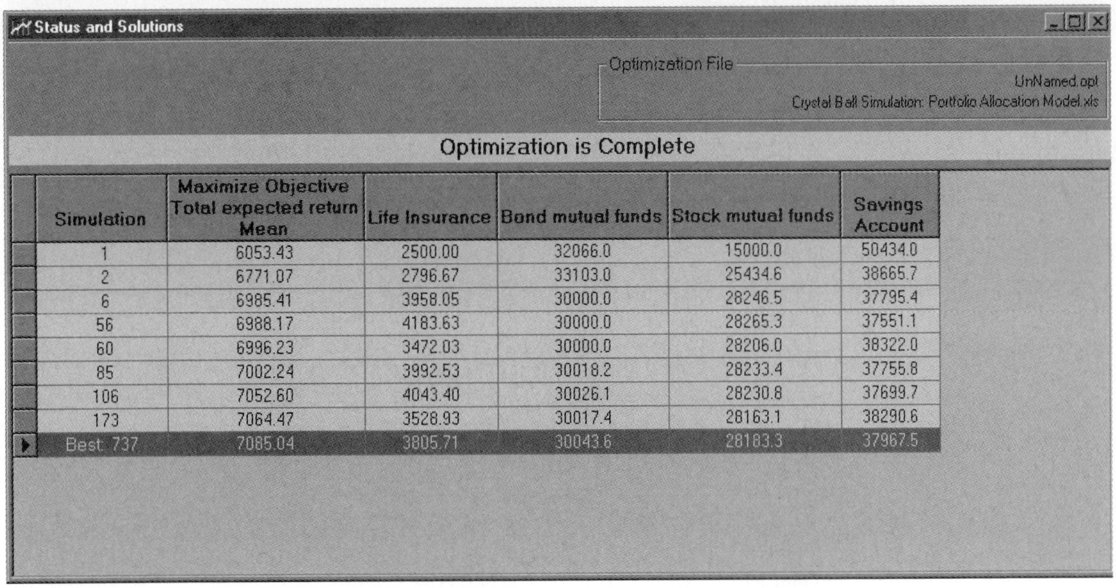

Optimization File

UnNamed.opt

Crystal Ball Simulation: Portfolio Allocation Model.xls

Optimization is Complete

Simulation	Maximize Objective Total expected return Mean	Life Insurance	Bond mutual funds	Stock mutual funds	Savings Account
1	6053.43	2500.00	32066.0	15000.0	50434.0
2	6771.07	2796.67	33103.0	25434.6	38665.7
6	6985.41	3958.05	30000.0	28246.5	37795.4
56	6988.17	4183.63	30000.0	28265.3	37551.1
60	6996.23	3472.03	30000.0	28206.0	38322.0
85	7002.24	3992.53	30018.2	28233.4	37755.8
106	7052.60	4043.40	30026.1	28230.8	37699.7
173	7064.47	3528.93	30017.4	28163.1	38290.6
Best: 737	7085.04	3805.71	30043.6	28183.3	37967.5

automatically given the extension name .OPT. The saved optimization file may be recalled by choosing *Open* . . . from the *File* menu.

Exit *OptQuest*

To exit, choose *Exit* from the *File* menu. *OptQuest* will now save the best simulations for you and will restore the one you select when you exit. After choosing *Exit* you will be given the opportunity to paste the best values found for the optimization variables in your *Crystal Ball* model. The results are shown in Figure 12.31. You can see that both constraints are satisfied (to within a small decimal fraction). Alternatively, other values can be pasted by highlighting the corresponding row on the *Status and Solutions* window accessible from the *View* menu.

Interpreting Results

You should note that the "best" *OptQuest* solution identified may not be the true optimal solution to the problem, but will, it is hoped, be close to the actual optimal solution. The accuracy of the results depends on the time limit you select for searching, the number of decision variables, and the complexity of the problem. With more decision variables, you need a larger number of simulations.

After solving an optimization problem with *OptQuest,* you probably would want to examine the *Crystal Ball* simulation using the optimal values of the decision variables in order to assess the risks associated with the recommended solution. Figure 12.32 shows the *Crystal Ball* forecast chart associated with the best solution. Although the mean value was optimized, we see that a high amount of variability exists in the actual return because of the uncertainty in the returns of the individual investments. In fact, the total returns varied from about $4,500 to over $12,000.

Adding a Requirement

A *requirement* is a forecast statistic that is restricted to fall within a specified lower and upper bound. The forecast statistic may be one of the following:

Mean
Median
Mode
Standard deviation
Variance
Percentile (as specified by the user)
Skewness

FIGURE 12.31 *OptQuest* Results for Portfolio Allocation Model

	A	B	C	D	E
1	Portfolio Allocation Model				
2		Annual			Risk factor
3	Investment	return	Minimum	Maximum	per dollar
4	Life Insurance	5.0%	$ 2,500.00	$ 5,000.00	-0.5
5	Bond mutual funds	7.0%	$ 30,000.00	none	1.8
6	Stock mutual funds	11.0%	$ 15,000.00	none	2.1
7	Savings Account	4.0%	none	none	-0.3
8	Total amount available	$100,000		Limit	100,000
9					
10		Amount			Total weighted
11	Decision variables	invested			risk
12	Life Insurance	$ 3,805.71			99,970.31
13	Bond mutual funds	$ 30,043.60			
14	Stock mutual funds	$ 28,183.30			Total expected
15	Savings Account	$ 37,967.50			return
16	Total amount invested	$ 100,000.11			$ 6,912.20

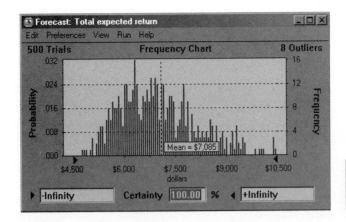

FIGURE 12.32 *Crystal Ball* Forecast Chart for *OptQuest* Solution

Kurtosis
Coefficient of variation
Range (minimum, maximum, and width)
Standard error

For example, to reduce the uncertainty of returns in the portfolio while also attempting to maximize the expected return, we might want to restrict the standard deviation to be no greater than 1000. To add such a requirement in *OptQuest,* select *Forecast* from the *Tools* menu. This will bring up the *Forecast Selection Screen.* Because we have only one forecast in the model, this row will be highlighted. The same cell may be simultaneously selected as an objective and as a goal. This can be achieved by highlighting the *Forecasts Name* in the *Forecast Selection* window and choosing *Duplicate* from the *Edit* menu. This creates a new row, with the forecast named Total Expected Return:2. From the drop-down menu in the first column, select *Requirement.* Click on the *Forecast Statistic* cell and using the drop-down menu, choose *Standard Deviation;* then set the upper bound to 1000. Finally, click OK.

You may now run the new model. The results are shown in Figure 12.33. The best solution among those with standard deviations less than or equal to 1000 is identified.

FIGURE 12.33   *OptQuest* Results with *Standard Deviation* Requirement

Status and Solutions

Optimization File
c:\documents and settings\james evans\desktop\statistics and data analysis 2e\optquest
Crystal Ball Simulation: Portfolio Allocation Model.xls

Optimization is Complete

Simulation	Maximize Objective Total expected return:1 Mean	Requirement Total expected return:2 Std_Dev <= 1000	Life Insurance	Bond mutual funds	Stock mutual funds	Savings Account
1	6874.53	1110.00 - Infeasible	3805.71	30043.6	28183.3	37967.5
3	6518.01	815.295	2891.15	42647.5	17091.0	37370.3
4	6678.43	932.994	2613.41	36571.6	22384.3	38430.7
12	6732.95	954.962	2585.76	34133.1	24174.4	39106.7
29	6772.92	912.327	3269.05	34381.1	24355.6	37994.2
107	6804.97	969.029	3233.15	34521.6	24185.8	38059.4
175	6823.83	991.276	4086.32	34257.5	24531.9	37124.3
408	6830.16	985.013	4075.83	34277.7	24503.3	37143.2
Best: 515	6842.10	987.485	4399.90	34196.9	24566.9	36836.3

Questions and Problems

1. Develop a spreadsheet model and solve the following linear programming problem using *Solver,* and interpret the results.

   Max $\quad\quad$ 6X + 7Y
   ST $\quad\quad$ 12X + 14Y ≤ 168
   $\quad\quad\quad\quad$ X $\quad\quad$ ≤ 10
   $\quad\quad\quad\quad\quad\quad$ Y ≥ 5
   $\quad\quad\quad\quad$ X, Y ≥ 0

2. Develop a spreadsheet model and solve the following linear programming problem using *Solver,* and interpret the results.

   Max $\quad\quad$ 3X + 7Y
   ST $\quad\quad$ X + Y ≤ 10
   $\quad\quad\quad$ 3X + Y ≥ 50
   $\quad\quad\quad\quad$ X, Y ≥ 0

3. Develop a spreadsheet model and solve the following linear programming problem using *Solver,* and interpret the results.

   Max $\quad\quad$ 3X + 7Y
   ST $\quad\quad$ X − Y ≤ 10
   $\quad\quad\quad$ 3X + 7Y ≥ 50
   $\quad\quad\quad\quad$ X, Y ≥ 0

4. Use the spreadsheet model you developed in Problem 23 of Chapter 11 to find an optimal solution for the media selection problem.
5. Use the spreadsheet model you developed in Problem 24 of Chapter 11 to find an optimal solution for the process selection problem.
6. Use the spreadsheet model you developed in Problem 25 of Chapter 11 to find an optimal solution for the blending problem.
7. Use the spreadsheet model you developed in Problem 26 of Chapter 11 to find an optimal solution for the production planning problem.
8. Use the spreadsheet model you developed in Problem 27 of Chapter 11 to find an optimal solution for the cash management problem.
9. Use the spreadsheet model you developed in Problem 28 of Chapter 11 to find an optimal solution for the distribution center location problem.
10. Use the spreadsheet model you developed in Problem 29 of Chapter 11 to find an optimal solution for the direct marketing problem.
11. Figure 12.34 shows the Answer and Sensitivity reports for the transportation model example formulated in Chapter 11. Answer the following questions, re-solving the problem only when necessary:
    a. What is the optimal solution?
    b. What would the shipping cost have to be for it to be profitable to ship from Marietta to Cleveland?
    c. The cost along the Minneapolis–Baltimore route has been reduced to $12.00. What is the new optimal solution and minimal cost?
    d. The cost along the Minneapolis–Baltimore route has been increased to $12.70. What is the new optimal solution and minimal cost?
    e. Explain why the allowable increase for the objective coefficient is infinity for all decision variables that have a final value of zero.
    f. If Marietta increases its supply availability by 100 units, what will happen? Re-solve the model to explain why the shadow price is zero.
    g. Why is the allowable increase for the constraint right-hand side zero for all demand constraints?
    h. Explain the shadow price associated with Minneapolis.

Target Cell (Min)

Cell	Name	Original Value	Final Value
$A$18	Total cost	$ -	$ 27,862

Adjustable Cells

Cell	Name	Original Value	Final Value
$B$13	Marietta Cleveland	0	0
$C$13	Marietta Baltimore	0	200
$D$13	Marietta Chicago	0	0
$E$13	Marietta Phoenix	0	1000
$B$14	Minneapolis Cleveland	0	150
$C$14	Minneapolis Baltimore	0	150
$D$14	Minneapolis Chicago	0	500
$E$14	Minneapolis Phoenix	0	0

Constraints

Cell	Name	Cell Value	Formula	Status	Slack
$B$15	Demand met Cleveland	150	$B$15=$B$8	Binding	0
$C$15	Demand met Baltimore	350	$C$15=$C$8	Binding	0
$D$15	Demand met Chicago	500	$D$15=$D$8	Binding	0
$E$15	Demand met Phoenix	1000	$E$15=$E$8	Binding	0
$F$13	Marietta shipped	1200	$F$13<=$F$6	Binding	0
$F$14	Minneapolis shipped	800	$F$14<=$F$7	Binding	0

Adjustable Cells

Cell	Name	Final Value	Reduced Cost	Objective Coefficient	Allowable Increase	Allowable Decrease
$B$13	Marietta Cleveland	0	1	12.6	1E+30	1.13
$C$13	Marietta Baltimore	200	0	14.35	1.13	0.02
$D$13	Marietta Chicago	0	2	11.52	1E+30	1.69
$E$13	Marietta Phoenix	1000	0	17.58	0.02	1E+30
$B$14	Minneapolis Cleveland	150	0	9.75	1.13	1E+30
$C$14	Minneapolis Baltimore	150	0	12.63	0.02	1.13
$D$14	Minneapolis Chicago	500	0	8.11	1.69	1E+30
$E$14	Minneapolis Phoenix	0	0	15.88	1E+30	0.02

Constraints

Cell	Name	Final Value	Shadow Price	Constraint R.H. Side	Allowable Increase	Allowable Decrease
$B$15	Demand met Cleveland	150	11	150	0	150
$C$15	Demand met Baltimore	350	14	350	0	200
$D$15	Demand met Chicago	500	10	500	0	200
$E$15	Demand met Phoenix	1000	18	1000	0	1000
$F$13	Marietta shipped	1200	0	1200	1E+30	0
$F$14	Minneapolis shipped	800	-2	800	200	0

FIGURE 12.34   *Solver* Reports for Transportation Model

12. Develop a spreadsheet model for Problem 10 in Chapter 11. Then answer the following questions independently of each other:
   a. There is a rumor that the market for Jalapeno Ham & Beans is changing. Would there be any change in recommendations if the price for this product changed from $2.00 to $2.05? How about a price drop to $1.95/can?
   b. If the price of Jalapeno Peppers increased to $1.40/can, would your recommendation change? Why or why not? What would the new daily profit be?
   c. Your ham supplier is willing to provide additional ham up to another 20,000 ounces per day at the price of $0.41/ounce. How many of these additional ounces do you recommend buying in addition to the normal daily purchase (which would still be $0.40/ounce)? Why or why not?
   d. The lima bean supplier is willing to provide up to 20,000 *additional* ounces per day at the price of $0.06/ounce. How many ounces do you recommend buying in addition to the normal purchase at the old price? Why or why not?
   e. There is a monthly sales meeting coming up. Do you have any recommendations concerning which products to advertise (increase demand) and which not to? Why?

13. Develop a spreadsheet model for Problem 11 in Chapter 11. Then answer the following questions independently of each other:
   a. How much would the cost of corn have to drop to make it worth adding more?
   b. If the cost of fishbones increased to $0.006 per pound, what would the impact be?
   c. If the cost of sawdust increased to $0.005 per pound, what would the impact be?
   d. If you reduced the advertised amount of protein from 200 grams/bag to 100 grams/bag, how much would that enable you to save? Why?
   e. If you increased the advertised proportion of fiber from 100 grams/bag to 200 grams/bag, how much would your cost increase? Why?

14. Develop a spreadsheet model for Problem 12 in Chapter 11. Then answer the following questions independently of each other:
   a. You may find a solution that doesn't use all available floor space. If you are trying to maximize profit, how can that be?

    b. What rate of interest should the chain consider for the opportunity to obtain additional investment capital? Note that the model deals with monthly operations. For how much additional money (per month) would that rate apply?

    c. If the chain obtains another $1 million of investment capital for stock, what would the solution be? (A new solution is required.) What would the marginal value of capital be in that case?

    d. (Return to the original model, with $20 million investment.) Some planning committee members are concerned about risk. Identify the solutions (to include investment, square footage, and risk ratio) if risk were to be limited to 10 percent of investment.

15. Develop a spreadsheet model for the Gulf Coast Oil Company problem (Problem 13) in Chapter 11. Solve the model and interpret the sensitivity report.

16. Develop a spreadsheet model for the Liquid Gold, Inc. problem (Problem 14) in Chapter 11. Solve the model and interpret the sensitivity report.

17. Develop a spreadsheet model for Problem 15 in Chapter 11. Solve the model as an integer optimization problem.

18. Develop a spreadsheet model for Problem 16 in Chapter 11. Solve the model as an integer optimization problem.

19. Develop a spreadsheet model for Problem 17 in Chapter 11. Solve the model as an integer optimization problem.

20. Use *Solver* to find an optimal solution to finding the optimal price that maximizes revenue for the function $-2.6556*(Price)^2 + 3016.2*Price$ as discussed in the Introduction to Chapter 11.

21. Solve the Markowitz portfolio model we formulated in Chapter 11 using *Solver*. Interpret the sensitivity report.

22. For the optimization model you developed for Kern's Meats (Problem 21, Chapter 11), compare solutions for the following probability levels (some of which may be infeasible): 0.5, 0.6, 0.7, 0.8, 0.9, and 0.95. Discuss the impact of higher probabilities of satisfying the meat requirement. You may use the function NORMSINV(probability) to get the appropriate z-value from Excel. (As a check, the z-value for a probability of 0.6 is 0.253347.)

23. Develop a spreadsheet model for Problem 22 in Chapter 11. Solve the model as a nonlinear optimization problem and interpret the Sensitivity Report from *Solver*.

24. Use *OptQuest* with the deterministic option to find a solution to the product mix example in Chapter 11. Does it give the optimal solution that *Solver* found?

25. For the project selection model in Chapter 11, suppose that the returns in the objective function are normally distributed with means as given by the expected returns and standard deviation equal to 10 percent of the mean. However, also assume that each project has a success rate modeled as a binomial distribution. That is, the return will be realized only if the project is successful. Success rates for the five projects are 0.80, 0.70, 0.90, 0.40, and 0.60, respectively. Modify the spreadsheet model in Chapter 11, and use *OptQuest* to find a solution that maximizes the mean return.

C A S E

DISTRIBUTION CENTER LOCATION FOR TRACWAY

Solve the optimization model you developed for the Tracway case in Chapter 11 to find the best location for the new distribution centers. Write a report to Henry Hudson explaining your solution and any recommendations you may develop by conducting appropriate sensitivity analyses with the model. Verify your solution by solving individual transportation problems for all combinations of two new distribution centers among the four potential locations. ■

APPENDIX

z	.00	.01	.02	.03	.04	.05	.06	.07	.08	.09
0.0	.0000	.0040	.0080	.0120	.0160	.0199	.0239	.0279	.0319	.0359
0.1	.0398	.0438	.0478	.0517	.0557	.0596	.0636	.0675	.0714	.0753
0.2	.0793	.0832	.0871	.0910	.0948	.0987	.1026	.1064	.1103	.1141
0.3	.1179	.1217	.1255	.1293	.1331	.1368	.1406	.1443	.1480	.1517
0.4	.1554	.1591	.1628	.1664	.1700	.1736	.1772	.1808	.1844	.1879
0.5	.1915	.1950	.1985	.2019	.2054	.2088	.2123	.2157	.2190	.2224
0.6	.2257	.2291	.2324	.2357	.2389	.2422	.2454	.2486	.2518	.2549
0.7	.2580	.2612	.2642	.2673	.2704	.2734	.2764	.2794	.2823	.2852
0.8	.2881	.2910	.2939	.2967	.2995	.3023	.3051	.3078	.3106	.3133
0.9	.3159	.3186	.3212	.3238	.3264	.3289	.3315	.3340	.3365	.3389
1.0	.3413	.3438	.3461	.3485	.3508	.3531	.3554	.3577	.3599	.3621
1.1	.3643	.3665	.3686	.3708	.3729	.3749	.3770	.3790	.3810	.3830
1.2	.3849	.3869	.3888	.3907	.3925	.3944	.3962	.3980	.3997	.4015
1.3	.4032	.4049	.4066	.4082	.4099	.4115	.4131	.4147	.4162	.4177
1.4	.4192	.4207	.4222	.4236	.4251	.4265	.4279	.4292	.4306	.4319
1.5	.4332	.4345	.4357	.4370	.4382	.4394	.4406	.4418	.4429	.4441
1.6	.4452	.4463	.4474	.4484	.4495	.4505	.4515	.4525	.4535	.4545
1.7	.4554	.4564	.4573	.4582	.4591	.4599	.4608	.4616	.4625	.4633
1.8	.4641	.4649	.4656	.4664	.4671	.4678	.4686	.4693	.4699	.4706
1.9	.4713	.4719	.4726	.4732	.4738	.4744	.4750	.4756	.4761	.4767
2.0	.4772	.4778	.4783	.4788	.4793	.4798	.4803	.4808	.4812	.4817
2.1	.4821	.4826	.4830	.4834	.4838	.4842	.4846	.4850	.4854	.4857
2.2	.4861	.4864	.4868	.4871	.4875	.4878	.4881	.4884	.4887	.4890
2.3	.4893	.4896	.4898	.4901	.4904	.4906	.4909	.4911	.4913	.4916
2.4	.4918	.4920	.4922	.4925	.4927	.4929	.4931	.4932	.4934	.4936
2.5	.4938	.4940	.4941	.4943	.4945	.4946	.4948	.4949	.4951	.4952
2.6	.4953	.4955	.4956	.4957	.4959	.4960	.4961	.4962	.4963	.4964
2.7	.4965	.4966	.4967	.4968	.4969	.4970	.4971	.4972	.4973	.4974
2.8	.4974	.4975	.4976	.4977	.4977	.4978	.4979	.4979	.4980	.4981
2.9	.4981	.4982	.4982	.4983	.4984	.4984	.4985	.4985	.4986	.4986
3.0	.49865	.49869	.49874	.49878	.49882	.49886	.49889	.49893	.49897	.49900
3.1	.49903	.49906	.49910	.49913	.49916	.49918	.49921	.49924	.49926	.49929
3.2	.49931	.49934	.49936	.49938	.49940	.49942	.49944	.49946	.49948	.49950
3.3	.49952	.49953	.49955	.49957	.49958	.49960	.49961	.49962	.49964	.49965
3.4	.49966	.49968	.49969	.49970	.49971	.49972	.49973	.49974	.49975	.49976
3.5	.49977	.49978	.49978	.49979	.49980	.49981	.49981	.49982	.49983	.49983
3.6	.49984	.49985	.49985	.49986	.49986	.49987	.49987	.49988	.49988	.49989
3.7	.49989	.49990	.49990	.49990	.49991	.49991	.49992	.49992	.49992	.49992
3.8	.49993	.49993	.49993	.49994	.49994	.49994	.49994	.49995	.49995	.49995
3.9	.49995	.49995	.49996	.49996	.49996	.49996	.49996	.49996	.49997	.49997

Entry represents area under the standardized normal distribution from the mean to z

TABLE A.2 The Cumulative Standardized Normal Distribution

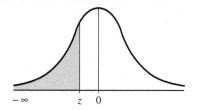

z	.00	.01	.02	.03	.04	.05	.06	.07	.08	.09
−3.9	.00005	.00005	.00004	.00004	.00004	.00004	.00004	.00004	.00003	.00003
−3.8	.00007	.00007	.00007	.00006	.00006	.00006	.00006	.00005	.00005	.00005
−3.7	.00011	.00010	.00010	.00010	.00009	.00009	.00008	.00008	.00008	.00008
−3.6	.00016	.00015	.00015	.00014	.00014	.00013	.00013	.00012	.00012	.00011
−3.5	.00023	.00022	.00022	.00021	.00020	.00019	.00019	.00018	.00017	.00017
−3.4	.00034	.00032	.00031	.00030	.00029	.00028	.00027	.00026	.00025	.00024
−3.3	.00048	.00047	.00045	.00043	.00042	.00040	.00039	.00038	.00036	.00035
−3.2	.00069	.00066	.00064	.00062	.00060	.00058	.00056	.00054	.00052	.00050
−3.1	.00097	.00094	.00090	.00087	.00084	.00082	.00079	.00076	.00074	.00071
−3.0	.00135	.00131	.00126	.00122	.00118	.00114	.00111	.00107	.00103	.00100
−2.9	.0019	.0018	.0018	.0017	.0016	.0016	.0015	.0015	.0014	.0014
−2.8	.0026	.0025	.0024	.0023	.0023	.0022	.0021	.0021	.0020	.0019
−2.7	.0035	.0034	.0033	.0032	.0031	.0030	.0029	.0028	.0027	.0026
−2.6	.0047	.0045	.0044	.0043	.0041	.0040	.0039	.0038	.0037	.0036
−2.5	.0062	.0060	.0059	.0057	.0055	.0054	.0052	.0051	.0049	.0048
−2.4	.0082	.0080	.0078	.0075	.0073	.0071	.0069	.0068	.0066	.0064
−2.3	.0107	.0104	.0102	.0099	.0096	.0094	.0091	.0089	.0087	.0084
−2.2	.0139	.0136	.0132	.0129	.0125	.0122	.0119	.0116	.0113	.0110
−2.1	.0179	.0174	.0170	.0166	.0162	.0158	.0154	.0150	.0146	.0143
−2.0	.0228	.0222	.0217	.0212	.0207	.0202	.0197	.0192	.0188	.0183
−1.9	.0287	.0281	.0274	.0268	.0262	.0256	.0250	.0244	.0239	.0233
−1.8	.0359	.0351	.0344	.0336	.0329	.0322	.0314	.0307	.0301	.0294
−1.7	.0446	.0436	.0427	.0418	.0409	.0401	.0392	.0384	.0375	.0367
−1.6	.0548	.0537	.0526	.0516	.0505	.0495	.0485	.0475	.0465	.0455
−1.5	.0668	.0655	.0643	.0630	.0618	.0606	.0594	.0582	.0571	.0559
−1.4	.0808	.0793	.0778	.0764	.0749	.0735	.0721	.0708	.0694	.0681
−1.3	.0968	.0951	.0934	.0918	.0901	.0885	.0869	.0853	.0838	.0823
−1.2	.1151	.1131	.1112	.1093	.1075	.1056	.1038	.1020	.1003	.0985
−1.1	.1357	.1335	.1314	.1292	.1271	.1251	.1230	.1210	.1190	.1170
−1.0	.1587	.1562	.1539	.1515	.1492	.1469	.1446	.1423	.1401	.1379
−0.9	.1841	.1814	.1788	.1762	.1736	.1711	.1685	.1660	.1635	.1611
−0.8	.2119	.2090	.2061	.2033	.2005	.1977	.1949	.1922	.1894	.1867
−0.7	.2420	.2388	.2358	.2327	.2296	.2266	.2236	.2006	.2177	.2148
−0.6	.2743	.2709	.2676	.2643	.2611	.2578	.2546	.2514	.2482	.2451
−0.5	.3085	.3050	.3015	.2981	.2946	.2912	.2877	.2843	.2810	.2776
−0.4	.3446	.3409	.3372	.3336	.3300	.3264	.3228	.3192	.3156	.3121
−0.3	.3821	.3783	.3745	.3707	.3669	.3632	.3594	.3557	.3520	.3483
−0.2	.4207	.4168	.4129	.4090	.4052	.4013	.3974	.3936	.3897	.3859
−0.1	.4602	.4562	.4522	.4483	.4443	.4404	.4364	.4325	.4286	.4247
−0.0	.5000	.4960	.4920	.4880	.4840	.4801	.4761	.4721	.4681	.4641

TABLE A.2   *(Continued)*

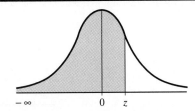

z	.00	.01	.02	.03	.04	.05	.06	.07	.08	.09
0.0	.5000	.5040	.5080	.5120	.5160	.5199	.5239	.5279	.5319	.5359
0.1	.5398	.5438	.5478	.5517	.5557	.5596	.5636	.5675	.5714	.5753
0.2	.5793	.5832	.5871	.5910	.5948	.5987	.6026	.6064	.6103	.6141
0.3	.6179	.6217	.6255	.6293	.6331	.6368	.6406	.6443	.6480	.6517
0.4	.6554	.6591	.6628	.6664	.6700	.6736	.6772	.6808	.6844	.6879
0.5	.6915	.6950	.6985	.7019	.7054	.7088	.7123	.7157	.7190	.7224
0.6	.7257	.7291	.7324	.7357	.7389	.7422	.7454	.7486	.7518	.7549
0.7	.7580	.7612	.7642	.7673	.7704	.7734	.7764	.7794	.7823	.7852
0.8	.7881	.7910	.7939	.7967	.7995	.8023	.8051	.8078	.8106	.8133
0.9	.8159	.8186	.8212	.8238	.8264	.8289	.8315	.8340	.8365	.8389
1.0	.8413	.8438	.8461	.8485	.8508	.8531	.8554	.8577	.8599	.8621
1.1	.8643	.8665	.8686	.8708	.8729	.8749	.8770	.8790	.8810	.8830
1.2	.8849	.8869	.8888	.8907	.8925	.8944	.8962	.8980	.8997	.9015
1.3	.9032	.9089	.9066	.9082	.9099	.9115	.9131	.9147	.9162	.9177
1.4	.9192	.9207	.9222	.9236	.9251	.9265	.9279	.9292	.9306	.9319
1.5	.9332	.9345	.9357	.9370	.9382	.9394	.9406	.9418	.9429	.9441
1.6	.9452	.9463	.9474	.9484	.9495	.9505	.9515	.9525	.9535	.9545
1.7	.9554	.9564	.9573	.9582	.9591	.9599	.9608	.9616	.9625	.9633
1.8	.9641	.9649	.9656	.9664	.9671	.9678	.9686	.9693	.9699	.9706
1.9	.9713	.9719	.9726	.9732	.9738	.9744	.9750	.9756	.9761	.9767
2.0	.9772	.9778	.9783	.9788	.9793	.9798	.9803	.9808	.9812	.9817
2.1	.9821	.9826	.9830	.9834	.9838	.9842	.9846	.9850	.9854	.9857
2.2	.9861	.9864	.9868	.9871	.9875	.9878	.9881	.9884	.9887	.9890
2.3	.9893	.9896	.9898	.9901	.9904	.9906	.9909	.9911	.9913	.9916
2.4	.9918	.9920	.9922	.9925	.9927	.9929	.9931	.9932	.9934	.9936
2.5	.9938	.9940	.9941	.9943	.9945	.9946	.9948	.9949	.9951	.9952
2.6	.9953	.9955	.9956	.9957	.9959	.9960	.9961	.9962	.9963	.9964
2.7	.9965	.9966	.9967	.9968	.9969	.9970	.9971	.9972	.9973	.9974
2.8	.9974	.9975	.9976	.9977	.9977	.9978	.9979	.9979	.9980	.9981
2.9	.9981	.9982	.9982	.9983	.9984	.9984	.9985	.9985	.9986	.9986
3.0	.99865	.99869	.99874	.99878	.99882	.99886	.99889	.99893	.99897	.99900
3.1	.99903	.99906	.99910	.99913	.99916	.99918	.99921	.99924	.99926	.99929
3.2	.99931	.99934	.99936	.99938	.99940	.99942	.99944	.99946	.99948	.99950
3.3	.99952	.99953	.99955	.99957	.99958	.99960	.99961	.99962	.99964	.99965
3.4	.99966	.99968	.99969	.99970	.99971	.99972	.99973	.99974	.99975	.99976
3.5	.99977	.99978	.99978	.99979	.99980	.99981	.99981	.99981	.99982	.99983
3.6	.99984	.99985	.99985	.99986	.99986	.99987	.99987	.99988	.99988	.99989
3.7	.99989	.99990	.99990	.99990	.99991	.99991	.99992	.99992	.99992	.99992
3.8	.99993	.99993	.99993	.99994	.99994	.99994	.99994	.99995	.99995	.99995
3.9	.99995	.99995	.99996	.99996	.99996	.99996	.99996	.99996	.99997	.99997

(handwritten annotation near 1.1 row, .08/.09 columns: "closest to .9")
(handwritten circle around .8997 in the 1.2 row, .08 column)

Entry represents area under the cumulative standardized normal distribution from $-\infty$ to z

TABLE A.3   Critical Values of *t*

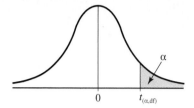

Degrees of Freedom	Upper Tail Areas					
	.25	*.10*	*.05*	*.025*	*.01*	*.005*
1	1.0000	3.0777	6.3138	12.7062	31.8207	63.6574
2	0.8165	1.8856	2.9200	4.3027	6.9646	9.9248
3	0.7649	1.6377	2.3534	3.1824	4.5407	5.8409
4	0.7407	1.5332	2.1318	2.7764	3.7469	4.6041
5	0.7267	1.4759	2.0150	2.5706	3.3649	4.0322
6	0.7176	1.4398	1.9432	2.4469	3.1427	3.7074
7	0.7111	1.4149	1.8946	2.3646	2.9980	3.4995
8	0.7064	1.3968	1.8595	2.3060	2.8965	3.3554
9	0.7027	1.3830	1.8331	2.2622	2.8214	3.2498
10	0.6998	1.3722	1.8125	2.2281	2.7638	3.1693
11	0.6974	1.3634	1.7959	2.2010	2.7181	3.1058
12	0.6955	1.3562	1.7823	2.1788	2.6810	3.0545
13	0.6938	1.3502	1.7709	2.1604	2.6503	3.0123
14	0.6924	1.3450	1.7613	2.1448	2.6245	2.9768
15	0.6912	1.3406	1.7531	2.1315	2.6025	2.9467
16	0.6901	1.3368	1.7459	2.1199	2.5835	2.9208
17	0.6892	1.3334	1.7396	2.1098	2.5669	2.8982
18	0.6884	1.3304	1.7341	2.1009	2.5524	2.8784
19	0.6876	1.3277	1.7291	2.0930	2.5395	2.8609
20	0.6870	1.3253	1.7247	2.0860	2.5280	2.8453
21	0.6864	1.3232	1.7207	2.0796	2.5177	2.8314
22	0.6858	1.3212	1.7171	2.0739	2.5083	2.8188
23	0.6853	1.3195	1.7139	2.0687	2.4999	2.8073
24	0.6848	1.3178	1.7109	2.0639	2.4922	2.7969
25	0.6844	1.3163	1.7081	2.0595	2.4851	2.7874
26	0.6840	1.3150	1.7056	2.0555	2.4786	2.7787
27	0.6837	1.3137	1.7033	2.0518	2.4727	2.7707
28	0.6834	1.3125	1.7011	2.0484	2.4671	2.7633
29	0.6830	1.3114	1.6991	2.0452	2.4620	2.7564
30	0.6828	1.3104	1.6973	2.0423	2.4573	2.7500
31	0.6825	1.3095	1.6955	2.0395	2.4528	2.7440
32	0.6822	1.3086	1.6939	2.0369	2.4487	2.7385
33	0.6820	1.3077	1.6924	2.0345	2.4448	2.7333
34	0.6818	1.3070	1.6909	2.0322	2.4411	2.7284
35	0.6816	1.3062	1.6896	2.0301	2.4377	2.7238

TABLE A.3 *(Continued)*

Degrees of Freedom	Upper Tail Areas					
	.25	.10	.05	.025	.01	.005
36	0.6814	1.3055	1.6883	2.0281	2.4345	2.7195
37	0.6812	1.3049	1.6871	2.0262	2.4314	2.7154
38	0.6810	1.3042	1.6860	2.0244	2.4286	2.7116
39	0.6808	1.3036	1.6849	2.0227	2.4258	2.7079
40	0.6807	1.3031	1.6839	2.0211	2.4233	2.7045
41	0.6805	1.3025	1.6829	2.0195	2.4208	2.7012
42	0.6804	1.3020	1.6820	2.0181	2.4185	2.6981
43	0.6802	1.3016	1.6811	2.0167	2.4163	2.6951
44	0.6801	1.3011	1.6802	2.0154	2.4141	2.6923
45	0.6800	1.3006	1.6794	2.0141	2.4121	2.6896
46	0.6799	1.3002	1.6787	2.0129	2.4102	2.6870
47	0.6797	1.2998	1.6779	2.0117	2.4083	2.6846
48	0.6796	1.2994	1.6772	2.0106	2.4066	2.6822
49	0.6795	1.2991	1.6766	2.0096	2.4049	2.6800
50	0.6794	1.2987	1.6759	2.0086	2.4033	2.6778
51	0.6793	1.2984	1.6753	2.0076	2.4017	2.6757
52	0.6792	1.2980	1.6747	2.0066	2.4002	2.6737
53	0.6791	1.2977	1.6741	2.0057	2.3988	2.6718
54	0.6791	1.2974	1.6736	2.0049	2.3974	2.6700
55	0.6790	1.2971	1.6730	2.0040	2.3961	2.6682
56	0.6789	1.2969	1.6725	2.0032	2.3948	2.6665
57	0.6788	1.2966	1.6720	2.0025	2.3936	2.6649
58	0.6787	1.2963	1.6716	2.0017	2.3924	2.6633
59	0.6787	1.2961	1.6711	2.0010	2.3912	2.6618
60	0.6786	1.2958	1.6706	2.0003	2.3901	2.6603
61	0.6785	1.2956	1.6702	1.9996	2.3890	2.6589
62	0.6785	1.2954	1.6698	1.9990	2.3880	2.6575
63	0.6784	1.2951	1.6694	1.9983	2.3870	2.6561
64	0.6783	1.2949	1.6690	1.9977	2.3860	2.6549
65	0.6783	1.2947	1.6686	1.9971	2.3851	2.6536
66	0.6782	1.2945	1.6683	1.9966	2.3842	2.6524
67	0.6782	1.2943	1.6679	1.9960	2.3833	2.6512
68	0.6781	1.2941	1.6676	1.9955	2.3824	2.6501
69	0.6781	1.2939	1.6672	1.9949	2.3816	2.6490
70	0.6780	1.2938	1.6669	1.9944	2.3808	2.6479
71	0.6780	1.2936	1.6666	1.9939	2.3800	2.6469
72	0.6779	1.2934	1.6663	1.9935	2.3793	2.6459
73	0.6779	1.2933	1.6660	1.9930	2.3785	2.6449
74	0.6778	1.2931	1.6657	1.9925	2.3778	2.6439
75	0.6778	1.2929	1.6654	1.9921	2.3771	2.6430
76	0.6777	1.2928	1.6652	1.9917	2.3764	2.6421
77	0.6777	1.2926	1.6649	1.9913	2.3758	2.6412
78	0.6776	1.2925	1.6646	1.9908	2.3751	2.6403
79	0.6776	1.2924	1.6644	1.9905	2.3745	2.6395
80	0.6776	1.2922	1.6641	1.9901	2.3739	2.6387

(Continued)

TABLE A.3 *(Continued)*

Degrees of Freedom	Upper Tail Areas					
	.25	.10	.05	.025	.01	.005
81	0.6775	1.2921	1.6639	1.9897	2.3733	2.6379
82	0.6775	1.2920	1.6636	1.9893	2.3727	2.6371
83	0.6775	1.2918	1.6634	1.9890	2.3721	2.6364
84	0.6774	1.2917	1.6632	1.9886	2.3716	2.6356
85	0.6774	1.2916	1.6630	1.9883	2.3710	2.6349
86	0.6774	1.2915	1.6628	1.9879	2.3705	2.6342
87	0.6773	1.2914	1.6626	1.9876	2.3700	2.6335
88	0.6773	1.2912	1.6624	1.9873	2.3695	2.6329
89	0.6773	1.2911	1.6622	1.9870	2.3690	2.6322
90	0.6772	1.2910	1.6620	1.9867	2.3685	2.6316
91	0.6772	1.2909	1.6618	1.9864	2.3680	2.6309
92	0.6772	1.2908	1.6616	1.9861	2.3676	2.6303
93	0.6771	1.2907	1.6614	1.9858	2.3671	2.6297
94	0.6771	1.2906	1.6612	1.9855	2.3667	2.6291
95	0.6771	1.2905	1.6611	1.9853	2.3662	2.6286
96	0.6771	1.2904	1.6609	1.9850	2.3658	2.6280
97	0.6770	1.2903	1.6607	1.9847	2.3654	2.6275
98	0.6770	1.2902	1.6606	1.9845	2.3650	2.6269
99	0.6770	1.2902	1.6604	1.9842	2.3646	2.6264
100	0.6770	1.2901	1.6602	1.9840	2.3642	2.6259
110	0.6767	1.2893	1.6588	1.9818	2.3607	2.6213
120	0.6765	1.2886	1.6577	1.9799	2.3578	2.6174
∞	0.6745	1.2816	1.6449	1.9600	2.3263	2.5758

For particular number of degrees of freedom, entry represents the critical value of t corresponding to a specified upper tail area (α)

Upper Tail Areas (α)

Degrees of Freedom	.995	.99	.975	.95	.90	.75	.25	.10	.05	.025	.01	.005
1			0.001	0.004	0.016	0.102	1.323	2.706	3.841	5.024	6.635	7.879
2	0.010	0.020	0.051	0.103	0.211	0.575	2.773	4.605	5.991	7.378	9.210	10.597
3	0.072	0.115	0.216	0.352	0.584	1.213	4.108	6.251	7.815	9.348	11.345	12.838
4	0.207	0.297	0.484	0.711	1.064	1.923	5.385	7.779	9.488	11.143	13.277	14.860
5	0.412	0.554	0.831	1.145	1.610	2.675	6.626	9.236	11.071	12.833	15.086	16.750
6	0.676	0.872	1.237	1.635	2.204	3.455	7.841	10.645	12.592	14.449	16.812	18.548
7	0.989	1.239	1.690	2.167	2.833	4.255	9.037	12.017	14.067	16.013	18.475	20.278
8	1.344	1.646	2.180	2.733	3.490	5.071	10.219	13.362	15.507	17.535	20.090	21.955
9	1.735	2.088	2.700	3.325	4.168	5.899	11.389	14.684	16.919	19.023	21.666	23.589
10	2.156	2.558	3.247	3.940	4.865	6.737	12.549	15.987	18.307	20.483	23.209	25.188
11	2.603	3.053	3.816	4.575	5.578	7.584	13.701	17.275	19.675	21.920	24.725	26.757
12	3.074	3.571	4.404	5.226	6.304	8.438	14.845	18.549	21.026	23.337	26.217	28.299
13	3.565	4.107	5.009	5.892	7.042	9.299	15.984	19.812	22.362	24.736	27.688	29.819
14	4.075	4.660	5.629	6.571	7.790	10.165	17.117	21.064	23.685	26.119	29.141	31.319
15	4.601	5.229	6.262	7.261	8.547	11.037	18.245	22.307	24.996	27.488	30.578	32.801
16	5.142	5.812	6.908	7.962	9.312	11.912	19.369	23.542	26.296	28.845	32.000	34.267
17	5.697	6.408	7.564	8.672	10.085	12.792	20.489	24.769	27.587	30.191	33.409	35.718
18	6.265	7.015	8.231	9.390	10.865	13.675	21.605	25.989	28.869	31.526	34.805	37.156
19	6.844	7.633	8.907	10.117	11.651	14.562	22.718	27.204	30.144	32.852	36.191	38.582
20	7.434	8.260	9.591	10.851	12.443	15.452	23.828	28.412	31.410	34.170	37.566	39.997
21	8.034	8.897	10.283	11.591	13.240	16.344	24.935	29.615	32.671	35.479	38.932	41.401
22	8.643	9.542	10.982	12.338	14.042	17.240	26.039	30.813	33.924	36.781	40.289	42.796
23	9.260	10.196	11.689	13.091	14.848	18.137	27.141	32.007	35.172	38.076	41.638	44.181
24	9.886	10.856	12.401	13.848	15.659	19.037	28.241	33.196	36.415	39.364	42.980	45.559
25	10.520	11.524	13.120	14.611	16.473	19.939	29.339	34.382	37.652	40.646	44.314	46.928
26	11.160	12.198	13.844	15.379	17.292	20.843	30.435	35.563	38.885	41.923	45.642	48.290
27	11.808	12.879	14.573	16.151	18.114	21.749	31.528	36.741	40.113	43.194	46.963	49.645
28	12.461	13.565	15.308	16.928	18.939	22.657	32.620	37.916	41.337	44.461	48.278	50.993
29	13.121	14.257	16.047	17.708	19.768	23.567	33.711	39.087	42.557	45.722	49.588	52.336
30	13.787	14.954	16.791	18.493	20.599	24.478	34.800	40.256	43.773	46.979	50.892	53.672

For a particular number of degrees of freedom, entry represents the critical value of χ^2 corresponding to a specified upper tail area (α).

For larger values of degrees of freedom (df) the expression $Z = \sqrt{2\chi^2} - \sqrt{2(df) - 1}$ may be used, and the resulting upper tail area can be obtained from the table of the standardized normal distribution (Table A.2a).

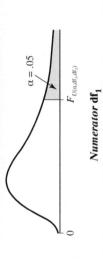

$\alpha = .05$

$F_{U(\alpha, df_1, df_2)}$

Numerator df_1

Denominator df_2	1	2	3	4	5	6	7	8	9	10	12	15	20	24	30	40	60	120	∞
1	161.4	199.5	215.7	224.6	230.2	234.0	236.8	238.9	240.5	241.9	243.9	245.9	248.0	249.1	250.1	251.1	252.2	253.3	254.3
2	18.51	19.00	19.16	19.25	19.30	19.33	19.35	19.37	19.38	19.40	19.41	19.43	19.45	19.45	19.46	19.47	19.48	19.49	19.50
3	10.13	9.55	9.28	9.12	9.01	8.94	8.89	8.85	8.81	8.79	8.74	8.70	8.66	8.64	8.62	8.59	8.57	8.55	8.53
4	7.71	6.94	6.59	6.39	6.26	6.16	6.09	6.04	6.00	5.96	5.91	5.86	5.80	5.77	5.75	5.72	5.69	5.66	5.63
5	6.61	5.79	5.41	5.19	5.05	4.95	4.88	4.82	4.77	4.74	4.68	4.62	4.56	4.53	4.50	4.46	4.43	4.40	4.36
6	5.99	5.14	4.76	4.53	4.39	4.28	4.21	4.15	4.10	4.06	4.00	3.94	3.87	3.84	3.81	3.77	3.74	3.70	3.67
7	5.59	4.74	4.35	4.12	3.97	3.87	3.79	3.73	3.68	3.64	3.57	3.51	3.44	3.41	3.38	3.34	3.30	3.27	3.23
8	5.32	4.46	4.07	3.84	3.69	3.58	3.50	3.44	3.39	3.35	3.28	3.22	3.15	3.12	3.08	3.04	3.01	2.97	2.93
9	5.12	4.26	3.86	3.63	3.48	3.37	3.29	3.23	3.18	3.14	3.07	3.01	2.94	2.90	2.86	2.83	2.79	2.75	2.71
10	4.96	4.10	3.71	3.48	3.33	3.22	3.14	3.07	3.02	2.98	2.91	2.85	2.77	2.74	2.70	2.66	2.62	2.58	2.54
11	4.84	3.98	3.59	3.36	3.20	3.09	3.01	2.95	2.90	2.85	2.79	2.72	2.65	2.61	2.57	2.53	2.49	2.45	2.40
12	4.75	3.89	3.49	3.26	3.11	3.00	2.91	2.85	2.80	2.75	2.69	2.62	2.54	2.51	2.47	2.43	2.38	2.34	2.30
13	4.67	3.81	3.41	3.18	3.03	2.92	2.83	2.77	2.71	2.67	2.60	2.53	2.46	2.42	2.38	2.34	2.30	2.25	2.21
14	4.60	3.74	3.34	3.11	2.96	2.85	2.76	2.70	2.65	2.60	2.53	2.46	2.39	2.35	2.31	2.27	2.22	2.18	2.13
15	4.54	3.68	3.29	3.06	2.90	2.79	2.71	2.64	2.59	2.54	2.48	2.40	2.33	2.29	2.25	2.20	2.16	2.11	2.07
16	4.49	3.63	3.24	3.01	2.85	2.74	2.66	2.59	2.54	2.49	2.42	2.35	2.28	2.24	2.19	2.15	2.11	2.06	2.01
17	4.45	3.59	3.20	2.96	2.81	2.70	2.61	2.55	2.49	2.45	2.38	2.31	2.23	2.19	2.15	2.10	2.06	2.01	1.96
18	4.41	3.55	3.16	2.93	2.77	2.66	2.58	2.51	2.46	2.41	2.34	2.27	2.19	2.15	2.11	2.06	2.02	1.97	1.92
19	4.38	3.52	3.13	2.90	2.74	2.63	2.54	2.48	2.42	2.38	2.31	2.23	2.16	2.11	2.07	2.03	1.98	1.93	1.88
20	4.35	3.49	3.10	2.87	2.71	2.60	2.51	2.45	2.39	2.35	2.28	2.20	2.12	2.08	2.04	1.99	1.95	1.90	1.84
21	4.32	3.47	3.07	2.84	2.68	2.57	2.49	2.42	2.37	2.32	2.25	2.18	2.10	2.05	2.01	1.96	1.92	1.87	1.81
22	4.30	3.44	3.05	2.82	2.66	2.55	2.46	2.40	2.34	2.30	2.23	2.15	2.07	2.03	1.98	1.94	1.89	1.84	1.78
23	4.28	3.42	3.03	2.80	2.64	2.53	2.44	2.37	2.32	2.27	2.20	2.13	2.05	2.01	1.96	1.91	1.86	1.81	1.76
24	4.26	3.40	3.01	2.78	2.62	2.51	2.42	2.36	2.30	2.25	2.18	2.11	2.03	1.98	1.94	1.89	1.84	1.79	1.73
25	4.24	3.39	2.99	2.76	2.60	2.49	2.40	2.34	2.28	2.24	2.16	2.09	2.01	1.96	1.92	1.87	1.82	1.77	1.71
26	4.23	3.37	2.98	2.74	2.59	2.47	2.39	2.32	2.27	2.22	2.15	2.07	1.99	1.95	1.90	1.85	1.80	1.75	1.69
27	4.21	3.35	2.96	2.73	2.57	2.46	2.37	2.31	2.25	2.20	2.13	2.06	1.97	1.93	1.88	1.84	1.79	1.73	1.67
28	4.20	3.34	2.95	2.71	2.56	2.45	2.36	2.29	2.24	2.19	2.12	2.04	1.96	1.91	1.87	1.82	1.77	1.71	1.65
29	4.18	3.33	2.93	2.70	2.55	2.43	2.35	2.28	2.22	2.18	2.10	2.03	1.94	1.90	1.85	1.81	1.75	1.70	1.64
30	4.17	3.32	2.92	2.69	2.53	2.42	2.33	2.27	2.21	2.16	2.09	2.01	1.93	1.89	1.84	1.79	1.74	1.68	1.62
40	4.08	3.23	2.84	2.61	2.45	2.34	2.25	2.18	2.12	2.08	2.00	1.92	1.84	1.79	1.74	1.69	1.64	1.58	1.51
60	4.00	3.15	2.76	2.53	2.37	2.25	2.17	2.10	2.04	1.99	1.92	1.84	1.75	1.70	1.65	1.59	1.53	1.47	1.39
120	3.92	3.07	2.68	2.45	2.29	2.17	2.09	2.02	1.96	1.91	1.83	1.75	1.66	1.61	1.55	1.50	1.43	1.35	1.25
∞	3.84	3.00	2.60	2.37	2.21	2.10	2.01	1.94	1.88	1.83	1.75	1.67	1.57	1.52	1.46	1.39	1.32	1.22	1.00
1	647.8	799.5	864.2	899.6	921.8	937.1	948.2	956.7	963.3	968.6	976.7	984.9	993.1	997.2	1001	1006	1010	1014	1018

(Continued)

$\alpha = .025$

$F_{U(\alpha,df_1,df_2)}$

Numerator df$_1$

Denominator df$_2$	1	2	3	4	5	6	7	8	9	10	12	15	20	24	30	40	60	120	∞
2	38.51	39.00	39.17	39.25	39.30	39.33	39.36	39.37	39.39	39.40	39.41	39.43	39.45	39.46	39.46	39.47	39.48	39.49	39.50
3	17.44	16.04	15.44	15.10	14.88	14.73	14.62	14.54	14.47	14.42	14.34	14.25	14.17	14.12	14.08	14.04	13.99	13.95	13.90
4	12.22	10.65	9.98	9.60	9.36	9.20	9.07	8.98	8.90	8.84	8.75	8.66	8.56	8.51	8.46	8.41	8.36	8.31	8.26
5	10.01	8.43	7.76	7.39	7.15	6.98	6.85	6.76	6.68	6.62	6.52	6.43	6.33	6.28	6.23	6.18	6.12	6.07	6.02
6	8.81	7.26	6.60	6.23	5.99	5.82	5.70	5.60	5.52	5.46	5.37	5.27	5.17	5.12	5.07	5.01	4.96	4.90	4.85
7	8.07	6.54	5.89	5.52	5.29	5.12	4.99	4.90	4.82	4.76	4.67	4.57	4.47	4.42	4.36	4.31	4.25	4.20	4.14
8	7.57	6.06	5.42	5.05	4.82	4.65	4.53	4.43	4.36	4.30	4.20	4.10	4.00	3.95	3.89	3.84	3.78	3.73	3.67
9	7.21	5.71	5.08	4.72	4.48	4.32	4.20	4.10	4.03	3.96	3.87	3.77	3.67	3.61	3.56	3.51	3.45	3.39	3.33
10	6.94	5.46	4.83	4.47	4.24	4.07	3.95	3.85	3.78	3.72	3.62	3.52	3.42	3.37	3.31	3.26	3.20	3.14	3.08
11	6.72	5.26	4.63	4.28	4.04	3.88	3.76	3.66	3.59	3.53	3.43	3.33	3.23	3.17	3.12	3.06	3.00	2.94	2.88
12	6.55	5.10	4.47	4.12	3.89	3.73	3.61	3.51	3.44	3.37	3.28	3.18	3.07	3.02	2.96	2.91	2.85	2.79	2.72
13	6.41	4.97	4.36	4.00	3.77	3.60	3.48	3.39	3.31	3.25	3.15	3.05	2.95	2.89	2.84	2.78	2.72	2.66	2.60
14	6.30	4.86	4.24	3.89	3.66	3.50	3.38	3.29	3.21	3.15	3.05	2.95	2.84	2.79	2.73	2.67	2.61	2.55	2.49
15	6.20	4.77	4.15	3.80	3.58	3.41	3.29	3.20	3.12	3.06	2.96	2.86	2.76	2.70	2.64	2.59	2.52	2.46	2.40
16	6.12	4.69	4.08	3.73	3.50	3.34	3.22	3.12	3.05	2.99	2.89	2.79	2.68	2.63	2.57	2.51	2.45	2.38	2.32
17	6.04	4.62	4.01	3.66	3.44	3.28	3.16	3.06	2.98	2.92	2.82	2.72	2.62	2.56	2.50	2.44	2.38	2.32	2.25
18	5.98	4.56	3.95	3.61	3.38	3.22	3.10	3.01	2.93	2.87	2.77	2.67	2.56	2.50	2.44	2.38	2.32	2.26	2.19
19	5.92	4.51	3.90	3.56	3.33	3.17	3.05	2.96	2.88	2.82	2.72	2.62	2.51	2.45	2.39	2.33	2.27	2.20	2.13
20	5.87	4.46	3.86	3.51	3.29	3.13	3.01	2.91	2.84	2.77	2.68	2.57	2.46	2.41	2.35	2.29	2.22	2.16	2.09
21	5.83	4.42	3.82	3.48	3.25	3.09	2.97	2.87	2.80	2.73	2.64	2.53	2.42	2.37	2.31	2.25	2.18	2.11	2.04
22	5.79	4.38	3.78	3.44	3.22	3.05	2.93	2.84	2.76	2.70	2.60	2.50	2.39	2.33	2.27	2.21	2.14	2.08	2.00
23	5.75	4.35	3.75	3.41	3.18	3.02	2.90	2.81	2.73	2.67	2.57	2.47	2.36	2.30	2.24	2.18	2.11	2.04	1.97
24	5.72	4.32	3.72	3.38	3.15	2.99	2.87	2.78	2.70	2.64	2.54	2.44	2.33	2.27	2.21	2.15	2.08	2.01	1.94
25	5.69	4.29	3.69	3.35	3.13	2.97	2.85	2.75	2.68	2.61	2.51	2.41	2.30	2.24	2.18	2.12	2.05	1.98	1.91
26	5.66	4.27	3.67	3.33	3.10	2.94	2.82	2.73	2.65	2.59	2.49	2.39	2.28	2.22	2.16	2.09	2.03	1.95	1.88
27	5.63	4.24	3.68	3.31	3.08	2.92	2.80	2.71	2.63	2.57	2.47	2.36	2.25	2.19	2.13	2.07	2.00	1.93	1.85
28	5.61	4.22	3.63	3.29	3.06	2.90	2.78	2.69	2.61	2.55	2.45	2.34	2.23	2.17	2.11	2.05	1.98	1.91	1.83
29	5.59	4.20	3.61	3.27	3.04	2.88	2.76	2.67	2.59	2.53	2.43	2.32	2.21	2.15	2.09	2.03	1.96	1.89	1.81
30	5.57	4.18	3.59	3.25	3.03	2.87	2.75	2.65	2.57	2.51	2.41	2.31	2.20	2.14	2.07	2.01	1.94	1.87	1.79
40	5.42	4.05	3.46	3.13	2.90	2.74	2.62	2.53	2.45	2.39	2.29	2.18	2.07	2.01	1.94	1.88	1.80	1.72	1.64
60	5.29	3.93	3.34	3.01	2.79	2.63	2.51	2.41	2.33	2.27	2.17	2.06	1.94	1.88	1.82	1.74	1.67	1.58	1.48
120	5.15	3.80	3.23	2.89	2.67	2.52	2.39	2.30	2.22	2.16	2.05	1.94	1.82	1.76	1.69	1.61	1.53	1.43	1.31
∞	5.02	3.69	3.12	2.79	2.57	2.41	2.29	2.19	2.11	2.05	1.94	1.83	1.71	1.64	1.57	1.48	1.39	1.27	1.00

(Continued)

$\alpha = .005$

$F_{U(\alpha, df_1, df_2)}$

| Denominator df_2 | \multicolumn{19}{c}{Numerator df_1} |
	1	2	3	4	5	6	7	8	9	10	12	15	20	24	30	40	60	120	∞
1	16211	20000	21615	22500	23056	23437	23715	23925	24091	24224	24426	24630	24836	24940	25044	25148	25253	25359	25465
2	198.5	199.0	199.2	199.2	199.3	199.3	199.4	199.4	199.4	199.4	199.4	199.4	199.4	199.5	199.5	199.5	199.5	199.5	199.5
3	55.55	49.80	47.47	46.19	45.39	44.84	44.43	44.13	43.88	43.69	43.39	43.08	42.78	42.62	42.47	42.31	42.15	41.99	41.83
4	31.33	26.28	24.26	23.15	22.46	21.97	21.62	21.35	21.14	20.97	20.70	20.44	20.17	20.03	19.89	19.75	19.61	19.47	19.32
5	22.78	18.31	16.53	15.56	14.94	14.51	14.20	13.96	13.77	13.62	13.38	13.15	12.90	12.78	12.66	12.53	12.40	12.27	12.14
6	18.63	14.54	12.92	12.03	11.46	11.07	10.79	10.57	10.39	10.25	10.03	9.81	9.59	9.47	9.36	9.24	9.12	9.00	8.88
7	16.24	12.40	10.88	10.05	9.52	9.16	8.89	8.68	8.51	8.38	8.18	7.97	7.75	7.65	7.53	7.42	7.31	7.19	7.08
8	14.69	11.04	9.60	8.81	8.30	7.95	7.69	7.50	7.34	7.21	7.01	6.81	6.61	6.50	6.40	6.29	6.18	6.06	5.95
9	13.61	10.11	8.72	7.96	7.47	7.13	6.88	6.69	6.54	6.42	6.23	6.03	5.83	5.73	5.62	5.52	5.41	5.30	5.19
10	12.83	9.43	8.08	7.34	6.87	6.54	6.30	6.12	5.97	5.85	5.66	5.47	5.27	5.17	5.07	4.97	4.86	4.75	4.64
11	12.23	8.91	7.60	6.88	6.42	6.10	5.86	5.68	5.54	5.42	5.24	5.05	4.86	4.76	4.65	4.55	4.44	4.34	4.23
12	11.75	8.51	7.23	6.52	6.07	5.76	5.52	5.35	5.20	5.09	4.91	4.72	4.53	4.43	4.33	4.23	4.12	4.01	3.90
13	11.37	8.19	6.93	6.23	5.79	5.48	5.25	5.08	4.94	4.82	4.64	4.46	4.27	4.17	4.07	3.97	3.87	3.76	3.65
14	11.06	7.92	6.68	6.00	5.56	5.26	5.03	4.86	4.72	4.60	4.43	4.25	4.06	3.96	3.86	3.76	3.66	3.55	3.44
15	10.80	7.70	6.48	5.80	5.37	5.07	4.85	4.67	4.54	4.42	4.25	4.07	3.88	3.79	3.69	3.58	3.48	3.37	3.26
16	10.58	7.51	6.30	5.64	5.21	4.91	4.69	4.52	4.38	4.27	4.10	3.92	3.73	3.64	3.54	3.44	3.33	3.22	3.11
17	10.38	7.35	6.16	5.50	5.07	4.78	4.56	4.39	4.25	4.14	3.97	3.79	3.61	3.51	3.41	3.31	3.21	3.10	2.98
18	10.22	7.21	6.03	5.37	4.96	4.66	4.44	4.28	4.14	4.03	3.86	3.68	3.50	3.40	3.30	3.20	3.10	2.99	2.87
19	10.07	7.09	5.92	5.27	4.85	4.56	4.34	4.18	4.04	3.93	3.76	3.59	3.40	3.31	3.21	3.11	3.00	2.89	2.78
20	9.94	6.99	5.82	5.17	4.76	4.47	4.26	4.09	3.96	3.85	3.68	3.50	3.32	3.22	3.12	3.02	2.92	2.81	2.69
21	9.83	6.89	5.73	5.09	4.68	4.39	4.18	4.01	3.88	3.77	3.60	3.43	3.24	3.15	3.05	2.95	2.84	2.73	2.61
22	9.73	6.81	5.65	5.02	4.61	4.32	4.11	3.94	3.81	3.70	3.54	3.36	3.18	3.08	2.98	2.88	2.77	2.66	2.55
23	9.63	6.73	5.58	4.95	4.54	4.26	4.05	3.88	3.75	3.64	3.47	3.30	3.12	3.02	2.92	2.82	2.71	2.60	2.48
24	9.55	6.66	5.52	4.89	4.49	4.20	3.99	3.83	3.69	3.59	3.42	3.25	3.06	2.97	2.87	2.77	2.66	2.55	2.43
25	9.48	6.60	5.46	4.84	4.43	4.15	3.94	3.78	3.64	3.54	3.37	3.20	3.01	2.92	2.82	2.72	2.61	2.50	2.38
26	9.41	6.54	5.41	4.79	4.38	4.10	3.89	3.73	3.60	3.49	3.33	3.15	2.97	2.87	2.77	2.67	2.56	2.45	2.33
27	9.34	6.49	5.36	4.74	4.34	4.06	3.85	3.69	3.56	3.45	3.28	3.11	2.93	2.83	2.73	2.63	2.52	2.41	2.29
28	9.28	6.44	5.32	4.70	4.30	4.02	3.81	3.65	3.52	3.41	3.25	3.07	2.89	2.79	2.69	2.59	2.48	2.37	2.25
29	9.23	6.40	5.28	4.66	4.26	3.98	3.77	3.61	3.48	3.38	3.21	3.04	2.86	2.76	2.66	2.56	2.45	2.33	2.21
30	9.18	6.35	5.24	4.62	4.23	3.95	3.74	3.58	3.45	3.34	3.18	3.01	2.82	2.73	2.63	2.52	2.42	2.30	2.18
40	8.83	6.07	4.98	4.37	3.99	3.71	3.51	3.35	3.22	3.12	2.95	2.78	2.60	2.50	2.40	2.30	2.18	2.06	1.93
60	8.49	5.79	4.73	4.14	3.76	3.49	3.29	3.13	3.01	2.90	2.74	2.57	2.39	2.29	2.19	2.08	1.96	1.83	1.69
120	8.18	5.54	4.50	3.92	3.55	3.28	3.09	2.93	2.81	2.71	2.54	2.37	2.19	2.09	1.98	1.87	1.75	1.61	1.43
∞	7.88	5.30	4.28	3.72	3.35	3.09	2.90	2.74	2.62	2.52	2.36	2.19	2.00	1.90	1.79	1.67	1.53	1.36	1.00

For a particular combination of numerator and denominator degrees of freedom, entry represents the critical values of F corresponding to a specified upper tail area (α).

Source: Reprinted from E. S. Pearson and H. O. Hartley, eds., *Biometrika Tables for Statisticians*, 3d ed., 1966, by permission of the *Biometrika* Trustees.

TABLE A.6 Critical Values[a] of the Studentized Range Q

UPPER 5% POINTS ($\alpha = 0.05$)

v\\n	2	3	4	5	6	7	8	9	10	11	12	13	14	15	16	17	18	19	20
1	18.00	27.00	32.80	37.10	40.40	43.10	45.40	47.40	49.10	50.60	52.00	53.20	54.30	55.40	56.30	57.20	58.00	58.80	59.60
2	6.09	8.30	9.80	10.90	11.70	12.40	13.00	13.50	14.00	14.40	14.70	15.10	15.40	15.70	15.90	16.10	16.40	16.60	16.80
3	4.50	5.91	6.82	7.50	8.04	8.48	8.85	9.18	9.46	9.72	9.95	10.15	10.35	10.52	10.69	10.84	10.98	11.11	11.24
4	3.93	5.04	5.76	6.29	6.71	7.05	7.35	7.60	7.83	8.03	8.21	8.37	8.52	8.66	8.79	8.91	9.03	9.13	9.23
5	3.64	4.60	5.22	5.67	6.03	6.33	6.58	6.80	6.99	7.17	7.32	7.47	7.60	7.72	7.83	7.93	8.03	8.12	8.21
6	3.46	4.34	4.90	5.31	5.63	5.89	6.12	6.32	6.49	6.65	6.79	6.92	7.03	7.14	7.24	7.34	7.43	7.51	7.59
7	3.34	4.16	4.68	5.06	5.36	5.61	5.82	6.00	6.16	6.30	6.43	6.55	6.66	6.76	6.85	6.94	7.02	7.09	7.17
8	3.26	4.04	4.53	4.89	5.17	5.40	5.60	5.77	5.92	6.05	6.18	6.29	6.39	6.48	6.57	6.65	6.73	6.80	6.87
9	3.20	3.95	4.42	4.76	5.02	5.24	5.43	5.60	5.74	5.87	5.98	6.09	6.19	6.28	6.36	6.44	6.51	6.58	6.64
10	3.15	3.88	4.33	4.65	4.91	5.12	5.30	5.46	5.60	5.72	5.83	5.93	6.03	6.11	6.20	6.27	6.34	6.40	6.47
11	3.11	3.82	4.26	4.57	4.82	5.03	5.20	5.35	5.49	5.61	5.71	5.81	5.90	5.99	6.06	6.14	6.20	6.26	6.33
12	3.08	3.77	4.20	4.51	4.75	4.95	5.12	5.27	5.40	5.51	5.62	5.71	5.80	5.88	5.95	6.03	6.09	6.15	6.21
13	3.06	3.73	4.15	4.45	4.69	4.88	5.05	5.19	5.32	5.43	5.53	5.63	5.71	5.79	5.86	5.93	6.00	6.05	6.11
14	3.03	3.70	4.11	4.41	4.64	4.83	4.99	5.13	5.25	5.36	5.46	5.55	5.64	5.72	5.79	5.85	5.92	5.97	6.03
15	3.01	3.67	4.08	4.37	4.60	4.78	4.94	5.08	5.20	5.31	5.40	5.49	5.58	5.65	5.72	5.79	5.85	5.90	5.96
16	3.00	3.65	4.05	4.33	4.56	4.74	4.90	5.03	5.15	5.26	5.35	5.44	5.52	5.59	5.66	5.72	5.79	5.84	5.90
17	2.98	3.63	4.02	4.30	4.52	4.71	4.86	4.99	5.11	5.21	5.31	5.39	5.47	5.55	5.61	5.68	5.74	5.79	5.84
18	2.97	3.61	4.00	4.28	4.49	4.67	4.82	4.96	5.07	5.17	5.27	5.35	5.43	5.50	5.57	5.63	5.69	5.74	5.79
19	2.96	3.59	3.98	4.25	4.47	4.65	4.79	4.92	5.04	5.14	5.23	5.32	5.39	5.46	5.53	5.59	5.65	5.70	5.75
20	2.95	3.58	3.96	4.23	4.45	4.62	4.77	4.90	5.01	5.11	5.20	5.28	5.36	5.43	5.49	5.55	5.61	5.66	5.71
24	2.92	3.53	3.90	4.17	4.37	4.54	4.68	4.81	4.92	5.01	5.10	5.18	5.25	5.32	5.38	5.44	5.50	5.54	5.59
30	2.89	3.49	3.84	4.10	4.30	4.46	4.60	4.72	4.83	4.92	5.00	5.08	5.15	5.21	5.27	5.33	5.38	5.43	5.48
40	2.86	3.44	3.79	4.04	4.23	4.39	4.52	4.63	4.74	4.82	4.91	4.98	5.05	5.11	5.16	5.22	5.27	5.31	5.36
60	2.83	3.40	3.74	3.98	4.16	4.31	4.44	4.55	4.65	4.73	4.81	4.88	4.94	5.00	5.06	5.11	5.16	5.20	5.24
120	2.80	3.36	3.69	3.92	4.10	4.24	4.36	4.48	4.56	4.64	4.72	4.78	4.84	4.90	4.95	5.00	5.05	5.09	5.13
∞	2.77	3.31	3.63	3.86	4.03	4.17	4.29	4.39	4.47	4.55	4.62	4.68	4.74	4.80	4.85	4.89	4.93	4.97	5.01

(*Continued*)

UPPER 1% POINTS ($\alpha = 0.01$)

v\\η	2	3	4	5	6	7	8	9	10	11	12	13	14	15	16	17	18	19	20
1	90.00	135.00	164.00	186.00	202.00	216.00	227.00	237.00	246.00	253.00	260.0	266.00	272.00	277.00	282.00	286.00	290.00	294.00	298.00
2	14.00	19.00	22.30	24.70	26.60	28.20	29.50	30.70	31.70	32.60	33.40	34.10	34.80	35.40	36.00	36.50	37.00	37.50	37.90
3	8.26	10.60	12.20	13.30	14.20	15.00	15.60	16.20	16.70	17.10	17.50	17.90	18.20	18.50	18.80	19.10	19.30	19.50	19.80
4	6.51	8.12	9.17	9.96	10.60	11.10	11.50	11.90	12.30	12.60	12.80	13.10	13.30	13.50	13.70	13.90	14.10	14.20	14.40
5	5.70	6.97	7.80	8.42	8.91	9.32	9.67	9.97	10.24	10.48	10.70	10.89	11.08	11.24	11.40	11.55	11.68	11.81	11.93
6	5.24	6.33	7.03	7.56	7.97	8.32	8.61	8.87	9.10	9.30	9.49	9.65	9.81	9.95	10.08	10.21	10.32	10.43	10.54
7	4.95	5.92	6.54	7.01	7.37	7.68	7.94	8.17	8.37	8.55	8.71	8.86	9.00	9.12	9.24	9.35	9.46	9.55	9.65
8	4.74	5.63	6.20	6.63	6.96	7.24	7.47	7.68	7.87	8.03	8.18	8.31	8.44	8.55	8.66	8.76	8.85	8.94	9.03
9	4.60	5.43	5.96	6.35	6.66	6.91	7.13	7.32	7.49	7.65	7.78	7.91	8.03	8.13	8.23	8.32	8.41	8.49	8.57
10	4.48	5.27	5.77	6.14	6.43	6.67	6.87	7.05	7.21	7.36	7.48	7.60	7.71	7.81	7.91	7.99	8.07	8.15	8.22
11	4.39	5.14	5.62	5.97	6.26	6.48	6.67	6.84	6.99	7.13	7.25	7.36	7.46	7.56	7.65	7.73	7.81	7.88	7.95
12	4.32	5.04	5.50	5.84	6.10	6.32	6.51	6.67	6.81	6.94	7.06	7.17	7.26	7.36	7.44	7.52	7.59	7.66	7.73
13	4.26	4.96	5.40	5.73	5.98	6.19	6.37	6.53	6.67	6.79	6.90	7.01	7.10	7.19	7.27	7.34	7.42	7.48	7.55
14	4.21	4.89	5.32	5.63	5.88	6.08	6.26	6.41	6.54	6.66	6.77	6.87	6.96	7.05	7.12	7.20	7.27	7.33	7.39
15	4.17	4.83	5.25	5.56	5.80	5.99	6.16	6.31	6.44	6.55	6.66	6.76	6.84	6.93	7.00	7.07	7.14	7.20	7.26
16	4.13	4.78	5.19	5.49	5.72	5.92	6.08	6.22	6.35	6.46	6.56	6.66	6.74	6.82	6.90	6.97	7.03	7.09	7.15
17	4.10	4.74	5.14	5.43	5.66	5.85	6.01	6.15	6.27	6.38	6.48	6.57	6.66	6.73	9.80	6.87	6.94	7.00	7.05
18	4.07	4.70	5.09	5.38	5.60	5.79	5.94	6.08	6.20	6.31	6.41	6.50	6.58	6.65	6.72	6.79	6.85	6.91	6.96
19	4.05	4.67	5.05	5.33	5.55	5.73	5.89	6.02	6.14	6.25	6.34	6.43	6.51	6.58	6.65	6.72	6.78	6.84	6.89
20	4.02	4.64	5.02	5.29	5.51	5.69	5.84	5.97	6.09	6.19	6.29	6.37	6.45	6.52	6.59	6.65	6.71	6.76	6.82
24	3.96	4.54	4.91	5.17	5.37	5.54	5.69	5.81	5.92	6.02	6.11	6.19	6.26	6.33	6.39	6.45	6.51	6.56	6.61
30	3.89	4.45	4.80	5.05	5.24	5.40	5.54	5.65	5.76	5.85	5.93	6.01	6.08	6.14	6.20	6.26	6.31	6.36	6.41
40	3.82	4.37	4.70	4.93	5.11	5.27	5.39	5.50	5.60	5.69	5.77	5.84	5.90	5.96	6.02	6.07	6.12	6.17	6.21
60	3.76	4.28	4.60	4.82	4.99	5.13	5.25	5.36	5.45	5.53	5.60	5.67	5.73	5.79	5.84	5.89	5.93	5.98	6.02
120	3.70	4.20	4.50	4.71	4.87	5.01	5.12	5.21	5.30	5.38	5.44	5.51	5.56	5.61	5.66	5.71	5.75	5.79	5.83
∞	3.64	4.12	4.40	4.60	4.76	4.88	4.99	5.08	5.16	5.23	5.29	5.35	5.40	5.45	5.49	5.54	5.57	5.61	5.65

[a]Range/$S \sim Q_{1-\alpha;\eta,v}$. η is the size of the sample from which the range is obtained, and v is the number of degrees of freedom of S.

Index

Boxes are indicated by the italicized letter *n*, figures are indicated by the italicized letter *f*, and tables are indicated by the italicized letter *t* following the page number.